THE ANTHROPOLOGY OF MEDICINE

THE ANTHROPOLOGY OF MEDICINE

—————— From Culture to Method

Second Edition

Edited by
Lola Romanucci-Ross
Daniel E. Moerman
Laurence R. Tancredi

BERGIN & GARVEY
NEW YORK • WESTPORT, CONNECTICUT • LONDON

Library of Congress Cataloging-in-Publication Data

The Anthropology of medicine : from culture to method / edited by Lola
Romanucci-Ross, Daniel E. Moerman, Laurence R. Tancredi. — 2nd ed.
    p.   cm.
    Includes bibliographical references and index.
    ISBN 0-89789-262-3 (alk. paper). — ISBN 0-89789-263-1 (pbk. :
alk. paper)
    1. Medical anthropology.   2. Folk medicine.   3. Materia medica,
Vegetable.   4. Mental illness—Social aspects.   5. Psychiatry,
Transcultural.   I. Romanucci-Ross, Lola.   II. Moerman, Daniel E.
III. Tancredi, Laurence R.
    [DNLM: 1. Anthropology, Cultural.   2. Medicine, Traditional.   WB
50.1 A628]
GN296.A63   1991
306.4'6—dc20
DNLM/DLC   91-21999

British Library Cataloguing in Publication Data is available.

Library of Congress Catalog Card Number: 91-21999
ISBN: 0-89789-262-3
      0-89789-263-1 (pbk.)

First published in 1991

Bergin & Garvey, One Madison Avenue, New York, NY 10010
An imprint of Greenwood Publishing Group, Inc.

Printed in the United States of America

The paper used in this book complies with the
Permanent Paper Standard issued by the National
Information Standards Organization (Z39.48-1984)

10   9   8   7   6   5   4   3   2   1

CONTENTS

PREFACE: THE CULTURAL CONTEXT OF MEDICINE AND THE BIOHUMAN PARADIGM

Medical systems emerge from human attempts to survive disease and surmount death, and from social responses to illness and the sick role. Descriptions and analyses of this process within the variety of world cultures define a field known as medical anthropology. Although this process is an ancient one—perhaps 60,000 years old—with roots in the middle Paleolithic, the field of study is a relatively new one that began with systematic inquiries by anthropologists into health practices and explanations of disease in technologically primitive and peasant cultures.

This volume represents various aspects of the state of the art of medical anthropology, emphasizing what we have called the anthropology of medicine: a study of medical thought and problem solving, the acculturation process of the healer and physician in diverse cultural settings, and the social and cultural context of medicine. Our approach is through the perspective of cultural and medical anthropologists who have taught and worked with Western-educated physicians immersed in clinical and research medicine, as well as those who have worked with other healers and patients outside the bounds of modern biomedicine and surgery. One of us provides, in addition, the perspective of a physician.

Anthropological field research is an experience in abstraction; it is an exercise in putting particulars into brackets as we search for universals in elements and the relations among them. In this sense we have chosen to fuse the particulars of Western medicine with those from other cultures for conceptual analysis in what we have called the anthropology of medicine. Beyond the surface differences, we try to expose similarities of deep structure, to demonstrate that there is a path beyond culture and that one may focus on method.

We believe that medicine, in a very real sense, stands astride both the cultural and the biological dimensions of humankind, and we elaborate on this in particular in one chapter of Part V. We believe that medicine is a kind of applied anthropology in the broadest sense of the term: action for human beings. As anthropologists who have learned a great deal from physicians and surgeons, we hope that the perspective we can bring to this complex cultural and biological exchange will be of value to those who, so much closer to the action, are in the very trenches we learn so much by observing.

This book, then, is designed for physicians and medical students, public health administrators and workers, and students in related health-science fields, as well as students and professionals in anthropology and social science who are interested in the practice of theory of health and healing. It is, in brief, a text for both the health sciences and anthropology.

For a century in the West, there have been two literatures regarding the health sciences. They have represented two different canons, or paradigms: the approaches of biomedical science and of behavioral science. To simplify somewhat, the biomedical paradigm tells us that, for example, tuberculosis is "caused" by *Mycobacterium tuberculosis*, whereas the behavioral-science paradigm tells us that tuberculosis is "caused" by poverty and malnutrition. It is our contention that these two approaches can be integrated into one biohuman paradigm; further, we contend that the unifying factor is the concept of culture. By culture we mean the system of meaning—belief, knowledge, and action—by which people organize their lives. Such organization structures the diseases to which people are subject: As a simple case, schistosomiasis is a disease of irrigation agriculture; as a less simple case, the *windigo* psychosis of Algonquian Indians is a disease (characterized by homicidal behavior and cannibalistic fears) of a hunting people subject to great environmental fluctuations.

Diseases, however, are never experienced directly; illnesses, cultural constructs of "dis-ease," are what people experience. Illnesses are constructed of belief and knowledge, which vary with both space and time. A contemporary example might be hyperactivity, an illness with associated treatment(s) that did not exist before the 1970s. People debate whether it is a new "disease," a response, perhaps, to new environmental toxins (i.e., food additives), or whether it was "always there" but not recognized. *Either case* provides an example (slightly different ones, to be sure) of the role of the cultural process in sickness and health. If it was always there but not recognized, then we have a case of an invented illness. If it is a new disease, we have a case of cultural concerns (for foods with this color or that) that have created a novel physiological disorder.

The theoretical value of such an approach seems evident. Human beings are simultaneously cultural and biological creatures, and these two dimensions necessarily interact. The historical concern of (at least North American) anthropologists with these two factors—differentiating anthropology from sociology or history, on the one hand, and from psychology or biology, on the other—means that the study of human health and healing in which people *attempt to influence directly the relationship between biology and culture*, is one rich with potential for learning fundamental things about what it means to be a human being.

Perhaps the greatest difference between these two paradigms and the greatest obstacle to their resolution lies in the notion of efficacy. What on earth is there to learn, the biomedical scientist wants to know, from the bizarre medical practices of the past? Grounded in the history of Western medicine, such a scientist is aware of the awesome array of tortures perpetrated on sick people in the past thousand years: bleeding and purging, whipping devils out of the insane, the presumably medicinal use of bat's blood and bear feces, or frog sperm and earthworms, gruesome tales of septic surgery on nonanesthetized patients, and so on.

We do not deny the terrifying state of medicine in Europe between the twelfth and eighteenth centuries. The difference lies in the fact that the anthropologist takes a broader view of the world, and sees pre-modern Europe as a very unusual and special case—one of the least healthy societies in human history—subject to dozens of new and terrifying diseases as a consequence essentially of the great growth of the population of both humans and domesticated animals. This "one-two punch" of domestication and urbanization created conditions for the evolution and communication of infectious disease organisms on a scale unprecedented in human history, well beyond the abilities of the best-intentioned physician to control or prevent.

Consider, as an ideal comparison, the health status of Europeans and Native Americans in the year 1480. Paleopathological evidence indicates that the Native Americans were extremely healthy: they had a life expectancy longer than that of Europeans of the time. Life was difficult, and they suffered from accidents, fractures, rheumatic conditions, and, perhaps, trichinosis contracted from animals that they hunted. Scholarly debate rages regarding the origins of syphilis; some argue that it was introduced into Europe from America by members of Columbus's crew, while others state that it was an Old World disease. It is, however, the *only* ambiguous case; all the other diseases transmitted from one continent to the other went westward: smallpox, measles, typhoid, tuberculosis, cholera, diphtheria, plague—the list seems endless. These diseases had ravaged Europe for generations. They were also the single most important cause of the cataclysmic drop in Native American population. The most recent available estimates suggest that between 1490 and 1890, the native population of the forty-eight contiguous United States dropped 90 percent, from 1.9 million to 200,000 (Thornton and Marsh-Thornton 1981). Similarly, it is estimated that the Australian aboriginal population dropped by four-fifths between 1788 and 1933 (White 1977). The poor health status of native peoples in colonial times was a consequence of colonialism, not a measure of indigenous health.

That Native Americans or aboriginal Australians had little medical where-withal when confronted with cancer or influenza seems a misplaced criticism. What is most striking about non-Western medicine is how much people did with what they had. That many of the herbal remedies of the past have been supplanted by synthetic ones—many of which are, after all, modified natural products (for example, aspirin)—should not detract from the per-spicacity of the original discoverers; and, as Chapter 12 attests, there may be much more of value that we can learn from non-Western medicine to enhance the biochemical basis of modern medicine.

But, perhaps because of the relative lack of powerful specific drugs in the non-Western pharmacopoeia, it is clear that many of these peoples were far more sophisticated and far more inventive than we in manipulating the social and human dimensions of medicine. This aspect of non-Western medicine may ultimately have the most to teach us about healing. Once one recognizes that the *form* of medical treatment affects the *outcome* of treatment, one can hardly leave it to chance, any more than one can prescribe drugs (however effective) by chance. The chapters in this book demonstrate that this *is* the case, and they show some of the forms that medical treatment can take; they show as well how deeply medical systems are embedded in culture.

Human beings are simultaneously biological and cultural organisms. For physicians to achieve their goal—to optimize human health—they must be intensely aware of this human duality. Our purpose is not to undercut the grounding of medicine in biology (tuberculosis *is* caused by a bacillus) but to assert that medicine has two feet, and that the other foot is grounded in culture (tuberculosis is *also* caused by poverty and malnutrition); moreover, and most importantly, these two dimensions are interconnected in many and complex ways.

As a very specific example, consider the character of medical diagnosis. Physicians, during the long years of training in which they gain their ex-pertise, increasingly become members of the medical subculture—with a language, a system of values, and a conceptual framework for decision mak-ing—and, at least for a time, are separated from the arena in which they are later to be effective. Moreover, physicians must learn how to cope with the inevitable internal duality of medicine as both scientific and clinical. Whereas scientific medicine involves public research on aggregates, clinical medicine involves private treatment of individuals; the former is statistical, the latter is idiosyncratic; the former is concerned with the course of a disease, the latter with the history of an illness. As clinicians confront patients they have to mold them into categories, transforming unique constellations of experience, notions, beliefs, symptoms, and disease into types, a "case of the measles," the proverbial "liver in Room 446." For the clinician this is almost a necessity, but for patients it is simultaneously clarifying and dehumanizing: Whatever they "have" rules out another thousand possibilities, but the price they pay is that they are no longer discrete sufferers but members of a class.

And likewise for the physician: To diagnose is to classify and to predict a course and a treatment based on the vagaries of statistics and experience; it is to take what can always be a very serious risk. This risk has both structural and statistical dimensions. It is a structural risk in that validation is essentially derived from the response to treatment, which is temporally remote. It is a statistical risk in that "classic cases" are rare, in that medical theory must be manipulated to fit the unique characteristics of infinitely varying patients. To do this at all is to *ignore* much of what patients present and to select as *meaningful* a segment of their existence that is particularly diagnostic, that is, to ignore things that patients think are important, to dismiss some (perhaps much) of their lives as *unimportant*; this is by its nature a dehumanizing process. A mutual commitment of patient and physician to an intrinsically categorical process, an intrinsinically dehumanizing process, is necessarily disconcerting; the process must inhibit people from acting in concert. And this must occur regardless of the cultural distance between physician and patient. Indeed, the experience of many physicians is that among the most difficult patients are other physicians; perhaps it is only that here the physician can more easily translate the patient's discontent—and, perhaps, less easily ignore it. This dehumanization can only be exacerbated by additional cultural differences in general education, class, ethnic origins, and so on.

Whatever else diagnosis may be, it is first a social process based on interpersonal communication between the scientifically knowledgeable physician and the concerned patient. The physician should understand why and when a person seeks medical attention, how the patient views his or her own sickness, how the patient reports his or her symptoms and interprets his or her feelings, and what changes occur in the patient's life because of the illness or treatment. These factors are always influenced by the cultural backgrounds of patient and physician. Wide variation in patients' backgrounds and the cultural differences between doctor and patient may profoundly influence the diagnostic process and therapeutic course (Romanucci-Ross and Tancredi 1987).

Yet if the patient cannot act in concert with the physician, how is the physician to control the course of the patient's disease? As the patient gives up uniqueness for a diagnosis, he or she also gives up independence. And the new dependence is on the physician. Dependence can take many forms. The skill with which the physician projects an appropriate, empathetic concern and strikes a responsive chord in the patient will affect the richness and utility of the interchange. If the process is to be dehumanizing, it may as well be as useful as possible. The therapeutic exchange can be so structured that the patient can develop a sense of trust and security while the physician can develop a sense of responsibility and confidence; this reciprocity can replace the prior independence and uniqueness of patient and physician. Trust and security in return for responsibility and confidence can only facilitate healing.

This relationship aside, the physician must remember that when a diagnosis is pronounced, there should be no assumption that the patient understands it in the same way the physician does. The patient may never have heard the word before; or, if he or she has, it is inconceivable that he or she understands the term as the physician does. And it is the patient's *understanding* that will influence the response to treatment.

Furthermore, there is increasing evidence that a significant group of patients, even those among the highly educated lay public, are unable to comprehend the nature of the medical information provided in order to obtain an informed consent (Tancredi 1982). Many of these patients may simply be inattentive during the session with the physician. This attitude may reflect either that patients desire to place the responsibility for critical decisions about their care on the physician, thereby effectively waiving the requirements of informed consent, or, more likely, that during a health crisis, patients are so distraught that they are incapable of making objective decisions concerning their medical care. The physician has to be sensitive to the many medical and emotional factors affecting the patient and make the necessary adjustments in the flow of communication to enhance the patient's understanding of the medical information that is being given.

The technique of patient interviewing can be a highly honed skill—focused but not rigidly structured; flexible, to adjust to the patient's perhaps abnormal attitudes and behavior (the patient is, after all, at least by his or her own definition, sick) but organized to elicit sufficient pertinent information in the available time to allow the physician room to take the diagnostic risk; and so organized that the patient has an *appropriate understanding* of the diagnosis.

It is ultimately only the pathologist who can know for sure what the patient had. By then, of course, it is too late. This is not to deny biological mortality; it is, rather, to assert the need for more than simply biological medicine.

This book is comprised of chapters on research in medical anthropology that we believe will provide a foundation for a biohuman medical paradigm by demonstrating how culture—human belief, knowledge, and action—structures the human experience of disease, affects the ways in which *both physicians and patients* perceive and define illness, and influences the matrices of decision making in the subcultures attempting to communicate about problems of health care.

REFERENCES

Romanucci-Ross, L., and L. R. Tancredi. 1987. "The Anthropology of Healing."
    In *In Search of the Modern Hippocrates* (Roger J. Bulger, ed.). Iowa City: University of Iowa Press, pp. 127–46.

Tancredi, L. R. 1982. "Competency for Informed Consent: Conceptual Limits of Empirical Data." *International Journal of Law and Psychiatry* 5:51–63.

Thornton, R., and J. Marsh-Thornton. 1981. "Estimating Prehistoric American Indian Population Size for United States Area: Implications of the Nineteenth Century Population Decline and Nadir." *American Journal of Physical Anthropology* 55:47–54.

White, I. M. 1977. "Pitfalls to Avoid: The Australian Experience." In I. M. White, *Health and Disease in Tribal Society.* Amsterdam: Elsevier.

PART I

INTERACTION OF MEDICAL SYSTEMS

The exchange of ideas concerning health and illness between cultures is no simple matter, and the interacting of medical systems provides a rich context for understanding the relationships between biology and the culture of medicine. In any particular case, how and which specific disease and disease concepts, and specific medicines and ideas about their use and effectiveness, are exchanged is an empirical question. But models for the nature of the exchange and the historicocultural context for the exchange provide an important focus for analyses that can (and often do) make prediction, and therefore health planning, possible.

The common conceit of the West—that the benefits of scientific medicine are obvious, as are the truths on which those benefits are based—is a conceit held by all peoples regarding their own medical systems. It was as true for the bleeding and purging physicians of the nineteenth century as it is for the neurosurgeons and cardiologists of the twentieth. These ideas, associated with fundamental principles of belief about the major cosmological issues of life and death, generally are very deeply held. In the United States in recent years, major political and social conflicts have raged over what can be narrowly conceived as medical issues. Abortion, the definition of death (or medical death), and the notion of "death with dignity" are examples of such issues where broad, deeply held beliefs influence medical matters.

Medical systems are, of course, part of the larger cultural system of any group. Ideas about sickness and health and curing constitute a system—that is, one can consider the parts and analyze the relations among the parts. Such beliefs within cultural systems in contact are reinforced or become diminished or distorted; the reason for this is that the system must, and does, include those persons whose perception and cognition conceptualize about the system. A dramatic example of this involves the enormous social and ecological changes undergone by the northeastern subarctic Algonquian Indians in response to the introduction of European diseases (Martin 1978). Martin, in what is nominally a history of the fur trade, argues that the commercial involvement of Indians in the fur trade was more apparent than real. For a people whose essential notion of all illness was that it represented retaliation by the spirits of mistreated prey animals, the vast epidemics of European diseases (often occurring long before the Indians actually encountered Europeans) presented a serious enigma. They had not mistreated the animals; why, then, were the animals killing them? Martin's argument is, in effect, that the Indians decided that, for unknown reasons, the animals had declared war on them. Adopting, when available, the providential armaments of the newly appearing Europeans (guns and steel traps), they fought back. The result was the Indian involvement in the fur trade and, not incidentally, the extermination of much of the animal life of North America.

The most extraordinary aspect of this case appears in ethnographic accounts of the descendants of these fur traders (Tanner 1979). They are today returning to a pattern very similar to the one they pursued four centuries ago, carefully harvesting animals with appropriate reverence and ceremony. The great epidemics of the past are, of course, gone, and (vaccinated) hunters may be as healthy as their ancestors were. The war, it seems, is over; and, after four centuries of incomprehensible social change, at least some essential notions of health for these people are unchanged.

The chapters in this section all focus on the ways in which the conceptual portions of medical systems change (or do not change) as a result of culture contact.

Romanucci-Ross's discussion of medicine in Italy describes the medicalization of folk medicine by Western medicine—the active attempt by official providers of health care to impose a standard structure on diagnostic and curing practices. Despite massive propaganda, and even apparent complicity—seen in repeated visits to state insurance doctors—traditional ideas of body image and dysfunction prevail. Here a population is engaged in creating a grammar and rhetoric of a health culture and life-style that begins to link its traditions to what it learns of medical scientific method, both in practice and from the media. Conjoining these modalities, the people explore therapeutic choices and evolve new ethnotherapies.

In Kidwell's account of the relationship between Aztec and Spanish medicine, we find that these systems exchanged a broad range of items that facilitated the identification and cure of a variety of diseases. Indigenous plants were used by the conquerors for the diseases they found in the New World; more problematical for the host populations were the diseases brought to them. Analysis of the Spanish and Aztec sources from the period can isolate features of the cross-cultural transactions in cognition. Upon what bases could the exchange of information occur? In this case, herbal medicine became a primary focus of exchange. Even though the Spanish had the Galenic binary structure of hot and cold, whereas the Aztecs classified plants by their uses, both groups found plants useful as food, medicine, and ornament. Aztec epidemiology and pharmacology fused with Greek and Galenic views; in time, the Mexican folk-medicine system emerged, perhaps the most fully syncretic medical system known.

As the Spanish incorporated Aztec medicines into their conceptualization of medicine, the Ningerum of Papua New Guinea are shown by Welsch to be incorporating Western medicine into their system. Western medicine plays a complementary rather than a competitive role, and Welsch sees the emergent system as integrative. Looking at the distribution of therapeutic knowledge and expertise in the Ningerum community and the locus of diagnostic and therapeutic decision making, this process is placed in Watson's (1980) broader social theory of consensual complementarity. Welsch demonstrates that the process of syncretization, as well as the resultant system, can be documented, if one can talk with individuals to assess motivation and thereby specify the operation of belief in individual instances.

Welsch's observations and interpretations differ from an earlier anthropological study in another part of New Guinea. In the Admiralty Islands (Manus) during the 1960s, curative practices appeared to involve a critical usage of Western medical resources that fell into patterns of acculturative and counteracculturative sequences (see Romanucci-Ross 1977). For the more traditional Manus, Western medicine excelled in lower-level descriptions of disease; it was, however, incomplete and did not admit of a multiple etiology in a bio-social-moral frame. One could predict which cures would be selected by knowing where the family or individual stood on the acculturation gradient. There was also a general attempt to match "whiteman's medicine" with "whiteman's diseases."

The Ostiak of Siberia have had a rather different response to the external alteration of their medical culture, under the pressure of Soviet antireligious and public-health programs. Here we find the original shaman, a prototype used by many anthropologists to describe curers in other cultures. The Ostiak differentiate three kinds of practitioners: the family shaman, a sort of general practitioner; the trance shaman; and the "big man," whose spiritual travels take him far and wide. The shaman's patient is a colleague in the medical event and helps by confessing wrongdoing; cure comes through abreaction and transference. Since the entire community participates in the process, this is a sort of community mental-health approach to individually focused group therapy. In this case, a deliberate attempt by the Soviet authorities to extinguish an indigenous system has succeeded to the degree that the systems have developed an antagonistic, rather than complementary or syncretic, relationship. During collectivization in the 1930s, shamans were characterized as "deceivers"; the campaign was successful enough that they are now characterized by many as "drunks" capable of doing evil. This example matches the traditional notion of acculturation: Ostiak notions of health today generally mirror those of the Soviet public-health movement. Even such distinctive aspects of the traditional system as the manipulation of altered states of consciousness are now widely disparaged.

These cases represent a wide range of medical interaction. If the Mexican case represents a fully syncretic system, the Siberian case represents a more nearly acculturated one. If the Ningerum case represents an emerging syncretism, the Italian case represents a stable, unshakable one. Exactly what determines the ultimate outcome of the interaction of medical systems is not yet clear. However, it *is* clear that this interaction is a complex and difficult one, not susceptible to facile prediction.

REFERENCES

Martin, C. 1978. *Keepers of the Game: Indian-Animal Relationships and the Fur Trade.* Berkeley: University of California Press.

Romanucci-Ross, Lola. 1977. "The Hierarchy of Resort in Curative Practices: The Admiralty Islands, Melanesia." In *Culture, Disease, and Healing*, David Landy, ed., pp. 481–86. New York: Macmillan.

Tanner, Adrian. 1979. *Bringing Home Animals: Religious Ideology and Mode of Production Among Mistassini Cree Hunters.* New York: St. Martin's Press.

Watson, James B. 1980. "Protein and Pigs in Highland New Guinea." Paper presented to the American Anthropological Association, 79th annual meeting.

1

CREATIVITY IN ILLNESS: METHODOLOGICAL LINKAGES TO THE LOGIC AND LANGUAGE OF SCIENCE IN FOLK PURSUIT OF HEALTH IN CENTRAL ITALY

LOLA ROMANUCCI-ROSS

For primitive societies and for folk or peasant cultures in the Europeanized world, including the United States, we have access to a considerable body of literature on health-seeking behavior and the contexts in which therapeutic decisions are made (Landy 1977; Logan and Hunt 1978). Investigators of illness and healing in different cultures have tended to agree on the universality of some aspects of health-seeking behavior regardless of other manifest differences in those cultures: One of the areas of agreement concerns client management of alternative systems of curative practices. Strategies employed by patients and/or their families on their behalf range from serial exclusion of one system in preference for another to the making of decisions that combine elements of several systems. Such combinations appear to the patient to maximize medical effectiveness.

The serial exclusion principle was well exemplified in the search for cures in a primitive group in the Admiralty Islands of Melanesia, where I was able to observe and record traditional medicine and the very beginnings of Western medicalization. What could be described here were shifting game strategies in curing events when the choices were multiple and the choosers were persons whose behavior ranged from traditional to "deculturated" to somewhat well adapted to living between two cultural models. Depending on the locus of the person on the acculturation continuum, the series of resort to curing practices in health-seeking behavior was predictable. Among the somewhat acculturated, Western medicine was chosen first; when this failed, traditional medicine was sought. The reverse was true for the traditional individual. The patterning became more complex in response to external political events, but the choices remained serial and temporally mutually exclusive (Schwartz 1969).

Such a process in a society based on kinship relationships provides a sharp contrast to a society that functions primarily through political and economic institutions. In the United States, groups pressuring public opinion regarding proper professional help in regaining health were instrumental in institutionalizing the historical defeat, so to speak, of many alternative systems of health care so that allopathic medicine won the field. It did so, shortly after the turn of the century, by marshaling all the strategic resources at its command: the political, the judicial, the scientific (including technological advances), and the growing public confidence in the idea of progress and expertise (Cohen 1983).

The culture under discussion in this chapter includes some elements and some combinatorial rules similar to those in both the above-mentioned groups. Aspects of a process of what might appear to be an eclectic approach to health-seeking behavior will be examined. We will consider similarities and differences between the country folk and the urban dwellers in assumptions about the body and body image and in uses of ecological resources such as plants, animals, other persons, and "natural laws." We will explore the roles of healer and client and indicate borrowed models for behavior from other spheres and arenas in the culture. In particular, we emphasize that in this culture we find a manner of creating a grammar from sectors of experience, a grammar that poses no difficulty in combining mythology, religion, "natural law," and the logic and language of modern science.

We focus on a rural area of small villages (with a large town, Ascoli Piceno, included as a reference point) in the eastern-central portion of Italy (Romanucci-Ross 1983). Ascoli Piceno, the town, is in the province of Ascoli Piceno and in the region of the Marches, which is surrounded by Tuscany, Umbria, Lazio, Abruzzi, and the Adriatic Sea. Ascoli Piceno, the province, contains both rural and urban communes (*comuni*) further divided into *frazioni* or smaller units, of which the urban *comune* of Ascoli has fifteen. Less than one-fourth of the communal populations are now engaged in agriculture, with the rest in small businesses or service and other industries that include power plants, metallurgy, engine repairs, textiles, paper, and chemical products. Agricultural activities include the raising of grain and grapes, and animal husbandry. Among the rural population, less than half own their own farmlands; the others are part of the *mezzadria*, a sharecropping system, and about 6% are hired laborers (see *Monografia Regionale* 1977). Many of the people living in the town either have migrated from the countryside or have relatives there.

Although there is a slow but continuous flow of rural people into the town, the past several years have witnessed a slow but steady flow of town people moving into country houses (sometimes within the villages); they drive to work each day. Not only do rural areas maintain their own dialects in an energetic bilingualism that small children can negotiate, but the town has its own dialect, Ascolano.

Ascoli had its own identity prior to commercial and political exchanges with Rome. There is early archaeological evidence that the Sabines from the north and the Illyrians from the coast came and settled among early Neolithic inhabitants (Balena 1979). Ascoli was dominated and culturally influenced by the French, under both Charlemagne and Napoleon. The period from 300 to 800 has been called by some "the abortive Germanization of Italy" (Pulgram 1958). Early German dialects left some traces, particularly in this area, and the patron saint of Ascoli is Saint Emidio, one of its early bishops of German provenience. Except for a brief period as a republic, Ascoli was a papal possession for hundreds of years (Berselli 1961).

At the present time, ethnomedicine in the region appears eclectic, and we will examine the process leading to such an end point. As for the basic features of what might be called folk medicine (see below), these are more akin to Sebald's description of its rural German counterparts (Sebald 1980) than they are to the system described by De Martino (1961) for a region of southern Italy. In the South, De Martino found the rich symbolism of the bite of the tarantula, aesthetic uses of color and music in cures, and possession, all within a cultural-historical context of early Greek versions of Christianity. We do not intend to describe in detail the folk medicine of Ascoli and its *frazioni*, for this has, in part, been done elsewhere (Romanucci-Ross 1982, 1983), and a description of folk medical practices for a nearby region in the Abruzzi is also available (Moss and Cappannari 1960). As indicated earlier, we will focus on continuity and change in health care.

Many features of the folk medical model in this area, it should be noted, are shared by both urban and rural populations. In the countryside one can still see red ribbons on oxen, strands of garlic on some entry doors, sprigs of rue on windows, a branch of pine in a child's bedroom. The sprigs and branches can be found in some urban houses also, just as the red or gold horns worn as amulets are found everywhere, for fear of the evil eye is not just a rural phenomenon. If, in the country, one fears the destruction of crops or animals by the evil eye, in the town one fears that the *mal occhio* will cause a son to fail an examination at a professional school or ruin a daughter's chances for a good marriage. In both rural and urban groups one finds healing and curing attended to through the uses of the rituals of religion (Catholicism), fear of witches, use of healers, uses of herbals,[1] foods as medicinals, and cures at spas and other watering places.

The folk medical model makes the following assumptions about illness and curing: Illness can occur through indifference to the "natural law" of the need for psychosomatic system balance, that is, all things should be done or consumed in moderation. One must not exert oneself physically or emotionally, for too much passion can be ruinous. (Common target organs are the liver, and the gastrointestinal tract for excesses of emotion.) One must avoid extremes of temperature or sudden temperature change. Too much air is harmful, especially for small children. The image of the body in good health is one that has a sufficient mass and density that it cannot "waste away" easily, hence being somewhat overweight is considered a sign of good health. The blood can become "impure" of course, through the lack of attention to system balance.

An individual does have control over illness caused by this lack of attention, and the remedies are to be found in nature itself through foods as medicinals, plants, mountain air, sulfurous waters, sunshine, ocean and shore and mineral waters. Privileged natural states can be used to bring relief from pain: A man with rheumatism can be stepped over many times by a pregnant woman who recites a formula. Honored moral states are curative: A man afflicted with a mental or "nervous" illness can regain his normal mental state by giving a shirt of his to a "man of virtue" to wear and to return to him, then wearing that shirt. A privileged genealogy can heal: One can go to the town of Amatrice to a family that, having in the distant past hosted St. Peter, has had, and still has, the power to heal (with oil and salt) the effects of the bite of a viper both in sheep and in humans. There is healing to be found in a town with deep mythico-historical roots: Offida, named after *ophis*, which means "snake" in Greek, has a long tradition of venerating serpents and has long had a sanctuary for cures.

But there are illnesses for which one is not expected to assume responsibility, and over these one has little control. Being victimized by ghostly or spiritual phenomena is considered an external cause, as is a soured social relationship. If one is dealing with a witch, these two causes can coalesce. Persons who possess the "evil eye" are often not to blame for the strong gaze that harms others, but one must try to avoid them. One also can try not to be too successful or talk too much about one's success, for that will attract envy and the evil eye. The witch (*strega*) appears to be an ordinary person going about her business, but she can be causing harm to you or your animals. A bewitched horse, ill, sweating, and with braided mane, has been ridden (and braided) by a witch who just keeps working at the washing fountain as though it had nothing to do with her. Against such incursions one has only the "horn" or medals or prayers, the touching of iron, and the knowledge instilled in every child that to be overtly and conspicuously successful is to invite disaster through illness or loss. Animal spirits can bring illness or bad luck, but this seems to be a function of the happenstance of being at the wrong place at the wrong time.

Remedies for the above are uses of the healers (women) and the *mago* (a male herbalist and magic-worker who can counter the wickedness of female witches and restore good health or good fortune), for healer and witch are never the same person. Preventive medicine in the folk medical model exhorts one to obey "natural laws" of avoiding excess, and the rules of social relationships exhort one to avoid envy, although it is acknowledged to be almost impossible.

The folk model is ideologically shared by healer and patient. Nevertheless, the Western allopathic physicians in the city seek to restructure the interpretation of health and illness through use of their professional model, which is in constant transformation because of scientific innovations (Romanucci-Ross 1982). These physicians are consulted from time to time and, at first glance, there appears to be an affinity in behavior among the village people in this area and what others do elsewhere concerning health-seeking behavior. Such behavior does follow the pattern of a hierarchy of resort in curative practices (Schwartz 1969), but the combinatorial aspects of the process in this region of Italy were unlike those I had observed in other cultures.

Through the local pathologist and general practitioner in the large town, I began to find a number of healers and diagnosticians who were active in the referral group that linked folk and Western medicine that is, their patients were (and often correctly) sent to a specialist in Ascoli Piceno. This referral pattern tends to foster meaningful information exchanges among the strata of healers. The patient never feels he or she is abandoning an ideological system because it is the healer or diagnostician who refers the patient to the allopathic physician; and the physician does not belittle the gifts of the healer who sent him the patient. These healers were referred to (by clients) as "the one who can be trusted" or "the one who knows."[2]

Clients of folk practitioners and healers represent a diversity of socioeconomic backgrounds. Among those who spoke freely and at great length to me of their hierarchies of resort in curative practices were middle-class housewives and wives of professionals, entrepreneurs, or other businessmen. Some of the clients were men; among them were a judge, a lawyer, a businessman, and a schoolteacher. In short, the sometime clients of folk healers are by no means characterized as rural and/or poor.

The three individuals named below, in particular, were frequented by a large number of persons in the urban and rural area.

Pasqualina, a diagnostician and healer, was called a *paragnostica* ("she who knows what is adjacent or peripheral"); she diagnosed by auscultation and by almost—but not quite—touching soft body parts, with trance behavior signaling the end of the physical examination. Her calling is considered scientifically validated because psychologists from the University of Bologna and other parapsychologists presumably had studied her. Her waiting room is usually overflowing with patients, who busily diagnose each other's presenting symptoms as they wait.

Another healer is called Maria La Santa. She appeared to me to be a living example of the syntactic structuring of folk symbols uniting religious passion, illness, and healing. She was described to me by some physicians as a "true hysteric"; her stigmata, covered by bandages or gloves, are said to bleed on certain Fridays preceding religious holidays.

The latest fad in healers is Olga, a pranotherapist; she has strong "electrical forces" in her hands and heals by touching. Patients bring her bottles of mineral water that she tosses into a vat. After washing her hands with baking soda, she runs her hands through the water and pours it back into bottles. This water has restored appetites and "cured malignant tumors." Through her thoughts, she resurrected her aunt in Philadelphia, and cured a child in New York City by sending a packet in the mail. Laws of time and space do not exist for magic, anywhere. Olga has printed a book at her own expense, *Io ti segno, dio ti cura* (I mark you, God cures you), which her clients feel privileged to purchase. This story of her life and healing contains photographs of her curing practices, including one of her aunt rising from the casket. The iconography is religious but the language is "scientific"; she speaks of forces, vectors, and gravity. "Before" and "after" X-ray pictures of Olga's cures are included, yet she wants patients to be religious believers.

These three healers represent others who are referred to as mystic or *sensitiva*. Some, but not all, of the following qualifications need to be present in such a healer: stigmata on the palms of the hands, visions, revelations, clairvoyant episodes, out-of-body experiences, hyperesthesia, and a profoundly altered sense of time. Any or all of these validate divine power, and they usually appear after a long and painful illness. Often the voice of a dead father provides the final incentive to use the power. But the power is not always welcome. The provocation in an unprepared person of the sudden emergence of paranormal faculties is thought to cause mental illness. Hence, dealing with psychic healers is not without risk. One woman was told by her summoned mother's spirit, "Maria, stop this nonsense and learn to live *in the world*!" Efficacy and power of healers are a function of distance from the patient; the further the distance to be traveled, the greater the belief in curative powers. Maria La Santa was highly touted by those who came from Abruzzi to be healed; and reaching Olga and Pasqualina required a drive of some eighty kilometers. Some patients go to the Black Madonna, which requires several hours' driving. Her miracles are particular for certain illness and infertility (Moss and Cappannari 1953).

Such healers function in a culture in which there is a great interest in emotional states and, as for Wilhelm Reich, the language of emotions is the language of the body (Reich 1969). Ecstatic, hysterical, or dream states, hypnotic states, meditative states, and trances are not considered irrelevant to the business of life in the world, but are viewed as central to meaning in the teleological unraveling of one's destiny. These states are grounded in the religious experience. In addition, and in the present time, however, we find a configuration also deeply embedded in Italian culture, the language and logic of science, from which those who create new epistemes in health can borrow in abundance. Both in verbal communication and in journalistic writings, individuals and groups adopt the language of science to describe healing techniques. For example, emotional states create "bioenergetics" that allow the healer to absorb energy from the universe that can be transmitted to others. "Bioenergetics" can also be absorbed from archaeological sites; it provides power to cure rheumatics and arthritics in a process known as bioradiant therapy or biomagnetic therapy. Such healers allow themselves to be studied "so that science might learn" about the natural laws expressed in their persons. These studies provide a scientific testimonial for these powers.

Folk healers, then, have been affected by the media and have joined a syncretic movement to link proofs of treatment efficacy from religion, medicine, and technology. Although there have been many cultural exchanges between nation-state and peasant enclaves, the nature of the exchange has been transformed radically. In the past it was occasioned mainly through migratory movements or administrative contact. In recent times the media-mediated information has blitzed the countryside as well as urban centers, engendering a syncretism of rational and metaphorical thought in reconstructing the path from illness to health.

Pharmacists in the region have joined the syncretic revolution and sell not only pharmaceuticals from commercial laboratories but also herbals and plant medicinals. With the client (patient) they discuss the virtues, the drawbacks, and the side effects of natural and of synthetic compounds from the pharmaceutical firms. Many pharmacists and some others interested in medical care are part of a *farmacognosia* movement whose members hold congresses and publish materials on all aspects of the study of drugs of plant origin. Gathered and classified are any materials dealing with the morphology and physiology of medicinal plants, pharmacological properties of botanicals and their active ingredients, or the gathering, conserving, or preparing of medicinals from botanicals. Old folk remedies once scoffed at are believed if read about in the newspaper. It is thought quaint and authenticating to read that "animals go for certain plants when sick" or a biblical tale about curing an ulcer with a poultice of figs. But such deference to ingenuity will not be shown to one's own folk predecessors. Through the young, the folk are once again learning to use words such as *decotto* (decoction) and *infuso* (infusion), and there are small lexicons of the most used medicinal terms. They are read to from dictionaries of infirmities with corresponding herbal remedies, and once more become believers. This goes beyond the reinforcement of traditional culture. In reversing the path of learning by going from younger to older, and by learning from print and other media, the tradition changes, yet elements that might have dropped out are preserved.

In the conscious models of thought about natural healing, some plants are considered to be only medicinal, but some are used both as food and as medicinals simultaneously (see Table 1.1). For example, onions, garlic, almonds, chestnuts, lettuce, rice, and many other everyday foods are consciously included in meals for their medicinal properties. One or more family members may need temporary relief from distressing symptoms or a minor

affliction. A continuum exists from nutrient to medicinal usage, de
on the framing and context. A nutrient in one meal may be a medi
another. Table 1.1 indicates that most disturbances are gastrointe
These somatic expressions relate to a loss of control over interperson
lations (Romanucci-Ross 1983).

Since the mid-1980s an interest in psychotherapy and psychoanalysis
existed in this region. A psychoanalyst from Rome came to give classes in
analysis to a group of five or six people in the city. Psychoanalytic percepts
have filtered into the reports of workers in the child welfare center. Wayward
children are often described in Freudian terms, and so are their performances
on the Rorschach, Thematic Apperception, or other projective tests. Several
rural people have begun to send problem children to a young psychoanalyst
at his residence in the country. In his opinion, these people probably would
not go to his office in the city.[3]

The incipient practice of psychoanalysis has had the curious effect of
providing more clients to the healers like Pasqualina, Maria La Santa, and
Olga. Their therapies inform bored and disaffected middle-class, middle-
aged housewives of former lives they have lived in Egypt or India, or the
Himalayas. "Pasts" are described in great detail, with the appropriate psychological terminology for the reasons and the meanings of their experiential
transformations through time. The clients I have interviewed seemed very
pleased with healers in this respect. Why are they pleased? First of all, what
does classic or neoclassic Freudian analysis purport to do for the patient? It
rephrases the problem (the neurosis, the psychosis, the malaise, the mal-
functioning) experientially and existentially. You are not who you think you
are, precisely, nor have you understood the nature of the bonding to those
who have caused or are causing your grief. You are told that some of these
present relationships are transferences of an earlier unconscious or subcon-
scious life. (Since you are not aware of them, they might just as well have
been in another life, in another epoch.) So, not unlike the psychoanalyst,
this type of healer provides the fantasy framework within which these women
can formulate and try to resolve their problems.

This method of the *sensitiva* provides her patient with an extraordinary
advantage, for this cultural group, of not calling into question the virtues of
the constellations of bondings known as the family. Here the patient is not
an oppressed individual seeking liberation from the constraints of the nuclear
family at a certain stage of development. The problem pinpointed is that a
dyad or constellation of characters from former times must patiently work
out a solution. No one here and now is at fault. Regardless of the etiology
of the fantasy therapy, we have sufficient evidence from psychologists to
assert that positive attitudes emerge and multiply between parties who engage in exchange behavior that is mutually rewarding (Byrne and Rhamey
1965).

The above creative synthesis, in trying to grapple with pathology and

Table 1.1
Conscious Models of Plants Used Both as Foods and as Medicinals

Name		Scientific Name	Local Usage	Parts Used
Almond	mandorlo	Prunus amygdalus Batsch	constipation, digestion, burns	fruit
Anise	anice	Pimpinella anisum L.	indigestion, stomach, spasms, cough, toothache	seeds
Apple	melo	Malus communis Poir	convalesence, constipation, diarrhea, stomach, hypertension	fruit
Asparagus	asparago	Asparagus officinalis L.	liver, intestinal cleaning, lungs, anemia	plant
Barberry	crespino (uva de la Madonna)	Berberis vulgaris L.	constipation, appetite, menstruation, as scorbutic	fruit, leaves
Basil	basilico	Ocinum basilicum L.	nervousness, cough, cold, spasm	plant
Beet	bietola	Beta vulgaris L.	anemia, cystitis, kidney, constipation	fruit, leaves
Carob	carrubo	Ceratonia siliqua L.	diarrhea, weight reduction	seeds, fruit
Chestnut	castagno	Castanea sativa Mill	diarrhea, cough	fruit, young leaves
Chicory	cicoria	Cichorum intybus L.	appetite, anemia, liver, skin, constipation, spring tonic	leaves, roots
Chili pepper	peperoncino	Capiscum annum L.	rheumatism, diarrhea, lungs	fruit
Coriander	coriandolo	Coriandrum sativum L.	digestion, spasm, dizziness	leaves
Cucumber	cetriolo	Cucumis sativus L.	colic, pruritis, skin problems	fruit

Table 1.1 (*Continued*)

Name	Scientific Name		Local Usage	Parts Used
Elder tree	sambuco	Sambucus nigra L.	hemorrhoids, nervousness, constipation, colds	flowers, leaves fruit
Fennel	finoccio	Foeniculum vulgare (Mill) Gaertn	bronchitis, diarrhea, impotence, cough, nursing mothers	fresh leaves, roots
Fig	fico	Ficus carica L.	constipation, cough, pregnancy	fruit
Garlic	aglio	Allium sativum L.	parasites, thought to have antibiotic qualities, prevents respiratory illnesses	bulb
Hazelnut	nocciolo	Corylus avellana L.	fever, circulatory problems	leaves, seeds, fruit
Lemon	limone	Citrus limon L.	cleansing, skin, hair, teeth; digestion, diarrhea	fruit
Lettuce	lattuga	Lactuca sativa L.	skin problems, nervousness	leaves
Licorice	liquirizia	Glycyrrhiza glabra L.	stomach, spasm, cough	roots, rhizome
Mallow	malva	Malva silvestris L.	constipation, appetite, menstruation, as scorbutic	roots, leaves, flowers
Marjoram	maggiorana	Origanum majorana L.	nervousness, stomach problems, dizziness	plant
Medlar tree	nespolo	Mespilus germanica L.	stomach, skin, diarrhea	fruit, nuts, leaves
Mint	mente	Mentha rotundifolia L.	appetite, digestion, mouth cleanser, cough, hiccups, convulsions	leaves, flowerets

14

Mustard	senape	Brassica nigra L.	bronchitis, respiratory illness	seeds
Oats	avena	Avena sativa L.	diabetes, skin disorders	seeds
Olive	olivo	Olea europea L.	hypertension, rheumatism, burns, hair care, liver, constipation	fruit
Onion	cipolla	Allium cepa L.	cleansing of respiratory system	bulb
Orange	arancio	Citrus simensis Osbeck	appetite, digestion, nervousness	fruit
Parsley	prezzemolo	Petroselinum sativum Hoffm.	anemia, digestion, rheumatism	plant
Rice	riso	Oryza sativa L.	diarrhea and other gastro-intestinal problems	grain
Rosemary	rosmarino	Rosmarinus officinalis L.	heart, liver, nervousness	flowering plant, leaves
Sage	salvia	Salvia officinalis L.	depression, impotence, frigidity, menstruation, gums, emphysema	leaves, flowerets
Strawberry	fragola	Fragaria vesca L.	angina, diarrhea, kidneys	fruit, young leaves
Sunflower	girasole	Helianthus annus L.	fever, hypertension, nervousness	leaves, flowers, seeds
Wheat	frumento	Triticum vulgare vill	pregnancy, impotence	grain

disordered states, contrasts with our (American) system, in which many consult chiropractors, osteopaths, and others who are not in the standard referral system and whose healing techniques have a history of conflicting claims to legitimacy (Morley and Wallis 1978).

Festinger (1957) held that when several conflicting cognitions are held at the same time, an individual or group is motivated to abolish or weaken the dissonance. Actually, the contrary may obtain, as demonstrated by research on religious cult behavior in Melanesia (Schwartz 1962), where it was shown that dissonance (i.e., ritual observed but no promised cargo) only served to fortify an even stronger belief in the eventual arrival of the cargo. The total commitment of believers was put in doubt by failure, not the relationship between the ritual behavior and the material goods that should have appeared because of it. We can transfer this lack of falsifiability of the tenets of a belief system to the belief of the patient in the healer, regardless of results. But, in addition to such adherence to faith in all cultures, we find the resort to curative practices fluid and vacillating for an even more pragmatic reason: The parameters of assessment are many, and an outcome may or may not be related to following or not following the doctor's advice.

So, too, in this Italian community the failure of cure did not call into question any of the components of the constantly emerging system, or the manner in which the elements were articulated. Information on health and illness in this culture is structured from metaphors in Catholicism and the language of science as it appears in newspapers, magazines, film, and theater. In this manner the nodes (a node is a nexus of information) provide centers for linkages of information systems for the new grammar to be used in the emergent discourse about health and illness. Included are the results of inductive, deductive, and analogic methods from medical science, as well as the revisionist thrust of alternative healing systems. Neologisms accrue throughout the entire network of the referral system.

The result is both agglutinative and assimilative, but the method represents a pulling away from the power holders of allopathic medicine. It is a centrifugal model and much like the model for local politics. It is good, it is thought, when no one gets the absolute majority of votes. It is good that no one school has the monopoly on restoring health to the body or the mind.

Folk practitioners aid communication between patients and modern providers of health care as the latter try to interpret the way patients report symptoms as well as responses to diagnoses and prescriptions. Folk practitioners do this through the referral system of which they are a part, and thus lessen the burden of the health care providers. Along with the patient they explore feedback loops linking new knowledge systems to the old ones; when the new and the old are similar, this validates the entire system of the old.

Unlike health care providers in the United States, neither these healers nor the allopathic physicians have strategic resources to employ as a political pressure group, as the latter group has in the United States. Yet the health seeker and the health care provider in our Italian model are more aware than their American counterparts that medicalization implies social control and that science is a socially negotiated and politically contested enterprise. Confronted with the discourse and the knowledge structures for management of health, the folk of this area, informed by tradition and the media, continually create an event-based grammar. New information about health and illness stimulates continuous restructuring of all the information, slowly changing the discourse as grammatical elements are added, deleted, or reenvironed. As knowledge structures are dismantled, their complexity is ignored and the discourse surrounding them is mapped onto new events, as we have described for evolving therapeutic choices in diagnostics, in ethnopharmacology, in psychoanalytic therapies, and in modifications of notions of nutrition and of preventive medicine.

At any point in time the health care system for any individual or group is metastable. What remains relatively stable is the mechanism that generates change. For Ascoli Piceno and environs these generators are grounded in the religion (Catholicism), in attitudes toward authority, and in the cultural-historical substratum of ideology and values regarding health and illness. Since January 1980 all Italians have been entitled to health insurance under the provisions of the Servizio Sanitario Nazionale. The persistent distrust of government, indifference to politics, and lack of belief in the honesty and capability of bureaucrats (Banfield 1958) should interest observers as physicians, patients, and their families negotiate the new health care system.

NOTES

1. For examples of uses of herbs as medicinal plants, see mint, rosemary, sage, basil, coriander, majoram, and mallow in Table 1.1.

2. "One who knows" and shared his knowledge with me was Gaetano Mari, who in daily life is an agricultural worker for an order of *frati* (brothers) in the city. In preparing a compress for rheumatic pains he will take equal parts of corn flour, mustard seeds (*Brassica nigra L.*), juniper (*Juniperus communis L.*), dried figs, and the flax plant (*Linum angustifolium Huds*), boil them in vinegar, and apply the compress. Men who are thus afflicted should also eat celery leaves; women, parsley. For eczema he will burn grapevines, boil the ashes and apply them. As gargle for a sore throat he boils the tender needles from the tip of the pine tree. He has many other such remedies that he assured me are effective; he has "believers" in the city and the country who follow his advice, as well as the advice they receive from physicians.

3. I am grateful to Dr. Francesco Giovanozzi, psychologist and psychoanalyst in Ascoli Piceno and Pedana, for giving me access to professional reports and discussing, in a general way, the nature of his relationship with his patients.

REFERENCES

Balena, Secondo. 1979. *Ascoli nel Piceno*. Ascoli Piceno: Edizioni Turistiche. Pp. 97–100.

Banfield, Edward. 1958. *The Moral Basis of a Backward Society*. Glencoe, Ill.: Free Press.

Berselli, Aldo. 1961. La Restaurazione e le società Segrete nelle Marche. In *L'Apporto delle Marche al Risorgimento Nazionale. Atti del Congresso della Storia. 30 Settembre–2 Ottobre 1960*. Ancona: Comitato Marchigiano per le Celebrazioni del Centenario dell Unita d'Italia. Pp. 69–91.

Byrne, D., and R. Rhamey. 1965. Magnitude of Reinforcement as a Determinant of Attraction. *Journal of Personal and Social Psychology* 2:889–99.

Cohen, Marcine. 1983. Medical-Social Movements in the United States (1840–1980): The Case of Osteopathy. Doctoral dissertation, University of California, San Diego.

De Martino, Ernesto. 1961. *La Terra del Rimorso: Contributo a una Storia Religiosa del Sud*. Milan: Il Saggiatore.

Fabiani, Giuseppe. 1958. *Collana di Pubblicazioni Storiche Ascolane. Ascoli nel Quattrocento*. 2 vols. Ascoli Piceno: Societa Tipolito-grafica Editrice.

Festinger, Leon. 1957. *A Theory of Cognitive Dissonance*. Evanston, Ill.: Row, Peterson.

Foster, George M., and Barbara Gallatin Anderson. 1978. *Medical Anthropology*. New York: John Wiley and Sons.

Landy, David. 1977. *Culture, Disease and Healing*. New York: Macmillan.

Logan, Michael H., and E. E. Hunt, Jr. 1978. *Health and the Human Condition: Perspectives on Medical Anthropology*. North Scituate, Mass.: Duxbury Press.

Lott, B., and J. Lott. 1969. Liked and Disliked Persons as Reinforcing Stimuli. *Journal of Personal and Social Research* 11:129–37.

Monografia Regionale per la Programmazione Economica Marche. 1977. Coordinated by Vincenzo de Nardo. Varese: Editrice Giuffre.

Morley, Peter, and Roy Wallis. 1978. *Culture and Curing*. London: Peter Owens.

Moss, Leonard W., and Stephen C. Cappannari. 1953. The Black Madonna: An Example of Culture Borrowing. *Scientific Monthly* 73:319–24.

———. 1960. Folklore and Medicine in an Italian Village. *Journal of American Folklore* 73, no.288:95–102.

Pelto, Pertti J., and Gretel H. Pelto. 1983. Culture, Nutrition and Health. In *The Anthropology of Medicine: From Culture to Method*. Lola Romanucci-Ross, Daniel E. Moerman, and Laurence R. Trancredi, eds. South Hadley, Mass.: Bergin Publishers.

Pulgram, Ernst. 1958. *The Tongues of Italy*. Cambridge, Mass.: Harvard University Press.

Reich, Wilhelm. 1969. *Character Analysis*. T. Wolfe, trans. New York: Farrar, Straus, and Giroux. 1969.

Romanucci-Ross, Lola. 1982. Medicalization and Metaphor. In *The Use and Abuse of Medicine*. Marten W. de Vries, R. L. Berg, and Mack Lipkin, Jr., eds. New York: Praeger Scientific. Pp. 171–182.

———. 1983. Italian Ethnic Identity and Its Transformations. In *Ethnic Identity: Cultural Continuities and Change*. George de Vos and Lola Romanucci-Ross, eds. Chicago: University of Chicago Press. Pp. 198–226.

Schwartz, Lola Romanucci (aka Lola Romanucci-Ross). 1969. The Hierarchy of Resort in Curative Practices: The Admiralty Islands, Melanesia. *Journal of Health and Social Behavior* 10:201–9.

Schwartz, Theodore. 1962. *The Paliau Movement in the Admiralty Islands: 1946–1954*.

Anthropological Papers of the American Museum of Natural History 49, pt. 2. New York: The Museum.

Sebald, Hans. 1980. Franconian Witchcraft: The Demise of a Folk Magic. *Anthropological Quarterly* 53:173–87.

2

Aztec and European Medicine in the New World, 1521–1600

CLARA SUE KIDWELL

Spanish settlers in the New World came bringing with them their customs, their foods, and their diseases. The New World represented a strange and even exotic place. It was primarily of interest to the Spaniards because of the material wealth of gold and silver that they dug from its bowels. However, although the gold and silver of the New World mines had a tremendous impact upon the role of Spain as a world power and upon the course of European history, the most lasting contributions of the North and South American continents to the European civilizations were not the minerals that represented wealth. Instead, it was the plants, primarily in the form of foodstuffs but also in the form of herbs for medical use, that were ultimately to provide a wealth far greater than the mineral wealth of the New World continents.[1]

In return for that wealth, the Spaniards gave to the native peoples of the New World many diseases—e.g., smallpox, typhus, cholera, and measles—and a life of slavery in the mines that largely decimated the Indian populations within approximately 50 years of the conquest.[2] Although there are many problems in calculating exact numbers of native populations at the time of conquest from which to calculate a rate of decline, the fact of the population decline due to disease is readily apparent.

The Spaniards, in their turn, suffered from what is often called "Montezuma's revenge," that is, gastrointestinal distress, as well as respiratory ailments induced by the living conditions in the New World. Agustin Farfan, a Spanish physician writing in Mexico in 1579, listed the principal afflictions of the Spanish residents of the New World as "flaqueza y indigestión del estómago" (weakness and indigestion of the stomach), "tauardete" [sic] (typhus), "dolor de costado" (tuberculosis), and "de la colica passion y del dolor de Ijada" (appendicitis).[3] Juan de Cardenas also devoted a chapter to the subject of Spanish ills in his *Primera Parte de los Problemas y Secretos Maravillosos de la Indias*. Those ills included stomach problems, menstrual difficulties, rheumatism, liver trouble, and urinary difficulty.[4] Native populations were also subject to respiratory and gastrointestinal diseases, of course, but the Spanish seemed much more susceptible to the illnesses of the New World.[5] One disease with major social and economic importance for the Spanish was syphilis.[6] One of the important export items from New Spain to Europe was guaiacum, highly touted in Europe as a cure for syphilis.[7] The theory seemed to be that syphilis was indeed a New World disease, and thus its cure should be a New World plant.

ACCULTURATION AND MEDICAL PRACTICE

It was in the area of medical practices that early forces of cultural assimilation began to affect both cultures, European and native. The tradition of medical "simples" was well known to European settlers in the New World, and since herbal medicines formed an important part of the medical practices of the Aztecs, Incas, and other native peoples with whom the Europeans were coming into contact, it can reasonably be assumed that at least some of these herbal remedies were adopted by the Spanish colonists and thus constituted a case of reverse acculturation, the adoption of native practices by the conquering civilization.[8] But the differences in basic premises of culture underlying the methods of treatment in the European and the Aztec societies were so different in so many respects that one would expect much less exchange of therapeutic methods outside of herbal medicines.

A body of writings by European physicians and Aztec writers (or information supplied by Aztecs) concerning materia medica in sixteenth-century New Spain shows some of the processes of acculturation that were going on in medical practice. These writings are sources of medical information that demonstrate the differing viewpoints of two cultures toward medical practices (and, as well, the viewpoint of one culture toward another). From these writings one can determine the interaction that was going on between native and European physicians, the differences and similarities of their viewpoints, and the extent to which any true influences were being exchanged in the first 80 years of contact between the cultures.

The body of writings under discussion comprises the following: from the Europeans, the *Opera Medicinalia* of Francisco Bravo (1525?–1594?), published in 1570 in Mexico;[9] the great work on New World plants compiled by Francisco Hernández (1517–1578) and published in part in 1628 under the title *Rerum Medicarum Novae Hispaniae Thesaurus* . . . ;[10] the *Tractado Breve de Anathomia y Chirugia* . . . , published in Mexico by Agustin Farfan (1531?–1604) in 1579 (with a second edition, *Tractado Breve de Medicina*, in 1592);[11] and *Summa y Recopilacion de Chirugia* . . . , by Alonso López Hinojosos (1535–1597), published in Mexico in 1578 (with a second edition in 1595).[12] And from the Aztecs *Libellus de Medicinalibus Indorum Herbis* . . . , written by Martin de la Cruz and translated from Aztec to Latin by Juan Badianus (both authors were Aztecs),[13] and the *Historia General de las Cosas de Nueva Espana*, compiled by Bernardino de Sahagun, a Franciscan priest, from Aztec informants.[14] The intricate relationship among these various works provides a fascinating insight into the differences between New World native medical practices and European concepts of medicine, and the bases upon which exchanges of information could be made. The convergences and divergences of viewpoints constitute an important chapter in the development of medicine in sixteenth-century colonial America.

COMMUNICABLE CONCEPTS IN AZTEC AND EUROPEAN MEDICINE

Aztec medicine was deeply embedded in the matrix of a culture that was highly religious in nature. Erwin Ackerknecht has commented on so-called primitive medicine that it is based essentially on supernaturalism with some rational elements, whereas modern medicine is based essentially on rationalism in spite of its magical elements.[15] An important aspect of medical practice among the Aztecs, for instance, was the ascription of causes of disease to the wrath of various deities. Xipe Totec caused skin diseases and was appeased in a yearly ceremony, in which sufferers of skin diseases walked in procession wearing the skins of sacrificial victims who had been flayed.[16] European medicine, on the other hand, was firmly rooted in the rational traditions of the Greeks, and the Galenic theory of the mechanism of the four humors and their balances in the body prevailed among European physicians. Attribution of qualities of hot and cold, wet and dry, was part of the Galenic tradition and linked European medicine with Aristotelian thought. Certainly all of the European physicians discussed here—Bravo, Farfan, López de Hinojosos, and Hernández—were firmly within the Galenic tradition of medicine. The Aztec writers, Badianus and de la Cruz, and the Aztecs upon whose information Sahagun based his work, represented a world view based upon the actions of the deities and their role in causing disease, as well as certain definite Aztec cultural values concerning fear, anxiety, and other emotional states that might be said to constitute illness.

Of the possible points of communication between the two systems of medical thought, two seem to be particularly important. The most obvious point of communication was a common belief in herbal medicines. The tradition of medical simples was well established in Europe, and the use of

New World plants for therapeutic purposes would seem obvious. A second point of communication, which bears on the first, is the pragmatic nature of medical practice in the New World, where there were few physicians and where the Spaniards were confronted with new conditions relating to their health. Of the works under consideration, those of Bravo and Hernández are most strongly based in the theoretical Galenic and Aristotelian tradition of European thought, whereas those of Farfan and López de Hinojosos, although they subscribe to Galenic doctrines, represent more the orientation of the practicing physician confronted with new situations in a land where traditional European physicians were not readily available to large parts of the colonial population. In many ways the Badianus-de la Cruz manuscript, with its almost cookbook-like approach to medical prescriptions, is closer to the Farfan and López de Hinojosos books than it is to the work by Sahagun, which sought to reflect the Aztec world view as a whole, which devotes limited attention to specific medical practices (book 10), and which treats the role of physicians (book 10), the nature of herbal medicines (book 11), and the role of deities as causes of illness (book 1) in different parts of the final version of the work.[17]

In terms of the historical connections among all of the works under discussion, there is evidence that the writers could have been in contact with one another in various ways, either directly or indirectly. Connections among the works by Bravo, Farfan, and López de Hinojosos are established in the prefatory material of the three books. Bravo wrote endorsements for both Farfan's *Tractado Breve de Anathomia y Chirugia* and López de Hinojosos's *Summa y Recopilacion de Chirugia*.[18] His endorsements may have been sought because of his reputation, which had been established with publication of his *Opera Medicinalia* (generally considered the first medical work published in the New World). Farfan also endorsed López de Hinojosos's work.[19] López de Hinojosos, in turn, was associated with Francisco Hernández at the Royal Hospital for Indians in Mexico, where he practiced for 14 years.[20] The connection between Hernández and Bernardino de Sahagun is very tenuous, but it appears that Hernández might have used a section of Sahagun's work in his own book (although without proper attribution).[21] Sahagun, in his turn, was for a time associated with the College of Tlalolco, where Juan Badianus and Martin de la Cruz were students. Sahagun was at the college from 1536 to 1540 and again in 1545. There is no indication that he was directly associated with de la Cruz and Badianus, whose work, the *Libellus*, was completed in 1552.[22] However, Sahagun's interest in the collection of Aztec materials may well have indicated a more general interest in writings by Aztecs at the college.

Despite the historical conjunction of these writers, there is very little evidence that transmission of knowledge from Aztec to European sources, or from European to Aztec sources, was taking place during the first century of contact. Rather, the conjunction is more evidence that differing cultural traditions were coming into contact but that, except in the area of herbal medicine, little exchange was taking place between the two cultures in medical practices.

European Physicians and Their Interpretations

Of the writers under consideration, Francisco Bravo seems most clearly the European physician. His work is divided into four major parts: a discussion of typhus (which he calls "tauardeste" [sic]) and its treatments; a disputation in the form of a dialogue concerning the uses of venesection to treat the disease; a discussion of the doctrine of critical days in the treatment of disease; and a description of sarsaparilla, with a discussion of its qualities . (Bravo maintained that the plant is hot and dry, rather than being cold as some maintained).[23] Bravo makes numerous references to Galen and also to Arabic writers—Avicenna and Rhazes—as well as to Fracastorio and Laguna, his closer contemporaries.[24] He makes no mention of native medical practices, and the herbal remedies that he does mention (except sarsaparilla) are of European origin. For example, a remedy for plague includes "rosis, violis, hordeo, lactucis, capitiabus papaveris, soliis salicis, et cannarum et cucurbitae" mixed in water.[25]

Francisco Hernández, physician to Philip II of Spain, was sent by Philip to the New World to collect material on natural history. His work is more in the encyclopedic tradition of natural histories and herbals that were appearing in Europe during the sixteenth and seventeenth centuries. Although he used the Aztec names of plants, reflecting a classification system based on use (*quilitl* as a suffix referred to plants used as foods; *yochitl* referred to ornamental plants; *patli* referred to medicinal plants; and economic plants useful for building and material objects were referred to by several suffixes),[26] Hernández introduced his discussion with reference to the classification system of Theophrastus, who classified plants according to form: *arbor*, *herba*, *suffrutex*, and *frutex*.[27] Hernández is much more concerned with description of the form of plants, although he does include medicinal properties in some descriptions (*texaxapotla*, for example, when burned and its vapors breathed, cured sneezing and dried up phlegm in the eyes, nose, and mouth).[28] The drawings of plants in his work are much more naturalistic than those in the *Libellus* of Badianus and de la Cruz. His work is an important source of information on Aztec plants and, in some cases, their medicinal uses. However, it remained very much in the European tradition of descriptive natural history.

Farfan and López de Hinojosos both follow European traditions in their references to humors, and to Galen and Guido as authorities.[29] However, both also made reference to herbal medicines used by Aztec healers. In the 1579 edition of Farfan's work, he mentions, for instance, xoxocoyoles (for stomach disorders),[30] mechoacan (*iopmoea jalapa*, *Bryonia mechoacana*, as a purgative),[31] guayacan (*guaiacum officinale*, for "mal de Bubas"),[32] and sarsaparilla (which, in agreement with Bravo, he describes as hot, its heat moving vapors in the body).[33] In the 1592 edition of the work, which is indeed more a major expansion of the section of medical practices than simply a new edition, he includes 59 native plants as remedies.[34]

López mentions remedies newly described and discovered by experiments.[35] He mentions specifically guayacan, sarsaparilla, canafistola, and chichimecapatle as ingredients in a cure for *alferezia* (epilepsy).[36] In regard to specific medical practices, both Farfan and López mention bleeding as a curative technique, but López says that he has not seen bloodletting as a practice among the natives.[37] However, specific mention of bleeding as a practice in the cure of headaches is made in Sahagun's work.[38]

As their treatises indicate, both Farfan and López de Hinojosos are much more concerned with experience than theory. The endorsements for Farfan's book speak of his long years of experience as a physician (he evidently obtained his medical degree on 20 July 1567 from the Real y Pontificia Universidad de Mexico).[39] Farfan and López both describe their books as being intended for those who are far from cities and need to learn about remedies for illness and medical practices.[40]

In its general nature, the *Libellus de Medicinalibus* of Badianus and de la Cruz is similar to the works of Farfan and López de Hinojosos. It, too, is a description of medical practices, primarily based on herbal medicines. Its intended audience was Don Francisco de Mendoza, son of the viceroy of New Spain. The title of the book can be translated as "A Little Book of Indian Medicinal Herbs Composed by a Certain Indian, Physician of the College of Santa Cruz, Who Has No Theoretical Learning, but Is Well Taught by Experience Alone."[41] The emphasis is upon experience rather than upon theory, and the approach of the book is purely descriptive, including extensive recipes of herbal medicines. The book is organized in a straightforward head-to-foot manner, following the organization of the human body. The dedication of the work is very revealing in the attitudes of native physicians toward their Spanish overlords. Badianus and de la Cruz were, of course, educated at the College of Santa Cruz at Tlalolco, which was established by Franciscan missionaries to educate the sons of Aztec nobles. De la Cruz includes in the dedication the following statement:

Indeed I suspect that you ask so earnestly for this little book of herbs and medicaments for no other reason than to commend us Indians, even though unworthy, to His Holy Caesarian Catholic Royal Majesty. Would that we Indians could make a book worthy in the King's sight, for this is certainly most unworthy to come before the sight of such great majesty. But you will recollect that we poor unhappy Indians are inferior to all mortals, and for that reason our poverty and insignificance implanted in us by nature merit your indulgence.[42]

The *Libellus* is enlivened with colored drawings of the herbs that are described, and the work contains such typical Aztec remedies as acozoyatl for treatment of one affected by a whirlwind.[43] It is interesting to note that conditions such as "fatigue, . . . lassitude suffered by officials holding public office," "fear . . . or faintheartedness," and "mental stupor"[44] are included as conditions to be treated with herbal remedies. Although the work reflects Aztec traditions, it contains nothing of the rich religious traditions that underlay the practice of Aztec medicine. It reflects a European bias in its statements concerning the lowly status of the natives. Its concern for practical treatment rather than theory may represent a European orientation (Sahagun's book 10 follows the same head-to-foot orientation and statement of specific treatments) that ignored the religiously based aspects of Aztec medicine, but it may also reflect a kind of pragmatic orientation toward treatment of illness that is somewhat similar to the works of Farfan and López de Hinojosos.

Conflict Between Rationality and Religion

If Bravo and Hernández represent the purely rational and theoretical tradition of European medicine, and Farfan and López de Hinojosos represent both the rational and pragmatic aspects, Bernardino de Sahagun represents the conflict of rational thought and religious belief, belief in both Christian and Aztec culture. The initial charge to Sahagun, given by the provincial father Francisco de Toral, was that Sahagun should write in the Nahuatl language those things that he considered useful for the maintenance of Christianity and the work and ministering of Christian doctrines.[45] Sahagun gathered information from Aztec informants and cross-checked his information with Aztecs in various parts of the country. But his original intent was to use the information to convince the Aztecs of the errors of their past ways. He thus included after his description of major deities a tract condemning the worship of those deities:

My children, perceive God's word, which is God's light. Thus will see those who live in darkness, who have lost the way; those who worship idols, who go with the sins of the devil, who is the father of lies. And thus will be known to them their gods and their lords which the word of God, which here, lying unfolded, revealeth how idolatry began. Likewise here are revealed many things concerning the error, misery, and blindness into which the worshippers of idols fell.[46]

Sahagun's work remains the standard source for descriptions of Aztec medical practices. It is interesting to note, however, that, like the work by de la Cruz and Badianus, Sahagun's work was not published in his lifetime. Indeed, it was not until 1830 that even a partial edition of the work was published.[47]

Medical Knowledge from the New World

In the contacts between medical practices in the New World and the Old, the major point at which exchange of information took place was in the area of herbal medicines. Indians were certainly treated by European practitioners in hospitals such as the Royal Hospital for Indians, where Hernández and López de Hinojosos worked together. But in terms of the overall structure of medical practices, European physicians did not adopt any of the religiously based ideas of the Aztecs concerning medical practices, and Aztecs did not immediately adopt any European practices that they did not already have.

An interesting example of the transmission of knowledge from Aztec to European sources is the plant *cacaloxochitl*, which is mentioned in Hernández's *De Rerum Medicarum*, the *Libellus*, and Sahagun's *Historia General*. The physical description of the plant differs in the *De Rerum Medicarum* and the *Historia General*. The physical description in Hernández reads as follows:

It is a tree of medium size with leaves like citrus, but much larger and with abundant veins which run from the center vein to the edges. The fruits are one pod, very large and red; the flowers are large, beautiful and of pleasing, pleasant scent, and are the only part that is used; they are used to make nosegays, garlands and crowns, things much used among the Indians and held in such esteem that they never appear before a head person without offering beforehand some of these offerings. It makes milk. Cooled and congealed, and applied, it is a cure for the illness of the breast which comes from heat. Its marrow, taken in a dose in two drachms, cleanses the stomach and the intestines.[48]

Sahagun describes the plant in the following terms:

It is a bush that they call cacaloxochitl; it has leaves that are somewhat broad, and somewhat long, and downy. It has branches straight and spongy, and the leaves and branches sometimes make milk, and this milk is sweet as honey. The flowers of this tree are beautiful. They are called also cacaloxochitl. They are bronze colored, of red, yellow and white. They have a delicate odor, and they comfort the spirit with their odor. Through the districts of Mexico one has these flowers, but those which come from warm lands are better; some are black. In former times these flowers were reserved for the lords.[49]

Badianus and de la Cruz do not give a written description of the plant, but their drawing shows a plant with red flowers and long, slender leaves. The veins mentioned in Hernández's description do not appear in the drawing.[50] The flowers of the plants are part of a very elaborate herbal formula entitled "Trees and Flowers for the Fatigue of Those Administering the Government and Holding Public Office."[51] That the plant is the same in all three sources, despite the discrepancies in written description, can be determined primarily by the fact that all three sources mention the same use for the plant, i.e., in relation to lords or high government officials. However, Badianus and de la Cruz mention a specific condition of those persons, fatigue related to holding high office, and the plant is thus treated as part of a remedy that would drive weariness away and would drive out fear and fortify the heart.[52] Hernández and Sahagun do not attribute any medicinal properties to the plant in its use as an offering to high officials. They do mention other medicinal uses, however.

In the contracts between medical practices in the New World and the Old, the only major point at which exchange of information took place was in the area of herbal medicines. Those were adopted by Europeans seemingly as a matter of the practical necessities of dealing with the diseases and health conditions in the New World. Interest in Aztec culture was primarily ethnographic in nature (as in Sahagun's work), or was firmly embedded in the natural-history tradition of European academic inquiry (as in Hernández's work). The very pragmatic nature of medical practice provided the only real point of contract between two very disparate systems of medical treatment. The importation of New World plants (such as guaiacum) to the Old World, and of Old World plants to the New World, and a mutual concern with the efficacy of herbal remedies, provided the only substantial evidence of cross-cultural medical practices.

NOTES

1. See Alfred W. Crosby, Jr., *The Columbia Exchange: Biological and Cultural Consequences of 1492* (Westport, Conn.: Greenwood Press, 1972), pp. 165–208, for a discussion of New World plants and Old World demography. See also Francisco Guerra, "Drugs from the Indies and the Political Economy of the Sixteenth Century," *Analecta medico—historica*, 1 (1966): 29–54.

2. William M. Denevan, ed., *The Native Population of the Americas in 1492* (Madison: Univ. of Wisconsin, 1976), 7.

3. Agustin Farfan, *Tractado breve de anathomia y Chirugia, y de algunas enfermedades, que mas comunmente suelen hauer en esta nueua Espana. Compuesto por el muy reuerendo padre Fray Augustin Farfan, Doctor en medicina, y religioso de la orden de Sant Augustin. Dirigido al muy reuerendo padre maestro Fray Martin de Perea, Prouincial de la dicha orden de Sant Augustin.* (Mexico: Casa de Antonio Ricardo, 1579), 223–64.

4. Juan de Cardenas, *Primera parte de los problemas y secretos marauillosos de las Indias* (Mexico: Casa de Pedro Ocharte, 1591; reprinted Mexico City: Imprenta del Museo Nacional de Arqueologia, Historia y Etnologia, 1913), 185–86, 191, 193.

5. See Sherburne F. Cook, "The Incidence and Significance of Disease Among the Aztecs and Related Tribes," *Hispanic American Historical Review*, 26 (1946): 320–35.

6. Crosby, *Columbia Exchange*, pp. 122–64; Francisco Guerra, "The Problem of Syphilis," in Fredi Chiappelli, ed., *First Images of America* (Berkeley: Univ. of California, 1976), 2:845–51.

7. Charles H. Talbot, "America and the European Drug Trade," in Chiappelli, ed., *First Images of America*, 2:834–36.

8. Juan Comas, "Influencia Indigena en la medicina hipocratica en la Neuva Espana del siglo XVI," *America Indigena*, 14 (1954):329.

9. Francisco Bravo, *Opera medicinalia in quibus plurima extant scitu medico necessaria in 4 li. digesta, que pagina versa cotinentur, Authore Francisco Bravo Ofunesi doctore, ac Mexicano Medico* (Mexico): Apud Petrum Ocharte, 1570). A facsimile reprint edition of Bravo's work, *The Opera Medicinalia* (Folkestone and London: Dawsons of Pall Mall, 1970), with an introduction by Francisco Guerra, makes the work available for scholarly study. Guerra cites the *Opera* as the earliest medical work published in the New World (see his introductory statements, p. 2).

10. Francisco Hernández, *De Rerum Medicarum Novae Hispaniae Thesaurus seu Plantarum Animalium Mineralium Mexicanorum Historia ex Francisci Hernandi Novi Orbis Medici Primarij relationibus in ipsa Mexicana Urbe conscriptis a Nardo Antonio Recchio Monte Coriunate Cath. Maiest. Medico et Neap. Regni Archiatro Generali Iussu Philippi II Hisp. Indar. Regis Collecta ac in ordinem digesta a Ioanne Terrentio Lynceo Constantiense Germ. Pho. ac Medico Notis illustrata Nunc primum in Naturaliũ rerũ Studiosor gratia et utilitatê studio et impensis Lynceorum. Publici iuris facta Philippo IV Magno Dicata* (Rome: Iacobi Mascardi, 1628). A new printing of the work, with a new title page, appeared in 1651. See Francisco Hernández, *Nova Plantarum, animalium et mineralium mexicanorum historia A Francisco Hernández primum compilata, dein a Nardo Antonio Reccho in volumen digesta, a Jo. Terentio, Io. Fabro, et Fabio Columna Lynceis notis, & additionibus longe doctissimis illustrata. Cui demum accessere aliquot ex principio Federici Caesi frontispiciis Theatri naturalis phytosophicae tabulae una com quamplurimus iconibus ad octigentus, quibus singula contemplanda graphica exhibentur* (Rome: V. Mascardi, 1651). The 1651 printing is much more readily available than the 1628. Hernández, during his stay in Mexico, collected 17 volumes of material, which he transmitted to Spain, where Philip II deposited them in the Escorial. A fire in the Escorial destroyed the manuscript in 1671. A version of the manuscript was derived from a copy left in the mission at Huaxtepec and was published in 1615 by Francisco Ximenez under the title *Quatro libros de la naturaleza, y virtudes de las plantas, y animales que estan recevidos en el uso de Medicina en la Neuva Espana, y la Methodo, y correccion y preparacion, que para ad mimmallas se requiree con lo que el Doctor Francisco Hernandez escrivio en lengua Latina. Muy util Paratodo Generode gente q vive en estacias y Pueblos, de no ay Medicas, ni Botica. Traduzido y aumentados muchos simples, y compuestos y muchos secretos curativos, por Father Francisco Ximenez, hijo del Conuento de S. Domingo de Mexico, natural de la Villa de Luna del Reyno de Aragon. A Nro R. P. Maestro Father Hernando Bazan, Prior Provincial de la Provincia de Sactiago de Mexico, de la Orden de los Prelicadores, y Cathedratico Iubilado de Theologia en la Universidad Real.* (Mexico: Casa de la Viuda de Diego Lopez Davalos, 1615). Further published versions of Hernández's work are based primarily on the 1628 (or 1651) edition of the summary by Reccho. The two modern editions of the work are *Historia de las plantas de Nueva Espana*, 3 vols. (Mexico: Imprenta Universitaria, 1942–46); and Francisco Hernández, *Obras completas*, 5 vols. (Mexico City: Universidad Nacional de Mexico, 1960), which includes not only the Mexican work but Hernández's translation of Pliny's *Natural History*. In 1790, an edition of Hernández's work, based on the Reccho manuscript, appeared as *Opera, cum edita, tum inedita, ad autographi fidem et integritatem expressa, impensae el jussu regio* (Matriti: Ibarrae Heredum, 1970).

11. Farfan, *Tractado Breve*. The 1595 edition is *Summa y recopilación de chirugia, compuesto por mestro Alonso López de Hinofosos, con un arte para Sangrar, y examen de*

Barberos, va anadido en esta segunda impression el origen y nascimientes de las reumas y las enfermedades que dellas proceden, con otras cosas muy provechosas para acudir al remedio dellas, y del otras muchas enfermedades (Mexico: Pedro Balli, 1595).

12. Alonso Lopez de Hinojosos, *Summa y recopilacion de chirugia, con un arte para sagrar muy util y prouechosa. Compuesta por maestre alonso Lopez, natural de los Inojosos. Chirugano y enfermero del Ospital de S. Iosephus de los Indios, destra muy insigne Ciudada de Mexico. Dirigido al Lii. Y. R. S. Don P. Moya de Contreras, Arcobispe de Mexico y del cocejo de su Magest.* (Mexico: Antonio Ricardo, 1578). See note 11 for 1595 edition.

13. *Libellus de medicinalibus Indorum herbis, quem quidam Indus Collegii sancte Crucis medicus compusuit, nullis rationibus edoctus, sed solis experimentis edoctus, Anno domini sexuatovis 1552.* The manuscript was discovered in the Vatican library and finally published, first as *The de la Cruz-Badiano Aztec Herbal of 1552,* trans. William Gates (Baltimore, Md.: The Maya Society, 1939), and then as *The Badianus Manuscript (Codex Barberini, Latin 241), Vatican Library, an Aztec Herbal of 1552,* introduction, translation, and annotations by Emily Walcott Emmart (Baltimore, Md.: John Hopkins, 1940).

14. Bernardino de Sahagun, *Historia general de las cosas de nueva España,* 5 vols. (Mexico Editorial Pedro Robredo, 1938). See also Fray Bernardino de Sahagun, *A History of Ancient Mexico (1547–1577),* trans. Fanny R. Bandelier from the Spanish version of Carlos Maria de Bustamenta, vol. 1 (Nashville: Tenn.: Fisk University, 1932). Subsequent editions of the work include *Historia general de las cosas de nueva Espana, escrita por Fr. Bernardino de Sahagun Franciscano y fundada en la documentacion en lingua mexicana recogida por los mismos naturales. La dispuso para la prensa en esta nueva edicion, con numeracion anotaciones y apendices Angel Maria Garibay K.,* 4 vols. (Mexico: Editorial Porua, 1956); *Historia general de las cosas de nueva Espana,* 5 vols. (Mexico: Editorial Pedro Robredo, 1938); and *General History of the Things of New Spain,* trans. Charles E. Dibble and Arthur J.Q. Anderson. Monographs of the School of American Research and the Museum of New Mexico, part 13 (Santa Fe, N.M.: 1950–65).

15. Erwin H. Ackerknecht, "Problems of Primitive Medicine," *Bulletin of the History of Medicine,* 2 (1942): 504.

16. Sahagun, *General History,* 2:16. See also Francisco Guerra, "Aztec Medicine," *Medical History,* 10 (1966): 320, for a general discussion of Aztec medical practices.

17. Sahagun, *General History,* part 11:139–63, 53; part 2:1–24.

18. Farfan, *Tractado breve* (1579), 17; and López de Hinojosos, *Summa y Recopilacion* (1578), 1–2.

19. López de Hinojosos, ibid., 3.

20. Joaquín García Icazabalceta, *Bibliografia mexicana del siglo XVI. Catalogo razonado de libros impresos en mexico de 1539 a 1600 con biografias de auteres y otras ilustraciones* (Mexico: Fondo de Cultura Economica, 1954), 235–36.

21. The connection between Hernández and Sahagun is established in Ioannis Nieremberg's *Historia naturae maxime peregrinae: Libris XVI distincta: In quibus rarissima Naturae arcana, etiam astronomica, & ignota Indarum animalia describuntur; Accedunt de miris et miraculosis naturis in Europa libri duo; item de iisdem in terra Hebraeis premissa liber unus* (Antverpiae: Ex Officina Plantiniana Balthasaris Moreti, 1635). Nieremberg attributed part of his book 2 directly to Hernández. The manuscript source from which he drew these chapters seems to be no longer extant. However, the chapters in Nieremberg's book are virtually identical to the appendix to book 2 of Sahagun's

Historia general. The material is a listing of religious ceremonies. See Nieremberg, pp. 142–44, and Sahagun, *General History*, 3:165–71. Leon Portilla asserts that Nieremberg took the material from Hernández without realizing that Hernández had in turn copied it from Sahagun's manuscripts. It is surprising then that there are not more correspondences between the descriptions of plants in the Hernández and Sahagun works. See Miguel Leon-Portilla, *Ritos, sacerdotes y atavios de los dioses: Introduccion, paleografia, version & notas de Miguel Leon-Portilla* (Mexico: Universidad Nacional Autonoma de Mexico, Instituto de Historia; Seminario de Cultura Nahuatl, 1958), 21.

22. Sahagun, *History of Ancient Mexico*, 3–9.

23. Bravo, *Opera medicinalia*, 2v–3, 167v, 273–74, 295v.

24. Ibid., 4, 8, 273–74.

25. Ibid., 79.

26. De la Cruz, *The de la cruz-Badiano aztec herbal*, xvii.

27. Hernández, *De rerum medicarum*, 8–9.

28. Ibid., 29–30.

29. See, for example, Farfan, *Tractado breve* (1579), pp. 2, 4v, 107; López de Hinojosos, *Summa y recopilación* (1578), 1, 2.

30. Farfan, ibid., 7r.

31. Ibid., 55v.

32. Ibid., 217v.

33. Ibid., 87.

34. Comas, "Influencia indigena," 345–61.

35. López de Hinojosos, *Summa y recopilacion* (1578), 16.

36. Ibid., 70.

37. Farfan, *Tractado breve* (1579), 77; López de Hinojosos, *Summa y recompilación*, 34v.

38. Scarification and bleeding were known to the Aztecs. The Badianus manuscript mentions a cure for veins swelling because of bloodletting, p. 281, in the heading of chapter 10, but the text does not include a specific cure as indicated by the heading of the chapter. Sahagun, *General History*, mentions bleeding the scalp as a cure for headache, 2:140.

39. Farfan, *Tractado breve* (1579), 1–2; Comas, "Influencia indigena," 344.

40. López de Hinojosos, *Summa y recopilacion* (1578), 16; Farfan, *Tractado breve*, 17.

41. De la Cruz, *Libellus*, 205.

42. Ibid.

43. Ibid., 306.

44. Ibid., 207–8.

45. Sahagun, *History of Ancient Mexico*, 3–9.

46. Sahagun, *General History*, 2:34.

47. Sahagun, *History of Ancient Mexico*, 13–14.

48. Hernández, *Historia de las plantas*, 3:806.

49. Sahagun, *Historia general*, 3:276.

50. De la Cruz, *Badianus Manuscript*, 276–77.

51. Ibid.

52. Ibid.

3

Traditional Medicine and Western Medical Options among the Ningerum of Papua New Guinea

Robert L. Welsch

> The practices of these peoples in relation to disease are not a medley of disconnected and meaningless customs, but are inspired by definite ideas concerning the causation of disease. Their modes of treatment follow directly from their ideas concerning etiology and pathology. From our modern standpoint we are able to see that these ideas are wrong. But the important point is that, however wrong may be the beliefs of the Papuan and Melanesian concerning the causation of disease, their practices are a logical consequence of those beliefs.
>
> W. H. R. Rivers, 1924

This chapter considers the expectations, attitudes, and beliefs about Western medicine held by the Ningerum people of Papua New Guinea. My concern here is to show how the Ningerum perceive interrelationships between traditional and recently introduced Western curative practices. In particular I will argue that the Ningerum people's extensive use of Western medicine is closely related to their understanding of disease processes.

The Ningerum, a lowland rainforest people, became aware of the outside world barely 30 years ago. With the arrival of government, missions, and mineral explorations teams, the Ningerums' familiarity with Western ways has expanded rapidly. Despite a certain amount of ambivalence, they have endorsed the government's rule of law, their own local government council, national and local elections, wage labor, money, and economic development. Although economic development has been minimal (see Jackson, Emerson, and Welsch 1980) and money is scarce, they have access to government and mission stations, trading stores and imported goods, shotguns, primary schools, and Western-style medical care.

The Ningerum are a very traditionally oriented society. They have no cash crops, they send few of their children to school, few men are employed as wage laborers, and subsistence activities remain largely as they were before government control. Their pig feasts and other ceremonies are frequent social occasions, practiced very much in their traditional ways. In contrast to their response to other innovations, the Ningerum have rapidly and eagerly accepted Western medicine. Every Ningerum person uses Western medicine—although not necessarily for every illness. Moreover, if one considers villages with easy access to an aid post, one finds that the aid post orderly (APO) provides more medical treatments than all traditional practitioners combined.

COMPARATIVE RESPONSE TO WESTERN MEDICINE OF NINGERUM AND BAKONGO

Prior to the arrival of the Australian Administration, the Ningerum had an extensive repertoire of curative and diagnostic practices. Although they are now regular and heavy users of government- and mission-sponsored health-care services, they continue to use most of their traditional medical practices. Ningerum acceptance of Western medical care is fairly typical of what has occurred in other non-Western communities. Janzen's (1978:3) description of BaKongo responses to Western medicine is equally applicable to the Ningerum.

The people of Zaire recognize the advantages of Western medicine and seek its drugs, surgery and hospital care, but contrary to what might have been expected, native doctors, prophets, and traditional consultations among kinsmen do not disappear with the adoption of Western medicine. Rather a modus vivendi has developed in which different forms of therapy play complementary rather than competitive roles in the thoughts and lives of the people.

Whereas the BaKongo response to Western medicine is the result of nearly a century of contact with introduced medical practices, the Ningerum response reflects barely a decade of regularly available Western medicines. In less than a generation the Ningerum have substantially changed their methods of treating a variety of illnesses. They have tried Western medicine, assessed its strengths and weaknesses, and incorporated Western medical services into a number of different treatment strategies. These strategies include both traditional and introduced treatments and regularly employ them together in a complementary fashion.

NON-WESTERN ASSIMILATION OF WESTERN MEDICINE: OVERVIEW

To the Ningerum, Western medicine initially appeared as an incomprehensible, alien, and perhaps undifferentiated means of dealing with sickness. But after fifteen years of more or less regular access to aid posts and small rural hospitals, they no longer view Western medicine in these ways. In assessing the strengths and limitations of Western care, they have integrated aid-post and hospital treatment with their own traditional practices. In short, Ningerum people—as opposed to Western health workers—do not see Western and traditional medicine as in competition, in conflict, or contradictory. Instead of being an intrusive, discrete medical system that is poorly integrated into the local society and culture, Western medicine is part of a differentiated but nevertheless integrated system of health care, one that relies heavily upon both Western and traditional practices.

Analytically, many studies of illness behavior in rural non-Western settings implicitly (if not explicitly) consider Western medicine on the one hand and indigenous curing practices on the other as essentially discrete medical systems that in one way or another are in competition or conflict. The labels used to describe these medical practices, such as modern medicine, cosmopolitan medicine, folk medicine, and primitive medicine, imply fundamental differences between traditional and introduced practices, just as they suggest that each operates as a separate medical system. Such studies frequently view patients as deciding among alternative medical systems—rather than choosing from among alternative treatments—as if each were an undifferentiated system of treatment practices.

Medical professions in Western countries encourage this view of practitioners as working within different "medical systems." From the practitioners' perspective, their practices often do have a certain coherence that may justify labeling each as a separate medical system. They may, for example, have professional trade secrets, professional economic interests, and esoteric theories of pathology and etiology. Thus an anthropology of comparative medical systems is possible (e.g., Leslie 1976; Kleinman et al. 1976; Morley and Wallis 1978).

My concern here is with users rather than with practitioners. If we want to understand how users conceptualize different therapeutic options and select from among these options, we cannot assume that users distinguish between medical systems in the same ways as practitioners, or even that they necessarily distinguish between medical systems at all (which is not to say that they do not distinguish among different therapies and different therapeutic goals).

Treatment Choices in Western Medicine

The structure of Western medical consultation also encourages a view of medical systems as undifferentiated systems of treatment practices. Physicians generally make their own diagnoses and prescribe treatment in terms of these diagnoses; patients merely recognize and present complaints. Given such a situation, the patient's decision to consult a physician is logically the same whether the doctor prescribes antibiotics, a diuretic, or confinement. Where self-diagnosis is more typically the rule, as in Ningerum, these same treatments may constitute quite different courses of action for the patient. This is particularly true when patients select practitioners for specific kinds of treatment, based on their own self-diagnosis.

Attempts to account for observed treatment choices generally stem from a single kind of explanation, namely, that because Western medicine is an introduced medical system, it is in some way less well integrated into the society and culture of the users than traditional practices. The usual task in explaining underutilization, noncompliance, and delays in seeking Western treatment has been to identify those areas where local beliefs and values, practices, role relationships, or economic requirements conflict with those of the Western system. There are many examples of this approach to treatment decisions: Adair and Deuschle (1970), Clark (1959), and Garrison (1977) consider a range of conflict areas; Cassel (1955), Carstairs (1955), Gonzalez (1966), Rubel (1960), L. Schwartz (1969), and Young (1976) examine conflicting beliefs, values, and expectations; Mitchell (1976) looks at differences between the general practice of medicine in the traditional and introduced medical systems; and Madsen (1964), Marriott (1955), Peck (1968), Press (1969), and Stanhope (1968) consider role relationships and socioeconomic factors. Each of these studies looks to one conflict area or another to demonstrate the poor integration of Western medicine within the local setting and thus explain underutilization as an artifact of the intrusive nature of Western medicine.

Although these studies offer valuable insights into how introduced medical practices do not always meet the needs of the users, their authors tend to have difficulty explaining how introduced medicine can and often does meet local users' needs. Explaining the tenacity of traditional beliefs and expectations in terms of the meaning system of the community does not help to clarify why non-Western peoples typically make heavy use of the Western medical system.

Paradoxically, studies accounting for the regular use of Western medicine for certain classes of illness often assume the same things about Western medicine's poor integration within the non-Western setting. They agree that Western and traditional medical systems differ in theory, in practice, and in practitioners' style, but argue that patients use Western medicine in spite of these differences—because they observe the empirical results of the superior Western medicine.

The strongest proponents of this view have been Erasmus (1952) and Foster (e.g., 1958), both of whom have argued that "in all societies people are remarkably pragmatic in testing and evaluating new alternatives, in deciding whether it is to their advantage to innovate" (Foster and Anderson

1978:245). While I do not for a moment doubt that people evaluate their available treatment options, I do question whether this evaluation is made without reference to indigenous illness beliefs. Foster and Anderson in essence argue that these practices are—for the users—a hodgepodge of poorly understood and meaningless practices. They say that the decision to use new practices is a pragmatic one, thus a decision made without reference to theory. Such decisions are "exercised on a situational basis" (1978:248), and subsequently, "all kinds of accommodations are made and all manner of rationalizations appear to justify continuing faith in the old system while simultaneously accepting the new" (1978:251). In short, because of their pragmatism when confronting new practices, non-Western people make decisions to use Western medicine in a haphazard and ad hoc way. Foster ends up in this untenable position because he insists that a community must view its own traditional practices and the newly introduced ones as discrete theoretical and practical systems. Underutilization is the result of slowly changing beliefs (and thus a conflict between the two systems) while the use of Western medicine is the result of empirical observations and human pragmatism that leave these introduced practices poorly integrated with the older, more traditional, practices.

My own observations of treatment choices in the Ningerum area suggest that introduced Western medicine is highly integrated into the local setting. Ningerum people have very definite ideas about how Western medicine works. These understandings are different from the theories of Western physicians, but are no more disconnected from Ningerum illness beliefs than are traditional medical practices. The observed pattern of aid-post and hospital attendance, including regular use of Western medicine as well as delays, noncompliance, and occasional nonuse, can best be explained in terms of the integration of the two medical traditions and in terms of the differing expectations that the Ningerum have of different kinds of treatment. Differences between Western and traditional Ningerum theories of illness exist, but Ningerum people are largely unaware of such differences. A single theory of illness accommodates Western as well as more traditional medical practices.

If we are to understand medical practices and thus the particular treatments that patients seek when they are sick, we must consider their beliefs about illness causation and pathology. But unlike Rivers, who was little concerned with the introduction of Western medicine in non-Western communities, I feel we should first seek explanations of *all* treatment choices in these same indigenous illness beliefs—whether the treatments chosen have their origins in indigenous or introduced medical traditions. The issue is not to show how indigenous and Western medical practices or principles are different: rather, our task should be to examine how non-Western peoples interpret and then make use of the new practices available to them.

To assume that Western medicine somehow stands apart from traditional curative practices and is poorly integrated within the local setting tends to lead analysis away from any understanding of how users actually conceptualize Western medicine and how these conceptualizations influence actual treatment choices. In short, I suggest a model of illness behavior that assumes a local interpretation of medical events and syncretism rather than conflict between a well-integrated traditional medical system and a poorly integrated new one.

NINGERUM CONTACT WITH EUROPEAN MEDICINE

Approximately 4,500 Ningerum people inhabit the hilly country immediately to the south of the Star Mountains on both sides of the border between Papua New Guinea and Indonesia. They are an interior lowlands people, practicing shifting cultivation and pig husbandry in a dense rainforest environment. Sago and bananas, the staple foods, are supplemented with tubers. Prior to European contact, the settlement pattern was one of individually dispersed homesteads, each containing a single extended family related by marriage and kinship ties to neighboring family groups. At the encouragement of both the government and the mission, the Ningerum formed villages, but continue to spend the larger portion of their time on their own family territories, away from the villages. These "bush houses" continue to be the families' primary residences, providing privacy and easy access to gardens and hunting territories.

Although some Ningerum were aware of Europeans in the early 1920s, government control and regular contact with Europeans did not begin until after 1950. During the early years following government control, many men had the opportunity to visit other parts of the country, working for wages as casual or contract laborers. Many were carriers for government and petroleum exploration patrols; others worked on plantations near Sorong, Port Moresby, and other centers; still others helped open government stations at Kiunga in 1951, Nomad River in 1962, and Ningerum in 1964. Today few have regular employment, per capita income is less than K10 ($15) per year, and the economy continues to be subsistence oriented. Knowledge of and interest in the outside world remain very limited.

Prior to the opening of Ningerum patrol post, access to Western medicine was minimal, consisting largely of infrequent patrols to control yaws or immunize the people against cholera and smallpox. Government administrative patrols gave routine treatments during their annual visits and contract laborers generally had regular access to medical care. About 1960 the government opened an aid post in the neighboring Yongom area, which was accessible to some Ningerum people.

Creation of Aid Posts

Partly as a response to a localized but serious dysentery outbreak, the Australian Administration opened the first aid post in Ningerum Census Division in 1963. The aid post orderly (APO) was reposted within the first year and was not replaced until about 1965. Staffing continued to be irregular until 1968, but since then APO postings have been continuous. Permanent staffing does not mean, however, that an APO is always present in the village to treat the sick. APO visits to Ningerum station for supplies, recreation leave, in-service training, and other absences typically leave the aid post unstaffed for three to six months each year.

This original aid post was located at Bwakim village, half an hour's walk from Hukim village, where I lived for two years. Large numbers of deaths due to dysentery and influenza epidemics led Bwakim people to relocate both their village and aid post three times in the following ten years. In 1976 the villagers decided to move the aid post to Hukim, where most of the original Bwakim families now reside. Despite the periodic relocation of this aid post, it continues to serve the same families as it did in 1963.

In 1964 the government opened an aid post at Ningerum patrol post. About the same time the Unevangelised Fields Mission opened the third aid post serving Ningerum Census Division. At this time all of the APOs were Papuans from Western Province but none were Ningerum. Their training was fairly basic; they were expected to treat the most common medical problems, viz., malaria, acute respiratory infections, gastroenteritis and diarrheal diseases, cuts and sores. As the first level of rural health care, they were expected to refer more serious conditions to rural hospitals.

The aid post at Ningerum patrol post was eventually upgraded to a rural health center, which made referrals from the village aid posts more convenient than the three- or four-day walk to Kiunga Health Centre. Staffing at Ningerum Health Centre increased steadily during the 1970s, and in 1979 there was a staff of ten, all Papua New Guineans. Maternal-child health (MCH) clinics began in the area about 1970. These clinics are held in the villages; patrols visit the villages three to six times a year, providing prenatal examinations for pregnant women as well as immunizations and regular exams for children up to five years. Before 1978 these patrols were conducted by European nurses, but at present, nurses and APOs conduct alternate patrols. MCH patrols have been the only area of health care provided directly by Europeans rather than by Papua New Guineans.

Perhaps the most significant change in health care delivery has been the training of local people from the Ningerum area as health workers. Since 1972 four Ningerum men have completed APO training and one woman has recently finished nurse aide training. One of these APOs and the nurse aide are from Hukim village.

For the village people, training Ningerum men as APOs has led to a stronger identification with the aid post and has added to the feeling that the aid post is a Ningerum institution. Training as a health worker is highly valued and many young men are seeking sponsorship for APO training. Local people take a keen interest in the selection and sponsorship of APO trainees by their elected local government council.

THE ORGANIZATION OF TRADITIONAL MEDICAL PRACTICES

Before considering the ways that Ningerum people interpret aid-post medical services, I want to examine, briefly, two aspects of how Ningerum curative practices are organized: (1) the distribution of therapeutic knowledge and expertise in the community; (2) the locus of diagnostic and therapeutic decision making. The organization of medical care structures the social production of knowledge about illness and its treatment. It provides culturally meaningful guidelines for how medical decisions ought to be made and who should make these decisions.

Every society has a certain body of medical knowledge readily available to anyone who cares to know about it. This is the basis of nonspecialist treatment, practices that have often been called "home remedies," but are more usefully considered as "individual and family based care" (Kleinman 1976). The Ningerum have many "self-help" therapies that require no special skills or abilities, no special training, and no specialized knowledge. Anyone may perform them for themselves or their relatives.

These treatments include topical herbal preparations, warm baths, rest, healthful foods, and nettles, or the proper ways to stop external bleeding, dress cuts, and treat fainting. Family-based care often includes the use of simple divinations and rituals that will identify and banish attacking ghosts. It often uses ritual techniques having to do with men's cult secrets (these secrets are not available to women, but are part of the standard repertoire of male knowledge).

The Ningerum also have a variety of specialized therapeutic and diagnostic practices. These are used for illnesses that people fear might lead to permanent disability, chronic weakness, or death. A practitioner must be expressly instructed in the proper procedures, ingredients, and ritual formulae if the treatment is to be effective.

These medical treatments require a certain amount of skill that can come only with experience. As with other skills—including successful gardening, pig tending, hunting, feasting, and control over valuables—the Ningerum believe that therapeutic abilities require jealousy guarded esoteric knowledge if they are to be done well. Individual aptitude is important, but uncommon, secret knowledge is essential.

Esoteric Knowledge

Esoteric knowledge is a source of power or control over external forces, and its possession makes one person's gardens more productive than another's, and some people's pigs fatter and less likely to run away. Access to uncommon knowledge produces fine hunters; it gives some men the means to put on fantastically successful feasts, allows some the ability to ensorcell their enemies or to change into various animals or to perform other extraordinary feats. Esoteric knowledge allows some men to acquire more wealth than others or to perform one of these specialized curative practices.

Instruction in the details of sucking out tiny ghost arrows or removing sorcery packets from a patient's body can come only from another specialist practitioner. Similarly, in order to perform an *anggun* ("burning bark") divination, or any of a dozen other therapeutic and diagnostic practices, one must be taught properly by someone who has the esoteric knowledge. Each skill is totally independent of all others, and, like all esoteric knowledge among the Ningerum, is customarily passed on from father to son. Men do not always teach their sons these closely guarded secrets, however, sometimes because they die first, but often for their own idiosyncratic reasons. As with other kinds of magic, therapeutic knowledge is property that can be given away or sold.

Ningerum society lacks "big men" in the classic New Guinea sense, just as traditionally there were no villages or other bounded political units larger than the extended family. Everyone engages in the same economic and social activities, and there is little in the ordinary pattern of daily life to distinguish one man from another. In a social field consisting of men who are virtually identical to himself, a Ningerum man can individuate himself only through his own outstanding abilities and esoteric knowledge.

From the Ningerum point of view, individuals are born with nearly identical capabilities, but as children mature, subtle personal differences lead them to develop their own aptitudes and interests, eventually leading them into particular fields of individuation or specialization through the acquisition of esoteric knowledge and expertise. Uncommon knowledge is power; it is implicitly magical and extraordinary, even when it includes no ritual formulae and has purely instrumental goals. This knowledge rather than innate ability is what makes a fine hunter or a therapeutic specialist.

Individuals cultivate these extranormal abilities and learn the esoteric things they can from their fathers or whoever will teach them. They acquire reputations for having narrowly defined specialties, expertise that surpasses what others are able to do in activities in which everyone has some ability. They keep their uncommon knowledge secret, unless they decide to train someone else. On occasion others call upon them for assistance that requires their particular abilities; when someone is ill, the patient or close relatives will send for a friend or relative who knows the necessary curative practice.

What emerges is a pattern that Watson (1980) describes as "consensual complementarity." Through a general consent, individuals have their own specialties, and everyone knows who possesses what special types of knowledge. Ningerum people frequently would say about one practice or another, "*De kaa, ne kaa duwam*" ("He knows [how to do it]; I don't know").

While control over esoteric knowledge and consequent control over others has many implications for Ningerum social dynamics—which I will not go into here—the implications for Ningerum medical care are striking. While everyone in the community shares the ability and knowledge of nonspecialized treatment, only a select few can perform any particular treatment that might be used with very serious illnesses. Everyone understands the general principles and methods of specialist therapy.

Specialization of Traditional Practice

Ningerum practitioners are specialists with one or perhaps two therapies. They are not general practitioners in the way that practitioners appear to be in other parts of Papua New Guinea (cf. Johannes 1980; Glick 1967; Nelson 1971; Luzbetak 1958). They do not have a broad inventory of curative practices available to them. Instead, Ningerum practitioners are selected because they can perform certain specialties; they are not consulted to make a diagnosis and then prescribe the appropriate therapy.

No Ningerum practitioner could treat every kind of illness, nor would a practitioner be asked to do so. Patients and their families must seek the treatments they feel are most appropriate to the condition: they must send for a practitioner—often a friend, relative, or affine. By selecting the practitioner they are thus selecting the kind of treatment that will be performed. This places the diagnostic burden on the patient and the family; it makes self-diagnosis an inherent part of traditional practice. Without self-diagnosis or a family-based diagnosis a patient could not get appropriate treatment.

Ningerum individual and family-based care, then, penetrates into the more specialized sector of the overall system of health care. The patient and family manage the illness and take over much of the responsibilities we are accustomed to expect a practitioner to handle. The extended family, as the "therapy managing group" (Janzen 1978), makes nearly all of the diagnostic and therapeutic decisions—though it should be noted that the patients often make many decisions themselves unless the illness is particularly disabling. Unless the practitioner is a member of the extended family, the Ningerum practitioner merely performs the requested treatment and then leaves the patient. Subsequently, when it comes to evaluating the results of treatment, it is the patient and family that share this burden; a practitioner seldom makes further comment on the results of treatment. Everyone in the Ningerum community is free to speculate on the cause and nature of any symptomatic episode; there is no one to legitimate a diagnosis. For example, when Okmun (a woman in her 30s) came down with gastroenteritis after eating some pork that had been given by her affines, she was able to diagnose the condition herself. With the help of her family, she performed a nonspecialist ghost divination that indicated an affinal ghost was responsible for the illness. The family performed the appropriate nonspecialized ritual to send the angry ghost away and Okmun recovered the following day. Many other people in the village—who had not shared the pork and were somewhat jealous about it—had a different view. Several people confided to me that Okmun's illness was due to having eaten spoiled pork; in their view the illness had nothing to do with ghosts.

In other cases, where the symptoms are more threatening, a specialist may be called for immediately. When Akorem (a man of about 40) came down suddenly with bronchopneumonia, high fever, and chest pains, he immediately diagnosed his condition as ensorcellment. He sent word to his classificatory brother to come and remove the sorcery packet lodged in his chest. When the brother did not arrive by the second day, a classificatory uncle arrived to perform the treatment. This uncle had not been asked to come; rather, he had heard that the illness was due to sorcery and came to assist when he heard that Akorem's brother was unavailable. The uncle said very little to Akorem or his family; after asking where the pain was, he smeared clay on Akorem's chest and removed the tiny sorcery packet, handing it to Akorem's wife. He waited until Akorem's wife began to wash the packet and study its contents, but then left without commenting on the contents or who might have been responsible. The packet contained tobacco and thus did not point to any one suspect, since many people could have stolen a discarded cigarette butt. Akorem had his suspicions as to the sorcerer's identity, but other people suspected a number of other people. Akorem went to the aid post twice during this episode, once before his uncle arrived, and then the day after the packet's removal. His subsequent recovery made the sorcerer's identity a moot point.

What is interesting in this example—although in no way unusual—is that Akorem's uncle, who was acting in the capacity of a specialist, did nothing to define or diagnose the illness condition. He merely performed the desired treatment and left, spending a total of ten minutes with his patient. The initial diagnosis and subsequent discussion of the sorcerer's identity were left entirely to Akorem and his family.

THE USE OF TRADITIONAL AND WESTERN MEDICINE

Ningerum people, old and young, educated and uneducated, continue to use traditional forms of treatment and feel that they are effective. This has not impeded their use of the aid post's medicines, which they also believe are quite effective. During the two years I lived in Hukim village, every person in the resident population used the aid post, and most attended quite regularly and frequently. Aid-post attendence did not lessen the importance of most kinds of traditional therapy, although several herbal treatments were used less frequently than in the past. In short, everyone used both traditional and aid-post treatments. Accepting one did not weaken their belief in the effectiveness of the other. While recognizing the separate origins of customary and aid-post treatments, the Ningerum never felt that one contraindicated the other. As in Akorem's case of bronchopneumonia, their treatment strategy was to employ treatments from both traditions together. I will consider this treatment strategy shortly.

Conditions treated at the aid post ranged from cuts, sores, coughs, headaches, and fever to more serious conditions, such as pneumonia, gastroenteritis, malaria, tuberculosis, and other disorders, some of which proved fatal. They used the aid post most frequently for minor complaints—but, of course, these are statistically the most common. The Ningerum used the aid post for chronic as well as acute illnesses, for internal as well as external conditions, for both mild and serious complaints, and for conditions that they explained as the result of both social and natural causes. There is no single criterion that correlates with the exclusive use of treatments from one or the other tradition, except availability.

Only conditions that persisted for several days—particularly if accompanied by much pain, disability, or worsening symptoms—generally received both traditional and aid-post treatment. With these more serious and persisting conditions, there was a noticeable tendency for patients to receive initial treatment from APO rather than from a traditional specialist or family member, particularly if the patient developed symptoms while in the village.

A hierarchy-of-resorts model of treatment selection—such as that suggested by Romanucci-Ross (Schwartz 1969; Romanucci-Ross, in the present volume)—is relevant here, though the Ningerum hierarchy of resorts should be examined carefully before assuming it is identical to hierarchies found elsewhere. Superficially, the Ningerum data resemble the "acculturative sequence" of treatment choices that Romanucci-Ross observed in Manus as one of several treatment strategies (Schwartz 1969:204). The acculturative sequence in the Manus case begins with European treatment and proceeds to traditional therapies. Although it is tempting to interpret Ningerum interventions in this way, such an analysis would be overly simplistic and, more important, it would not elaborate upon local understandings of Western medicine. Thus, it would ignore the very aspects of treatment selection that Romanucci-Ross and others have attempted to elucidate by considering treatment sequences as hierarchies of resorts.

We cannot assume, as some researchers have done (e.g., Woods 1977), that the sequential order of treatment always reflects a ranking of treatment preferences. Similarly, we should not assume, as Kunstadter (1976) does, that different treatments are always therapeutic alternatives: they can easily be therapeutic supplements. There is no a priori reason why treatment strategies must follow an ordered sequence of trial and error, trying first one treatment and then another as different practices fail to cure the condition.

In cases such as Akorem's, the strategy was to use both a traditional specialist and the aid post simultaneously. Akorem would have preferred to have the customary treatment first, immediately followed by a course of treatment at the aid post. During the actual episode, he started treatment at the aid post while waiting for his classificatory brother to arrive. It was only by happenstance that he used the APO's medicine first; therefore one cannot assume that Western practice was the first resort; for the patient both *Western and traditional* practices were part of the same resort.

Treatment Strategies as a Function of Severity of Problem

Ningerum treatment strategies vary according to the degree of severity of the illness. Generally speaking, there are three levels of severity: trivial, serious, and life-threatening. Defining different levels of severity are different thresholds of pain, disability, and suddenness of onset. In addition, there are a number of culturally marked "significant symptoms"—such as vomiting, fainting, noticeable weight loss or swelling, and profuse bleeding— that indicate a serious or perhaps life-threatening condition regardless of the accompanying symptoms.

The Ningerum language does not have labels for these different levels of severity. Nevertheless, there are marked differences in people's responses to illnesses at each level of severity. Patients demonstrate the severity of their condition by the kind of sick role they assume. At the same time, relatives and friends respond to increasing severity by taking on more and more responsibility for therapy management and treatment decision making. For each level of severity there are different treatment options, and at each level these treatment options include both European and customary treatments. Treatment options for trivial conditions never include specialized traditional therapy. They may be either aid-post or customary treatments, although nowadays there is a heavy emphasis upon the APO's medicines.

Once a condition is defined as serious, the course of treatment nearly always includes some kind of traditional specialized therapy, although in most cases the treatment strategy includes other kinds of treatment that Ningerum people see as complementing the specialist's efforts. If the condition persists, a series of specialists may be called in each with a separate treatment strategy that may include complementary nonspecialist care.

When a patient is in extremis, lying in his house recumbent and helpless, treatments of all kinds are administered in rapid succession by many different individuals. Each relative will offer whatever treatment he knows, whether specialist or nonspecialist, and the APO will usually make house calls to offer his own medications. Each individual may have his own diagnosis.

Thus, by their nature, treatment sequences during life-threatening episodes lack a coherent treatment strategy, being more a collage of many individuals' last-resort efforts.

The Ningerum hierarchy of resorts does not emphasize the many differences between introduced and customary treatments: either or both may be used at each level of severity. The specific course of treatment has much to do with the nature of the symptoms experienced and the ways that the Ningerum people understand different etiologies and pathological processes.

Serious illnesses do not always develop dramatic symptoms suddenly, and life-threatening conditions almost never do. What initially appears as a simple headache may develop over several days into a high fever, *rigors*, and chest pain. In such cases the patient will initially seek treatment at the aid post for his headache. When debilitating symptoms develop, the patient and his family will redefine the condition as serious and will decide upon a new treatment strategy that includes specialist treatment (although often it will include a mix of aid-post and nonspecialist treatments as well). Patients do not say that the aid-post medication was ineffective; rather, they say that it was insufficient. In short, the Ningerum hierarchy of resorts consists of a progression of increasingly complex treatment strategies that correspond to increasingly threatening illness conditions.

THE RELATIONSHIP BETWEEN TRADITIONAL AND WESTERN MEDICINE

Like other researchers in similar settings, I was struck initially by the many differences between Western medical practices and the more dramatic traditional forms of treatment, which included the magical removal of sorcery packets, divination, and exorcism of spirits. I recognized many differences between traditional and Western theories of illness causation and of how treatments were supposed to effect cures. After I had spent about six months in the village, it became increasingly apparent to me that many of these differences went unnoticed by the Ningerum. Such differences were not what they saw as most significant about the two medical traditions.

Villagers were largely unaware of Western biomedical theories of illness causation and the logic of Western treatments. They recognized differences between the two sets of practices in their materials and techniques, in the kinds of training required, and in their origins, but they seldom mentioned these differences. Instead, they repeatedly stressed the similarities and interchangeability of customary and aid-post medicine. Later it became clear to me that only certain traditional and aid-post treatments were fully comparable. In general, they felt that aid-post therapies were highly effective in assisting the body's ordinary regenerative process. In terms of what Ningerum see as the goals of treatment, Western medicines are virtually identical to many of their own nonspecialist treatments, treatments that are aimed at strengthening the body, restoring internal tissue damage, lessening pain, and so forth. The APO's medicines are not, according to the Ningerum, effective in exorcising spirits or in removing sorcery packets. The APO performs no treatments involving the men's cult, just as he never identifies ghosts.

APOs often come from other ethnic groups in the region, but they all share many of the Ningerum people's understandings about ghosts, sorcery, and the men's cult. APOs frequently attend men's cult feasts, divinations, and other rituals, just as I did. They are interested in learning Ningerum beliefs about these phenomena, and often participate in village conversations about them. Like the village people, APOs fear ambush from killers, assault sorcerers that are called *vada* in Motu and *sanguma* in Pidgin (see Williams 1932:124 and Glick 1973). Moreover, APOs observe many of the same precautions concerning ghosts, spirits, and sorcerers that village people do.

As I have discussed elsewhere (Welsch 1979), APOs seldom talk with patients about the theoretical basis of their treatments, nor do they tell their patients the specific effects they hope to achieve with any particular course of treatment. In most cases they merely administer the necessary medication, with instruction—or sometimes orders—to return if a second dose is required. Insofar as APOs discuss their medicines at all, it is to describe their treatments in terms of strengthening the body or the symptom-specific effects of various drugs. They never discuss aid-post medicines in terms of ghosts or sorcery, although patients are well aware that APOs know about these phenomena and that APOs do talk about ghosts and sorcery in other contexts. Thus, it is not surprising that villagers interpret aid-post medicines as aimed only at strength-giving and symptom-specific relief—that is to say, restoring ordinary body functions.

Some traditional treatments, such as nettles and certain ritual preparations, are intended to promote the patient's overall strength. Others, including several herbal preparations, venesection, and dressings for wounds, are topical; their objective is the relief of localized pain or, alternatively, the restoration of impaired organs or tissues. Other treatments aim at etiologic agents responsible for the condition; for example, divination and exorcisms are intended to identify and send away attacking ghosts. Finally, some therapies, particularly men's-cult curing rituals, strive for all three of these effects at once; simultaneously they send off ghosts, relieve localized pain, and promote the patient's general strength.

The Ningerum insistence that Western and traditional treatments are essentially the same is a manifestation of their view that the two traditions are not discrete medical systems. Both Western and traditional practices are heterogeneous, and the selection of specific therapies is made in terms of the specific effects patients want to achieve. In the past, Ningerum people chose only traditional treatments—since that was all that was available. But they did not choose treatments randomly. They had specific goals in mind when selecting from the assortment of possible treatments. But the recognition persists that only traditional medicine can deal with ghosts, spirits, and sorcery.

If we consider the therapeutic objectives of Western and traditional practices (as the Ningerum understand them), there is only one medical theory and only one medical system. The concerns of Western therapies (as APOs present these concerns to the users) are easily subsumed into the traditional medical theory.

The Ningerum recognize differences in the ingredients and forms of treatment in the two medical traditions, but they also see similar differences among customary treatments. Despite the many differences, all customary medical practices have one or more of the same three therapeutic goals. In the same way, Ningerum people interpret Western medical practices to have these same ends, and this is what people meant when they said that Western and traditional medicine are the same.

Selection of Appropriate Treatment

Traditionally, there are more or less standardized associations between certain symptoms (or combinations of symptoms) and various etiologies and pathological processes.

Fever, for example, unaccompanied by any other symptom, suggests exposure to intense sunlight, ghost attack, and several other possible explanations, but it is not a manifestation of sorcery. Accompanied by chest pain and coughing, a high fever might be explained as a secondary sign of sorcery. I regularly encountered patients with simple fever and would ask if anyone had treated the patient to remove a sorcery packet. Not surprisingly, I never encountered a case of simple fever treated in this way. Although I continued to inquire about this treatment option, just to be certain, my field assistants were puzzled by my questions. Finally, they asked me, "Why do you always ask about that? You have been here two years already; you know we never try to remove a sorcery packet for a fever."

This example is not unique. Most traditional treatments are used for a specified range of illness conditions. Ningerum people, like Americans, have very definite ideas about what kinds of treatments would be appropriate for any particular illness condition. Removing a sorcery packet from a febrile Ningerum patient is as inappropriate as prescribing laxatives for Americans suffering from migraine or decongestants for patients with swelling in their legs.

Since a range of medical treatments is available from the APO, one might assume that this unifying factor would lead the Ningerum to identify all Western treatments as part of a single alternative medical system. But their use of the aid post suggests that they differentiate aid-post treatments according to the conditions for which they are most appropriate, just as they differentiate traditional practices. Villagers make fewer distinctions among aid-post medications than do APOs, but they clearly recognize certain categories of treatment, each appropriate for particular kinds of illness conditions. These categories of APO medication include the following: cough mixture, stomach mixture, injections, tablets, ointments, bandages, liniment, iodine, and *tinea* paint. Very few people could name any of the different kinds of tablets available at the aid post, although everyone was aware of differences in size, shape, color, taste, and dosage. They also know from the APO that some tablets are for pain, some are for fever, some for pregnant women, and so forth.

Patients regularly asked for a particular kind of medication by name, rather than describing their symptoms or case history. This was particularly true when they wanted cough mixture, stomach mixture, liniment, bandaging, and occasionally even tablets and injections. When patients did describe their condition and mentioned particular symptoms, they often discussed the symptoms in a way that suggested they had a particular treatment in mind; they were not seeking a diagnosis and corresponding treatment from the APO. Patients occasionally told me before they went to the aid post the kind of medication they were going to get.

On numerous occasions a patient would mention only one or two symptoms when he was experiencing other symptoms as well. Unaware of other symptoms and assuming that the patient was suffering only from the symptoms mentioned, the APO usually gave the patient precisely the kind of treatment he sought. A full listing of symptoms might not be given, even when the APO took some interest in the case and asked many questions about the history. In some cases, patients had experienced chest pains and coughing or fever, and a relative had removed a sorcery packet the previous day. Although the patients still felt chest pain, they mentioned only the cough or fever; in such cases patients viewed the APO as a pharmacist or dispenser of medications, which patients had already decided they needed. Only in a few cases, where the illness exhibited unusual or puzzling symptoms, was the APO consulted in the role of diagnostician.

The APO is a single practitioner, but the Ningerum pattern of utilization would scarcely be altered if there were ten different APOs, each with a single specialty.

CAUSATION AND TREATMENT STRATEGIES

In selecting and following a treatment strategy, Ningerum people also consider agents responsible for their discomfort and symptoms. These causal agents may be either natural or social—what Ackerknecht (1971) and others have seen as a contrast between natural and "supernatural" or natural and "sociomoral" causes. From the Ningerum point of view, both natural and social agents influence the body in much the same ways, and an analytical preoccupation with whether the cause of an illness is seen as natural or social merely confuses our understanding of Ningerum illness behavior. Analytically, what is more significant is how the Ningerum understand these agents to affect the body to produce illness.

In the Ningerum view, all causal agents originate outside the body and damage or obstruct normal functioning in some direct way. The agent may be ethereal or tangible, but the effects are always physiological. Food sorcery uses a magical technique to implant a foreign object within the body, and this sorcery packet damages tissues in much the same way that an axe or fire can damage skin and flesh. Eating rotten food or too much pig fat disrupts ordinary digestion, leading to diarrhea and nausea. Spirits and ghosts can cause pain, disable limbs, or disrupt digestion by striking, strangling, or binding their victim's limbs and internal organs. They can also implant foreign objects within the victim's body to cause pain and internal damage. The smells of sexual secretions and menstrual blood create within the body reactions that produce midline hernias and chronic hoarseness, respectively. Spirits can come at night, while people sleep, to consume their victims' vital fluids, producing fever and weight loss. Whatever the agency, all illness is the direct result of some physiological disruption.

The Ningerum recognize the regenerative ability of the human body and expect their bodies to gradually repair most damage inflicted by external agents. These regenerative powers cannot, however, eliminate a causal agent that continues to obstruct normal functioning. Thus, they perceive a fundamental difference between illnesses due to agents acting continuously over a period of time and those due to an agent like a knife cutting the body, which has only a temporary effect. Once the knife is removed from a wound, the body can begin to repair the damage. Similarly, spirits sometimes capriciously cause pain, fever, or other discomfort, but, for reasons known only to the spirits themselves, they do not always continue their attacks. In such an instance, the body will return to normal over a relatively short period of time without intervention.

In contrast, a sorcery packet, once implanted, remains inside the body until it is removed. It will continue to disrupt normal functioning and will cause further internal damage. If left intact, the sorcery packet will cause irreparable internal damage, ultimately resulting in death.

Spirits may repeatedly consume a victim's vital fluids; if the spirit is not identified and sent away, it will persist until the victim's condition degenerates to an irreversible and terminal state. Natural agents can also repeatedly impair the body; for example, chronic coughs were sometimes attributed to smoking, and several men had given up tobacco so that they would not exacerbate the condition.

"Negative" and "Positive" Treatments

The Ningerum understand all medical treatments to act in one of two ways: the treatment either checks the continued effect of the attacking agent or it helps promote the body's normal regenerative processes. The Ningerum distinction, thus, resembles what Glick (1967:44f.) describes for the Gimi as the "negative" and "positive" mobilizations of power; the former aims at weakening the cause, while the latter enhances the patient's ability to resist these causal influences (see also Johannes 1980:51ff.).

From the Ningerum perspective these two treatment actions are fully complementary. Removal of a sorcery packet merely eliminates the source of internal damage and stops the damage from becoming worse. This treatment does nothing to help the body return to normal. Rubbing the same patient with stinging nettles strengthens the body but does nothing to remove a sorcery packet.

During the cool rainy season many people in the village, including myself, developed symptoms of head cold. The Ningerum believed head cold to be caused by eating too many okari nuts, which have their season at this time. They feel that the soft husk around the nut irritates the membranes at the back of the throat, producing congestion and coughing. Repeatedly they told me that if I wanted to get rid of the condition, I would have to stop eating okari nuts for a few days. I suggested going to the aid post for cough mixture, a very popular medication despite its unpleasant taste. They laughed at me and said that if I did not leave the okari nuts alone for a while, nothing that I did would alleviate my condition. There was, thus, a clear distinction between treatments that dealt directly with the agents causing an illness and those that helped restore normal body functions.

Traditional treatments were sometimes aimed at the agents and sometimes at restoring the body, but aid-post treatments were nearly always discussed in terms of restoring normal functions. Ningerum people thus never viewed any aid-post treatment as the functional equivalent of removing a sorcery packet or an exorcism. Aid-post medications never competed with these kinds of treatments but were instead regularly used to complement such treatments.

While aid-post medicines do not compete with traditional treatments for ghosts or sorcery (although some APOs think they do), they do compete with a variety of treatments aimed at restoring body functions. Since aid-post medications are so convenient, they have in some cases lessened the importance of many herbal, nonspecialist preparations for trivial and moderately serious conditions. For this reason, young men today are frequently unfamiliar with many of the herbal preparations.

Patients often told me that after a sorcery packet had been removed, they went to the aid post to make their recovery faster; they would probably get better in any event, but the APO's medicines helped the process.

Multiple Treatments

When patients are gravely ill and show little sign of improvement, the treatment strategy changes again: many infrequently used treatments are performed, to remove a series of causal agents as well as to help restore the body with as many techniques as possible. Nearly all of the therapeutic repertoire of the Ningerum was used in such cases, both traditional and introduced practices—that is, those of the APO's medicines that the APO would administer. In these cases the Ningerum are not trying to find one treatment that will cure the patient; rather, they are using a variety of different therapies together to help the patient's body in every possible way: increase strength, repair localized dysfunction, and deal with all possible causal agents that might be involved. Again, the emphasis is on complementary use of medical options.

APOs often complain that patients on a three- or five-day course of medication for malaria or pneumonia do not return for the full treatment; such patient noncompliance can be explained in terms of Ningerum ideas about the objectives and effects of treatment. As I have discussed elsewhere (Welsch 1979), Ningerum people generally expect any treatment to bring noticeable signs of improvement over a period of 24 to 36 hours (cf. Mitchell 1976 for a discussion of similar expectations among the Lujere). After receiving the first dose of antimalarial medicine or penicillin, patients often begin to feel better—particularly if a traditional specialist has also performed some treatment. In these cases patients often do not return for the full course of aid-post medication, explaining that they are feeling better and that their illness is finished. Once they are recovering from the illness, they believe that their bodies will return to normal as a matter of course. They experience signs of improvement and feel certain that the original causal agents no longer have a detrimental influence upon them. If persistence of symptoms is not very troublesome, further restorative treatment is considered unnecessary.

CASES OF CONJUNCTIVITIS

The following three episodes of conjunctivitis illustrate how traditional and aid-post treatments can be either functional equivalents or complements.

Case 1. Tenong (a man in his early 30s) came down with conjunctivitis in both eyes. He attended the aid post regularly for several days, until the condition cleared up. When I interviewed him, Tenong was uncertain as to how he had come to develop the condition, nor was he particularly interested in speculating about its cause. He assured me that he had performed no other treatment and that the aid-post ointment had helped his eyes considerably.

Case 2. Several months later Tenong again came down with a similar infection in one eye. Again, the condition was neither debilitating nor very painful; it was probably less troubling than his earlier episode. During this episode Tenong developed the symptoms when he was away from the village, and he treated himself with the sap from a certain succulent shrub generally regarded by the Ningerum as an effective restorative for eye conditions. By the time he had returned to the village, the illness was much better, and Tenong sought no further treatment. When I asked about this traditional treatment, Tenong insisted that it was the same kind of treatment as the APO's ointment. He told me that the two worked in the same way and that there was really no difference between the two. Tenong also explained that had the condition started when he was in the village, he would have gone to the aid post because it was more convenient; but since the eye infection had begun when he was away from the village, he used the customary treatment.

Case 3. Timop (a man in his late 20s) developed a more painful and debilitating case of conjunctivitis in both eyes, which he described in the same terms that Tenong had. Timop also sought treatment first at the aid post, when the pain was limited. He, like Tenong, received ointment. When the condition worsened, Timop continued to attend the aid post each day, but he decided that something more serious was wrong. Assisted by his wife, he performed a divination to determine whether ghosts were causing his illness. It indicated that three particular ghosts were responsible for his symptoms and that they were repeatedly poking him. The ghosts were angry and jealous about several minor incidents in the village. The ghosts were related to Timop's wife, and she performed the rituals necessary to expel each of the ghosts in turn. Timop's condition did not improve significantly over the next few days, during which time he had walked to Ningerum station for a meeting. At Ningerum he continued his treatment at the health center, and by this time his treatment included penicillin. Again he experienced no improvement and so performed another divination, which identified yet a fourth ghost. Timop sent this ghost away as he had the others. After several more injections his condition improved considerably and he resumed ordinary activities.

His explanation of the entire episode was that a relative's ghost had gotten angry and had begun the episode by poking him in the eyes. Other ghosts noticed Timop's weakened condition and began to do the same. The aid-post treatments would have helped his condition early on, he felt, except that every time he sent one ghost away, another started aggravating his condition, giving him no rest. After sending all of the ghosts away, the medicines from the aid post and health center began to take effect and his condition returned to normal.

These three cases illustrate how some traditional treatments are functional equivalents to aid-post medicines, whereas others are not. Cases like these show that the major factors in deciding between functional alternatives are accessibility and convenience. In contrast, divinations and aid-post medications are functional complements that people use together for the best results. They are not therapeutic alternatives in the way that treatments aimed at symptom-specific effects often are. Moreover, these three cases illustrate how the degree of disability and pain is related to different treatment strategies, according to the Ningerum hierarchy of resorts and differential diagnoses of similar conditions. Timop's condition required some explanation in order to control the persistent causes of the symptoms, because the persistence of symptoms indicated continued influence from (in this case) ghosts.

There are, of course, conflicts between Western and customary Ningerum medical practices. APO complaints about noncompliance are only one of several possible examples. But if we emphasize the conflicts between Western and traditional practices we tend to lose sight of this syncretic integration of older and newer practices. Specifically, if we uncritically assume that Western and traditional medical theories are different, we may lose sight of how users conceptualize their medical options. We stand to learn a lot more about treatment decision making by examining the ways that people in non-Western communities conceptualize and integrate practices which, on the surface, would appear to be quite distinct. Once we have examined the ways that different communities interpret introduced medical practices and how they integrate these practices with basic ideas about illness, we can begin to understand the typical treatment choices. At that point in our analysis we will be in a position to understand the limited ways that conflicting medical theories and practices can modify more basic treatment strategies.

REFERENCES

Ackerknecht, Erwin H. 1971. *Medicine and Ethnology: Selected Essays*. Baltimore: Johns Hopkins Press.

Adair, John, and Kurt Deuschle. 1970. *The People's Health: Anthropology and Medicine in a Navaho Community*. New York: Appleton-Century-Crofts.

Carstairs, G. Morris. 1955. "Medicine and Faith in Rural Rajasthan." Benjamin D. Paul, ed., *Health, Culture and Community*. New York: Russell Sage Foundation.

Cassel, John. 1955. "A Comprehensive Health Program Among South African Zulus." Benjamin D. Paul, ed., *Health, Culture and Community*. New York: Russell Sage Foundation.

Clark, Margaret. 1959. *Health in the Mexican-American Culture: A Community Study*. Berkeley: Univ. of California Press.

Erasmus, John Charles. 1952 "Changing Folk Beliefs and the Relativity of Empirical Knowledge." *Southwestern Journal of Anthropology*, 8:411–28.

Foster, George M. 1958. *Problems in Intercultural Health Programs*, SSRC pamphlet no. 12. New York: Social Science Research Council.

Foster, George M., and Barbara Gallatin Anderson. 1978. *Medical Anthropology*. New York: John Wiley & Sons.

Garrison, Vivian. 1977. "Doctor, *Espiritista* or Psychiatrist?: Health-Seeking Behavior in a Puerto Rican Neighborhood of New York City." *Medical Anthropology*, 1:65–180.

Glick, Leonard B. 1967. "Medicine as an Ethnographic Category: The Gimi of the New Guinea Highlands." *Ethnology*, 6:31–56.

———. 1973. "Sorcery and Witchcraft." Ian Hogbin, ed., *Anthropology in Papua New Guinea: Readings from the Encyclopedia of Papua New Guinea*. Melbourne: Univ. of Melbourne Press.

Gonzalez, Nancy Solien. 1966. "Health Behavior in Cross-Cultural Perspective." *Human Organization*, 25(2):122–25.

Jackson, Richard, Craig Emerson, and Robert L. Welsch. 1980. *The Impact of the Ok*

Tedi Project. Konedobu, Papua New Guinea: Papua New Guinea Department of Minerals and Energy.

Janzen, John M. 1978. *The Quest for Therapy in Lower Zaire*. Berkeley: Univ. of California Press.

Johannes, Adell. 1980. "Many Medicines in One: Curing in the Eastern Highlands of Papua New Guinea." *Culture, Medicine and Psychiatry*, 4:43–70.

Kleinman, Arthur M. 1976. "Social, Cultural and Historical Themes in the Study of Medicine in Chinese Societies: Problems and Prospects for the Comparative Study of Medicine and Psychiatry." Arthur M. Kleinman et al., eds., *Medicine in Chinese Cultures*. Bethesda, Md.: National Institutes of Health.

Kleinman, Arthur; Peter Kunstadter; E. Russell Alexander; and James L. Gale. 1976. "Medicine in Chinese Cultures: Comparative Studies of Health Care in China and Other Societies" (Papers and a discussion from a conference held in Seattle, Washington, February 1974). Publication of Geography and Health Studies, John Fogarty International Center for Advanced Studies in U.S. Dept. of Health, Education and Welfare, Public Health Service, National Institute of Health DHEW, publ. no. (NIH) 75–6530. Washington, D.C.: Supt. of Documents, U.S. Govt. Printing Office.

Kunstadter, Peter. 1976. "Do Cultural Differences Make Any Difference? Choice Points in Medical Systems Available in Northwestern Thailand." Arthur M. Kleinman et al., eds., *Medicine in Chinese Cultures*. Bethesda, Md.: National Institutes of Health.

Leslie, Charles. 1976. *Asian Medical Systems: A Comparative Study*. Berkeley: Univ. of California Press.

Lewis, Gilbert. 1975. *Knowledge of Illness in a Sepik Society: A Study of the Gnau, New Guinea*. London: Athlone Press.

Luzbetak, L. J. 1958. "The Treatment of Disease in the New Guinea Highlands." *Anthropological Quarterly*, 31(2):42–55.

Madsen, William. 1964. "Value Conflicts and Folk Psychotherapy in South Texas." Ari Kiev, ed., *Magic, Faith and Healing*. Glencoe, Ill.: Free Press.

Marriott, McKim. 1955. "Western Medicine in a Village of Northern India." Benjamin D. Paul, ed., *Health, Culture and Community*. New York: Russell Sage Foundation.

Mitchell, William E. 1976. "Culturally Contrasting Therapeutic Systems of the West Sepik: The Lujere." Thomas R. Williams, ed., *Psychological Anthropology*. The Hague: Mouton.

Morley, Peter, and Roy Wallis, eds. 1978. *Culture and Curing: Anthropological Perspectives on Traditional Medical Beliefs and Practices*. Pittsburgh: Univ. of Pittsburgh Press.

Nelson, Harold E. 1971. "The Ecological, Epistemological and Ethnographic Context of Medicine in a New Guinea Highlands Culture." Ph.D. diss., University of Washington.

Peck, John. 1968. "Doctor Medicine and Bush Medicine in Kaukira, Honduras." Thomas Weaver, ed., *Essays on Medical Anthropology: Southern Anthropological Society Proceedings*, no. 1:78–87.

Press, Irwin. 1969. "Urban Illness: Physicians, Curers, and Dual Use in Bogota." *Journal of Health and Social Behavior*, 10:209–18.

Rivers, William H. R. 1924. *Medicine, Magic and Religion.* New York: Harcourt & Brace.

Rubel, Arthur J. 1960. "Concepts of Disease in Mexican-American Culture." *American Anthropologist,* 62:795–814.

Schwartz, Lola. 1969. "The Hierarchy of Resort in Curative Practices: The Admiralty Islands, Melanesia." *Journal of Health and Social Behavior,* 10:201–9.

Schwartz, Theodore. 1963. "Systems of Areal Integration: Some Considerations Based on the Admiralty Islands of Northern Melanesia." *Anthropological Forum,* 1(1):56–97.

Stanhope, John. 1968. "Competing Systems of Medicine Among the Rao-Breri, Lower Ramu River, New Guinea." *Oceania,* 39:339–45.

Turner, Victor. 1968. *The Drums of Affliction: A Study of Religious Processes Among the Ndembu of Zambia.* Oxford: Clarendon Press.

Wagner, Roy. 1972. *Habu: The Innovation of Meaning in Daribi Religion.* Chicago: Univ. of Chicago Press.

Watson, James B. 1980. "Protein and Pigs in Highland New Guinea." Paper presented to the American Anthropological Association, 79th annual meeting.

Welsch, Robert L. 1979. "Barriers to the Aid Post: Problems of the Very Isolated Community." Ralph Premdas and Stephen Pokwin, eds., *Decentralisation: 1978 Waigani Seminar.* Waigani, Papua New Guinea: Univ. of Papua New Guinea.

Williams, F. E. 1932. "Sex Affiliation and Its Implication." Reprinted in F. E. Williams, *The Vailala Madness and Other Essays,* ed. Erik Schwimmer. Honolulu: Univ. Press of Hawaii, 1977.

Woods, Clyde. 1977. "Alternative Curing Strategies in a Changing Medical Situation." *Medical Anthropology,* 3(1):25–54.

Young, Alan. 1976. "Some Implications of Medical Beliefs and Practices for Social Anthropology." *American Anthropologist,* 78:5–24.

4

DOCTORS OR DECEIVERS?
THE SIBERIAN KHANTY SHAMAN AND
SOVIET MEDICINE

MARJORIE MANDELSTAM BALZER

In a new spirit of respect for indigenous medicine, the United Nations World Health Organization has instituted a policy of training traditional medical practitioners in hygiene and midwifery, while at the same time encouraging certain ancient "folk" herbal and shamanic cures (Bannerman 1977:16–17). Without denial of the real benefits of modern psychiatry and medical technology, health problems are increasingly studied in their historical, social, and symbolic contexts (Gillin 1948; Turner 1964; Romanucci-Ross 1977:481–87; Ohnuki-Tierney 1976, 1980; Kleinman 1979). It is especially appropriate to undertake such a study in Siberia, where "classical" shamanism has long and diverse roots.[1]

This chapter examines multiple ways in which illness is cognitively and behaviorally coped with by the Siberian Khanty, Ob Ugrians often termed "Ostiak" in Western literature.[2] Although Khanty ideas about sickness have been changing rapidly with the arrival of Soviet doctors, some traditional ideas about health and how to obtain it are still alive. These ideas center on the dramatic role of shamans, whose ecstatic trance journeys enable some Khanty to believe they can communicate with and control the supernatural.

Khanty concepts of health as essentially spiritual help to explain both traditional curing and modern attitudes toward medicine. Shamanic cures are directed at "spiritual" ailments of patients, usually believed to take the form of lost or stolen souls. In treating such afflictions, shamans have sometimes managed to get at the heart of interlocked physical and psychological problems. The success of a shaman in doing this, however, depends upon his or her stature in a given community, and, given Soviet anti-religious propaganda, this stature is changing.

To put these changes in perspective, Khanty soul belief and correlations of moral behavior with health are discussed. Shamans and seances are then described, to illustrate the importance of shamanism in community relations and to illuminate how the symbolism of shamanic trance may contribute to curing. Ideas of Shirokogoroff (1935), Turner (1964, 1977) and Lévi-Strauss (1967) are adapted, and recent responses to Soviet medicine are analyzed. Modern Soviet attitudes have frequently undermined precisely the elements of shamanism which may have made it effective in traditional contexts, but key aspects of the Khanty shamanic symbol system survive.

THE RELATION OF SOULS AND MORALITY TO HEALTH

Khanty souls have contrasting named functions and locations, which have led to categorizations of souls as "dual" (Karjalainen 1921:21; Raun 1955:50–71) or "multiple" (Chernetsov 1963:5; Sokolova 1976:57). The Soviet scholar Chernetsov (1963:5) argues that it is impossible to squeeze all Khanty concepts of the soul into a dualistic framework. I would add that we have yet to understand the scope of soul belief, given indications of "souls" or soul-aspects residing in many parts of the body (head, hair, skin, liver, heart), plus indications that souls guide human conscience, dreaming, sickness, and reincarnation (see Table 4.1).

Chernetsov (1963:3–45) has classified four main Ob-Ugrian souls as those representing material being, sickness, dreaming, and reincarnation. He suggests that a fifth soul, enabling physical strength, is exclusively the province of men (1963:5).[3] The sickness soul, *iləs*, is believed to live either in the head or "on the surface" of the body (Chernetsov 1963:13–14).

Khanty claim that when a person is awake and healthy, the sickness soul is invisible. However, when an individual is ill or asleep, this soul takes on the form of an insect or a bird. In sleep, the sickness soul naturally wanders. Usually this is considered safe, but sometimes the soul can be stolen, resulting in illness involving weakness, lethargy, and unconsciousness (Chernetsov 1963:15). Additional danger occurs if the sickness soul leaves while a host is not sleeping, as when someone has chills, sneezes, or takes fright. Shamans can see and recover sickness souls by letting their own *iləs* leave their bodies in trance.

According to Khanty consultants, most of the dangers that can befall a soul are considered unavoidable by the unfortunate victim. Soul theft is often attributed to a recently deceased relative longing for the company of the patient. Nonetheless, some examples of soul loss have traditionally been

Table 4.1
Khanty Soul Beliefs

Soul or Soul Aspect	Gloss	Location	Image	Function
Is-chor *Is*	Material or shade	Shadow	Shadow	To stay with a person in life and stay with the grave in death; can cause nightmares; may be the conscience
Ilas Is-ilt	Sickness	Head or body surface	Mosquito; cuckoo; swallow; magpie	Health; stays with person while awake; leaves in sleep and can be stolen to cause sickness; shaman causes this soul to leave at will in trance
Uləm is	Dreaming	Head in sleep; forest in waking hours	Wood grouse; black cock	To enable dreaming, visions, and life; can cause nightmares
Lil	Reincarnation; breath	Head or hair	Bird: falcon?	Ancestral Khanty spirit enabling perpetuation of Khanty clans; can warn master in times of danger; is basis for divination of *liaksys* (ancestral namesake) name

Sources: Chernetsov (1963); Karjalainen (1921); Raun (1955); Tegy and Karym consultants.

related to a patient's morality. Such concepts were common through the 1930s, and have limited currency today.

Khanty considered themselves safe from spiritual and therefore bodily harm only when ancestral idols had been treated well, when rules regarding ritual purity had been obeyed, and when ceremonies had been performed properly. Ancient concepts of well-being merged good health and fertility with fishing and hunting gains, since success in these goals reflected oneness with propitiated ancestors. Ancestral patrilineal clan spirits, called *menk* and *mis*, were believed capable of chastising Khanty for sins of disregard by soul theft. Evidence from early ethnographers Gondatti (1887:84) and Nosilov (1904:14) indicates that epidemics of smallpox were believed by Ob Ugrians to result from grave disrespect for spirits, possibly incurred by too much contact with Russians. Traditionally defined sins worthy of bringing on illness thus concerned both human-supernatural transgressions and interpersonal human relations. Serious crimes, such as incest or murder, were particularly considered to invite retaliation by ancestral spirits (cf. Bartenev 1896:85, 95).

Occasionally, health was thought to depend on maintenance of rapport with shamans. Revengeful shamans were believed capable of sending disease in the form of a physical object—like entrails, a worm, or hair—into their victim's body (cf. Shashkov 1864:99; Startsev 1928:93). But shamans, especially those known personally in a given community, were usually considered to be more doctor than witch. (A popular turn-of-the-century shaman assured Alexander Brem [1897:378] that, although his spirit helpers could be used to do evil, the shaman himself endeavored only to cure and to protect his community from "unclean powers.")

Shamans were traditionally able to attribute the sickness to the patient's own behavior, to someone else, or to a dead relative. To accomplish this attribution, shamans solicited confessions from patients and family members. Such a confession was itself believed beneficial to health, and may indeed have had psychological benefits (cf. Frank 1961:51–52).

SHAMANS: DEFINITIONS AND CLASSIFICATIONS

Since shamans traditionally determined the nature of sickness and were major actors in seances to recover lost souls, Khanty considered them crucial for their personal well-being. But Khanty shamans, like most Siberian shamans, were more than medical practitioners. As mediators between the natural and supernatural, they made predictions, provided spiritual shields for the living in times of danger, acted as intelligence agents in times of interclan rivalry, and behaved as psychiatrists, entertainers, and judges.

Ugrian names for shamans reveal many nuances of meaning. The Northern Khanty call the shaman *semvojan*, or "seeing one," with suffixes *xo* or *ne* to denote man or woman. *Tsepanən-xoi* connotes a sorcerer as well as a medicine man in Vakh River dialects, while on the Vasyugan a shaman is referred to as a great or little magician, *jol* (Hadju 1968:170). Karjalainen (1927:245–305) mentions also *multə-xo* ("praying man") and *t'arttə-xo* ("prophet") for Tremyugan shamans. Still other widely used terms denote "men who fall into trances," with notions of heat and narcotic drunkenness as intrinsic to the trance state (Balazs 1968:53–57).

The traditional Khanty shaman was often a community leader, by virtue of personality, spiritual knowledge, and proven ability as a conductor of souls. But the degree to which shamans fulfilled leadership roles has varied according to the individual shaman. A classification of Khanty shamans should be based on their reputations and the range in which they operate, rather than on distinctions of "black" (evil) and "white" (good) identity.[4] Gradations of power can be seen to form a system over time whereby an apprentice shaman "graduates" to practice first in the family, then the locality (defined as extended patrilineal clan affiliations), and finally, in villages not affiliated by clan. While reality is undoubtedly not so systematic, descriptions of shamans by Khanty, Karjalainen (1927:245–95), Startsev (1928:90–91), and Minenko (1975:204) confirm this. Female shamans usually practice only at the family or local level (cf. Durrant 1979).

Training

Questions of shamanic power begin with who becomes an apprentice. Potential talent is believed inherent from birth, although it is often not discovered until the teens, when it is manifest in nervousness, dreaming, and sickness (Khanty consultants; cf. Dunin-Gorkavich 1911:48). While shamanic status is not necessarily hereditary, usually close older relatives who are themselves shamans discover and informally coach their sometimes reluctant candidates. Primarily, training involves learning how to send one's sickness soul into the world of spirits. To achieve a trance state, traditional shamans were taught how to use dried mushrooms, *Amanita muscaria*; alcohol and physical exertion seem to be more current (although less effective) means to alter consciousness.[5]

The apprentice learns how to control specific helper spirits, which come in trance—usually as animals and birds, but also as ancestral forest spirits. Soviet anthropologist Sokolova (1971:224) associates such helpers with clan "totems" of particular shamans (cf. Ridington and Ridington 1975:190–204). Through dreams or trance, the shaman also discovers how to obtain necessary magical accoutrements, such as reindeer-skin drums, felt hats, and iron or brass ornaments.

The most structured aspect of training involves memorizing songs and prayers, passed down by the shaman with whom an apprentice eventually works as an assistant. Service to a master shaman includes maintaining seance equipment and sometimes translating the shaman's trance exploits from mumblings into a dramatic story for the audience. This can give an assistant considerable power as well as practice.

There is no formal initiation or fixed training time for the Khanty shaman, although part of the trance process may involve the symbolic flesh cutting and bone reorganizing torture of an apprentice by spirits, to signify death and rebirth (Siikala 1978:22; cf. Eliade 1974:62–95; Nachtigall 1976:320). When a master considers an apprentice ready to perform, a small extended family seance is arranged for curing or prediction. Word of success spreads rapidly, making for a flexible system.

Family shamans are available on call for relatives and are rarely felt to be spiritually threatening to members of their community. Ugrian specialist Hajdu (1968:147) defines such shamans of lesser strength as "people with sensitive nervous systems who distinguish themselves by their skills in dream reading and in healing minor diseases." This kind of shaman might have some herbal knowledge, but little seance paraphernalia. Family shamans usually live from subsistence activities, rather than seance commissions. The Soviet ethnographer Startsev (1928:89) knew two such family shamans in the 1920s, one a young hunter of 26, the other an older head of a large household, "who hunted, made bows and arrows and boats, and in nothing differed from others." Most shamans alive today are probably on this level. One example is a Tegy woman, considered by several Russians as well as Khanty to be a shaman. She has little contact with Russians, refusing to learn their language, and is reputedly well versed in shamanic lore.

A more powerful type of shaman, operating at the local level, has a reputation for prediction and healing through trance with helping spirits. Such shamans would probably own a drum, bells, hats, and some metal ornaments, depending on their location within Khanty territory and on possible Samoyed influences. They can control only a few helping spirits, making for modest seances devoid of "miracles" or prolonged trances. Shamans of this caliber usually have neither the desire nor the personality for broader practice. (A supplementary explanation might be that they do not use intense trance-producing narcotics, because of restricted access to them or to the knowledge involved in using them.) A current example of a shaman with a local reputation is a Tegy recluse in his 40s who lives in the forest and is feared by many but still summoned by a few Khanty believers.

The true shaman of wide reputation and power does not necessarily appear in every community or in every lifetime. This "big man" travels widely, in both this world and the spirit world. Hajdu (1968:147) defines a shaman of great repute to be one "who excels in communicating with spirits and superior beings and who practices magic and produces wonder-working powers." Such Khanty shamans are perceived capable of visiting both the upper and lower worlds of Khanty cosmology, of manipulating in one seance as many as seven spirit helpers including the bear, and of controlling the emotions of a large audience for two or three consecutive evenings.[6] They have many professional secrets, enabling them to perform logic-defying feats of physical endurance, ventriloquism, and dancing.

A "big man" shaman is a true man of iron, wearing a cloak filled with dangling metal ornaments calculated to attract helper spirits (cf. Businsky 1893:35; Prokof'yeva 1971:5–10). He beats an enormous drum, *koim*, which is believed to be transformed in trance into a horse or reindeer (cf. Roheim 1954:49; Dioszegi 1968:260–61). He "rides" his drum into mountainous upper and lower worlds, sometimes depicted in symbolic form on the drum itself (Czaplicka 1914:222). Often the back, handle, and beater of the drum are decorated with iron rings and figures representing spirit helpers. Iron, as a multifaceted symbol of strength, longevity, and spiritual power, is particularly appropriate for the shaman.[7]

Examples of "big man" shamans are rare today, because the climate of adulation required for a shaman to build a following is lacking. On the Vakh River, in the 1960s, a great shaman named Jorgen was buried by his clients, mostly old men who came from 150 kilometers around (Sokolova 1971:224). I heard of one shaman reputed to have been a phenomenal miracle worker operating out of Beriosovo. He was the father of the current local Tegy shaman. In addition, several Salekhard shamans have wide reputations for curing.

TRADITIONAL KHANTY SHAMANISM

Complex beliefs enable performances of seances and help shape not only the personality and power of individual shamans, but also the culture of curing in a given community. Many researchers focus on the psychology and "miracles" of a shaman, rather than on the reasons these "miracles" are or were impressive to clients.[8] During a traditional seance, an enormous amount of communal energy was directed at solving a spiritual emergency, with an extended family often actively participating in chants and dancing (cf. Startsev 1928:94–96). The Khanty shaman, whether male or female, was and to some extent still is able to fulfill mediating roles and to manipulate important Khanty symbols of communication by being an artist and impresario, transforming a small hut into a scene of moving dramatic action (cf. Charles 1953:95–122; Revunenkova 1974:110).

There are often two stages to a Khanty shamanic cure. The first is a diagnosis stage, involving confessions and the summoning of spirit helpers to the cabin of a patient to discover the causes of the illness. The second stage consists of a shamanic trance journey into the upper or lower world. A trance journey may not be necessary if helping spirits are able to accomplish a cure or suggest a sacrifice in the first stage.

A mid-nineteenth-century student of Siberian shamanism, Shashkov (1864:97–99) witnessed a Khanty seance that culminated in a sacrifice. The shaman's helping spirits directed him to order several reindeer from the patient's family as their price for a cure. The reindeer were dragged directly into the yurt of the patient:

To the leg of one deer they fasten one end of a rope, the other end is held by the patient, and when the latter pulls the rope, they kill the deer. The head and horns are laid on the floor, the flesh is eaten and the sick man is anointed with fat. (Shashkov 1864:98–99)

This sacrifice is significant because the patient took an active part in his cure. Anointing the patient is itself similar to the smearing of idols with fat and blood during shaman-led sacrifices to ancestors. Thus this patient was given the same kind of concerned attention that sacred ancestral idols were given. Today—because of Soviet restrictions against killing collective animals—animal sacrifices for curing, burial ritual, or ancestral grove worship are rare, but they are not entirely unknown (Balzer 1980:82).

Patient participation during traditional curing sessions was, and to some extent still is, also accomplished by confessions. A story told by Khanty to Obdorsk resident Bartenev (1896:85) illustrates the high value Khanty place on confession, although the story itself is probably apocryphal. During a difficult childbirth, female relatives of an expectant mother sent for a renowned shaman in panic and concern. The shaman entered the darkened, ritually prepared birth hut and began to beat his drum, asking the unhappy patient in what way she had "sinned." She first said she had "masturbated," then that she had had "a relationship with a dog," and finally that she had "slept with her father" (Bartenev 1896:85). Only after this ultimate confession was the shaman satisfied, and the mother safely delivered of her child. This story probably served Khanty as a morality play, demonstrating graphically the necessity of full confession. A more current description of Ob Ugrian birth rituals by Mansi ethnographer Rombandeeva (1968:80) stresses confessions of both mothers and fathers.

While confession of culturally defined "sins" by a patient or family members might help clear the air for a cure, further information regarding sources of sickness was acquired supernaturally. At the turn of the century, the Finnish ethnographer Karjalainen (1927:310–15) witnessed an impressive summoning of helping spirits on the Vasyugan River. At nightfall the shaman placed himself in the darkest corner of a low, crowded yurt and began to play a native lyre, *narsus*. First he contacted a fierce and somewhat impertinent flying messenger called "Stern Woman with the Handled Stick." When she arrived, he began to shake and ordered her to summon underground spirits. With each helper's arrival, the shaman sang to his audience about the journeys the spirits had made. He announced a bear spirit, claiming, "I hear the hairy humped beast of the Great Earth coming from under the first layer of the earth to the water of the second" (Karjalainen 1927:311).

After helping spirits of the underground were assembled, the shaman began to call forth celestial helpers, using his lyre and metaphorical speech. Each time a spirit entered the yurt, the shaman shook with its power and then renewed the music and rhythm of his dialogues. After seven spirits were called, one of them an important celestial horse that nearly knocked the shaman out with its cold breath, the shaman announced that a second evening would be required for him to travel on the grey horse to the spirit world (Karjalainen 1927:313).

Karjalainen (1927:318) stresses that the Vasyugan shaman was not possessed by spirits, but rather was inspired by their whispering in his ear. During seances, shamans were likely to sing praises of special spirits, to challenge them, and to advertise control over a range of spirit types. A song fragment collected by H. Paasonen on the Konda, at the turn of the century, brags, "I spirits (*tonxət*) a hundred, forest goblin (*menk*) a hundred have conjured" (Vertes 1968:119). Two kinds of classic song-myths were folk models for shamanic trance, one in which the shaman rescued a lost soul from greedy, fighting underworld spirits of the dead; and a second in which the shaman either flew by horse or turned himself into a white-winged bird to negotiate with sky deities (cf. Karjalainen 1927:245–331; Senkevich 1935:158).

In the 1920s, Khanty seances were still widely believed capable of solving spiritual problems. The skeptical Startsev (1928:94–96) saw a Vakh River seance intended to recover the lost soul of a young child. The tightly packed session continued until 5 in the morning, with seven seances. During breaks, the shaman told his audience which spirits had come to him. With each seance, he became more energetic and "ferocious," while dancing, reeling, and tossing his drumsticks to the audience. He brought himself and his audience to a fever pitch with the ever-louder intensity of his drumbeats.[9] "Characteristic moments occurred when the shaman put the edge of his drum on the small of his back, on his left leg, and on his torso. He would touch family members [of the sick child] and yell" (Startsev 1928:95–96). When the sessions were over, the shaman had barely enough strength to promise that the child would be well.

MULTIPLE DIMENSIONS OF SHAMANISM

Given the importance of patient and audience participation in seances, it is logical to view shamanism as potentially effective for community cohesion as well as individual health (see Table 4.2). Shirokogoroff's monumental work on Siberian Tungus psychology stresses the responsiveness of shamanism to community stress; he calls "the treatment of psychic troubles . . . the practical aim of shamanism" (1935:422). His analysis can be compared with that of Turner on the African Ndembu (1964:230–63), particularly because each sees curing complexes as aiding adaptive responses to tensions produced during culture change (cf. Shirokogoroff 1935:393).

For both Shirokogoroff and Turner, major benefits of Tungus and Ndembu seances are assumed to stem from improvements in community relations that result from confessions and symbolic enactments of emotional group solidarity. Turner (1964:237) concludes that Ndembu doctors "are well aware of the benefits of their procedures for group relationships, and they go to endless trouble to make sure that they have brought into the open the main sources of latent hostility in group life."

This applies to Khanty curing, although it is unwise to attribute to shamans control over all latent social problems. Social control varies with the personality, experience, and stature of a shaman. What the nonlocal shaman gains through a reputation as a "big man," he loses in lack of intimacy regarding local affairs. To compensate, a shaman's assistants and in-laws can act as informants, explaining marital problems, hunting shortages, and extended-family tensions in a given community.

Theories About Shamanic Cures

Although traditional shamanism does indeed seem to be a form of group therapy, its successful treatment of individuals is more problematic. The intense communal and spiritual activity of seances can provide an incredible psychological boost by increasing self-confidence and jolting a patient out of depression (cf. Gillin 1948:387–400). Creatively handled symbols of common cultural experience, whether coded in shamanic paraphernalia or speech, can also help define and channel individual problems, beginning with diagnosis of afflictions, peaking in trance journeys, and ending with

Table 4.2
Khanty Shamanism: A Feedback System of Symbolic Action

Players	SHAMAN →		PATIENT →			COMMUNITY →		
Definitions	Mediator between natural and supernatural worlds		Sufferer from culturally defined and/or transcultural afflictions			Loose grouping of extended patrilineal families		
Potential Benefits	Increased Reputation		Cure			Cohesion		
Level of Effectiveness	Personal	Technique	Physical	Psychological	Social	Problem Solving	Values	Cosmology
Descriptions	Unusual confidence in self, system	Controlled trance: *Amanita muscaria* hemp?; alcohol; dance	Endorphin trigger?	Abreaction	Confession	Social resentments aired	Taboos enforced: clan; sexual	Beliefs enacted: layered universe
	Leadership ability	"Miracles"	Herbal medicine	Transference	Group attention: calling shaman; in seance	Hunting, fishing, reindeer losses explained	Respect: ancestors; animals; spirits; elders; shamans	Spirit helpers: bear; lizard; birds; *menk*; *mint*; *tonx*
	Creativity	Costume: color; symbols; metal	Massage	Suggestion		Individual restored to group	Soul belief	Ancestral power
	Nervousness	Drum: cosmology model; transport metaphor; seance intensifier		Hypnosis?		Sorcery discovered, punished		Sacrifices: horse; reindeer
	Remuneration			Dream analysis		Culture change tensions eased, explained?		Offerings: cloth; coins
				Shock therapy?				

various prescribed postseance tasks. Whether this psychological effect is enough to unblock mental or physical anguish depends greatly on the patient and the complaint.

Lévi-Strauss (1967), stressing the value of repetitive, emotion-laden symbolism in shamanic chants, has provided an explicit discussion of how individual cognition may be shaped by culture in the curing process. The crux of curing is that a chaotic and painful experience is reorganized by the shaman for the patient, through processes of abreaction and transference, and fitted into a comprehensible familiar mythical system. This reorganization "induces the release of the physiological process" (p. 193). While Lévi-Strauss suggests that polynucleids in brain nerve cells could be affected, newer research indicates that brain chemicals such as endorphins (Beeson et al. 1979) may be triggered in the brain to willfully control pain.[10]

Curative Procedure

The details with which Khanty shamans regale their audiences may have a focusing effect on patients, similar to that which Lévi-Strauss suggests for Cuna Indians. As the shaman overcomes an obstacle-filled topography of the lower world, with a powerful bear spirit as a guide, the patient anticipates recovery of a lost sickness soul. When the shaman finally confronts a spirit of the dead with soul theft and offers the spirit food, money, and valuable cloth, it may be an enormous relief to the patient to know that the soul has been pinpointed. If a battle ensues, between shamanic helpers and spirits of the dead, this battle may be mirrored in the mind of a patient struggling with pain or drowsiness. Finally, when the shaman flies back to earth with the prized soul clenched firmly in his fist, the patient may sense a renewal of energy and confidence, made concrete when the shaman blows the soul back into the patient's ear (cf. Karjalainen 1927:305–15).

Generalizations about what goes on in a patient's mind are highly speculative, but in traditional contexts of faith and communal concern, some shamans were able to cure, at least temporarily, a respectable portion of their patients. It is possible that this was accomplished with the aid of tremendously powerful symbol manipulation. Shamans themselves may have had no inkling of specifically how their ecstatic journeys produced bodily cures. They were just as likely to go into trance for the lost soul of an infant, who could not mentally follow their exploits, as for an adult, who could. Thus, I am not attributing clairvoyance of scientific principles to shamans, but simply saying that the effect of their ecstasy was sometimes positive.

Although Lévi-Strauss's thesis is perhaps furthered by discovery of endorphins, aspects of his structural assumptions are still questionable. As his articulate critic Jerome Neu (1975:285–92) has pointed out, there is no direct homology, even for the Cuna, between the physical body and the supernatural world, so that there is little proof of universal structuralism by reference to either physical or "fantasy-physical" parallels with shamanic mythology. Similarly, "limited laws" of symbolism cannot be derived from physical correspondences (cf. Lévi-Strauss 1967:199).

Assuming that processes of abreaction and transference do occur during some shamanic cures, they undoubtedly are managed in different ways, with numerous powerful, culturally defined metaphors. For Khanty, abreaction could result from confession of cultural or even clan-specific taboos; from adroit removal of bloody hair out of a patient's body as evidence of sorcery; or from the blowing of a lost soul into a patient's ear. Transference could be accomplished not only during seances, but throughout a patient's potentially lifelong relation with a family or local shaman (cf. Beck 1967:317, 321).[11]

Worldviews reaffirmed in seances are also significant. The cosmology of a soul's journey or a shamanic initiatory trance may be similar for a number of Siberian peoples, but it differs considerably from that of the Cuna. Thus, a balance should be kept between awareness of similar widespread and effective forms of psychotherapy, and an understanding of the multiple symbol systems which are tapped in the process of therapy.

Indigenous views of health and of shamanic behavior may vary in their congruence with interlocked psychophysiological curing mechanisms. Thus success rates for cultures in which mythological chants are loudly dramatized and shamans are widely respected may be greater than for cultures where shamanic cures are secretly mumbled away from the patient (cf. Fortune 1932:144–47). Since cultures also emphasize different styles of curing, ranging from the more individually oriented to the more communal, there is further scope for variations in effectiveness. This in turn can change over time, as our own psychiatry reveals. Finally, various kinds of illnesses may lend themselves differently to symbolic manipulation. Difficult childbirth may be more susceptible to cure through psychologically triggered release of brain chemicals than tuberculosis.

In sum, shamanism can cure certain kinds of social and personal ills, working at once on the body politic, ancestral relations, and, perhaps, the culturally influenced mind of a patient.

CULTURE CHANGE

An absolute prerequisite for an effective shamanic cure is faith, and this is difficult, but not impossible, to find today. Much belief in shamanism that currently exists in Northern Khanty villages seems to be a negative belief in the power of shamans to do evil. Whereas many Khanty shamans were traditionally thought to be restrained in misuse of their spirit powers, heightened community tensions—with increased Russian contact and antishaman propaganda—seem to have exacerbated Khanty ideas of the shaman as a sorcerer. This trend was particularly marked in the 1930s through the 1950s.[12]

Any previous ability of shamans to restore community equilibrium in times of trouble, as suggested by Turner (1964) and Shirokogoroff (1935), was often overwhelmed by Sovietization, serious losses in World War II, displacement of Khanty communities, and efforts to settle nomadic Khanty reindeer breeders. This does not mean that Khanty culture has disintegrated, but rather that new emphases are being developed in other areas of cultural life, including rituals (Balzer 1980, 1981; Sokolova 1976).

A Contemporary Shamanic Treatment

Today many Soviet officials deny the existence of Khanty shamans, and, indeed, belief in shamans as either curers or sorcerers is waning. However, I was able to get the following account of a curing attempt in Tegy:

There is a shaman, about 41 years old, who lives not far from here, separate, with his family. He has daughters who study. He is always drunk, and has been in jail. He came to this house one time and tried to cure an old woman who was living here. Everyone ran away when he came, except one woman who was very drunk, and a small child. The shaman cut the sick woman who had called for him. He cut her on the side of the neck, and blood ran down to her stomach. He stood at the door so no one could see just what he did. He raised his hands and motioned to the sky, to call his special evil spirits. You can tell he is a shaman by his evil eyes. Everyone knows he is a shaman. He takes an ax and shakes, when the spirits come to him, as he crouches on the ground.

There is much that is unconventional about this account. Shamans are not known for extreme bloodletting or for covert seances. The shaman's helping spirits are referred to here as "evil," whereas once only a few in uncontrolled contexts were considered frightening. A medium of divination (the ax) has become a weapon, while other crucial symbols of shamanic power (the drum, iron ornaments, special clothing) are missing from the account. The story of this disreputable shaman continues:

This same man, earlier, lived in this very house. He tortured us. He was always drunk, and broke furniture. He speaks in shaman's tongues, and knows all the old shaman songs. He sometimes did not let us into our own home. He stood straight at the door, and stared, and said: "The spirits are helping me." The police chase him. He lived in Beriosovo, and his father was a big and very famous shaman. He is a swine shaman. He was kicked out of the Beriosovo collective and so he came here. His wife's brothers lived here . . . He lived there, but after a month and a half, they kicked him and his family out of their house. He cursed them, and I heard it: "From now on in this house, you will not live well, may there be blood on your floors." And after this, the brother of his wife shot himself and died . . . Then he moved in here . . . and finally the police chased him from here . . . He aided so many deaths . . . Probably one of his daughters too will become a shaman. How can people say there aren't shamans? Of course there are.

It is hard to measure how common such stories of shaman misbehavior and Khanty condemnation are, since there still seem to be a few shamans whom the Khanty revere and protect from prying ethnographers. This Tegy shaman seems to be disillusioned to the point of despair at the ridicule of his knowledge, but reputedly other shamans in the Arctic town of Salekhard have not lost their confidence. In general, the Soviet-spurred cycle of hiding and distrust has broken many of the mutually reinforcing bonds previously maintained by followers and shamans. Private seances are not necessarily effective, because an important aspect of curing involves the communal support given to patients and shamans. This kind of public-private distinction between effective hope-producing atmospheres in ritual curing is made by Frank (1961:62), who adds: "Even in private forms of healing, group and cultural factors are implicit" (cf. Kleinman 1979:364).

Shamans as Deceivers

The decline of shamanism among Northern Khanty began in the 1930s, with collectivization and agitation against shamans as "deceivers" (cf. Ankudinov and Dobriev 1939; Vdovin 1976:261–62). Soviet officials destroyed sacred idols (often of ancestral shamans) and took away drums and other equipment of shamans in raids. They used each illegal offense of shamans (for example, drunkenness, or kulak offenses of wealth and hoarding) as a reason to put them in jail. More positively, the government also initiated "red tents" with which doctors, nurses, and medical assistants traveled, giving modern medical aid. Earlier, distances required to reach hospitals were so prohibitive as to discourage their use by natives.

Judging by Startsev's accounts (1928:88–97), shamanism was alive and popular with both Khanty and Siberian Russian peasants in the 1920s. Senkevich, ten years later, had a much harder time trying to record shamanic songs: "The clever shamans not only don't want to sing them, but also in general hide their profession" (1935:158).

Looked at from the Soviet point of view, the campaign against shamans is understandable. Zealous revolutionaries from the south, bent on scientifically and collectively unlocking Siberian resources, had no use for the "wasteful" animal sacrifices encouraged by shamans. They considered shamans to be exploiters of peasants and natives, and accused them of demanding too much payment for services or forcing sacrifices solely for their share of meat. Such "kulak-shamans" were condemned at regional Communist Party meetings in the 1930s, which were geared toward training young Siberian natives to reject traditional political-religious elders.

It is logical in these conditions that some shamans went underground, others became alcoholics, and a few revolted. In the 1930s, under the leadership of the shaman Yarkin of Narikarsky, a huge sacrifice of horses was organized, in an effort to prevent collectivization (Kartsov 1937:120). Such activism was especially great on the Kazym and Sosva rivers, where there was even shaman-led destruction of Soviet encampments as well as more common refusals to attend schools. In addition, authorities claimed to have uncovered a plot to kill Communist party workers, which led to arrests and court sentencing for many shamans and their followers (Kartsov 1937:120). Persecution turned the tradition which made shamans great into a dangerous badge of religious conservatism.

Today, local log-cabin hospitals are available in villages as small as Kazym.[13] Hospitals are accessible—even to nomadic breeders of reindeer—by helicopter and Ob River hydrofoil. Focus for curing is on hygiene, drugs, and surgery. Although modern medicine has been introduced, psychological roots of illness are rarely explored, and the shared worldview on which shamanic mythology was based is being discredited. Communist ideology, although not totally rejecting psychiatry, precludes most psychological explanations of illness, whether Freudian or native. In the context of modern diseases, both Khanty and Siberian Russian villagers realize that Soviet medicine is often more effective than shamanic seances. Nonetheless, Soviet methods are not always chosen by the Khanty.

THE KHANTY RESPONSE

The first point to be made about current Khanty responses to Soviet medicine is that choices of cures are open to experimentation. If a local shaman is more accessible than a Soviet doctor, that shaman might be tried before the patient bothers to apply to a hospital. If a Soviet cure has failed, a Northern Khanty family might try to send for a nonlocal Salekhard shaman with a wide reputation. Recourse to shamans is kept a family secret, if possible, to avoid the displeasure of Soviet authorities. I learned of one blind woman who, having been treated unsuccessfully by both Soviet and Khanty practitioners, was putting her final faith in a new Soviet medicine which she had heard cured reindeer of eye problems. A progression of medical alternatives can theoretically lead to a systematic study of the "hierarchy of resort" (Romanucci-Ross 1977:481–87).[14]

A second factor, concerning contrasts in the curing milieu, partially explains Khanty difficulties in adjusting to Soviet medicine. The power of traditional focus on spirit-oriented cures, confession, drama, and communal participation in seances has been stressed. In Soviet hospitals, the family is confined to formal visits, and the patient is likely to feel isolated. There is an unaccustomed discomfort in the clean white rows of beds and the unfamiliar faces of other patients and staff. A modern cure entails the reverse of concerned group solidarity, which engulfs the patient in goodwill in an otherworldly, darkened, and impassioned atmosphere. It involves the crisp professional relationship of the patient with a usually Russian doctor and a few medical assistants.

I met a young woman in Kazym who was awkwardly waiting out an illness of her mother in the hospital, while her reindeer-breeding father stayed behind in their reindeer-skin tent. She told me she longed for the tundra and for her family, and that her mother also wished to go home. They, like most Khanty, had some confidence in the ability of Soviet doctors, but they resented the situation in which their family was placed. It was hard for them to understand why a cure for the body had to be divorced from cures for the souls of the mother and her family. It was likely that, when they returned to the tundra, a shaman would be asked to make sure that not only the symptoms but also the cause of the sickness had been treated.

Third, it has taken a long time for the level of confidence in Soviet medicine to be built to its current point. When Soviet doctors first came to the north, they were resented as part of the collectivization effort. They were confusing foreign figures, curing without communal ritual. They were also actively opposed by Khanty shamans who believed sincerely in their own abilities. In the early Soviet period, shamanic self-assurance was still nurtured by community approval, in a complex feedback system (cf. Boas 1930:20–41; Lévi-Strauss 1967:169–75; Table 4.2). Any defect of Russian medicine became a victory for shamanism. Startsev (1928:90) tells of a Russian medical assistant whose death was popularly attributed by Vakh River villagers to revenge taken by the local shaman for trifling with his drum. This very polarization prevented shamans, often especially intelligent and creative individuals, from becoming "culture brokers" in the new political and medical atmosphere (cf. Landy 1977:468–81).

FAITH IN MEDICAL SYSTEMS

Even Western medicine requires some faith to be effective, particularly if cures entail the regular taking of drugs. The transfer of faith can involve an intense conversion with a successful cure, or more commonly a slow process of trial, suspicion, pain, and reward (cf. Frank 1961:76, 81, 98). Failures of "foreign" medicine when Russians were trying to win over the populace could not have helped the Soviet cause. Just as "red-tent" programs were beginning to be accepted, World War II, with its terrible losses of Siberian natives, occurred. "Why couldn't Russian medicine have saved more Khanty soldiers?" Khanty asked.

The issue of change in medical faith leads to a hypothesis concerning the ways Khanty think about medical problems. This suggestion is derived from Goodenough (1963:152) and Romanucci-Ross (1977:481–87). Goodenough notes that some Pacific natives coping with acculturation have cognitively divided sickness into white man's and native categories. When they have a white man's sickness, it can be treated with white man's medicine. Otherwise, native cures will suffice. I believe that the Khanty similarly differentiate choices about cures, but that not all sickness can be neatly pigeonholed into Soviet and Khanty categories. Thus, in practice Khanty may combine Western and native cures. Illnesses likely to be treated with native medicine are menstrual, birth, and sexual difficulties, as well as depression, lethargy, dizziness, blindness, soreness, and arthritis.

Syncretism, the merging of beliefs or symbolic actions from different cultures, is a natural part of cognitive adjustment, especially during intense periods of culture change. Its patterning often reveals a logic of its own, as when a prerevolutionary Khanty shaman painted images of St. Nicholas on his drum, claiming that the Russian Orthodox saint, renowned for his curing ability, had become the shaman's helping spirit (Shukhov 1916:31). Today, when Khanty combine respect for Soviet surgery with belief in lost souls, they may be demonstrating an underlying awareness that illness often involves the whole self—both body and mind. Shamanic theories and their accompanying symbolic actions are, as Lévi-Strauss (1967:173–74) has shown, relatively false, but they reach, nonetheless, important symbolic realms rarely glimpsed by modern medicine.

For many Khanty, these realms are based upon sacred correlations, such as birds and hair with souls; bears, horses, and reindeer with spirit messengers; and iron with strength and longevity. These Khanty symbols seem to be both multifaceted and dominant, rendering them flexible and long-lasting, with potential to take on new meanings (cf. Turner 1977:77). Other representations of the sacred, such as clan-related forest spirits (*menk* and *mis*) seem to have less meaning in the Soviet social environment. It is difficult to determine the degree to which ancient shamanic myths have meaning and power in new, limited curing contexts. There is still belief in shamanic ability to turn into a bird, and there is a continuing memory of marathon legends dealing with the travels of shamanic ancestors. I was told one myth about a shamanic cat ancestor who founded a forest grove still revered by some Kazym Khanty. Thus, a few key sacred symbols and myths have maintained a vitality enabling shamanism to survive "underground," but the richness of Khanty symbolism wanes with the death of each shamanic elder.

CONCLUSION

In conclusion, Khanty are increasingly turning to Soviet medicine. The communal atmosphere required for effective symbol-manipulating shamanic seances has been undermined both by Soviet persecution of shamans and by the advances of Soviet medicine. Faith in shamanic power has sometimes turned to fear, making failure of traditional medicine as self-fulfilling a prophecy as success once was. With changing worldviews have come syncretism and increased choice. A combination of factors governs Khanty choices about cures, including issues of convenience, family attention, shamanic reputation, and definitions of sickness as Soviet or native. Khanty consider shamans to be both doctors and deceivers.

ACKNOWLEDGMENTS

I am indebted to the International Research and Exchanges Board, which made 13 months in the Soviet Union (1975–76) possible, and also to IREX for providing preparatory fellowship funds in the summers of 1973 and 1974. Participation in a summer field trip to the Khanty-Mansisk area of northern Siberia (1976) was made possible through Leningrad University. The American Association of University Women (Helen Wood-Pearl Hogrefe Fellowship), the Washington, D.C., Alumnae Association of Bryn Mawr, Sigma Xi, and the Harvard Russian Research Center have generously provided additional support. I wish to acknowledge helpful comments on portions of this material by Professors Frederica de Laguna and Jane C. Goodale of Bryn Mawr and by Professors Demitri B. Shimkin (University of Illinois), Jonathan Andelson (Grinnell), Michael Harner (New School for Social Research), Lydia Black (Providence), Evon Z. Vogt (Harvard), and Michael Fischer (Harvard). Doctors Ronald Dubner and Candace Pert of the National Institute of Health and Curator Ildiko Lehtinen (National Museum of Finland) deserve special thanks for their aid. I am also grateful to the Soviet scholars Rudolf Ferdinandovich Its (head and founder of Leningrad University's anthropology department) and Valery Alexandrevich Kozmin (expedition leader and professor at Leningrad University). They are not, however, responsible for my non-Marxist interpretations of data.

NOTES

1. "Classical" forms of shamanism are recognized to be rooted in Siberia, especially among Tungus-Manchu peoples (Laufer 1917; Nowak and Durrant 1977:38; Harner 1973: xii; Siikala 1978:14–15), although the linguistic origins of the Tungus word *saman* are also sought in more southern, Turkic, traditions, in Sanscrit *sramana*, and Vedic *sram* (Shirokogoroff 1935:270; Demitri Shimkin, personal communication April 1979). The Ob Ugrian (Khanty and Mansi) shamanism described here reveals both northern and southern influences (cf. Dioszegi 1978:135–62).

2. This chapter combines ethnohistorical research with limited field data. For further information about sources, see Balzer (1979). Leningrad University's eight-member student-oriented 1976 ethnographic expedition to the Northern Ob River area (near the Arctic Circle) stayed in two Khanty villages: Tegy, a fishing collective, and Kazym, a reindeer-breeding center. Although Russian was the main means of communication, I learned key concepts in Khantesky and was able to seek my own consultants.

3. Given the complexity of Ob Ugrian soul beliefs, the question becomes whether Khanty have one soul with many aspects or separate souls. Lydia Black believes that multiple manifestations of souls in Siberia represent "the relationship of parts to the whole" (personal communication 16 Feb. 1978). Named distinctions are nonetheless made, and when asked about a gender-based discrepancy in souls, an elderly Tegy woman explained: "Males are higher and females are lower. Males are stronger."

4. In some areas of Siberia, especially among the Mongolic Buriat and the Turkic Yakut, shamans are divided into "black," dealing with lesser and evil spirits of the lower or eastern world; and "white," dealing with major, pure spirits of the upper

or western world (Krader 1954:334–37; Krader 1978:192; Zelenin 1936:294–98). Both can cure, but black shamans are also sorcerers.

5. I have no evidence of *Amanita muscaria* use today, but did see it growing near Kazym. Khanty consultants loathed all mushrooms and were appalled at the large numbers eaten by expedition members, but a few Khanty shamans may secretly maintain the mushroom tradition. Eyewitness evidence for Ugrian shamanic use of *Amanita muscaria* comes from Munkasci (1907), reprinted in Wasson (1960:306), Dunin-Gorkavich (1904:95), and Patkanov (1897:121). Czigany (1980:213) confirms the antiquity of mushroom use by Ob Ugrians. Khanty shamans may also have used hemp seeds thrown in fires to produce intoxication and a blue smoke (Balazs 1968:59–61; Zuev [1771–72] 1947:45). This is documented for Central Asia (Shimkin 1967:624).

6. The importance of the number seven and of a multilayered cosmology in Khanty shamanism may reveal Tatar influences (Karjalainen 1927:245–331; Siikala 1978:224). Ob Ugrian myths describe seven layers of the universe: three upper and three lower worlds, with the earth as central (Chernetsov 1935). Bears, key symbols of supernatural mediation, are still greatly revered throughout Siberia. In Tegy, I was told: "The bear understands everything. He is older than us all. He is the biggest, most important being in the world." (See also Balzer 1979; Hallowell 1926.)

7. Iron and other metals may have once been impressive markers of trade wealth. The religious significance of metal in Khanty symbolism has been shown by Sokolova (1978) and Moszynska (1968), and is studied by Ugrian specialist Ildiko Lehtinen. Shaman accoutrements in National Museum of Finland collections are from Potanin, Alquist, and Karjalainen (e.g., numbers 4866:6; 1870:22; and 4934:216). Metal images of spirit helpers, associated either with shaman equipment or idols, include a bear, lizards, and birds.

8. There is a large literature on whether the shaman is "neurotic" or "schizophrenic." Proponents include Czaplicka (1914), Bogaras (1909), Zelenin (1936), Devereux (1961), and, with reservations for "shaman-saviors," LaBarre (1972). Opponents include Ackerknecht (1943), Honigman (1960), Nordland (1967), Opler (1959, 1961), and Murphy (1964). Beck (1967) and Torrey (1974) argue that the shaman is more psychiatrist than psychotic, whereas Eliade (1974) believes that shamans are cured psychotics. Silverman (1967) stresses that technically schizophrenic tendencies are put to good supportive-creative use in shamanist cultures (cf. Revunenkova 1974; Hultkranz 1978; and Peters and Price-Williams 1980).

9. Neher (1962) suggests that there are important trance-inducing effects of near-alpha brain wave frequencies in shamanic drumming, but the French ethnomusicologist Rouget (1980) forcefully refutes Neher's "reductionist" claims.

10. I am grateful to Doctors Ronald Dubner and Candace Pert at NIH for providing me with leads to possible biochemical responses of patients during shamanic seances. For discussion of endorphins, see Snyder (1977) and Foster and Anderson (1978:99–100). In fall 1980, the Mental Hygiene Institute, R.M. Bucke Memorial Society, and Department of Psychiatry of McGill University sponsored a conference in Montreal entitled "Shamans and Endorphins." Linkages of endorphins with pain control, memory, acupuncture, and shamanic trance were explored.

11. Theories of Freud (1949) and Sargant (1964) are not directly applicable, although abreaction, transference, and heightened suggestibility seem to occur during seances. Cathartic acting out of suppressed desires by a Khanty patient is rare. Other

psychological techniques which may apply to Khanty shamanism include shock therapy (during sorcery object removal); hypnosis (from repetitive shamanic recitations of spirit arrivals); dream interpretation (during diagnosis and in shamanic training); and social reintegration (showing to a patient group concern). Similar native therapies are suggested by E. Fuller Torrey (1974:330–37) and Vincent Crapanzano (1973:212–29), with each cultural context altering the healing process (cf. Kleinman 1979:363–65).

12. A similar increase in "witch-fear" during a period of intense cultural change has been described among the Eskimo by Edmund Carpenter (1961:508–15).

13. In 1976, Kazym had about 270 families with a population of roughly 1300. Such figures are fluid because many Kazym Khanty use their houses as bases from which to go hunting, fishing, or reindeer breeding. There were 466 people in Tegy, living in about 180 houses. They had access to a small medical center in the village and a hospital in Beriosovo. For statistics on modern medical improvements, see Diachkov (1979:20–24).

14. Lola Romanucci-Ross (1977) explains that Manus frequently choose native medicine, basing decisions on a moral component of sickness, whereas choices of European medicine are often last resorts (cf. Landy 1977; Nichter 1978). Studies of "resort" must cope with haphazard elements of choice, and with sampling accurately enough to reflect cultural trends and change (Jon Andelson, personal communication, November 1979).

REFERENCES

Ackerknecht, Erwin H. 1943. "Psychopathology." *Bulletin of the History of Medicine*, 14:30–67.

———. 1958. "Problems of Primitive Medicine [1942]. W. A. Lessa and Evon Z. Vogt, eds., *Reader in Comparative Religion*. Evanston, Ill.: Row Peterson & Co., 342–53.

Ankudinov, N., A. Dobriev, and K. S. Sergeeva. 1939. *Shamany Obmanshchiki* [Shamans as Deceivers]. Leningrad: Glausevmorputi.

Balazs, J. 1968. "The Hungarian Shaman's Technique of Trance Induction," trans. Stephen Dunn. V. Dioszegi, ed., *Popular Beliefs and Folklore Tradition in Siberia*. Uralic and Altaic Studies, vol. 57. Bloomington: Indiana Univ. Press, 53–57.

Balzer, Marjorie Mandelstam. 1979. "Strategies of Ethnic Survival: Interaction of Russians and Khanty in Twentieth-Century Siberia." Ph.D. diss., Bryn Mawr College. Ann Arbor: Univ. of Michigan Microfilm.

———. 1980. "The Route to Eternity: Cultural Persistence and Change in Siberian Khanty Burial Ritual." *Arctic Anthropology*, 17:77–90.

———. 1981. "Rituals of Gender Identity: Markers of Siberian Khanty Ethnicity, Status and Belief." *American Anthropologist*, 83(4):850–67.

Bannerman, R.H. 1977. "W.H.O.'s Programme." *World Health*, Nov.:16–17.

Bartenev, Victor. 1896. *Na Krainem Severe-Zapade Siberia* [In the Far North of Siberia]. Saint Petersburg: M.F. Paukina.

Beck, Robert J. 1967. "Some Proto-Psychotherapeutic Elements in the Practice of the Shaman." *History of Religions*, 6(4):303–27.

Beeson, Paul B., Walsh McDermott, and James B. Wyngaarden. 1979. *Cecil Textbook of Medicine*. Philadelphia: W.B. Saunders Co.

Boas, Franz. 1930. "The Religion of the Kwakiutl." *Columbia University Contributions to Anthropology*, 10(2).

Bogaras, Waldemar. 1909. *The Chukchee*. Memoirs of the American Museum of Natural History, no. 11. New York: Stechert.

Brem, Alexander, 1897. "Ostiaki-Idolpolkoniki" (Ostiak Idol Worshippers). *Ezhemesiachnyia Literaturnyia Prelozheniia k Nive*, 2:347–83.

Businsky, P. O. 1893. *Kreschenie Ostiakov i Vogulov Pre Petre I* [Christianization of Ostiak and Vogul Under Peter I]. Kharkhov: Gub. Pravleniia.

Carpenter, Edmund S. 1961. "Witch-Fear Among the Aivilik Eskimos." Yehudi A. Cohen, ed., *Social Structure and Personality*. New York: Holt, Rinehart and Winston, 508–15.

Charles, Lucile Hoerr. 1953. "Drama in Shaman Exorcism." *Journal of American Folklore*, 66:95–122.

Chernetsov, Valery Nikolaevich. 1935. *Vogul'skie Skazki* [Vogul Tales]. Leningrad: Soslitizdat.

———. 1963. "Ideas of the Soul Among Ob-Ugrians," trans. Ethel Dunn and Stephen Dunn. Henry Michael, gen. ed., *Studies in Siberian Shamanism: Anthropology of the North*, vol. 4. Toronto: Univ. of Toronto Press, 3–45. (Original: "Predstavleniia o Dushe u Obskikh Ugrov." *Trudy Instituta Etnografiia*, 51 [1959]:114–59.)

Crapanzano, Vincent. 1973. *The Hamadsha: A Study in Moroccan Ethnopsychiatry*. Berkeley: Univ. of California Press.

Czaplicka, Marie A. 1914. *Aboriginal Siberia*. London: Oxford Univ. Press.

Czigany, L. G. 1980. "The Use of Hallucinogens and the Shamanistic Tradition of the Finno-Ugrian People." *Slavonic and East European Review*, 58:212–17.

Devereux, George. 1961. "Shamans as Neurotics." *American Anthropologist*, 63:1088–90.

Diachkov, V. I. 1979. "Sostoianie i Perspektivy Razvitiia Zdravookhraneniia v Iamalo-Nentskom i Khanty-Mansiiskom Avtonomykh Okrugakh Tumenskoi Oblasti" (Condition and Perspectives on the Growth of Health Care in the Iamal-Nenet and Khanty-Mansi Autonomous Districts of the Tumen Region). *Zdravookhranenie Rossiskoi Federastii*, 4:20–24.

Dioszegi, Vilmos. 1968. *Tracing Shamans Through Siberia*, trans. Antia Rajkay Babo. Oosterhout, The Netherlands: Anthropological Publications. (Original: *Samanok Nyomaban Sziberia foldjen*. Budapest, 1960.)

———. 1978. "Pre-Islamic Shamanism of the Baraba Turks and Some Ethnogenetic Conclusions," trans. S. Simon. V. Dioszegi and M. Hoppal, eds., *Studies in Seberian Shamanism*. Budapest: Akademiai Kiado, 83–167.

Dunin-Gorkavich, A. A. 1904, 1910, 1911. *Tobol'skii Sever* [The Tobol'sk North], vols. 1–3. Tobolsk: Gub. Tip.

Durrant, Stephan. 1979. "The Nisan Shaman Complex in Cultural Contradiction." *Signs*, 5(2):338–47.

Eliade, Mircea. 1974. *Shamanism: Archaic Techniques of Ecstasy*. Princeton: Princeton Univ. Press.

Fortune, Reo. 1932. *Sorcerers of Dobu*. New York: Dutton & Co.

Foster, George M., and Barbara Gallatin Anderson. 1978. *Medical Anthropology*. New York: John Wiley & Sons.

Frank, Jerome. 1961. *Persuasion and Healing*. Baltimore: Johns Hopkins Univ. Press.

Freud, Sigmund. 1949. *An Outline of Psychoanalysis*, trans. James Strachey. New York: Norton. (Original: *Abriss der Psychoanalyse*, 1940.)

Gillin, John. 1948. "Magical Fright." *Psychiatry*, 11:387–400.

Gondatti, N.L. 1887. "Sledy Iazycheskikh Verovanii u Mansov" (Traces of Pagan Belief Among Mansi). *Trudy Obshchestva Estestvenii Antropologii i Etnografii*, 8:49–93.

Goodenough, Ward. 1963. *Cooperation in Change*. New York: Russell Sage Foundation.

Hajdu, Peter. 1968. "The Classification of Samoyed Shamans," trans. Stephen Dunn. V. Dioszegi, ed., *Popular Beliefs and Folklore Tradition in Siberia*. Uralic and Altaic Series, vol. 57. Bloomington: Indiana Univ. Press, 147–73.

Hallowell, A. Irving. 1926. "Bear Ceremonialism in the Northern Hemisphere." *American Anthropologist*, 28:1–175.

Harner, Michael. 1973. *Hallucinogens and Shamanism*. London: Oxford Univ. Press.

Honigman, John J. 1960. "Review of *Culture and Mental Health*, ed. Marvin Opler." *American Anthropologist*, 62:920–23.

Hultkrantz, A. 1978. "Ecological and Phenomenological Aspects of Shamanism," trans. S. Simon. V. Dioszegi and M. Hoppal, eds., *Shamanism in Siberia*. Budapest: Akademiai Kiado, 27–58.

Karjalainen, K. 1921, 1922, 1927. *Die Religion der Jugra-Volker*, 3 vols. Folklore Communications 41, 44, 63. Porvoo: Finnish Academy of Sciences.

Kartsov, V. G. 1937. *Ocherk Istorii Narodov Severo-Zapadnoi Sibiri* [Essay on the History of the Peoples of Northwest Siberia]. Moscow-Leningrad: Gos. Sots.-Ekon. Izdat.

Kleinman, Arthur. 1979. *Patients and Healers in the Context of Culture*. Berkeley: Univ. of California Press.

Krader, Lawrence. 1954. "Buryat Religion and Society." *Southwestern Journal of Anthropology*, 10:322–51.

———. 1978. "Shamanism: Theory and History in Buryat Society," trans. S. Simon. V. Dioszegi and M. Hoppal, eds., *Shamanism in Siberia*. Budapest: Akademiai Kiado, 181–233.

LaBarre, Weston. 1972. "Hallucinogens and the Shamanic Origins of Religion." Peter Furst, ed., *Flesh and the Gods: The Ritual Use of Hallucinogens*. New York: Praeger, 261–78.

Landy, David. 1977. "Role Adaptation: Traditional Curers Under the Impact of Western Medicine." David Landy, ed., *Culture, Disease and Curing*. New York: Macmillan.

Laufer, Berthold. 1917. "Origin of the Word Shaman." *American Anthropologist*, 19:261–71.

Lévi-Strauss, Claude. 1967. *Structural Anthropology*, trans. Claire Jacobsen and Brooke G. Schoepf. New York: Anchor Books.

Minenko, Nina Adamova. 1975. *Severo-Zapadnaia Sibir'* [Northwest Siberia]. Novosibirsk: Nauka.

Moszynska, V. 1968. "On Some Ancient Anthropomorphic Images from West Siberia," trans. Stephen Dunn. V. Dioszegi, ed., *Popular Beliefs and Folklore*

Tradition in Siberia. Uralic and Altaic Series, vol. 57. Bloomington: Indiana Univ. Press, 93–101.

Murphy, Jane. 1964. "Psychotherapeutic Aspects of Shamanism on St. Lawrence Island, Alaska." Ari Kiev, ed., *Magic, Faith and Healing*. New York: Free Press, 53–83.

Nachtigall, Horst. 1976. "The Cultural-Historical Origin of Shamanism." A. Bharati, ed., *The Realm of the Extra-Human: Agents and Audiences*. The Hague: Mouton, 315–22.

Neher, Andrew. 1962. "A Physiological Explanation of Unusual Behavior in Ceremonies Involving Drums." *Human Biology*, 34:151–60.

Neu, Jerome. 1975. "Lévi-Strauss on Shamanism." *Man*, 10(2):285–92.

Nichter, Mark. 1978. "Patterns of Resort in the Use of Therapy Systems and Their Significance for Health Planning in South Asia." *Medical Anthropology*, 2(2):29–56.

Nordland, Odd. 1967. "Shamanism as an Experiencing of 'the Unreal.' " C. Edsman, ed., *Studies in Shamanism*. Stockholm: Almqvist & Wiksell, 166–85.

Nosilov, K.D. 1904. *U Vogulov* [Among the Voguls]. Saint Petersburg: Suvorin.

Nowak, Margaret, and Stephen Durrant. 1977. *The Tale of the Nisan Shamaness: A Manchu Folk Epic*. Seattle: Univ. of Washington Press.

Ohnuki-Tierney, Emiko. 1976. "Shamanism and World View: The Case of the Ainu of the Northwest Coast of Southern Sakhalin." A. Bharati, ed., *The Realm of the Extra-Human: Ideas and Actions*. The Hague: Mouton, 175–200.

———. 1980. "Ainu Illness and Healing: A Symbolic Interpretation." *American Ethnologist*, 7:132–51.

Opler, Marvin K. 1959. *Culture and Mental Health: Cross Cultural Studies*. New York: Macmillan.

———. 1961 "On Devereux' Discussion of Ute Shamanism." *American Anthropologist*, 63:1091–92.

Patkanov, S. K. 1897. *Die Irtysch Ostyaken und ihre Volkspoesie*. Saint Petersburg: Suvorin.

Peters, Larry G., and Douglass Price-Williams. 1980. "Towards an Experiential Analysis of Shamanism." *American Ethnologist*, 7:397–418.

Prokof'yeva, E. E. 1971. "Shamanskie Kostiumy Narodov Sibiri" [Shaman Costumes of Peoples of Siberia]. *Sbornik Museia Antropologii i Etnografii*, 27:5–10.

Raun, Alo. 1955. *The Ostyak and the Vogul*. New Haven: Human Relations Area File.

Revunenkova, E. V. 1974. "O Lichnosti Shamana" [On the Personality of the Shaman]. *Sovetskaia Etnografiia*, 3:104–11.

Ridington, Robin, and Tonia Ridington. 1975. "The Inner Eye of Shamanism and Totemism" (1970). Denis Tedlock and Barbara Tedlock, eds., *Teachings from the American Earth*. New York: Liveright, 190–204.

Roheim, Geza. 1954. *Hungarian and Vogul Mythology*. Monographs of the American Ethnological Society, vol. 23. New York: Augustin.

Romanucci-Ross, Lola. 1977. "The Hierarchy of Resort in Curative Practices: The Admiralty Islands." David Landy, ed., *Culture, Disease and Healing*. New York: Macmillan, 481–87.

Rombandeeva, E. I. 1968. "Some Observances and Customs of the Mansi (Voguls) in Connection with Childbirth," trans. Stephen Dunn. V. Dioszegi, ed.,

Popular Beliefs and Folklore Tradition in Siberia. Uralic and Altaic Series, vol. 57. Bloomington: Indiana Univ. Press, 77–83.

Rouget, Gilbert. 1980. *La Musique et la Trance.* Paris: Gallimard.

Sargant, William. 1964. *Battle for the Mind.* London: Pan Books.

Senkevich, V. 1935. "Skazka i Pesni Khantov" [Khanty Tales and Songs]. *Sovetskii Sever,* 6(3–4):151–59.

Shashkov, S. 1864. *Shamanstvo v Sibiri* [Shamanism in Siberia]. Saint Petersburg: Morichegovskogo.

Shimkin, Demitri. 1967. "Pre-Islamic Central Asia." *Canadian Slavic Studies,* 1(4):618–39.

Shirokogoroff, Sergei. 1935. *Psychomental Complex of the Tungus.* London: Kegan Paul, Trench, Trubner.

Shukhov, I. N. 1916. "Reka Kazym i ee Obitateli" [The River Kazym and Its Inhabitants]. *Ezhegodnik Tobol'skogo Gubernskogo Muzeia,* 26:1–57.

Siikala, Anna-Lenna. 1978. *The Rite Technique of the Siberian Shaman.* Folklore Communications 220. Helsinki: Finnish Academy of Science.

Silverman, Julian. 1967. "Shamans and Acute Schizophrenia." *American Anthropologist,* 69:21–31.

Snyder, Solomon H. 1977. "Opiate Receptors and Internal Opiates." *Scientific American,* 236(3):44–57.

Sokolova, Z. P. 1971. "Perezhitki Religioznykh Veronanii u Obskikh Ugrov" (Survivals of Religious Belief Among the Ob Ugrians). *Sbornik Muzeia Antropologii i Etnografii,* 27:211–39.

———. 1976. *Strana Ugrov* [The Country of the Ugrians]. Moscow: Mysl'.

———. 1978. "The Representation of a Female Spirit from the Kazym River," trans. S. Simon. V. Dioszegi and M. Hoppal, eds., *Shamanism in Siberia.* Budapest: Akademiai Kiado, 491–501.

Startsev, Georgi. 1928. *Ostiaki: Sotsial'no-Etnograficheskii Ocherk* [The Ostiak: A Social-Ethnographical Study]. Leningrad: Priboi.

Torrey, E. Fuller, M.D. 1974. "Spiritualists and Shamans as Psychotherapists: An Account of Original Anthropological Sin." Irving I. Zaretsky and Mark P. Leone, eds., *Religious Movements in Contemporary America.* Princeton: Princeton Univ. Press, 330–37.

Turner, Victor W. 1964. "An Ndembu Doctor in Practice." A. Kiev, ed., *Magic, Faith and Healing.* New York: Free Press, 230–63.

———. 1977. "Process, System and Symbol: A New Anthropological Synthesis." *Daedalus,* 106(3):61–80.

Vdovin, I. S. 1976. "The Study of Shamanism Among the Peoples of Siberia and the North." A. Bharati, ed., *The Realm of the Extra-Human: Agents and Audiences.* The Hague: Mouton, 261–73.

Vertes, E. 1968. "On the Trail of Ostyak (Khanty) Mythical Songs." V. Dioszegi, ed., *Popular Beliefs and Folklore Tradition in Siberia.* Uralic and Altaic Series vol. 57. Bloomington: Indiana University Press, 113–22.

Wasson, Robert Gordon. 1960. *Soma: The Divine Mushroom of Immortality.* New York: Harcourt, Brace Jovanovich

Zelenin, D. K. 1936. *Kul't Ongongov v Sibiri* [Cult of Idols in Siberia]. Moscow-Leningrad: Akademii Nauk.

Zuev, Vasilii F. 1947. "Opisanie Zhivushchikh Sibirskoi Gubernii v Beriosovskom Uezde, Inovercheskikh Narodov Ostiakov i Samoyedov" (Notes on the Inhabitants of Siberia in Beriosovo, the Natives Ostiak and Samoyed) (1771–1772). *Trudy Instituta Etnografii*, 5(1):1–95.

PART II

SYMBOLS AND HEALING

Relationships between specific medical systems were presented and discussed in Part 1. We presented health care system types to show that outcomes can differ radically in terms of syncretism or acculturation. In Part 2 we will discuss illness as symbol and healing as influenced by symbolic behavior as well as by symbol. This is a more reflexive aspect of negotiating illness and cure; it is perhaps more visible to us in exotic cultures but is not absent in our own, as we shall see.

Lévi-Strauss (1967) describes in some detail how the shaman and the mythology shared by him and the patient alter physiological processes through the control of mental processes, dissolving the boundary between self and other, and offering reintegration to the patient. The "shaman provides a language" (p. 198) and, like the psychoanalyst, allows the conscious and the unconscious to merge. He does this through a shared symbolic system, and that is why a cured individual improves the mental health of the group. Because of this, the patient performs a very important social function; he provides a definition for normalcy and validates the system by calling into play the group's sentiments and symbolic representations to have them "become embodied in real experience" (pp. 180–82). For these healers, the mind, the body, and the experiential field are one.

The key to this social process is the relationship between the process and the consequences of healing, one of the great foci from which we have much to learn from non-Western medicine. Figure II.1 sketches a few of the paths

Figure II.1
Paths of Consequence in the Healing Process

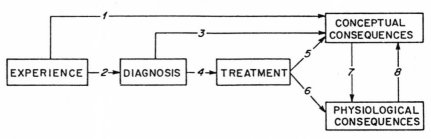

of consequence in the healing process. The patient experiences something amiss: his stomach hurts, he feels lonely and depressed, he develops a sore on his lip or a pain in his head. These symptoms may well, by themselves, have a series of consequences for the patient (path 1)—in the simplest case, they may frighten him and cause stress. In Figure II.1, this fear is a "conceptual consequence," and the stress is a "physiological consequence" of the fear (path 7). Stress, producing an experience itself (path 8), can compound fear; the system contains a feedback loop. The universal human response to such a situation is a kind of analysis we call diagnosis. Either alone, or in consultation with family or therapist, the patient develops an explanation for his experience (path 2). Diagnosis has two types of consequence. The first is directly conceptual (path 3) and may vary greatly in degree. The diagnosis may be soothing ("Oh, it's just a fever sore") or terrifying ("Oh, it's skin cancer"). A soothing diagnosis may "damp down" the feedback loop, whereas a terrifying one may intensify it.

The second consequence of diagnosis (path 4) is treatment, which has two types of consequences, conceptual and physiological. The variation in conceptual responses is great, ranging from minor ("It's just a fever sore— use this ointment on it twice a day") to major ("It's skin cancer—let's try radiation and chemotherapy"). And, of course, different treatments can have different kinds and degrees of physiological consequences. There is here, however, a particularly interesting interaction between the two types of consequences. The ointment may contain an astringent that will help heal the sore; the evidence of healing can encourage the patient, reducing his anxiety via pathways 6–8–7. This process is often generalized so that people develop a kind of faith—"Ointments heal sores"—which can itself be generalized—"Medications heal illnesses"—which can simultaneously induce healing via pathways 5–7–8.

This entire process is deeply embedded in culture. Sickness, a fundamental assault on person and society, is a matter of the deepest human concern: affecting life and death, it can induce deep emotional arousal. Not surprisingly, the act of healing, often including intensely dramatic ritual, shares qualities of the "numinous" in religious experience—it can be ineffable, absolute, and undeniable (Rappaport 1979: 211–16). In simpler terms, the experience of healing can be highly marked.

But sickness raises other issues as well, less emotional, more cosmological. Undeniable experience combined with ultimate cosmology can simultaneously account, in cultural terms, for both. This fact is amply demonstrated in the chapters that follow. Crandon-Malamud gives us an illustration of illness and medicine as a trope to make statements about social relations. Medical dialogue occurring in a pluralistic and stratified society may often provide a context for the construction and negotiation of ethnic identity among Aymara Indians and mestizos in a rural Bolivian village on the altiplano. Diagnostic opinions are simultaneously statements about a condition, the sick person, the person delivering the opinion, and nosological and etiological categories deriving from the various medical traditions in the culture (Indian, folk, and Western). Roberts develops a persuasive argument for the symbolic character of medicines, showing how a specific agent (the charred bones of immolated arsonists) represents a vast cosmological system in Tabwa therapeutics and witchcraft. In Lévi-Straussian terms mentioned above, we find an actual representation of metaphors for illness and cure acted upon to restore harmony to the community; disharmony or disorder had resulted from deviant behavior. Moerman considers the conceptual and subsequent physiological consequences of medical treatment by examining the placebo in Western biomedicine.

None of this is to say that the physiological consequences of medical treatment are not important; path 6 of Figure II.1, the central domain of biomedicine, is a fundamental one (see Part 3 of this book for detailed treatments of this path in non-Western medical traditions). It *is* to say that paths 1, 3, 5, and 7—that is, the conceptual consequences of sickness, diagnosis, and treatment—and their interactions are extremely important in understanding and controlling sickness. An integrated biohuman medical paradigm requires that all of these relationships be understood simultaneously. And biohuman medicine requires that they all be controlled to optimize the healing process.

REFERENCES

Lévi-Strauss, C. 1967. *Structural Anthropology.* Garden City, New York: Doubleday.
Rappaport, R. 1979. *Ecology, Meaning, and Religion.* Richmond, CA: North Atlantic Books.

5

PHANTOMS AND PHYSICIANS: SOCIAL CHANGE THROUGH MEDICAL PLURALISM

LIBBET CRANDON-MALAMUD

Vicente Callisaya, an elderly rural Bolivian Aymara man, was obviously sick in 1977, but everyone in town had a different opinion about what he had. He himself considered all possibilities, and finally determined he had a fatal disease that, according to local belief, affects only Indians. Another opinion was anemia that, consensus had it, cosmopolitan medicine could cure; but he rejected it. Why he made such a choice had little to do with his frame of mind, his access to medicine, or with Aymara beliefs as such. Nor was it due to race, although Doña Teresa, the self-appointed town aristocrat, held that it was. Rather, Vicente's choice was related to the use of the concept of ethnicity and race in Bolivian society and history, and to the use of medicine to create social change.

Doña Teresa's convictions about the "Indian race" are hardly peculiar. In the Bolivian popular mind, as throughout much of the Western world, ethnically defined indigenous populations are considered racially distinct.[1] On those grounds, Indian labor has been exploited since the conquest. Those segments of Bolivian society which have regarded the nation as backward

This chapter is an expanded version of "Medical Dialogue and the Political Economy of Medical Pluralism: A Case from Rural Highland Bolivia." Reproduced by permission of the American Antropological Association from *American Ethnologist* 13:3, August 1986. It includes text from my *From the Fat of Our Souls* University of California Press, (Berkeley: 1991). Clotilde in this chapter is Doña Antonia de Villazon in *From the Fat*; Vicente Callisaya and Doña Teresa are Edegon and Doña Ana in "Medical Dialogue."

have blamed the lack of national progress on the Indian—along with U.S. imperialism when the Indian vote was desirable. Although there is much to support the latter assertion, its periodic appearance contrasts with the consistency of the former explanation.[2]

Following the concept of ethnicity as racially based, mestizos are thought to be of mixed Spanish and Indian ancestry. Among the Aymara and Quechua Indians and the *mestizos* of the highlands, medicine supports these racial categories when indigenous medical ideology defines certain illnesses as visited solely upon Indians, and when cosmopolitan medical records confirm that Indians suffer greater incidence of disease than mestizos or elites. When indigenous medical ideology ascribes disease suffered by Indians to mestizo and upper-class elements, however, medicine does just the opposite: Because it can conquer the disease, it thereby empowers resistance to oppression. Thus medicine plays a role in the formation (and reformation) of the meaning of ethnicity, and in effecting social change, particularly in an environment that is medically pluralistic and socially diverse. One way to examine how medicine can both reinforce social structure and support social change is to examine the changes in medical ideology itself. The history of the *karisiri* is a case in point.

MEDICAL IDEOLOGY AS HISTORY: THE *KARISIRI*

The *karisiri*, or *karikari*, and the illness it causes have been noted in Andean chronicles and by priests and anthropologists in the region since the colonial conquest (Oblitas Poblete 1963;[3] La Barre 1948;[4] Tschopik 1951;[5] Aguilo 1982[6]). It is the robed and bearded apparition of a Jesuit priest that, for over four hundred years, was said to inflict death upon the Aymara and Quechua by stealing the fat from their kidneys. Such fat was given to the bishop, who made holy oil from it that sanctified the non-Indian population.

During the 1960s and the Alliance for Progress years, when much of the blame for the failure of the 1952 Movimiento Nacional Revolucionario (MNR) revolution to modernize the country was placed on U.S. imperialism, some anthropologists and priests[7] reported that the *karisiri* was said to sell the oil to North Americans, who used it to generate electricity.

In the village on the Bolivian altiplano where I did my research for eighteen months between 1976 and 1978, Indians and *mestizos* alike agreed that the *karisiri* is not an apparition but, rather, a skill that any village mestizo can learn. Such a mestizo steals the fat with instruments clandestinely obtainable in pharmacies in La Paz. The fat is sold at huge profits to factories that make perfumed luxury soaps for the European and North American markets. Significantly, the affliction is no longer considered fatal.

In this explanation of illness,[8] what people say about their social world through the idiom of medicine are statements about political and economic realities, and the meaning of ethnic relations; the shifts in that explanation, or medical theory, reflect changes in Bolivian society. Since the Bolivian revolution of 1952, which instituted a land reform and destroyed the hacienda system established under colonialism, landownership and increased market participation among the Aymara have resulted in decreasing rates of malnutrition and consequent reduction in mortality from infectious diseases and parasites. To be Indian is no longer to be completely at the mercy of demonic beings, the agricultural or mining elite, and the rural *mestizos* who served the interests of those elites in the countryside before 1952. Among the mestizos, however, the revolution and land reform took away the land and the power they had wielded over the Indians. The loss of rural power led to divisions among the mestizos as they suddenly found it necessary to compete against one another for the few resources that could be used for social mobility and eventual migration to the city. Within the village this once cohesive and locally powerful group is now politically and economically marginal.

Following the theoretical contributions of such authors as Emily Martin (1987), Susan Sontag (1978), and Nancy Scheper-Hughes and Margaret Lock (1987) the *karisiri* myth is another example of medicine as metaphor for social relations. The *karisiri* example, however, is more amenable to Foucault's line of reasoning (e.g., 1965, 1973) insofar as changes in its interpretation can be seen over time as concurrent with changes in the political economy, in ethnic affiliation with that economy, and in the effects of that political economy on the content of ethnic identity. The significance of the *karisiri* belief, then, is the question it raises: How medicine as metaphor changes over time, and what role it plays in interethnic relations and in the formation of social relationships.

MEDICAL PLURALISM, SOCIAL DIVERSITY, AND SOCIAL CHANGE

In an environment that is diverse in ethnicity and class, and is also medically pluralistic, people draw on multiple medical ideologies. As they do so, their medical dialogue reflects, involves, and contributes to the construction of political, economic, ideological, and social relations. Through medical dialogue, ethnic groups negotiate the meaning of ethnic identity and affiliation, and therefore of interethnic relations.[9] Consequently, medical dialogue is a medium through which we can see political and economic processes as they pertain to the nature of interethnic relations. Simultaneously it is an arena in which those interethnic relations are negotiated and played out. Hence medical ideology and dialogue are both an arena for change and a window on the politicoeconomic relationship between medicine and ethnicity (and social class).

An examination of actual use of medical ideology and medical dialogue between and among Indians and mestizos in a rural highland Bolivian village can move us beyond the view of medicine as metaphor to an understanding of how medicine changes in the short run, is constantly reinterpreted by different social segments as a means for the exchange of political and economic resources, and as a mechanism to facilitate or impede change, particularly the reformation of social relations. How people talk about illness is a means by which the symbolic content of ethnic identity is interpreted, and the nature of social relationships is defined.

This examination is dependent on a focus on dialogue about medical beliefs as symbols both within and between ethnic and class groups.[10] As such, the focus is not upon symbols that express group unity but, rather, on symbols through which communication is made across ethnic and class lines and therefore permits or facilitates opposition, conflict, and change.

Field research took place in a small, biethnic rural Bolivian village on the altiplano that serves as the center of the canton of Omasullu. Here approximately a thousand Aymara and mestizos inhabit the *municipio* that serves some sixteen thousand Aymara in thirty-six surrounding *aldeas*. During my stay there, a number of people in the village became ill; each time, everyone in town knew every symptom and detail of the illness that the victim suffered and, as often as not, a number of details that he or she did not. People voiced their opinions vociferously as to what they thought a patient had, and consequently what ought to be done about it. To do so, they drew upon nosological and etiological categories that derive from Indian, folk, and cosmopolitan medical traditions, categories that carry social significance depending on the context in which they are used. Each diagnostic opinion was a statement about the sick person, the person delivering the opinion, and the relationship between the two. The social relationship being expressed was often that among the several parties discussing the illness and a person not present. Although conversations were ostensibly debates about what a patient suffered from, the fundamental issue under negotiation concerned the power to monopolize the construction of the meaning of the illness, and hence to define the relationship between the parties engaged in the dialogue. The outcome of the discussion had multiple political and economic implications in village life.

VICENTE

When Vicente became ill in 1977, he sought out several *yatiris*, Aymara shamans. They provided various diagnoses but did not make him feel any better. Vicente's son told me that Vicente had told him he had *limpu*, a fatal condition caused by witnessing an Indian stillbirth. The *limpu* is the soul of a stillborn who, having died before baptism, is prohibited from entering heaven and therefore seeks to continue its existence on earth. This soul enters the body of a witness to the birth, and since the soul survives by consuming the victim, the victim—or host—grows thinner and thinner until death occurs.

One analysis of this etiology discloses *limpu* as a statement of Indian identity that differentiates Indian oppression from non-Indian or mestizo domination and points to the inequality of access to resources of the two ethnic groups. Mestizos neither cause *limpu*—because they do not live like or are not Indians—nor get it—because they never attend Indian births. Furthermore, the key element in the transmission of the disease—the absence of baptism—is an element of Catholicism, and until the 1970s the local Catholic church was controlled by mestizos and elites, served their interests at the expense of those of the Aymara, and subsisted on Indian labor. Moreover, Indians do grow "thinner and thinner" and die from anemia or malnutrition much more often than do mestizos.

The mestiza Clotilde, mother of four, wife of an itinerant schoolteacher, and landless, agreed with Vicente's son that Vicente probably had *limpu*. She allowed that her judgment rested on the fact that she herself had had experience with the illness in her family. However, she urged Vicente to see the physician just in case it was something that a physician might treat. She appeared concerned about his health and agreed that his own choice of diagnosis was reasonable. She further shared the sense of victim implied by the illness even though, as a mestiza, she belonged to a class of people who deny vulnerability to Indian illnesses such as *limpu*.

Over the many years they had known each other, Clotilde had frequently sympathized with Vicente when he recalled the brutality of hacienda life before 1952. The patron of the hacienda to which Vicente had been attached, a wealthy mestizo who was able to migrate to the city after the land reform, is now a professional in La Paz and calls himself white. He has spurned Clotilde's family's overtures for aid, which were first made on the basis of old *compadrazgo* (fictive kin ties).[11] His denial was based on the defense that the ties were his father's, not his, and were therefore no longer valid. Clotilde's family, reasonably well-to-do in 1952 had by the 1970s dropped into the village's lowest socioeconomic stratum. Now landless, Clotilde is unable to support her four children on her husband's salary, much of which goes for his own support away from home.

In 1977, Clotilde increased her contact and exchange with Vicente's family, initially on the basis of *compadrazgo* ties and later on a vague claim to kinship. However, unlike the earlier mestizo-Indian *compadrazgo* bond that had joined the two ethnic groups in a dependent relationship of unilateral exploitation, Clotilde and Vicente's relationship is equilateral. Clotilde's mestizo class no longer has the power to sanction labor exploitation, and Vicente's fellow Aymara have the freedom to bypass many local mestizos in order to get access to resources from the urban or national domain. Indeed, Clotilde needs Vicente and access to his agricultural produce as much as he needs her for the social ties he can gain through her. Hence, when he falls sick, Clotilde delivers an opinion and a little aid in a mode that denotes the egalitarian nature of their relationship, and aligns herself with Indian ethnicity.

The one physician in town was from La Paz and an aspirant to the urban elite, serving his year of required rural duty. He examined Vicente and described his health as "perfect." Vicente was "old and anemic," he explained, and he prescribed vitamins and rest. Of significance, however, is the similarity between anemia and *limpu*; the symptoms are identical. The significant difference is that *limpu* is usually fatal, as is implied by its etiology, adding a political dimension to the illness by underlining Indian/mestizo inequality.

The mestiza Doña Teresa, keeper of the town archives, virtual head of the most prestigious mestizo family in town, godmother to perhaps a hundred Aymara children, and *comadre* or godmother to a number of well-placed families in La Paz, thought that both diagnoses were preposterous. She found Clotilde's medical opinions scandalous, although they confirmed what she had suspected all along: that there were Indians in Clotilde's family. That would account for Clotilde's degenerate behavior of associating beneath her class and ethnic group, disgracing the *gente decente*, as well as her lack of wealth, power, and good connections. Teresa determined to cease extending credit to Clotilde or even selling her items from Teresa's family's *tienda*.[12]

Teresa also knew better than the physician. He was, she claimed, a young fellow from the city who lacked her experience with Indians in the countryside. Her family had been godparents to Vicente's family for many generations. Yet in recent decades his family had not honored the *compadrazgo* relationship sanctioned before 1952 by providing her family with agricultural goods and services. This delinquency had produced a hardship on Teresa's household, which had lost much of its land to the reform. Teresa sees Vicente as lazy, poorly behaved, and sick because of the degeneracy of his moral constitution. Moral decrepitude leading to poor health is a folk illness derived from Euro-Christian folk tradition, and is a form of moral retribution for which there is no remedy. Consequently, Teresa had no therapeutic recommendation to offer. In her opinion, Vicente ate quite adequately. At least he had sufficient resources on his land. Her medical opinion makes it quite clear and nonnegotiable that she no longer has any obligation to Vicente.

Vicente died twenty-four hours after his visit to the physician, convinced that he had *limpu*. The cause of death was never determined in a manner that would be satisfactory to this audience, although I noted he was quite elderly and suspect he died of heart failure. As in the process of diagnosis, everyone in town held an opinion about the cause of Vicente's death. The *limpu*/anemia/moral decrepitude complex employed in this case and the particular issues involved are merely examples of a variety of options and issues employed in a given illness incident by which individuals define and display their relationships to each other. The potential of such medical dialogues for the reformation of social relations is always manifest.

UNDERSTANDING THE DIALOGUE ABOUT VICENTE

An explanation of how and why this dialogue exposes social processes requires an understanding of five dimensions of Bolivian social life that, according to popular belief, do not exist: (1) the social construction of ethnicity and race; (2) the political economy of Bolivia that facilitates or compels social mobility across ethnic boundaries; (3) the downward as well as upward social movement as a consequence of that political economy;[13] (4) the confluences of culture that are shared by different ethnic groups[14] and permit that movement; and (5) the political economy of medical pluralism which facilitates that movement. The argument here is not that medicine is a metaphor for social relations embedded in a political economy, as has been argued elsewhere (e.g., Sontag 1978; Taussig 1980). Rather, medical dialogue is a means by which political and economic resources are exchanged, and is thus a mechanism that facilitates or inhibits change.

The Social Construction of Ethnicity

Contrary to Doña Teresa's convictions, racial integrity never existed in Upper Peru[15] or Bolivia. During the colonial era, many descendants of the Spanish experienced downward economic mobility and some were even designated Indians, while many Indian elites wore European dress, were educated in Europe, and married the Spanish (Abercrombie 1986; Crandon-Malamud 1991; Platt 1978a, 1978b, 1982a; 1982b; Rasnake 1988). Mestizos constituted that population—both Spanish and Indian—which served the interests of the elite by controlling Indian labor, particularly in the rural areas, until the MNR revolution of 1952.[16] Today they compose the middle classes—the working classes and the service sector—who are excluded from the moneyed elite. Neither Indian nor elite, they were, and remain, despised by both (Carter 1958:52).

Ethnicity is thus the product of class conflict, exploitation, and resistance, justified by concepts of race, to permit the mobilization of labor on behalf of the state or the elite. For the agriculturally based Aymara and Quechua who maintain an indigenous social organization, legal system, and economy—albeit within the national domain—the construct of ethnicity has facilitated their oppression, opposition, defiance, and survival. For Spanish *and* Indians who became mestizos, the myth that they were a mixed race justified their exclusion from the elite but their social class position as supervisors of Indian labor. Since both mestizos and Indians managed to join the ranks of the elite over the past four centuries, and many of the elite lost wealth and position and were excluded from that social class, Indians, mestizos, and elites all share confluences of the same culture; and a principal cultural domain they all share is medical ideology.

Thus, contrary to popular opinion, an enormous amount of shift in ethnic and class membership has taken place since the sixteenth century, and medical ideology has facilitated that social change as much as it has supported the myth of race. A brief reference to Bolivian political and economic history[17] and an analysis of interethnic relations reveals why this movement takes place. Specifically, it shows why Clotilde wants to befriend Vicente on the basis of mutual friendship and give up the privileges of her superordinate ethnic group.

Political Economy and Movement across Ethnic Boundaries

Seen as a nation of two distinct cultures—the "traditional Indian" and the "modern"—Bolivia has fallen prey to the "dual economy" dichotomy and related concepts that mask the essentiality of Indian labor, first to the colonial crown and then to the nation-state; the participation of both in the world economy (Dunkerley 1984; Wallerstein 1974; Wolf 1982); the links that articulate them; and the consequent confluences of culture that they of necessity share. The two primary related concepts are modernization and development, both of which obfuscate the confluences of culture that Indian, mestizo, and elite share.

"Modernization" refers to the transformation of social organization and worldview into that of an industrialized middle class (e.g., Valenzuela and Valenzuela 1978). "Development" refers to economic diversification, industrialization, and participation in a world market in a manner that is decreasingly "dependent" or "peripheral" (Muñoz 1981). The general position is that development, if it does not destroy indigenous culture, at least modernizes it in such a way that—if it is Western-oriented—the population should increasingly aspire to the principles of science and commerce, court modern medicine, and decry the "superstition of magic."[18]

However, the political economy that articulates Bolivian elites, mestizos, and Indians is as much a product of the detrimental effects of efforts to modernize and develop as it is of Bolivia's colonial and prerevolutionary legacy. That legacy was a political arena in which caudillismo (rule by a strongman) was the principle by which power was obtained, and *personalismo* or privilege that by which access to resources and power was gained. Ever since the Spanish conquest, Bolivia has been a country characterized by extreme poverty of the vast majority of the population, scarcity of resources[19] caudillo rule,[20] and the exchange of goods and power through *personalismo*.

Personalismo ties are established through kinship and *compadrazgo*. They do not follow ethnic or class divisions but are specifically constructed to cross cut them, vertically linking segments of all social sectors. They thus oppose ethnic and class interests as players struggle to create and manipulate ties to gain access to limited resources and to reinforce highly centralized rule.

Contemporary Bolivia's political economy continues to be based on an increasing scarcity of resources that perpetuates those very principles. This is so in spite of many attempts to create class interests and political parties based on a more equitable distribution of wealth and the destruction of the principle of *personalismo*, particularly since 1952. In that year the MNR revolution destroyed the hacienda system, initiated an agrarian reform, armed the peasant masses, established unions (including peasant unions), and instituted universal suffrage.[21] The hacienda Indian attachment to a patron through labor obligations in exchange for rent was transformed into a land-owning peasantry of campesinos that now has access to some education and some economic, even entrepreneurial, opportunity.[22] By the 1970s postrevolutionary colonization and development of the state of Santa Cruz had led to exports of gas, cotton, and sugar that appeared to be benefiting the middle and upper classes.

In spite of these great economic and social changes, a commercial class has not been able to establish itself as a dominant sector in Bolivia, and proletarianization of the peasantry on the altiplano has been slow or absent (Mendelberg 1985). Only the mining unions were able to unify a socioeconomic sector with a political platform that reflected its social interests as a class (Nash 1979). The unions accounted, however, for only 3 percent of the population and dispersed when the mines were closed in the mid-1980s.[23]

Virtually none of the development activity had a negative effect on *personalismo*, and the particular formation of the contemporary cocaine economy may well be a product of it. *Personalismo* and caudillo activity undermined the campesino unions established in the 1950s by the revolution, as campesino leaders competed for scarce resources within a divided government; these unions were dismantled before the campesinos ever perceived themselves to be in any way unified (Heath 1969b). By 1980 gas, cotton, and sugar had failed to accumulate capital. On the contrary, they escalated an already extraordinary national debt, and in the 1980s they were replaced by cocaine as Bolivia's principal export (Canelas O. and Canelas Z. 1983; Dunkerley 1984). Since the late 1970s, Argentina has virtually inhaled Bolivia's gas exports, the price of which, General Videla pointed out as he tore up his gas bill in November 1982, did not cover the interest on the loan that Bolivia received from Argentina in 1980. While the development of the lowland area has indeed diversified national production that had previously been limited to tin, the benefits have accrued solely to a particular segment of the lowland society and to the military, and have rarely, if ever, been reinvested in Bolivia. Between 1980 and 1983 national production decreased between 2 and 10 percent annually. The national debt is so great that what production there is does not begin to erase it.

In the spring of 1984, Bolivia was the first developing country to default on its loans. The government declared that it would pay nothing toward the interest until 1987; and North American banks, terrified of the precedent this would set, quietly let it pass (Gwynne 1987).[24] Although the subject of considerable debate, it appears that the cocaine economy has benefited no sector of Bolivian society except the narcotraffickers and those segments of the military which are involved with them. Most evidence reveals its social, economic, and politically destructive, if not devastating, consequences (Aguilar personal communication; Malamud-Goti 1990). Ecologically and environmentally it has been catastrophic. Initially the major economic impact from increased coca production was inflation, calculated for 1983 at 25,000 percent.[25] During most of this time, salaries—except those of the military— were frozen.[26] Consequently, both economic and political resources are scarcer than ever for the vast majority of the Bolivian population, and *personalismo* remains the most effective, if not the only, means by which one gains access to resources.[27]

Concomitantly the democratic experiment degenerated into military rule in 1964, and although democracy appeared momentarily for elections in 1978, 1979, and 1980, the latter election resulted in the flight of the elected president and congress from military coups engineered by fortune-seeking caudillos. Although Hernán Siles Suazo, after coming in first in all those elections in the 1970s, finally took office in 1983, he held it for less than the full term and with considerable difficulty.[28]

This situation has impeded any political unification of classes; and the rigidity of ethnic boundaries remains a useful myth to explain the limited strategies available for gaining access to resources in such a system. Little remains changed or exchanged, from onions to presidents, except through *personalismo*. Among kin and *compadres*, aid, security, wealth, and privilege are exchanged for loyalty. Certainly employment in the public sector and political power are contingent on personal ties. So it is that when interim president Lydia Gueiler Tejada reprimanded her renegade nephew Luis Garcia Meza for attempting a military coup in 1979, she did not take strong legal action against him, such as imprisonment or exile. Likewise, when he successfully seized the government a year later, he liberally supplied his followers and relations with contracts in the cocaine trade and exclusive rights to diamond fields in the interior, manipulating the legislative process for his personal interests much like his caudillo predecessors.[29]

Even the Bolivian military does not compose a class or body with shared interests. Rather, it is composed of a loosely connected series of pyramidal structures, each internally organized according to the principles of *personalismo*, and each led by a general who competes with the other generals to dominate military and political activities for his own economic gain and for the benefit of his relatives and his followers, according to the ideal of the good patriarch. Such a system provides upward mobility only to the privileged—those with the right connections. For those without those connections, not only is downward mobility a necessity, but affiliation with Indian ethnicity is an advantage.

Upward and Downward Mobility

Following the myth that ethnic boundaries are rigid—a myth that is being unmasked and addressed in some contemporary anthropological literature on the area (e.g. Abercrombie 1986; Platt 1978a Rasnake 1988)—is the further assumption, both popular and anthropological, that what social movement does occur across ethnic lines is only upward from Indian to mestizo to white. This assumption emerged from the belief in Western hegemony and faith in "modernization" and "development" ubiquitous among non-Indians, and is reinforced by the presence of both indigenous and national economies and modes of exchange and the nature of their articulation. To the crises of history, Bolivia has adapted by continuing to maintain the indigenous peasant economy.[30]

The peasant or *ayllu* economy of the agriculturally based Aymara and Quechua campesino is a precolonial structure: a subsistence agricultural economy that articulates multiple ecological zones through reciprocity of goods and labor. It lies primarily outside the cash economy although it supplies much of Bolivia's domestic agricultural produce, and is locally governed or facilitated by its own elected officials (Abercrombie 1986; Buechler and Buechler 1971; Carter 1982; Rasnake 1988). It thus can provide subsistence when the national economy collapses[31] Within and between Aymara and Quechua communities, exchange is based on egalitarian social relations and reciprocity usually defined by the *ayllu*—the extended family in which reciprocity of productive labor is obligatory.

Although *ayllu* is based on a fundamentally different mode of production relations (see Wolf 1982:23) than that of the national economy, these two economies are tightly integrated; the dominance and wealth of the non-Indian domain have been, and remain, based on the oppression and isolation of the Indians, particularly as agricultural producers. Indian participation in the cash economy as agricultural producers is limited to favor the urban sector and elites and to subsidize their modernization and development. At least through the 1970s,[32] the price of all domestic agricultural goods was fixed by the government, inhibiting the development of both the market sector of Aymara and Quechua entrepreneurs and the new campesino landowners who, long since abandoned by the government as a sector worthy of investment or support, cannot make a meaningful profit by marketing or producing agricultural goods at levels much greater than subsistence (International Work Group on Indigenous Affairs 1978; Morales 1966; Malloy 1970; Nash 1979. See also Malloy 1971; Arnaude 1957; Alexander 1958; Heath 1969a; McEwen et al. 1969; Preston 1969).

On the one hand, this policy accentuates the dependency of the national economy on that of the Indian. Taken together, they constitute a single system at the political and economic peripheries of the world economic system (Dunkerley 1984; Frank 1966, 1971; Mayorga 1987; Quiroga Santa Cruz 1973; Roxborough 1979). The myth that ethnic boundaries are rigid and permit only occasional upward mobility structures economic relations and exchange between these two economic domains hierarchically along ethnic and class lines, and reinforces the principle of privilege as a means of access to resources and power within the national domain.

On the other hand, this policy is facilitated by the fact that the *ayllu* economy, being independent of cash and highly adapted over thousands of years to the Andes, provides subsistence to its participants and affiliates when the national economy collapses—which it has on many occasions over the last four centuries. As the peasant economy coexists with Bolivia's non-industrialized and frequently ailing economy, the peasant economy is discerned, particularly by the poorer classes, as a flexible resource that enables one to ride out a national economic crisis. Thus, in spite of continued oppression of the Indians and the use of ethnicity to justify and perpetuate it, being Indian, or being accepted by Indians, has its advantages. Downward mobility is a serious option for many poor mestizos like Doña Clotilde.

Crossing ethnic boundaries in Bolivia is overtly prohibited but covertly institutionalized and follows a specific set of rules. Rules for upward mobility include the change in language, dress, and comportment that Harris refers to in his seminal work on race in Latin America (1964), and the mythification of one's heritage, as Teresa's comment about Clotilde's genealogy indicates. Downward mobility requires involvement in campesino production and egalitarian social relations with campesinos. However, accessibility to it is problematic: one has to enter the peasant economy by its own social rules of egalitarianism. Movement in either direction is not achieved by the individual but negotiated within the community. One must convince the others to treat him or her accordingly. A principal way to do so is through the use of medical dialogue and the manipulation of ideologies inherent in medical pluralism. This is possible because everyone in Bolivia shares confluences of the same culture.

Confluences of Culture

As we are here conceiving of Bolivia as a single population organized into a series of interrelated hierarchical sectors corresponding to access to economic and political resources, which sectors in turn define ethnic identities between which there is bilateral movement, we are necessarily presupposing confluences of culture that are shared by all three ethnic and class groups in spite of separate ethnic, political, and social identities. This view permits one to examine how a society that perceives itself as rigidly divided ethnically has such considerable movement across ethnic boundaries, and to incorporate the data that a llama fetus and other magical items are buried under the four corners of the foundations of every modern building in downtown La Paz, including the Chase Manhattan Bank and the old Gulf Oil building,[33] that the wealthy often trust the reading of the coca leaves more than their financial advisers (Press 1969, 1971; Bastien 1981), and that *yatiris* are including intravenous solutions and antibiotics in their treatment of "magical" disorders (Bastien 1981; see also Romanucci-Ross 1986).

While in the Indian domain the earth mother Pachamama reigns supreme over a pantheon of magical and supernatural entities that control and manipulate the destinies of human lives, Indians share with the mestizos and elites these same symbols, using them in different ways, often to define, create, or solidify social ties that link those domains. Actual ancestry and kinship ties are less significant than recognized heritage and kinship ties; kinship ties are manipulable (Strickon and Greenfield 1972); and heritage is constructed and mythified to fit social and political needs. Ties that are recognized or acknowledged define those social relations through which power and wealth are exchanged and, hence, ethnic identity and affiliation. One way to acquire acknowledgment is through the use of medical discourse.

More significantly, the view of Bolivia as a single system permits us to examine the movement across ethnic boundaries as a negotiated process that in turn permits the consideration of how medical dialogue plays a role in these negotiations. Hence we see in the mestiza Teresa's dialogue that she knows very well what *limpu* is and means, and uses that knowledge to assert her social superiority over Vicente.

Clotilde's efforts to establish an egalitarian relationship with Vicente required that she both adopt some elements of Aymara identity (vulnerability to *limpu*) and be willing to sacrifice ties with and respect from some of the more prestigious mestizos. Her conversation with Vicente is an example of one means by which the process of crossing ethnic boundaries and establishing affiliation takes place.

The Political Economy of the Content of Ethnic Identity

The rural mestizos in Omasullu who were also mestizos in 1952 still maintain as much as possible of the pre-1952, prerevolution colonial heritage that established them as overlords of the rural Indian population. But the foundation upon which that heritage was maintained was destroyed with the land reform of 1953 and the collapse of the hacienda system. These highland rural mestizos try not to work the land themselves and do not participate in the new entrepreneurial activities. They survive instead as proprietors of *tiendas* that originally operated on the principle of debt peonage; the debtors were Indians with whom the mestizo *tienda* owner had *compadrazgo* ties. The *tienda* constituted the local form of patriarchal *personalismo* exchange that has broken down since 1952.

Entrepreneurial activities are now monopolized by *cholos*, nonsubsistence-based Indians, many of whom aspire to be urban mestizos. Today rural mestizos also survive on government salaries as schoolteachers and rural officials. Their main objective and that of upwardly mobile *cholos* is to try, through their personal contacts in the city, to establish their children there, not only because they have always emulated the urban elite but also because the contemporary rural mestizo has lost almost all the means by which to directly extract a subsistence from the Indian population. Consequently, unless one is willing and able to do subsistence agriculture or to engage in entrepreneurial activities, there is little for a mestizo to do today on the rural Bolivian altiplano. Government salaries are paltry and are dependent upon *personalismo* ties with government officials that, if not prestigious, may result in the rural employee being sent to the least desirable region of the country.

Some mestizos have successfully moved to the city or, like Doña Teresa, formed ties there, while others have not. Consequently, while many rural mestizos look to the city to establish ties with which to improve their condition, those whose strategies have been unsuccessful, like Doña Clotilde, look down, as it were, toward egalitarian relations with Indians as a means of survival in a contracting economic environment. Such a move, toward egalitarian relations with Indians in a patriarchal society, requires a renegotiation of the content of ethnic identity and affiliation.

MEDICAL DIALOGUE AND THE NEGOTIATION OF DOWNWARD MOBILITY

In the Omasullu village where this research was carried out, a substantial number of poor mestiza women whose families had lost their *tiendas* and their land since 1952 were, in 1976–1978, bartering magical and medicinal items and spices in the peasant market in return for agricultural produce and eggs. The agricultural produce was their family's source of subsistence; the eggs were sold in La Paz for cash that served as their capital with which the items and spices were resupplied. Many of these women had sought Indians as godparents to their children, looking "down" rather than "up" the *compadrazgo* network, contrary to usual mestizo practice. By doing so, they established egalitarian rather than hierarchal relationships with Indians.

The Indian and mestizo modes of existence in the rural altiplano and the political significance of their hierarchal relationship, as well as the fact that that relationship is changing, not only are expressed in indigenous medical ideology to which both Indians and mestizos subscribe, but also are initiated through medical dialogue. The participants thereby acknowledge that they share confluences of culture as they conflate two previously distinct domains of economy and ethnic affiliation.

Between 1970 and 1977 in this village, six mestizo youths in their late teens and twenties suffered severe illnesses that would appear to have, in scientific terms, both nutritional and psychological complications.[34] All six came from families that had once been among the most prestigious in the area. Since the revolution they had all lost nearly everything of value they had once owned, and were now among the poorest of village mestizo society. The first four of these illnesses were treated by Western medical and psychiatric therapies based on a village consensus that the youths suffered from scientifically identifiable disorders. All four died from these illnesses. In 1976 and 1977, the last two of these six ailing youths turned instead to Aymara *yatiris*, and most villagers concurred that they suffered from Indian diseases.[35]

The last two youths survived their illnesses. Both of these youths were siblings of two of the four who had died earlier of ostensibly similar but differently diagnosed illnesses. The fathers of both youths had died years earlier and the young men were supported by mothers who were landless or nearly so, and who made a living by bartering in the Indian peasant market. Both women had established relations with Indians on an egalitarian basis, even claiming kinship. One was denounced as the town "crazy lady"; the other was ostracized by the better-off mestizos, who continued to aspire to the economic and political life of the patriarchal domain of the urban sector. While sufficient data are unavailable to establish causes of illness in each case, the decisions made about treatment, regardless of pathology, show a group of families choosing one medical tradition over another in these specific cases. The significant variable in their condition appears to be whether they had suffered rather than gained by the revolution, whether they had been unsuccessful in the non-Indian domain, whether they had inadequate personal ties and had thus been excluded from a world to which they aspired, and whether they then perceived non-Indians as oppressing them, much as the Aymara see the mestizos oppressing Indians.

In all cases there had been a subtle change in ethnic identification and affiliation toward "Indianness," to participation in the Indian economic exchange, and away from dependency on *personalismo* ties in the patriarchal domain of the center. Most significantly, those who take this latter course also have a self-perception of vulnerability to Indian diseases. That is, in all cases there has been a change in the content of ethnic identity. Analysis of a conversation between Doña Clotilde and several Aymara concerning a physician reveals how medical dialogue not only reflects but also implements changes in the content of ethnic identity and, as a result, incremental social change.

HOW IT WORKS: INCREMENTAL SOCIAL CHANGE
THROUGH MEDICAL DIALOGUE

Like many physicians throughout the world, Dr. Tallacagua explicitly used exclusively cosmopolitan medicine to achieve upward mobility, which for him meant crossing the ethnic boundary that divides the Aymara from the Bolivian upper classes. He had been born an Aymara Indian in one of the outlying communities, then had attended a Methodist Indian school, where he won a church scholarship that put him through medical school. In 1978 he returned for two months to the village as part of his medical training. The town clinic, founded by Methodist missionaries, is jointly controlled by the local Aymara and the Bolivian Methodist Church, and is perceived as an Indian institution that receives "gringo" financial support.

Everyone in town interpreted what Dr. Tallacagua said about medicine and how he talked in the clinic—his medical dialogue—as rejection of his Aymara ethnicity; and they resented it. As they discussed this resentment, they created an alliance between themselves that led to incremental steps in the creation of social change: Tallacagua's loss of status and early departure from town, the reinforcement of Aymara control and use of indigenous medicine in the clinic.

As Clotilde saw it, the trouble with Tallacagua was that he refused to speak Aymara at the clinic except with monolingual Aymara speakers. He was brusque and uncommunicative, and intimidated Clotilde. He had reduced her salary for washing linens from one peso per item to one peso per six items. Her work at the clinic was already a social disgrace among the village mestizos. But, landless and *tienda*-less, Clotilde and her four children could not subsist on the remittances her husband sent home. Ashamed that he could not send her more, her husband often called her a spendthrift and threatened to leave her for another woman who would be more financially responsible. When she took him seriously, she feared he would throw her and the children out of the house to starve. Her poverty and emotional outbursts were a source of shame to the other mestizos, who felt she reflected badly on them, particularly by being employed as a laundress at the clinic— even though most of them are just as poor. Doña Teresa thought Clotilde behaved like an Indian. Worse, her current employer, Tallacagua, was an Indian! Clotilde frequently had "attacks" and initially turned to the clinic for tranquilizers. In 1978, however, she was afraid to request them from Dr. Tallacagua.

Clotilde received more from her association with the Aymara, in or outside of the clinic, than she did from her association with mestizos. They had given her a job. And as she benefited more and more from the Aymara, she found herself suffering more and more from disorders that Doña Teresa insisted afflict only Indians.

The Aymara campesino Eugenio didn't like Tallacagua at all. He said

Tallacagua had mistreated him and his five-year-old daughter when he brought her to the clinic with severe pains in her lower abdomen. He complained that the doctor was apparently of the opinion that everyone should learn to speak Spanish and that Tallacagua should facilitate that by being a role model. He refused to accept payment in kind. He told his patients bluntly not to come to the clinic unless they were prepared to pay for services in cash. These policies, explained Eugenio, were condescending assertions of superiority that Tallacagua wielded now that he had a medical degree and presumably consequential access to Bolivian elite society. Previous physicians had spoken a few words of Aymara, accepted payment in kind, explained diagnoses in detail, been sympathetic to the Aymara worldview, respected indigenous medicine, and permitted *yatiris* to practice in the clinic. Tallacagua, said Eugenio in more complicated terms, was trying to negotiate a new identity, and Eugenio wasn't buying.

In this case Dr. Tallacagua had diagnosed appendicitis and strongly recommended immediate surgery. Eugenio insisted on postponing such a drastic measure until he could discuss it with the rest of the family. Tallacagua must have been anxious for the child's health and angry that his medical authority carried so little weight when the problem was so urgent. He angrily warned that the child had only hours to live, that the operation was so serious that it would cost five hundred pesos (twenty-five dollars), an enormous sum; that the child was so sick because Eugenio had waited so long to bring her in; that surgery would be risky; and that he could not even guarantee its success at that time—let alone later if the father delayed changing his mind!

To Eugenio these words further confirmed Tallacagua's exploitative intents. He interpreted the doctor's words as lies designed to abuse and exploit Eugenio. He argued that as an Aymara campesino he had virtually no cash. He reasoned that being an Aymara himself, Tallacagua was fully aware of that. Cash greases the mestizo and elite worlds Eugenio saw as oppressing his own, and now Tallacagua asked him to deliver an outrageous sum to a man who had betrayed his Aymara identity and community to join those worlds. Given the more liberal clinic policy that had obtained before Tallacagua's arrival, his demand for cash seemed unnecessary, intended to serve Tallacagua's personal interest at Eugenio's expense, consistent with mestizo interests pursued at Aymara expense. His accusation of irresponsibility and ignorance for bringing the child in at such a late state in the illness furthered Eugenio's suspicions. The timing felt quite reasonable to Eugenio, who, like everyone else in town, could not easily afford either the clinic or a *yatiri* as a first course, and waited until home remedies proved ineffective.

Eugenio interpreted Tallacagua's warning of the child's possible death as a threat. To Eugenio, Tallacagua behaved exactly like a *karisiri*. Furthermore, Tallacagua had told Eugenio that the operation might not be successful, insisting that Eugenio openly acquiesce and reaffirm Dr. Tallacagua's newfound ethnic affiliation by agreeing to accept nothing in return should the treatment fail and the child die. That the words the doctor probably intended as sincere warnings were interpreted by Eugenio as threats, is based upon Eugenio's definition of Tallacagua's chosen identity—the way he discussed medicine—which Tallacagua substantiated by maintaining a social distance from the Aymara, by living apart from them, and by making no compromising gestures to reform that identity.

Miraculously, the child survived. Maybe Tallacagua's diagnosis was wrong.

From another perspective Tallacagua was not the evil character the towns-people made him out to be. They had their own reason for doing so: to create an alliance against his shift in ethnic identity through medicine, which they saw as being at their expense. Admittedly the analysis that Tallacagua was abandoning his Aymara identity to become a member of the elite appears to be correct. His implication that the local folk could not or should not understand cosmopolitan medical information is the first evidence to that effect. However, an attempt to understand Tallacagua's own strategy reveals a very different picture, and exposes another role ethnicity plays in medicine and medicine plays in ethnic identity. The use of medical ideology leads to incremental social change.

Tallacagua saw himself as an ambitious Aymara with a medical degree: as forging a new frontier, and thus an anomaly in Bolivia. The only one of his kind in medical school, he finished six years in five and graduated near the top of his class, yet friends I had attending medical school at that time assured me that Tallacagua had not done well and was a fool. No one, least of all Tallacagua, knew what to do with a professional Indian. Upward mobility, while it occurs all the time, is covert, as was the Indians' arrangement of their entry into the town's mestizo class at the turn of the century. Tallacagua, however, came directly from the countryside, offending everyone by breaking the rules.

As a professional in La Paz, everything that revealed the immediacy of his Aymara Indianness worked against Tallacagua. At the same time, scientific medicine was good to him, He did well in school. One of his teachers referred to him as brilliant. He felt that were he not discriminated against, he could enjoy a successful life and help lift his family out of poverty. They were expecting him to do so, and he honored his familial obligations. However, finding himself alienated from both the Aymara and the Bolivian upper classes, Tallacagua wanted to go to Brazil, where he believed his Indianness would have no negative significance and his talents would be appreciated.

In order to do so, however, he had to play by Bolivian rules. He had to show the people with power in La Paz what he thought they wanted to see before they would help him secure a job elsewhere. So he perfected his Spanish. He distanced himself socially from the Aymara, whose association he thought would jeopardize him. He changed hospital policy to approximate as much as possible the policy of the teaching hospital in La Paz, and in ways that emphasized efficiency and the importance of scientific medicine.

Aymara medicine was not tolerated. Neither was payment in kind. Given that most of the drugs in the dispensary had surpassed their stipulated shelf life, cash was desperately needed. Any step toward financial self-sufficiency would reduce dependency on "gringo charity" and make the hospital stronger. Tallacagua felt he was contributing to the modernization of the clinic. He also hoped to capitalize on those efforts. An article appeared in the La Paz newspaper referring to his work at "Tallacagua's clinic." That reference offended many in town, and after two months Tallacagua left, much to the relief of all parties, particularly himself.

In stark contrast with Dr. Tallacagua, Felipe Apaza, a proud Aymara and head nurse at the clinic, employed the ethnic dimension of medicine to his social and financial benefit by taking advantage of medical pluralism. Trained at the clinic by Methodist missionaries, he came to town from one of the surrounding communities. He maintained great respect for Aymara medicine, although he was less skilled at it than in referring patients to *yatiris*. Medicine provided him with multiple incomes at the clinic because he was administrator, nurse, radiologist, and laboratory technician. He also picked up extra cash by running a private practice out of his home for people who didn't wish to go to the clinic, either because he could treat some cases less expensively or because, unlike Tallacagua, he drew on Aymara medical ideology and incorporated indigenous medical resources into his cosmopolitan medical skills. During his long and successful career he had covertly become the primary authority at the hospital, although he carefully allowed the doctors who came and went to take credit for decisions that he himself supervised. Through the deft use of both medical traditions, he cultivated himself as cultural ambassador but definitively Aymara. As such he gained enormous stature throughout Omasullu and not a little wealth.

Everyone in town, Aymara and mestizos alike, looked up to Felipe. In the 1970s he was voted president of the local PTA.[36] He also was the only person in town to actively pursue the negotiation of a settlement between ethnic and religious groups, and the development of a single united community. When Father Christian called a meeting to castigate his Catholic flock for not attending church, not fulfilling their obligations to the church, and letting the building fall into disrepair, it was the Methodist Aymara Felipe who was the first to donate money to repair the padre's roof. He insisted the church repair was a community issue, not a Catholic one, and in so doing he renegotiated mestizo-Aymara relations so that both had equal civic responsibility—at least for a while. Facilitating that community unity was Felipe's staunch defense and use of Aymara medical beliefs. The Aymara said proudly, "Felipe Apaza is the hospital administrator." As such he wielded a lot of power in town. He is very proud of the Aymara medical tradition and wants someday to write a book on it. "Perhaps you can help me write them down," he said to me once, "I want to preserve them before they disappear." Because Felipe's strategies at the clinic were successful and Dr. Tallacagua's were not, he does not have to worry about the disappearance of Aymara medicine.

THE MORE PRACTICAL ARGUMENT

The relationship between ethnic identity and medical traditions is more than ideological. The diagnosis of an Indian illness, which today is more or less a diagnosis that involves some component of what cosmopolitan practitioners might decry as "magic," has a number of implications that are related to the political economy of the mestizo and Indian modes of existence.

Belief in the magical component involves accepting that one shares a vulnerability with Indians and an acceptance of a sanction which ensures that the appropriate therapy *will* be followed. Indian illnesses are usually caused by one of a pantheon of phantasms and spirits who are hungry, and will be pacified only with a meal. Refusal to feed them results not only in death of the victim but also in further inflictions on the victim's relatives. An unfed demonic being is a public menace. Consequently, when the doctor diagnoses anemia and insists the patient eat meat daily, the desperately poor mestizo or Indian patient places his concern for personal well-being far behind the welfare of his family and, like Vicente, does not eat the meat. Protein-rich foods, mostly guinea pigs, eggs, chicken, and pork, are usually the only source of cash, and there are numerous expenses that have greater priority to the poor of the Bolivian altiplano than the vague symptoms of a chronic illness. But when the *yatiri* says the patient is a victim of a hungry spirit that demands to be fed, and that the patient must make a *mesa*[37] and sacrifice pigs, guinea pigs, chickens, and eggs every Tuesday and Thursday for six Tuesdays and Thursdays, the patient and his extended family sacrifice pigs, guinea pigs, chickens, and eggs every Tuesday and Thursday for six Tuesdays and Thursdays. This explains in part why the doctor's diagnosis of anemia held so little weight for Vicente.

Sacrifices are made along with a vast number of herbal treatments that are quite likely effective because they derive from the Callaguaya medical tradition (Bastien 1987; Oblitas Poblete 1963). The sacrificed animals are expensive; the herbs come from all over Bolivia and are Indian property. Treatment, then, often requires both wealth and the mobilization of social relationships with Indians who have access to herbs. For the wealthy in La Paz, this presents little problem; for the rural mestizos who are poor, despised by elites and Indians alike, such resources may be hard to find. Isolated from both groups in the postrevolutionary era, mestizos who are unable to join the urban elite find some rewards in discarding their superordinate status and allying themselves with the Aymara. For Felipe Apaza it is good business. Though paradoxical from the perspectives of both modernization theory and cosmopolitan medical wisdom, one consequence of this downward mobility may be improved health care.

WHAT ALL THIS MEANS

The focus of this study has been the anthropology of medical ideology and medical dialogue in a medically plural environment: how such social change takes place through medicine and how social analyses of medicine and medical dialogues can contribute to the study of social change. This analysis generates a reexamination of the popular dichotomy in medical anthropology between traditional and modern medical systems, and the relatively new notion of medical pluralism.

The dichotomy between traditional and modern medical systems still obtains in the anthropological literature in spite of its inaccuracies (cosmopolitan medicine has a tradition; the *yatiri*'s medicine is modern) and misleading connotation (not all traditional systems are alike). It implies that the two are discrete and that the latter will eradicate the former over time (Foster and Anderson 1978). This study is one of many that have demonstrated the fallacy of that assumption. The concept of medical pluralism (e.g., Leslie 1979; Elling 1980) refers instead to an environment in which there is more than one medical tradition. This conceptual change has permitted a shift toward examination of several coexisting medical traditions and how they interact. Nevertheless, within this concept the focus remains on medical traditions as bounded systems rather than as social institutions (Paul Unschuld is a noted exception—e.g., 1975, 1985). The major questions in this area today include the following: What is of medical or therapeutic value, and hence what is retainable of traditional systems according to cosmopolitan standards? How can medical systems that are of nationalistic or symbolic value be upgraded to meet Western standards through education, licensing, and incorporation into the Western medical model? How can such systems coexist and interact with cosmopolitan medicine?

While these are essential questions, they cannot adequately explain the persistence of medical traditions, their significance, the ways in which they change, and their relations to other dimensions of social change. An understanding of the political economy of medical traditions in a pluralistic environment, however, reveals something about the composition and dynamics of social change within that environment, and hence the nonmedical significance of medical traditions. Because of the politicoeconomic nature of the Bolivian indigenous medical tradition and the cosmopolitan medical tradition as it exists in Bolivia, the deployment of those medical traditions, the use of medical ideology, and medical dialogue—how people talk about who has what disease or illness and what should be done about it—all constitute a social idiom through which Bolivians negotiate the content of ethnic identity, and thereby facilitate or impede movement of economic and political resources across ethnic boundaries.

An analysis of the political economy of Bolivia at large, of the relations between mestizos and Indians within that context, of the contemporary directions that social change has been taking in Bolivia, and of the way that affects community life, clarifies the parameters of the negotiation of identity that takes place through the idiom of medicine. If we look at the confluences of culture in Bolivia, we see a population that encompasses several economic and ethnic domains, but also shares the same symbolic system, in such a way that symbols can be manipulated and negotiated. The use of ideologies that pertain to medical pluralism then becomes both a reflection of social processes taking place as well as a means by which they do so. And medicine is also a necessary idiom with which to negotiate identity, because the political economies of the various medical traditions involve the same social relations that define a person's identity and social and economic standing on the altiplano of Bolivia.

NOTES

1. Marvin Harris's seminal treatment of race in Latin America (1964) argues that the concept there differs fundamentally from that in the United States. In Latin America race is culturally based, defined by language, dress, and comportment, not by phenotypic or genetic characteristics, as it is in the United States. All evidence I encountered leads to the somewhat different interpretation that, while etically speaking, Harris is right, discourse engages the concept of genetics. In this article I contend that there is no "racial integrity" whatsoever in Bolivia, that race is a mask for social class, but that the genetic or racial argument inherent within the concept of ethnicity is ubiquitously evident, particularly in medical ideology.

2. The most comprehensive histories of twentieth-century Bolivia, are Dunkerley 1984; Klein 1969; and Kelley and Klein 1981. All three cover the rise of American imperialism as an issue in the MNR revolution of 1952 and its aftermath for very concrete reasons, including the manipulation of the world tin market by the United States to the detriment of Bolivia just after the nationalization of the Bolivian tin mines in 1953. They argue as well, however, that blaming U.S. imperialism for Bolivia's poverty was effectively employed to deflect attention from the demands of the Indians and from the resistance of the revolutionary government to meeting them.

3. Oblitas Poblete 1963, p. 112: the *khariciri* takes the image of a priest, steals fat from the navel, and sells it to indigenous medicine men (*callaguayas*) who can cure or ensorcell with it.

4. La Barre 1948, p. 167: the *q'ariq'ari* is "an evil spirit incarnated in a body, with a penchant for cutting open the neck of a person and stealing his soul, after which that person sickens and dies." Another version, he says, is that it is "frequent in August . . . steals the heart and puts sand in its place."

5. Tschopik 1951, p. 204: the karikari "are spirits of deceased Catholic priests . . . [who] take away all of a man's fat and make soap out of it. They look like Franciscan Fathers."

6. Aguilo 1982, p. 122: the "Karisiri" is a white man, a priest or engineer who at night steals blood or fat, for holy oil and for curing.

7. Personal communication with anthropologists and priests in Peru and Bolivia.

Bastien came across the *kharisiri* among the Kallawaya (1987:71) but limits his discussion to how the fat is believed to be extracted.

8. Here and throughout most of the chapter, the dialogue presented constitutes statements made by individuals, rather than linguistic interchanges between two or more people. That is, the data presented here are statements rather than discussions. However, the fact that these statements are "consumed" or accepted by the parties to whom they are directed implies the nature of the response to the statements presented here and of the discussions that ensued. On that basis I use the term "dialogue." I thank Alexander Alland, Jr., for bringing the possible ambiguity of my usage to my attention.

9. The same argument can be made for class. While the focus of this article is ethnicity, its premise is that ethnicity in Bolivia is in fact a mask for social class.

10. I am arguing here that ethnicity is a mask for social class. However, not all social classes are distinguished by ethnicity. Ethnicity permits both oppression and resistance. Thus, while one often constitutes the other, the two terms are not synonymous.

11. The significance of fictive kin or *compadrazgo* ties in Bolivia and throughout most of Latin America is its subscription to patronage and clientage; godparents serve as patrons to the parents of godchildren (*compadres*), who in turn—in Bolivia—provide the godparents with agricultural resources and services. This obligation was often inherited over several generations (see Strickon and Greenfield 1972).

12. A *tienda* is a small store which sells the same items that all other *tiendas* sell: canned goods, noodles, sugar and other staples, alcohol, beer, and magical items for curing. Running a *tienda* is a mestizo occupation and, until recently, one of a very few ways of generating some cash. Since all the *tiendas* sell the same items, customers are won through *compadrazgo* ties and goodwill, not through competitive marketing.

13. Some people might find my description of shifts between Indian, mestizo, and elite as upward and downward mobility offensive. Economically and politically, however, the use of these terms is accurate.

14. Since the argument here is that ethnicity is a mask for social class, what pertains to ethnicity, such as social movement and use of medical ideology and dialogue, also pertains to social class.

15. Until independence from Spain, what is now Bolivia was referred to as Upper Peru.

16. The revolution of 1952 engineered by the Movimiento Nacional Revolucionario (MNR), under the leadership of Victor Paz Estensorro and Hernán Siles Suazo, brought an end to the hacienda system instituted under colonialism, nationalized the mines that supported the state, and transformed the rural countryside. It was unable, however, to modernize Bolivia as it intended.

17. The intent of this chapter is not to do an analysis of Bolivia's political economy or to review the outcome of the 1952 revolution, except insofar as some analysis and review will clarify the context of medical dialogue. Hence this analysis and review are considerably simplified to suit the purposes of the chapter. Those interested in such an analysis are referred to Kelley and Klein 1981.

18. This is, naturally, the basis of all efforts in applied medical anthropology. For a splendid example of effective work, see World Health Organization 1975, concerning the Carroll Behrhorst program in Chimaltenango, Guatemala, and publications of the National Council for International Health. The Andean Rural Health

Care Program in Bolivia is introducing revolutionary changes in the delivery of health care to the rural sector.

19. Though Bolivia is rich in natural, particularly mineral, resources, these have always been expensive to tap.

20. Caudillos were strongmen who cultivated and developed power domains based on personal favors and loyalty, and who fought one another to expand their spheres of influence. This decentralized and competitive political structure was originally encouraged by the Spanish crown as a means of maintaining royal control over an independent-minded population far from home. Upon independence, the competitive caudillo structure merely fitted itself to the new parameters of independence. Between 1825 and 1984, Bolivia experienced over 260 successful coups d'état. Many of the early presidents who seized office looked on Bolivia as their personal property (Carter 1971:39); Garcia Meza's behavior from 1980 to 1982 strongly suggests that he felt the same way.

21. Many of these gains, particularly universal suffrage, have had very little exercise since 1952.

22. One response to this change was the development of peasant entrepreneurs and middlemen, (cholos), who dominate the internal market for small goods and agricultural produce and transportation.

23. The most recent and valiant attempt to organize a political platform and pursue economic goals for political (in this case national) rather than personal ends was President Hernán Siles Suazo's presidency. Prevented from carrying out needed reforms in a divided nation under severe strain, he resigned halfway through his presidency. The Reagan administration's grinding pressure on Siles to take action against the drug trade came at a time when the state's economic resources were thoroughly depleted and social needs were at an all-time high. Further, Siles had just been kidnapped by the special drug forces—the Leopardos—that the Reagan administration, through the Drug Enforcement Agency, had organized. Indeed, the history of that administration gives solid credence to the argument that much of Bolivia's inability to modernize is related to U.S. policies.

24. This policy was reversed under Paz Estensorro, elected president in 1985, who immediately approached the International Monetary Fund to resume negotiations.

25. The dollar, worth 20 pesos bolivianos in 1979 after nearly a decade of stability, and 25 pesos bolivianos from 1979 to 1982, was being bought officially for 1,500,000 in September 1985. Whether inflation was due to the booming cocaine economy or to other factors is the subject of great debate.

26. President Siles, upon taking office in 1983, reduced government salaries; when President Victor Paz Estenssoro assumed office, he froze all wages until 1986.

27. The United States and the world economy played major roles in Bolivia's economic crisis during the 1980s. The return to democracy in 1983 also occurred under extraordinary circumstances.

28. Referring to Bolivia's history before 1952, Carter wrote that "for many decades it was a notable event for a Bolivian president to finish his term of office alive" (1971:39). Possibly the one achievement of the replacement of caudillo rule by military dictatorship is the contemporary fate of deposed presidents: exile instead of execution. However, Siles Suazo's successor, Paz Estenssoro, elected in 1985, was successfully succeeded in 1989 by Jaime Paz Zamora.

29. Historian Herbert Klein situates the end of caudillismo in Bolivia in the last century with the rise of republicanism. I do not dispute him in any way by pointing out that contemporary politics maintains many of the characteristics of its heritage. Klein has agreed to let me get away with this interpretation.

30. There is yet another mode pertaining to the *cholo* population that has developed since 1952. Likewise, yet another mode has recently developed in the Santa Cruz and Chapare areas that pertains to the cocaine economy. Neither is relevant to the case discussed here.

31. These two economies, the national or cash economy and the *ayllu*, do, of course, articulate in multiple arenas. During the colonial era they were specifically articulated to serve the interests of capital accumulation and labor (Ainger 1990).

32. They may still be; I have not investigated this issue since 1978, at the conclusion of the research discussed in this chapter. Shifts in the 1980s in many Latin American economies toward unfettered free market principles have led to the elimination of such controls. Peru is a case in point (Ainger 1990).

33. Personal communication with numbers of members of the commercial and elite classes in La Paz.

34. I have written on this series of cases elsewhere: see Crandon 1983; Crandon-Malamud 1991: chs 9–11.

35. One of these cases is the focus of Crandon 1983; two more, of Crandon 1986. All are examined in Crandon-Malamud 1991.

36. The local PTA is called the Padres de Familia.

37. A *mesa* is the prepared offering to the designated spirit and is composed of a variety of items carefully arranged on a cloth or table.

REFERENCES

Abercrombie, Thomas. 1986. The politics of sacrifice: An Aymara cosmology in action. Ph.D. dissertation, University of Chicago.

Aguilar, Anibal. 1990. Personal communication.

Aguilo, Federico. 1982. *Enfermedad y Salud*. Sucre, Bolivia: Los Talleres Graficos Qori Llama.

Ainger, Hilary. 1990. Agrarian structure and local experience: Continuity and change in Peru's southern sierra 1560–1982. Ph.D. dissertation, Teacher's College, Columbia University.

Alexander, Robert J. 1958. *The Bolivian National Revolution*. New Brunswick, NJ: Rutgers University Press.

Arnaude, Charles. 1957. *The Emergence of the Republic of Bolivia*. Gainesville: University of Florida Press.

Bastien, Joseph. 1981. Evaluation of herbal curing among the Callaway Indians. Paper presented at the 41st meeting of the Society for Applied Anthropology, Edinburgh.

———. 1987. *Healers of the Andes: Kallawaya Herbalists and Their Medicinal Plants*. Salt Lake City: University of Utah Press.

Buechler, Hans, and Judith-Maria Buechler. 1971. *The Bolivian Aymara*. New York: Holt, Rinehart & Winston.

Canelas Orellana, Amado, and Juan Carlos Canelas Zannier. 1983. *Bolivia: Coca Cocaina*. La Paz: Los Amigos del Libro.

Carter, William. 1958. Kachitu: Change and conflict in a Bolivian town. Master's Thesis, Columbia University.

———. 1971. *Bolivia: A Profile.* New York: Praeger

———. 1982. *Irpa Chico: Individuo y Comunidad en la Cultura Aymara.* La Paz, Bolivia: Libreria Editorial "Juventud."

Crandon, Libbet. 1983. Between shamans, doctors and demons: Illness, curing and cultural identity midst culture change. In *Third World Medicine and Social Change*, John Morgan, ed., pp. 69–84. Lanham, MD: University Press of America.

———. 1986. The political economy of medical dialogue in rural highland Bolivia. *American Ethnologist* 13 (3):463–476

———. 1989. Changing times and changing symptoms: The effects of modernization on mestizo medicine in rural Bolivia, *Medical Anthropology* 10(4):255–264.

Crandon-Malamud, Libbet. 1991. *From the Fat of Our Souls: Social Change, Political Process, and Medical Pluralism in Bolivia.* Berkeley: University of California Press.

Dunkerley, James. 1984. *Rebellion in the Veins: Political Struggle in Bolivia 1952–1982.* London: Verso Press.

Elling, Ray, ed. 1980. Medical sociology: Traditional and modern medical systems. Special Edition of *Social Science and Medicine* 15A(2).

Foster, George, and Barbara Anderson. 1978. *Medical Anthropology.* New York: Wiley.

Foucault, Michel. 1965. *Madness and Civilization: A History of Insanity in the Age of Reason.* Translated by Richard Howard New York. Random House.

———. 1973. *The Birth of the Clinic: An Archaeology of Medical Perception.* Tr. by A.M. Sheridan Smith. New York: Vintage.

Frank, Andre Gunder. 1966. The development of underdevelopment. *Monthly Review* 18:17–31.

———. 1971. *Capitalism and Underdevelopment in Latin America.* New York: Monthly Review Press.

Gwynne, S. C. 1987. *Selling Money.* New York: Viking Penguin.

Harris, Marvin. 1964. *Patterns of Race in the Americas.* New York: Walker.

Heath, Dwight. 1969a. *Land Reform and the Social Revolution in Bolivia.* New York: Praeger.

———. 1969b. Bolivia: Peasant syndicates among the Aymara of the Yungas: A view from the grass roots. In *Latin American Peasant Movements*, H. Landsberger, ed., pp. 170–209. Ithaca, NY: Cornell University Press.

International Work Group on Indigenous Affairs. 1978. *The Indian Liberation and Social Rights Movement in Kollasuyu (Bolivia).* Copenhagen: IWGIA.

Kelley, Jonathan, and Herbert Klein. 1981. *Revolution and the Rebirth of Inequality.* Berkeley: University of California Press.

Klein, Herbert. 1969. *Parties and Political Change in Bolivia 1880–1952.* New York: Cambridge University Press.

La Barre, Weston. 1948. The Aymara Indians of the Lake Titicaca Plateau, Bolivia. *American Anthropologist* 50(1, Pt. 2).

Leslie, Charles, ed. 1979. Medical anthropology: Medical pluralism. Special Edition of *Social Science and Medicine* 14B(4).

Lomnitz, Larissa. 1977. *Networks and Marginality.* New York: Academic Press.

McEwen, William, et al. 1969. *Changing Rural Bolivia*. New York: Research Institute for the Study of Man.

Malamud-Goti, Jaime. 1990. Politics, cops, soldiers and drugs in Bolivia. Department of Anthropology, Columbia University. Unpublished manuscript.

Malloy, James M. 1970. *Bolivia: The Uncompleted Revolution*. Pittsburgh: University of Pittsburgh Press.

———. 1971. *MNR: A Study of a National Popular Movement in Latin America*. Council on International Studies. Buffalo: State University of New York. ·

Martin, Emily. 1987. *The Woman in the Body; a Cultural Analysis of Reproduction*. Boston: Beacon Press.

Mayorga, Rene A. 1987. *Democracia a la Deriva: Dilemas de la Participación y Concertación Social en Bolivia*. La Paz: CERES.

Mendelberg, Uri. 1985. The impact of the Bolivian agrarian reform on class formation. *Latin American Perspectives* 46(12):45–58.

Morales, Ramiro Condarco. 1966. *Zarete el "Temible" Willka, Historia de la Rebelion Indigena de 1899*. La Paz: Talleres Graficos Bolivianos.

Muñoz, Geraldo. 1981. *From Dependency to Development*. Boulder, CO: Westview Press.

Murra, John. 1975. El Control Vertical de un Maximo de Pisos Ecologicos en la Economia de las Sociedades andinas. In *Formaciones Economicas y Politicas del Mundo Andino*, pp. 59–116. Lima: Instituto de Estudios Peruanos.

Nash, June. 1979. *We Eat the Mines and the Mines Eat Us*. New York: Columbia University Press.

Oblitas Poblete, Enrique. 1963. *Cultura Callaguaya*. La Paz: Talleres Graficos Bolivianos.

Platt, Tristan. 1978a. Symetries en miroir. Le concept de yanantin chez les Macha de Bolivie. *Annales, E..S.C.* (Paris) 33(5–6):1081–1107.

———. 1978b. Acerca del sistema tributario pre-toledano en el Alto Peru. *Avances* (La Paz) no. 1:33–46.

———. 1982a. *Estado Boliviano y Ayllu Andino: Tierra y Tributo en el Norte de Potosí*, Historia Andina 9. Lima: Instituto de Estudios Peruanos.

———. 1982b. The role of the Andean ayllu in the reproduction of the petty commodity regime in northern Potosí (Bolivia). In *Ecology and Exchange in the Andes*, David Lehmann, ed., pp. 27–69. Cambridge: Cambridge University Press.

Press, Irwin. 1969. Urban illness: Physicians, curers and dual use in Bogota. *Journal of Health and Social Behavior* 10(3):209–218.

———. 1971. The urban curandero. *American Anthropologist* 73:741–756.

Preston, David. 1969. The revolutionary landscape of highland Bolivia. *The Geographic Journal* 135:1–16.

Quiroga Santa Cruz, Marcelo. 1973. *El Saqueo de Bolivia*. La Paz: Ediciones Puerta del Sol.

Rasnake, Roger. 1988. *Domination and Cultural Resistance: Authority and Power Among an Andean People*. Durham, NC: Duke University Press.

Romanucci-Ross, Lola. 1986. Creativity in illness: Methodological linkages to the logic and language of science in folk pursuit of health in central Italy. *Social Science and Medicine* 23(1):1–7.

Roxborough, Ian. 1979. *Theories of Underdevelopment*. Atlantic Highlands, NJ: Humanities Press.

Scheper-Hughes, Nancy, and Margaret Lock. 1987. The mindful body: A prolegomenon to future work in medical anthropology. *Medical Anthropology Quarterly* 1(1):6–41.

Sontag, Susan. 1978. *Illness as Metaphor*. New York: Farrar, Straus & Giroux.

Stein, Stanley J., and Barbara H. Stein. 1970. *The Colonial Heritage of Latin America*. New York: Oxford University Press.

Strickon, Arnold, and Sidney Greenfield, eds. 1972. *Structure and Process in Latin America: Patronage, Clientage and Power Systems*. Albuquerque: University of New Mexico Press.

Taussig, Michael. 1980. *The Devil and Commodity Fetishism*. Chapel Hill: University of North Carolina Press.

Tschopik, Harry, Jr. 1951. *The Aymara of Chucuito, Peru*. Anthropological Papers of the American Museum of Natural History. New York: The Museum.

Unschuld, Paul. 1975. Medico-cultural conflicts in Asian settings: An explanatory theory. *Social Science and Medicine* 9:303–312.

———. 1985. *Medicine in China: A History of Ideas*. Berkeley: University of California Press.

Valenzuela, J. Samuel, and Arturo Valenzuela. 1978. Modernization and dependency: Alternative perspectives in the study of Latin American underdevelopment. *Comparative Politics* 10(4):535–557.

Vincent, Joan. 1974. The structure of ethnicity. *Human Organization* 33(4):375–379.

Wallerstein, Immanuel. 1974. *The Modern World-System: Capitalist Agriculture and the Origins of the European World Economy in the Sixteenth Century*. New York: Academic Press.

Wolf, Eric. 1982. *Europe and a People Without History*. Berkeley: University of California Press.

World Health Organization. 1975. *Health by the People*. Geneva: WHO.

6

ANARCHY, ABJECTION, AND ABSURDITY: A CASE OF METAPHORIC MEDICINE AMONG THE TABWA OF ZAIRE

ALLEN F. ROBERTS

In memory of Minnie G. Curtis

THE EVENT

On 10 October 1960, two young men named Kiyumba and Mulobola[1] rode their bicycles from Kirungu to Chief Kaputo's village, ostensibly to purchase reed mats to resell at Kirungu market. In fact, their intention was to steal tax moneys held by the chief's clerk; Kiyumba would set fire to the chief's residence, and while everyone's attention was fixed on the blaze, Mulobola would break into the clerk's and steal the funds. Kiyumba did his part, without realizing that the chief himself was napping inside. Women saw him do this, and sounded the alert. Mulobola, frightened by the ensuing commotion, took flight, while Kiyumba was captured by the chief's men. Kiyumba was thrashed till he admitted his plan and told where his partner would probably be waiting for him, on the road back to Kirungu. Mulobola, too, was apprehended, and both were beaten senseless. Chief Kaputo sent his car to fetch his judge, then visiting a nearby village; the judge later told me that by the time he arrived at the chief's, the thieves were in a pitiful state. He could do nothing, at that point, to alter the course of the event.

Accounts vary as to what occurred next. The official inquest[2] found that "in a paroxysm of anger," Chief Kaputo Lambo ordered that the two men be burned alive. As though summing up the event, the report concludes that "a very important detail should not be overlooked . . . : Kiyumba was found bearing an MNC Lumumba card." My informants skipped over this detail. The judge said that he saw Kanengo, the chief's counselor and a noted practitioner of traditional medicine (*mfumu*, pl. *wafumu*), take a long, sharp knife and lead young men from the village in carrying the two thieves to the bridge across a nearby stream. The judge later learned that the two had been burned alive. As Nzwiba, another practitioner and close informant, said, "This [the culprits' ashes] is what is called *kapondo*. *Wafumu* practitioners from all over went and got *vizimba* medicines then. Many, many went there, and those who have *kapondo* will show it to you if you ask, and will say it came from that time at Chief Kaputo's. If you say you want to buy some, ah, you buy it."[3]

THE HISTORICAL CONTEXT

With Independence on 30 June 1960, the Congo began a series of convulsions, relatively mild at first, that would lead to unparalleled tragedy. A week after Independence, the Force Publique mutinied; several days later, before a rumored intervention by the Soviet Union could occur, United Nations troops arrived in the Congo; and almost concurrently, Katanga seceded. Through July and August, Katangans lived in fear of an expected invasion by the Congolese National Army (ANC); in August, Kasai also seceded and sought federation with Katanga. In September, the ANC occupied several key centers in Kasai, and many civilians were killed. President Kasavubu divested Prime Minister Lumumba of his powers, and vice versa; Colonel Mobutu declared both parties "neutralized" till the end of the year. On 10 October, Lumumba was confined to his official residence, with UN troops assuring his security by occupying the gardens around the house, while ANC forces menaced all within the periphery of the property they surrounded.

Tabwa living along the southwestern shores of Lake Tanganyika were within the old province and new state of Katanga, and were among the earliest and most ardent supporters of Tshombe's breakaway government, providing several of its first ministers and other high officials. The tumultuous nature of these first months of double independence was the backdrop for the questioning of much more local authority; unrest would grow among Tabwa around Kirungu, as factions long denied power within the colonial hierarchy of chiefs attempted to wrest control from their adversaries. With international, national, regional, and local tensions so high, an attempted robbery was not especially remarkable; the judiciary could not focus attention upon such an event in such times. Instead, the Belgian Magistrat Instructeur noted that one of the perpetrators had allegedly possessed the party identity card of those against whom Katangans were fighting for independence, and the matter was dropped without Chief Kaputo, his counselor Kanengo, or anyone (but the two thieves) receiving the least punishment.

THE ACTORS

It is difficult to say much about the two thieves. Present-day residents of Chief Kaputo's village remember the event, but nothing of the young men; I did not contact their families. Although others in the area who engaged in overtly political, insurrectionist actions during these same years are well known and still celebrated locally, these two are not. It seems most likely that the general state of alarm prevailing throughout Katanga and the attraction of a strongbox containing 8,000 francs in tax receipts proved too great a temptation for the two, who sought only private gain. They were not (or were not allowed to become) "social bandits"—men acting with public (or at least factional) approbation in social protest against forces commonly perceived as "the oppressor" (see Hobsbawn 1965, 1981). The magistrate, trying to justify (or at least to pass over) both their assassinations and the lack of pursuit by an overtaxed Katangan judiciary, seems to imply that they *were* social bandits, acting in the name of a political party subversive to the Katangan state. Rather, they were deemed criminals by Chief Kaputo's people, men without regard for order as personified by the chief whose life they had wantonly threatened in the course of their attempted robbery.

Chief Kaputo Lambo (dead in the mid-1960s) was known as an irascible fellow whose ambitions for power within his local political arena knew few bounds. He tried to replace an inferior chief in the colonial hierarchy whose insistence of superiority by tradition and precolonial history had long chafed him; when this effort was foiled, with great loss of face, Kaputo saw to it that he was physically abused by soldiers. It is still believed that Kaputo had great medicines at his disposal, including an ability to send "lion" to maim or kill his enemies. Such powers are associated with Kanengo, his closest henchman.

Until his death in the late 1970s, Kanengo was widely renowned for two capacities: his knowledge of Chief Kaputo's history, for which he was consulted in all affairs in which the legitimacy of the chief's rule was questioned; and his knowledge of medicines. When my wife and I knew him, he was living in exile from Kaputo's chiefdom, after protracted quarrels with the man who succeeded to the chair at the death of Kaputo Lambo. As a gauge of his marginality, Kanengo's house—far from any village and located deep in a swamp—was the only round (hence, "traditional") one we saw in four years among the Tabwa. He was known as the greatest practitioner of *mfumu* in the area, and the most difficult cases were taken to him. A kinsman of his who had violent psychotic episodes was kept in stocks in the same yard in which others—there for treatment, or living with Kanengo—were seated or seeing to everyday chores. Kanengo told us that he had tried all his means to heal the young man, but was resisted at every turn; we were left with the distinct impression that the old man would "solve" the problematic case whether or not the disturbed nephew survived his cure. He suggested that my wife (an anthropologist studying traditional medicine, who as a paramedic ran a small clinic of Western medicine) give injections of his traditional medicines to his kinsman and other difficult cases. This and his attempt to involve us in his conflict with the seated Chief Kaputo (by telling others *we* wanted to divest him of power, and as expatriates would see that it happened) left us very uneasy in our dealings with Kanengo.

Kanengo was also one of only two Tabwa we ever knew who was reputed to have been (or still be?) in the Kazanzi society (BaKazanzi). This society was introduced to the central Luba around the turn of the nineteenth century by Luba traders visiting the Songye (Reefe 1981:118) and spread to the lands along the Luvua and Lukuga rivers (Lebaigne 1933).[4] It was popular among northern Tabwa (or "Holoholo") at the turn of the present century (Schmitz 1912:278) and was encountered among ("Luba-ized") western Tabwa (or "Hemba") slightly thereafter (Colle 1913:528). An elderly informant once came upon a seance of the society at Chief Rutuku's near the Lubilaye (and counts himself lucky to have escaped unscathed!), but said that the society never spread farther south than that. The BaKazanzi may have survived the first decades of the 1900s, but in an attenuated form, being replaced by new religious organizations more apt in the context of established colonialism (e.g., BuGabo, Ukanga). It did not disappear altogether. As one old man remarked with acerbity, "It lasted long after the Belgians came; even when they finally left [in 1960], they didn't know how to 'see' sorcerers, so how could they 'see' Kazanzi adepts?"

Among Luba, the Kazanzi eliminated avenging ghosts by disinterring corpses, burning fagots in the opened graves to prevent the spirits' return, and incinerating the remains for later use as medicines (Lebaigne 1933; Joset 1934). All Tabwa I questioned contended that Kazanzi adepts among them killed and ate sorcerers identified by diviners and/or the poison oracle (and denied that war enemies, the elderly, slaves, or others of "lowly condition" would also be consumed, as stated in Colle 1913:540). With macabre detail, Tabwa recount how adepts would be summoned by a chief to eliminate one designated a sorcerer. Using the strength of their medicine called *niembo* or *buyembe* (as in Colle 1913:541; Burton 1961:171), they would secrete medicines in the headpad the victim used to carry loads, and this would cause the soul (*roho* in Swahili, *mutima* in KiTabwa) to leave the body. The sorcerer would be powerless against this, and his/her body would then go to the Kazanzi camp. The adepts, their faces crimson with *nkula* powder ground from Pterocarpus bark (this a "symbol of blood" [*mfano ya damu*], as I was told), would dance about and begin to dissect the victim, beginning with the legs, as the victim looked on vacuously. When the sorcerer finally fell, his/her flesh would be eaten, openly, it was said, in contrast to the secret manner in which sorcerers consume the flesh of their victims. Colle reports that as they did this, they would imitate the hyena's cry (1913:539). The bones would be burned and used as medicines. BaKazanzi also danced publicly performing incredible feats such as piercing their cheeks. In the past, they held regular ceremonies during the dark of the moon (Schmitz 1912:281).

THE ACTION

The execution of the two thieves at Chief Kaputo's is most easily explained as the result of "a paroxysm of anger"; that the chief's house was set afire, and that he himself was asleep inside at the time, would seem due cause for retribution. The severity and form of the method, the choice of executioner, and the ultimate meaning of the act as reflected in what became of the relics are not so simply explained.

A common Tabwa adage is that "theft and sorcery are of one path." The perpetrators of either manifest a disregard for others' sanctity, act in contradiction to community, and therefore taunt and threaten social life. Sorcery for Tabwa is a "solar" activity; God and the sun are both said to be sorcerers in their lack of limit (hence, figuratively, of pity [uruma]) and through their association with death. God is said to feast upon humans "like goats," and the sun kills crops (and hence humans) when it shines unabated. Yet the sun is recognized as necessary to life, the order of which is synonymous with a god called Leza Malango ("Almighty Intelligence").

Opposed to these phenomena is the marked discontinuity of the life cycle. Kinship is considered a phenomenon expanding outward from a central point where there emerged, either from a deep body of water or a subterranean passage, the first human beings. As generations passed, humankind spread out to populate the lands surrounding this point. Such a concept is given representation (or found) in spirals such as that of mpande conus shell disks, once an important symbol of chiefship and still revered as an ancestral shrine item.[5] The mpande is of a paradigm with the moon, as is most clearly indicated in a Tabwa myth in which they can be interchanged (A.F. Roberts 1980:426–27). Each turn of its spiral is analogous to the "belt" of a chief; succession is called "to wear the belt" (kuvaa mukaba), and the succession of generations can be imagined as concentric circles, each succeeding generation encompassing previous ones. A paradox of existence is that while life is eternal, in that the "belt" is always inherited (except in the case of executed sorcerers), it is finite in that each individual is born and dies (ibid.:98–101). Sorcery is an action opposing such expansion, as those who superficially appear supportive kinsmen or neighbors nefariously rob their victims of vitality and finally "eat their flesh." Sorcerers, when caught and executed, are not succeeded, and every attempt is made to obliterate them physically and from memory (kufuta). Thieves with so little regard for life and property would be meted out condign punishment, and Tabwa are hard pressed or loath to draw a distinction between sorcerers and thieves in cases of the sort.

Kanengo was the executioner of the two young men, a role for which his cultic background had prepared him technically and for which his personality was attuned. Several of the traits characteristic of Kazanzi adepts are especially apt in this case, and may be elaborated.

Colle reported that as the BaKazanzi partook of their ghastly repast, they uttered the cry of the hyena. A reference to this animal, in turn, allows a clearer understanding of the place of Kazanzi adepts in their contemporary society. Specifically, *baendo* joking partners, who see to the burial of members of their opposite clans, are called "hyena"; and the classificatory grandchildren who orchestrate the burial of a chief are assigned the term even more explicitly. Those who act as *baendo* and bury someone one day, will receive the same service from their opposites another. The cutting insults they offer must be tolerated, as they, too, will be returned on a later occasion. This sort of exchange is called *vizambano*, and the image Tabwa evoke in explaining the term is of boys wrestling, first one on top of and pinning the other, then the one on the bottom reversing his partner. Such alternation finds its obvious analogy in that of the seasons, and the fierce but jocular behavior of the "hyena" is that of dry-season heroes seeing to the bloody business of change.

The burial of a chief is performed in a lunar idiom, the period of his reign analogous to the light of the moon, his death to the tenebrous two or three days prior to the new moon. It is no coincidence that the Kazanzi adepts, too, chose this time for their celebrations. For Tabwa, moonlight is thought auspicious, as it allows one to discern predators lurking on the periphery of the community or along one's path; on the other hand, the dark of the moon, called *kamwonang'anga*, is a liminal time, fraught with danger. The name means "the one seen by the *ng'anga* or practitioner": the moon is "still there," but can only be seen by those with supernatural vision. The moon is a *mulozi* or sorcerer then, as it effects its apparent journey from the east, where its final sliver was seen, to the west, where it will newly appear; during *kamwonang'anga*, Lake Tanganyika, whipped by high winds, unleashes its most treacherous furies, and the most pernicious beasts are in evidence. In contrast, game and fish may be seen in especially large numbers, but they will elude their pursuers; they have been "closed" by the moon, as people say (A.F. Roberts 1980:111–18). The moon, then, usually lights a person's way, or "leads" the person, just as a chief is ordinarily the "father of his people" and looks to their succor. Yet, on a regular basis, the hidden side of the moon—like that of a chief—will predominate. As Father Theuws has written of beliefs held by people closely related to the Tabwa, "the moon is ambiguous as is life itself: . . . to be and become, to live and to die are but two faces of the same reality" (1968:11). Tabwa chiefs are leaders of their people but they are also deemed the greatest sorcerers of the land.

Theirs is the marginality of privilege. They do not kill and eat victims like other sorcerers, but they do condone the practice in their community. It is said that sorcerers will bring a portion of the meat of their victim to the chief, who will sell it to other sorcerers, thus drawing a direct profit. For Tabwa, lunar and solar tropes are used to order and understand life, but neither is univocal; each has two sides, and when the positive of one predominates, often it does so in contradistinction to the other, and vice versa.

THE HYENA AND ITS METAPHORIC SIGNIFICANCE

The spotted hyena, *Crocuta crocuta*, is a *solar* animal, and so opposed to the moon and those of its idiom. A Tabwa myth tells of a hyena fetching the sun and bringing it to the universe. The sun is said to be unchanging, hence unmarked (whereas the moon has phases and period); it is sexless, and not personified, as is the moon. The trait of the spotted hyena making it most sunlike through metaphor is its apparent lack of sexual dimorphism. Observers as early as Aristotle commented upon this, and as noted in the twelfth-century *Bestiary*, the spotted hyena's "nature is that at one moment it is masculine and at another moment feminine, and hence it is a dirty brute" (White 1960:3).[6] Beidelman has reviewed the spotted hyena's other odd characteristics noticed by many African observers and given moral sense via metaphor: they have an odd posture and gait, with front legs longer than back; their "grotesque and somewhat humanoid calls [have been] described by some writers as demonic"; they "paste" an odoriferous substance from anal glands to mark territory; and they chew up and digest bones left as refuse by other predators, so that their droppings may be white—and "hot," as Tabwa say—as a consequence (Beidelman 1975:190; see also Sapir 1981). Important for Tabwa in conjunction with this last is the hyena's *malosi*, the singular vision that they believe allows the beast to see carrion at great distances; metaphorically, this would assist "hyena" in perceiving sorcerers. Like hyenas, Kazanzi adepts are reputed to have exhumed corpses, especially of those "proven" sorcerers by the poison oracle, and to have obliterated them (just as hyenas consume bones, the final vestige of vital form). Finally, hyena anal hairs *may* have been a transform for the *kizimba* of the rainbow-producing serpent, Nfwimina. If for Kaguru such "liminal qualities make hyena the witches of the animal world" (Beidelman 1975:190), for Tabwa these same allow "hyena" to turn *against* the sorcerers with whom they are somewhat consonant. Sorcerers in the social realm, like hyenas in the natural, are betwixt or altogether outside of the categories by which life is ordered (cf. Turner 1967:97 and passim). Being quintessentially "between," they bespeak transition, both negative (sorcerers robbing crops' or kin's vitality) and positive ("hyena" restoring order by destroying sorcerers).

After a Tabwa chief is buried,[7] classificatory grandchildren—whose "souls are red" like the camwood powder and Lady Ross's turaco plumes they sport—are said to lust for blood, and a moment called *kisama* is begun. All goods on their way back from the watercourse beside or under which they have buried the chief are broken or confiscated; chickens, goats, and even small children are slaughtered; and adult kinsmen of the chief are captured, mistreated, and held for ransom. The chief's surviving kinsmen hasten to placate them, and, their rampage stopped, the same "grandchildren" choose a successor. It is they who sing "he returns, he awakens, he awakens" as they circle the hut where the successor is hidden, bidding him to "reappear" like the new moon.

In this act they echo the role of the cosmic serpent Nfwimina, which stops the rains with the rainbow, yet assures their return with the smoke of the dry season's last and most important bushfires. Tabwa place a medicine bundle at a point in the woods which they intend to make the center of a fire lit from several sides; it is hoped that all four cardinal winds will join to bring the fire to a flaming circle, trapping game at the center where the medicines have been hidden. An element of this *nsipa* bundle[8] is the belt of an executed sorcerer (*mukaba wa mulozi*), and the pyric circle of the bushfire repeats its message of destruction and contraction, so opposed to the expansion of the generations. Another *kizimba* used in the bundle is that of Nfwimina, the solar serpent; and when the circle closes, annihilating all brought within its constricting perimeter, the column of smoke that rises above the point is said to be Nfwimina itself, standing on the tip of its tail, its head toward the heavens. This moment is one of several vital transformations: wild animals become meat (even "cooked" meat!), and the column of smoke causes clouds to "build" (*kujenga*), carrying the first rains, which will in turn extinguish the bushfires.

The "hyena" have staged the death of the chief (which is hidden from the populace till the decomposition of the corpse is such that the skull falls from the body), the *kisama* interregnum, and the reapparition, just as the dry-season heroes bring back the wet. "Hyena" had other roles in Tabwa society, in which their dread propensities had an ultimately moral denouement. One didactic tale recorded by Schmitz among northern Tabwa recounts how Kimbwi, the hyena, changed into a person and accepted a baby from a negligent mother intent on going off dancing, only to smash the baby's head on a rock (1912:268). Although there were theriomorphic lions (and Tabwa terrorists who assumed this disguise), aside from random stories in which an odd circumstance might be explained (unconvincingly for many listeners) by sorcerers assuming some other animal's form, Tabwa do not speak of hyena-men. That is, when they speak of "hyena," this is a figurative term, one with social connotations for Tabwa, but not evidence of a belief in metempsychotic transformation to this beast.

As "hyena," then, the Kazanzi adepts—like classificatory grandchildren burying a chief—oversaw a transformation important to the continuity of social life. As a "stabilizing institution," they were " 'saviors to the whole community' " (Reefe 1981:205 citing W.F.P. Burton, p.118). Unlike the "grandchildren," they were summoned by will rather than circumstance, by a desire to eliminate a sorcerer rather than by the death of a chief. They reduced the sorcerer to nothing. It is not clear whether they engaged in the anthropophagous orgies early missionaries did, and Tabwa still do, attribute to them; this may have been feigned as a part of their showmanship, of which the piercing of their cheeks while they danced was another example. A few colonial authorities denied the existence of the practice (Lebaigne 1933), but most repeated or rephrased the ghoulish details of Father Colle and other missionaries as though absolute truth (e.g., Administrateur Territorial 1919). Such a clear-cut "failure to comprehend that they were dealing with inverted moral orders, rather than descriptions of concrete happenings" (Arens 1979:153), had political motivations and consequences best elaborated elsewhere.[9] More significant was the adepts' obliteration of the sorcerer, their dismembering of the cadaver (or, perhaps, of the yet-living), incineration of its bones, and their transmutation of the circumstance and substance into an elemental meaning for use in medicines. The disruptive were then brought back into order and put to the service of the community, I would suggest, in the same way that the smoke from the last and most intense bushfires, catalyzed by the *nsipa* bundle with its *vizimba* of a sorcerer's belt and Nfwimina, brings the clouds of the season's first rains.

THE MEANING

The elements of Tabwa traditional medicine are of two clear-cut categories, *miti* ("trees" in KiTabwa) plant substances, and *vizimba* (s. *kizimba*), or what Richards has called "activating agents" (1969). These latter are mostly parts of animals, references to place (e.g., a pebble from the mountaintop wherein resides an Earth spirit) or to circumstance (e.g., a piece of root traversing a path upon which one has tripped). A few may be termed relics, in that they are parts of human beings whose essence or history may be typified. To possess knowledge of these is suspicious; to *use* them, much more so, and always subject to situational interpretation, either condemned as sorcery or deemed pardonable when resorted to in "self-defense."

As C.D. Roberts has written, "the transformative capacity of any kizimba is referred to by people not as its 'strength' (*nguvu*), but as its 'meaning' (*maana* in Swahili)" (1981). When the two thieves were burned alive, their bones were taken and used as the *kapondo kizimba*. Different informants explain *kapondo* in various ways, according to their level of esoteric knowledge and their descriptive flair; an overarching or underlying meaning can be discerned in them all. Kiuma, a chief's son in his 60s who is *not* a practitioner, said that *kapondo* is when someone dies alone in the bush of hunger or lack of care; this, he stated, is what Nfwimina is, and furthermore both are the same as a woman who has never menstruated or had children, a "woman—man." Others, among them practitioners, articulate this knowledge, distinguishing among these parts; all *are* related, and a relic of a *musala* or amenorrheal woman *is* a transform of the *kizimba* of Nfwimina, the rainbow-breathing solar serpent (whose story Kiuma did not know; see A.F. Roberts 1980:244–49). These are related to but not the same as *kapondo*. Another nonpractitioner said that this was someone who lives alone in the woods without fields or a house, and who steals from others; such a person's "head is not right" (*kichwa si sawa, hata*). He went on to describe a case of this when he was a boy, of a woman who lived in the hills like an animal, with hair and fingernails exaggerated to the point of bestiality. As an aside, it may be added that Kanengo (the executioner of the two thieves) once said that crazy people are like Mbote "pygmies": they run about in the woods and will sleep anywhere.

Other Examples of Alienation

Practitioners offered more elaborated explanations. Kabemba (the only person with *muyembe* medicines like Kanengo's whom we ever met) said *kapondo* is a person walking alone, fallen upon and killed for no reason. Kalwele (a renowned practitioner living at Chief Kaputo's) said this is someone who has been "taken" by a possessing spirit *(pepo)*, a usage repeated by others (see C.D. Roberts 1981); when I said that the same term had been used in reference to the two thieves, he noted that to burn a chief's house, one must have been possessed by a bad spirit or *shetani* (from "Satan"). All of these explanations bespeak mental and/or social alienation, hence absurdity, discordance. Yet by being contrary to reason, by being antistructural, they are part of a greater whole demanding dialectic to define reason.

The word *kapondo* is from a verb meaning to pound, grind, or crush, as one does with manioc or corn in a mortar.[10] Derivatives bridging metaphorically from this root range in sense: "to dispirit," "to be shunned," "a night thief," "a woman who eats well without the knowledge of her husband" (who presumably does not!), "din or tumult." All touch upon reduction and disindividualization.

Most informants' exegeses, like these dictionary definitions, deal with solitude, isolation, or seclusion. Dying alone is absurd, since a "proper" death is in the arms of kinswomen whose warmth and ministrations reflect the afflicted person's lifelong participation in kinship and other close relations. Dying of hunger while alone underscores the abjection, for Tabwa are diligent farmers and responsible providers who would not be so careless with self or others—even complete strangers—except in the most dire of circumstances. Such a person is *lost*, from human contact and the succor it implies. Being killed while a solitary traveler, for no reason due to past history, is equally absonant with a social universe in which all acts are willed and have a history that is determinable through divination, if not already common knowledge. Kiuma's assertion that *kapondo*, Nfwimina the solar serpent, and the amenorrheal woman are all the same plays upon the unmarked nature of them all.

The alienation in the examples given is more evident when individuals are deranged (their "heads are not right") or possessed by spirits to the exclusion of an ordinary self. Eating alone is a rejection of the commensal norm important to Tabwa for everyday survival and proclaimed as an attribute of Tabwa chiefs (Kaoze 1950) as opposed to Luba or Luba-ized ones, who eat in seclusion. Tabwa see this as the height of greed, which, as a threat to life, is a definitive characteristic of sorcery; to choose to eat alone, then, is evil, while to be forced to eat alone is pitiable. Din and tumult are opposed to harmony in the aural realm, just as solitude is a "pounding down" (also from *kaponda*) of the obligations and prerogatives that make an individual *distinctive* within a community interrelated by kinship, marriage, and neighborliness.[11]

The two thieves at Chief Kaputo's displayed a singular disregard for person and property. The firing of *anyone's* house is a heinous act, and when the residence is the chief's, brings an added sense of anarchy. Solitude, eating alone, and din are all of a paradigm with anarchy, each having its own context against which it is the disorderly foil. The thieves' anarchy was checked, however, by the old "hyena," Kanengo the aged Kazanzi adept, and his young followers. *Kapondo*, too, represents this completion, this ultimate restoration of order after absurdity.

The substances which are made *vizimba* are employed as I understand tropes in rhetoric to be used.[12] Roots by the thousand cross one's path, yet a particular one on a particular occasion "causes" one to stumble; a piece of this root is taken for use in medicines, as the reduction of that set of circumstances which includes the trip and the tripping, but also such other elements as a sense of destiny, the interference of vengeful ghosts or sorcerers, pain (in the toe), and the knowledge that such a seemingly inconsequential injury can lead (through secondary infection) to eventual loss of limb or life. Through a synecdochal process, the particular root is chosen that represents the whole of these circumstances, and it will "foreground those aspects of the whole that are not only distinctive but are also taken as essential or directly relevant to the topic" (Sapir 1977:16). It is still a piece of root (without regard to botanical identity) and as such metaphorically joins the separate domains "root" and "fate" or whatever ultimate meaning the *kizimba* possesses.

The charred bones of the two thieves are still just that as well: charred bones like all other; but their transmutation has led to a sense beyond that of ordinary skeletal remains. This is a sense which may be derived from other circumstances than the anarchic threat as in the event described here. Each of these others will be synecdochically reduced, then each stands

Figure 6.1
Origins of the Kapondo Kizimba

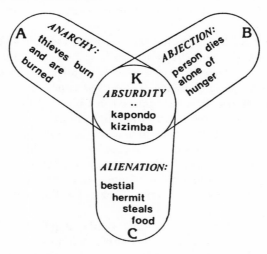

metaphorically in relation to the others, through the common mediator of the kizimba (see Figure 6.1: A:K, B:K, C:K = synecdoche; AK:BK:CK = metaphor; K + L + M + other vizimba: amulet X = metonomy). The kizimba has a single meaning (in this case, kapondo's is absurdity, I would assert), although each kizimba is a paradigm for its various sources; kapondo can then be mixed metonymically with other vizimba/paradigms in the preparation of complex medicines (where "metonym" implies the juxtaposition within a single domain—the medicine bundle or amulet—of distinct items).

THE EVENTUAL USE

Substances used as vizimba are often difficult to obtain, and may be purchased from distant practitioners at significant expenditure of money, time, and energy. Only a tiny quantity is required (perhaps a cubic centimeter of charred bone, for instance) and this will serve many, many times, since each medicine bundle or amulet contains the merest shaving of the bone, a dusting from something else, a smudge of yet another. In other words, these elements or their combination are not iconic, and one cannot know their identity and meaning unless told.

The *kapondo kizimba* is an ingredient in important concoctions, the constitutions of which were revealed to us only after several years of working with the same practitioners. It is an element of the *kiito* medicine horn of Tabwa snare hunters, and used to be employed in the *kinkungwa* horn of members of the now-defunct Mowela big-game hunting guild. It is added to medicines prepared "to throw someone in the bush" (*kumutupa mutu mu pori*), that is, to rid the patient of an avenging ghost. It can be employed in the *mwanzambale* protective amulet, as *muyembe* practitioner Kabemba explained, and this *kizimba* in conjunction with the many others of the device will make a solitary person seem as though many. "If you are alone and someone comes to test (*kupima*) the strength of his medicines against the strength of yours [as sorcerers do in trying to conquer even the hardiest of practitioners], they will see that in your medicines many things are mixed, each and every quality or meaning." In other words, the solitude of the *kapondo*'s source is put to use, to make hunted animals bereft of direction or wiles, or to thwart aggressive sorcerers by having "solitude" under control and "closed" within one's amulet.

There are other, less salubrious uses. As Nzwiba explained,

Now these *vizimba* that they go and take from your fellow man, ah we see this tends to be sorcery. For they take the kizimba from that one who has died, and they invoke it: "Now, you kizimba, I want so-and-so to be killed." So it is certain that afterwards he will die, the kizimba will agree that the person will die. . . . For instance, if he had taken a kapondo kizimba, a bone or something of someone who has died, he puts this with other medicines and begins to invoke there, saying, "This man has not done right by me, I want him to die the same way you died," then won't he die? Because he has prayed to the person who has already died to do this, he [the victim] will die or have another kind of accident. . . . because the one who died agrees to the business for which it has been called.[13]

Any of these uses may be deemed sorcery, depending upon the situation. Hunters are said to ensorcell (*kuloga*) their game, and amulets like *mwanzambale* are considered to be protective by their possessors, but offensive by critics. The absurdity of *kapondo*—its meaning (*maana*) as a constituent of medicines—is brought to bear on animal or human targets, plucking them from their apparent destinies and assuring them another fate they desire less, yet one which allows the greater community to continue in restored harmony. Individuals who possess and deploy *kapondo* are intervening in the course of events, and such hubris must always have its detractors as well as its supporters among those denied and gaining advantage, respectively. The hubristic, in turn, are *of* society but not altogether *in* society. Like the hyena, they are masters of transformation and transition, necessary yet dread.

ACKNOWLEDGMENTS

Four years' anthropological fieldwork was undertaken from late 1973 to late 1977 with financial support from the National Institute of Mental Health (no. 1-F01–55251–01-CUAN), the Committee on African Studies and the Edson-Keith Fund of the University of Chicago, and the Society of the Sigma Xi. A first draft of this paper, entitled "*Kapondo*: The Use of Political Synecdoche in Tabwa Traditional Medicine," was prepared for the "Sovereignty, Sickness and Health in Africa" panel of the 1981 African Studies Association meetings, chaired by Randall Packard. As this work has evolved, helpful comments have been received from J. Knight, O. Kokole, D. Merten, D. Moerman, R. Packard, T. Reefe, and C. Roberts, some of which have been incorporated here. Despite such generosity, all responsibility for this paper's content remains my own.

NOTES

1. All names have been changed except that of Kirungu, the central town of Tabwa lands along the southwestern shores of Lake Tanganyika in the Zaire Republic. Common Tabwa names have been chosen, and are employed in the writing of C.D. Roberts (1980, 1981) and of the present author to refer to the same individuals.

2. A single document concerning this incident was discovered quite by chance in the archives of the Bureau des Affaires Culturelles, Division Régionale des Affaires Politiques in Lumbumbashi: W. DeBruyn, Magistrat Instructeur, "Avi d'ouverture d'instruction," Parquet du Tanganika, Etat du Katanga, 7 Nov. 1960.

3. Nzwiba, interview of 14 May 1976 at Nanga; other relevant interviews with the chief's judge, Kanengo, and other interested parties were conducted on a visit to Chief Kaputo's in March 1977.

4. I disagree with Reefe's assertion that "the presence of the bambudye and bakasandji secret societies and subsequent transformation of oral traditions in frontier areas to the Luba, like those of northern Tabwa suggest that the loyalty of distant client-lineages and villages was changing into a more substantial sense of belonging to a common polity" (1981:153). Although there *is* a linguistic and cultural *aire* of which Luba, Tabwa, and other groups are members, among whom ideas and practices have long been traded easily, evidence that these chiefdoms (e.g., Tumbwe's) were "client-lineages and villages" of a centralized Luba empire is scant and unconvincing. Rather than belonging to "a common polity," that there were Tabwa Kazanzi adepts may reflect the borrowing of beliefs and behavior patterns deemed powerful because of their alien origin. The most effective medical practitioners, practices, and substances known to Tabwa my wife and I consulted still come from Luba beyond the hills and rivers to the west (or, less frequently, from across Lake Tanganyika).

5. Other spirals important to Tabwa cosmology are discussed in A. F. Roberts (1980:353–74).

6. Female spotted hyenas have an elongated clitoris visually identical to the male's penis, and a sham scrotum; the clitoris becomes erect during greeting, as does a male's penis, and field biologist Kruuk admits that he can distinguish between male and female adolescents only through close anatomical inspection (1974:210–11). The vagina is at the end of the clitoris, and coitus occurs when, in estrus, the entrance swells and the clitoris does not become erect; these points are reviewed in A. F. Roberts 1980:265–74.

7. Although many Tabwa ceremonies and rituals are no longer practiced as they were precolonially, most informants believe that chiefs are still buried in the manner mentioned here, and a *kisama* interregnum follows; no direct observation was possible.

8. *Nsipa* is a term used for the bundle of medicines buried in a central place in a new village, to attract residents and to keep them content in staying. Cunnison (1956) has described these among southern Tabwa along the Luapula.

9. In a future paper, tentatively entitled " 'Sinister Caricatures': 'Cannibalism' Among Belgians and Africans in the Congo," the Kazanzi society among colonized and the Mitumbula among colonizers will be contrasted as to political history and essence.

10. Van Acker 1907:54; Van Avermaet and Mbuya 1954:533–34; White Fathers 1954:619; Kajiga 1975:611; Johnson 1971:384. In KiTabwa-*ponda* can also mean "to insult, to dance fast"; *muponda* is the wild dog, *Lycaon pictus*, and *kiponda* a "night thief," according to Van Acker. In both KiLuba and CiBemba (which in turn are closely related to KiTabwa), derivatives refer to rebellion, insurrection, and the "underground" (*maquis*).

11. Not coincidentally, Tabwa and others in the area used to create a din when the moon was "eaten" during eclipse. See Heusch 1972:72–82, for an elegant discussion of how this is an action to "separate the sky and the earth," to maintain the discrete nature of cosmic principles.

12. I rely here upon J. David Sapir's "Anatomy of Metaphor" (1977), in which he holds that "metaphor states an equivalence between terms taken from separate domains"; "metonymy replaces or juxtaposes contiguous terms that occupy a distinct and separate place within what is considered a single semantic or perceptual domain"; and "synecdoche, like metonymy, draws its terms from a single domain; however, one term always includes or is included by the other" (p.4). Figure 6.1 is also derived from his (p. 20).

13. The place and meaning of invocation in the Tabwa medical process, as well as the usefulness of the rhetorical analogy in the explication of the process, will be expounded upon in the writings of C. D. Roberts.

REFERENCES

Administrateur Territorial. 1919. Untitled administrative report from Albertville, 22 Jan. 1919. Archives of Sous-Région du Tanganika, Kalemi (Zaire).

Arens, W. 1979. *The Man-Eating Myth*. New York: Oxford Univ. Press.

Beidelman, T. 1975. "Ambiguous Animals: Two Theriomorphic Metaphors in Kaguru Folklore." *Africa*, 45(2):183–96.

Burton, W. F. P. 1961. *Luba Religion and Magic in Custom and Belief*. Tevuven: Annales du Musée Royal de L'Afrique Centrale, Sciences Humaines, no. 35.

Colle, P. 1913. *Les Baluba*. 2 vols. Anvers: Albert Dewit.

Cunnison, I. 1956. "Headmanship and the Ritual of Luapula Villages." *Africa*, 26(1):2–19.

DeBruyn, W. 1960. "Avis d'ouverture d'instruction." Judicial report, Parquet du Tanganika, Etat du Katanga, 7 Nov. 1960. Archives du Bureau des Affaires Culturelles, Division Régionale des Affaires Politiques, Lubumbashi.

Heusch, L. de. 1972. *Le roi ivre, ou l'origine de l'état*. Paris: Gallimard.

Hobsbawm, E. 1965. *Primitive Rebels*. New York: Norton.

———. 1981. *Bandits*. New York: Pantheon.

Johnson, F. 1971. *A Standard Swahili-English Dictionary*. London: Oxford Univ. Press. (1st ed., 1939.)

Joset, G. A. 1934. "Etude sur les sectes secretes de la circonscription de Kinda, district du Lomami—territoire des Baluba." *Bulletin de la Société Royale Belge de Géographie*, 58(1):28–44.

Kajiga, B. 1975. *Dictionnaire de la langue swahili*. Goma: Librarie des Volcans.

Kaoze, S. 1950. "Histoire des Bena-Kilunga." G. Nagant, ed., *Une société de l'est du Zaire, les Tusanga depeints par eux-mêmes*. Paris: Ecole Pratique des Hautes Etudes.

Kruuk, H. 1974. *The Spotted Hyena: A Study of Predation and Social Behavior*. Chicago: Univ. of Chicago Press.

Lebaigne, L. 1933. "Sectes Secretes." Administrative report from Albertville, 13 July 1933. Archives of Sous-Région du Tanganika, Kalemie.

Reefe, T. 1981. *The Rainbow and the Kings: A History of the Luba Empire to 1891*. Berkeley: Univ. of California Press.

Richards, A. 1969. *Land, Labour and Diet in Northern Rhodesia*. London: Oxford Univ. Press.

Roberts, A. F. 1980. "Heroic Beasts, Beastly Heroes: Principles of Cosmology and Chiefship Among the Lakeside BaTabwa of Zaire." Ph.D. diss., University of Chicago.

――――. 1982. " 'Comets Importing Change of Times and States': Ephemera and Process Among the Tabwa of Zaire." *American Ethnologist*, 9(4)712–29.

Roberts, C. D. 1980. *"Mungu na Mitishamba*: Illness and Medicine Among the BaTabwa of Zaire." Ph.D. diss., University of Chicago.

――――. 1981. "*Kutambuwa Ugonjuwa*: Concepts of Illness and Transformation Among the Tabwa of Zaire." *Social Science and Medicine*, 15B:309–16.

――――. In press. "Emblems and Imagery: Analysis of a Tabwa Diviness Headdress." D. Ben-Amos, ed. *Verbal and Visual Arts in Africa*. Bloomington, Indiana: Indiana University Press.

Sapir, J. D. 1977. "The Anatomy of Metaphor." J. David Sapir and J. Christopher Crocker, eds., *The Social Use of Metaphor: Essays on the Anthropology of Rhetoric*. Philadelphia: Univ. of Pennsylvania Press, 3–32.

――――. 1981. "Leper, Hyena, and Blacksmith in Kujamaat Diola Thought." *American Ethnologist*, 8(3):526–41.

Schmitz, R. 1912. *Les Baholoholo*. Anvers: Albert Dewit.

Theuws, T. 1968. "Le Styx ambigu." *Bulletin du Centre d'Etudes des Problémes Sociaux Indigénes*, 81:5–33.

Turner, V. 1967. *The Forest of Symbols*. Ithaca, NY: Cornell Univ. Press.

Van Acker, A. 1907. *Dictionnaire kitabwa-francais, francais-kitabwa*. Musée Royal du Congo Belge, *Annales*, series 5, Ethnographie-Linguistique.

Van Avermaet, E., and B. Mbuya. 1954. *Dictionnaire kiluba-francais*. Musée Royal du Congo Belge, *Annales*, Sciences de l'Homme, Linguistique.

White, T. 1960. *The Bestiary*. New York: Putnam.

White Fathers. 1954. *Bemba-English Dictionary*. Capetown: Longmans, Green.

7

Physiology and Symbols: The Anthropological Implications of the Placebo Effect

Daniel E. Moerman

How can we account for the effectiveness of non-Western medical treatment? What can we learn about the effectiveness of Western healing through comparative study?

One of the foremost dilemmas in ethnomedicine is understanding how the manipulations of the shaman or healer actually influence the physiological state of the patient. Many studies, including several of my own, have devoted much energy to investigating the effectiveness of native pharmacology. The standard exercise is to show that pharmaceuticals in use have "appropriate" physiological impact. Many tribal peoples cooperate with this exercise by having enormous pharmacopoeias at their disposal. Wyman and Harris (1941) reported 515 species of medicinal plants for the Navajo alone. My compilation of native American medicinal plants includes 2,147 different plant species from 760 genera used by 123 different cultures in 17,634 different ways (Moerman 1986).

In a less standard exercise, comparing those medicinally *used* plants with *available* plants, I have been able to demonstrate substantial selectivity among families by Native Americans. The three most heavily utilized families (Asteraceae, Rosaceae, Lamiaceae) account for 27 percent of medicinal items in my compilation, but only 19 percent of the species in the Flora North America (FNA) list of some 17,000 species (Shetler and Skog 1978). The three least heavily used families, in terms of their availability (Poaceae, Cyperaceae, and Fabaceae) account for 4 percent of items in my list but 21 percent of the genera in FNA (Moerman 1989). But we can also be certain that neither native therapists nor their patients saw pharmaceuticals as any more important in therapy than the song, dance, and din that accompanied treatment. While several investigators (most notably Victor Turner) have provided brilliant symbolic analyses of these more dramatic aspects of treatment, few have attempted to understand the healing quality of such symbolic dimensions of treatment.

This bimodal quality of native treatment often baffles Western observers. One notes approvingly the intelligent study, the deliberate consideration, and the long empirical tradition employed as the Navajo healer gathers thirty or forty herbal medicines—many of them "rational," "effective" drugs. But despair follows when the subsequent infusion is fed to and washed over the patient—*and* a dozen singers and friends who are participating in the ritual. What kind of effectiveness is this? The Navajo healing ritual, focused on a sweat-emetic rite, coupled with chants and beautiful sand paintings, is said by Reichard to be like "a spiritual osmosis in which the evil in man and the good of deity penetrate the ceremonial membrane in both directions, the former being neutralized by the latter" (1970:112). Such a rich metaphorical structure, part of the Navajo cosmological system, is simultaneously healing and barely intelligible to the Western "biomedical" understanding.

BIMODAL QUALITY OF WESTERN BIOMEDICINE

Yet there is an impressive array of evidence of similar processes, with similar effects, in our medical practice. This bimodality in treatment is probably universal. My argument is

- That the *form* of medical treatment as well as its content can be effective medical treatment
- That medical treatment must be understood bimodally, in terms of both its specific and its general dimensions
- That we have only a rudimentary capacity for simultaneously understanding both modes.

In Western medical and surgical contexts, what I refer to as "general medical therapy" is usually referred to as the "placebo effect." Various investigators (Beecher 1961; Frank 1975:195) attribute between 35 percent and 60 percent of the effectiveness of contemporary biomedicine to this placebo effect. In the shaman's context, some investigators attribute *all* effectiveness to general medical therapy, although this clearly devalues empirical pharmacological traditions dating back to middle Paleolithic times (Solecki 1965).

Even though the general effectiveness of treatment is occasionally recognized as a substantial component of the healing process, biomedicine founders in its attempts to account for the phenomenon. This follows, I suggest, from the naive dualism of contemporary medical science, which characteristically assumes a fundamental mind-body dichotomy in its conceptualization of the human organism. And since disease is an affliction of the body, whereas perception (of treatment) is an aspect of the mind, and since the only available mediators of this dichotomy are as ineffable and "unscientific" as the "soul", biomedicine tends simply to ignore, or even deny, the significance of general medical therapy (see Engel 1977; Goodwin, Goodwin, and Vogel 1979).

Even in neuroendocrinology, where recent ingenious work has shown that the hypothalamus, a central portion of the brain, is simultaneously a central portion of the endocrine system (the body), authors insist on maintaining this naive dualism; the hypothalamic neurons that produce hormones (which regulate pituitary function) are routinely called "transducer cells" (Wurtman 1971). There is a wide range of phenomena that compels us to reject this dualism. In addition to the findings of neuroendocrinology, we might mention phenomena as diverse as psychosomatic illness, biofeedback (Stoyva et al. 1972), host-pathogen interaction (Solomon 1969), Eastern meditative techniques (Datey et al. 1969) and, just for fun, fire handling (Brown 1984; Kane 1976). General medical treatment as I have defined it falls within this class where conceptual, meaningful, cultural, categorical events influence physiological processes.

Anthropologist James Fernandez has eloquently demonstrated the power of the metaphor, a "strategic predication" that can move us—that is, change our behavior (1971:43). I argue that metaphor can heal, that meaning mends. I will consider in some detail one case where we can see some consequences of meaningful human performance in Western biomedicine.

Placebo Surgery

One of the most common causes of death in the United States is myocardial infarction, or heart attack. The traditional biomedical understanding of this disease is that it is caused by ischemia, a lack of adequate blood flow to some region of the heart, which in turn is caused by atherosclerosis, which is a buildup of lipids or fatty tissues in the arteries that carry blood to the heart. The lipid buildup or atherosclerotic plaque causes lesions on the blood vessels. The heart attack is typically understood to be caused by thrombosis, that is, blockage of the narrowed artery by a blood clot (a thrombus). The clots are said to form near sites of such fixed lesions; they are often not actually seen, since, it is said, "spontaneous thrombolysis" (breakdown of the clots) occurs in two-thirds of cases. In any event, these clots block the artery; heart muscle, deprived of oxygenated blood, dies. The heart goes into fibrillation, and the patient dies.

In milder forms, coronary arteriosclerosis may lead to angina pectoris, a pressing pain beneath the sternum that often radiates out to the left arm. Small doses of nitroglycerin dissolved under the tongue provide dramatic and rapid relief from the severe pain of angina. This has been the medical treatment of choice for over a century. The drug has a potent relaxing effect on smooth muscle tissue, notably of the blood vessels; it rapidly reduces blood pressure. In addition, recent research shows that the drug seems to mimic the action of an endogenous "relaxing factor," comprised largely of nitric oxide and produced by the endothelial cells, a component of the vascular tissue (Abrams 1988; Ignarro 1989). The relaxation of the blood vessels presumably allows blood to flow more freely to the heart, alleviating the pain.

But angina pectoris, a grave and dangerous symptom of serious underlying pathology, is highly responsive not only to nitrates but to inert treatment as well. This is quite surprising since the theory of sclerotic arteries and blood clots would seem to leave little place for such unlikely findings. Benson and McCallie (1979) reviewed the literature on placebo effectiveness in angina; examining the histories of a series of treatments subsequently demonstrated to be inactive and then abandoned, they noted a consistent pattern: "The initial 70 to 90 percent effectiveness in the enthusiasts' reports decreases to 30 to 40 percent 'base-line' placebo effectiveness in the skeptics' reports" (Benson and McCallie 1979:1424). Thus, for this grave condition, skeptics can heal 30 to 40 percent of their patients with inert medication; enthusiasts, 70 to 90 percent. Either case, given the standard explanation of lesions, clots, and epithelium, seems remarkable.

The logic of this theory has yielded several other interesting approaches to angina. The surgical metaphor, by analogy with the manipulation characterized by splinting limbs, removing broken teeth, or cleaning wounds, is a powerful one for people confident of the physical basis of illness. The placebo consequences of surgery were noted by Beecher (1955, 1961), and have more recently been elaborated by Frank (1975). And, in recent years, a number of surgical procedures have been developed to deal with angina. Since the problem (pain and ultimately infarction) is presumed to be due to a constricted blood supply, why not reroute some blood supplies, bypassing the constricted areas and revascularizing the muscles at risk?

Several indirect revascularization techniques involving rerouting various arteries were developed, in the 1930s by Beck and in the 1940s by Vineburg (Meade 1961:480–515). Although Beck's procedure attained modest popularity, the first widely used surgical approach to angina was the bilateral internal mammary artery ligation (BIMAL). The internal mammary (or thoracic) arteries arise from the aorta and descend just inside the front wall of the chest, ultimately supplying blood to the viscera. Following anatomical research by Fieschi, an Italian surgeon, which indicated connections between various ramifications of these arteries and the coronary circulation, several other Italian surgeons developed a procedure in which the arteries were

Table 7.1
Improvement of Patients Undergoing Actual and Sham Bilateral Internal
Mammary Artery Ligation

Improvement	Actual				Sham			
	Study Number		Row		Study Number		Row	
	1	2	Total	Pct.	1	2	Total	Pct.
Substantial	5	9	14	67%	5	5	10	83%
Slight	3	4	7	33%	2	0	2	17%
Total	8	13	21	100%	7	5	12	100%

Sources: Study 1: Cobb et al. 1959 ("Substantial Improvement" = subjective improvement greater than 40%); Study 2: Diamond et al. 1960 ("Substantial improvement" = subjective improvement greater than 50%).

ligated below the point where these branches presumably diverged to the myocardium, in order to enhance this flow and supplement the blood supply. The operation was first performed in the United States by Robert Glover and J. Roderick Kitchell in the late 1950s (Glover 1957; Kitchell, Glover, and Kyle 1958). It was quite simple and, since the arteries were not deep in the body, could be performed under local anesthesia. The physicians reported symptomatic improvement (ranging from slight to total) in 68 percent of their first sample of fifty patients, in a two-to-six-month follow-up. The operation quickly gained some popularity.

This situation—a simple technique requiring only local anesthesia to treat a grave disease—laid the basis for a remarkable scientific study. Two research teams independently carried out double-blind studies comparing the BIMAL with a sham procedure in which the entire operation was carried out except that the arteries were not ligated (Cobb et al. 1959; Dimond et al. 1960). In both studies, patient follow-up was carried out by cardiologists unaware of which patients had undergone arterial ligation and which had not. In both studies the sham-procedure patients reported the same substantial subjective relief from angina as BIMAL patients (see Table 7.1). Most patients, with ligation or without, reported substantially reduced need for nitroglycerin. Both studies concluded that the results of the operation could be accounted for by placebo effects, and therefore should be discontinued. It was; Dr. Dimond reported subsequently that his paper was "generally credited with the successful burial of internal mammary artery ligation" (Dimond 1978).

In sum, the surgery did not work for the reasons that it was performed, and it quickly disappeared from the surgeon's repertoire. The question for *us* is, how *did* it work, how did it relieve this severe systemic pain?

A major breakthrough in the surgical approach to angina came in the 1960s with the development of direct revascularization, in which veins from elsewhere in the body (now routinely the saphenous vein from the leg) are grafted directly into the aorta and then into the appropriate coronary arteries beyond their obstructions.

Contemporary Use of Coronary Bypass Surgery

While it is hard to know exactly how many coronary bypasses are done, authoritative estimates suggest that some 228,000 were performed in 1986, up from 114,000 in 1979 (Feinleib et al. 1989). Given the increasing rate at which the operation is being repeated a second or even a third time for the same person—currently 10 to 20 percent of the caseload at many large centers (Grondin et al. 1989)—and given the increasing proportion of the population that is in the greatest risk years, and that these operations cost in the vicinity of $20,000 each, this is at least a $5 billion-a-year business, and growing. Although the operation has become very popular, it remains highly controversial. Many surgeons are, clearly, deeply committed to the tremendous value of the procedure. Its logic is obvious; its effects, dramatic.

Numerous studies indicate that the operation is highly successful, reducing symptoms (i.e., pain) in 80 to 90 percent of patients with severe stable angina pectoris. However, there are other measures of the effectiveness of such a procedure. In several very large controlled trials, only small subsets of surgically treated patients have been shown to survive longer than medically treated patients. In a trial carried out by the Veterans' Administration, survival after seven years of surgically treated patients was 77 percent and of medically treated patients 70 percent; that difference was not statistically significant. After eleven years even that difference had narrowed; surgical patient survival was 58 percent and medical patient survival was 57 percent. Similar results were achieved in the more recent European Coronary Surgery Study. After seven years the surgical group survival rate was 87 percent and the medical group survival rate was 79 percent; after twelve years surgical patient survival was 71 percent and medical group survival was 67 percent (Gersh et al. 1989). There are a few subgroups of patients—for instance, those with restrictions of the left main coronary artery or those with three-vessel disease and left ventricular dysfunction—for whom surgery improves chances of survival. Unfortunately, the degree of left ventricular dysfunction is the best predictor of death during surgery (Bonow and Epstein 1985). One large study has shown that although the operation clearly alleviates symptoms, it has little rehabilitative effect on patients. Among 350 patients studied, "There was no improvement in return to work or hours worked after surgery" (Barnes et al. 1977; see also Smith, Frye, and Peihler 1983 for a review of several such studies, all with similar results). Another study has shown that of a group of eighty-eight patients recommended for bypass graft surgery, seventy-four were referred for continued medical treatment in a second-opinion program. "Sixty of these 74 patients chose this option and continued to receive medical therapy without any fatalities during a follow-up period of 27.8 months" (Graboys et al. 1987:1611; see also McIntosh 1987).

But the most interesting aspect of coronary artery bypass surgery is that several authors have noted that "some patients undergoing coronary artery bypass have improvement of angina despite the fact that all grafts are occluded" (Gott et al. 1973:30). A study examined 446 bypass patients who underwent coronary arteriography subsequent to their surgery. Of these, fifty-four had no functioning, patent grafts. Both groups displayed similarly impressive functional improvement. The authors concluded that coronary bypass surgery patients

experience impressive symptomatic improvement regardless of completeness of revascularization . . . [and] the late survival of unsuccessful revascularization patients is more favorable than predicted from previous natural history data. [This] suggests that factors other than coronary bypass surgery may play a role in the long-term survival of coronary artery disease patients undergoing surgery. (Valdes et al. 1979)

One authority concluded, gently enough, that "the situation is complex and . . . increased blood flow to the ischemic [occluded] region is not the only possible explanation for symptomatic improvement" (Ross 1975:503). Other explanations have been proposed, including the notions that surgery actually causes minor myocardial infarctions (heart attacks) and that surgery denervates the angina-producing region.

How Does Heart Surgery Work?

This means that although the surgery works, *it does not necessarily work for the reasons that it is done.* The rationality of the procedure for the preponderance of patients is apparently unconnected with its effectiveness. In the 1880s, when James Mooney analyzed the use of a series of Cherokee drugs, he concluded, "We must admit that much of their practice is correct, however false the reasoning by which they have arrived at this result" (Mooney 1891:328). A similar situation apparently applies to these cases of heart surgery.

How can cutting two little incisions over the second intercostal space alleviate the pain of angina pectoris? How can coronary bypass patients with occluded grafts experience this profound relief? The logic of these procedures is persuasive, if erroneous. And it is this logic that is propounded to the patient by the surgeon. And, thereby, an obvious remaining explanation for the effectiveness of bypass surgery, or BIMAL, is general or placebo effectiveness. Bypass surgery, especially, is, from a patient's point of view, a cosmic drama following a most potent metaphorical path. The patient is rendered unconscious. His heart—source of life, fount of love, racked with pain—is stopped. He is, by many reasonable definitions, dead. The surgeon restructures his heart, and the patient is reborn, reincarnated. His sacrifice (roughly $20,000) may hurt as much as his incisions. Remembering that angina can be a remarkably stable nonfatal condition (Gott et al. 1973) and considering the substantial subjective components in pain itself, it seems reasonable to conclude that the general metaphorical effects of this surgery are as decisive in its anomalous effectiveness as are graft-patency rates (Frank 1975).

Research on the etiology of coronary artery disease has shown that angina and infarction may be caused by coronary artery spasm (Maseri et al. 1978; see also Goldberg 1983), which may in turn be caused by neurological impulses or emotional stresses. Angina and heart attacks are not random mechanical events but, rather, the results of neurological or mental processes—the process is a complex one open to cortical influence, increasing our confidence that it is subject to symbolic and meaningful influences.

In modern Western biomedicine as well as in tribal healing, whether by design or default, the *form* of medical treatment, internal or surgical, can be effective medical treatment. Recall the characteristic American medical treatments of the period immediately preceding the biomedical revolution of the 1880s: most conditions were treated with calomel (mercurous chloride), a powerful purgative, or with venesection, minimally a symbolic operation, the laying on of steel (Shryock 1966:245). These two treatments probably had some specific physiological impact, as may modern medical treatments for cancer that employ powerful purgatives. Such stress might trigger a general immunological response. But in all likelihood, the decisive elements in any effectiveness the physician had were a consequence of the dramatic, general, and metaphorical elements these treatments contained. Such effectiveness adheres to modern treatment.

HEALING AND PHILOSOPHY

We have no generally accepted theoretical paradigm within which we can evaluate and interpret such human experience. Even the growing literature on holistic medicine seems essentially empirical, cataloging experience on biofeedback, host-pathogen interactions, "stress" and illness, and so on (Pelletier 1977). And consonant with that empiricism is a kind of religiosity: those who venture beyond the empirical seem almost inevitably to begin speaking of archetypes, gods, or souls (Hillman 1964). Even the more scholarly of them, we feel, are straining against the temptation to break into song.

Dualism

This follows, I think, from a naive dualism, the ethnometaphysic of our time. With a thinking and unextended mind, and an unthinking and extended body, in Descartes's formulation, there is no ground for interaction of these human quanta, or onta, save some ephemeral, mystical, spiritual soul (Stent 1975). A variant and, I suggest, increasingly popular variation of this dualism involves a more complex conceptualization of the organism, one where the person has a "mind and a body" but the body also has a "mind of its own." A student once explained the placebo effect to me in this way: "The mind tells the body what to do," she said. The body, presumably listening with its own mind, did what it was told. Much current speculation about "visualization," "body imagery," and the like employs similar language; for a critique of such thinking, see Chapter 17 in this volume.

Philosophical attempts to resolve the dilemma of dualism come in many forms, one as likely as the next, each one reasonable in its own terms, each one fundamentally flawed in terms of the others. Idealism and behaviorism are two very powerful monisms, each denying one or the other of mind and body. Although idealism resolves the mind-body dilemma by denying body, it also denies the reality of the external world; solipsism seems too high a price to pay for this solution. Much more popular is behaviorism, which resolves the dilemma by denying mind, by denying mental life. Among the strongest of such positions is that taken by the philosopher J. J. C. Smart: "When I 'report' a pain, I am not really reporting anything . . . but am doing a sophisticated sort of wince" (Smart 1959:141). Such a position denies the existence of an autonomous inner life, not to mention the possibility of culture.

Among several more sophisticated varieties of dualism are parallelism and interactionism, and several combinations of them. They all seem similarly open to critical challenge. For a classic philosophical dogfight on the matter, see Globus et al. 1976.

Person Theory

A very interesting philosophical consideration of this problem is Brody's (1977) defense of Strawson's (1958), Kenny et al.'s (1973), and Grene's (1976) "person theory." This theory simultaneously meets many of the challenges of the standard philosophical positions and can be extended to meet many of the concerns of the anthropologist. It is one philosophical position in this debate that has a central role for culture. At the risk of oversimplifying, I will briefly summarize Brody's argument and indicate how it meets the anthropological requirements of a cultural epistemology, and how it provides a framework for understanding what I have called general medical therapy.

Denying the primitive qualities of the quanta "mind" and "body," this theory asserts that there are two kinds of entities, "material bodies" and "persons," to which two kinds of predicates, "mental" and "physical," can be attached. "Material bodies can correctly have ascribed to them only physical predicates, while persons can have applied to them both physical and mental predicates" (Brody 1977:93). Kenny says, "To have a mind is to have the capacity to acquire the ability to operate with symbols in such a way that it is one's own activity that makes them symbols and confers meaning upon them" (quoted in Grene 1976:178). The critical logical feature of this position is that "the concept of person is more basic than the physical and mental predicates ascribed to it" (Brody 1977:93). This is a unitary conceptualization of the human organism that does not have to account for either of those quanta in terms of the other, yet lets us talk about human beings in an intuitively familiar manner. In this formulation, "persons" are understood as animals possessing the capacity to use symbols in special ways, specifically in structuring experience and generally in participating in culture, an anthropological commonplace. In this context, there is no longer in principle an anomaly in understanding how performance can influence physiological state:

If being a dweller within culture is a special way of being an animal, it should not be anomalous if this characteristic were found to influence other animal capacities— including the capacities to undergo changes in bodily status and function. Experiencing symptom change due to the placebo effect is therefore the bodily expression of the person's participation in the healing context as a culturally determined, symbolic phenomenon. (Brody 1977:102–3)

To be a person is to have a mind. To have a mind is to be able to use symbols. Symbols are most evident in language. Private symbols are impossible in the same sense that private language is impossible—were it private, it would not be language. Therefore, being a person is essentially a *social* phenomenon and requires the prior existence of other persons. (I note parenthetically that the quantum "person" need not necessarily be confined to one individual body [Crocker 1976].) "One can ascribe states of consciousness to oneself only if one can ascribe them to others" (Strawson 1958:339); "The ability to use [mental] predicates self-referentially follows from the ability to use them at all" (Brody 1977:111), that is, to use them regarding others. Hence, self-consciousness is a differentiating process, a process of noting meaningful contrasts, of noting, in Bateson's phrase, differences that make a difference, not merely an indexing or naming process.

Using Kleinman's contrast (1973), we equate "disease" with "difference," and "illness" with "a difference that makes a difference," that is, a meaningful difference. It is at this point that diagnosis, either by the patient (based on widely shared symbolic norms) or by the healer (based on more private, technical, professional, or sacred norms), becomes critical. For it is at this point that the inchoate disease becomes a meaningful quantum "illness," hence understandable and, within the limits of animal mortality, finally controllable. And likewise for the treatment of illness through performance, remembering Fernandez (1971), medical metaphors are those strategic mental predications that can "move" us, that is, manipulate physical predications, in a process we call "healing."

Objections

Consider a curious and poetic objection in an essay by Erde, a philosopher of medicine. He contrasts some contemporary dualisms with a variation of this person theory in a sort of double reductio ad absurdum proof. He argues that dualism commits us to much that is incredible, a position with which I would agree. But he further argues that a unitary position does likewise:

It implies that the body is animate. . . . [I]f the body is also a character within the drama, if we personify the body and it becomes an agent unto itself, we might understand that it could produce physical illness from within. . . . [T]he implication is that what we call "bodily illness" may be meaningful in the sense made current by Freud regarding neuroses, dreams, and slips of the tongue. . . . [I]f a man is a unity, somatic illness is as meaningful as any illness . . . and should be understood by the sick individual and by the physician even before it is determined whether it should be treated by . . . secondary material means. . . . (Erde 1977:187, 189)

This, Erde concludes, is "incredible."

It seems to me to be eminently credible, and even, from an anthropological and semiotic point of view, properly intuitive.

MEDICAL THERAPY, SPECIFIC AND GENERAL

From this perspective, I propose these somewhat more formal definitions of specific and general medical therapy. Specific therapy is that healing activity influencing the physical predicates of persons; general therapy is that influencing (wittingly or otherwise) the mental predicates of persons. Such a view places these alternative experiences on an equal ontological footing, compatible and comparable in effect. It also affords a guide to clear talk about such experiences. Thus the sentence "I feel better; I have less heart pain" breaks down into "I feel better because I have more blood in my myocardium and because I have a restructured heart." The relative impact of these two predicates on the subject is, in any individual case, open to analysis and, before the fact, each is open to manipulation, control, and skill.

Of course, this does not solve the problem of general effectiveness in detail any more than it does for specific effectiveness; how a given drug precisely influences a given organ is a complex research question, and the same complexity may be expected in understanding the particular influence of any general therapy. But it does mean that there is no obstacle *in principle* to understanding such effectiveness through properly designed studies. Work by Levine and others (1978) implicating endorphins in placebo analgesia is a brilliant example of the beginnings of such work.

Meaning mends. Study meaning, and learn about mending. But study mending, and we might learn about meaning. These are some of the implications of the study of physiology and symbols.

ACKNOWLEDGMENTS

I am indebted to John Ross, Jr., MD, who advised me on the details of coronary artery disease and its treatments. Diane Lintner read the manuscript and made very helpful suggestions. Of course, all responsibility for the interpretations put forth here is mine.

REFERENCES

Abrams, J. 1988. "Nitrates." *Medical Clinics of North America* 72:1–35.

Barnes, Glenda K., M.J. Ray, A. Oberman, and N.T. Kouchoubos. 1977. "Changes in Working Status of Patients Following Coronary Bypass Surgery." *Journal of the American Medical Association* 238:1249–52.

Beecher, H. K. 1955. "The Powerful Placebo." *Journal of the American Medical Association* 159:1602–6.

———. 1961. "Surgery as Placebo." *Journal of the American Medical Association* 176:1102–7.

Benson, Herbert, and David P. McCallie. 1979. "Angina Pectoris and the Placebo Effect." *New England Journal of Medicine* 300(25):1424–29.

Bonow, Robert O., and Stephen E. Epstein. 1985. "Indications for Coronary Artery Bypass Surgery in Patients with Chronic Angina Pectoris: Implications of the Multicenter Randomized Trials." *Circulation* 72 (supp. V): V23–30.

Brody, Howard A. 1977. "Persons and Placebos: Philosophical Dimensions of the Placebo Effect." Ph.D. dissertation, Michigan State University, East Lansing. Ann Arbor: University Microfilms.

Brown, Carolyn Henning. 1984. "Tourism and Ethnic Competition in a Ritual Form: The Firewalkers of Fiji." *Oceania* 54:223–44.

Cobb, L. A., G. I. Thomas, D. H. Dillard, K. A. Marendino, and R. A. Bruce. 1959. "An Evaluation of Internal Mammary Artery Ligation by a Double Blind Technic." *New England Journal of Medicine* 260:1115–18.

Crocker, J. Christopher. 1976. "The Mirrored Self: Identity and Ritual Inversion Among the Eastern Bororo." *Ethnology* 15:129–45.

Datey, K. K., S. N. Deshmukh, and C. P. Dalvi. 1969. " 'Shavasan': A Yogic Exercise in Management of Hypertension." *Angiology* 20:325.

Dimond, E. G. 1978. Personal communication.

Dimond, E. G., C. F. Kittle, and J. E. Crockett. 1960. "Comparison of Internal

Mammary Artery Ligation and Sham Operation for Angina Pectoris." *American Journal of Cardiology* 5:483–86.

Engel, George. 1977. "The Need for a New Medical Model: A Challenge for Biomedicine." *Science* 196:129–36.

Erde, Edmund L. 1977. "Mind-Body and Malady." *Journal of Medicine and Philosophy* 2:177–90.

Feinleib, Manning, R. J. Havlik, R. F. Gillum, R. Pokras, E. McCarthy, and M. Moien. 1989. "Coronary Heart Disease and Related Procedures: National Hospital Discharge Survey Data." *Circulation* 79 (6): Suppl I, I13–I18.

Fernandez, James. 1971. "Persuasions and Performances: Of the Beast in Every Body . . . and the Metaphors of Everyman." *Daedelus* 110:39–60.

Frank, Jerome. 1975. "Psychotherapy of Bodily Illness: An Overview." *Psychotherapy and Psychosomatics* 26:192–202.

Gersh, Bernard J., Robert M. Califf, Floyd D. Loop, Cary W. Atkins, David B. Pryor, and Timothy C. Takaro. 1989. "Coronary Bypass Surgery in Chronic Stable Angina." *Circulation* 79 (6) Suppl I:I46–I59.

Globus, Gordon G., Grover Maxwell, and Irwin Savodnik. 1976. *Consciousness and the Brain: A Scientific and Philosophical Inquiry*. New York: Plenum.

Glover, Robert P. 1957. "A New Surgical Approach to the Problem of Myocardial Revascularization in Coronary Artery Disease." *Journal of the Arkansas Medical Society* 54:223–34.

Goldberg, Sheldon (ed.). 1983. "Coronary Artery Spasm and Thrombosis." *Cardiovascular Clinics* 14(1): 1–281.

Goodwin, James S., Jean M. Goodwin, and Albert V. Vogel. 1979. "Knowledge and Use of Placebos by House Officers and Nurses." *Annals of Internal Medicine* 91:106–10.

Gott, Vincent L., J. S. Donahoo, R. R. Brawley, and L. S. Griffith. 1973. "Current Surgical Approaches to Ischemic Heart Disease." *Current Problems in Surgery* V. 1973 no. 10.

Graboys, Thomas B., Adrienne Headley, Bernard Lown, Steven Lampert, and Charles M. Blatt. 1987. "Results of a Second-Opinion Program for Coronary Artery Bypass Graft Surgery." *Journal of the American Medical Association* 258:1611–14.

Grene, Marjorie. 1976. " 'To Have a Mind . . . .' " *Journal of Medicine and Philosophy* 1:177–99.

Grondin, C. M., Lucien Campeau, J. C. Engle, F.S. Cross and H. Schreiber. 1989. "Coronary Artery Grafting with Saphenous Vein." *Circulation* 79 (6) Suppl I: I24–I29.

Hillman, James. 1964. *Suicide and the Soul*. New York: Harper & Row.

Ignarro, L. J. 1989. "Endothelium-derived Nitric Oxide: Pharmacology and Relationship to the Actions of Organic Nitrate Ester." *Pharmaceutical Research* 6:651–59.

Kane, Stephen. 1976. "Holiness Fire Handling: A Psychophysiological Analysis." Paper presented at the annual meeting of the American Anthropological Association, Washington, D.C.

Kenny, A. J. P., H. C. Longuet-Higgins, J. R. Lucas, and C. H. Waddington. 1973. *The Development of Mind*. Edinburgh: Edinburgh University Press.

Kitchell, J. F., R. P. Glover, and R. H. Kyle. 1958. "Bilateral Internal Mammary Artery Ligation for Angina Pectoris." *American Journal of Cardiology* 1:46–50.

Kleinman, Arthur. 1973. "Medicine's Symbolic Reality." *Inquiry* 16:206–13.

Levine, J. D., N. C. Gordon, and H. L. Fields. 1978. "The Mechanisms of Placebo Analgesia." *Lancet* 2:654–57.

McIntosh, Henry D. 1987. "Editorial: Second Opinions for Aortocoronary Bypass Grafting Are Beneficial" *Journal of the American Medical Association* 258:1644–45.

Maseri, Attilio, A. L'Abbate, A. Baroldi, G. Chierchia, S. Marzilli, M. Ballestra, A.M. Severi, S. Parodi, O. Biagini, A. Distante and A. Pesola. 1978. "Coronary Vasospasm as a Possible Cause of Myocardial Infarction." *New England Journal of Medicine* 229:1271–77.

Meade, Richard H. 1961. *A History of Thoracic Surgery.* Springfield, Ill.: Charles C. Thomas.

Moerman, Daniel E. 1986. *Medicinal Plants of Native America.* Technical Reports, No. 19. University of Michigan Museum of Anthropology.

————. 1989. "Poisoned Apples and Honeysuckles: The Medicinal Plants of Native America." Washington, D.C.: *Medical Anthropology Quarterly* 3:52–61. (Included as Chapter 8 in this volume.)

Mooney, James. 1891. "The Sacred Formulas of the Cherokees." *Seventh Annual Report of the Bureau of American Ethnology*, pp. 301–97. Washington, D.C.: Smithsonian Institution.

Pelletier, Kenneth R. 1977. *Mind as Healer, Mind as Slayer: A Holistic Approach to Preventing Stress Disorders.* New York: Delta.

Reichard, Gladys. 1970. *Navajo Religion.* New York: Bollingen Foundation.

Ross, Richard S. 1975. "Ischemic Heart Disease: An Overview." *American Journal of Cardiology* 36:496–505.

Shetler, S., and L. Skog. 1978. *A Provisional Checklist of Species for Flora North America.* Monographs in Systematic Botany, vol. 1. St. Louis: Missouri Botanical Garden.

Shryock, Richard H. 1966. *Medicine in America: Historical Essays.* Baltimore: Johns Hopkins University Press.

Smart, J. J. C. 1959. "Sensations and Brain Processes." *Philosophical Review* 68:141–56.

Smith, Hugh C., Robert L. Frye, and Jeffrey Peihler. 1983. "Does Coronary Bypass Surgery Have a Favorable Influence on the Quality of Life?" *Cardiovascular Clinics* 13:253–64.

Solecki, Ralph S. 1965. "Shanidar IV, a Neanderthal Flower Burial in Northern Iraq." *Science* 190:880–81.

Solomon, George F. 1969. "Emotions, Stress and the Central Nervous System." *Annals of the New York Academy of Science* 164:335–42.

Stent, Gunther S. 1975. "Limits to the Scientific Understanding of Man." *Science* 187:1052–57.

Stoyva, Johan, T. X. Barber, L. V. DiCara. 1972. *Biofeedback and Self Control, 1971.* Chicago: Aldine.

Strawson, P. F. 1958. *Persons.* Minnesota Studies in the Philosophy of Science, vol. 2. Minneapolis: University of Minnesota Press.

Valdes, M., B. D. McCallister, D. R. McConahay, W. A. Reed, D. A. Killen, and

M. Arnold. 1979. " 'Sham Operation' Revisited: A Comparison of Complete vs. Unsuccessful Coronary Artery Bypass." *American Journal of Cardiology* 43:382.

Wurtman, R. 1971. "Brain Monoamines and Endocrine Function." *Neuroendocrine Research Program Bulletin* 9:172.

Wyman, Leland C., and Stuart K. Harris. 1941. *Navaho Indian Medical Ethno-Botany.* University of New Mexico Bulletin no. 336. Albuquerque: University of New Mexico Press.

PART III

EMPIRICAL ANALYSES OF NON-WESTERN MEDICAL PRACTICES AND MEDICAL ECOLOGY

Non-Western folk or tribal medical systems use a broad range of botanical and other elements in the treatment of the sick. That these herbal systems may reside within complex and medically significant ideologies in no way mitigates the fact that the herbs themselves are significant as medicines.

Humans have been experimenting with medicinal plants for a long time. Indeed, although one cannot be certain that they were used medicinally then, the fact that most of the pollens found by Solecki with the middle Paleolithic burial of Shanidar IV were from plants still in use medicinally by the local Iraqi population suggests that they were so used. One of the plants identified was *Ephedra*, source of ephedrine, a substance widely used in modern medicine as an antihistamine. Several of the other plants also have substantial demonstrable active principles (Solecki 1975).

That cases like these are not simple luck, that people carefully select medicinal plants and do not merely choose them at random, has been demonstrated twice, by independent researchers, in analyses of different continents. But, Hu, and Kong (1980), analyzing the use of 4,941 species of Chinese medicinal plants, and Moerman in Chapter 8, analyzing the use of 2,143 species of North American medicinal plants by Native Americans, have both concluded (by somewhat different techniques) that medicinal plants used are nonrandom selections of plants available. In addition, Moerman has shown that the plants selected tend to come from groups which produce biologically active substances to protect themselves against competition from other plants or from browsing by insects or vertebrates. These approaches show that it is possible to make sense of the enormous botanical pharmacopoeias of tribal peoples in theoretically interesting ways, not just empirically.

But there is more to health than medicines used to improve it. Bogin, in his comprehensive review of the evolution of human nutrition, demonstrates clearly that human health is a consequence of nutrition, and that nutrition is a consequence of culture. He also demonstrates the much less obvious notion that changes in the human diet since the end of the Upper Paleolithic, and especially since the development of agriculture and the consequent reduction in both the variety and the quality of foodstuffs, have led to a general decline in the state of human health. Similarly, in an only somewhat narrower framework, Van Blerkom shows how the great preponderance of infectious diseases were transferred from animals, primarily domesticated animals. This argument follows from a comparison of the extraordinarily different disease histories of Europeans and Asians, on the one hand, and Native Americans, on the other; the latter suffered very few infectious diseases because they had no domesticated animals of significance.

In a closer analysis of one West African society, Etkin and Ross argue that diet is tied not only to the maintenance of health but also to the amelioration of disease, as they argue that a number of elements in the Hausa diet can actually affect the course of malaria. The difference between "drugs" and "food" is ultimately one of concept, not of content. In a similar vein, Keith and Armelagos demonstrate the widespread incidence of therapeutic quantities of naturally occurring antibiotics in various non-Western diets.

There is a wealth of knowledge and belief, explicit and implicit, in the non-Western world regarding healing. Not all, or perhaps even much, of it may ever be of significance for Western medicine—but some of it may be. All of it is useful in our attempt to understand how humans live. The combination of such possibility with such certainty is sufficient reason to continue the serious pursuit of understanding of these other systems of health care.

REFERENCES

But, P. P., S. Y. Hu, and Y. C. Kong. 1980. "Vascular Plants Used in Chinese Medicine." *Fitoterapia*, 51:245–64.

Moerman, D. 1979. "Symbols and Selectivity: A Statistical Analysis of Native American Medical Ethnobotany." *Journal of Ethnopharmacology*, 1:111–19.

Solecki, R. 1975. "Shanidar IV, a Neanderthal Flower Burial in Northern Iraq." *Science*, 190:880–81.

8

POISONED APPLES AND HONEYSUCKLES: THE MEDICINAL PLANTS OF NATIVE AMERICA

DANIEL E. MOERMAN

A decade ago, I reported a statistical analysis of the medicinal uses of plants by Native Americans (Moerman 1979). This chapter updates that analysis on a much larger sample, using data comprising very nearly a complete census of the medicinal plants of North America. Ten years ago it seemed reasonable to focus on the issue of "efficacy," to attempt to demonstrate that Native American botanical medicine was not "only placebo medicine," simply the result of random activity. While this sort of demonstration is still useful, the field of ethnobotany and the world around it has changed enough so that other emphases now seem more interesting. The primary questions addressed here are the following: What sorts of plants were Native Americans most or least likely to select for use as medicines? Why is it that these choices were effective ones? Alternatively, why is it that plants have medicinal value, and how did people figure this out?

THE DATA BASE

My earlier analysis was based on a sample of 4,869 uses of 1,288 species of plants. That data base is referred to as *American Medical Ethnobotany* (AME) (Moerman 1977). Since then, a much larger data base, *Medicinal Plants of Native America* (MPNA), has been constructed (Moerman 1986). The complete data set includes 17,634 uses of 2,397 taxa. The present report is based on an analysis of 15,843 uses of 2,143 species for which complete taxonomic

Table 8.1
Comparison of the Data Bases

	American Medical Ethnobotany (AME)	Medicinal Plants of Native American (MPNA)	MPNA[a] AME
Items	4,869	15,843	3.25
Cultures	48	123	2.56
Species	1,288	2,143	1.66
Genera	531	735	1.38
Families	118	141	1.19

[a]This column represents the second column of figures dvided by the first.

and botanical data are available (see Table 8.1).[1] As in the earlier paper, botanical information is derived from the provisional checklist of species from the *Flora North America* (FNA) (Shetler and Skog 1978).

MPNA includes all the data in AME (all checked against the original sources, and corrected accordingly). It is worth noting that tripling the number of items in the data base increased the number of species by only 66% and the number of genera by only 38%. This can be taken as evidence that MPNA is less a sample than a census of the medicinal plant species of the continent. Substantially increasing the number of items would thus be unlikely to increase the number of medicinal taxa markedly.

This chapter develops a technique of regression residual analysis for selecting portions of the data for further examination. A particular benefit of this method is that it permits us to isolate not only the plants that are used frequently, but also the ones used infrequently or not at all.

ANALYSIS

There is a challenging methodological problem in pursuing this analysis. How can one actually analyze 15,843 uses of 2,143 species at the same time? Recognizing that botanists sort plant species into families (232 of them in North America), we might try to compare those families having many medicinally used species with those having only a few. The three families with the largest number of medicinal species in North America are Asteraceae (the sunflowers) with 345, Rosaceae (the roses) with 115, and Fabaceae (the beans) with 108. But these are also very large families (Asteraceae has 2,231 species in *Flora North America*, while Rosaceae has 577 and Fabaceae has 1,225). These facts suggest that we should consider not the number of medicinal species but rather the proportion or percentage of medicinally used species out of the total number of species in the family. Listing our 232 families this way, the three large families noted above become lost in the crowd: Rosaceae is in 70th position, Asteraceae in 89th, and Fabaceae, 115th.

While simple counts of medicinal species thus overemphasize large families, percentages or indices overemphasize small ones. For example, there are seven families with only one, two, or three species, all of which are used medicinally and would therefore place these families at the top of any use list by percentage. (Among these families are the Datiscaceae with one species, Saururaceae with two, and Calycanthaceae with three.) The percentage method also presents problems at the other extreme. For example, no species of Agavaceae or Zingiberaceae is used medicinally by Native Americans. These two families would thus share the same ranking on a list by either gross count or percentage—both zero. There are, however, 86 species in the former family and only one in the latter. It seems somehow more significant that none of Agavaceae's 86 species is used medicinally than that Zingiberaceae's one is not.

An alternative approach to the data that addresses most of these dilemmas and that still allows us to stratify the sample in anthropologically interesting ways is based on regression analysis (Snedecor and Cochran 1967:135–71; Runyon and Haber 1984). In our case, the number of species per family used medicinally (MPNASPE) is regressed on the total number of species in each family as recorded in the *Flora North America* (FNASPE). The results are shown in Tables 8.2 and 8.3. The regression equation is

$$\text{MPNASPE} = 1.21 + (.1115 \times \text{FNASPE})$$
$$\text{with } r = .876.$$

Thus, to predict the number of species used medicinally from a given family, one multiplies the total number of species in the family by .1115 and adds 1.21. The analysis indicates that this is a "good" regression because the correlation (r) is high. This means that the number of species in a family used medicinally is well predicted by the number of species in that family. This could be taken as evidence that the selection of medicinal plants was more or less random; that is, it was not very selective at all.

An analysis of the residuals, however, shows that selection was *not* random. In a regression analysis, the residual is defined as the actual value of the dependent variable minus the predicted value of the variable. Consider a case: we have already noted that the Asteraceae family has 2,231 species in North America, according to FNA. Multiplying the number of species by .1115 and adding 1.21, we get 250 as the predicted number of species used medicinally. MPNA indicates, however, that 345 species were used medicinally. The residual then is 95 (actual minus predicted = 345 − 220 = 95).

Table 8.2

Subsequent Regressions of Number of Species in MPNA on Number of Species in FNA[a]

Case	N	r	Coeff.[b]	Const.[c]	S.E.	Residuals Min.	Max.	Skewness	Kurtosis
1	232	.875	.111	1.21	13.2	-129	95	-2.43	52.1
2	226	.891	.121	.96	5.4	-15	25.3	1.81	7.39
3	209	.908	.115	.67	2.8	-	11.2	.93	2.62

[a]These figures represent three successive regressions. The first case represents the regression on the entire set of 232 families. In the second case, six families have been eliminated from the set because their residuals were greater than twice the standard error (S.E.); these are the three high-use families and the three low-use families shown as Case 1 in Table 8.3. This process was repeated twice more to identify a total of three groups ("cases") of most and least-used plant families.

[b]The coefficient or slope of the regression equation.

[c]The constant or intercept of the regression equation.

Ninety-five more species were used medicinally than the regression predicted.

Another measure of a "good" regression, in addition to the correlation coefficient, is one where these residuals are all small. A standard measure of the size of the residuals is their standard deviation, called here the "standard error of the regression" (S.E. in Table 8.2). To be confident of the predictive value of a regression, the collection of residuals should also be distributed normally about the mean. Two measures of normality are skewness and kurtosis. Skewness measures whether values are distributed symmetrically about the mean. Positive (or negative) values indicate that the distribution is disproportionately greater than (or less than) the mean; a value of 0 indicates a symmetrical distribution. Kurtosis, roughly speaking, measures the shape of the distribution. Kurtosis of 0 represents a normal distribution; positive values indicate sharply peaked distributions while negative values indicate flat distributions. These values are shown in the first row of Table 8.2; they indicate some negative skewness and a high value for kurtosis, indicating a peaked distribution. Plant families with particularly large positive residuals indicate that they are selected for medicinal usage far more often than is ordinarily the case; cases with large negative residuals indicate selection less often than expected. The great value of residual analysis is that we can easily identify these important outliers.

Note that the predictive value of regression is not of great interest here. We have little need to predict how many taxa from some family will be used medicinally, because we already know that: the data are very nearly a census

Table 8.3
Families by Residual from Regression Analysis

Case	Family	Flora North America		Medicinal Plants of Native America			
		Genera	Species	Genera	Species		
					Actual	Predicted	Residual
		High-use families					
1	Asteraceae	296	2231	99	345	249.88	95.12
	Rosaceae	53	577	28	115	65.53	49.47
	Lamiaceae	56	320	30	64	36.88	27.12
2	Pinaceae	7	71	6	35	9.62	25.38
	Caprifoliaceae	7	77	7	35	10.36	24.64
	Ranunculaceae	24	294	17	60	36.81	23.19
	Salicaceae	2	131	2	40	16.94	23.06
	Apiaceae	79	319	30	58	39.86	18.14
	Liliaceae	59	393	27	67	48.89	18.11
	Corylaceae	5	33	5	21	4.99	16.01
	Saxifragaceae	34	260	17	46	32.67	13.33
	Ericaceae	30	180	16	36	22.91	13.09
	Solanaceae	23	129	6	28	16.70	11.30
3	Cupressaceae	5	27	5	15	3.79	11.21
	Cornaceae	1	17	1	12	2.64	9.36
	Fagaceae	5	140	4	26	16.82	9.18
	Pyrolaceae	12	27	5	12	3.79	8.21
	Berberidaceae	7	29	6	12	4.02	7.98
	Aceraceae	1	15	1	10	2.41	7.59
	Polypodiaceae	44	215	17	33	25.47	7.53
	Araliaceae	4	10	3	8	1.83	6.17
	Asclepiadaceae	10	97	1	18	11.86	6.14
	Polygonaceae	20	413	5	54	48.31	5.69
	Araceae	13	16	6	8	2.52	5.48
		Low-use families					
1	Poaceae	206	1477	24	37	165.84	− 128.84
	Cyperaceae	27	718	5	22	81.24	− 59.24
	Fabaceae	118	1225	39	108	137.75	− 29.75
2	Scrophulariaceae	66	632	17	63	78.03	− 15.03
	Caryophyllaceae	36	287	7	22	35.96	− 13.96
	Boraginaceae	33	304	12	25	38.03	− 13.03
	Juncaceae	2	123	2	4	15.96	− 11.96
	Agavaceae	9	86	0	0	11.45	− 11.45
	Hydrophyllaceae	16	183	5	12	23.28	− 11.28
	Brassicaceae	85	510	23	52	63.15	− 11.15
3	Acanthaceae	19	65	0	0	8.17	− 8.17
	Euphorbiaceae	33	264	10	23	31.12	− 8.12
	Cactaceae	22	180	6	14	21.44	− 7.44
	Malvaceae	32	213	8	19	25.24	− 6.24
	Onagraceae	16	247	6	23	29.16	− 6.16

of the situation, and prediction is not really necessary. The analysis of residuals, however, gives us an elegant way to identify families that are particularly interesting in one way or another, by a method that avoids the ambiguities of ranking by number or percent.

Recalling that our intent is to stratify the sample into some interesting subgroups that we can compare with one another, a simple iterative process was used to identify the "most used" and the "least used" families. Families with residuals either more than or less than twice the value of the standard error were eliminated from the sample, and the regression was repeated. This was done twice, yielding three regression equations on successively smaller samples (shown in Table 8.2). This process allowed us to identify six sets of families of particular interest to ethnobotany: three sets that are intensively used as the source of medicine, and three sets that are infrequent sources of medicines (Table 8.3).

DISCUSSION

The 24 "high-use" families in Table 8.3 comprise 37% of the species in *Flora North America*, but they constitute 55% of the species used medicinally by Native Americans. The 15 "low-use" families likewise comprise 40% of the species in FNA, but only 20% of species in MPNA. What differences exist between the high- and low-use families? I cannot consider all 39 of these families in detail here, but some observations suggest broader generalizations and future research.[2]

The Edible Grasses

The Poaceae, the grass family, stands apart from all the rest as being by far the least used medicinally. This is a very large and complex family; in North America, it has some 206 genera and 1,477 species, nearly 10% of the species of the continent. Only 24 of the genera and 37 of the species are used medicinally (in 107 ways). A number of these uses are quite distinctive. The Blackfoot, Cheyenne, Dakota, Omaha, Pawnee, Ponca, and Winnebago all use *Hierochloe odorata*, sweet grass, as an incense to purify, beautify, or otherwise enhance a variety of healing and other activities. The Thompson Indians of British Columbia use an infusion or decoction of the plant as a pleasant wash for the body or hair. Other grass species are used similarly; thus, while these plants play a part in medical activities, the grasses are rarely used internally as medicines. We also note, however, that the grass family is the source of the vast majority of human food—wheat, corn (maize), oats, rye, and barley are only a few of the many seed grains that feed most people and their domesticated animals.

To understand these facts, one needs to answer a more general question, namely, why do plants produce medicines at all? What is it that leads poppies to produce chemicals that mimic the biological activity of vertebrate endorphins? More generally, why do plants produce substances that have biological activity? In detail this is a very difficult question to answer, although in broad strokes it seems apparent that most such substances, often termed "secondary metabolites,"[3] have the effect of minimizing browsing, reducing botanical competition (by inhibiting the growth or germination of other plants), or enhancing pollination or seed dispersal. Speaking ecologically, these botanical activities can be seen as similar to a K-strategy of investment, in which animals devote energy to enhancing the survival of individual offspring (MacArthur and Wilson 1967). The grasses, it seems, do not produce a significant number of these chemicals and are, therefore, not useful sources of medicines; the reaction of many grasses to being browsed (or mowed) is simply to grow back. (One might note that grasses seem to adopt an r-strategy, rather in the manner of oysters—i.e., they produce a great many seeds, and invest little in them.) Some species of this great family have made themselves so nontoxic and nutritious that one curious vertebrate species has for the last 8,000 years made it its business to tend these grasses until they have become the dominant plant species over vast regions of the temperate zones.

Given the large size of the grass family, it is not surprising to find exceptions to the general principle outlined above. Several species of the genus *Andropogon*, bluestem, are formulated as analgesics, diuretics, stimulants, and the like and are administered internally by the Chippewa, Omaha, Comanche, Houma, Catawba, and others. At least one species of this genus (*A. nardus*) produces the fragrant oil citronella, which is to some degree toxic or noxious to insects (Claus, Tyler, and Brady 1970:179); related species may produce similar substances.

Poisoned Apples

What is hinted at by the Poaceae is much more clearly exemplified in other families. The Rosaceae demonstrates the point in a very intriguing way. This family, which includes apples (*Pyrus*), pears, peaches, cherries, and almonds (all *Prunus*), seems to combine both K-and r-investment strategies, creating what we can refer to as the "poisoned apple syndrome." Many members of the rose family produce nutritious and attractive fruits, as do the grasses; many species also produce quite toxic substances in the leaves, bark, and pits. People have died eating apple seeds, for example. Amygdalin is one of a number of cyanogenetic glucosides produced by various species of Rosaceae which

can give rise to cyanide poisoning. Usually this is only moderate, with distress, but occasionally more serious poisoning gives rise to loss of consciousness and serious

Table 8.4
Characteristics of Genera in *Caprifoliaceae*

Genus	FNA species	MPNA species	Uses	Common name
Diervilla	2	1	18	Bush honeysuckle
Linnaea	1	1	8	Twinflower
Lonicera	29	8	77	Honeysuckle
Sambucus	14	8	170	Elder
Symphoricarpos	10	7	70	Snowberry
Triosteum	2	1	26	Feverwort
Viburnum	19	9	79	Viburnum

respiratory trouble. Apnoeia and fatal collapse are exceptional, but have occurred. [Bodin and Cheinisse 1970:162]

The fruits of these plants attract various browsers to aid in dispersion of the seeds, but the poison simultaneously protects the seeds from being destroyed. At the same time people have made medicinal use of these chemicals in moderation. Of the species of Rosaceae, 20% are used medicinally by Native Americans (in 1,038 ways, according to *Medicinal Plants of Native America*), notably for treatment of gastrointestinal, dermatological, and gynecological problems of many sorts.

The Honeysuckle Family

Useful as my approach may be for sorting out useful plant families, no ethnobotanist is going to be surprised to see Asteraceae, Rosaceae, and Lamiaceae (mints) on a list of highly used medicinal plants. Identification of other outliers like the Caprifoliaceae (the honeysuckle family), however, demonstrates the utility of the method. All seven genera in this family were used medicinally by Native Americans, as were 35 of its 77 species in nearly 450 ways (see Table 8.4). Looking at the table, one observes that elder (*Sambucus*) is the most heavily utilized of the seven genera.[4] Elder is an interesting genus; like members of the Rosaceae, this genus provides edible berries.[5] Most elderberries must be cooked, dried, or fermented before they are eaten, however, to ameliorate the effects of several emetic alkaloids that they contain, probably to inhibit excessive browsing by birds. These substances (and others) are responsible for the preponderant use of the genus as an emetic, cathartic, and laxative (40 of the 170 uses in MPNA).

The next major grouping of uses of *Sambucus* is in various preparations for external application to sprains, bruises, or swellings (by the Cherokee, Delaware, Houma, Iroquois, and Paiute); on cuts, wounds, boils, or sores (by the Iroquois, Rappahannock, Makah, and Pomo); and to the head for headaches (by the Chickasaw and Iroquois). While the basis for these sorts of actions is not as clear as the plant's emetic qualities (it probably produces tannin), many other peoples around the world have discovered these properties as well, whatever their origin. Hartwell (1982:105–6) lists two pages of similar topical uses of elder from sources that range from Chile to Belgium, and from Dioscorides to Lord Bacon. Furthermore, Duke and Ayensu (1985:236) note the use of the genus in China for, among other things besides emesis and diuresis, "injuries, skin diseases, swellings . . . sprains . . . and traumatic injuries."

Moreover, these two major categories of use (laxative/emetic and discutient) are the same as those recommended in the *United States Pharmacopoeia* (USP), in which elder was listed one way or another from 1820 until 1905 and in the *National Formulary* from 1916 until 1947. The first revision of the USP said of *Sambucus canadensis*: "The flowers are diaphoretic and discutient; the fruit, laxative and sudorific" (United States Pharmacopoeia 1830:55).[6]

CONCLUSION

There is no single explanation for how Native Americans or others learned the medicinal values of plants. Yet at least one category of biologically active plants is composed of those that have produced substances to protect themselves from browsing. Clearly the effectiveness of such protection would be enhanced if the plants could somehow signal, and browsers could somehow detect their presence before too much was eaten—perhaps through a distinctive odor or taste.

It seems plausible to suggest that people have used these same signals as evidence of potentially valuable medicines, and over millennia, human knowledge of the subject has accumulated. "Knowledge" is a complex phenomenon with both historical and cultural dimensions: "In their practical projects and social arrangements, informed by the received meanings of persons and things, people submit . . . cultural categories to empirical risks" (Sahlins 1985:ix). In the process, the explanations for things may change; but a kernel of truth, a sort of natural object (e.g., that *Sambucus* heals sores), may remain, even though it may be accounted for in a multitude of ways. The initial experiments by which this natural object became "known" need not have been repeated many times; things only have to be learned once. Similar kernels of truth may apply to *Pyrus* and *Prunus* and perhaps even to sweet grass.

ACKNOWLEDGMENTS

The data base MPNA was produced with the support of the National Endowment for the Humanities, grant number RT–20408–04. This article was written with support from the National Science Foundation, grant number BNS–8704103. Stanwyn Shetler of the Smithsonian Institution Museum of Natural History provided the computer tape with the indispensable *Flora North America* data. Special thanks to Barry Bogin, Katie Anderson-Levitt, Charlotte Gyllenhaal, and Sally Horvath for providing extremely helpful criticisms of earlier drafts of this article. The University of Michigan-Dearborn has supported me in uncounted ways for more than a decade.

Correspondence may be addressed to the author at the Department of Behavioral Sciences, University of Michigan-Dearborn, College of Arts, Sciences, and Letters, Dearborn, MI 48128.

NOTES

1. Several hundred items in MPNA, identified only by genus, are excluded here, as are a small number of domesticated species with anomalous distributions (e.g., chamomile, mustard, cabbage, and cotton).

2. A monograph dealing with these matters, among others, is currently in preparation.

3. Primary metabolites are those that are commonly used and synthesized throughout the biological world like nucleic, amino, and fatty acids. Secondary metabolites constitute that great range of substances—terpenes, alkaloids, phenols, saponins, and so on—that differ from one species to the next. Etkin has criticized this distinction in a helpful fashion (1988:32).

4. One can use the same sort of regression/residual analysis with the elder as done earlier on families. In this case, regressing the number of uses on the number of species used medicinally (MPSPE) gives

$$\text{USES} = 6.5 + (11.5 \times \text{MPSPE})$$
$$r = .79$$

The predicted number of uses for elder by that equation is 98.5; the actual value is much greater: residual = $170 - 98.5 = 71.5$

5. The earliest recipe I am aware of that uses elder is from Apicius's cookbook, written during the reign of Tiberius in the first century. He recommended a sort of omelet of eggs, elderberries, and liquamen (a sauce made of fish and salt, on the order of Worcestershire), with pepper and wine (Flower and Rosenbaum 1958).

6. So far I have only applied this method to ethnologically derived data from native North America. But, Hu, and Kong (1980), however, note that Graminea (e.g., Poaceae, the grasses), Cyperaceae, and Juncaceae all produce low percentages of medicinal plants in China. These are also on our list of low-use plants. Among highly used families But, Hu, and Kong list Compositae (i.e., Asteraceae), Rosaceae, and Labiatae (i.e., Lamiaceae, the mints), as do I. They do not provide data sufficient for a regression analysis, but if these similarities, like those mentioned by Duke and Ayensu (1985:42–47), indicate a comparable selection pattern on two continents, it will be notable indeed.

REFERENCES

Bodin, F., and C. F. Cheinisse. 1970. *Poisons.* H. Oldroyd, trans. New York: McGraw-Hill.

But, Paul Pui-Hay, Shiu-Ying Hu, and Yun Cheung Kong. 1980. Vascular Plants Used in Chinese Medicine. *Fitoterapia* 51:245–64.

Claus, Edward P., Varro E. Tyler, and Lynn R. Brady. 1970. *Pharmacognosy.* Philadelphia: Lea & Febiger.

Duke, James, and Edward Ayensu. 1985. *Medicinal Plants of China.* 2 vols. Algonac, MI: Reference Publications.

Etkin, Nina L. 1988. Ethnopharmacology: Biobehavioral Approaches in the Anthropological Study of Indigenous Medicines. *Annual Review of Anthropology* 17:23–42.

Flower, Barbara, and Elisabeth Rosenbaum. 1958. *The Roman Cookery Book.* London: Harrap.

Hartwell, Jonathan L. 1982. *Plants Used Against Cancer.* Lawrence, MA: Quarterman Publications.

MacArthur, Robert H., and Edward O. Wilson. 1967. *The Theory of Island Biogeography.* Princeton, NJ: Princeton University Press.

Moerman, Daniel. 1977. *American Medical Ethnobotany: A Reference Dictionary.* New York: Garland Publishing.

————. 1979. Symbols and Selectivity: A Statistical Analysis of Native American Medical Ethnobotany. *Journal of Ethnopharmacology* 1:111–19.

————. 1986. *Medicinal Plants of Native America.* 2 vols. Technical Reports, no. 19. Ann Arbor: University of Michigan Museum of Anthropology.

Runyon, Richard P., and Audrey Haber. 1984. *Fundamentals of Behavioral Statistics.* 5th edition. Reading, MA: Addison-Wesley.

Sahlins, Marshall. 1985. *Islands of History.* Chicago: University of Chicago Press.

Shetler, Stanwyn G., and Laurence E. Skog, eds. 1978. *A Provisional Checklist of Species for Flora North America.* Monographs in Systematic Botany, vol. 1. St. Louis: Missouri Botanical Garden.

Snedecor, George W., and William G. Cochran. 1967. *Statistical Methods.* 6th edition. Ames: Iowa State University Press.

United States Pharmacopoeia. 1830. *The Pharmacopoeia of the United States of America.* 2nd edition. New York: S. Converse.

9

THE EVOLUTION OF HUMAN NUTRITION

BARRY BOGIN

During a lifetime a human being will eat thousands of pounds of food. The body will use this food to grow, to repair damaged tissue, and to maintain organs, such as the brain and the heart. Some of these foods will be enjoyable to eat because they are perceived as looking appetizing and tasting delicious. Other foods may not be enjoyable to eat but will be consumed anyway because they are "good for the body or the spirit."

Biochemically, the body does not distinguish between foods that are liked and disliked, for the human body does not use food; rather the body requires the biological nutrients contained in food. Biology, however, is not the entire story of human nutrition. Cultural variables, such as the type of food eaten, its manner of preparation, and the social context in which it is consumed, often determine the efficacy of that food to meet human needs for health and well-being. It is the purpose of this chapter to explore the evolution of some of the biological and cultural requirements of human nutrition. Although at times the biology and culture of nutrition will be treated separately, the major theme of this chapter is to view human nutrition holistically as a biocultural phenomenon.

Nutritional biochemists have determined that there are forty-five to fifty essential nutrients required for growth, maintenance, and repair of the body. Essential nutrients are those substances which the body needs but cannot manufacture. These substances are divided into six classes: protein, carbohydrate, fat, vitamins, minerals, and water. Table 9.1 lists the essential

Table 9.1
Essential Nutrients of the Human Diet

Essential Nutrients as Classified in 1985		
Carbohydrate	**Minerals**	**Vitamins**
Glucose	Calcium	Fat-soluble
	Phosphorus	A (retinol)
Fat or Lipid	Sodium	D (cholecalciferol)
Linoleic acid	Potassium	E (tocopherol)
	Sulfur	K
Protein	Chlorine	Water-soluble
Amino acids	Magnesium	Thiamin
Leucine	Iron	Riboflavin
Isoleucine	Selenium	Niacin
Lysine	Zinc	Biotin
Methionine	Manganese	Folacin
Phenylalanine	Copper	Vitamin B_6
Threonine	Cobalt	Vitamin B_{12}
Tryptophan	Molybdenum	Pantothenic acid
Valine	Iodine	Vitamin C
Histidine	Chromium	
Nonessential nitrogen	Vandium	**Water**
	Tin	
	Nickel	
	Silicon	

Source: Guthrie 1986.

nutrients in these categories. Nutrients are proven to be essential for people by experiments with animals. An animal, such as a young rat or pig, is fed a diet that includes all the known nutrients except the one being tested. If the animal gets sick, stops growing, loses weight, or dies, it usually means that the missing nutrient is essential for that animal. The nutrient is next tested on a young monkey or chimpanzee to see if that animal stops growing or dies. Such experiments do not prove that the same nutrient is needed for people, but to be safe, any nutrient essential for nonhuman primates is probably essential for the human primate.

We do not usually eat these essential nutrients directly as pure chemicals;

rather, we eat food. This was certainly true for all of our animal ancestors throughout evolutionary history. Human foods come from all the kingdoms of living organisms: plants, animals, fungi (e.g., mushrooms), protists (e.g., bacteria used in fermented foods), and monereans (e.g., species of algae referred to as "seaweed"). These organisms present us with a dazzling array of colors, flavors, odors, textures, shapes, and sizes.

EATING A BALANCED DIET

How does a person know which foods to eat so that all of the essential nutrients are consumed in required amounts? Animals in the wild, laboratory rats, and human infants all share the ability to eat a balanced diet. Wild animals seek out and eat foods that supply them with all the essential nutrients they need. To what extent that ability is innate or the result of experience is difficult to determine. Under experimental conditions, rats can learn to select a balanced diet. If fed a diet deficient in one or more nutrients, the rats become ill and develop an aversion to that diet. If presented with the choice of foods to balance the diet, the rats will, over time, come to eat the required foods (Rodgers 1967; Rozin 1967). One interpretation of these experiments is that the nature of food-seeking behavior is to learn to avoid diets that produce illness or malaise and search for foods that reduce the feeling of malaise, thus fulfilling nutritional requirements (Franken 1988:107). In an oft-quoted but unreplicated study, Davis (1928) found that newly weaned human infants can learn to select a balanced diet when presented with an array of foods. As with the rats, this learning takes time and may be explained as a strategy to reduce the feeling of discomfort. More recent research shows that the control of food intake by human infants is related to calories and not to specific nutrients in food. Infants may be offered as many bottles of nutritionally complete formula as they can drink, but they will drink only until their need for energy is satiated (Bergmann and Bergmann 1986). Infants fed low-energy-containing formulas (e.g., skim milk or low-fat formulas) will ingest a greater quantity of formula than infants fed a balanced diet (ibid.). These results may indicate that people have evolved an innate capacity to seek and eat those foods which satisfy some basic nutrient requirements.

Findings such as these point out a curious and paradoxical problem: If human infants and other animals can, somehow, know how much to eat and what to eat, why are so many children and adults in the United States overweight? Why do so many people in Africa, Asia, and Latin America suffer from malnutrition and starvation? These are not easy questions to answer.

Leaving aside these evolutionary aspects of feeding behavior for a moment, we may note that during human ontogeny, children learn what to eat because their parents, or other adults, prepare their food. By tasting these foods, and watching older people prepare them, children acquire patterns of food preferences, including what should not be eaten, under what social conditions a food should be eaten, and the ways to prepare foods. Not all people eat all the same foods. For instance, some people in the United States eat chocolate-covered ants, but most Americans do not think of insects as food. In parts of Africa and South America, however, insects such as ants, termites, and beetle larvae are food—in fact, they are considered delicacies! Yanomamo Indians of southern Venezuela cultivate certain plants in which they know beetles will lay their eggs. The Yanomamo harvest the beetle larvae and eat them raw or roasted (Chagnon 1983). From a nutritional point of view, insects are excellent sources of protein, fats, and some minerals. In fact, pound for pound, grasshoppers have more protein than cattle or hogs, yet this fact is unlikely to encourage the sale of "grasshopper nuggets" at fast-food outlets in the United States.

Every group of people has developed a cuisine, an assortment of foods and a style of cooking that is unique to that culture. Some examples are Italian cooking, Chinese cooking, and Mexican cooking. Even Americans have a cuisine, including foods such as corn on the cob and hamburgers. Despite the differences in specific foods, the cuisine of each human culture provides all the essential nutrients. One fascinating aspect of food preferences in different cultures is the way two or more foods are combined and eaten together to increase the nutritional value of both—for example, complementary proteins. Table 9.1 shows that there are eight amino acids (the building blocks of proteins) that are essential nutrients. Not all foods contain all eight amino acids, so we must eat several foods to get them all, with the proteins in one food complementing those lacking in the other food. Cereal grains, such as wheat and rice, lack some of the amino acids that are found in beans, peas, milk, and cheeses. Conversely, beans, peas, milk, and cheeses lack the amino acids found in cereal grains. By eating these foods together at the same meal, people can ensure themselves of an adequate supply of all the essential amino acids. In the Middle East many people eat wheat and cheese in the same dish. In Mexico beans, tortillas, and rice are popular, while on the island of Jamaica peas and rice is the national favorite. In the United States cereal (grains) and milk are complementary protein sources popular at breakfast. The biochemistry of complementary protein foods has been discovered only recently, yet the cultural history of this food practice is ancient.

Each culture developed its own cuisine for many reasons. Not all foods grow in all countries—for instance, corn originally comes from Central and South America; rice, originally from Asia. But most food preferences cannot be so easily explained. The isolation of each human culture, exploration and contact between cultures, and many other unknown factors occurring during thousands of years of human history are responsible.

From the foregoing, two general observations about human nutrition can be made:

1. All people have the same basic biological requirements for nutrients.
2. Each culture has a unique cuisine that has the potential to satisfy these nutrient requirements.

Some additional universal features of human food systems, compiled by Pelto and Pelto (1983), extend this list.

3. People are omnivorous, eating hundreds of different species of plants, animals, fungi, bacteria, and even algae.
4. People depend on transport systems to move food from the place where it is found or acquired to the place of consumption.
5. People use systems of food storage that protect the nutritional quality of foods from the time of their acquisition until the time of their consumption. That time period may be months, even in premodern societies.
6. People expend great effort in food preparation—such as cooking, mixing, flavoring, and detoxifying natural ingredients—and depend on technology to do this (e.g., the hand axes and fire used by *Homo erectus*, the food processors and microwave ovens of *Homo sapiens*).
7. People share and exchange food regularly, and have cultural rules that order such sharing and exchanges.
8. People have food taboos, that is, social proscriptions against the consumption of certain foods based on age, sex, state of health, religious beliefs, and other culturally defined reasons.

One final item must be included in this list of human food behavior.

9. People use foods for nonnutritional purposes, such as for medicine to cure or cause disease and as offerings in ritual or religious behavior (see Chapter 12 in this volume). In these contexts food may have some physiologic function (plants do contain active pharmaceutical compounds), but the foods also have symbolic meaning for the people using them.

Evidence from fossil and archaeological remains of human ancestors indicates that these nine universal features of human nutrition and food have been in existence for at least thirty-five thousand years, and possibly more than one hundred thousand years. Yet until the twentieth century, most foods were acquired locally. The most parsimonious way to account for these biological and cultural universals relating to food is to hypothesize that a common evolutionary history for all people shaped human nutritional requirements, food acquisition and processing systems, and food behavior. This is a hypothesis that can be verified or rejected by research.

SOURCES OF KNOWLEDGE

Several kinds of data may be considered in the study of the evolution of human nutrition. Archaeological and paleontological evidence provides the only direct data on what our ancestors ate and what effect diet may have had on our physical and behavioral evolution. However, studies of living primates and other mammals, living hunter/gatherer societies, and cross-cultural comparisons of cuisines provide indirect evidence that is useful in reconstructing human nutritional history.

Primate Studies

The living primates include prosimians, New World monkeys, Old World monkeys, Asian and African apes, and people. Fossil evidence indicates that all primates evolved from insectivore-like mammals that lived some seventy-five million years ago. The geological context of these fossils indicates that the general habitat was tropical forest. Primate ancestors may have been those insectivores which moved into the flowering trees of these tropical forests to exploit insects associated with the flowers and fruits of the trees (Cartmill 1974). The flowering plants and trees, called angiosperms, appear in the fossil record about one hundred million years ago, and they opened up new habitats and ecological niches that promoted the coevolution of other species, including the primates.

The earliest primates exploited an insect-eating niche. They had jaws that moved in a scissorlike motion and teeth with pointed cusps, both features well suited for catching insects by rapid mouth "snapping," then piercing their chitinous exoskeletons to extract internal tissues and fluids. An extinct primate group, the plesiadapids, evolved sixty-five million years ago with dental specializations for gnawing tough plant material. Possibly they were specialized for eating large seeds, but they clearly were not restricted to insects. By about fifty-five million years ago, primate fossils show changes in jaws and teeth toward those of living forms, with jaws adapted for greater power in biting and chewing. It seems that by that time some primates were eating fruits, leaves, and seeds as well as insects.

Thus, the general primate dietary pattern is ancient. That pattern is based on the ability to eat a wide variety of foods in order to meet nutritional requirements. Primate nutritional requirements are highly varied; the higher primates, including humans, may be the animals with the longest list of essential nutrients. The reason for this may be our tropical origins. Today, tropical forests are characterized by a high diversity of species but a low density of any given species. There are thousands of species of tropical trees, and at any one site there may be between 50 and 100 different species per hectare (Oates 1987), but only a few trees of the same species may be growing on that hectare. In contrast, temperate and montane forests are often char-

Table 9.2
Dietary Frequency and Major Diet Components of 131 Primate Species

Food Category	Dietary Frequency	Major Component[1]
Fruit	90	45
Soft plant foods	79	9
Mature leaves	69	15
Invertebrates	65	23
Seeds	41	2
Hunted and scavenged vertebrates	37	0
Tree parts	34	0
Grasses and roots	13	5

[1]Percentage of species for which this category was identified as the major food.

Source: Harding 1981.

acterized by a few tree species, such as pine-oak forests, but large numbers of trees of those species. The diversity and density of animal species in tropical forests follow the pattern for plant life. There is no reason to expect that ancient tropical forests were different from modern tropical forests in terms of species diversity. Ancestral primates capable of eating a wide variety of foods would have had a veritable smorgasbord of choices, and judging by their descendants, the living primates, many food types were consumed.

Using published data, Harding (1981) divided naturally occurring tropical forest foods into eight categories and calculated the dietary frequency of each category for 131 species of primates, from all families excluding humans (Table 9.2). The dietary frequency is defined as the percentage of those species surveyed, "for which a given food category was listed in the diet" (p. 206). The data show that variety is the rule, and most species included seven of the eight food categories in their diets ("grasses and roots" was the category most often missing). The chimpanzee, our closest living primate relative, eats foods from all eight categories. It is worth noting, at this point, that on a worldwide basis, living people eat more grasses, such as wheat and corn, and roots, such as potatoes and manioc, than any other foods listed in the table.

Some selectivity in diet is seen in the major components of the diet, with fruits, invertebrates, and mature leaves being the most common items. Meat from vertebrates, either hunted or scavenged, and tree parts (e.g., bark, cambium) are not reported as major components for any nonhuman primate species. Thus, it might be best to characterize primates not as omnivores but as selective omnivores. There are several reasons for this selectivity.

First, primates are, with few exceptions, diurnal and highly active. Second, primates have brains that are about four times larger, relative to body size, than the brains of other mammals. Third, primates have relatively long gestations and nurse on demand for a relatively long period after birth. Each of these traits places a high metabolic demand on an animal to maintain activity, to supply the brain with energy and oxygen (the human brain uses 20 percent of the body's energy and oxygen), and to meet the nutritional needs of a female primate and her fetus or infant.

Accordingly, primates must select foods that are dense in essential nutrients. Fruits and invertebrates are such foods; fruits are dense in carbohydrates, minerals, and vitamins; invertebrates are rich in fats and proteins (remember those grasshoppers!). Soft plant foods are mostly water, and tree parts are mostly cellulose or lignin, all of which are low in nutrients. Grasses and roots are good foods for those species which live in savanna-woodland habitats where grasses are abundant (e.g., baboons), but most primates live in the tropical forests. Vertebrate meat and seeds are also nutrient dense, but require hunting skills or specialized mastication or behavior to make use of them. Of the 131 species surveyed, only some baboons and chimpanzees regularly hunt mammalian prey (Strum 1981; Teleki 1981), and only two monkey species, *Cercopithecus neglectus* and *Colobus satanas*, include seeds as major foods. Chimpanzees and baboons have been seen to use rocks to break open seeds to eat the contents, but this requires much effort and time that could be spent feeding on more easily acquired foods.

The human primate, not included in Harding's survey, is unusual in that vertebrate meat and seeds are major components of both modern and ancient diets. We, and our hominid ancestors dating back to *Australopithecus*, possess teeth and jaws that allow for rotary grinding (small canines, flattened molars, and enlarged pterygoid muscles) and a dependence on tools for food processing. Rotary grinding and tools are biological and behavioral specializations that allow the hominid reliance on meat and seeds.

A second reason for selectivity is the coevolution of primates and their foods. Coevolution refers to the interactions of different species of living organisms that exist in the same community; these interactions result in genetic change in those organisms over time. Predator-prey relationships are a common example of coevolution. Animals can move, and animal prey may run, jump, or fly away to avoid capture. Over time there will be selection for predators that are better suited to capture their prey and selection for prey that are better able to avoid capture. In contrast, plants are stationary but not defenseless. They produce a host of noxious or toxic substances (called secondary compounds), such as tannins and alkaloids, to discourage their predators. Plants may also evolve edible parts with low nutritional content (Hladik 1981), or seeds and fruits with coverings too hard to pierce (Kinzey and Norconk 1990), thus making those parts less attractive as food to primates. In a review of the literature on secondary compounds, Glander (1982) found that the rich appearance of the tropical forest may be deceptive, for many primate species avoid a large percentage of potential plant foods. Glander concludes that the selectivity of primates for plant species and parts of plants must be viewed as a strategy balancing "the nutrient and secondary compound content variation in these foods"(p. 1).

A third reason for selectivity is that primates have a worldwide distribution as an order but are localized as genera into dozens of populations restricted to species-specific habitats. Thus, it is not surprising that many primates, despite their evolutionary heritage of an eclectic food base, have, in practice, species-specific diets. The tamarins and marmosets of South America, for example, eat insects, fruit, and foliage, which are food items common to most primate diets, but also require tree sap for survival. The tree sap is the major source of calcium in their diet (Sussman and Kinzey 1984). These primates have clawlike nails used to cling to tree trunks and procumbent lower incisors used to gouge bark and release sap. No other group of primates has this suite of anatomical specializations for tree sap consumption.

Some species of Old World monkeys, such as the langur of Asia and the colobus of Africa, have anatomical specializations for eating large quantities of high fiber plant foods. These monkeys, and others like them belonging to the subfamily Colobine, have stomachs that are pouched ("sacculated" is the anatomical term). In those pouches live colonies of bacteria that have a commensal relationship with the monkey. The primate eats large quantities of leaves and other vegetable material, the cells of which are covered by cellulose, a substance that is not easily digested by mammals. The bacteria can and do digest the cellulose, thereby thriving and reproducing in the monkey's stomach. The primate digests and absorbs some of the contents of the cellulose-covered plant cells and also the bacteria. This commensal relationship is so efficient that some colobines can subsist on diets with a leaf intake as high as 75 percent of total intake (Struhsaker and Leland 1987). Noncolobine primates would die on such a high-cellulose diet.

Comparisons of this sort point out the nutritional and dietary differences between primate species, but they also help define the unique requirements and specializations of human nutrition. The large number of essential nutrients required in the human diet is a consequence of the tropical primate diet. With a wide variety of food resources, especially fruit, foliage, and insects, ancestral primates were able to obtain many vitamins, minerals, protein, carbohydrates, and fats from their diet. It is metabolically expensive, in terms of energy consumption, for an organism to manufacture its own nutrients (a process called autotrophism). Thus, through mutation and selection those early primates which reduced autotrophism and shifted to a dependency on dietary intake to meet nutrient needs would have gained an energy advantage, one that could be put to use, for instance, to increase reproduction. All mammals, for example, require vitamin C for maintenance and repair of body tissue, but only in some mammals, all members of the primate order, is vitamin C (ascorbic acid) an essential nutrient. About twenty-five million years ago a mutation occurred in the metabolic pathway that produces vitamin C in primate ancestors of living monkeys, apes, and humans. The glucose (carbohydrate energy) needed to convert biochemical precursors to ascorbic acid was released for use by other body systems (Scrimshaw and Young 1976). The wide distribution of vitamin C sources in tropical environments, and the ability of primates to utilize these sources, assured that this nutrient could be supplied by the diet alone.

Human Nutrition Research

The vitamin C story has particular relevance to human nutrition. Humans live in many nontropical habitats and will suffer from scurvy when vitamin C is absent from the diet. Eskimo and Inuit obtain some ascorbic acid by eating the skin of marine mammals, such as narwhal, and boreal forest Indians of North America made infusions of pine tree bark to concentrate vitamin C. Ascorbic acid is only one essential nutrient, and human cuisines developed, in part, to assure that all essential nutrients would be consumed. This development occurred over the past thirty thousand to one hundred thousand years, and most of it is lost in the prehistory of our species. However, methods of prehistoric research "flesh out" details of the early human diet.

Archaeology and Fossil Studies

Archaeological methods "include the identification of edible materials, functional analyses of artifacts employed in food preparation, coprolite [fossil feces] analysis, information on paleohabitat, and analyses of [hominid] skeletal material" (Sillen and Kavanagh 1982). Paleontological data are derived from the kinds and percentages of fossil remains found at a site. Each type of evidence contributes some knowledge, but each has serious limitations. The association of hominid fossil remains with the skeletal remains of other fossil vertebrates may result from geologic forces, such as rivers carrying carcasses to a central location or a volcanic eruption simultaneously burying a community of animals, rather than hominid food-gathering behavior. Early speculation by Dart (1957) that the bone accumulations at the South African cave sites of *Australopithecus* represented hominid hunting activity are now considered incorrect. Rather, Brain (1981) argues that the fossil remains, including the hominids, represent the activity of nonhominid carnivores, especially leopards, and geological forces. Dr. Brain names his book on this subject, aptly, *The Hunters or the Hunted*, and his conclusion is that the early hominids were the prey of the leopards.

The 1980s saw a 180 degree shift in opinion about the fossil evidence for the evolution of human hunting. In the 1960s the book *Man the Hunter* (Lee and DeVore 1968) represented majority opinion that uniquely human characteristics, such as bipedalism, large brains, division of labor, sharing, and intense parental investment in offspring, were the consequence of hunting and carnivorousness (see especially Washburn and Lancaster 1968). Implicit in this argument is the notion that the type of diet consumed by human ancestors played a significant role in the evolution of human biology and behavior. This notion is reasonable, but the explicit assumption of carnivorousness and hunting became less acceptable as new paleontological evidence was discovered. The newer evidence is based on analyses of bone and stone tool material associated with early hominids. Potts and Shipman (1981) used scanning electron microscope images of mammalian long bones dating to 1.7 million years ago to show that cut marks produced by stone tools were incised on top of those made by carnivore teeth and the teeth of known scavengers, such as porcupines. Assuming that the order of markings reflects the order of use by hunters and scavengers, the hominids were the last to have at the bones, even after porcupines!

Subsequent analysis shows that hominids may have been collecting bones for their marrow rather than for any meat remaining on the surface of the bone (Binford 1987). Marrow is high in fat and protein, but few carnivores have the morphology necessary to break open large long bones. Hyenas do have the ability to exploit marrow and are formidable predators and scavengers, but are most active at night (Schaller and Lowther 1969). Hominids are diurnal, and the invention of stone tools, first manufactured by hominids about two million years ago, may have been a dietary adaptation. Stone tools would allow early hominids to exploit animal foods by extracting marrow, with little competition from other meat eaters. Of course tools may also have been used to process hard-to-chew plant foods, such as seeds. Walker (1981) and Kay (1985) studied the finer details of early hominid dental structure and tooth wear, using the scanning electron microscope and tooth wear experiments. These researchers propose that the diet of the early hominids, including *Australopithecus* and *Homo habilis*, was largely herbivorous, including softer plant foods (leaves, fruits) as well as the tougher seeds and tubers. Perhaps it is safest to say that the gathering of plants, insects, birds' eggs, and other relatively immobile foods and the scavenging of marrow from carnivore kills typified early hominid food behavior.

Binford (1987) reanalyzed fossil material from Torralba, a *Homo erectus* site in Spain, and Zhoukoudian, a cave site near Beijing, China, spanning the period from *H. erectus* to *H. sapiens*. During the *H. erectus* period of occupation (250,000 to 450,000 years B.P.), both sites show a continuation of the early hominid dietary pattern, that is, gathering plant foods and scavenging rather than hunting. The animal bones at these sites appear to have been processed and consumed on the spot, rather than carried to any sort of base camp. If this is so, then past theories about the evolution of human biology and behavior, including bipedalism, large brains, division of labor, sharing, and intense parental investment in offspring, which depended on hunting and "family style dining" at home bases, have to be rejected. Binford (1984) states that convincing evidence for the regular hunting of big game does not appear in the fossil record until ninety thousand years B.P. at the earliest.

A type of big-game scavenging may have occurred much earlier in hominid evolution. One of the oldest, and the most complete, *H. erectus* skeletons provides indirect evidence of an increase in meat in the diet. The skeleton is from the Koobi Fora formation, located on the eastern shore of Lake Turkana, Kenya, and is dated to 1.6 million years B.P. (Walker et al. 1982). Analysis of the skeleton indicates that it was female and has "striking pathology" in the long bones of the limbs. These bones have a deposit of abnormal coarse-woven bone, up to seven millimeters thick in places, above the normal skeletal tissue on the outer surface of the bone. Walker and his colleagues consider many possible causes for this pathological bone growth and conclude that an overconsumption of vitamin A (hypervitaminosis A) is the most likely cause. Similar cases of hypervitaminosis A have occurred in arctic explorers who consumed the livers of polar bears and seals. The liver stores vitamin A; and the livers of carnivores, who are at the top of the food chain, usually contain the greatest amounts of this vitamin. Walker et al. suggest that the cause of the bone pathology in this specimen of *H. erectus* was due to eating the liver of carnivorous animals.

How these livers were acquired is not known. One may speculate that *H. erectus* scavenged them from the carcasses of carnivores that died from disease, old age, or competition with other carnivores. Another, rather intriguing speculation is offered by Cavallo (1990), an anthropologist who has been studying the ecology and behavior of leopards in Tanzania. Most carnivores, such as lions and hyenas, leave their prey on the ground and consume most of the internal organs and limb meat within a few hours after the kill. Leopards, in contrast, carry their kills into trees and consume their prey over several days. The kill may even be left unattended for several hours, for other terrestrial carnivores ignore the carcasses hanging in trees. Cavallo believes that human ancestors may have scavenged these arboreal caches of meat. This speculation is supported by the South African cave evidence of Brain (1981) showing that australopithecines and leopards lived together and that the hominids were often the prey of the carnivores. Cavallo argues that by the time of the appearance of *Homo*, some hominids may have reversed the predator-prey relationship. There are reports that groups of baboons have killed leopards, and confirmed observations of chimpanzees scavenging tree-cached leopard kills and taking and eating leopard cubs (Cavallo 1990). Would stone-tool-wielding hominids have been any less likely to have done the same on occasion? Perhaps it was the occasional (or regular?) consumption of leopard, including its liver, that caused the hypervitaminosis A of *H. erectus*. Cavallo's research may lead to yet another revision in the "hunting" hypothesis for human evolution.

H. erectus added fire to its repertoire of technology. Fire, which may have been used as early as 1.4 million years ago and was certainly controlled by 750,000 years B.P., provided warmth, light, protection, and a new way to process foods. Where and how cooking was invented is a matter for speculation. Cooking, by roasting or boiling, increases the nutritional benefit of many vegetable foods by helping to break down the cellulose of those foods, which is indigestible by humans. Fire may be used to open large seeds that resist even stone tools. Cooking, especially drying or smoking, helps to preserve foods for storage. Fire may also be used to get foods, especially by driving game toward a convenient killing site. All of these uses of fire did not appear simultaneously, and many appear to be the invention of *H. sapiens* rather than of *H. erectus*. What is certain is that the controlled use of fire was a significant addition to hominid technology with profound consequences for nutritional status.

Fossilized Feces

Coprolite analysis might seem to provide unequivocal evidence of dietary habits, but it too is subject to misinterpretation. First, the coprolite must be identified unambiguously as being from a hominid. Second, coprolites can only verify that a particular substance was eaten. That substance may or may not have been a food item itself; it may have been ingested coincidentally along with a food, such as a seed or insect clinging to an animal or a plant. Third, only indigestible substances will be found in feces, and those substances must be suitable candidates for fossilization in order to be preserved in a coprolite. Thus, coprolite analysis may provide a very biased picture of the true dietary intake. Even so, considerable information has been obtained about the diet of prehistoric humans and limited information about the diet of hominid ancestors of modern humans.

The animal affinity of desiccated coprolites can be determined by placing the specimen in a trisodium phosphate solution for seventy-two hours. Human coprolites turn the solution an opaque dark brown or black; no other species produces this effect (Bryant and Williams-Dean 1975). Other characteristics of human feces are inclusions of charcoal and the presence of undigested animal parts from a wide variety of species. Charcoal comes from cooking food over a wood fire. Since humans cook their food and other animals do not, the presence of charcoal in feces is indirect evidence for a unique human behavior. Humans also have an eclectic diet compared with most other mammals, so undigested parts from a wide variety of species is another indirect indicator of the human affinities of a coprolite. More than one thousand Paleo-Indian coprolites from the American Southwest have been identified and analyzed. One group of specimens was collected from Texas sites that date from 800 B.C. to A.D. 500, representing the temporary camps of hunting and gathering peoples (Bryant 1974). By comparing the pollen content of the coprolites with that found in the adjacent soils, it was determined that the people had consumed large quantities of flowers. Because the physical characteristics of flower pollens are unique to each species, it was possible to determine that flowers of agave, sotol, yucca, prickly pear cactus, gilia, and leadtree were popular foods. Also found were remains of wild onion bulbs, bark, grasshoppers, fish, small reptiles, and snails. Although not the current cuisine of Texas, this diet is typically human in its diversity of species. The flower pollen even provides a time frame for the occupation of the sites, spring and early summer.

Coprolites from Paleo-Indian sites in New Mexico, Arizona, and Texas contain pollen from plants of known pharmacological value, suggesting that people have a long history of consuming plants as medicines as well as foods (Reinhard 1989). Willow, an analgesic with essentially the same active ingredient as in aspirin; ephedra, an antihistamine; and creosote, an antidiarrheal, are the most concentrated pollens in the samples. Ethnographic evidence shows that these three species were, and still are, widely used as medicines by Native Americans (Moerman 1986, 1989). Willow tea is used to treat many aches and pains, ephedra tea is prescribed to relieve the stuffy nose of the common cold, and creosote is indicated for any type of loose bowels. Reinhard states that the analysis of these coprolites "demonstrates the antiquity of folk remedies and provides circumstantial evidence of certain disorders suffered by prehistoric peoples" (p. 2).

The oldest verified coprolites of a hominid species are from the *Homo erectus* site of Terra Amata located on the French Mediterranean. These coprolites may be as old as 300,000 B.P., and they are heavily mineralized. They have only a slight reaction to trisodium phosphate rehydration (Bryant and Williams-Dean 1975). The specimens contain sand grains, charcoal, and mollusk shell fragments. The sand and shell are expected, since Terra Amata is a beach site, and the charcoal helps establish that foods were cooked before consumption (is this evidence for a prehistoric clambake?).

Older coprolites usually are completely mineralized, which makes them impossible to rehydrate. A method to identify the species affinity of mineralized coprolites was offered by Spencer and Boaz (1983). They collected desiccated feces from seventeen living species of African animals and classified them into three groups, depending on the particle size of food material. Particle size was measured from scanning electron microscope photographs. The large-particle group included large herbivores—giraffes, bovids, zebras—and hyenas. The medium-particle group included smaller bovids, large felines, and some primates (gorilla, chimpanzee, and baboon). The small-particle group included small felines, pigs, weasels, and modern humans. When the form and particle size of coprolites dating from the Plio/Pleistocene boundary from East Africa were compared with these categories, it was possible to identify several types of mammals, "including probable hominids." Identification of specific food remains in the specimens has not been published.

Trace Element Analysis

A more general picture of the relative amounts of plant and animal food in the diet may be available from chemical analyses of trace elements in skeletal materials. The ratio of strontium to calcium (Sr/Ca) in animal bone is the most widely used technique at present. Sillen and Kavanagh (1982) reviewed the use of Sr/Ca analysis in paleodiet research; the following is a brief summary of that review. Strontium and calcium resemble each other chemically and, if both are present in the soil, plants will assimilate and utilize both. Animals eating these plants can digest and absorb both chemicals, up to 80 percent of ingested calcium and up to 40 percent of ingested strontium. Calcium is an essential nutrient for mammals, but strontium is not. Once food is digested and absorbed, mammals eliminate strontium from the blood circulation in two ways: excretion from the kidney and sequestration in bone, where the strontium is stored and inactive metabolically. Given this, the Sr/Ca ratio in organisms should decrease from plants (no discrimination against Sr), to herbivore mammals (initial discrimination against Sr), to carnivore mammals (secondary discrimination against Sr). Thus, the Sr/Ca ratio in bone from living or extinct mammals, including hominids, could serve as an indicator of the relative amounts of plant food versus meat in the diet.

The Sr/Ca method shows some promise for paleodiet research, but unfortunately there are a number of factors that can influence Sr/Ca ratios in bone that are not due to diet. The amount of calcium and strontium in groundwater affects uptake by plants and herbivores. The age of a mammal influences the absorption of both chemicals. Young animals, growing bone tissue rapidly, absorb more strontium than older animals. Deficiencies of other nutrients, such as vitamin D, may impair digestion and absorption of calcium and strontium. Pregnancy and lactation also are factors. Laboratory animal research and human clinical studies show that pregnant and lactating females store more strontium in bone than males or postreproductive females (Blakely 1989). Finally, the geological context of preservation and fossilization of bone may enhance or deplete the Sr/Ca ratio.

Although caution must be exercised in the interpretation of Sr/Ca ratios in living or fossil bone, the technique has proven useful in some cases. In archaeological samples of human skeletons from Mexico, Schoeninger (1979) found a strong negative correlation between indicators of social status and strontium in bone. Burials with greater amounts of high-status grave goods had lower Sr/Ca ratios than burial with fewer or no high-status grave goods. This suggests strongly that high-status individuals consumed more meat and lower status individuals consumed more plant foods. Schoeninger (1982) also applied the Sr/Ca method to the analysis of fossil material of archaic and modern *Homo sapiens* from sites in Israel dating between seventy thousand and ten thousand years ago. The purpose of the study was to see if a change in diet, from relatively more meat to relatively more plant food consumption, correlates with the change in human form from archaic to modern (e.g., modern humans have more gracile skeletal features than archaic forms). Care was taken to control for differences in the amount of calcium and strontium in the soils of different fossil sites and other confounding geological variables. It was found that Sr/Ca ratios in bone increased with time, suggesting more plant food in the diet, but the increase occurred twenty thousand years after the modern human form appears in the fossil record. Schoeninger concludes that the morphological transition from archaic to modern *H. sapiens* was not due to the utilization of new foods; rather it was due to "alterations in the means of procuring or processing the same kinds of foods that had been utilized earlier in time" (1982:37). If this interpretation is correct, changes in cultural behavior relating to food may have had more of an influence on human biology than the biochemistry of the foods per se.

The Sr/Ca ratio technique offers some idea of the relative amounts of meat and plant foods in the diet of our prehistoric ancestors. To date, hominid fossils older than about fifty thousand years B.P. have not been analyzed due to difficulties in the application of trace-element analysis to this older fossil material and the reluctance of researchers to submit fossil material for analysis (requiring destruction of that material) until the results of the technique are more reliably interpretable. Efforts continue toward this goal (e.g., Sillen 1988; Blakely 1989).

Studies of Living Hunters and Gatherers

Today, 99.9 percent of people derive their food from some form of agriculture. However, from the time of the *Australopithecus* until about ten thousand years ago, a time period that covers 99 percent of human evolution, hominids lived by foraging—the gathering and hunting of wild foods. As explained above, most meat eating was based on small-game hunting and scavenging. Big-game hunting, and a diet providing regular consumption of game meat, evolved after ninety thousand years ago. Most human physical traits, and perhaps many behavioral propensities, evolved during the time that hominids lived as hunters and gatherers. That biobehavioral evolution includes current human dietary requirements, adaptations for food acquisition and processing, and biocultural responses to food intake. Studies of the few remaining cultures of hunting and gathering peoples offer an indirect view of that style of life, now nearly extinct. These ethnographic and ecological studies complement the information derived from paleontological and archaeological sources.

Foragers are a diverse group geographically and culturally, ranging from the arctic Inuit (Eskimo), to the tropical forest Ache (Paraguay), to the dry scrub San (Africa), and the desert Australian aborigines. Yet the research shows some consistencies in behavior and diet. The diversity of food resources utilized is high among gathering and hunting peoples compared with agriculturalists. The !Kung San of southern Africa, for instance, eat 105 species of plants and 144 species of animals (Lee 1984). The Australian North Queensland aborigines exploit 240 species of plants and 120 species of animals (Gould 1981). The Ache forage on fewer species, about ninety types of plants and animals (Hill and Hurtado 1989). Even the Dogrib, residing in the subarctic of Canada, gather ten species of plants and thirty-three species of animals (Hayden 1981). That is a small food base for hunters and gatherers, but still a large number relative to agriculturalists, who, on a worldwide basis, subsist largely on four species of plants—wheat, rice, potatoes, and corn—and two species of animals—cattle and hogs—which account for 80 out of every 100 metric tons of domesticated animal meat. Poultry, lamb, goat, buffalo, and horse make up the bulk of the remaining 20 metric tons (Bogin 1985).

A second common feature is that gathered foods (plants, insects, birds' eggs, turtles, etc.) are the primary subsistence base in most foraging societies. Lee (1968) compared fifty-eight forager groups and found that the primary subsistence source was gathering for twenty-nine, fishing for eighteen, and hunting for eleven. Ten of the hunting groups and sixteen of the fishing groups lived north or south of the fortieth parallel. Thus, not only is gathering the most common subsistence pattern, it is correlated with tropical, subtropical, and low temperate habitats. Such habitats were the home for all species of hominids until the middle to late Paleolithic.

Often the use of many species for subsistence is correlated with the high diversity, low density, or seasonality of food items in the environment. In habitats where low density is combined with the wide dispersal of foods, foragers must be mobile and live in small groups. Thus, a small, mobile social group is a third typical feature of forager societies but, as shown in Table 9.3, it is not a universal feature. Leaving aside the Nootka, average group size ranges from nine to fifty-five, and average densities range from one to two hundred people per one hundred square miles. Mobility ranges from daily movement from camp to camp in the case of the Ache to seasonal sedentariness at one camp (e.g., a winter lodge) in the case of the Mistassini (hunters of the Canadian boreal forests).

The Ache are unusual in their daily movement, but contemporary Ache live at agricultural mission settlements and travel on foraging trips only 25 percent to 35 percent of the year (Hill and Hurtado 1989). Based on foods consumed, the purpose of these trips appears to be hunting, with up to 66 percent of calories consumed while traveling coming from mammalian meat. Thus, their daily movement may be the result of intense hunting in a short period rather than a typical pattern of mobility. The Nootka are also unusual due to both large group size and high density. The Nootka lived on the Pacific coast of Canada. Oceanic conditions, high rainfall, and varied terrestrial topography make this region extremely abundant in plants and animals.

Table 9.3
Demographic Characteristics of Forager Groups

Group (location)	Group Size	Population Density/100 square miles	Frequency of Moves
Nootka (Canada)	1,500	200	seasonal
Western Desert Australians	20	3	1-2 weeks
Mistassini (Canada)	15	1	seasonal
G/wi San (Africa)	55	16	3 weeks
Guayaki (S. America)	16	7	3 days
!Kung San (Africa)	20	41	2-3 weeks
Andamanese (Asia)	45	200	2-6 months
Hazda (Africa)	9	40	2 weeks
Paliyans (India)	24	200	as needed
Ache[1] (S. America)	48	8	daily

[1]From Hill and Hurtado 1989.

Source: Hayden 1981.

The Nootka had available a nearly inexhaustible supply of food, so much that of sixteen forager groups studied by Hayden (1981), they have the longest list of edible plants and animals that were avoided. Their diverse and reliable food base allowed the Nootka to form large camps to exploit seasonal foods (such as salmon and whales) and maintain permanent villages.

The high density of the Andamanese and Paliyans is due to their being restricted to relatively small areas. The Andamanese live on an island rich in food resources from both land and sea. The Paliyans (of southern India) live in a rich habitat capable of supporting high densities and are surrounded by agriculturalists, which means they live, effectively, within an ecological island. All the other groups have much lower population densities.

A fourth common feature is that all foragers depend on complex technology to procure, process, and store food. Technology ranges from simple to complex, both in amount and in sophistication. Savanna and desert foragers, such as !Kung and Australians, use a digging stick to get at roots and tubers that are hidden from view or not possible to extract by hand. The digging stick seems simple, but that tool significantly increases the calories available to the people who use it, compared with nonhuman primates living in similar habitats (Washburn and Moore 1980). At the other extreme are the Eskimo, who possess dozens of pieces of equipment for hunting or fishing, including hooks, spears, sleds, knives, and specialized clothing. The !Kung use bow and arrow to hunt large game. The bow is lightweight and not, by itself, capable of delivering a lethal blow to prey. Rather, the shaft of the arrow carries a dose of a neurotoxin that paralyzes the animal without poisoning the meat. The toxin is derived from the larva of a beetle that must be specially processed to be effective. The simplicity of the material culture of the !Kung belies the effectiveness and sophistication of their system of hunting.

Food preparation techniques include cooking (e.g., boiling, steaming, roasting, frying), soaking, grinding and grating, pounding, drying, fermenting, and putrefying (as in "aged" meat). Many human foods are poisonous prior to preparation by one or more of these techniques. Acorns and horse chestnuts, eaten by many North American Indian foragers, are toxic when raw. The toxins in these foods are removed by leaching, that is, by boiling them in water and then allowing the food to dry prior to consumption. Rhubarb and cashews, eaten by some people in modern industrial societies, are toxic until cooked by boiling or roasting. Finally, food storage by drying, caching, and, where possible, freezing or salting is common to many forager groups. It is essential to remember that dependence on technology for food procurement, food processing, and food storage are all behaviors unique to the human species and are found universally in all known human cultures.

Sharing and the division of labor comprise a fifth characteristic of foragers. Much has been made of both food sharing and division of labor because these two behaviors were considered necessary consequences of the "hunting hypothesis" for human evolution (Washburn and Lancaster 1968; Issac 1978). The basic premise is that male hominids ranged widely to hunt large game while female hominids, encumbered by pregnancy and dependent children, gathered plant foods in a smaller area. Both sexes returned to a home base and shared the fruits (and ribs) of their labor with each other and the children. That hypothesis is currently out of favor because there is no fossil evidence for the type of big-game hunting that requires sharing and division of labor to be effective prior to the appearance of *Homo sapiens*. Nevertheless, the fact that all known living hunters and gatherers share food, even small game and vegetables in many cultures, and have some division of labor indicates that this is a universal human nutritional adaptation that may have its evolutionary origin in pre-*H. sapiens* times.

Although sharing is universal, the degree to which it occurs is not constant in all cultures. Some forager groups share food regularly and have cultural rules to encourage food exchange. The !Kung and Ache, for example, prohibit hunters from keeping their own kills; rather, the meat must be given to others, often a respected elder, for distribution to all members of the band. Ache women who share plant food are given praise by others, and "children are taught that stinginess is the worst trait a person can have" (Hill and Hurtado 1989:439). In contrast, several Australian groups and the Paliyans share less regularly. Hayden's (1981) review of these cultures shows that Australian men usually ate all the game they hunted in the bush, rarely bringing meat back to camp for their wives and daughters. Women and children might eat more than 50 percent of their total food intake while foraging (Hayden calls this "snacking"), and would bring back to camp only those foods needing processing. The Paliyans also practiced snacking while foraging and brought back little food to be shared at the camp.

Sharing and division of labor may best be viewed as behaviors that (1) reduce the effects of unpredictability and variance in food supply, and (2) increase reproductive fitness. By dividing the social band into working groups based on sex and age, more of the necessary subsistence tasks may be accomplished in a shorter period of time. Adults may gather plant foods, honey, insects, and other small animal foods, and hunt larger animal prey. Children may remain at the camp in age-graded play groups, with older children caring for younger children, or may accompany their parents in order to learn foraging techniques (Bogin 1988a). Men often range over larger areas in search of food and hunt larger prey than do women, and this serves further to increase the total supply and diversity of food. Using statistical analysis and mathematical models of food behavior among the Ache, Hill and Hurtado (1989) find that division of labor and sharing results in an 80 percent increase in nutritional status and nearly a threefold increase in the predictability and regularity of daily food intake (that is, a reduction in the daily variance of calories consumed by the average nuclear family from 13,243 calories to 4,863 calories).

Reproductive fitness, measured by the number of offspring who survive to reproductive age, is increased by division of labor and sharing. Most animals must acquire all their own food. A few primates, including baboons and chimpanzees, are known to share some food, but only in a limited way compared with humans. Chimpanzees are more like humans in terms of reproductive biology, that is, both species take a relatively long time to reach sexual maturity and typically bear one offspring at a time. This places a tremendous reproductive constraint upon the chimpanzee. Chimpanzee females in the wild reach menarche (the first menstruation) at ten to eleven years of age (Goodall 1983). The average period between successful births in the wild is 5.6 years, and young chimpanzees are dependent on their mothers, which precludes a subsequent pregnancy, for about 4.5 years (Teleki et al. 1976; Goodall 1983). Just to reproduce herself and one of her mates, a female must live to be about twenty-five years old. This is a long time for the animal to struggle for its own existence, find food, avoid predators, and compete with conspecifics. It is more time than most chimpanzees live; Teleki et al. (1976) and Goodall (1983) estimate that in one African game reserve only about 35 percent of all live-born chimpanzees survive to their mid-twenties. Even so, it is a significantly greater percentage of survival than for most other species of mammals. Lions, another social mammalian species, successfully rear about 14 percent to 16 percent of their offspring to adulthood (Lancaster and Lancaster 1983). The female chimpanzee's parental investment of time and energy is efficient when viewed in this context.

Humans living in traditional hunting and gathering societies delay reproductive age even longer than chimpanzees, but do not wait as long between successful births. The best-documented example is the !Kung of southern Africa. A woman's age at her first birth averages 19 years; subsequent births follow about every 3.6 years, for an average of 5.1 births per woman (Howell 1976, 1979; Short 1976). Like all human children, the !Kung child is dependent on its parents, or other adults, for at least a decade. The traditional !Kung lived under relatively austere ecological conditions, including moderate malnutrition during childhood (Tobias 1975). Thus, it may be safe to assume that for earlier hominids, living under better conditions, the average amount of time between successful births was no longer than for the !Kung. Indeed the Ache, foragers of a tropical rain forest and living part-time on mission settlements, average only 3.1 years between births and 7.2 births per woman (Hill and Hurtado 1989). This presents a paradox: human birth spacing is shorter than that for the chimpanzee, but human childhood dependency is longer and development is slower. How can hunting and gathering people have it both ways, when for all other primates dependent young preclude another birth?

To have it both ways requires some assurance that the birth of a new child will not result in the death of an earlier-born child (or children) still receiving basic care. Human parents solve part of this problem by provisioning all their children with food. Lancaster and Lancaster (1983) call this type of parental investment "the hominid adaptation." Some female nonhuman primates will share food items with their young, although complete provisioning is extremely rare. Male nonhuman primates do not share vegetable food with their mates or with their young; male chimpanzees will share meat with other adult males and estrous females. Human parents, male and female, regularly share food with their offspring, and this may be viewed ecologically as both a feeding and a reproductive strategy. Monkeys and apes, with less parental investment than humans, successfully rear between 12 percent and 38 percent of their offspring to maturity. "Human hunter-gatherers, even without benefit of modern medicine, successfully raise to adulthood about one out of every two children born to them" (Lancaster 1985). Food provision by adults to the young is part of the reason for lower infant and child mortality in humans, but food sharing does not solve the problem of caretaking for children who are still dependent after a newborn arrives.

The age-graded play group, part of the division of labor found in many forager societies, provides for both the caretaking and enculturation of the young, freeing the adults from these tasks so that they may provide food, shelter, and other necessities for the young who may be at various stages of development. A woman may simultaneously be pregnant, have a child weaned within the past year, and one or more older offspring. Thus, adults may be able to increase their net reproductive output during a relatively short period of time. In this way, sharing leads to greater reliability and predictability of food intake, better nutritional status, and increased reproduction and survival of the young. It is easy to see how these behaviors would have evolved by natural selection during the course of human history.

Sharing also may help us to understand the nature of human food taboos. Hunters in many societies are prohibited from eating their own kills (Hayden 1981), thus ensuring that sharing will occur. The extent to which taboos increase sharing in other contexts, such as foods to be eaten only by men, women, or infants, is unknown. Also in need of study is the consumption of plants, fungi, and animals for nonnutritional purposes. The use of potential foods as medicines or for the symbolic properties ascribed to them by hunting and gathering peoples is not well documented. The archaeological evidence for medicinal plant use by foragers, from coprolite analysis and other sources, is compelling, and ethnographic documentation from nonforaging societies is copious (e.g., Moerman 1986).

SUMMARY OF EVIDENCE FOR THE EVOLUTION OF HUMAN NUTRITION

Table 9.4 lists the nine universal features of human nutrition and food behavior. Also in the table are the sources of evidence that allow an understanding of the origin and function of these universals. The human place in nature among the primates explains our broad requirements of essential nutrients. Fossil and archaeological evidence accounts for the development of cuisines and the technology for food acquisition, preparation, and storage. The study of living hunting and gathering peoples complements and supports these other sources of evidence. Five features of food and behavior are typically found in hunting and gathering societies: a high diversity of food types, greater dependence on gathering rather than hunting, small, mobile social groups, dependence on complex technology for acquiring and processing foods, and division of labor and sharing. Additionally, forager studies detail the nature of human food transport for exchange and sharing, and provide some information on the origin of food taboos and nonnutritional uses of foods.

"CAVEMAN CUISINE"

For millions of years all humans and human ancestors lived as hunters and gatherers. Only in the last eight thousand years have agriculture and animal domestication become major sources of food. The biological and psychological makeup of the human being is still adapted for the ancient pattern and

Table 9.4

The Nine Universal Features of Human Nutrition and Food Behavior and the Sources of Evidence Used to Study Their Evolution

Universal Features	Sources of Evidence
1. Large numbers of essential nutrients	Primate studies
2. Each culture has a cuisine	Archaeology, living cultures
3. Extreme omnivorousness	Primate studies, hunters and gatherers
4. Transport of foods	Archaeology, living cultures
5. Storage of foods	Archaeology, living cultures
6. Complex technology for acquisition and preparation	Hunters and gatherers and other living cultures
7. Sharing and division of labor	Primate studies, hunters and gatherers
8. Food taboos	Living cultures
9. Non-nutritional use of potential foods	Archaeology, living cultures

diet of a hunting and gathering life-style. Eaton and Konner (1985) used archaeological evidence, ethnographic studies of living hunting and gathering people, and the nutritional analysis of wild plant and animal food to reconstruct the diet of Paleolithic people living about fifteen thousand years ago. Table 9.5 compares the Paleolithic diet with that of modern Americans and U.S. government recommendations for a safe and healthy diet. Our ancestors ate more protein and less fat than we do. Eaton and Konner's analysis of living foragers indicates that the average diet consists of 35 percent of calories from meat and 65 percent of calories from carbohydrates. Plants contribute protein to the diet, but these estimates indicate that most of the protein was from animals, including fish, insects, and other invertebrates. Fat intake was lower in the Paleolithic due to the low content of fat in wild game. The average carcass fat content of fifteen species of wild herbivores surveyed by Eaton and Konner is 3.9 percent, compared with an average of 25 percent to 30 percent in domesticated animals. Moreover, compared with domesticated meat, the fat of wild game is about five times higher in the polyunsaturated form. Along with plant foods rich in polyunsaturated fats, the Paleolithic diet has a high ratio of polyunsaturated to saturated fats. Cho-

Table 9.5
The Paleolithic Diet of 15,000 Years B.P., the Current American Diet, and
Dietary Recommendations for the United States

	Paleolithic	American	Recommended[1]
Total Dietary Energy (%)			
Protein	34	12	12
Carbohydrate	45	46	58
Fat	21	42	30
P:S Ratio[2]	1.41	0.44	1.00
Daily Intakes			
Cholesterol (mg)	591	600	300
Fiber (g)	46	20	30-60
Sodium (mg)	690	2300-6900	1100-3300
Calcium (mg)	1580	740	800-1200
Ascorbic acid (mg)	392	88	45
Simple sugars (g)	trace	95	44

[1]Recommendations of U.S. Senate Select Committee and Food and Nutrition Board, National Academy of Sciences.

[2]Ratio of polyunsaturated to saturated fats from all foods.

Source: Eaton and Konner 1985.

lesterol intakes appear not to differ very much between the ancient and modern diet. Animal meat, both wild and domestic, contains similar amounts of cholesterol.

The reconstruction also indicates that our ancestors ate much more fiber (from plant foods), calcium (from meat), and vitamin C, but far less sodium. Our ancestors ate simple sugars only in natural forms—for instance, in fruits; today we each eat about seventy-six pounds of refined sugar a year. Paleolithic foragers consumed no dairy products, except for mother's milk during infancy. Neither did they eat many cereal grains, for the abundance of these plant foods in our diet today is the result of agriculture. Indeed, Paleolithic people would have gathered a wide assortment of wild plant foods, ensuring variety in both vitamin and mineral content, and in taste and appearance.

In contrast, the modern American diet is extremely narrow in food options. Modern people eat more wheat, rice, potatoes, and corn than the next twenty-six most often consumed plants combined (when did you last eat a turnip?). Survey a supermarket for the variety of animal protein sources, and a similar lack of diversity will be found (when did you last eat a squirrel or rabbit?). The uniformity and limited variety of offerings available at fast-food restaurants depicts the current American diet very well. Apparently Americans are aware of a problem, for millions of dollars are spent annually to purchase nutritional supplements and special "health foods." The U.S. Food and Drug Administration (note that foods and drugs are lumped together by American culture) estimates that 40 percent of adults regularly take at least one vitamin or mineral product (Moss et al. 1989). Taking vitamin pills to compensate for a narrow diet was not the nutritional behavior followed by our ancestors. There are attempts today to promote more eclectic diets and alternative food resources, but so far none has proved to be popular or commercially successful.

AGRICULTURE AND THE DECLINE OF HUMAN NUTRITION AND HEALTH

Some of the nutritional problems of the modern world are (1) a narrow food base, leading to deficiencies in some essential nutrients; (2) an inadequate supply of energy (i.e., total calories from all food sources) for about 60 percent of the world's population, especially the poor in the least developed countries; and (3) an oversupply of energy, leading to obesity and other diseases, in the developed nations and, increasingly, among the more affluent in the developing nations. The immediate causes of these problems include a host of social problems, such as poverty, political unrest (such as civil wars), inadequate water management, and unregulated population growth, as well as natural phenomena such as drought, floods, and cold weather. Although these are significant proximate causes for the world's current nutritional crisis, there is a more fundamental explanation that had its origin at the end of the Paleolithic.

The major culprit of the nutritional dilemma is agriculture. More recently, industrialization and urbanization have compounded the effects of agriculture on the health of human populations. Agriculture, industrialization, and urbanization are often stated to be the hallmarks of "progress" of the human species. Though progressive in a technological sense, each of these achievements has had negative consequences for human nutrition and health.

Studies of ancient populations show that several indicators of biological stress increase with the transition from foraging to horticulture and agriculture (Cohen and Armelagos 1984). These stress indicators include lines of arrested growth on long bones, deficits in enamel formation in teeth, loss of bone tissue from the skeleton, bone lesions due to infectious disease (e.g., tuberculosis), and reduced skeletal growth in children and adults (Goodman et al. 1988). The Dickson Mounds site in the Illinois River valley provides a classic example. From 950 to 1300 the human population of that area changed from mobile foragers to sedentary intensive agriculturalists. During this short time period,

The shift in subsistence led to a fourfold increase in iron deficiency anemia (porotic hyperostosis) and a threefold increase in infectious disease (periosteal reaction). The frequency of individuals with both iron deficiency and infectious lesions increased from 6% to 40%. (Goodman et al. 1988:180)

The incidence of enamel hypoplasias (malformations of the tooth crown that include pitting, linear furrowing, and complete lack of enamel) also increases from the forager to the agricultural period. These dental deficiencies occur when malnutrition or disease disrupts the secretion of enamel-forming material. For the permanent teeth, that process takes place during infancy and childhood. Thus, enamel hypoplasias leave a permanent record in the teeth of nutritional or disease stress that people experienced in early life. In the Dickson Mound skeletal material the prevalence of hypoplasia increases with time, going from 45 percent to 80 percent of individuals affected. Furthermore, the number of hypoplasias is correlated with mortality. Individuals with one hypoplasia died, on average, five years earlier than people with no hypoplasias. With two or more hypoplasias, age at death was reduced by nine years (Goodman et al. 1988:180). Since teeth form in a fixed pattern that is virtually the same in all human beings, it is possible to correlate the frequency of hypoplasias found on different teeth with the age of the individual when the disease stress occurred. At Dickson Mound that correlation indicates that infants and young children were especially subject to health stress at the age of weaning (about two to four years old). Deficiencies in the weaning diet, combined with weaning diseases, were very likely the cause of the hypoplasias (Goodman et al. 1988).

With the development of agriculture, the Dickson Mound people shifted from a diverse food base to one dependent on corn. The emphasis on monoculture reduced the supply of essential nutrients, especially amino acids and vitamins not found in corn, and this compromised the health of the people. Compounding these nutritional problems was rapid population growth. Despite a lowering in the average age at death at the Dickson Mound site, population sizes increased due to a shorter interval between births (about two years, compared with four years in forager populations). Larger populations and sedentarism gave rise to conditions favorable for the spread of infectious disease, and the poor nutritional state of the people made them more susceptible to these diseases.

Archaeological research on St. Catherines Island, one of the barrier islands off the coast of Georgia, shows how health of the native population declined after contact with Spanish conquistadores and a change in diet. Hutchinson and Larsen (1988) review the research and provide a new analysis of dental hypoplasia data. The early precontact native population were foragers utilizing a wide variety of foods collected and hunted from saltwater marshes, freshwater streams, and forests. Fish, shellfish, reptiles, birds, mammals, and many different plant species comprised the diet. The late precontact population practiced agriculture, and corn was the dominant plant food in the diet. After contact, the Spanish established mission sites and forced the settlement of some native people at these sites. Dependence on corn agriculture increased at the missions due to the forced abandonment of traditional life-style, including food practices, and in order to provide food for the growing Spanish population.

In the late precontact agricultural period, about 75 percent of the people had at least one hypoplasia. That percentage is similar to the Dickson Mound site, where 80 percent of the individual dentitions from the agricultural period had one or more hypoplasias. Thus, some of the disease stress associated with agriculture was already present on St. Catherines Island before the Spanish arrived. After contact the rate of individuals affected increased to about 95 percent of the population. Contributing to the nutritional causes of that stress were the infectious diseases that the Spanish introduced to the New World. These diseases "include smallpox, measles, bubonic plague, scarlet fever, whooping cough, malaria, typhus, diphtheria, cholera, and influenza" (Hutchinson and Larsen, 1988:102). Forced settlement at the mission agricultural sites increased the possibility for the transmission of these diseases from person to person.

A similar pattern of reduced dietary variety and decreased health status is seen in virtually all cases of the transition from hunting and gathering to agriculture. Colonization of the New World, Africa, and Asia by the Spanish and other Europeans exacerbated the local change in subsistence economy by introducing new diseases. The colonists, however, also suffered from the introduction of new foods. Pellagra is a nutritional disease caused by a lack of niacin (vitamin B_3). The word "pellagra" is Italian and was used to describe that disease when it first appeared in the eighteenth century in Italy. In Spain the same disease appeared at that time, but was called *mal del sol* (sun disease). Pellagra's classic symptoms are the four D's—dermatitis, diarrhea, depression, and dementia. The early symptom of light-sensitive dermatitis gave the condition its Spanish name. However, sunlight only aggravated the real cause, a diet based on the consumption of highly refined corn. Corn was domesticated in the New World and exported to Europe after contact with native American people. Corn grew well in Europe and quickly became an abundant and inexpensive food that replaced many traditional grains. This was true especially in the diet of the poor of southern Europe, which by the 1700s was predominantly based on corn, molasses, and salt pork.

Corn is naturally low in the amino acids lysine, tryptophan, and cystine, and in the vitamin niacin. Molasses and salt pork are deficient in the same nutrients. Milling the corn removes the husk and germ, further reducing the niacin content, from 2.4 milligrams per cup to 1.4 milligrams per cup. The minimum daily need for niacin in adults is set at 13 milligrams per day by the World Health Organization. For cultural reasons, Europeans preferred the bleached white appearance of the highly milled corn and, for the poor who followed a monotonous diet of corn, pellagra was the result. Pellagra spread to the United States as European people, and diets, became dominant. It was confined to cotton-producing and cotton-milling areas in the southern states, where the corn, molasses, and salt pork diet was common. Even as late as 1918 an estimated ten thousand deaths from pellagra occurred in the United States, and one hundred thousand cases were reported. Hospitals and mental institutions treated the disease as an endemic condition (endemic diseases are peculiar to a people or a region). At that time the cause of pellagra was believed to be heredity, unsanitary living conditions, or an infectious agent in spoiled corn (Guthrie 1986).

In an experiment conducted in 1917, inmates in a U.S. prison were asked to switch from the normal prison diet to the pellagragenic corn-based diet in exchange for reprieve. After five months the prisoners developed pellagra, and the nutritional cause of the disease was established. Not until 1937, however, was the specific cause, niacin deficiency, discovered.

In the Americas, when corn was first domesticated, some populations received 80 percent of their total caloric intake from corn. Yet pellagra was unknown in the New World prior to European contact. The reason for this is that New World people used the whole grain of the corn, including the germ, and prepared the corn in a manner that enhanced the tryptophan content and the available niacin. Throughout Central America, Mexico, and those regions of the United States where corn was (or is) the dietary staple, the following method of preparation was commonly used. Ears of corn were dried and the kernels removed from the cob. The kernels were ground by hand (minimal milling) and placed in a pot of water. Ground limestone (calcium carbonate) was added to the pot and the contents were boiled. The mixture was removed and dried until it formed a malleable dough (called *masa* in Latin American Spanish) that could be shaped into foods such as tortillas and tamales. The limestone is an alkali and reacted chemically with the corn and the water to increase the tryptophan content of the corn by hydrolysis (Katz et al. 1974). In turn, tryptophan is a precursor for niacin, that is, in the human body tryptophan can be converted into niacin by metabolic processes. The rate of conversion is about 60 milligrams of tryptophan for 1.0 milligram of niacin (Guthrie 1986). Thus, a diet in which 80 percent of the calories are derived from *masa*-based foods provides sufficient niacin.

INDUSTRIALIZATION, URBANIZATION, AND THE FURTHER DECLINE OF NUTRITION AND HEALTH

Industrialization, and its concomitant urbanization, compounded the problems started with the introduction of agriculture. Industrial peoples are removed yet another step from their food sources, and often become more dependent on a limited variety and quality of food. Industries and cities divert vast amounts of water from agriculture and food production, to be used instead for power generation and, more recently, for processing and cooling materials. Industrial processes cause pollution of the environment— that is, they concentrate naturally occurring, but widely dispersed, substances that are toxic to people, such as lead, coal dust, and hydrocarbons, into small areas. Industrial processes also create new substances that are toxic to people, such as polychlorinated biphenyls (PCBs) and dioxin. Industrialization further concentrates people in smaller areas, increasing the opportunity for transmission of infectious disease. Finally, industrialization increases sedentarism, restricts outdoor activity, breaks up traditional kinship-based societies, and increases socioeconomic stratification. The sharing of food, and other goods and services, also decreases. Each of these changes in behavior and social organization has the potential to impact negatively on human nutrition and health.

Historical records for the population of the Connecticut River valley during the eighteenth and nineteenth centuries show that as a market economy and industrialization increased, so did the incidence of tuberculosis and diarrheal infections (Meindl and Swedlund 1977; Swedlund et al. 1980). Infectious disease can impair nutritional status by curtailing appetite and food intake, impairing the absorption of nutrients by the digestive system, and, at the same time, increasing the body's need for nutrients, especially protein (Scrimshaw and Young 1976). Poor nutrition may make a person more susceptible to disease by depressing the body's immune responses. This synergism between malnutrition and infection shows up clearly in records of physical growth in height and weight of individuals or populations. Since growth is dependent on an adequate supply of all essential nutrients, malnutrition and infection work against optimal growth. Public health workers, epidemiologists, anthropologists, economists, and historians use records of physical growth to measure the health and well-being of human populations (Schell 1986).

A recent example of using height growth to investigate well-being that is relevant to this discussion of the health effects of industrialization is the work of Paigen and colleagues (1987) at Love Canal. The site of the research was a residential neighborhood in Niagara Falls, New York, that was constructed above a three thousand-meter-long unfinished canal. Prior to building homes and a school at the site in the 1950s, the canal "was used as a burial site for 19,000 metric tons of organic solvents, chlorinated hydrocarbons, acids, and other hazardous waste during the 1940's" (Paigen et al. 1987:490). By 1977 the presence of unsafe levels of chemicals in the groundwater, the soil of the school playground, and the indoor air of homes was established. In 1978, due to an excess of miscarriages by women from Love

Canal, the state of New York evacuated 235 families. In 1980 the U.S. government evacuated the remaining 800 families.

Prior to the 1980 evacuation, Paigen and colleagues measured the height and weight of 921 children between the ages of 1.5 and 16.99 years, from 424 Love Canal households. A control sample of 428 children from Niagara Falls were also measured. The children of the control sample were from homes in noncontaminated neighborhoods but were similar to the Love Canal sample in terms of socioeconomic and ethnic backgrounds. No difference in weight was found between the Love Canal and control samples. However, children born and residing in Love Canal for at least 75 percent of their lives were significantly shorter than control children. That difference could not be accounted for by statistically controlling the effect of parental height, socioeconomic status, nutritional status, birth weight, or history of chronic illness. The authors of the report conclude that chronic exposure to the toxic industrial wastes is a likely cause of the growth retardation of Love Canal residents.

During the years 1750 to 1900, the time of the industrial revolution in the Western world, the growth in height of people living in industrialized areas was less than that of people living in agricultural areas (Bogin 1988b). In a study of eighteenth-century British military recruits, Steegmann (1985) found that men from rural areas averaged 168.6 centimeters and the average height of men born in urban areas was 167.5 centimeters, a statistically significant difference. Steegmann noted that during the 1700s Britain was a developing nation. Industrializing urban regions were becoming increasingly dependent on food supplies from rural areas. Crop failures, unreliable transportation, lack of food storage and preservation techniques, and demand from higher-paying external markets resulted in periodic food shortages in cities. Figure 9.1 illustrates the relationship of food availability and the stature of military recruits, based on the year of birth of those men, for all of England and Ireland between 1750 and 1778. The average heights of men born in "bad" years (food shortages) are significantly less than those of men born in "good" years (food adequacy). Industrializing areas were particularly hard pressed in bad years, and in 1753 and 1757 there were food riots in some cities. Research with modern populations shows that severe malnutrition during infancy and childhood has a permanent stunting effect on human growth in height (Bogin 1988b). Steegmann's British data for the 1700s conforms with undernutrition as the cause for the reduced height of men born during periods of food shortages.

DIET AND THE DISEASES OF MODERN LIFE

After 1900 the affluent people of industrial areas in Britain and other Western nations began to achieve adult heights greater than those of people in rural

Figure 9.1

The Adult Stature of Military Recruits from England and Ireland Born Between 1749 and 1795

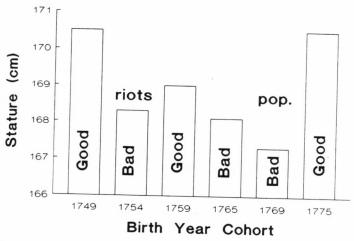

Note: The dates of each birth year cohort begin with the year indicated and continue until the next birth cohort: the earliest cohort was born between 1749 and 1753, the next cohort was born between 1754 and 1758, etc. "Good" and "Bad" are relative terms that refer to historical estimates of food availability in England. "Riots" refers to years of food shortages so severe as to cause riots and "pop." indicates a period of rapid population growth (after Steegmann, 1985).

Source: Steegmann 1985.

areas. The technology of the Western nations, including efficient transport of regional and nonnative foods, refrigeration, nutritional supplementation, treated water, and public sanitation, allowed their people to overcome some of the nutritional and health deficits of agriculture, industrialization, and urbanization (Bogin 1988b). Other evidence for the improving conditions of life in the developed nations comes from mortality statistics. Prior to 1850, epidemic diseases were a leading cause of mortality in the cities of Europe and North America. Death rates were so high that urban populations required massive migration from rural areas just to maintain constant numbers (McNeill 1979). Between 1850 and 1900 death rates in urban and rural areas began to equalize, and since 1900 urban mortality rates, at all ages, have been lower, generally, than rural mortality rates. The process of modernization in the developed counties that resulted in better physical growth and lower rates of mortality for urban populations is now taking place in the developing nations. Conditions of life in many Third World cities are still abominable for the poor underclass. However, current trends in some Third World countries indicate that these nations may follow the historical path toward modernization that occurred in the Western nations (Bogin 1988a).

Improved physical growth and longer life do not mean that modern urban populations are free of the specter of malnutrition and disease. Rather, as the threat of undernutrition and infectious disease eased, a suite of new diseases related to diet and life-style of industrialized/urbanized people developed to burden modern affluent people. Cardiopulmonary disease and cancer are the two leading causes of death in the developed nations today. They are followed by accidents (mostly motor vehicle accidents) and diabetes. The literature on the relationship of diet to heart disease, cancer, and diabetes is abundant and controversial. At the very least, there is a nutritional connection to each disease, in that people in extreme positive energy balance (i.e., obese people), have a significantly increased risk for heart disease, diabetes, and certain types of cancer. Alcohol, a dietary component as well as a drug, contributes substantially to accidents.

Overnutrition, especially of certain foods, may be a specific cause of some modern diseases. Both heart disease and diabetes are linked, in some studies, with a high consumption of sugar (as are dental decay and gum disease). Diabetes is a disease of glucose regulation. Glucose is one of the major sources of energy used by the body to maintain metabolism. Normally the amount of glucose in the bloodstream and in body cells is regulated by food intake and insulin. The carbohydrates in food are converted by the body into glucose, and insulin, secreted by cells in the pancreas, triggers body cells to absorb the glucose. Type I diabetes, which occurs in about 20 percent of people with the disease, is due to the lack of insulin production. In type II diabetes, the type found in about 80 percent of diabetes sufferers, the body cells become resistant to insulin and blood levels of glucose stay too high. This leads to hypertension, kidney disease, general circulatory disease, blindness, and death.

As shown in Table 9.5, the average American consumes ninety-five grams of sugar per day, or about seventy-six pounds per year! At the turn of the twentieth century the average sugar intake was about twenty pounds per year, mostly from whole-food sources. Half of the sugar in the modern diet comes from refined white sugar (sucrose) and corn syrup (fructose), both of which are added to virtually all processed foods as sweeteners and preservatives. There are many hereditary and environmental factors that contribute to diabetes and heart disease, but a diet with high sugar content is often a leading factor. Long-term studies find that since World War II, as industrialization, sedentary life-styles, and sugar consumption increased in Japan, Israel, many African countries, Polynesia, Micronesia, and among Native Americans and Eskimos, so did the incidence of obesity, diabetes, and cardiovascular disease (Weiss et al. 1984; Hamilton et al. 1988). Of course, these associations are only correlations and do not prove that sugar itself is among the causes of these diseases. Indeed, other populations have not responded to increased sugar consumption in the same manner. What seems clear, however, is that in susceptible populations there is a synergistic interaction between industrial/urban life-styles and diet, and metabolic diseases (Weiss et al. 1984).

A relationship between diet and cancer is well founded but, as with metabolic diseases, the exact causes are unclear. Takasaki and colleagues (1987) studied the rates for different types of digestive system cancer in the Japanese population during the period 1950 to 1983. The researchers argue that between 40 percent and 60 percent of the incidence of cancer may be attributable to diet, especially in those cases where carcinogens come into direct contact with the gastrointestinal tract. In the earlier years, the typical Japanese cuisine was based on rice seasoned with highly salted condiments, some green and yellow vegetables, and very little milk or dairy products. Takasaki et al. report that research links this diet to stomach cancer, and stomach cancer is the most frequent type of digestive system cancer in Japan. During the 1960s the postwar industrialization and economic recovery of Japan proceeded rapidly. One of the consequences of that expansion was a shift in cuisine from the traditional to one that included significantly more dairy products and fat. Between 1965 and 1983 rice consumption dropped from about 300 grams per person per day to about 200 grams. Milk and dairy products increased from about 75 to 150 grams per person per day. Diets high in fat are associated with cancers of the intestine and colon. In Japan mortality rates (age adjusted) per 100,000 population for stomach cancers dropped from about 37 to 22, while the same rates for intestinal cancer increased from about 2 to 4.5.

Epidemiological studies, such as Takasaki and colleagues' Japanese research, show many links between cancer and specific foods or cuisines. The same holds true for heart disease, diabetes, and the other diseases of modern life. This research negates the belief that these diseases are the natural consequence of aging. Rather, these diseases are potential indicators of the environmental quality of life and the well-being of human populations. Today, researchers use physical growth in height as a measure of the adequacy of the biological, social, and economic environment. These causes of growth failure are well understood and preventable. Sadly, however, about three-fourths of the world's children—more than 1.5 billion— are still at risk for growth retardation due to economic and social inequities that the affluent populations are unwilling to change. In the future, experimentation, field studies, and clinical research will determine the cause-and-effect relationships among diet, life-style, and diseases such as cancer and diabetes. When that happens, these modern diseases will be preventable as well. Researchers will use the incidence of these diseases, just as growth data are now used, as economic and social markers distinguishing those who have access to an environment that promotes health from those people who do not.

CONCLUSION

This chapter offers one perspective on the evolution of human nutrition. The mammalian and primate background for human nutrition, the hominid fossil and archaeological evidence, the behavior and diet of human foraging societies, and the development of modern foods and life-styles are treated in some depth. Other aspects of human evolution related to food and nutrition are neglected here, such as the spread of malaria to human populations following the introduction of agriculture in Africa (Livingston 1958) and the development of lactose tolerance in people dependent on animal domestication and herding (Kretchmer 1972). These and other topics dealing with human nutritional biochemistry, genetics, history, ethnology, and psychology relating to food may be pursued in other sources of reference, including other chapters in this book. The central message of all these sources, and of this chapter, is that food is central to human life. From a biological perspective food is central because of the essential nutrients needed for growth, repair, and maintenance of the body. From a sociocultural perspective food is central because of the behaviors that have evolved around foods and their use. From a medical perspective food is central because of the consequences of diet and food behavior for human health. Combining these discrete perspectives into a single holistic framework leads to the conclusion that human nutrition is a biocultural phenomenon, and requires a biocultural approach for its study.

ACKNOWLEDGMENTS

Daniel Moerman and Alan Goodman read earlier versions of this chapter, offering many suggestions to improve the presentation and to correct errors of fact. Their help and friendship are much appreciated.

REFERENCES

Bergmann, R. L., and K. E. Bergmann. 1986. Nutrition and Growth in Infancy. Frank Falkner and J. M. Tanner, eds., *Human Growth*, 389–413.

Binford, L. R. 1984 *Faunal Remains from the Klasies River Mouth*. New York: Academic Press.

———. 1987. American Association of Physical Anthropologists Annual Luncheon Address, April 1986: The Hunting Hypothesis, Archaeological Methods, and the Past. *Yearbook of Physical Anthropology*, 30:1–9.

Blakely, M. 1989. Bone strontium in pregnant and lactating females from archaeological samples. *American Journal of Physical Anthropology*, 80: 173–85.

Bogin, B. 1985. The Extinction of Homo Sapiens. *Michigan Quarterly Review*, 24: 329–43.

———. 1988a. Rural-to-Urban Migration. C. G. Mascie-Taylor and G. W. Lasker, eds., *Biological Aspects of Human Migration*, 90–129. Cambridge: Cambridge University Press.

———. 1988b. *Patterns of Human Growth*. Cambridge and New York: Cambridge University Press.

Brain, C. K. 1981. *The Hunters or the Hunted? An Introduction to African Cave Taxonomy*. Chicago: Chicago University Press.

Bryant, V. M., Jr. 1974. Prehistoric Diet in Southwest Texas: The Coprolite Evidence. *American Antiquity*, 39:407–20.

———., and G. Williams-Dean. 1975. The Coprolites of Man. *Scientific American*, 232:100–109.

Cartmill, M. 1974. Rethinking Primate Origins. *Science*, 184:436–43.

Cavallo, J. A. 1990. Cat in the Human Cradle. *Natural History*, (2):52–60.

Chagnon, N. A. 1983. *Yanomano–The Fierce People*. George Spindler and Louise Spindler, eds., New York: Holt, Rinehart and Winston.

Cohen, N. and G. Armelagos. 1984. *Paleopathology at the Origins of Agriculture*. New York: Academic Press.

Dart, R. A. 1957. *The Osteodontokeratic Culture of* Australopithecus Prometheus. Pretoria: Transvaal Museum Memoirs, No. 10.

Davis, C. M. 1928. Self Selection of Diet by Newly Weaned Infants. *American Journal of Diseases of Children*, 36:651–79.

Eaton, S. B., and M. Konner. 1985. Paleolithic Nutrition. *The New England Journal of Medicine*, 312:283–89.

Franken, R. E. 1988. *Human Motivation*, 2nd ed. Pacific Grove, CA: Brooks/Cole.

Glander, K. E. 1982. The Impact of Plant Secondary Compounds on Primate Feeding Behavior. *Yearbook of Physical Anthropology*, 25:1–18.

Goodall, J. 1983. Population Dynamics During a 15-year Period in One Community of Free-living Chimpanzees in the Gombe National Park, Tanzania. *Zeitschrift für Tierpsychologie*, 61:1–60.

Goodman, A. H., R. B. Thomas, A. C., Swedlund, and G. J. Armelagos. 1988. Biocultural Perspectives on Stress in Prehistoric, Historical, and Contemporary Population Research. *Yearbook of Physical Anthropology*, 31:169–202.

Gould, R. A. 1981. Comparative Ecology of Food-Sharing in Australia and Northwest California. Robert S. O. Harding and Geza Teleki, eds., *Omnivorous Primates*, 422–54. New York: Columbia University Press.

Guthrie, H. 1986. *Introductory Nutrition*. 6th Edition. St, Louis: Mosby.

Hamilton, E. M. N., E. N. Whitney, and F. S. Sizer. 1988. *Nutrition: Concepts and Controversies*, 4th ed. St. Paul, MN: West.

Harding, R. S. O. 1981. An Order of Omnivores: Nonhuman Primate Diets in the Wild. Robert S. O. Harding and Geza Teleki, eds., *Omnivorous Primates*, 191–214. New York: Columbia University Press.

Hayden, B. 1981. Subsistence and Ecological Adaptations of Modern Hunter/Gatherers. Robert S. O. Harding and Geza Teleki, eds., *Onmivorous Primates*, 344–421. New York: Columbia University Press.

Hill, K., and A. M. Hurtado. 1989. Hunter-Gatherers of the New World. *American Scientist*, 77:436–43.

Hladik, C. 1981. Diet and the Evolution of Feeding Strategies Among Forest Primates. Robert S. O. Harding and Geza Teleki, eds., *Omnivorous Primates*, 215–54. New York: Columbia University Press.

Howell, N. 1976. *The Population of the Dobe Area !Kung*. Cambridge: Cambridge University Press.

———. 1979. *Demography of the Dobe !Kung*. New York: Academic Press.

Hutchinson, D. L., and C. S. Larsen. 1988. Determination of Stress Episode Duration from Linear Enamel Hypoplasias: A Case Study from St. Catherines Island, Georgia. *Human Biology*, 60:93–110.

Issac, G. L. 1978 The food sharing behavior of proto-human hominids. *Scientific American*, 238(4):90–108

Katz, S. H., M. L., Heideger, and L. A. Valleroy. 1974. Traditional Maize Processing Techniques in the New World. *Science*, 184:765–73.

Kay, R. F. 1985. Dental Evidence for the Diet of *Australopithecus*. *Annual Review of Anthropology*, 14:315–41.

Kinzey, W. G., and M. A. Norconk. 1990. Hardness as a Basis of Fruit Choice in Two Sympatric Primates. *American Journal of Physical Anthropology*, 81:5–15.

Kretchmer, N. 1972. Lactose and Lactase. Norman Kretchmer and William van B. Robertson, eds., *Human Nutrition*. 130–38. San Francisco: W. H. Freeman.

Lancaster, J. B. 1985. Evolutionary Perspectives on Sex Differences in the Higher Primates. In *Gender and the Life Course*. A. S. Rossi ed., New York: Aldine.

———., and C. S. Lancaster. 1983. Parental Investment: the Homin. *How Humans Adapt*. D.J. Ortner ed. Washington, D,C.: Smithsonian Institute Press, 33–65.

Lee, R. B. 1968. What Hunters do for a Living, or, How to Make Out on Scarece Resources. In *Man the Hunter*. R.B. Lee and I. Devore eds. Cambridge, Mass.: Harvard University Press.

———. 1984. *The Dobe !Kung*. New York: Holt, Rinehart and Winston.

———., and Devore, I. 1968. *Man the Hunter*, Cambridge, Mass.: Harvard University Press.

Livingstone, F. B. 1958. Anthropological Implications of Sickle Cell Gene Distribution in West Africa. *American Anthropologist*, 60:533–62.

McNeill, W. H. 1979. Historical Patterns of Migration. *Current Anthropology*, 20:95–102.

Meindl, R. S. and A.C. Swedlund. 1977. Secular Trends in Mortality in the Connecticut Valley, 1700–1850. *Human Biology*, 49:389–414.

Moerman, D. E. 1986. *Medicinal Plants of Native America*, 2 volumes. Ann Arbor: University of Michigan Museum of Anthropology.

———. 1989. Poisoned Apples and Honeysuckle: the Medicinal Plants of Native America. *Medical Anthropology Quarterly*, 3:52–61.

Moss, A. J., A. S. Levy, I. Kim, and Y. K. Pak. 1989. Use of Vitamin and Mineral Supplements in the United States. *Advance Data from Vital and Health Statistics*, 174, Washington, D.C.: National Center for Health Statistics.

Oates, J. F. 1987. Food Distribution and Foraging Behavior. Barbara B. Smuts, Dorothy L. Cheney, Robert M. Seyfarth, Richard W. Wrangham, and Thomas T. Struhsaker, eds., *Primate Societies*, 197–209. Chicago: University of Chicago Press.

Paigen, B., L. R. Goldman, M. M. Magnant, J. H. Highland, and A. T. Steegmann, Jr. 1987. Growth of Children Living Near the Hazardous Waste Site, Love Canal. *Human Biology*, 59:489–508.

Pelto, J. P., and G. H. Pelto. 1983. Culture, Nutrition, and Health. In *The Anthropology of Medicine*, 173–200. New York: Praeger.

Potts, R. B. and P. Shipman. 1981. Cutmarks Made by Stone Tools on Bones from Olduvai Gorge, Tanzania. *Nature*, 291:577–80.

Reinhard, K. J. 1989. Coprolite Evidence of Medicinal Plants. presented at the annual meetings of the Paleopathology Association. Plattsburgh, New York.

Rodgers, W. L. 1967. Specificity of Specific Hungers. *Journal of Comparative and Physiological Psychology*, 64:49–58.

Rozin, P. 1967. Specific Aversions as a Component of Specific Hungers. *Journal of Comparative and Physiological Psychology*, 64:237–42.

Schaller, G. B. and G. R. Lowther. 1969. The Relevance of Carnivore Behavior to the Study of Early Hominids. *Southwest Journal of Anthropology*, 25:307–41.

Schell, L. M. 1986. Community Health Assessment through Physical Anthropology: Auxological Epidemiology. *Human Organization*, 45:321–27.

Schoeninger, M. J. 1979. Diet and Status at Chalcatzingo: Some Empirical and Technical Aspects of Strontium Analysis. *American Journal of Physical Anthropology*, 51:295–310.

———. 1982. Diet and the Evolution of Modern Human Form in the Middle East. *American Journal of Physical Anthropology*, 58:37–52

Scrimshaw, N. S., and V. R. Young. 1976. The Requirements of Human Nutrition. Norman Kretchmer and William van B. Robertson, eds., *Human Nutrition*, 156–70. San Francisco: W. H. Freeman

Short, R. V. 1976. The Evolution of Human Reproduction. *Proceedings, Royal Society*, Series B, 195:3–24.

Sillen, A. 1988. Elemental and Isotopic Analyses of Mammalian Fauna from Southern Africa and their Implications for Paleontodietary Research. *American Journal of Physical Anthropology*, 76:49–60.

———., and M. Kavanagh 1982. Strontium and Paleodietary Research: A Review. *Yearbook of Physical Anthropology*, 25: 67–90.

Spencer, F., and N. T. Boaz. 1983. Form and Particle Size as Determinants of Taxonomic Affinities in Plio-Pleistocene Mammalian Coprolites. *American Journal of Physical Anthropology*, 60:256.(Abstract.)

Steegmann, A. T., Jr. 1985. 18th Century British Military Stature: Growth Cessation, Selective Recruiting, Secular Trends, Nutrition at Birth, Cold and Occupation. *Human Biology*, 57:77–95.

Struhsaker, T. T., and L. Leland. 1987. Colobines: Infanticide by Adult Males. Barbara B. Smuts, Dorothy L. Cheney, Robert M. Seyfarth, Richard W. Wrangham, and Thomas T. Struhsaker, eds., *Primate Societies*, 83–97. Chicago: University of Chicago Press.

Strum, S. 1981. Processes and Products of Change: Baboon Predatory Behavior at Gilgil, Kenya. Robert S. O. Harding and Geza Teleki, eds., *Omnivorous Primates*, 255–302. New York: Columbia University Press.

Sussman R. W., and W. G. Kinzey. 1984. The Ecological Role of the Callitrichidae: A Review. *American Journal of Physical Anthropology*, 64:419–49.

Swedlund, A. C., R. S. Meindl, and M. I. Gradie. 1980. Family Reconstitution in the Connecticut Valley: Progress on Record Linkage and the Mortality Survey. B. Dyke and W. Morril, eds. *Geneological Demeography*. New York: Academic Press, 139–55.

Takasaki, Y., C. Pieddeloup, and S. Anzai. 1987. Trends in Food Intake and Digestive Cancer Mortalities in Japan. *Human Biology*, 59:951–57.

Teleki, G. 1981. The omnivorous diet and eclectic feeding habits of chimpanzees in Gombe National Park, Tanzania. Robert S. O. Harding and Geza Teleki, eds., *Omnivorous Primates*, 303–43. New York: Columbia University Press.

———., E. Hunt, and J.H. Pfifferling. 1976. Demographic Observations (1963–1973) on the Chimpanzees of the Gombe National Park, Tanzania. *Journal of Human Evolution*, 5:559–98.

Tobias, P. V. 1975. Anthropometry among Disadvantaged Peoples: Studies in Southern Africa. E.S. Watts, F.E. Johnston, and G.W. Lasker, eds., *Biosocial Interrelations in Population Adaptation*. The Hague: Mouton, 287–305.

Walker, A.C. 1981. Dietary hypotheses and human evolution. *Philosophical Transactions of the Royal Society*, B292:58–64.

Walker, A., M. R. Zimmerman, and R. E. F. Leakey. 1982. A Possible Case of Hypervitaminosis A in Homo Erectus. *Nature*, 296:248–50.

Washburn, S. L. and C.H. Lancaster. 1968. The Evolution of Hunting. R. B. Lee and I. Devore, eds., *Man the Hunter*, 293–303. Cambridge, Mass.: Harvard University Press.

———., and R. Moore. 1980. *Ape Into Human: A Study of Human Evolution*, 2nd edition, Boston: Little, Brown.

Weiss, K. M., R. E. Ferrell, and C.L. Hanis. 1984. A New World Syndrome of Metabolic Diseases With a Genetic and Evolutionary Basis. *Yearbook of Physical Anthropology*, 27:153–78.

10

ZOONOSES AND THE ORIGINS OF OLD AND NEW WORLD VIRAL DISEASES

LINDA M. VAN BLERKOM

INTRODUCTION

Disease affects culture, and culture in turn affects disease. Acquired immune deficiency syndrome (AIDS) illustrates this well. This disease changed sexual practices and values while cultural responses to it, such as screening blood and using condoms, slowed its spread. The causative agent, human immunodeficiency virus (HIV), also changed, with several new strains evolving since the beginning of the epidemic (Yokoyama et al. 1987; Yokoyama and Gojobori 1987). AIDS is still an important public health problem, and a powerful reminder that we do not completely control our environment and cannot prevent threats to human health from new infectious diseases.

The appearance of new human infections is dependent on a number of factors that favor transmission and endemicity. Social factors such as population size and density, and interaction with other populations are important because causative agents need a minimum host population size in order to continually find new susceptibles. This size varies with the requirements and characteristics of each disease. *Varicella zoster* virus (chickenpox) remains latent throughout its host's life, often causing painful eruptions of shingles in old age. This virus requires only a few thousand people in contact for its persistence, while measles, with its short, virulent infection resulting in lifelong immunity or death, must have a host population of at least half a million (Black 1966). More densely settled societies suffer more frequent epidemics, as do those with extensive trade and communication networks including other large societies. The presence of several civilized centers in the Old World and their increased interaction contributed to the many epidemics that have plagued Europeans since the Roman era (McNeill 1976).

The presence of pathogens in the environment, and climatic and cultural factors that affect their survival, virulence, and transmission, also affect infectious disease evolution. Many infections require vectors such as mosquitos for transmission. Arthropod vectors are sensitive to temperature, humidity, and altitude, and they must have suitable breeding places (often unwittingly supplied by humans). Especially important sources of human disease are the infections of other animals and cultural practices that put humans in infectious foci or in contact with infected animals or vectors. Unlike human epidemic infections such as influenza or AIDS, which are widely distributed and somewhat independent of environment (like their host), most wild animal diseases are localized in more or less defined niches, called foci or nidi (Pavlovsky 1966). Human contact with such foci may result in the interspecific transmission of infection. For example, sylvatic yellow fever in South America is usually found only in the upper canopy inhabited by the monkeys and mosquitos it infects. People can acquire the infection by felling trees, which brings the mosquitos temporarily to ground level (Fiennes 1964:55). Clearing new land for agriculture is notorious for its association with zoonotic diseases. Other human cultural activities, such as trapping and skinning infected animals or living with domesticated and commensal species, also contribute to the potential for infection with zoonoses, animal infections that can also affect humans.

Once a person is infected with a zoonosis, the potential exists for adaptation to human hosts and person-to-person transmission. The more frequently human infection occurs, the greater the likelihood of the zoonosis evolving into a new, specifically human disease. Most of our infectious diseases came to us recently in our evolution, and from other animals (Table 10.1). Some infections (e.g., herpes, colds, malaria, poxvirus infections) evolved along with us, with related strains in other primates. But entirely new human diseases are most likely to be either new strains of existing human pathogens (by mutation or infection of bacteria such as staph or strep by toxin-producing bacteriophages) or microorganisms acquired from an animal population. Therefore cultural practices that favor the transmission of zoonoses should also favor the evolution of new human infections. The Old World's greater reliance on domesticated animals and higher tolerance of large commensal rodent and primate populations in human settlements contributed to the large number of epidemic diseases native to that hemisphere (Table 10.2; Van Blerkom 1985).

These are the same diseases that killed a major portion of the population of the Americas in the first century after contact. Estimates range as high as 95 percent for some areas (Dobyns 1966), and while the extent of depopulation is disputed, most agree that Native Americans were unfamiliar with

Table 10.1
Common Diseases of Probable Zoonotic Origin

Human Diseases	Related Animal Diseases
Measles*	Canine distemper, bovine rinderpest
Influenza*	Swine, equine, or wild bird influenza
Smallpox*	Poxvirus infections in many primates and domesticates
Dengue fever* and urban yellow fever*	Sylvatic yellow fever
AIDS*	Retrovirus infections of other primates
Plague	Rat plague
Tuberculosis	Bovine and avian TB
Relapsing fever (louse-borne)	Sylvatic relapsing fever (tick-borne)
Typhus (louse-borne)	Murine typhus (flea-borne)
Trypanosomiasis (African sleeping sickness, Chagas' disease in New World)	Trypanosomiasis in wild herd animals in Africa; American reservoir still unknown

*Human viral infections.

most of these infections from Europe and Africa. For the paleoepidemiologist or medical historian, this is no surprise, because the two hemispheres had had no substantial contact for at least twelve thousand years, and most epidemic diseases appeared after the development of large sedentary populations in the Neolithic (Armelagos and McArdle 1975; Armelagos and Dewey 1978). The surprise is that Native Americans appear to have had so few epidemics of their own with which to ravage their conquerors. This is especially hard to explain in Mesoamerica, where population densities were comparable with those in the Old World and should have been sufficient to sustain a chain of infection (Van Blerkom 1985).

The epidemic diseases that killed so many Native Americans after European contact probably had zoonotic origins. The biggest killers appear to have been smallpox, measles, typhus, and influenza (Ashburn 1947). Native Americans may have had their own strains of influenza A, as this virus is carried by migrating wild birds of both hemispheres. New and unfamiliar strains coming from other populations can still have severe consequences, however—for example in the 1918 influenza pandemic.

Cultural differences can help explain why fewer infectious diseases evolved in the New World. Different styles of interaction with animals led to unequal numbers of infectious diseases in the precolumbian Old and New worlds. Less dependence on domesticated animals, especially herd animals that are milked and stalled in human habitations, and the hunting of rodents

Table 10.2
Pre-Columbian Distribution of Major Human Infections

	Old World	Both	New World
Viral diseases	Dengue fever	Chickenpox	Changuinola fever
	Measles	Colds	
	Mumps	Hepatitis	
	Rubella	Herpes	
	Smallpox	Influenza	
	Yellow fever	Polio	
		Trachoma	
Bacterial	Diphtheria	Pertussis	Bartonellosis
	Gonorrhea	Salmonellosis	Pinta
	Leprosy	Shigellosis	Syphilis
	Relapsing fever	Staph infections	
	Scarlet fever	Strep infections	
	Typhoid fever	Tuberculosis	
	Yaws		
Rickettsial	Typhus		
Protozoal	Amoebiasis	Giardiasis	Chagas' disease
	Malaria		
	African trypanosomiasis		
Fungal		Candidiasis	
		Piedra	
		Ringworm	
Helminths	Guinea worm	Hookworm	
	Filariasis	Pinworm	
	Loiasis	Roundworm	
	Onchocerciasis	Tapeworm	
	Schistosomiasis	Trichuriasis	

and primates attracted to human structures and activities (which kept these animals' populations below epizootic levels) are among the factors that decreased Native Americans' potential for acquiring new infections. But this supposedly more "healthy" state of affairs had tragic consequences during contact with Europeans and Africans.

Three of the four major killers of Native Americans are viral diseases. Table 10.2 shows that the distribution of viral infections was particularly skewed toward the Old World before contact. The only human virus to evolve in the pre-Columbian New World is the Changuinola fever virus of humans and sand flies (phlebotomus) in Central America. This arbovirus, which produces a three-to-four-day fever and malaise, probably infected Spanish invaders, but as death from this infection is unknown (Benenson 1985:38–39), it would have had little effect on the conquest. Most viruses

Table 10.3
Viral Zoonoses with Pre-Columbian Worldwide Distribution

Infection	Reservoir	Transmission
Encephalomyocarditis	Commensal rats (Old World _Rattus_ and New World _Sigmodon_) and other rodents	Ingestion of infected meat, urine, or feces
Influenza type A	Migratory waterfowl; also turkeys, ducks, chickens, swine	Direct contact or inhalation of airborne droplets
Kemerovo virus infection	Many animals and birds	Tick
Phlebotomus fever	Gerbils (Old World); arboreal rodents and monkeys (New World)	Sandfly
Psittacosis (Ornithosis)	Parakeets, parrots, pigeons, turkeys, ducks, and other birds	Inhalation of dessicated droppings
Rabies	Dogs, cats, wild carnivores (esp. Eur. foxes, Asian wolves), bats, N. Am. raccoons and skunks	Bite

are host-specific, so their zoonotic sources can be determined. For these reasons, and to keep the scale of this study manageable, it is limited to analysis of viral zoonoses and the evolution of human viral diseases. The study suggests that the New World contained no important indigenous human viruses because its inhabitants were less likely to acquire zoonotic viral infections.

METHOD OF ANALYSIS

Tables 10.3 to 10.5 include all zoonoses listed in the volumes on viral zoonoses in *Handbook Series on Zoonoses* (Beran 1981). The infections are organized by hemispheric distribution before contact, along with their reservoirs and most frequent sources of human disease. This information came primarily from the *Handbook Series*, with help from other sources (Benenson

1985 especially; also Bisseru 1967; Fiennes 1967; Hubbert et al. 1975; Schwabe 1984).

Some zoonoses, especially those with wide host ranges or carried by migrating birds, were probably found in both hemispheres before contact (Table 10.3). They are few, however, compared to the longer lists of viral zoonoses found in each hemisphere alone (Tables 10.4 and 10.5). Inhabitants of the New World were more likely to acquire zoonotic infections from the bites of arthropod vectors (arboviral infections) or while hunting, while Old World people suffered from many more diseases requiring proximity with infected animals.

Tables 10.3–10.5 are summarized in Table 10.6, which shows there was little difference in the pattern of animal involvement for vector-borne zoonoses in the two hemispheres. Transmission of these infections does not require direct contact with their reservoir hosts, so most of these diseases are maintained in wild animals. While activities that take people into the foci of these diseases are still a factor, these diseases are more independent of culture and custom concerning the uses and treatment of animals. Domesticated animals are involved in four of the Old World's thirty-three arboviral infections and are amplifying hosts for five others (and three New World arboviruses since European contact). An amplifying host is a species that, while not the usual reservoir, can support a chain of infection and propagate the causative agent such that the probability of human infection is greatly increased.

Diseases requiring contact with an infected vertebrate or its discharges are more frequent in the Old World (Table 10.6), supporting closer relationships between humans and other species in that hemisphere. Domesticates and commensal rodents (rats and mice attracted to human settlements and dependent on human activities) contribute all the New World diseases of this type and almost all in the Old World, where primates are also a disease risk. Domesticates involved in the Americas were mostly turkeys and dogs, while cattle, sheep, and goats are implicated in most Old World zoonoses of domesticated animals. Today these three important multipurpose animals act as amplifying hosts in the western hemisphere as well.

The frequency of Old World contact infections acquired from domesticates, commensal rodents, and primates suggests that the difference in infectious disease load carried by inhabitants of the two hemispheres can be explained at least in part by differences in types and frequency of interactions with animals.

DISCUSSION

New viral infections continue to appear, and virologists can observe their evolution and measure mutation rates. Recently, novel strains of influenza have caused local epidemics every one to three years, and major pandemics every decade (Benenson 1985:194; Fenner et al. 1974:627–29). An important new public health problem in the United States today is AIDS. Almost half

Table 10.4
Viral Zoonoses Indigenous to the Western Hemisphere

Infection	Reservoir	Transmission
Arenaviral hemorrhagic fevers	Field rodents (Calomys) of Argentina & Bolivia	Ingestion or inhalation of dust contaminated by rodent urine or feces
Bussuquara fever	Rodents (Proechimys) of Panama, Columbia, and Brazil	Mosquito
California encephalitis	Squirrels and chipmunks, U.S. and Canada	Mosquito
Colorado tick fever	N. Am. ground squirrels (Citellus), chipmunks (Eutamias), deer mice (Peromyscus), porcupines	Tick
Eastern equine encephalitis	Wild passerine birds, esp. pheasants; amplifying host, horses, since conquest	Mosquito
Group C bunyaviral fevers	Cental and South American rodents	Mosquito
Mayaro fever (Uruma)	New World monkeys and marmosets	Mosquito
Mucambo fever	South American rodents (Oryzomys)	Mosquito
Oropouche fever	Monkeys (Alouatta and Cebus) of Trinidad and Brazil	Midge (Culicoides)
Piry fever	Amazon opossums or other wild animals	Mosquito
Powasson encephalitis	Canadian and U.S. squirrels and groundhogs	Tick
Rocio encephalitis	Wild birds of coastal Brazil	Mosquito
St. Louis encephalitis	Wild birds	Mosquito
Venezuelan equine fever	Wild rodents; amplifying hosts: dogs; horses, and other domesticates since conquest	Mosquito

Table 10.4 *(Continued)*

Infection	Reservoir	Transmission
Vesicular stomatitis	Arboreal & semi-arboreal mammals in tropics; horses, cattle, and swine since conquest	Sandfly
Western equine encephalitis	Wild birds, esp. blackbirds, swallows, U.S. and Canada	Mosquito

Source: Platt and Dufrenoy (1953), except as otherwise indicated by footnotes.
* Korzybski et al. (1967).
∞ Böttcher (1964).
Δ Majno (1975).
§ Rosett and Hodges (1980).
** Kinosita and Shikata (1965).

the Center for Disease Control's 1990 budget is devoted to its surveillance and control. And while several drugs hold some promise of keeping AIDS patients alive a little longer, we still cannot completely protect ourselves from it or keep AIDS patients from dying sooner and younger than people with heart disease or cancer. Where did AIDS come from, and how did it evolve?

A zoonotic origin for HIV is not as recent as many thought when a similar virus (SIV_{AGM}) was isolated from healthy African green monkeys. Thirty to 50 percent of monkeys caught in the wild are seropositive for this virus (Mulder 1988), so it was a good candidate for an HIV ancestor. But comparison of their nucleotide sequences shows that these viruses are too different to have diverged during this century (Fukasawa et al. 1988). All the human and simian immunodeficiency viruses have been sequenced, resulting in the phylogenetic reconstruction in Figure 10.1. HIV-1 is the family of strains found in Central Africa, Europe, and the United States, while HIV-2 is a West African variant (found occasionally in the United States). HIV-2 is closely related to a virus, SIV_{SM}, of sootey mangabeys (Hirsch 1990). SIV_{AGM}, SIV_{MAC}, and SIV_{MND} are viruses from wild green monkeys, laboratory rhesus macaques, and mandrills, respectively. The latter two cause AIDS-like diseases in monkeys, while SIV_{AGM} infection of green monkeys is asymptomatic. With the exception of SIV_{SM} and SIV_{MAC}, which are more closely related to HIV-2, all the primate AIDS viruses are equally related, so the best family tree is a bush branching out from a common lentivirus ancestor.

Retroviruses mutate at a rate of approximately 10^{-3} nucleotide substitution per site per year (Yokoyama and Gojobori 1987). This is about one million times faster than rates for DNA genomes, and helps explain why new viral

Table 10.5
Viral Zoonoses Indigenous to the Eastern Hemisphere

Infection	Reservoir	Transmission
Banzi fever	Unknown (Africa)	Mosquito
Bunyamwera fever	Unknown (Africa)	Mosquito
Bwamba fever	Unknown (Africa)	Mosquito
Central European tick-borne encephalitis	Wild vertebrates (hedgehogs, shrews, voles, etc.); amplifying hosts: cattle, sheep, goats	Tick or infected goat's milk
Chikungunya fever	Old World canopy monkeys; amplifying host: baboon (Papio)	Mosquito
Crimean-Congo hemorrhagic fever	Hares (Lepus) and other small Eurasian mammals; amplifying hosts: sheep, goats, horses, cattle	Tick or nosocomial; migrating birds carry infected ticks to Africa
Dengue fever	Canopy primates of W. Malaysia and W. Africa	Mosquito
Dugbe viral fever	West African cattle	Tick
Ebola-Marburg virus disease	Unknown (Africa)	Nosocomial (contact with infected blood, semen, secretions, or organs)
Far Eastern tick-borne encephalitis	Eurasian rodents	Tick
Foot and mouth disease	Cloven-footed animals, incl. cattle, sheep, goats, swine, camels	Inhalation of aerosol droplets or contact with discharges
Germiston fever	Unknown (Africa)	Mosquito
Getah virus infection	Domestic mammals and fowl, Malaysia and Australia	Mosquito
Japanese encephalitis	Herons, egrets in Asia & Pacific; amplifying hosts: swine	Mosquito
Keterah virus infection	Asian bats	Tick

Table 10.5 *(Continued)*

Infection	Reservoir	Transmission
Korean hemorrhagic fever	Eurasian field mice (<u>Apodemus</u>) and voles (<u>Clethrionomys</u>); urban rats and mice (<u>Rattus</u> and <u>Mus</u>)	Aerosol transmission from rodent excreta
Kunjin fever	Unknown (Australia and Malaysia)	Mosquito
Kyasanur Forest disease	Indian rats, shrews (<u>Suncus</u>), cattle	Tick
Langat virus infection	W. Malaysian wild rats	Tick
Lassa fever	African multimammate mouse (<u>Mastomys</u>)	Ingestion or inhalation of infected urine
Louping ill	Ticks, sheep, red grouse (<u>Lagopus</u>) and deer in the U.K.	Tick
Lymphocytic choriomeningitis	House mouse (<u>Mus</u>); also found in hamsters (<u>Mesocricetus</u>)	Ingestion or inhalation of infected urine, or bite
Murray Valley encephalitis	Water birds of N. Australia, New Guinea	Mosquito
Newcastle disease	Chickens, other birds	Contact with infected carcasses
Omsk hemorrhagic fever	Siberian muskrats and other rodents	Tick
O'nyongnyong	Unknown (Africa)	Mosquito
Orf virus disease	Sheep, goats, reindeer, and musk oxen	Contact with infected animals
Poxvirus infections: Cowpox Horsepox Monkeypox Pseudocowpox Tanapox Yabapox	Cattle Horses W. African monkeys Cattle African primates W. African monkeys	Contact with respiratory discharges or skin lesions
Quaranfil	African herons	Tick

Table 10.5 *(Continued)*

Infection	Reservoir	Transmission
Rift Valley fever	Wild res. unknown; amplifying hosts sheep and cattle, Africa	Mosquito, or handling infected carcasses
Ross River fever	Australian rodents and marsupials	Mosquito
Scrapie	Sheep and goats	Ingestion or contact with infected brains
Semliki Forest viral fever	Wide variety of African birds and animals	Mosquito
Sendai virus infection	Mice (Mus)	Droplet spread or contact with respiratory secretions
Simian B virus disease	Old World monkeys	Bite or contact with infected saliva or tissue cultures
Simian parainfluenza virus infection	African green (Cercopithecus) and rhesus monkeys (Macacus)	Droplet spread or contact with respiratory secretions
Sindbis fever	Wild birds	Mosquito
Spondweni fever	Unknown (Africa)	Mosquito
Tahyna virus infection	Small mammals of Europe and Africa	Mosquito
Tanjong Rabok viral infection	W. Malaysian arboreal mammals	Unknown arthropod vector
Wesselsbron fever	Unknown (Africa); amplifying host sheep	Mosquito or handling infected carcasses
West Nile fever	Birds of Africa, Europe, and Asia	Mosquito
Yellow fever	African primates; New World primates since conquest	Mosquito
Zika Forest fever	Old World monkeys	Mosquito
Zinga fever	Large wild mammals and monkeys of Central Africa	Mosquito

Table 10.6
Animals Most Frequently Involved in Viral Zoonoses

	Old World	Both	New World
Vector-borne viral diseases:			
Reservoir: wild animals	29*	2	15
(includes primates)			
Reservoir: domesticates	4	0	0
(cattle, sheep, goats)	(3)**		
Amplifying hosts: domesticates	5	0	3
(cattle, sheep, goats)	(4)		(2)
Amplifying host: baboon	1		
Total	33	2	15
Nonvector-borne diseases:			
Reservoir: domesticates	7	3	0
(cattle, sheep, goats)	(6)		
Reservoir: commensal rodents	4	1	1
Reservoir: primates	5	0	0
Reservoir unknown	1		
Total	17	4	1
Grand Total	50	6	16

*Reservoirs of nine unknown, presumably in nondomesticated animals.

**Numbers in ( ) equal zoonoses of dometicates involving cattle, sheep, and goats.

infections are more likely to be caused by RNA viruses. The changeability of RNA viruses was first discovered in influenza, which undergoes this process of mutational drift as well as antigenic shifting caused by recombination between strains of different species. The dramatic epidemic of 1918 is now believed to have been the result of recombination between human and swine strains (Fenner et al. 1974:629–30). A similar event during Columbus's second voyage may have produced a flu epidemic that killed Indians, Spaniards, and their horses in 1493–1494 in Santo Domingo. Apparently, Columbus's ships carried both men and hogs infected with their own species' specific viruses. Coinfection of man or beast with both strains and recombination between them may have resulted in a new, more virulent pathogen, because human antibodies would not recognize its swine influenza antigens. This new virus was therefore also able to overcome European immunity, infecting even Columbus himself (Guerra 1987). Another possible origin of this epidemic is that European and American strains of influenza recombined into a strain virulent for both humans and animals (human influenza can also infect horses).

Lentiviruses also may recombine. Recombination, both between viral

Figure 10.1
Molecular Phylogeny of HIV

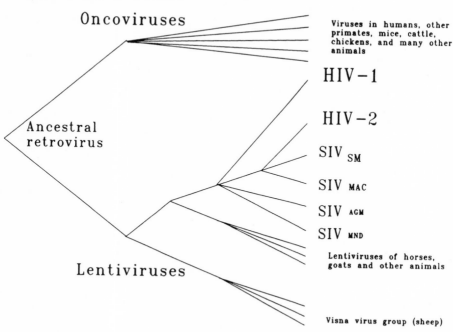

strains and between viral and host cell DNA, occurs in oncoviruses; (Sonigo et al. 1986; Thayer et al. 1987). This process may be involved in the origin and variation of other retroviruses as well, and produces bigger changes than point mutations. The potential of RNA viruses to change rapidly by both mechanisms explains why humans can contract frequent colds and influenza infections, in spite of host immunity. Antigenic changes in the coat proteins of these viruses prevent efficient host protection by antibodies. Most of our pathogenic viruses, including zoonoses, are RNA-containing viruses (see Table 10.7).

The amino acid substitution rate of retroviruses is also on the order of 10^{-3} change per site per year (Yokoyama and Gojobori 1987; Yokoyama et al. 1987). Comparison of viral polypeptide sequences furnishes a molecular clock allowing us to estimate divergence times and reconstruct the evolution of AIDS. Depending on the protein chosen (different loci do not mutate at the same rate), the primate AIDS viruses diverged between 200 and 325 years ago (mean value 275 years), with the HIV-2/SIV$_{MAC}$ split occurring 60 to 200 years ago (140 mean; all estimates based on extent of amino acid homology reported in Fukasawa et al. 1988). Hirsch (1990) estimates HIV-2 split from SIV$_{SM}$ within the last century. Others have stated that the ancestor of HIV separated from nonprimate lentiviruses (e.g., visna virus of

Table 10.7
Human Viruses and Related Strains in Animals

Viral Family	Viruses of Humans	Animal Viruses
RNA Viruses		
Arenaviridae	Zoonotic only	Rodent arboviruses of Lassa fever, lymphocytic choriomeningitis, arenaviral hemorrhagic fevers, and others
Bunyaviridae	Human phlebotomus fever virus	Arboviruses such as California encephalitis Crimean-Congo hemorrhagic fever Phlebotomus fever Rift Valley fever Bunyamwera fever Nairobi sheep disease, and more than 200 others
Coronaviridae	Respiratory viruses (colds)	Respiratory viruses of many species
Orthomyxoviridae	Influenza types A,B, and C (many strains of each)	Influenza type A of horses, swine, birds, and fowl Other arboviruses of Africa and Europe
Paramyxoviridae	Parainfluenza viruses Mumps Measles Human respiratory syncytial virus	Simian parainfluenza Newcastle and other parainfluenza viruses of birds Sendai (mice and pigs) Canine distemper Bovine rinderpest Peste de petits ruminants (rodents) Bovine respiratory syncytial virus Mouse pneumovirus
Picornaviridae	70 enterovirus such as Polioviruses Coxsackie A and B viruses Echoviruses Hepatitis A Human cardioviruses More than 100 rhinoviruses (colds)	Enteroviruses of cattle, pigs, and other animals Swine coxsackie Foot-and-mouth disease Primate echoviruses Duck hepatitis Encephalomyocarditis in rodents and birds Rhinoviruses in chimps and gibbons Perhaps also caliciviruses of sea lions, swine, and cats; bacterial ribophages
Reoviridae	Human rotavirus (infantile diarrhea) Reoviruses of enteric tract Changuinola virus	Rotaviruses of cattle, swine, mice, monkeys Reoviruses in many animals Colorado tick fever and some arboviruses of Europe and Africa Sheep blue tongue African horse sickness
Retroviridae	Human AIDS viruses (HIV-1 and 2) Human T-cell leukemia (HTLV-1 and 2) and possibly other oncogenic human viruses Foamy agents, perhaps Hepatitis C	SIV and AIDS viruses of other animals Equine infectious anemia virus Caprine arthritis encephalitis virus Visna virus of sheep Simian AIDS ("D-type") viruses Oncogenic and leukemia viruses of many animals and birds Simian foamy agents
Rhabdoviridae	Humans are now a reservoir for Piry virus	Rabies viruses Piry virus of opossums Lagos bat virus Some viruses of fish, insects, and plants Vesicular stomatitis

Table 10.7 *(Continued)*

Viral Family	Viruses of Humans	Animal Viruses
RNA Viruses		
Togaviridae	Rubella virus	Group A arboviruses (Alphaviruses) such as Venezuelan, Eastern, and Western equine encephalitis viruses
	Dengue virus	Group B arboviruses (Flaviviruses) including yellow fever and dengue in primates Tick-borne encephalitis viruses (rodents) Louping ill of sheep Bat salivary gland virus Japanese and St. Louis encephalitis viruses and many others, especially in bats and rodents Hog cholera and other pestiviruses of cattle and swine
DNA Viruses		
Adenoviridae	33 human respiratory viruses, some oncogenic	Adenoviruses of primates, other mammals, and birds
Herpesviridae	Human herpesviruses: Types 1 and 2 (Herpes simplex) Type 3 (Varicella zoster)	Simian B virus and other alphaherpesviruses of Old and New World primates, cattle, horses, dogs, cats, fowl Pseudorabies of swine and cattle
	Type 4 (Epstein-Barr virus)	Gammaherpesviruses of primates Lymphoproliferative viruses of turkeys and rabbits
	Type 5 (Cytomegalovirus)	Betaherpesviruses in primates, mice, and swine
Iridoviridae	No human forms at present	Insect iridescent viruses African swine fever Viruses in frogs, and fish
Papovaviridae	Human SV40 virus, a polyomavirus (tumorigenic viruses) At least 24 human papillomaviruses (warts)	Polyomaviruses of monkeys, mice, rabbits Papillomaviruses of rabbits, cattle, dogs, sheep, goats, horses, hamsters, deer, and many other species
Parvoviridae	Adeno helper viruses	Adeno-associated viruses in primates, dogs, cattle, horses, and birds Insect densoviruses
	Norwalk and other gastroenteritis viruses Erythema infectiosum, and perhaps, Hepatitis B	Parvoviruses of many species worldwide
Poxviridae	Smallpox Vaccinia	Poxviruses of monkeys and cattle are most closely related; poxviruses also found in sheep, goats, birds, water buffalo, camels, swine, and most other animals, including insects
	Molluscum contagiosum	Milker's nodule virus Orf virus Myxomatosis in New World hares

sheep and related viruses in goats and horses) between three hundred and five hundred years ago, or about twice as long as since the primate lentivirus radiation (Yokoyama and Gojobori 1987).

Natural selection favors parasites that don't kill their hosts (although lentiviruses, by their very slowness, overcome many obstacles to transmission not faced by more rapid agents such as smallpox or measles). This means that infectious agents which are not vector-borne tend to attenuate with time in their most important host, as both host and pathogen evolve toward commensalism. The molecular phylogeny and pathogenicity of the primate lentiviruses suggests their derivation from a common ancestral form once found in African green monkeys. The lack of clinical symptoms in SIV infection in these animals, unlike that in any other primate studied so far, suggests that this species has probably harbored lentiviruses the longest. AIDS was probably a zoonosis several hundred years ago, when social disruption and cultural change accompanying the slave trade, conquest, and colonialism may have contributed to human infection and transmission. Note that the simian lentiviruses isolated so far are found in terrestrial or laboratory species that are more likely to come into contact with people than are exclusively arboreal monkeys or reclusive apes. The primate AIDS viruses, including two human strains, remained localized in West and Central Africa until social change, migration, prostitution, and international jet travel increased the incidence of infection and spread HIV-1 out of Central Africa. The West African variant, HIV-2, remained more localized (Clavel et al. 1987). HIV-1, on the other hand, as it spread around the world, gave rise to several new strains in Europe and on the east and west coasts of the United States.

The AIDS example illustrates how a viral agent evolves at the molecular level. The molecular mechanisms and phylogeny are worked out, but much more research is needed to fill in the historical and cultural factors that contributed to this evolution. Chances are that, when understood more completely, the evolution of AIDS will have involved interaction with other animals.

Zoonotic origins are likely for many viral infections, especially those caused by RNA viruses, because all human viruses have relatives in other animals (Table 10.7). This suggests two possibilities. First, all the members of a family are probably derived from a common ancestor, and given the rapid mutation rate of RNA viruses, this was probably more recent than the divergence of the host species. That is, there was probably relatively recent interspecies transmission leading to expansion of host range rather than origin in the common ancestor of the host animals and separate evolution of each virus as its host evolved. For example, HIV and SIV did not evolve along with their human and cercopithecoid hosts, because the thirty million years since the divergence of these two primate families would have produced a much greater degree of genetic variation in RNA viruses. A viral family that does appear to have evolved separately in different primate species is the herpes virus group. These are DNA viruses and have a millionfold slower mutation rate (Yokoyama and Gojobori 1987).

The second implication of the viral relationships shown in Table 10.7 is the potential for interspecific recombination in viruses with overlapping host ranges. This might occur when human and other strains coinfect the same person or animal. Recombination between host DNA and viruses that integrate their genetic material into host genomes or replicate in cell nuclei can also take place. In this process, too, infection of an other-than-normal host might lead to a new virus and a new disease. A multitude of viruses wait in wild animals, birds, fish, even insects and plants, many potentially capable of infection and transmission in human hosts.

We should not underestimate the influence of cultural and behavioral factors when assessing the potential for interspecies transmission of infection. Activities that favor outbreaks of viral zoonoses include forest work (yellow fever and other arboviral infections), clearing new agricultural areas (Eastern equine encephalitis), field work, especially during harvest season (hemorrhagic fevers, Lassa fever), crowding animals and people together in barns and peasant huts (influenza and other respiratory infections, cowpox), milking or drinking milk (milker's nodules, cowpox, Central European encephalitis), storing water in uncovered vessels (yellow and dengue fevers and other mosquito-borne arboviruses), medical work (Ebola/Marburg infections), laboratory use of monkeys (simian B virus infection, simian AIDS), irrigating rice paddies (Japanese encephalitis), butchering (Newcastle disease, Rift Valley fever, Wesselsbron fever), and eating sheep brains (scrapie). These are just some viral infections; cultural styles promote or protect from many bacterial, rickettsial, protozoal, fungal, and helminthic zoonoses as well.

Comparison of disease burdens and cultures of Old and New World civilizations suggests that differences in practices relating to animals contributed to the relative lack of epidemic disease in the Americas. Greater reliance on domesticated herd animals in the Old World, and more intensive contact with them (milking, stalling, often in the same structure as humans, riding, harnessing to vehicles and plows, etc.), provided many opportunities for communication of infection. Compare this with the Andean style of using camelids, in which llamas and alpacas are herded but never fed by humans or milked, only occasionally ridden, and eaten only after their useful lives as pack or fleece-bearing animals are over (Gade 1969). Furthermore, the relative lack of domesticated meat sources in the New World contributed to overhunting in some areas, which reduced the density and diversity of fauna near large settlements.

Cultural attitudes in Old World civilizations, such as the Hindu doctrine of ahimsa, or reverence for life, and a general reluctance to eat rodents, contributed to the buildup of commensal rats and mice, first in Asia, where many of our epidemic diseases were born, and eventually throughout the Old World (Zinsser 1934). Both *Rattus* and *Mus*, as well as these attitudes, were transplanted to cities of the New World. But indigenous reactions to rats and other rodents were to hunt, trap, and eat them, especially the large species of South America (Gilmore 1950; Linares 1976). Garden trapping resulted in lower commensal populations, and hunting may have contributed to the extinction of several species (Gilmore 1950). Diminished rodent populations not only reduce the likelihood of contacting a diseased one but also lessens the probability of rodent epidemics in the first place. It's interesting that domesticated guinea pigs did not contribute any viruses to the human disease pool. Being kept within Indian huts probably insulates them from most wild rodent diseases. They have recently been implicated in zoonoses of Old World commensal rodents, such as plague (Hubbert et al. 1975).

Ahimsa protects cattle and monkeys in India as well as rats. Cattle, like other milked domesticates, can carry many important zoonoses. People of India consider rhesus macaques and langurs sacred and tolerate a certain amount of mingling in Indian urban areas. This contrasts with tropical America, where monkeys are almost completely arboreal in their habits, and so in less intimate contact with humans. This even inhibits sharing of insect vectors, which are adapted to different heights in the canopy. Native Americans also hunt monkeys, which reduces the chance of infection for the same reasons their hunting of rodents does.

So humans in the eastern hemisphere were surrounded by animals with which they interacted closely at times, because of cultural differences more than environmental ones. Large populations of humans and their commensal and domesticated species, especially in southern Asia, where tropical latitudes provided high biodiversity, provided the perfect conditions for the evolution of viral epidemics. Population concentrations in the New World hunted rather than domesticated most of the animals of their environments. This kept animal densities low and afforded fewer opportunities for zoonotic infection and subsequent adaptation to a human host.

CONCLUSION

For a new human viral disease to arise, there must be a suitable virus available in the environment, humans must come into contact with it in a fashion conducive to transmission, and there must be enough new susceptibles in the human population to sustain a chain of infection. The virus also must adapt to human hosts, but since most viruses evolve rapidly, and because viral infections produce astronomical numbers of virus particles, this is easily accomplished.

Zoonoses are a frequent source of new human infections. Therefore, anything that increases animal population size, density, disease load, or contact with humans increases the chance of human disease, as veterinarians have been pointing out for a long time (Schwabe 1984). Differences in the disease burdens of the Old and New Worlds before contact are at least partly the result of differences in coresident animal populations and in attitudes and practices concerning them.

We must be aware of the continuing evolution of new human diseases in a global environment we cannot totally control. Just as AIDS seemed to come from nowhere, with terrible loss of life in Africa and in several risk groups in the United States, other infections will surface, especially those we can least control. The use of antibiotics sets up perfect laboratory conditions for the selection of drug-resistant strains. Our ability to influence so many aspects of our environment means that future plagues will be even harder to stop, as their epidemiology will increasingly involve factors we control the least (like human sexual and addictive behavior).

We are ourselves animals, part of the natural ecosystem, in spite of culture and our ability to mold our environments (our technology may be our biggest threat, for it now poisons nature and selects for those diseases we can least control). Infectious epidemics like AIDS still remind us of our species' vulnerability in evolution's cosmic game of chance.

APPENDIX: SHORT DESCRIPTIONS OF ANIMAL VIRUS FAMILIES

Viruses are classified according to morphology and serology rather than by mode of transmission, target organ, or type of disease.

Adenoviridae

Nonenveloped, icosahedral double-strand DNA viruses that replicate in cell nuclei. Associated with respiratory infections with prolonged latency in many mammals (Genus *Mastadenovirus*) and birds (*Aviadenovirus*). Some produce tumors.

Arenaviridae

Genus *Arenavirus:* Spherical enveloped viruses with segmented single-strand RNA genomes that replicate in the cytoplasm and mature by budding from the plasma membrane. Associated with chronic inapparent infections in rodents.

Bunyaviridae

Over 200 roughly spherical, enveloped arboviruses, with tubular nucleocapsids, single-strand RNA in three circular segments that replicate in the cytoplasm and mature by budding from intracytoplasmic membranes. Consists of the genus *Bunyavirus* and others as yet unclassified. All multiply in and are transmitted by arthropods.

Coronaviridae

Genus *Coronavirus:* Spherical enveloped single-strand RNA viruses with tubular nucleocapsids that replicate in the cytoplasm, bud from intracytoplasmic membranes, and cause respiratory disease in a variety of animals.

Herpesviridae	Enveloped, icosahedral, double-strand DNA viruses that replicate in the nucleus and bud from the nuclear membrane. Associated with latent or persistent infections in many animals, and often cause a vesicular rash; some are oncogenic.
Iridovidae	Genus *Iridovirus*: Large, nonenveloped, icosahedral, double-strand DNA viruses that replicate in the cytoplasm. Include insect iridescent viruses and viruses of fish, amphibians, and African swine fever. Vertebrate iridoviruses are enveloped.
Orthomyxoviridae	Genus *Influenzavirus*: Spherical enveloped viruses with segmented single-strand RNA and tubular capsids that multiply in the cytoplasm and mature by budding from the plasma membrane. Important cause of respiratory disease in animals and human beings.
Papovaviridae	Nonenveloped, icosahedral viruses with circular, double-strand DNA that multiply relatively slowly in the nucleus. Cause latent and chronic infections and tumors, mostly benign, in a variety of animals, if the viral genome becomes integrated into host cell DNA. Genera *Papillomavirus* (causative agents of warts) and *Polyomavirus* (oncogenic viruses of primates, mice, rabbits).
Paramyxoviridae	Genera *Paramyxovirus*, *Pneumovirus*, and *Morbillivirus*: Viruses similar to the Orthomyxoviridae, except the RNA genome is in one piece and does not recombine. Associated with respiratory disease and skin rashes.
Parvoviridae	Small, icosahedral, single-strand DNA viruses that multiply in the nucleus. Genera *Parvovirus* (many rodent and other viruses), *Densovirus* (in insects), and the adeno-associated virus group that replicates only in the presence of an adenovirus.
Picornaviridae	A large group of small, single-strand RNA viruses with no envelopes and icosohedral nucleocapsids that replicate in the cytoplasm and generally cause inapparent infection. Genera include *Enterovirus*, in the intestines of many animals; *Rhinovirus*, causing mild respiratory infections; *Calicivirus*, in swine, sea lions, and cats; *Cardiovirus*, in rodents mostly; and *Aphthovirus*, foot-and-mouth and equine rhinoviruses.

Poxviridae	Largest animal viruses. Brick-shaped, double-strand DNA viruses with a DNA-containing core surrounded by several envelopes of viral origin. They replicate in the cytoplasm and mature within cytoplasmic foci. Recombination can occur within genera. Involved in many diseases of mammals, birds, humans, often with vesiculo-pustular rash. Subfamilies Chordopoxviridae, in vertebrates, and Entomopoxviridae, in insects.
Reoviridae	Nonenveloped viruses with segmented double-strand RNA and icosahedral double capsids that replicate in the cytoplasm. Genera *Reovirus* and *Rotavirus*, found in human and animal enteric tracts, and *Orbivirus*, a group of arboviruses.
Retroviridae	Spherical, enveloped viruses with icosahedral inner shells, tubular nucleocapsids, and single-strand RNA that is transcribed, by viral reverse transcriptase, into DNA proviruses capable of integration into the cellular genome. Subfamilies Lentiviridae, slow viruses of sheep plus human AIDS and related viruses (all with long incubation periods before the onset of clinical symptoms); Oncoviridae, oncogenic and leukemia viruses of many species, including integrated genomes occurring naturally in normal cells; and Spumaviridae, or "foamy agents" causing inapparent infections in cats, monkeys, and cattle.
Rhabdoviridae	Enveloped single-strand RNA viruses with double-helical nucleocapsid inside a bullet-shaped shell. Replicates in the cytoplasm and buds from the plasma membrane. Genera *Lyssavirus*, rabies and related viruses with wide distribution in nature, including insects and plants; *Vesiculovirus*, vesicular stomatitis, related arboviruses, and some viruses of fish; and *Sigmavirus*, found in *Drosophila*.
Togaviridae	Spherical, enveloped, single-strand RNA viruses with icosahedral nucleocapsids that replicate in the cytoplasm. *Alphavirus* (Group A arboviruses, all mosquito-borne) and *Rubivirus* (rubella) mature by budding from the plasma membrane, while *Pestivirus* (found in cattle, pigs, horses) and *Flavivirus* (Group B arboviruses, mosquito- and tick-borne) bud from intracytoplasmic membranes. Purified RNA of this family is infectious.

REFERENCES

Armelagos, George J., and John R. Dewey. 1978. "Evolutionary Response to Human Infectious Diseases." In *Health and the Human Condition: Perspectives on Medical*

Anthropology, Michael H. Logan and Edward E. Hunt, Jr., eds., pp. 101–7. Belmont, Calif.: Wadsworth.

Armelagos, George J., and Alan McArdle. 1975. "Population, Disease, and Evolution." In *Population Studies in Archaeology and Biological Anthropology: A Symposium*, Alan C. Swedlund, ed. Memoirs of the Society for American Archaeology, No. 30 (American Antiquity 40, No. 2, Part 2):1–10.

Ashburn, P. M. 1947. *The Ranks of Death: A Medical History of the Conquest of America*, Frank D. Ashburn, ed. New York: Coward-McCann.

Benenson, Abram S., ed. 1985. *Control of Communicable Diseases in Man*. Washington, D.C.: American Public Health Association.

Beran, George W. 1981. *Viral Zoonoses*, vols. 1 and 2. In *Handbook Series in Zoonoses*, James H. Steele, editor-in-chief. Boca Raton, Fla.: Chemical Rubber Company Press.

Bisseru, B. 1967. *Diseases of Man Acquired from His Pets*. Philadelphia: J. B. Lippincott.

Black, Francis L. 1966. "Measle Endemicity in Insular Populations." *Journal of Theoretical Biology* 11:207–11.

Clavel, François, Kamal Mansinho, Sophie Chamaret, Denise Guetard, Veronique Favier, Jaime Nina, Marie-Odette Santos-Ferreira, Jose-Luis Champalimaud, and Luc Montagnier. 1987. "Human Immunodeficiency Virus Type 2 Infection Associated with AIDS in West Africa." *New England Journal of Medicine* 316:1180–85.

Dobyns, Henry F. 1966. "Estimating Aboriginal American Population, I: An Appraisal of Techniques with a New Hemispheric Estimate." *Current Anthropology* 7:395–416.

Fenner, Frank, Brian R. McAuslan, C. A. Mims, Joel Sambrook, and David O. White. 1974. *The Biology of Animal Viruses*, 2nd ed. New York: Academic Press.

Fiennes, Richard. 1964. *Man, Nature, and Disease*. London: Weidenfeld and Nicolson.

———. 1967. *Zoonoses of Primates: The Epidemiology and Ecology of Simian Diseases in Relation to Man*. Ithaca, N.Y.: Cornell University Press.

Fukasawa, Masashi, Tomiyuki Miura, Akira Hasegawa, Shigeru Morikawa, Hajime Tsujimoto, Keizaburo Miki, Takashi Kitamura, and Masanori Hayami. 1988. *Nature* 333:457–61.

Gade, Daniel W. 1969. "The Llama, Alpaca, and Vicuña: Fact vs. Fiction." *Journal of Geography* 68:339–43.

Gilmore, Raymond M. 1950. "Fauna and Ethnozoology of South America." *Handbook of South American Indians*, vol. 6, 345–464. Bureau of American Ethnology Bulletin 143. Washington, D.C.: American Ethnological Society.

Guerra, Francisco. 1987. "Cause of Death of the American Indians." *Nature* 326:449–50.

Hirsch, Vanessa M. 1990. "Origins of Human Immuno Deficiency Virus type 2 in Sootey Mangabeyes." Paper presented to the 1990 meeting of the Association for the Advancement of Science, New Orleans, February 16.

Hubbert, William T., William F. McCulloch, and Paul R. Schnurrenberger, eds. 1975. *Diseases Transmitted from Animals to Man*, 6th ed. Springfield, Ill.: Charles C. Thomas.

Linares, Olga F. 1976. " 'Garden Hunting' in the American Tropics." *Human Ecology* 4:331–49.

McNeill, William H. 1976. *Plagues and Peoples*. Garden City, N.Y.: Anchor Books.

Mulder, Carel. 1988. "Human AIDS Virus not from Monkeys." *Nature* 333:396.

Pavlovsky, Eugeny N. 1966. *Natural Nidality of Transmissible Diseases*. Frederick K. Plous, Jr., trans., N. D. Levine, ed. Urbana: University of Illinois Press.

Schwabe, Calvin W. 1984. *Veterinary Medicine and Human Health*, 3rd ed. Baltimore: Williams & Wilkins.

Sonigo, P., C. Barker, E. Hunter, and S. Wain-Hobson. 1986. "Nucleotide Sequence of Mason-Pfizer Monkey Virus, an Immunosuppressive D-type Retrovirus." *Cell* 45:375–86.

Thayer, R. M., M. D. Power, M. L. Bryant, M. B. Gardner, P. J. Barr, and P. A. Luciw. 1987. "Sequence Relationships of Type D Retroviruses Which Cause Simian Acquired Immunodeficiency Syndrome." *Virology* 157:317–29.

Van Blerkom, Linda M. 1985. The Evolution of Human Infectious Disease in the Eastern and Western Hemispheres. Ph.D. dissertation, University of Colorado, Boulder.

Yokoyama, Shozo, and Takashi Gojobori. 1987. "Molecular Evolution and Phylogeny of the Human AIDS Viruses LAV, HTLV-III, and ARV." *Journal of Molecular Evolution* 24:330–36.

Yokoyama, Shozo, Etsuko N. Moriyama, and Takashi Gojobori. 1987. "Molecular Phylogeny of the Human Immunodeficiency and Related Retroviruses." *Proceedings of the Japanese Academy of Science*, Ser. B, 63:147–50.

Zinsser, Hans. 1934. *Rats, Lice, and History*. Boston: Little, Brown.

11

NATURALLY OCCURRING DIETARY ANTIBIOTICS AND HUMAN HEALTH

MARGARET KEITH AND GEORGE J. ARMELAGOS

The widespread prescription of antibiotic drugs in the 1950s was expected to revolutionize Western medicine. The physician would no longer be servant to nature, but would become its master (Marti-Ibanez 1958:20). The term "magic bullet" was employed to describe the *specific* nature of microorganisms causing antibiosis; i.e., diseased cells were targeted for destruction by an antagonistic, but closely related, substance, whereas—ideally—healthy cells were left untouched. It was anticipated that these wonder drugs would cure all diseases: bacterial, fungal, and viral. Use of antibiotics in animal feeds would eradicate animal disease and close the gap between poor and wealthy nations.

That the expectations of the "antibiotic era" in Western medicine will never be realized is now apparent. Although many disease patterns were disrupted, the evolution of resistant strains of microorganisms was unforeseen. Researchers are now suggesting that overprescription of antibiotics itself has facilitated the development of resistance to antibiotics.

Failure to obtain the anticipated results was due to a misunderstanding of the nature of human–biotic relationships and to underestimation of exposure to antibiotics in supposedly virgin populations. Evidence for antibiotic resistance in virgin populations in Borneo (Davis and Anandan 1970), the Solomon Islands (Gardner et al. 1969), and other human and animal communities (Maré 1968) suggests the existence of naturally occurring antibiotics. Large-scale screening of plant material to determine antibiotic activity was undertaken as early in the "antibiotic era" as 1943 (Osborn), at which time 2300 species of plants were tested against pathogenic organisms, and 63 genera showed inhibitory action. It was subsequently pointed out that inhibitory activity was often accompanied by toxicity to humans and that plant material was therefore not as therapeutically valuable as substances of "microbial origin" (Nickell 1959:281—82); nevertheless, the rush was on to find naturally occurring substances that could be patented as human medicine. After systematic survey of the Pteridophytes (ferns and fern allies), it was reported that 64 percent of the sample examined had antibiotic activity (Banerjee and Sen 1980). Of these, 41 percent were inhibitory to Gram-positive bacteria alone, in agreement with the folk-medicine usage of ferns for staphylococcal and streptococcal infections (ibid.:292). In a study of Aztec medicinal plants, deMontellano (1975) found that 16 of the 25 plants analyzed were empirically effective (i.e., when evaluated within the Aztec medical paradigm). Another 4 plants "may possibly have been active" (p. 220)—an 80-percent concordance with the goals of the therapeutic measures.

Ivan Polunin (1976) cautions against the "moldy-bread-on-wounds-means-they-had-antibiotics" school, and claims that any medical practice must be judged within its own system. That is, its validity depends upon its ability to produce the results claimed within the context of the system itself. Frederick Dunn, on the other hand, points out that the system of primitive herbalists has evolved through centuries of trial and error, not differing qualitatively from the experimental procedures of modern chemotherapeutics (1976). Further, Laughlin states that the remarkable success of our species was due at least in part to local solutions of medical problems (Laughlin 1963:116–140). We do not here attempt to defend the empirical efficacy of any system. We are concerned with the effects of exposure to naturally occurring antibiotics, whether intentional or not. This approach gives rise to a different set of questions for anthropological populations.

What antibiotics exist in the natural environment of a given population? What cultural factors either buffer or enhance exposure? And what effect would exposure have on health and disease patterns, either short or long term?

Before concerning ourselves with cultural practices affecting exposure, a brief discussion of the ecological requirements of antibiotic-producing microorganisms themselves is in order.

ANTIBIOTICS

Antibiotics in the broadest sense of the term are substances that inhibit life processes. Their action ranges from disruptive (bacteriostatic) to fatal (bacteriocidal); effective dosage varies according to the source of the antibiotic and to the competing microorganism. They are, in fact, toxins—the antibiotic substance is produced to exclude competing species from a food source. The *toxicity* of a given substance, however, is a function of its capacity to produce a reaction when tested by itself. The anthropologist must be concerned with the *hazard* of the given toxic substance, i.e., its ability to produce a reaction under the conditions of exposure.

Antibiotics are generally classified according to the type of organism producing them, since the chemical structure is often unknown (Korzybski et al. 1967:8). More than one-half of all known antibiotics are derived from the Actinomycetes (soil microorganisms). This group includes streptomycin, the tetracyclines, erythromycin, and chlormycetin, the most active and, generally, the most effective of all antibiotics. They are a natural defense system against the thousands of soil microbes, each of which produces a specific toxin directed against its most likely natural competitor (ibid.:6). Approximately 100 million microbes exist in a single cubic centimeter of soil. They cause the decay of organic materials into inorganic forms, thereby performing the valuable function of removing dead bodies, garbage, and other wastes from the environment—and incidentally forming plant nutrients in the process. Antibiotics exhibiting antitumoral activity are derived from this group (ibid.:2).

Other sources of antibiotics include bacteria, *Fungi imperfecti*, basidiomycetes, algae, lichens, and higher plants and animals (ibid.:1). Penicillin is produced by the *Fungi imperfecti* group and is the least toxic to humans of the commercially utilized drugs. It does of course produce an allergic response in susceptible individuals.

Animal sources include maggots, insects, molluscs, blood, pigs' hooves, slime of snails, etc. (Korzybski et al. 1967:1535—46). Whether or not the active substance is then available to humans is dependent upon dietary restrictions, mode of preparation, etc.

The locus of action of antibiotics is the basis for its specificity of action and is essential to therapeutic use for humans (Woodruff 1980:1227). Antibiotics act by inhibition of cell-wall synthesis or protein synthesis, by disruption of bacterial membranes of nucleic acid polymers, or by enzymatic action (ibid.). Action on bacterial cells rather than mammalian cells is critical to its therapeutic value for human use.

Toxicity may also be due to interference with normal symbiotic relationships with human microflora, e.g., disruption of intestinal microorganisms, which are necessary for synthesis of vitamins. Extended exposure may result in deficiencies; broad-spectrum antibiotics such as tetracycline are particularly likely to cause such disruptions.

ECOLOGICAL AND METHODOLOGICAL CONSIDERATIONS

The study of Banerjee and Sen (1980) raises a number of areas of concern for investigators of archeological populations. They note that there is "considerable variation in the distribution of antibiotic substances within the plant" (p. 293); one must test the specified plant part to make definitive statements as to its efficacy. Seasonal variations in antibiotic activity were noted (p. 294), and ecological conditions were shown to modify activity; e.g., the *epiphytic* habit of the *Drynaria quercifolia* is responsible for its antibiotic activity. *D. quercifolia* growing on *Cocos nucifera* exhibit no activity, whereas *D. quercifolia* growing on *Strychnos nux-vomica* is active against tuberculosis, as claimed in the folk medicine of the region. State of maturity, genetic changes, and strains of test microorganisms contribute to test results. Discrepancy between laboratory results and the claims of folk medicine may even be due to the incorrect identification of plants by the herbalist (p. 296). Misidentification may have been a problem when a population migrated to a similar, but not identical, econiche.

In testing for antibiotic activity, the extracting solvent and dilution itself will affect results. For example, Bhakuni et al. (1969, 1971) and Dhawan et al. (1977) did not find any activity in the 42 species of ferns examined by them, in contrast to the 64 percent exhibiting antimicrobial properties when examined by Banerjee and Sen (1980). They claim that the discrepancy is because previous studies used only one solvent and at high dilution. The question remains: do the proper conditions for the antibiotic substance exist in a natural state? If extractable in an aqueous solution, for example, one might expect the method of preparation of foodstuffs or medicinal herbs to be boiling.

CULTURAL FACTORS INFLUENCING EXPOSURE TO AND EFFECTS OF ANTIBIOTICS

The ubiquitous nature of antibiotics might lead one to suspect that humans are constantly subjected to pharmacologically active substances; such is not the case. Many cultural factors influence both the growth of antibiotics and subsequent exposure to them.

The shift from a hunting-gathering mode of subsistence to agricultural, with the concomitant emphasis on food storage, greatly increased the possibilities for growth of antibiotic substances in dietary items. Both length and method of food storage affect the microclimates that affect the selective advantage of any given microorganism over another. Tetracyclines require a warm, dry, alkaline environment (Bassett et al. 1980). The introduction of metal bins for storage of coffee facilitates storage, but the resultant buildup of moisture increases the possibility of contamination by *Cladosporium* or *Aspergillius* (Hiscocks 1965:17). Relative humidity may also cause insect infestation, and the material of the storage bin itself may interact with microorganisms present (Majumder et al. 1965:30–32).

Food processing may either free a substance for absorption in the human gut or destroy it. Dietary antibiotics may also be antagonistic to one another.

Indeed, food items themselves may curtail action of an antibiotic, e.g., the well-known tetra-cycline-binding properties of dairy products effectively prevent absorption of tetra-cycline from the intestinal tract.

Pratt and Dufrenoy (1953) warn that "with the exception of the alkaloids, quinine and emetine, many natural compounds are not selective and are therefore too toxic for systemic use, since effective dosage would be expressed in milligrams rather than micrograms per ml." (p. 358). They suggest that the potential value of such substances would be in antifungal activity, particularly in the control of topical microflora (ibid.).

In the case of plant material it is necessary to know what parts are utilized. The alkaloid Tomatin is extractable from the leaves of certain varieties of tomato plants (ibid.). Tomatin is an active bacteriocide, but leaves are not generally consumed. One might then investigate their use as a topical antibiotic.

An analytical approach could then be applied to anecdotal evidence for antibiotic use in anthropological populations. Perhaps the radish-onions-garlic diet of workers in Cheops's pyramid was a key factor in preventing infectious disease. Perhaps heparin, an antimicrobial agent in liver tissue (Rosett and Hodges 1980:30), did affect the health of recipients of human gladiator liver (Majno 1975:401–2). Table 11.1 lists a variety of items commonly proposed as having antibiotic properties, along with the substances responsible for antibiotic activity.

That antibiotics were available to an archeological population and did influence health and disease patterns there is evidenced by tetracycline labeling in the skeletons of Sudanese Nubians, an agricultural population that cultivated the flood plains of the Nile A.D. 350–550 (Bassett et al. 1980). It had been stated in a previous study that the infectious disease rate of this group was notably low (Armelagos 1969).

THE NUBIAN EXAMPLE

When tetracycline enters the human digestive tract, it is bound by bivalent and trivalent metals (e.g., calcium, phosphorus) and absorbed as a salt onto those surfaces of bone that are actively mineralizing at the time of exposure. The compound so deposited then fluoresces indefinitely in the bone in discrete areas, including osteons, osteocyte lacunae, Volkmann's canals, and circumferential lamellae on the subperiosteal and endosteal surfaces. These represent areas of both primary and secondary mineralization; mature osteons remain unaffected. The fluorophors are then visible at 500 mm under a fluorescence microscope.

That the tetracycline in the Nubian sample was incorporated in vivo, and not as a postmortem mold infestation, is shown by several factors. First, the fluorescence occurs on discrete surfaces, corresponding exactly to those of clinically labeled bone, and not as the diffuse fluorescence resulting from

Table 11.1

Naturally Occurring Antibiotics Cited in Ethnopharmacopoeias and Tested for Biological Activity

Antibiotic	Biological Source	Entities Principally Active Against
Allicin*	Garlic, onion	Bacteria
Anacardiac acid	Cashew	
Anemonin (dimer of protoanemonin)	Pasque flower	Bacteria; fungi; yeast
Asiatic acid	Asiatic pennywort	Mycobacterium leprae
Asiatioside	Asiatic pennywort	Mycobacterium leprae
Benzoic acid	Urogenital gland of beaver	Bacteria
Benzoyl∞	Nasturtium	Staphylococci
Berberine	Barberry	Bacteria; fungi
Blood	Whole blood of dog (probably leukocytes that are active)	Brucella suis and some other bacteria
	Processed blood of human, cattle, or sheep	Bacteria
Cassic acid (see Rhein)		
Castoreum	Urogenital gland of beaver	Bacteria
Centellic acid	Asiatic pennywort	Mycobacterium leprae
Centelloside	Asiatic pennywort	Mycobacterium leprae
Centioc acid	Asiatic pennywort	Mycobacterium leprae
Cepnaranthine	Stephania cepharantha	Mycobacterium tuberculosois var. hominis and other bacteria
Cheiroline	Wallflower	Bacteria; fungi
Chlorophorin	Iroko fustictree	Bacteria
Coumarin (see Dicoumarin)		
Crepin	Hawksbeard	Bacteria
Curcumin	Turmeric	Bacteria; Trichophyton gypseum
Datiscetin	Datisca cannabina	Bacteria; Plasmodium sp.
Defensoate*	Garlic	Bacteria
Dicoumarin	Tonka bean, yellow sweet clover, common red clover	Bacteria
Dicoumarol (see Dicoumarin)		
Eriodin	Yerba santa	Bacteria
Erythrin	Red blood cells	Bacteria
Galangine∆	Honey	Bacteria
Gastric factor	Gastric contents of human, dog, rat, or mouse	Bacteria
Helicidin	Helix spp. (land snails)	Hemophilus pertussis
Heparin§	Liver	Bacteria; fungi
Humulon	Hop	Bacteria

224

Table 11.1 *(Continued)*

Antibiotic	Biological Source	Entities Principally Active Against
Juglone	Species of walnut	Bacteria
Kojic acid **	Rice mold	Bacteria
Lactenin	Milk	Lactobacilli and other bacteria
Lupulon	Hop	Bacteria
Lycopersicin	Currant tomato	Bacteria; fungi
Lysozyme	Egg albumen	Bacteria
Mammalian tissue factors	Extracts of various organs, such as cecum of rabbit and dog; thymus of dog, pig, cattle; pancreas of cattle and pig	Anthrax organism and other bacteria
Patasorbic acid	European mountain ash	Micrococcus phyogenes var. aureus; Trypanosoma equiperdum
Phenols	Urogenital gland of beaver	Bacteria
Phloretin	Apple	Bacteria
Pinosylvine	Scotch pine	Bacteria; fungi
Podophyllin	Common May apple	Fungi
Protoanemonin	Pasque flower	Bacteria; fungi; yeasts
Pterygospermin	Horseradish tree	Bacteria
Puchiin	Chinese water chestnut	Bacteria
Purothionin	Wheat flour	Bacteria; yeasts
Quercitin	Various higher plants	Bacteria
Quinine	Cinchona	Plasmodium vivax; P. falciparum
Raphanin*∞	Radish	Bacteria
Rhein	Senna, rhubarb	Bacteria
Rutin (rhamnoglycoside of quercitrin)	Buckwheat	Bacteria
Simaroubidin	Orinoco simaruba	Endamoeba histolytica
Solanine	Nightshade, potato, Jerusalem cherry	Fungi; yeasts
Spleen factor	Human beings and cattle	Streptococci
Tomatin (pure form of tomatine)	Currant tomato	Bacteria; fungi
Tomatine (formerly called Lycopersicin)	Currant tomato	Bacteria; fungi
Trilobin	Japanese snailseed	Mycobacterium tuberculosis var. hominis
Umbellatine	Himalayan barberry; Sikkim barberry	Paramecium sp.; Leishmania tropica
Urine, normal, fresh	Human beings	Bacteria

Source: Platt and Dufrenoy (1953), except as otherwise indicated by footnotes.

*   Korzybski et al. (1967).   §   Rosett and Hodges (1980).

∞   Böttcher (1964).   **   Kinosita and Shikata (1965).

Δ   Majno (1975).

mold infestation. Second, osteons were identified that were the result of interrupted dosage or interrupted growth, i.e., an unlabeled area is visible between labeled lamellae. Third, "feathered"—incompletely mineralized—osteons were identified. This phenomenon is the result of either an in-vivo diffusion barrier (Frost 1961) or osteocytic osteolysis (Hoshino and Nomura 1969), also an in-vivo process.

The Source of Tetracycline

Wheat, barley, and millet were staples of the Nubian diet, and beer and bread comprised 70 percent of their caloric intake, as it does today. It is interesting to note that Egyptian medical papyri have different names for those grains stored for making bread and those grains stored for making beer. Since the source of the grains was the same, the difference was either in the method of storage, length of storage, or both. We know that grains were stored in mud bins and clay pots (Adams 1977).

The source of contamination of the grains was the Nubian soil itself; streptomycetes (produced by actinomyces) comprise 60–70 percent of Nubian soil microorganisms (Waksman 1967). These are the moldlike bacteria from which nonsynthetic tetracyclines are derived. Streptomycetes have a selective advantage over other soil bacteria in a hot, very dry, alkaline environment—just the conditions that obtain inside the storage bins and pots. By culturing modern grains on Nubian soils under various experimental conditions, streptomycetes were isolated at 55°C., dry heat (Bassett et al. 1980); streptomycetes are sources of naturally occurring tetracyclines. Some cultures exhibited obvious antibiotic behavior.

Antibiotic activity would have been advantageous to the brewing process, since tetracycline kills off competing bacteria but allows fermentation by yeast. Modern German breweries take advantage of this fact by introducing tetracycline-impregnated filters into the brewing process. It is likely that over time the Nubians realized the adaptive nature of contaminated grain to the beer-making process, if not also to its effect on their health and disease parameters.

Removal of grain from storage on a frequent basis would also have contributed to the maintenance of the streptomycetes in an immature state; i.e., sporation would have been disrupted, and the antibiotic-producing phase would have been maintained by "shear" action.

The Effect of Antibiotic Exposure on the Nubian Population

The X group—that is, the population during the period of Sudanese Nubian development that occurred after the breakup of the Meroitic Kingdom and before the Christian unification, A.D. 350–550—is characterized by a high frequency of parasitic infestation, specifically head lice, the vector for typhus and relapsing fever (Armelagos 1969). Dietary iron deficiency is also well documented (Armelagos 1968; Carlson et al. 1974). One might expect then to find "normal" to high incidence of infection lesions, which are generally a correlate of parasitic and nutritional stressors. However, only about 8.5 percent of the X group exhibits infectious lesions (Armelagos 1968). Periodic ingestion of therapeutic levels of tetracycline could have affected infectious disease processes, as tetracycline is a broad-spectrum antibiotic effective against Gram-negative and Gram-positive Rickettsiae, spirochetes, bacteria, and some viruses.

Although periodic ingestion of small amounts of tetracycline would have had the most beneficial effect on infectious disease vectors, extended exposure of any given population to antibiotics may ultimately have deleterious effects. Modern studies have shown that side effects of tetracycline therapy include temporary inhibition of bone growth in infants, vitamin B depletion (Kucers and Bennett 1975), interference with phagocytic activity (ibid.), inhibition of spermatogenesis (Timmermans 1974), and interference with protein synthesis (Kucers and Bennett 1975; Jackson 1963).

Recent studies have also shown that extended exposure to an antibiotic results in the evolution of resistance factors (R factors), which negate the effects of the antibiotic. The occurrence of R factors in antibiotically virgin populations has been demonstrated (Davis and Anandan 1970; Gardner et al. 1969). Exposures to naturally occurring antibiotics are most likely responsible.

Periodic exposure to this broad-spectrum antibiotic may explain the observed low infectious disease rate in this population, which was subjected to a number of stressors usually resulting in a high rate of infectious disease. Continued exposure may have resulted in the evolution of R factors.

The Nubian study is but one possible approach to the problem of exposure to natural antibiotics. The investigator looking at disease patterns in anthropological populations must be aware of the environmental and cultural factors affecting exposure, as well as effects on demographic variables.

ACKNOWLEDGMENTS

The analysis of tetracycline in the skeletal series was partially funded by the University of Massachusetts Biomedical Research Support Grant RR07048. We would like to acknowledge the help of Mary Jane Saunders, Guy Marrocco, Peter Hepler, and Otto Stein.

REFERENCES

Adams, William Y. 1977 *Nubia*. Princeton: Princeton Univ. Press.
Armelagos, George J. 1968. "Paleopathology of Three Archeological Populations from Sudanese Nubia." Ph.D. diss., University of Colorado.

————. 1969. "Disease in Ancient Nubia." *Science*, 163:255–59.

Banerjee, R.D., and S.P. Sen. 1980. "Antibiotic Activity of Pteridophytes." *Economic Botany*, 34(3):284–98.

Bassett, E.J., M.S. Keith, G.J. Armelagos, D.L. Martin, and A.R. Villanueva. 1980. "Tetracycline-Labeled Human Bone from Ancient Sudanese Nubia (A.D. 350)." *Science*, 209:1532–34.

Bhakuni, D.S., M.I. Dhar, M.M. Dhar, F.N. Dhawan, and B.N. Mehrotra. 1969. "Screening of Indian Plants for Biological Activity. Part II." *Indian Journal of Experimental Biology*, 7:250.

————, M.I. Dhar, M.M. Dhar, F.N. Dhawan, B.N. Mehrotra, B. Gupta, and R.C. Srimal. 1971. "Screening of Indian Plants for Biological Activity. Part III." *Indian Journal of Experimental Biology*, 9:91.

Böttcher, Helmut. 1964. *Wonder Drugs: A History of Antibiotics*. Philadelphia: J.B. Lippincott.

Carlson, D.S., G.J. Armelagos, and D.P. Van Gerven. 1974. "Factors Influencing the Etiology of Cribra Orbitalia in Prehistoric Nubia." *Journal of Human Evolution*, 3:405–10.

Davis, C.E., and J. Anandan. 1970. "The Evolution of R Factor." *New England Journal of Medicine*, 282:117.

deMontellano, Bernard O. 1975. "Empirical Aztec Medicine." *Science*, 188:215.

Dhawan, B.N., G.K. Patnaik, R.P. Rastogi, K.K. Singh, and J.S. Tandon. 1977. "Screening of Indian Plants for Biological Activity. Part IV." *Indian Journal of Experimental Biology*, 15:208.

Dunn, Frederick. 1976. "Traditional Asian Medicine and Cosmopolitan Medicine as Adaptive Systems." C. Leslie, ed., *Asian Medical Systems: A Comparative Study*. Berkeley: Univ. of California Press.

Frost, H.M. 1961. "Feathering." *Henry Ford Hospital Medical Bulletin*, 9:103–14.

Gardner, P., D. Smith, H. Beer, and R.C. Moellering. 1969. "Recovery of Resistance (R) Factors from a Drug-Free Community." *Lancet*, 2:774.

Hiscocks, E.S. 1965. "The Importance of Molds in the Deterioration of Tropical Foods and Feedstuff." G.N. Wogan, ed., *Mycotoxins in Foodstuffs*. Cambridge: MIT Press.

Hoshino, T., and T. Nomura. 1969. "Feathering and Osteocytic Osteolysis." *Clinical Orthopedics*, 65:110.

Jackson, F.L. 1963. "Mode of Action of Tetracyclines." R.J. Schnitzer and I. Hawking, eds., *Experimental Chemotherapy*, vol. 3. New York: Academic Press, 103–17.

Kinosita, R., and T. Shikata. 1965. "On Toxic Moldy Rice." G.N. Wogan, ed., *Mycotoxins in Foodstuffs*. Cambridge: MIT Press.

Korzybski, T., Z. Kowszuk-Gindifer, and W. Kurylowicz. 1967. *Antibiotics: Origin, Nature and Properties*, vols. 1 and 2. Oxford: Pergamon Press.

Kucers, A., and N.M. Bennett. 1975. *The Use of Antibiotics: A Comprehensive Review with Clinical Emphasis*. London: William Heinemann Medical Books.

Laughlin, W. 1963. "Primitive Theory of Medicine: Empirical Knowledge." I. Gladston, ed., *Man's Image in Medicine and Anthropology*. New York: International Universities Press.

Majno, Guido. 1975. *The Healing Hand: Man and Wound in the Ancient World*. Cambridge, Mass.: Harvard Univ. Press.

Majumder, S.K., K.S. Narasimhau, and H.A.B. Parpia. 1965. "Microecological Factors of Microbial Spoilage and the Occurrence of Mycotoxins on Stored Grains." G.N. Wogan, ed., *Mycotoxins in Foodstuffs*. Cambridge: MIT Press, 27–47.

Maré, I.J. 1968. "Incidence of R Factors among Gram Negative Bacteria in Drug-Free Human and Animal Communities." *Nature*, 220:1046.

Marti-Ibanez, Felix. 1958. *Men, Molds and History*. New York: M.D. Pubs.

Nickell, Louis G. 1959. "Antimicrobial Activity of Vascular Plants." *Economic Botany*, 13:281.

Osborn, E.M. 1943. "On the Occurrence of Antibacterial Substance in Green Plants." *British Journal of Experimental Pathology*, 24(6):227.

Polunin, Ivan. 1976. "Disease, Morbidity and Mortality in China, India and the Arab World." Charles Leslie, ed., *Asian Medical Systems*. Berkeley: Univ. of California Press.

Pratt, Robertson, and Jean Dufrenoy. 1953. *Antibiotics*, 2d ed. Philadelphia: J.B. Lippincott.

Rosett, W., and G.R. Hodges. 1980. "Antimicrobial Activity of Leparin in Liver and Lung Tissue." *Journal of Clinical Microbiology*, 11(1):30.

Timmermans, L. 1974. "Influence of Antibiotics on Spermatogenesis." *Journal of Urology*, 112:348–49.

Waksman, S.A. 1967. *The Actinomycetes: A Summary of Current Knowledge*. New York: Ronald.

Woodruff, H. Boyd. 1980. "Natural Products from Microorganisms." *Science*, 208:1225.

12

Recasting Malaria, Medicine, and Meals: A Perspective on Disease Adaptation

NINA L. ETKIN AND PAUL J. ROSS

Once relegated to studies of the exotic, indigenous medicine has come to command a prominent and finally "legitimated" position in an anthropological discourse that seeks to comprehend from multi-cultural and cross-cultural perspectives how people conceptualize and manipulate health and illness. Intellectually, such inquiry is most cogently cast in the theoretical and conceptual idioms of human ecology and explores not only the cultural construction of therapeutics and other health-seeking behaviors but also their physiological outcomes. These are investigations that best embody the bio-behavioral perspective of medical anthropological inquiry (Etkin 1986a, 1986b, 1988, 1990; Franquemont et al. 1990; Johns 1990; Johns and Keen 1986; Macfoy and Cline 1990; Posey 1984), which is only intimated in other studies of ethnomedicine and diet. In a more narrow framework, phytochemists and pharmacologists are optimistic that study of indigenous medicines will expand the biomedical pharmacopoeia and contribute to basic scientific inquiry in therapeutics (e.g., Barton and Ollis 1986; Collins et al. 1990; Cox et al. 1989; Lydon and Duke 1989; Penso 1980; Phillipson and Anderson 1989). Compelled by more applied considerations, ministries of health and national governments have formalized policies that champion indigenous medicine, thereby serving as vehicles for promoting nationalism through reaffirmation of traditional institutions. Further, these polities emphasize that indigenous modalities constitute the principal form of primary health care for the majority of people in developing countries, and need to be assessed and appreciated in that regard as well (Akerele 1987; Bastien 1987; Donahue 1986; Oswald 1983). And in global schemes to promote "Health for all by the Year 2000," the World Health Organization and international donor agencies have made explicit recommendations to study indigenous medicines with a view toward both systematic investigations of efficacy and risk, and initiatives for the incorporation of indigenous medicines and healers into biomedically oriented care services (Good 1988; Green 1988; Last 1990; Last and Chavunduka 1986; Penso 1977; Pillsbury 1982; WHO 1978).

This chapter resonates all those concerns through a revised version of our contribution to the first edition of this volume. We present original data on Hausa medicine and diet and interpret those through a unique model of disease adaptation. For this updated version, we review findings from our field research on plants used in both diet and medicine during 1975–1976 and the laboratory investigations for antimalarial activity that followed. We also interpret preliminarily findings from a second field study during 1987–1988. Those observations will be elaborated elsewhere; the point here is to present sufficient detail for comparative purposes, to suggest the potentially temporal applicability of our model, and to underscore the dynamic nature of the interrelationships among medicines, foods, and illness.

Our model of disease adaptation is compiled from the constructs of ecological theory and is an interpretative framework onto which we project a constellation of data that draw on extensive ethnographic and environmental observations about plants used in the treatment of all and any symptoms of a particular disease—in this case, malaria; documentation of the multicontextual uses of those plants, especially in regular utilization of substantial volumes, such as in diet; and laboratory investigations and pharmacological assessments of those plants to evaluate efficacy in the prevention and/or treatment of the illness in question. The operationalization of those variables and specific methodology are described below.

STUDY SITE AND DATA COLLECTION

Our research was conducted among an agricultural Hausa-Fulani community fifty kilometers southeast of Kano in northern Nigeria. Hurumi (a pseudonym) comprises an administrative area of approximately four thousand residents, with a population of four hundred in its nucleated core. Its economy centers on intensive nonmechanized agriculture supplemented by livestock raising and trade in locally produced and exogenous commodities. The village, while less remote today than during our initial investigation, remains without a paved road and has neither electricity nor piped water.[1]

Data on Hausa medicine, diet, and health were collected first in the course of a twenty-two-month investigation during 1975–1976, a time when Hurumi residents relied almost exclusively on an extensive herbal pharmacopoeia for all manner of therapeutic and preventive measures. Plant utilization was mediated by a dynamic syncretism of four overlapping domains of knowledge that shape Hausa understandings of their physical and spiritual environment:

1. For conditions in which naturalistic etiology is invoked, plants are manipulated to effect balance along such tangible axes as cold-hot, dry-wet, sweet-salty, bitter-sweet, and permutations thereof.
2. Traditional Islamic medicines include plants, but more commonly take the form of invocations of Allah through prayer, recitation and writing of Koranic passages, and the fabrication of amulets and other propitiatory media.
3. Medicines derive as well from Bori, a religion that antecedes Islam and centers on the intercessions of spirits in human affairs.
4. Preventions and therapies also take the form of interventions directed at the malevolent actions of witches and the machinations of sorcery.

Information was collected regarding Hausa understandings of disease etiology and nosology in order to describe the most commonly perceived symptoms and their appropriate treatments. Extensive interviews were conducted with individuals who were identified by others, and who perceived themselves, as most conversant in matters related to health. Five women and nine men constituted a core of principal respondents and included among them a woman whose knowledge of plant medicines, and especially spirit medicines, earned her districtwide recognition as chief herbalist. Other respondents represented rather more narrow foci of medically related knowledge: a barber-surgeon, three midwives, and authorities in such specific areas as venereal diseases, jaundice, weaning medicines, and malfeasance among co-wives. Other interviews and observations throughout the village revealed that most adults are familiar with at least several medicines for a variety of common disorders, including gastrointestinal complaints, fevers, and dermatoses.

Interviews were loosely structured around a catalog of 637 plants, for each of which individuals described physical attributes, availability, and medicinal and other uses; and a catalog of 808 diseases, symptoms, and related terms for which respondents described commonly used medicines, including source, preparation, additional constituents of composite medicines, approximate dose and schedule of administration, and alternatives for circumstances in which that medicine is not available or does not produce desired results. Our data are largely concordant with observations in other parts of Hausaland; differences are of a magnitude one would expect given temporal and geographic distance, compounded by the varying methodologies of other reporters—for example, Adam et al. (1972), Busson et al. (1965), Dalziel (1937), Oliver (1986); Prietze (1913–1914), Stock (1980), Wall (1988).

A dietary survey of eight households was conducted to understand sources, distribution, and preparation of foods and to document consumption levels. This was implemented for twenty-four-hour periods, randomly selected twice per week per household, for forty-eight consecutive weeks to coincide with the end of one harvest and the beginning of the next, these being the most meaningful delineators of the annual agricultural cycle. Precise weight measures of unprocessed foods were augmented by extensive interviews and observations. The participating households contained a mean of forty-six residents and represented the full range of economic variation, taking into account all adult men and women for each unit. For each of the three daily meals, all foods were weighed prior to cooking and other preparation. Independent and repeated analyses of all food types and preparations consumed by the study population included weight and volume measures for all ingredients, tabulated sequentially through all stages of preparation to final cooked (or otherwise modified), consumable form. This permitted extrapolation from the household unprocessed weight measures to quantified approximations of nutrient values (of calories, protein, etc.). All foods, including snacks, consumed by adults and obtained from extrahousehold sources—such as market or gift—were recorded in the same way, using collateral data such as cost per unit of prepared food, fluctuating market prices, and so on.[2] A more detailed exposition of methods and results of the dietary survey will be presented elsewhere. For purposes of this chapter, we review only yearly fluctuations in relative quantities of different food types, particularly with reference to grain-based foods and those characterized more by inclusion of herbaceous plants and leaves ("vegetables").

In the course of the yearlong follow-up study in the same village during 1987–1988, we used a more rigorous methodology (Etkin et al. 1990) in order to extend the depth of our inquiry to understand better the antecedents and sequelae of plant use by Hausa and to collect additional antimalarial plants for further laboratory investigation. Again a dietary survey helped us to understand the multicontextual use of plants. Building on our initial dietary investigation, we extended our survey for the more recent period using the methodology outlined above: the same eight households (fifty-four residents) were monitored for a full forty-eight-week cycle covering the same period of time as the first dietary study. Our investigation of plant use was expanded to include a wider range of respondents and took the form of villagewide structured surveys that were systematically and regularly administered.[3] These were based on plant inventories that had been constructed from our earlier investigations and later amended as warranted. These data were further supplemented by field and market surveys to assess plant availability. The medical investigation was further elaborated by a monthly village health survey and a two-month investigation among patients and staff at the recently opened biomedical facility located eight kilometers from Hurumi.

In combination, this research established bases from which we could address questions concerning the direction and magnitude of changes that had occurred in local medicine and diet. The most conspicuous shifts in therapeutic strategies were related to increased availability of pharmaceuticals and other forms of biomedicine, although Hausa plants still figured prominently among the commonly used medicines (Etkin et al. 1990). The range of items that contribute to diet had expanded over the twelve-year period as a result of increased interregional and international communication and trade. In both medicine and diet more subtle changes were suggested by shifting environmental circumstances that affected the availability of medicinal and food plants.

During both studies voucher specimens were collected for as many plants as possible; they have been taxonomically identified by botanists at the Missouri Botanical Garden in St. Louis, Kew Royal Botanic Garden in London, and Ahmadu Bello University Herbarium in Zaria, Nigeria. The full catalog is now part of the permanent African reference collection of the Missouri Botanical Garden Herbarium. Plants designated for phytochemical and pharmacological investigation were collected in bulk, air-dried in the field, and sent to our laboratory in the United States.

HOW DOES ONE SELECT PLANTS FOR STUDY?

Conventionally, investigations of indigenous medicines have evaluated therapeutic efficacy on the basis of treatment for simple, discrete symptoms. Antimicrobial activity, especially, has been tested in plants used in the treatment of wounds (Macfoy and Cline 1990), tooth and gum disease (Elvin-Lewis 1986; Etkin 1981), dermatoses (Palanichamy and Nagarajan 1990), and gastrointestinal disorders (Caceres et al. 1990; Etkin and Ross 1982). Antipyresis and analgesia are targets for medicines used in the treatment of fevers (Agwu and Akah 1990). Effects on platelet and phagocyte function (Hammerschmidt 1986) and systemic arterial pressure (Singh et al. 1990; Stevenson 1986) define the core interest for plants used in the treatment of cardiovascular disorders. Studies of fertility-regulating plants center on estrogenic actions (Benie et al. 1990).

By contrast, our model for empirical evaluation of plant medicines directs attention to the potential efficacy of therapies used in the treatment of disorders characterized by interrelated and superficially indiscernible symptom complexes. As we have discussed elsewhere (Etkin 1979, 1981), investigation of indigenous treatments of symptom-complex disorders such as malaria is particularly important in view of the associated high morbidity and mortality, and because it is in the prevention and treatment of those complex diseases that one confronts the most misinterpretation and tension between biomedical and indigenous treatment modalities (Counts and Counts 1989; Etkin et al. 1990; Green 1988; Pillsbury 1982).

Pharmacological investigations of indigenous antimalarials have largely considered only those plants described specifically for the treatment of the malaria symptom complex in its entirety. We are not aware of studies that, in acknowledging potential lack of concordance between biomedical and other illness categories, have directed investigations of antimalarial activity toward plants used only for one or some of the symptoms or for emically nonmedical purposes such as alimentation, hygiene, and cosmetics. (We do not count here broad-spectrum screening of plants and compounds for antimalarial activity, since those studies tend to be informed by the paradigms of botany and phytochemistry and have little interest in cultural context, and thus virtually no bearing on ethnomedicine.)

The plants that we selected for our first laboratory investigations are among the more common Hausa medicines used in the treatment of one or more components of what biomedicine understands to be the malaria symptom complex. These include the characteristic intermittent fevers, as well as more equivocal markers such as anemia, hemoglobinuria, hepatosplenomegaly, and jaundice. In this way, our analysis incorporates medicines used to treat the full range of symptoms, singly or in some combination. This forestalls the problems inherent in restrictive analyses that study only those medicines used when all symptoms appear together as "malaria"—a biomedical construct that indigenous healers do not necessarily recognize as a discrete entity. The plants most commonly used during 1975–1976 in the treatment of malaria are listed alphabetically by genus in Table 12.1. An expanded inventory now in preparation will accommodate material from the follow-up study.

LABORATORY AND PHARMACOLOGICAL STUDIES OF HAUSA PLANTS

Investigations of Antimalarial Activity—Series 1

Rationale. Our first laboratory protocols drew conceptually on indirect measures of efficacy, specifically perturbations of red blood cell oxidation-reduction (redox) equilibrium. That approach was an important departure from conventional pharmacological studies, which until that time had been largely constituent analyses for quinine-like alkaloids or for compounds that mimic the structure, and presumably the activity, of known synthetic antimalarials (Peters and Richards 1984).

The significance of redox fluctuations in the course of malaria infection has been amply demonstrated (e.g., Bhattacharya and Swarup-Mitra 1987; Docampo and Moreno 1984; Eaton et al. 1976; Etkin and Eaton 1975; Vennerstrom and Eaton 1988); recently others have included redox phenomena in their investigations of antimalarial plants (e.g., Meshnick et al. 1989; Osoba et al. 1989). The most salient point for the present discussion is that increased oxidation compromises host red cell integrity and so interferes with plasmodial metabolism that parasite maturation is impaired and continued infection of new blood cells is interrupted.

Red blood cell integrity is dependent upon suppression of chemical equi-

Table 12.1
Commonly Used Hausa Antimalarial Plant Medicines

Genus species (Family)	Hausa Name	Medicinal application for Malaria	Dietary Use	A	B	C
Abrus precatorius L. (Papilionaceae)	IDON ZAKARA	Whole plant for periodic fevers and jaundice	Whole plant edible; sweet leaves used as flavoring	+	+	+
Acacia albida Del. (Fabaceae)	GAWO	Bark for fever and Jaundice	-	-	-	-
Acacia nilotica (L) Willd ex Del (Fabaceae)	GABARUWA	Fruit pulp and pods for fever	Leaves, fruit, and seed edible; gum is occasionally chewed	+	+	+
Adansonia digitata L. (Bombacaceae)	KUKA	Leaves, fruit, seeds, and bark for fever; bark for jaundice	Fruit, seeds, leaves, young root, and bark are edible	+	+	+
Amaranthus hybridus L. (Amaranthaceae)	ALAIYAHO	Leaves for anemia	Leaves are a vegetable	+	+	+
Anogeissus leiocarpus (DC) Guill & Perr (Combretaceae)	MARKE	Leaves for jaundice; bark for fever	Infusion of bark and stems is a beverage; gum is edible	+	+	-
Azadirachta indica A. Juss (Meliaceae)	DARBEJIYA	Leaves and bark for fevers; all parts for periodic fever	Flowers are stomachic and diuretic	+	-	-
Balanites aegyptiaca (L) Del (Zygophyllaceae)	ADUWA	Root for periodic fever; fruit for fevers; leaves for jaundice	Fruit, seeds, leaves, flowers, and occasionally rsin are eaten	+	+	+
Bauhinia reticulata DC B. thonningii Schum (Fabaceae)	KARGO	Leaves, root, and bark for fever; root for splenomegaly	Leaves and pods are edible; root bark chewed to impart red color to lips and teeth	+	+	+
Cadaba farinosa Forssk. (Capparaceae)	BAGAYI	Whole plant for anemia	Leaves in sweet snacks; stems are chewed for sweet taste	+	+	+
Cassia goratensis Fresen (Fabaceae)	RUNHU	Leaves and fruit pod for fever	Leaves and fruit are edible; leaf infusion is a refreshing beverage	+	+	+
Cassia occidentalis L. (Fabaceae)	MAJAMFARI	Leaves for periodic fever, jaundice, and fevers; roots for fever and hepatic disorders	Young leaves and unripe fruit edible; root decoction stimulates appetite; seeds in beverages	+	+	+
Cassia tora L. (Fabaceae)	TAFASA	Leaves for fever	Leaves are popular vegetable; seeds in beverages and are edible	+	+	+
Celosia trigyna L. C. isertii CC Townsend (Amaranthaceae)	NANNAHO	Whole plant for periodic and other fevers	Leaves for soup and are a vegetable	+	+	+

236

Table 12.1 *(Continued)*

Genus species (Family)	Hausa Name	Medicinal application for Malaria	Dietary Use	A B C
Chrozophora senegal-ensis (Lam) A. Juss. ex Spreng (Euphorbiaceae)	DAMAGI	Leaves for fever		- - -
Cochlospermum planchonii Hook (Cochlospermaceae)	BALAGANDE	Root for fever and jaundice	Seeds edible; root added to food to impart yellow color	+ + -
Cochlospermum tinctorium Rich. (Cochlospermaceae)	RAWAYA	Bark and root for jaundice	Root added to cooking oil and food for yellow color	+ + -
Commiphora kerstingii Engl. (Burseraceae)	DALI	Leaves for jaundice		- - -
Corchorus tridens L. (Tiliaceae)	TURGUNNUWA	Leaves and seeds for splenomegaly	Leaves in soup	+ + +
Eratrostis cilianensis Lutati (Poaceae)	BUNSURUM FAGE	Whole plant for fevers	Seeds are edible	+ + +
Ficus ovata Vahl. (Moraceae)	CEDIYA	Leaves for fevers and jaundice; bark for spleno- or hepato-megaly	Young leaves in soups; fruit edible	+ + +
Ficus polita Vahl. (Moraceae)	DURUMI	Leaves for fevers	Young leaves in soups	+ + +
Guiera senegalensis JF Gmel (Combretaceae)	SABARA	Leaves for fever and as vehicle for other medicines	Leaves in soups and in gruels as appetizer	+ + +
Hibiscus sabdariffa L. (Malvaceae)	YAKUWA	Seeds, fruit, and leaves for fevers	Leaves and calyces are vegetables; fruit, seeds and seed oil are edible	+ + +
Ipomoea asarifolia (Desr) Roem. & Schultes (Convolvulaceae)	DUMAN RAFI	Whole plant for fevers		- - -
Momordica balsamina L. M. charantia L. (Cucurbitaceae)	GARAHUNU	Whole plant for fevers and anemia	Leaves are vegetable	+ + +
Moringa oleifera Lam. (Moringaceae)	ZOGALE	Leaves for fever and jaundice	Leaves are vegetable and in soups; fruit pods, roots, and seed oil are edible	+ + +
Nauclea diderrichii (de Wild) Merr. (Rubiaceae)	TAFASHIYA	Leaves and root for fevers, jaundice, and hemoglobinuria; bark for periodic fevers and jaundice	Fruit is edible; stem infusion is a tonic beverage	+ - -

237

Table 12.1 *(Continued)*

Genus species (Family)	Hausa Name	Medicinal application for Malaria	Dietary Use	A B C
Parkia filicoidea Welw ex Oliv (Fabaceae)	DORAWA	Leaves and fruit pulp for fevers; bark for jaundice	Leaves, fruit pulp, seeds, and flowers are edible; bark infusion is a tonic	+ + +
Prosopis africana Taub. (Mimosaceae)	KIRYA	Leaves and bark for fevers	Seeds are edible	+ - -
Sclerocarya birrea (A Rich) Hochst (Anacardiaceae)	DANYA	Fruit for hemo-globinuria	Fruit and seeds are edible	+ + +
Securidaca longipedunculata (L) Livera ex Alston (Polygalaceae)	SANYA	Root for periodic fever; seeds and root for fevers	Bark infusion is a tonic beverage	+ + -
Sesamum radiatum Schum & Thonn (Pedaliaceae)	KARKASHI	Whole plant for jaundice	Leaves and seeds in soup	+ + +
Striga hermontheca (Del) Benth (Scrophulariaceae)	SOKI	Whole plant for anemia and jaundice	Whole plant cooked with vegetables and legumes to soften	+ + +
Strychnos spinosa Lam. (Loganiaceae)	KOKIYA	Fruit and roots for fevers	Fruit and leaves are edible	+ + +
Tamarindus indica L. (Fabaceae)	TSAMIYA	Leaves, fruit, bark, and root for fevers; leaves and bark for jaundice; flowers for hepatomegaly and jaundice	Leaves are vegetables and in soup; fruit, seeds, and flowers are edible; bark and pod infusions are tonics	+ + +
Ximenia americana L. (Olacaceae)	TSADA	Leaves, young stems, and roots for fevers	Leaves, fruit, and seed oil are edible	+ + +

In column A, + denotes that one or more parts of this plant are used as food.

In column B, + denotes that the same structure serves both as food and as medicine for one or more symptoms of malaria.

In column C, + denotes that the plant part from column B is maximally available during the period of high malaria risk.

Figure 12.1
Catabolism of Glucose in Human Erythrocytes

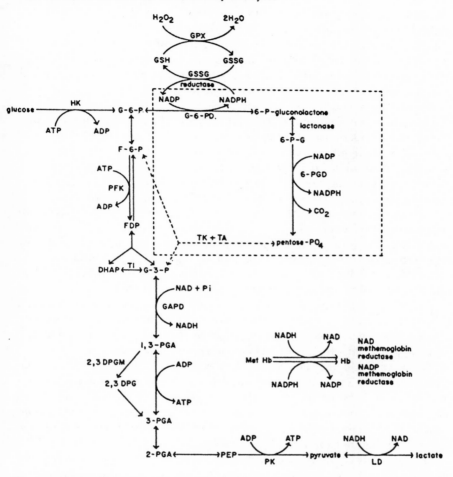

The pentose phosphate shunt is circumscribed by a broken line and is defined by these ab-
breviations: G6PD = the enzyme glucose-6-phosphate dehydrogenase; NADP/NADPH and
NAD/NADH = oxidized and reduced forms, respectively, of the enzyme cofactors nicotinamide adenine dinucleotide phosphate and nicotinamide adenine dinucleotide; GSSG/GSH =
oxidized and reduced forms of glutathioine; H_2O_2 = hydrogen peroxide, a potent oxidant; Hb
= hemoglobin; metHb = the oxidized methemoglobin.

Source: Harris and Kellermeyer 1970:47. Reprinted with permission.

librium with molecular oxygen, the transport of which, paradoxically, is the
red cell's principal function. That equilibrium is offset in normal cells by
redox reactions that are part of or integrally linked to the pentose phosphate
shunt, one of two alternative glucose-catabolizing pathways (Figure 12.1).

Levels of intracellular oxidation increase variably during the course of normal metabolic fluctuations, in certain inherited red cell anomalies (e.g., G6PD deficiency), consequent to ingestion of some foods (e.g., *Vicia faba*) and drugs (e.g., primaquine), and in reaction to certain infections. Potentially injurious redox status is reflected in high titers of methemoglobin and of enzyme cofactors and glutathione in their oxidized configurations relative to their reduced counterparts. Oxidation is reflected as well by diminutions of the hemoprotein catalase that mediates the decomposition of hydrogen peroxide to oxygen and water.

Our early investigations (Etkin and Eaton 1975) revealed that elevated intracellular oxidation attends malaria infection: in vivo methemoglobin concentrations are significantly higher in infected cells, which are markedly more sensitive to additional oxidant stress, and isolated parasite suspensions oxidize the enzyme cofactors NADH and NADPH. Moreover, in infected red cells catalase is irreversibly inhibited by aminotriazole, a suppression that absolutely requires presence of the oxidant H_2O_2. Other researchers have reported oxidant generation in malaria infection (reviewed in Vennerstrom and Eaton 1988), and the collective narrative that emerges explains how elevated intracellular oxidation, some of plasmodial origin, selectively renders infected cells more susceptible to hemolysis through peroxidation of membrane lipids and decomposition of sulfhydryl-containing enzymes, hemoglobin, and other key cellular constituents. This interrupts maturation of the plasmodium, which cannot survive extracellularly as an immature blood form. This helps to explain a range of circumstances that protect the human host against fulminant malaria infection: oxidant sensitivity in G6PD deficiencies (including "favism", a severe hemolytic episode following the ingestion of the fava bean) (Etkin and Eaton 1975) and some hemoglobinopathies (Hebbel et al. 1982), vitamin E deficiency (Eaton et al. 1976), free-radical intermediates in the metabolism of certain pharmaceuticals (Docampo and Moreno 1984), and naturally occurring endoperoxides (Meshnick et al. 1989; Vennerstrom and Eaton 1988).

In view of that cumulative evidence, we investigated the oxidizing potential of Hausa plant medicines used to treat one or more symptoms of malaria. We hypothesized that the combined effects of plant- and parasite-generated intraerythrocytic oxidation would overwhelm host cell oxidant defenses, resulting in lysis of infected red cells and release of immature parasites incapable of continuing the infection.

Methemoglobin generation is a sensitive indicator of erythrocyte oxidant damage and is determined through standardized assays (see Etkin and Eaton 1975 for details). Extracts were prepared from macerated plant materials in solutions of isotonic saline and neutralized to physiologic pH. Normal red cell hemolysates in dilute hemoglobin suspensions were incubated at 37°C in equivolume ratios with plant extracts, and metHb was determined after two hours' incubation. Control samples were identically prepared, sans plant

Table 12.2
Methemoglobin Generation by Plant Extracts

SAMPLE	Percent Hb → MetHb
Acacia nilotica (GABARUWA) root	56%
Azadirachta indica (DARBEJIYA) leaf	42%
Azadirachta indica (DARBEJIYA) bark	09%
Azadirachta indica (DARBEJIYA) root	07%
Cassia occidentalis (MAJAMFARI) root	78%
Cassia occidentalis (MAJAMFARI) leaf	68%
Cassia tora (TAFASA) leaf	35%
Cassia tora (TAFASA) root	29%
Cochlospermum tinctorium (RAWAYA) root	51%
Guiera senegalensis (SABARA) root	47%
Guiera senegalensis (SABARA) leaf	100%
Securidaca longipedunculata (SANYA) root	29%
Controls	00.5%

extract. Data are summarized in Table 12.2, with two-hour metHb concentrations expressed as percentages of original Hb converted to oxidized metHb. In this study *Guiera senegalensis* leaves appear to be the most potent oxidant generators, with 100 percent conversion of Hb ⟶ metHb.

Our second measure of oxidizing potential evaluated plant extracts for glutathione oxidation (GSH ⟶ GSSG). Extracts, hemolysates, and controls were prepared as for the metHb studies, with starting GSH concentration at 2.0 millimoles (mM). Samples were incubated for two hours at 37°C and residual GSH measured at thirty-minute intervals (methods as reported in Etkin and Eaton 1975). Results are summarized in Table 12.3, which indicates both the relative rates of depletion and glutathione residua for all samples. Highest oxidant activity is indicated for leaf extracts of *Guiera senegalensis*, *Azadirachta indica*, and *Cassia tora*, which had the lowest final GSH concentrations.

The results of these preliminary investigations of methemoglobin generation and GSH depletion suggest that some Hausa plant medicines have oxidizing activity, indirectly recommending their efficacy in the therapy of malaria infection. On this basis, we selected the best candidates for inclusion in direct, in vivo tests of efficacy against an analogue of human malaria, murine *Plasmodium berghei*, studies of which represent most of the basic experimental work in human malaria therapy (Peters and Richards 1984).

In vivo studies. Malaria infection is maintained in laboratory animals by

Table 12.3
Glutathione Oxidation: GSH → GSSG

SAMPLE	0 min.	30 min.	60 min.	120 min.
Acacia nilotica (GABARUWA) root	2.0 mM	1.3 mM	0.9 mM	0.2 mM
Azadirachta indica (DARBEJIYA) leaf	2.0	1.2	0.7	0.1
Azadirachta indica (DARBEJIYA) bark	2.0	1.7	1.6	1.4
Azadirrachta indica (DARBEJIYA) root	2.0	1.8	1.8	1.7
Cassia occidentalis (MAJAMFARI) root	2.0	1.9	1.7	1.5
Cassia occidentalis (MAJAMFARI) leaf	2.0	1.9	1.6	1.0
Cassia tora (TAFASA) leaf	2.0	0.4	0.4	0.1
Cassia tora (TAFASA) root	2.0	1.5	1.3	0.9
Cochlospermum tinctorium (RAWAYA) root	2.0	1.8	1.7	1.2
Guiera senegalensis (SABARA) root	2.0	1.8	1.5	1.5
Guiera senegalensis (SABARA) leaf	2.0	0.5	0.1	0.1
Securidaca longipedunculata (SANYA) root	2.0	1.8	1.7	1.5
Controls	2.0	1.9	1.9	1.9

intraperitoneal injection (IP) of healthy subjects with *Plasmodium*-infected red blood cells drawn from heavily parasitized animals. We interrupted this process with an incubation phase in order to expose parasites to extracts of the medicinals *Acacia nilotica* root, and leaves of *Azadirachta indica*, *Cassia tora*, and *Guiera senegalensis*. After two hours' incubation, infected blood was injected into healthy subjects; we monitored time elapsed before the infection reached patency and the duration of infection prior to death, two standard evaluations used in the testing of antimalarial drugs (Peters and Richards 1984). Toxicity of plant extracts to host was ruled out by a parallel series of investigations in which neutralized extracts were injected by same route of administration (IP) over a course of seven days. Results are summarized in Table 12.4. Exposure to extracts of *Acacia nilotica*, *Azadirachta indica*, and *Guiera senegalensis* clearly suppressed infection, while *Cassia tora* extended survival only insignificantly.

While it is difficult immediately to reconcile the findings of these preliminary investigations of Hausa antimalarial plants, this will be clarified when more rigorous laboratory protocols fractionate the specific constituents responsible for in vitro oxidant activity, establish whether ingestion of these oxidizing plants raises intraerythrocytic oxidation to levels that disrupt malaria parasite development, and determine whether the apparent in vivo effects against *Plasmodium berghei* are due to those and/or other constituents. Our preliminary findings were sufficiently promising as a prototype study to sustain our investigatory energy, and we reported those results in the first edition

Table 12.4
In Vivo Effects of Hausa Antimalarials

Sample	Parasitemia Day 7
Acacia nilotica root	0%
Azadirachta indica leaf	0%
Cassia tora leaf	83%
Guiera senegalensis leaf	1%
Controls	87%

of this volume principally to highlight a unique methodology for the evaluation of antimalarial plants.

Investigations of Antimalarial Activity—Series 2

Rationale. The argument is still compelling that the search for new antimalarials should include consideration of oxidant sensitivity of infected red cells and the efficacy of existing oxidant antimalarials (Vennerstrom and Eaton 1988:1277). Other directions need to be explored as well, including two important advances that have become available since the late 1970s, when we began our antimalarial studies.

Refinement of a continuous culture technique for *Plasmodium falciparum* (Trager and Jensen 1976) has made possible the propagation and ever more elaborate manipulation of human malaria parasites; and long-term maintenance of cultures provides a system for the direct and quantifiable measurement of in vitro antimalarial activity. We took advantage of this more rigorous protocol in our most recent assessments of the antimalarial potential of Hausa plants. Having expanded our original data base through the extensive follow-up study in 1987–1988, we tested 309 specimens representing 134 different species for activity against cultured *P. falciparum*. And to designate plants for further study, we again applied the criterion of multicontextual use and selected from among 126 Hausa febrifuges 82 plants that are used as well in diet, either as major meal constituents or as flavoring, garnish, and the like. These observations are summarized in Table 12.5 (Etkin and Eaton 1990). Primary aqueous/ethanol extractions (I) of these plants yielded positive results in twenty-four specimens (twenty-three species). Differential extraction with saline (II NaCl) and chloroform (II chlor), and finally extraction of the

Table 12.5
Activity of Plant Extracts Against Cultured *Plasmodium falciparum*

Genus, Species	Hausa	(Part)	I	II NaCl	II Chlor	III
Acacia nilotica (L) Willd ex Del	Gabaruwa	(root)	+	+	-	+
Agelanthus dodoneifolius (DC)	Kauci	(whole)	+	-	-	+
Artemisia maciverae Hutch & Dalz	Tazargade	(whole)	+	-	+	-
Cassia occidentalis L.	Majamfari	(root)	+	-	+	+
Cassia occidentalis L.	Majamfari	(leaves)	+	+	-	+
Centaurea perrottetii DC	Dayi	(while)	+	-	+	-
Chrozophora senegalensis (Lam)	Damagi	(whole)	+	+	-	+
Cyperus articulatus L.	Kajiji	(root)	+	-	+	+
Diospyros mespiliformis Hochst	Kanya	(leaves)	+	-	-	+
Erythrina senegalensis DC	Minjirya	(root)	+	-	+	-
Feretia apodanthera Del	Kurukuru	(leaves)	+	-	-	+
Ficus ingens (Miq) Miq	Kawari	(bark)	+	-	-	-
Ficus ovata Vahl.	Cediya	(bark)	+	-	+	+
Ficus polita Vahl.	Durumi	(leaves)	+	+	-	+
Momordica balsamina L.	Garahunu	(whole)	+	-	-	-
Piper guineense Schum & Thonn	Masoro	(fruit)	+	+	-	-
Psidium guajava L.	Gwaiba	(leaves)	+	+	-	+
Securinega virosa Baill	Tsa	(leaves)	+	+	-	+
Sorghum spp.	Dawa	(root)	+	-	-	-
Syzgium aromaticum (L) Merr & Perry	Kanumfari	(clove)	+	+	+	+
Terminalia avicennioides G & P	Baushe	(leaves)	+	+	-	+
Thonningea sanguinea Vahl	Kulla	(root)	+	+	+	+
Xylopia aethiopica (Dunal) A Rich	Kimba	(fruit)	+	-	+	-
Zingiber officinale Roscoe	Cittaraho	(rhizome)	+	-	+	+

remaining insoluble residue with ethanol (III), demonstrated antimalarial activity in additional fractions.

A second strategic advance for research on antimalarial plants is the availability of NAPRALERT, NAtural PRoducts ALERT, a unique natural products data base that distills the world literature on the chemical constituents, activity, and pharmacology—including human studies—of plant parts and extracts. Its capabilities are vast and replace the type of literature search that one used to do "by hand" or with weaker computer instruments. Ready access to those data greatly advance our knowledge of the specific plants on which our studies center, help us to understand more fully the physiological outcomes of plant use, and suggest direction for refining laboratory investigations.

INTERRELATIONS AMONG INDIGENOUS MEDICINES, DIET, AND DISEASE

In addition to pharmacological assessment of these plants through laboratory study and literature review, it is important to consider other contexts of use. Diet especially suggests overlapping categories and is important additionally because plants consumed as food tend to be ingested regularly and in relatively large quantities compared, for example, with use of those same plants as cosmetics or in occasional rituals (Etkin and Ross 1991).

Table 12.1 illustrates some of the multicontextual aspects of plant utilization. Of forty commonly used Hausa antimalarials, 90 percent (n = 36) also appeared in diet, and among those there was 92 percent concordance (n = 33) that the same plant structure (root, leaves, etc.) served as both medicine and food. Further, among those thirty-three plants, 88 percent (n = 29) were maximally available during the period of highest risk of malaria infection. Were we to extend this tabular presentation through inclusion of our most recent (1987–1988) observations, roughly the same proportions would obtain, illustrating once more the significant overlap between diet and medicine.

We now illustrate the physiological import of these overlapping contexts of use through review of some general interactions between nutrition and disease, followed by specific comments relevant to malaria infection.

Nutrition and Disease

The bulk of clinical, epidemiological, and biochemical evidence regarding interactions between nutrition and disease point to synergism between malnutrition and infection. This is recorded as increased susceptibility to infection through immune dysfunction, exacerbated symptomatology, anorexia-driven depression of nutrient intake, precipitation of frank nutrient deficits with increasing parasitemia, and increased mortality (Crompton 1986; Hoffman-Goetz 1986; Martorell 1980). These physiological parameters are overlaid by such cultural variables as conscious underfeeding of ill children and therapeutically inspired food proscriptions (e.g., Duggan et al. 1986; McKay 1980).

The significance of those interactions notwithstanding, we are concerned that there has been little systematic study of potentially antagonistic relationships—that is, circumstances in which nutrient imbalances antagonize infection. A number of special cases have been described. Diets consisting almost entirely of milk have been observed to suppress a variety of infections: rheumatic heart disease of streptococcal origin, likely attributable to the antimicrobial actions of oleic acid; malaria, due to low levels of PABA, riboflavin, and vitamin E; *Giardia lamblia*, due to a human-specific lipase; and malaria, tuberculosis, *Entamoeba histolytica*, and others due to the presence in milk of partially saturated lactoferrin and transferrin in sufficiently high concentrations to compete with parasites for iron. Similarly, low levels of iron and other nutrients have been implicated in suppression of those same infections among people experiencing temporary and long-term food shortages or outright famine (Bates et al. 1987; Eaton et al. 1976; Gillin et al. 1983; Harvey et al. 1989; Murray et al. 1982).

But what can one say of the pharmacological effects of routine dietaries on the occurrence or expression of infection? To this end we are informed by a disaggregated literature on "food pharmacology" which records physiological activities for specific foods and projects that information onto populations whose epidemiologic circumstances may not be known but who nonetheless consume those plants in food and/or medicine. For example, dietary ingestion of anthelmintic chenopod seeds (*Chenopodium ambrosioides*) has been invoked to account for the absence of intestinal worm infection that was adduced from studies of parasite-free coprolites of a prehistoric population in Lovelock Cave, Nevada (Kliks 1975) (although it appears to us equally plausible that *Chenopodium* was consumed medicinally). And the chewing of betel nut (*Areca catechu*) has been proposed to reduce intestinal vermiform parasites in some Melanesian populations (Wyatt 1977). Naturally occurring chelators such as tannins and phytates may sequester sufficiently large pools of serum iron (Disler et al. 1975; Graf and Eaton 1990) to suppress some infectious agents, an effect that might be offset in the case of malaria by the antioxidant actions of phytate, or enhanced by simultaneous consumption of vitamin C. The difficulty lies in tying these observations to real populations with known disease history and rigorously testing such hypotheses. The edited volume *Plants in Indigenous Medicine and Diet* (Etkin 1986a) is organized explicitly around this goal, and the studies reported therein provide direction for this type of inquiry. We use that same framework for reporting results of our investigations of Hausa plant medicines and foods.

Malaria in Northern Nigeria

Malaria is endemic throughout northern Nigeria, and in Hurumi the risk of infection is greatest during August–October, a pattern typical of much of the sub-Saharan savanna, which is dominated by a unimodal pattern of rainfall (Wernsdorfer 1980). In this region the annual cycle includes three to four months of rains and an eight-to-nine-month dry season. In most years the onset of rains in June is followed by the progressive development of microenvironments that support mosquito breeding, so that by August mosquitoes abound in numbers sufficient for the sustained growth of malaria parasites and their continued transmission to susceptible human hosts. Nonetheless, the reported incidence of fulminant and debilitating plasmodial infection is relatively low for this region.[4] This apparent suppression of malaria infection may be ascribed to a number of factors, one of which—the efficacy of indigenous antimalarials—was discussed earlier in this chapter. The potential contribution of diet to malaria suppression is discussed below.

Malaria Epidemiology and Dietary Patterns: 1975–1976

Reflecting a continued dependence on local agricultural produce through the 1970s, dietary patterns in Hurumi were distinguished by marked seasonal fluctuations in the availability of foodstuffs. For example, the principal staples millet (*Pennisetum* spp.) and guineacorn (*Sorghum* spp.) were sown in early June, harvested from approximately mid-September through November, and subsequently stored in granaries. The chief legumes cultivated are groundnuts (*Arachis hypogaea*) and cowpeas (*Vigna unguiculata*), generally sown in late June to early July and harvested at the same time as the later-maturing sorghums. Maximum availability and lowest market costs for all these products coincided with their harvest, and their supplies gradually diminished through the end of the dry season and beginning of the rainy months, with market prices for their replacement increasing commensurately. The exception to this pattern of fluctuating availability for the primary foodstuffs was cassava (*Manihot esculenta*), which was available year-round through xerophytic adaptations that permit its continuation as a transannual which can provide edible rootstock for as long as three years.

The patterning of types and quantities of foods consumed in Hurumi corresponded closely to fluctuations in availability and costs. Variability was greatly reduced just after the harvest, when grains were readily available for consumption in the form of thick porridges favored by Hausa as the appropriately energy-rich fundamental around which meals are designed. Dietary elaboration became increasingly pronounced through the progression of the dry season and commencement of rains, taking the form of an increased variety of foods eaten and of their sources and preparation forms. Figure 12.2 depicts the frequency with which nongrain foods contributed to total caloric intake, and illustrates the increasing dietary reliance on nongrain foods as the next harvest approached.

Explanation of this dietary elaboration invokes both ecological and cultural parameters, and its implications are several. The depletion of staples stored from the previous harvest forged a greater reliance on market purchases of raw grains and on foods purchased from extrahousehold sources, typically market vendors and village women who sell prepared main dishes and snacks. These sources amplified the range of variability in the household's diet beyond what would otherwise have been only those products reaped during the previous harvest. Moreover, the frequency and duration of market attendance increased during the dry season. The population was thereby exposed to a greater array of foods from other areas, and increased purchases

Figure 12.2
Caloric Sources Other Than Grains, 1975–1976

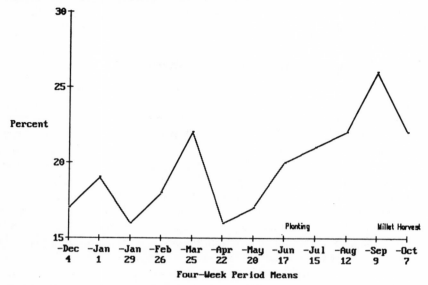

Note: The frequency with which nongrain foods contributed to diet is expressed as a percentage of total caloric intake. The mean caloric value of nongrain foods is 22 percent, ranging between 16 and 28 percent. Means are presented for four-week periods.

beyond necessities for household meals. Another factor that encouraged dietary variability toward the end of the dry season is a greater number of ceremonies that, in the public celebration of life-cycle events, involve intra- and intervillage food exchanges and redistributions. Although grains predominated in the diet throughout the year, the steady increase in market costs, which reached a maximum during the latter part of the rainy season, dissuaded many people from replacing their diminished grain stores; they relied more on other, less preferred but readily obtained, foods.

Another feature of dietary elaboration that characterized the rainy season was the increased availability of wild and semicultivated "vegetables," a collective term for various and principally nonligneous plants marked for Hausa food largely by their foliature, although young stems, calyces, buds, fruits, and flowers are indicated in some cases. These are to a large extent "free goods," since those growing on public grazing land, paths, and other nonprivatized property can be collected without permission or obligation. These plants were most prominent in diet during the last two months of the rainy season, although some were dried for consumption throughout the year. That timing can be explained by three interrelated factors. First, these plants were more readily available then; compared with grains, they matured and were available for collection or market purchase earlier and were less

Figure 12.3
Frequency of Vegetable Use in Diet, 1975–1976

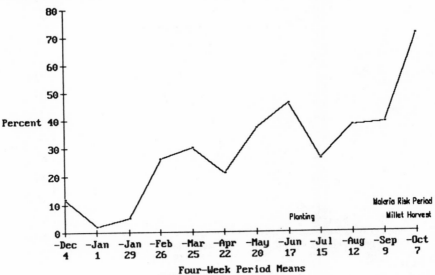

Note: This is expressed as a percentage of days in a four-week period on which vegetables appeared in household diets. The mean percentage is 28, ranging between 2 and 71. Grain in some quantity appeared in all household diets for every day examined and would, at 100 percent, appear above the top of the graph as a horizontal line.

expensive. Second, these vegetables helped to extend remaining grain stores during a period of shortest supply by addition to cereal-based mixtures. Third, they provided a welcome substitute for cassava, which remained readily available, became a substitute for the dwindling grains, and had become, by Hausa standards, tedious (*gundura*). Cereal-based dishes were augmented by the addition of vegetables and by the substitution of cassava for at least one meal, usually at midday, in order to reserve grain for the most important, evening meal. Vegetable dishes also were favored over cassava, which was itself a substitute. The aggregate effect was increased consumption of vegetables through the progression of the rainy months.

The leaves and nonligneous parts of some species were especially favored as the centerpiece of several popular dishes, including, from Table 12.1, *Amaranthus hybridus, Cadaba farinosa, Cassia tora, Celosia trigyna, C. isertii, Hibiscus sabdariffa, Momordica balsamina, M. charantia,* and *Moringa oleifera.* The leaves of other species that figure more prominently for soups and as seasonings include, from Table 12.1, *Adansonia digitata, Corchorus tridens, Celosia trigyna, Ficus ovata, F. polita, Guiera senegalensis, Parkia filicoidea, Sesamum radiatum,* and *Tamarindus indica.* Figure 12.3 demonstrates this

Figure 12.4
Grams of Grains and Vegetables Consumed Per Capita per Day, 1975–1976

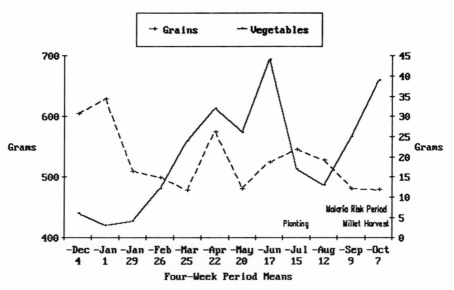

increased use of vegetable foods in household dietaries as the annual cycle approaches the next harvest.

Further, most of the plants listed in Table 12.1 are also used medicinally other than for antimalarial action. Most notable in this regard is *Guiera senegalensis*, one of whose Hausa names is "mother of medicines" (*uwar magunguna*), reflecting its common uses as both principal and vehicle in medicinal preparations. The likelihood that the use of this plant would influence malaria infection is heightened by its indication for the prevention and treatment of other rainy season diseases, such as *sanyi* and *raba*, complicated symptom clusters whose etiology is ascribed to dampness and the chill of wet clothing and house floors. Also of note in these examples of multiple exposure and maximal rainy season utilization is the dietary use of *Striga hermontheca*, which is used in cooking to soften vegetables.

As was noted earlier, during 1975–1976 the period of highest malaria risk coincided with the end of the rainy season, when increases in vegetable consumption and decreases in grain utilization were most marked. This is demonstrated in Figure 12.4, which shows that during the period of maximum malaria risk the quantity of grains consumed reached its lowest, and the amount of vegetables one of its highest, points. We suggest that these interrelated aspects of dietary patterning both may have antagonistic effects on malaria infection, thereby helping to explain why, despite the high risk, plasmodial infections that occurred tended to be relatively moderate.

From a pharmacological perspective, dietary and other uses of antimalarial plants should be interpreted as additional exposure to constituents of potential therapeutic efficacy. That is, the consumption of oxidizing and otherwise antiplasmodial plants in both medicinal and dietary contexts, during a time of year when risk of malaria infection was highest, may have had a compound effect in limiting this infection.

Additionally, the reduction in grain consumption that coincided with increased use of vegetables may contribute to reduced parasitemia. We draw here on the observations of Murray et al. (1982), who noted recrudescence of previously undetected plasmodial infections among populations whose impoverished diets were supplemented with grains. It is possible that the apparent protection against malaria occurred because of deficits in vitamin E (an antioxidant) (Eaton et al. 1976), and that this balance was overturned on supplying those populations with vitamin E-rich grains. Or perhaps the critical nutrient was iron. In any case, the observation holds that the circumstances of grain deprivation coincide with suppressed malaria infection.

We proposed that what appeared to be paradoxically low levels of fulminant malaria in Hurumi could be attributed at least in part to the combined effects of decreased consumption of grains rich in vitamin E and iron, and increased consumption of vegetables that generate oxidants and/or otherwise compromise plasmodial development.

Dietary Postscript: 1987–1988

During our follow-up study in Hurumi we noted marked diminution in the seasonal constraints on resource availability that characterized dietary patterns twelve years earlier. This is due in part to increased availability of a range of foodstuffs through expanded regional markets coincident with the growth of transportation and communication networks. There was substantial evidence of increasing participation of Hurumi residents in the larger economy: more took part in short-term migration to urban and periurban areas, bringing back to Hurumi cash and new dietary preferences; a greater number were selling *and* buying foodstuffs, both more often and throughout the year. Further, cassava cultivation and consumption declined dramatically for the most recent period: whereas cassava provided as much as 14 percent of all calories consumed during it peak consumption period during 1975–1976, it represented no more than 2 percent of all calories consumed during 1987–1988 (the respective weekly means being 6.1 percent and 1.6 percent). This reflects changes in food preferences as well as such ecological variables as unfavorable growing conditions and plant diseases. While the full impact of these dietary shifts is beyond the scope of this chapter, we need to underscore two aspects that are relevant for our earlier model of a cyclical dietary and its potential impact on malaria.

The first aspect of changing diet pertains to grain consumption. Although

Figure 12.5
Grams of Vegetables Consumed Per Capita per Day, 1975–1976, and 1987–1988

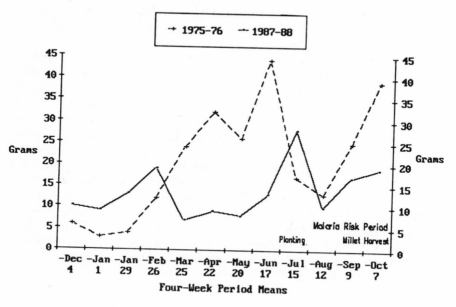

there were no marked cyclical reductions for the 1987–1988 research period, the overall yearly consumption of grain was relatively low, in fact comparable with the diminished rates of grain consumption that characterized the 1975–1976 high-risk malaria season. (The forty-eight-week mean was 450 grams per capita for 1987–1988.) The lower consumption of grain was accounted for in part by the year-round substitution of legume-based midday meals and the more frequent inclusion of imported, and costly, polished rice.

The second aspect of dietary change is of greater concern for the continued relevance of our model. Here we note for 1987–1988 a marked reduction in the quantity of wild and semicultivated vegetables consumed (Figure 12.5). This decrease, particularly during the period of malaria risk, can be partly attributed to replacement of cassava-based dishes with more favored legume- and grain-based dishes, and a concomitant reduction in vegetable-based dishes. Interestingly, while the quantity of vegetables in the diet diminished, the incidence of population exposure to at least some of these products remained relatively comparable for the two research periods, illustrating the continued importance of vegetables as dietary supplements. Whether this dietary change that attends economic and other changes portends a trend that may affect disease (malaria) expression is at this stage only conjecture. Still, the dietary and medicinal pharmacological model suggested by our earlier work continued to inform our investigations through the most recent field research and helps to shape future inquiry as well.

SUMMARY AND CONCLUSIONS

For the present discussion, a model that integrates features of disease and specific indigenous treatment modalities was applied to investigate how certain foods and medicines might interact with malaria infection. Elsewhere we used this framework to investigate how foods and medicines might influence gastrointestinal disorders (Etkin and Ross 1982), illustrating again how the pharmacological potential of botanicals is extended through their use in various contexts. By focusing on these plants for investigations of biocultural adaptations to disease, we conceptualize them broadly as ingestible plants, rather than as exclusively "medicines" or "foods." With this approach, we propose to extend considerations of ingestible plants beyond the disciplinary boundaries that have traditionally circumscribed nutritional/dietary studies, on the one hand, and examinations of medicine and infectious disease, on the other.

Our contribution to this volume embodies this approach. In sum, we note that a number of Hausa medicinal plants used to treat malaria infection also constitute important dietary elements. Laboratory investigations of Hausa antimalarials suggest their efficacy in the treatment of that infection. Moreover, the plasmodiostatic activity demonstrated for some of these plant materials might be augmented by a diminished consumption of grains. An examination of local diets during 1975–1976 revealed that both an elevated utilization of medicinal plants as dietary components and a diminished consumption of grains coincided with the period of heightened risk of malaria infection. From our more recent study, we document changes in the local diet—most noticeably a diminution in the quantities of plant materials that provided the focus of our earlier investigations. These observations, cast in a broad ecological framework, provide a basis from which we can explore the potential implications of other (perhaps more subtle) dimensions of change.

ACKNOWLEDGMENTS

Both studies benefited enormously from the contributions of Ibrahim Muazzamu and the participation and collective wisdom and goodwill of Hurumi village. This work was supported in part through grants awarded to Nina Etkin by the National Science Foundation (BNS-8703734), the Social Science Research Council, the Fulbright Senior Research Scholars Program, the Bush Foundation, the University of Minnesota, and the Social Science Research Institute of the University of Hawaii; to Paul Ross by the National Science Foundation (SOC 74–24412), Sigma Xi, and Washington University; and to Nina Etkin and Paul Ross by faculty research appointments in the Department of Pharmacognosy and Drug Development at Ahmadu

Bello University, Zaria, Nigeria. We also thank the Kano State Department of Health and Wudil Local Government. Dr. Daniel Klayman of the Walter Reed Medical Center generously provided samples of *Artemisia annua*, which we used as one of the controls for studies of antimalarial activity against cultured *P. falciparum*.

NOTES

1. During the intervening years, both a paved road and piped water have reached within two kilometers of the village center.

2. We are aware that a better research design would have used a larger, randomized survey sample and would have measured quantities of foods actually consumed by each individual. However, our experiences—including a pilot study—during six months' residence in the village prior to initiating the dietary survey showed us that the more rigorous methodology was simply impossible. This reflects the great amount of time entailed in conducting such surveys, the intrusive nature of such measures, and the marked emphasis on privacy that Hausa apply to eating. In light of this, the dietary survey proceeded with informed compromises; and any resultant shortcomings are offset by the depth of detail of the data and their high degree of reliability.

3. This villagewide protocol is a better vehicle than were specialist/practitioner interviews for eliciting exoteric knowledge and for understanding better the preventive and therapeutic modalities that affect the great majority of villagers on a day-to-day basis.

4. The scope and locus of this study made it impossible to include any clinical examination or to secure blood samples for parasite analysis. In view of that, conclusions regarding the prevalence and severity of malaria infection are drawn from reports of the Ministry of Health, the WHO Malaria Research Center in Kano, staff of the district hospital and dispensary, published studies of malaria epidemiology in northern Nigeria (e.g., Abudu 1983; Ayeni et al. 1987; Schram 1971; Stock 1983), and for 1987–1988 from our village and hospital epidemiological surveys.

REFERENCES

Abudu, F. 1983. "Planning Priorities and Health Care Delivery in Nigeria." *Social Science and Medicine* 17:1995–2002.

Adam, J. G., N. Echard, and M. Lescot. 1972. "Plantes Médicinales Hausa de l'Ader (République du Niger)." *Journal d'Agriculture Tropicale et de Botanique Appliquée* 19:259–399.

Agwu, I. E., and P. A. Akah. 1990. "*Tabernaemontana crassa* as a Traditional Local Anesthetic Agent." *Journal of Ethnopharmacology* 30:115–19.

Akerele, O. 1987. "The Best of Both Worlds: Bringing Traditional Medicine up to Date." *Social Science and Medicine* 24:177–81.

Ayeni, B., G. Rushton, and M. L. McNulty. 1987. "Improving the Geographical Accessibility of Health Care in Rural Areas: A Nigerian Case Study." *Social Science and Medicine* 25:1083–94.

Barton, D. H. R., and W. D. Ollis, eds. 1986. *Advances in Medicinal Phytochemistry*, pp. 1–194. London: J. Libbey.

Bastien, J. W. 1987. "Cross-Cultural Communication Between Doctors and Peasants in Bolivia." *Social Science and Medicine* 24:1109–18.

Bates, C. J., H. J. Powers, W. H. Lamb, W. Gelman, and E. Webb. 1987. "Effect of Supplementary Vitamins and Iron on Malaria Indices in Rural Gambian Children." *Transactions of the Royal Society of Tropical Medicine and Hygiene* 81:286–91.

Benie, T., A. El Izzi, C. Tahiri, J. Duval, and M.-L. Thieulant. 1990. "*Combretodendron africanum* Bark Extract as an Antifertility Agent. I: Estrogenic Effects in Vivo and LH Release by Cultured Gonadotrope Cells." *Journal of Ethnopharmacology* 29:13–23.

Bhattacharya, J., and S. Swarup-Mitra. 1987. "Reduction in Erythrocytic GSH Level and Stability in *Plasmodium vivax* Malaria." *Transactions of the Royal Society of Tropical Medicine and Hygiene* 81:64–66.

Busson, F., P. Jaeger, P. Lunven, and M. Pinta. 1965. *Plantes Alimentaires de l'Ouest Africain*. Paris: Ministère de la Coopération.

Caceres, A., O. Cano, B. Samayoa, and L. Aguilar. 1990. "Plants Used in Guatemala for the Treatment of Gastrointestinal Disorders. 1. Screening of 84 Plants Against Enterobacteria." *Journal of Ethnopharmacology* 30:55–73.

Collins, D. J., C. C. J. Culvenor, J. A. Lamberton, J. W. Loder, and J. R. Price. 1990. *Plants for Medicines: A Chemical and Pharmacological Survey of Plants in the Australian Region*. Melbourne, Australia: CSIRO.

Counts, D. R., and D. A. Counts. 1989. "Complementarity in Medical Treatment in a West New Britain Society." In *A Continuing Trial of Treatment: Medical Pluralism in Papua New Guinea*, S. Frankel and G. Lewis, eds., pp. 277–94. Dordrecht: Kluwer.

Cox, P. A., L. R. Sperry, M. Tuominen, and L. Bohlin. 1989. "Pharmacological Activity of the Samoan Ethnopharmacopoeia." *Economic Botany* 43:487–97.

Crompton, D. W. T. 1986. "Nutritional Aspects of Infection." *Transactions of the Royal Society of Tropical Medicine and Hygiene* 80:697–705.

Dalziel, J. M. 1937. *The Useful Plants of West Tropical Africa*. London: Crown Agents for Overseas Governments and Administrations.

Disler, P. B., S. R. Lynch, R. W. Charlton, J. D. Torrance, T. H. Bothwell, R. B. Walker, and F. Mayet. 1975. "The Effect of Tea on Iron Absorption." *Gut* 16:193–200.

Docampo, R., and S. N. J. Moreno. 1984. "Free Radical Intermediates in the Antiparasitic Action of Drugs and Phagocytic Cells." In *Free Radicals in Biology*, vol. 6, W. A. Pryor, ed., pp. 243–88. Orlando, Fl.: Academic Press.

Donahue, J. M. 1986. "The Profession and the People: Primary Health Care in Nicaragua." *Human Organization* 45:96–103.

Duggan, M. B., J. Alwar, and R. D. G. Milner. 1986. "The Nutritional Cost of Measles in Africa." *Archives of Disease in Childhood* 61:61–66.

Eaton, J. W., J. R. Eckman, E. Berger, and H. S. Jacob. 1976. "Suppression of Malaria Infection by Oxidant-Sensitive Erythrocytes." *Nature* 264:758–60.

Elvin-Lewis, M. 1986. "Therapeutic Rationale of Plants Used to Treat Dental Infections." In *Plants in Indigenous Medicine and Diet: Biobehavioral Approaches*, N. L. Etkin, ed., pp. 48–69. New York: Gordon and Breach Science Publishers (Redgrave).

Etkin, N. L. 1979. "Indigenous Medicine Among the Hausa of Northern Nigeria: Laboratory Evaluation for Potential Therapeutic Efficacy of Antimalarial Plant Medicines." *Medical Anthropology* 3:401–29.

————. 1981. "A Hausa Herbal Pharmacopoeia: Biomedical Evaluation of Commonly Used Plant Medicines." *Journal of Ethnopharmacology* 4:75–98.

————, ed. 1986a. *Plants in Indigenous Medicine and Diet: Biobehavioral Approaches.* New York: Gordon and Breach (Redgrave).

————. 1986b. "Multidisciplinary Perspectives in the Interpretation of Plants Used in Indigenous Medicine and Diet." In *Plants in Indigenous Medicine and Diet: Biobehavioral Approaches,* N. L. Etkin, ed., pp. 2–29. New York: Gordon and Breach Science Publishers (Redgrave).

————. 1988. "Ethnopharmacology: Biobehavioral Approaches in the Anthropological Study of Indigenous Medicines." *Annual Review of Anthropology* 17:23–42.

————. 1990. "Ethnopharmacology." In *Medical Anthropology: Contemporary Theory and Method,* T. M. Johnson and C. F. Sargent, eds., pp. 149–58. New York: Praeger.

Etkin, N. L., and J. W. Eaton. 1975. "Malaria-Induced Erythrocyte Oxidant Sensitivity." In *Erythrocyte Structure and Function,* G. J. Brewer, ed., pp. 219–32. New York: Alan R. Liss.

————. 1990. "Antimalarial Activity of Plant Medicines Against Cultured *Plasmodium falciparum.*" Unpublished results.

Etkin, N. L., and P. J. Ross. 1982. "Food as Medicine and Medicine as Food: An Adaptive Framework for the Interpretation of Plant Utilization Among the Hausa of Northern Nigeria." *Social Science and Medicine* 16:1559–73.

————. 1991. "Should We Set a Place for Diet in Ethnopharmacology?" *Journal of Ethnopharmacology* 32:25–36.

Etkin, N. L., P. J. Ross, and I. Muazzamu. 1990. "The Indigenization of Pharmaceuticals: Therapeutic Transitions in Rural Hausaland." *Social Science and Medicine* 30:919–28.

Franquemont, C., E. Franquemont, W. Davis, T. Plowman, S. King, C. R. Sperling, and C. Niezgoda. 1990. *The Ethnobotany of Chinchero, an Andean Community in Southern Peru.* Chicago: Field Museum of Natural History.

Gillin, F. D., D. S. Reiner, and C.-S. Wang. 1983. "Human Milk Kills Parasitic Intestinal Protozoa." *Science* 221:1290–92.

Good, C. M. 1988. *The Community in Primary Health Care.* Lewiston, N.Y.: Edwin Mellen Press.

Graf, E., and J. W. Eaton. 1990. "Antioxidant Functions of Phytic Acid." *Free Radical Biology and Medicine* 8:61–69.

Green, E. C. 1988. "Can Collaborative Programs Between Biomedical and African Indigenous Health Practitioners Succeed?" *Social Science and Medicine* 27:1125–30.

Hammerschmidt, D. E. 1986. "Chinese Diet and Traditional Materia Medica: Effects on Platelet Function and Atherogenesis." In *Plants in Indigenous Medicine and Diet: Biobehavioral Approaches,* N. L. Etkin, ed., pp. 171–85. New York: Gordon and Breach Science Publishers (Redgrave).

Harris, J. W., and R. W. Kellermeyer. 1970. *The Red Cell,* rev. ed. Cambridge, Mass.: Harvard University Press.

Harvey, P. W. J., P. F. Heywood, M. C. Nesheim, K. Galme, M. Zegans, J.-P. Habicht, L. S. Stephenson, K. L. Radimer, B. Brabin, K. Forsyth, and M. P. Alpers. 1989. "The Effect of Iron Therapy on Malarial Infection in Papua

New Guinea Schoolchildren." *American Journal of Tropical Medicine and Hygiene* 40:12–18.

Hebbel, R. P., J. W. Eaton, M. Balasingam, and M. H. Steinberg. 1982. "Spontaneous Oxygen Radical Generation by Sickle Erythrocytes." *Journal of Clinical Investigation* 70:1253–59.

Hoffman-Goetz, L. 1986. "Malnutrition and Immunological Function with Special Reference to Cell-Mediated Immunity." *Yearbook of Physical Anthropology* 29:139–59.

Johns, T. 1990. *With Bitter Herbs They Shall Eat It: Chemical Ecology and the Origins of Human Diet and Medicine.* Tucson: University of Arizona Press.

Johns, T., and S. I. Keen. 1986. "Taste Evaluation of Potato Glycoalkaloids by the Aymara: A Case Study in Human Chemical Ecology." *Human Ecology* 14:437–52.

Kliks, M. 1975. "Paleoepidemiological Studies on Great Basin Coprolites: Estimation of Dietary Intake and Evaluation of the Ingestion of Anthelmintic Plant Substances." Ph.D. dissertation, Department of Anthropology., University of California, Berkeley.

Last, M. 1990. "Professionalization of Indigenous Healers." In *Medical Anthropology: Contemporary Theory and Method*, T. M. Johnson and C. F. Sargent, eds., pp., 349–66. New York: Praeger.

Last, M., and G. L. Chavunduka, eds. 1986. *The Professionalisation of African Medicine.* Manchester: Manchester University Press.

Lydon, J., and S. O. Duke. 1989. "The Potential of Pesticides from Plants." In *Herbs, Spices, and Medicinal Plants: Recent Advances in Botany, Horticulture, and Pharmacology.* vol. 4, L. E. Craker and J. E. Simon, eds., pp. 1–41. Phoenix: Oryx Press.

Macfoy, C. A., and E. I. Cline. 1990. "*In vitro* Antibacterial Activity of Three Plants Used in Traditional Medicine in Sierra Leone." *Journal of Ethnopharmacology* 29:323–27.

McKay, D. A. 1980. "Food, Illness, and Folk Medicine: Insights from Ulu Trengganu, West Malaysia." In *Food, Ecology and Culture*, J. R. K. Robson, ed., pp. 61–66. New York: Gordon and Breach.

Martorell, R. 1980. "Interrelationships Between Diet, Infectious Disease, and Nutritional Status." In *Social and Biological Predictors of Nutritional Status, Physical Growth, and Neurological Development*, L. S. Greene and F. E. Johnston, eds, pp. 81–106. New York: Academic Press.

Meshnick, S. R., T. W. Tsang, F. B. Lin, H. Z. Pan, C. N. Chang, F. Kuypers, D. Chiu, and B. Lubin. 1989. "Activated Oxygen Mediates the Antimalarial Activity of Qinghaosu." In *Malaria and the Red Cell*, J. W. Eaton, S. R. Meshnick, and G. J. Brewer, eds. pp. 95–104. New York: Alan R. Liss.

Murray, M. J., A. M. Murray, N. J. Murray, M. B. Murray, and C. J. Murray. 1982. "Adverse Effects of Normal Nutrients and Foods on Host Resistance to Disease." In *Adverse Effects of Foods*, E. F. P. Jelliffe and D. B. Jelliffe, eds., pp. 313–21. New York: Plenum Press.

Oliver, B. 1986. *Medicinal Plants in Tropical West Africa.* Cambridge: Cambridge University Press.

Ortiz de Montellano, B. R., and C. H. Browner. 1985. "Chemical Bases for Medicinal Plant Use in Oaxaca, Mexico." *Journal of Ethnopharmacology* 13:57–88.

Osoba, O. A., S. A. Adesanya, and M. A. Durosimi. 1989. "Effect of *Zanthoxylum xanthoxyloides* and Some Substituted Benzoic Acids on Glucose–6-Phosphate and 6-Phosphogluconate Dehydrogenases in Hbss Red Blood Cells." *Journal of Ethnopharmacology* 27:177–83.

Oswald, I. H. 1983. "Are Traditional Healers the Solution to the Failures of Primary Health Care in Rural Nepal?" *Social Science and Medicine* 17:255–57.

Palanichamy, S., and S. Nagarajan. 1990. "Antifungal Activity of *Cassia alata* Leaf Extract." *Journal of Ethnopharmacology* 29:337–40.

Penso, G. 1977. "Problemi Relative all'Uso delle Piante Medicinali nel Mondo." *Bolletino Chimicofarmaceutico* 116:506–19.

———. 1980. *Piante Medicinale nella Terapia Medica*. Milan: Medico Farmaceutica.

Peters, W., and W. H. G. Richards, eds. 1984. *Antimalarial Drugs I: Biological Background, Experimental Methods, and Drug Resistance*. Berlin: Springer-Verlag.

Phillipson, J. D., and L. A. Anderson. 1989. "Ethnopharmacology and Western Medicine." *Journal of Ethnopharmacology* 25:61–72.

Pillsbury, B. L. K. 1982. "Policy and Evaluation Perspectives on Traditional Health Practitioners in National Health Care Systems." *Social Science and Medicine* 16:1825–34.

Posey, D. A. 1984. "A Preliminary Report on Diversified Management of Tropical Forest by the Kayapo Indians of the Brazilian Amazon." *Advances in Economic Botany* 1:112–26.

Prietze, R. 1913–1914. "Arzneipflanzen der Haussa." *Zeitschrift für Kolonialsprachen* 4:81–90.

Schram, R. 1971. *A History of the Nigerian Health Services*. Ibadan, Nigeria: Ibadan University Press.

Singh, G. B., S. Singh, S. Bani, and S. Malhotra. 1990. "Hypotensive Action of a *Coscinium fenestratum* Stem." *Journal of Ethnopharmacology* 30:151–55.

Stevenson, D. R. 1986. "High Blood Pressure Medicinal Plant Use and Arterial Pressure Change." In *Plants in Indigenous Medicine and Diet: Biobehavioral Approaches*, N. L. Etkin, ed., pp. 252–65. New York: Gordon and Breach Science Publishers (Redgrave).

Stock, R. 1980. "Health Care Behavior in a Rural Nigerian Setting, with Particular Reference to the Utilization of Western-Type Health Care Facilities." Ph.D. dissertation, Department of Geography, University of Liverpool.

———. 1983. "Distance and the Utilization of Health Facilities in Rural Nigeria." *Social Science and Medicine* 17:563–70.

Trager, W., and J. B. Jensen. 1976. "Human Malaria Parasites in Continous Culture." *Science* 193:673–75.

Vennerstrom, J. L., and J. W. Eaton. 1988. "Oxidants, Oxidant Drugs, and Malaria." *Journal of Medicinal Chemistry* 31:1269–77.

Wall, L. L. 1988. *Hausa Medicine: Illness and Well-Being in a West African Culture*. Durham, N. C.: Duke University Press.

Wernsdorfer, W. H. 1980. "The Importance of Malaria in the World." In *Malaria*, vol. 1, *Epidemiology, Chemotherapy, Morphology, and Metabolism*, J. P. Kreier, ed., pp. 1–93. New York: Academic Press.

WHO. 1978. *The Promotion and Development of Traditional Medicine*. World Health Organization Technical Report no. 622. Geneva: World Health Organization.

Wyatt, G. B. 1977. "Health in Melanesia." In *The Melanesian Environment*, J. H. Winslow, ed, pp. 459–62. Canberra: Australian National University Press.

PART IV

PSYCHIATRY IN MODERN MEDICINE: PROBLEMATICS FOR ITS TRANSCULTURAL APPLICATIONS

The intersection of cultural values with medicine is most pronounced in psychiatry. Other fields of medicine, such as internal medicine, rely on a relatively objective, statistically defined body of information for determining the difference between illness and health. Because it is concerned with disorders of mood, thought, and behavior, psychiatry must select from the panorama of everyday life, including social interactions, patterns of behavior that reflect psychological disturbances. These disturbances are often not obvious, because they involve an infusion of the symbols, imageries, and metaphors of the culture into the content of the specific patterns. This makes psychiatry problematic; the nature of the disorders that are the focus of its attention must inevitably involve manifestations of certain cultural characteristics. The dilemma is that of differentiating patterns involving cultural symbolism that are evidence of disorder from those which are merely idiosyncratic to the culture itself. From one perspective, it is as though one were looking at a colony of one thousand viruses in a petri dish and attempting, on the basis of physical characteristics alone, to determine which of these viruses are aberrant. The psychiatrist must examine certain personality features and behavioral patterns against the backdrop of a culture that enriches the patterns and, at the same time, separate basic divergences from the norm.

PROBLEMS OF INTERPRETATION
IN PSYCHIATRY

Unlike internal medicine or other fields of medicine, psychiatry cannot rely on laboratory tests to corroborate clinical symptomatology and evidences of deviation. It must rely almost totally on perceptions of the dissonances existing in the mood, thought, and behavior of the patient, as these are viewed against the fabric of culture. Slippage in perception and interpretation can occur at several points; two seem most germane. First, there is the margin of distortion of those who are in the position to determine what constitutes a statistical deviation. The perceiver involved in this determination, often the psychiatrist or psychiatric epidemiologist, stands back and observes the culture—devising, perhaps in part intuitively, some notion of normative standards of behavior—and then conceptualizes behaviors that are distinctly deviant. Second, there is the basic tension in the dynamics between culture and personality. This relationship of culture and personality poses many questions similar to those involving mind-body dualism. The most important of these is whether the personality deviation, though manifesting itself through cultural symbolism, represents something separate from culture; for example, does the presence of a mental disease or defect stand outside of the influences of culture? Or, perhaps, phrased another way: Does the notion of mental health inevitably involve culturally biased value judgments? And, in keeping with this argument, is it possible to conceptualize valid generalizations about defects in physiology or in the process of socialization that might produce similar psychological distress, might be called mental illness, and might be irrelevant to the culture of the individual?

Culture–Personality Dualism

As with the dualism of mind and body, the dualism of culture and personality is reinterpreted at every stage in history. As mind-body dualism is breaking down in contemporary times with new knowledge of the biochemistry and biophysiology of mental processes, so, too—through our expansion of anthropological knowledge—the presumed dualism of culture and personality is breaking down. We are learning more about the nature of the interaction of culture with pattern disorders. Many anthropological studies have addressed questions such as whether the symptoms that psychiatry conceptualizes as evidence of mental illness are invariant in their nature, or are culturally linked—if not culturally specific (De Vos 1961). Some studies have examined the extent to which a society may pattern the actual mental disorder or may produce the personality types through child rearing and subsequent development of the individual. Others, as demonstrated by Devereux (1945), have pointed out that the culture may actually perpetuate mental dysfunction in certain roles by rewarding it. Similarly, according to other investigations, a culture may produce psychiatric disorders differentially in segments of the population, perhaps by placing such segments in certain stressful roles. In *Civilization and Its Discontents*, Freud (1962) emphasized the complexity of culture and its relationship to the development of the personality. He recognized this complexity and in many respects set the stage for the development of a psychosocial notion of mental illness.

It seems clear from the work of both psychiatrists and anthropologists that there is a strong dynamic relationship between culture and the way in which mental illness is classified, as well as between culture and personality formation. The rapidly developing field of forensic psychiatry has rendered the relevance of cultural influences on personalities (of those labeled and those who label) compelling. The forensic psychiatrist, through his taxonomy of psychiatric diseases, helps to assess which "deviant behaviors" are the result of problems and which are the result of willful intention of the perpetrator. The psychiatrist is now often involved in competency cases (making of wills, refusing medical care, custody rights over children for the child's "best interest," etc.). Yet despite this formidable and expanding influence of a professional group, there has been little reflection about what occurs in other cultures concerning these matters. Afer all, it would appear there is much to be learned from understanding any society's process of defining the nature of deviance, in understanding how cultural rules and regulations have developed around such a concept, in understanding how any society determines personal growth and moral responsibility, in learning how decisions are made as to what is criminal, what is "civil," and which actions are properly and primarily the responsibility of the offenders.

Romanucci-Ross and Tancredi in the chapter "Psychiatry, the Law, and Cultural Determinants of Behavior" address some basic issues concerning the concept of deviance in various cultures, and particularly how deviance is handled in contemporary western European and American psychiatry. Conceptual problems of the Diagnostic Statistical Manual-III and the role of the psychiatrist as negotiator or mediator for establishing order in a disrupted society are considered, along with reflections on a few important cases that occurred in the 1980s. The cases demonstrate the cultural perception of the role of the forensic psychiatrist and the manner in which abuses occur in a field where the scientific approach is outdistanced by opinion and interpretation.

Jen-Yi Wang's chapter, "Psychosomatic Illness in the Chinese Cultural Context," demonstrates even more strikingly the degree to which the culture shapes individual responses to psychological problems. Wang examines the thesis that the Chinese have a strong inclination to deny psychological difficulties, expressing them instead as physiological disorders. Once reified into physiological symptoms, these emotional problems can be subjected to physical (medical) treatment.

Underlying the need to somatize psychological problems is the fact that

Chinese culture attaches a severe stigma to psychological or emotional problems. By treating mental disease with the same methods that would be used to treat physiological illness, the disease is seen as something outside of the purely emotional problems of the patient. Much of the reason for this stigma is the importance that the Chinese place on self-discipline and control. To accept psychological manifestations is to accept the notion that individuals might lack self-discipline, despite their desire to the contrary, or the social sanctions strongly pushing in the opposite direction. This introduces another important issue—the extent to which culture has an impact on psychiatric disorders through the sanctions and strictures that it imposes on acceptable behavior. By regulating acceptable behavior strictly, as in the case of Chinese culture, behavior would be viewed as inappropriate and as disordered even if it involved only a minimal deflection from self-control and would be considered appropriate behavior in other cultures with less rigid sanctions.

Radine indicates some of the social and political forces operating in the area of care for mentally and developmentally impaired patients. He analyzes a bureaucratic structure designed to protect the rights of these patients, examining the relationships among the central office, the field staff, and the hospital staff in terms of anthropological theories about pollution and anomaly, so that we can understand the strains within and between various belief systems and subsystems in the medical culture. The field staff of rights advisers, caught between the office and the hospital, are in an impossible position, neither this nor that; they are perceived as "polluted." Thus, the central office marshals a series of rituals of demarcation and control, limiting the effectiveness so deeply desired by the agency.

CULTURAL VALUES AND THE GOALS OF PSYCHIATRIC TREATMENT

In addition to the epistemological questions of the definition of mental illness, there is a close relationship between cultural values and the goals of psychiatric treatment. Tancredi and Weisstub examine the psychiatric instruments through which our courts have become substantially engaged in the practice of psychiatry. Epidemiological studies packaged into statistical pronouncements avoid conceptual issues and conceal their presuppositions in the framework of the studies. These are implicit but discoverable only by "internal critiques" for which both the framers of studies and, even more remarkably, those who use them are unprepared. Compared with therapies in other areas of medicine, the assessment of psychotherapy is considerably more subjective. When a patient suffers from diabetes and is shown by a laboratory test to have a blood sugar of over 120, the goal of medical treatment is clear: to reduce the blood sugar, to compensate for other metabolic changes, and to educate the patient in appropriate diet and self-treatment. In psychiatry, there are no laboratory tests that can act as barometers for establishing the degree of illness and the rate of improvement. Therefore, the criteria that have often been applied to the effectiveness of psychotherapy are highly value-laden, which makes it nearly impossible to assess its impact on patients.

The Four Major Goals of Psychiatric Treatment in Western Cultures

The four major goals of psychiatric treatment are to relieve symptoms, to provide support for the patient, to assist in the definition of identity and self-actualization, and to bring about an adaptation of the patient to the requirements of society. The first of these, relieving symptoms, would appear to be the least value-laden of the goals of psychiatric treatment. But, upon further analysis, it is apparent that values enter into the criteria for determining whether symptoms have been relieved. For example, the obsessive-compulsive patient who sees a psychiatrist because he is suffering from severe anxiety and "nervousness" might be quickly relieved of his symptoms by having a tranquilizer prescribed. From the long-term perspective, the psychiatrist might examine ways of altering the behavior of the patient so as to minimize the development of symptoms. Once this step of analysis occurs, biases will enter into how the psychiatrist shapes the therapeutic objectives. Those with obsessive-compulsive disorders, or those considered manic-depressive, may be viewed as the most highly productive members of society. The psychiatrist may be so strongly directed toward minimizing these characteristics that they are dealt with at the expense of the patient's creative productivity. Therefore, in treating the underlying disorder aggressively, the psychiatrist may actually regress the patient to the cultural norm, even though the purpose is simply to relieve symptoms.

In the goal of therapy to provide psychological support in, for example, treating the housewife-mother who is suffering from anxiety and doubts about her role, therapists who see their role as that of supporting the patient may be serving simply as a palliative. The value presupposition underlying such a therapeutic decision would be that it is good to be married, to be a mother, to assume all of the household tasks full time, and to be almost totally responsible for the care of one's children.

A goal of adaptation to society has been the object of considerable criticism by a wide range of thinkers. One difficulty, of course, has been that we have never really resolved the distinction between those behaviors which we view as flowing from mental illness and those—such as taking drugs, engaging in criminal or delinquent acts, and suicide, to name a few—which we view as relatively unrelated to mental illness. Many would argue that these latter behaviors are evidence of structural personality defects. Others, taking a more conservative position on free will, might argue to the contrary: that people who engage in such criminal activities have control over their conduct and do not operate under the influence of some mental disease. There is considerable overlap between behaviors labeled criminal and those labeled sick. On a less conspicuous level, decisions to force treatment on patients, that are designed to return them to a level where they can function within the social system also address the issue of conformity and social control.

EVALUATION OF EFFICACY OF TREATMENT

Another value-laden aspect of psychiatric therapy is the role of cultural notions in defining and assessing the efficacy and effectiveness of such therapy. Whether a treatment works on a mental patient depends on the extent to which that person is socializable. As has already been pointed out, we don't have any physiological or biochemical basis for differentiating mental diseases, let alone for determining whether the treatment course is efficacious. Hence the assessment of psychiatric treatments, both verbal and nonverbal, involves cultural values that determine the "conformity" of the individual. Is the patient in a position to be able to go out into society and to function, even in a minimal way? This decision must involve examining the patient's mood, thought, and behavior from the perspective of how it will engage with that of the society at large. Once again, societal values come directly into play in determining the destiny of those individuals who are considered outside the norm. In effect, culture is involved in the development of a psychiatric nosology, the understanding of the etiology of psychiatric diseases—perhaps through the nature of child-rearing behaviors in that society—and the devising of goals used to assess the effectiveness of various treatments employed by the psychiatric profession.

The chapters in Part IV address many of the issues that have been indicated in this brief introduction. By no means are the issues resolved. The nuances are made clear in many of the chapters but, at best, more questions are raised, any one of which could lead to a profound examination of anthropological, psychiatric, and philosophical issues. The main thrust of these chapters is an examination of the variety of ways that culture creates the expression of those behaviors designated as mental illness. Another important aspect is the delineation of the complexity between culture and personality development. A final important issue underlying much of the discussion is whether the concept of mental health inescapably involves culturally biased value judgments or whether it might be the result of valid generalizations of certain conduct and distresses that are separable from cultural bias. This question remains essentially unresolved. Increasingly, through psychiatric research, it appears that certain serious conditions may have a biogenetic basis, which would give greater weight to the separability of mental illness and culture. Research on the biological and genetic basis of schizophrenia and manic-depressive illness seems to suggest strongly that certainly these very serious psychiatric disorders may have their etiology in some biochemical aberration. This discovery does not negate the importance of culture as an etiological agent or as a factor that influences the patient's condition. With regard to the less serious mental diseases or emotional difficulties, such as character disorders, neurosis, and even problems with living, the relationship between culture and personality can be quite pronounced and may argue against the generalizability of these disorders separate from cultural influences.

REFERENCES

Devereux, George. 1945. The Logical Foundations of Culture and Personality Studies. Transactions of the New York Academy of Sciences. Series II, 7:110–30.
De Vos, George. 1961. "Symbolic Analysis in the Cross-Cultural Studies of Personality." In B. Kaplan, ed., *Studying Personality Cross-Culturally*. Evanston, Ill.: Rowe, Peterson.
Freud, Sigmund. 1962. *Civilization and Its Discontents*. Tr. James Strachey. New York: W. W. Norton.

13

Psychiatry, the Law, and Cultural Determinants of Behavior

LOLA ROMANUCCI-ROSS AND LAURENCE R. TANCREDI

Forensic psychiatry is always accompanied by a set of cultural attitudes. These attitudes represent an anthropology concerning the nature of man and the nature of culture, which can be recognized only on close scrutiny of the unexpressed presuppositions of the discipline. Although we consider ourselves far removed from our primitive antecedents and our primitive contemporaries, those who study cultures have demonstrated that primitive "science" is not without its empirically verifiable scientific aspects (Lévi-Strauss, 1966, p. 15–22), and that modern thought systems of our professions are not without ritual, magic, belief in incantations, and a certain amount of liturgy (Romanucci-Ross, Moerman, & Tancredi, 1983, p. 347–348).

What are some of the fundamental characteristics of primitive societies that might be contrasted with the complexities of our own? Such characteristics have been noted and accepted as absolute. Are they? Primitive societies appear to rest on a communalistic economic base. However, their members usually do own something in excess of their needs; their possessions include songs, myths, manufacturing processes, fishing rights, rights to the produce of trees, etc. These things are of great value, so the communal aspect of property, for example, might be misleading. Functions of leadership are traditional and communal, not usually political or secular. But politics often creeps into choice of succession, and power may often be achieved through skill or situation as well as through rank, status or age. Laws in the form we know them do not exist, but laws in the form of custom and informal sanctions are more than adequate in these population isolates. Deviance, therefore, is of much more serious consequence because of reliance on custom. The major institutions of a society are indistinguishable: religion, social structure and technology are integrated. An individual is always participating in a larger segment or social construct of the society; and if something goes wrong, all look for "error" in every part of the system: within kin groups, in forest and field, in the heavens, and in the universe of all living things through which social groups are linked in totemic relationships.

In these simple societies, a concept of the self connects inner and outer worlds; therefore, the burden that falls upon the individual in our society is shared by everyone in these societies. When not attributed to foreign evil spirits that attack the traveler, illnesses are believed to have been caused by sociomoral infractions (Romanucci-Ross, 1969, pp. 201–209). Medical events are transformed into "litigation proceedings" to discover who has not fulfilled obligations or who has flouted a moral code. (In many ways this system resembles the Salem witch trials in American colonial history.)

Within the great traditions of our Western cultures, we are pleased to note that generally we do not share this view of the universe and man's place within it. Our views of "order" and its complement "disorder" are based on values we have created from centuries of "science" and rationalism using a mode of thought that is primarily analytic. We do not tolerate disorder very well; hence, we classify endlessly, putting generations of doctoral candidates to work to extend taxonomies so that we might tuck away within our classifications all of the residuals.

On the other hand, works such as Biasin's *Literary Diseases* (1975) and Sontag's *Illness as Metaphor* (1977) suggest that Western cultures may not differ from so-called primitive societies in the way that they negotiate and resolve illness. Though they do have their complex scientific taxonomies, they are at the same time influenced by emotion-laden reactions to disease. The most recent example of this, Acquired Immune Deficiency Syndrome (AIDS), brings to light widespread "irrational" reactions to disease. This disease—like leprosy, the plague, and, in more recent times, cancer—evokes pejorative meanings or metaphors that in a very real way conflate illness with notions of immorality and sin. In the sophisticated halls of clinical medicine there is rarely direct allusion to this connection, but this is not the case in the community at large. Since the beginning of the AIDS epidemic in 1982, many statements that address the issue of immorality and the etiology of this disease have found their way into the media, *both* popular and scientific. Suspicions of causality are fostered by the knowledge that certain groups and certain types of behavior are associated with AIDS, and fueled by the fact that the disease evidences certain features such as skin lesions and other "stigmata" that represent signs of physical and, by association, spiritual and moral degradation. Even some of the scientific literature in the clinical journals addresses, if only obliquely, pejorative implications of this disease (Tancredi & Volkow, 1986).

Lévi-Strauss in *The Savage Mind* (1966) demonstrated that we can relate very well to "primitive thought," by paying attention not to our respective sciences of the "concrete," but rather to similarities in semiotics, systems of transformation, and the relationship of the universal to the particular. He asks us to alter our level of discourse so that we find sophistication in primitive thought and note the metaphoric, metonymic and other nonrational elements in our thought systems. He writes:

It will be objected that there remains a major difference between the thought of primitives and our own: Information theory is concerned with genuine messages whereas primitives mistake mere manifestations of physical determinism for messages. Two considerations, however, deprive this argument of any weight. In the first place, information theory has been generalized and it extends to phenomena not intrinsically possessing the character of messages, notably to those of biology; the illusions of totemism have had at least the merit of illuminating the fundamental place belonging to phenomena of this order, in the internal economy of systems of classification. In treating the sensible properties of the animal and plant kingdoms as if they were the elements of a message, and in discovering "signatures"—and so sign—in them, men have made mistakes of identification: the meaningful element was not always the one they supposed. But, without perfected instruments which would have permitted them to place it where it most often is—namely at the microscopic level—they already discerned "as through a glass darkly" principles of interpretation whose heuristic value in accordance with reality have been revealed to us only through very recent inventions: telecommunications, computers and electron microscopes. We have only been able to evolve information theory after the recognition that the universe of information is part of the natural world. (Lévi-Strauss, 1966, p. 269)

Lévi-Strauss goes on to affirm that some societies have approached the physical world from opposite ends, "one supremely concrete, the other supremely abstract; one proceeds from the angle of sensible qualities, and the other from that of formal properties. . . . the long separated paths have crossed by the detour of communication" (Lévi-Strauss, 1966, p. 269).

In this discussion we shall seek to examine if and how this meeting of different approaches to the law and psychiatry (our classificatory "fields") from selected cultures of the world can illuminate our unexpressed presuppositions in forensic psychiatry. We shall also note how, in the evolving discourse of psychiatry, binary oppositions have dominated the decision-making process in the legal appraisal of conduct, that is, sane: insane; criminal: noncriminal, etc. We shall examine the mediators of such binary opposition and how they serve to perpetuate what are perhaps questionable dichotomies.

THE CONCEPT OF DEVIANCE

Even in primitive societies in which a social and psychological typology unites inner and outer worlds of the person, the concept of cultural solidarity exists; it is the place of a selected individual to help "straighten out" those who have strayed from the path and threatened the unity and harmony of the social group. The shaman, or his equivalent healer by any other name, scans the universe and "travels" by trance and dance to its "outer rims" and returns with the solution to the problem. For his task is to heal not only the deviant, whose waywardness may be expressed by illness, but the society as well.

Lévi-Strauss describes how the shaman and the beliefs shared by him and his patient can alter physiologic processes through the control of mental processes, as the boundaries between self and others are dissolved in healing ceremonies. The "shaman provides a language" (Lévi-Strauss, 1966, p. 198) and, like the psychoanalyst, allows the conscious and unconscious to merge. Because this is done through a shared system of symbols, the healing of one individual revitalizes the group. The patient, therefore, performs a very important social function; he provides a definition of health (physical and mental) and normalcy, and validates the symbolic system by reifying its components and its grammar as they are "embodied in real experience" (Lévi-Strauss, 1966, pp. 180–182).

In this illustration we again meet the primitive world halfway on the information circuit. As Philip Rieff has pointed out, we are "a whole society dominated by psychotherapeutic links . . . in the emergent democracy of the sick, everyone can, to some extent, play doctor to others and none is allowed the temerity to claim that he can definitely cure or be cured. The hospital is succeeding the church and the parliament as the archetypal institution of Western culture" (Rieff, 1959, p. 355).

The psychiatrist or psychoanalyst, in the process of becoming a professional, spends many years learning how to join the medical subculture. Apparently in contrast to the symbolic language acquired for healing in a primitive culture, a new language has to be learned by our psychiatrist, which is obscure to those who are served by the psychotherapeutic method. This applies equally to new conceptual frameworks and the assumptions of new values for our psychotherapeutic healers. In the process of professionalization, the individual separates himself from the arena in which he is to be effective. In a primitive culture there appears to be much more sharing by the entire group in "the medical belief system." On the other hand, even in our culture, those who come to the medical professional for help already share in the physician's belief system; furthermore, they will be allowed into medicine's Eleusinian mysteries through "patienthood" and will subsequently convert significant others in their lives to the belief system. As for the curing process, both the psychiatrist and the shaman, in a deep structural sense, allow the conscious and unconscious mind to merge so that the patient can reassemble the experience (Romanucci-Ross & Tancredi, 1987).

Although it may not be obvious on first examination, in our advanced and complex society we do share something with the shaman and his retainers. The healed patient performs a very important service for the social group. He has validated an expression of deviance and, thereby, defines normalcy for the group (Romanucci-Ross, 1969). This process of concensualizing group identity has also been noted by Kai Erickson in a historical analysis of the witch trials in *Wayward Puritans* (1966). Both psychotherapist and shaman *validate* the symbolic system as they act out the healing process, of which the audience is part. Shaman and psychiatrist both "enjoy the status of interpreter of symbols, cultural instruments for the perceiving and arranging of reality. As interpreters in understanding manifold meanings of sign and signifying function, they also play a part in the integration of symbols as generators and stylizers of patterns of systems: religious, medical, social, and economic. They are, therefore, significant vectors of a force that produces configurations, a force that compels mind, matter, and experience" (Romanucci-Ross, 1985, p. ix).

The defining of illness is a group process. A person suffering from a sickness will ask himself, "Am I ill?" and will seek confirmation from others—from family and friends, and ultimately from professionals. It has been well documented that many cultures consider certain illnesses to be natural states and, conversely, see symptom and syndrome where we see only "anxiety" in human growth and development. As an example, a state involving certain situational emissions of semen, which we would consider normal, is a state which the Ayurvedic medical practitioner would consider abnormal and would therefore seek its etiology and its cure (Obeyesekere, 1976).

The intersection of cultural values with medicine is most pronounced in psychiatry. "Because it is concerned with disorders of mood, thought and behavior, psychiatry must eke out of the panorama of everyday life . . . disturbances which involve an infusion of the symbols, imageries and metaphors of the culture into the content of specific patterns of behavior" (Romanucci-Ross, Moerman, & Tancredi, 1983, p. 262). Problems of interpretation, of course, are abundant.

Foucault has noted that in Europe from the 13th to the 15th century, the virtual disappearance of leprosy left 20,000 leprosariums to be filled—with something. That something turned out to be "mental illness." The values and attitudes that had been ascribed to lepers were then directed towards "the mad" (Foucault, 1965). The "insane" were collected in these empty hospitals along with those who had run afoul of the law, the unemployed, and those who had bitterly disappointed their families. Foucault also documented how, as European cultures were busy classifying certain behaviors as undesirable and trying to determine the proper context for mad persons, physicians were attempting to develop an intellectual framework for understanding them. It was felt that nonreason had to relate to reason, and so the logic of the insane was considered a perversion of sane logic, but nonetheless based upon it—a fitting summary for the Age of Reason, according to Foucault.

From the 16th to the 18th century, we see the beginnings of the medicalization of mental states and behaviors, as well as personal interactions when these appear "strange" to significant observers. We had only to find "scientific" evidence evolving from readings of physiognomies to statistical skewings of behavior to decide when and where, who were the strange.

The NIMH-ECA (Eaton and Kessler 1985) put forth ideas for deviance in terms of mental health. This was based on a statistical survey of about 17,000 community residents and five sites in the United States to gain a representative sample large enough to study low frequency disorders. Results were based on the Diagnostic Interview Schedule that assesses the presence, duration and severity of individual symptoms. They were then analyzed to yield diagnoses based on explicit criteria such as those used in the Diagnostic Statistical Manual-III (DSM-III). For some reason, it does not seem to be recognized that the external codes, that is, criteria supplied by the "men of reason," are the main ingredient (not questioned) put into this "truth machine." This epidemiological catchment area study was characterized in a *Journal of the American Medical Association* article as reflecting "the progress made during the past decade in improving the reliability of psychiatric diagnosis" (Glass & Freedman, 1985). Alcohol abuse dependence was found to be the most common single disorder, followed in prevalence by the occurrence of a major depressive episode during an individual's lifetime (interestingly, more than half of these episodes in individuals studied had occurred within the preceding six months), other disorders such as anxiety and panic attacks, and finally, the least common, cognitive disorders. Considering cognitive disorders, Erich Fromm once queried—if a patient's situation because of social or interpersonal causes is indeed depressing, panic-creating, or threatening to the point where he reacts in a "paranoid fashion," is this personal pathology, or given a significant number of such cases, is this more a matter of the accuracy of the patient's report of his experience (personal communication, 1961)?

All cultural groups need to establish a place for madness in their socially approved behavioral repertoire. How a consensus may be reached is demonstrated in observations of a small primitive group in the Admiralty Islands of Melanesia in the South Pacific. This chapter will not provide the complete details of the months of observation by the anthropologist; they have been documented elsewhere (Romanucci-Ross, Moerman, & Tancredi, 1983, pp. 268–272). The process observed involved the dialectic between a "mad" woman and members of her family, and the family of her alienated husband, who was seeking for a proper way to legitimize his relationship with another woman. In this small primitive society there were certain forms of behavior that were traditionally standard for a mad person to assume. Examples included removing the *laplap* (loincloth) and running about naked, running towards another person with a fishing spear, uttering a curse on the children of one's brother, or breaking a taboo, possibly by speaking to a person one must avoid.

The woman in this illustration obliged the village by doing all of these things, except for removing her loincloth, but she performed each act only once. Having satisfied some requirements, she then began to pray in the church at night, to put flowers on the table before eating, and to talk to dogs in the village. All of these things she had learned at a Catholic junior high school in faraway New Britain. Yet, it was these particular, recently acquired behaviors that compelled the villagers to pronounce her insane. The degree to which she was publicly "certified" insane varied with the degree of kinship that certain individuals had with the mad woman, or the degree of kinship that they had with her now hostile husband and his would-be bride. They expected her to be particularly crazy during those times when the moon was full, and she did not disappoint them. In the old days she would have been killed, but at the time of these observations, the village chief asked the anthropologist to refer her to the psychiatrist so that she could be sent away. Western psychiatry provided a new acculturative method of ejecting a person who could disturb group homeostasis.

During the year in which consensus of the community regarding this woman's madness evolved, the anthropologist was given every possible etiological explanation. These ranged from her being affected by the full moon, inhabited by a bad tree spirit or exposed to Western culture and religion, to her having broken the taboos of the aboriginal culture. Full moons and bad tree spirits, of course, exculpated her from responsibility—a sort of "medicalized" view of madness. The latter two reasons put the onus on her for having been the moral agent of her misfortune. Needless to say, those who cared about her medicalized her condition, and others held her to blame. None appeared to be too sorry, however, when the psychiatrist medicalized in his own idiom and put her in a hospital in New Britain.

A more intensive and explicit model of the relationship between health and morality is to be found in an investigation of mental illness and the moral order among Yemenite Jews in Israel (Palgi, 1983, pp. 319–335). For these traditional folk, isolates within Yemen society, spirits are more numerous than humans and can fly anywhere. Good or evil, male or female, they can be evoked; they have ongoing deep involvements with human beings, preferring to play their most predominant role in sexual aspects of human interaction. For example, Lilith, the leading female demon, mentioned in both the Talmud and the Koran, is capable of causing a person's death. Because of Lilith and others like her, men are warned not to sleep alone away from home for fear of seduction.

Palgi's psychiatric case histories of the Yemenite Jews reflect a preoccupation with sexual misbehavior, even within marriages, and the invocation of evil spirits who are thought to swarm around "spilled" sperm. Phantom or real pregnancies caused by *shedim* (spirits) raise a very serious problem; how did these spirits enter the Holy Land? Such *shedim* are known to have inhabited a man's body and, because of a *shed*'s jealousy toward the man's wife, make it impossible for him to have intercourse with her. This is regarded simply as a supernaturally caused illness. In every case history, then, all share the burden of perpetuating the moral order. One might say, as in Melanesia, the illness and its diagnosis are the punishment and the judgment; the treatment is the chance for cure or redemption, and reaffirmation and strengthening of the moral order.

Among Yemenite Jews, as in other parts of the Mediterranean, the "evil eye," the gaze of another motivated by envy, whether noticed or not, may cause tragedy and destruction (Moss & Cappannari, 1960; Romanucci-Ross, 1986a). Palgi's work emphasizes the social structure-and-function aspects of the evil eye, for Judaic principles demand the avoidance of extreme emotions such as anger, jealousy or pride, which injure both the subject and object of such feelings. Modesty and what is considered appropriate sexual conduct reinforce the well-being and sanctity of home and community. Both the group concept of human nature and the ideal moral order are addressed in such a belief system (Palgi, 1983, p. 334).

In some folk cultures of Italy, honored moral states can be curative: for example, a man afflicted with a mental or "nervous" illness can give a shirt of his to a "man of virtue" to wear and then return to him so that he may regain his normal mental state (Romanucci-Ross, 1986a).

If Palgi's group in the Middle East illustrates an overt acknowledgment and expression of mental illness (mitigated by supernatural causes exculpating the afflicted), in the Chinese context the "patient" escapes personal responsibility by denial that the illness is mental at all. Kleinman's stimulating analyses (Kleinman, 1977, 1980), buttressed and enriched by the writings of cultural "insiders" (Wang, 1983; Tseng, 1972, 1974, 1975), have led us to an understanding of somatization of mental illness among Chinese cultural groups. Family members of patients with severe mental illness or minor emotional problems will most often deny the affliction and keep patients at home or take them to medical doctors. Tseng (1975) reports the results of a study indicating that 70% of patients later documented as suffering from mental illness initially presented to the psychiatry clinic at National Taiwan University with somatic complaints. In other similar studies the percentages in models of presentations and diagnoses were even higher, some as high as 88% (Tseng, 1975).

Wang (1983) examines the Chinese classification of "affective disorders," which includes problems ranging from emotional discomfort to severe mental illness, notes that these are masked by physiological complaints and tries to learn why this should be so. Childhood rearing practices stress interdependence, lack of privacy and place a high value on group conformity and familism, that is, learned social behavior stresses the manner in which one is to be a child or sibling, and to become a parent and a mature, senior member of the extended family. There are public spheres and private spheres of verbal, nonverbal and other social behavior, and they do not overlap. Wang points out that "in terms of the sick role, physiological sickness is the legitimate occasion for people to show affection. . . . It is always during one's sickness that one receives expressed concern and sympathy from others." Also, "when people discover that their social obligations are too hard to bear, some unconsciously escape to avoid their obligation" (Wang, p. 307). The Chinese moral order places great value on self-control, so that failure of self-control, implicit in any affective disorder, reveals a moral weakness.

Data on mental illness are always the product of deductions and analyses of *observers* of the mentally ill. Constructs of similar observations over history would inevitably lead to what Wallace has referred to as a frequency distribution of certain personality characteristics in a certain class of persons. This class of persons would be a cultural group or a subgroup within that culture; for example, "Japanese," "peasant culture," "the Plains Indians," "persons over 50," etc. (Wallace, 1970, p. 156). Personality characteristics carry behavioral expectations for both the "actor" and the "audience." The epidemiology of mental illness or deviant behavior would be concerned with those responses that would fall outside the socially acceptable range of appropriate responses for a "certain class of persons" to defined and recognizable event structures. The components that comprise "the appropriate," as we saw from several foregoing examples, are defined by variables that are not necessarily primarily individual-psychological, but include elements of the linguistic, the economic, and the religious within the state of integration or disintegration of a cultural group.

Another manner of defining deviance which is used by certain social scientists is description in terms of sociocultural correlates. This has been analyzed by Brudner-White, who uses core and periphery theory with "order" at the center and "disorder" at the margins. Amongst conflictful goals of class and ethnic groups, young marginal males fall through the cracks of social support systems in terms of careers and are centrifugally pushed to the periphery. Oscar Lewis (1957), in his study of Mexican families and later in his "culture of poverty" studies in the United States, described the phenomenon of low status sectors not being well linked into the dominant system. The poor and certain minority groups do not interact with institutions such as banks, universities, private clubs and so forth, but rather with institutions such as welfare agencies and prisons. Delinquency, then, is not only defined and perpetuated, but actually created as young males seek fulfillment in the only sociocultural niches where it is available to them.

We have seen from the above examples that deviance is not a phenomenon to be discovered, but rather a cultural construct that can be fashioned by consensual validation in a group experience. It is a statistical concept, an artifact produced by social theorists or an "empty set" waiting to be filled by behavioral residuals that the members of a society have not yet classified because of insufficient knowledge.

DEVIANCE AND AMERICAN-EUROPEAN PSYCHIATRY

Concepts of deviance in Western European and American psychiatry are the result of divergent views. Fundamentally, deviance is predicated on a statistical sense of certain behaviors and personality traits that are at variance with comparable characteristics in the majority. This notion of deviance, as we have seen in primitive cultures, is statistical rather than ontological, for differences in personality characteristics find their basis only in the significant deviations from the norm in behaviors and conditions in question (Slaby & Tancredi, 1977). The differences of deviance, therefore, cannot be traced to well-documented and understood disorders in the biochemistry and biophysiology of the individuals exhibiting the behavior. In some cases, biochemical and biophysiological differences *may* be established, but, in fact, the label of deviance is based on the manifest content of the individual's behavior rather than the presence of pathology in brain function. As a result, deviance as a psychiatric notion covers a wide range of behaviors. It can be applied to behaviors that might be classified as criminal by a society—as a murderer or rapist might be called deviant. The definition may also apply to a range of behaviors that are noncriminal because they do not infract on the rights of others or result in injury to persons or property. An example of the latter might be the behavior of an individual who derives sexual pleasure, perhaps to the point of orgasm, from rubbing his leg against a bed post. Few would argue that this fits within the norm of human psychosexual response, but the consequences (especially if the act is done in private) are not injurious to others and, therefore, would not be classified as criminal.

A second distinction for classification can also be applied to deviant behavior across the board. This distinction deals with the antipodes of sane and insane behavior. Mental illness, perhaps best exemplified by schizophrenic behavior, would be appropriately classified as deviance (Slaby & Tancredi, 1975). The paranoid schizophrenic patient, who interprets the blinking of lights when he rides on the New York subway as evidence of communication with Mafia figures who are about to enter his subway car and harm him physically, is participating in a thinking process and behavioral response that is not considered normal. An individual whom we define as mentally disturbed may behave in either what we define as a criminal or noncriminal manner. The fact that some criminal behavior may reflect mental illness has been the major point of diacritical focus for psychiatry in the criminal process. Stated another way, psychiatry has the function of establishing that an individual's deviance is evidence of "true" mental and emotional pathology, and that certain criminal acts flow from that pathology, in contrast to other forms of deviance in which criminal acts flow from the calculated intentions of a mind that is attuned to socially perceived and agreed upon reality. This point of distinction between "insane" and "sane" criminal (or deviant) behavior also relates directly to the conceptualization of some behaviors as exculpable and others as morally culpable.

The noncriminal sane deviants have not been the focus of significant attention from forensic psychiatry. On the other hand, general psychiatry[1] has been concerned with this group and has characterized noncriminal deviants who display no evidence of serious mental disorder as being afflicted with specific personality defects, or mild mental and emotional disorganization. Justification, then, for psychiatric intervention in this noncriminal sane group is predicated on the professional's perception of symptoms, that is, the belief that these individuals suffer from anxiety or phobic reactions that relate to behaviors viewed as deviating from the norm. This is in contradistinction to psychiatric perceptions of the criminal sane deviant for whom the basis of the symptomatology is important if linked to the nature of the criminal infraction. In other words, in the former situation, the modern psychiatric basis for classifying the group within the scope of mental and emotional disorders is that these individuals suffer from certain symptoms of a psychiatric nature. In the latter group, the same symptoms may be present to some degree, as in fact they may be present in the normal person in society, but the primary focus for distinction of the group is not the personally experienced symptoms as much as the nature of the criminal infraction. Hence, a calculating rapist may experience little personal discomfiture from his psychic condition, and in part this may be due to the fact that he is able to actualize internal desires, but he is labeled a deviant because he cannot "control" his behavior to fit within the rules and regulations of the social system, as evidenced by infraction of a criminal code.

In addition to the distinctions between criminal and noncriminal, and sane and insane, psychiatry is willing to admit that the normal individual, whether statistically or clinically defined, experiences some of the same feelings and thoughts as those who are classified as deviant (Slaby, Tancredi, & Lieb, 1981). The deviant, therefore, is not qualitatively different from the normal person. He does not experience feelings or thoughts different from those of an individual who lives a traditionally well-adjusted normal life. Rather the difference rests in the quantitative admixing of mental or psychic desires, needs and fears with a set of intense emotional reactions. It has often been said in classical psychiatry that all of us have elements of the full range of thoughts and feelings that are possible within human existence. At times our thoughts might be filled with evil and destruction, and at other times with good and the heroic. The difference between the normal and the deviant experience of extreme desires lies in the way in which the desires are integrated by the individual, his success in self-control, and the range and intensity of the feeling associated with his thoughts. With this basic paradigm for understanding deviance it is easy to appreciate why the 20-year-old who is "compelled" to engage in sexual behavior, even at the expense and overt rejection of a partner, is evidencing deviant behavior. The distinction rests in some ways on the capacity of the individual to control his behavior to comport with the majority's accepted patterns of conduct. This last point is particularly important because the basis for the identification of deviance is the outward manifestation of behavior, rather than a method that allows us to delve deeply into the internal mental and emotional typology of the individual.

The Diagnostic Statistical Manual III (DSM III, 1980), which serves as the primary manual for the psychiatric classification of illnesses, has various special categories of deviance which include clusters of behaviors that involve infractions of the rules of society, and also general noncriminal behavioral disorders. Some of these disorders are explicitly concerned with an individual's inability to control behavior. Others are focused on infrastructural personality defects, possibly related to the development of the individual, which result in characteristics that permit certain deviant responses. One of the most important issues to be considered in examining certain classifications in the Diagnostic Statistical Manual III is that the classification of a disorder tends to imply total understanding of an individual. When we diagnose, for example, an individual as suffering from kleptomania—a serious disorder of impulse control—we tend to forget that this represents only one feature, albeit a prominent one, of that individual's behavior, and that the remaining parts of the personality may allow for a whole range of behaviors that would be considered normal or within the socially acceptable range of responses. There is a way in which the psychiatric classification of deviance is "situation precise" and suggests a "part-whole" relationship which does not give justice to the complexity of an individual's personality (Slaby & Tancredi, 1975). A range of behaviors that results in a diagnostic label or the attribution of "criminal" may not provide insight into the personality of the offender or even the range of his moral reactions to his life and the world at large.

A second feature to be considered in examining the psychiatric definition of deviance as a general phenomenon is that there is a high relativity component in the way in which certain behaviors are classified or not classified as psychiatric. Probably the most conspicuous example of this in recent years concerns the decision in the early 1970s to remove homosexuality from the taxonomy of mental illnesses. This decision has been the object of much research and writing and has been attributed to certain important social/cultural developments that affected the community's view of homosexual behavior. This shift in classification from a behavior that demonstrated illness to one acceptable within the range of well or normal psychosexual adjustments required a vote by the members of the American Psychiatric Association. Therefore, the deviance previously associated with homosexuality was purely culturally based, as is its status of "normalcy" at the present time. With the change in cultural perceptions of this behavior, psychiatry was pressured to reconceptualize the condition so that it was no longer viewed as a disease.

What did result from this change in the classification of homosexuality was the development of the concept *ego-dystonic homosexuality* (DSM III, 1980, Sec. 302.00). This concept resulted in a more direct focus on the presence of symptoms or maladjustment *secondary* to the condition of homosexuality, rather than on homosexuality itself as the basis for a diseased condition. Hence, in the classification of ego-dystonic homosexuality, the Diagnostic Statistical Manual III focuses on the presence of an overpowering desire to acquire a heterosexual pattern of relationship (DSM III, 1980, Sec. 302.00). These patients are disaffected and distressed over their homosexual needs. The symptom, therefore, that is the focus of the definition of "deviance" or "illness" as it applies to homosexuality, is that of preoccupation with the desire to change sexual orientation and the presence of a range of emotions from guilt, anxiety, and depression to shame. So-called ego-syntonic homosexuality is not classified in the DSM III as a mental disorder. The DSM III (1980, Sec. 302.00) presents two diagnostic criteria for ego-dystonic homosexuality: first, a sustained pattern of homosexual arousal which the patient insists is a source of distress, and secondly, the presence of insufficient heterosexual arousal to allow for the initiation or maintenance of a heterosexual relationship.

The example of homosexuality is important not because it addresses the classification of a behavior that is currently viewed as criminal (for in most jurisdictions homosexuality is no longer classified as such) but because it clearly demonstrates some of the relativistic aspects of what is accepted as deviance. There are other disorders listed in the DSM III that are deviant and may involve behaviors that are clearly criminal, in the circumstance. One group of such behaviors would be disorders of *impulse control* (DSM III, 1980, Secs. 312.31–312.39). These disorders have various features that are in common. First, they involve failure of the individual to resist a temptation, a desire or an impulse to perform an act. The act may be injurious to others and may also be ego-syntonic with the participant; that is to say, the individual who engages in the act may shape the desire in his consciousness to engage in the behavior. Some examples of disorders of impulse control include pyromania (DSM III, 1980, Sec. 312.33), kleptomania (DSM III, 1980, Sec. 312.32), explosive disorders (DSM III, 1980, Sec. 312), and pathological gambling (DSM III, 1980, Sec. 312.31). The patient may or may not feel a sense of guilt or self-reproach following the act which he is unable to resist.

One of the most interesting acts is pathological gambling which, consistent with impulse disorders, involves the inability of the afflicted individual to resist the impulse to gamble, even in the face of compromising or harming family, personal resources or vocational plans. These patients experience a whole range of associated symptoms, such as an inability to function socially, loss of work, and inability to handle financial responsibilities, and engage in a range of secondary criminal behaviors such as forgery, fraud and embezzlement for the purposes of repaying the money that is lost from the gambling (DSM III, 1980, Sec. 312.31). The DSM III requires certain diagnostic criteria for pathological gambling. These include the inability to resist the impulse to gamble, and three of the following associated symptoms (see DSM III, 1980, Sec. 312.31): arrest for forgery, fraud or related white collar crime, default on debts, relationship problems with family and spouse, inability to account for money, loss of work and borrowing money.

In addition, the criteria include an exclusionary phrase specifying that the gambling is not due to an antisocial personality disorder. It is important to note that in all of these impulse control disorders, the emphasis is on the individual's inability to control the compulsiveness of his behavior. Certainly there may be individuals who do not desire to gamble all the time and can control their urges but, in fact, choose to gamble continuously. They would not be classified according to the DSM III as possessing an impulse control disorder. The impulse control disorders are particularly important because they represent important differential diagnoses of the cause and reasons for criminal behavior.

A diagnostic label that is frequently associated with much criminal behavior is the *antisocial personality disorder* (DSM III, Sec. 301.70). This condition is present in a diverse range of individuals viewed as deviant and criminal. More than simply an inability to control impulses, it includes a very basic structural disarrangement or defect in the individual's personality that results in behaviors that are unacceptable to society. This defect has often been explained in psychoanalytic terms as resulting from disturbances in the growth and development of the superego, allowing basic id desires to dominate the personality unimpeded, so that the individual is not informed of socially and morally acceptable behavior.[2] In the DSM III, antisocial personality disorder has various diagnostic criteria. Some of the most important include the requirement that the onset has to occur before the age of 15 as evidenced by a history of at least three of the following (DSM III, Sec. 301.70): truancy of a certain severity as established by the number of days per year, episodes of expulsion or suspension from school, running away from home overnight, persistent lying, repeated drunkenness or substance abuse, vandalism, initiation of fights and thefts, and delinquency and overall evidence of chronic violation of rules at home, at school and within other social institutions.

A second list of characteristics includes the manifestation after the age of 18 of certain behavioral patterns, such as inability to sustain a job, lack of responsibility as a parent, failure to accept norms of lawful behavior, inability to maintain an enduring relationship, failure to honor obligations of a financial or other nature, failure to plan ahead, a basic disregard for the truth, and finally, general recklessness. Another diagnostic criterion that must be present is continuous antisocial behavior that violates the rights of others with no period of time of at least five years when such behavior did not occur. Last is the provision that excludes those afflicted with severe mental retardation, schizophrenia or manic episodes.

The antisocial personality is particularly important to the law because many, if not most, of those who engage in repeated or recidivistic criminal behaviors are included in this class. Although this disorder is listed as a mental illness and classified as such in the DSM III, the law has not responded with sympathy to patients suffering from this condition. In the increasingly popular American Law Institute test for insanity, the second provision explicitly excludes consideration of recidivistic behavior alone as evidence of insanity (Brooks, 1974). By including this provision the American Law Institute is essentially excluding the antisocial personality from possible exculpation on the basis of insanity for criminal acts. The antisocial personality, therefore, is a psychiatric construct that represents individuals who are clearly deviant, likely to be criminal and perceived as possessing a serious personality disorder.

Equally important, this condition, as conceptualized in the DSM III, is global with respect to the individual's personality and psychic interests. Unlike pathological gambling, for example, the characterization of antisocial personality includes the full range of the ways in which the individual may react to his world and to his relationships. The pathological gambler may be compulsive and obsessed by his need to participate in gambling behavior, and this compulsiveness and obsessiveness may affect, by virtue of its occupation of the mind of the sufferer, his abilities to relate and to engage in other activities. But the pathological nature of the individual's condition is not so pervasive of his personality as it is in the case of the antisocial personality disorder. That the antisocial personality disorder does not render itself to specific pathology is in part the reason why the legal system has not accepted it as exculpatory of certain behavioral deflections that adversely affect society. Somewhere in the chorus of societal understanding of the antisocial personality disorder is the notion that the individual has control over his behavior, that he is capable of initiating and controlling his will. Self-knowledge and reflexivity, therefore, do characterize the antisocial personality disorder but must be viewed as descriptive rather than ontological or explanatory of any particular behavior. In this one example, we see how psychiatric understanding of a condition has had minimal influence on legal and moral attributions of responsibility for behavior.

Psychiatric representations of deviance, as we have discussed in the above examples from the DSM III, focus most particularly on what some might argue are objective data regarding an individual's external behaviors. Psychiatry has created a diagnostic or taxonomic system for understanding deviance, which essentially ends its inquiry into behavioral manifestations. It has created a classification of people based on behavioral patterns that may be suggestive of infrastructures of abnormality in the subjective parts of an individual's mind, but which do not require an understanding of such internal processes. Deviance, therefore, is not only situation-precise and culturally determined, even within psychiatry, but it requires certain patterns of behavior. Although these features may be important in developing a psychiatric taxonomy of deviant behavior, they provide us with little information regarding issues of personal responsibility. The focus on objective patterns gives us minimal insight into an individual's intent and his ability to construct a moral perception of reality, or into his ability to exert his will over behaviors that may be destructive or that involve infractions on the rights of others.

The law as it deals with criminal behavior will allow for the imputation of intent, but that imputation—however important for establishing responsibility, guilt or innocence—does not require a "scientific" assessment of subjective processes. The inference, in any event, is always from the objective external manifestation to the subjective, even if one relies on psychological tests. But the objective, when shaped by psychiatric diagnosis, is sufficiently far removed from the truth of subjective intent or desire that its accuracy for that purpose must be called into question. Personal responsibility in various cultures may be based wholly on the individual's behavior. There may be little effort to attempt to understand what we in Anglo-American law call mens rea or *criminal-mindedness*. Psychiatry attempts to do this to the extent that it interprets a cluster of behaviors as "revealing" of certain intent, but the phenomenology of psychiatric taxonomy does not suggest the cause, which would enable one to make precise statements about the intent of the deviant engaging in behaviors that are either criminal or noncriminal. Although it is assumed that deviant behaviors require conscious intent on the part of the actor, in very few circumstances is it possible to ascertain whether this exists. A theory of personhood, therefore, would have to incorporate power over behavior but would require much more to address an individual's range of feelings, thought processes and capacity to exert his will over thoughts and actions. This does not exist to any degree in the taxonomy of deviant behaviors, or in modern psychiatric understanding of the relationship of thought and feelings to action.

Psychiatry relies on statistical or predictable notions about personality characteristics. Even though the psychiatrist/patient relationship is on a one-to-one basis, and even though the origins of modern psychiatry rely on Freud's interpretations of single patients, the information gleaned from the one-to-one encounter has been abstracted and generalized in a type of pseudo statistic that is applied as a framework to understand patients' behavior. Furthermore, this overarching pattern involves imputing intent and other elements of personhood to patients or offenders in the criminal process. But by virtue of the phenomenological fields involved, these constructs are necessarily "objectively" derived. They are derived by abstraction from early case studies, augmented by interpretation of these abstractions through the history of modern psychiatry in the light of cultural notions of intentionality, good, evil and personal responsibility. These qualities, therefore, cannot be understood from the subjective state of the patient or offender in the criminal process. In fact, even the tests applied to glean information for understanding qualities such as intent and personal responsibility have the stamp of the objective or culturally derived notion of these qualities.

This is not to say that methods do not exist for better understanding the subjective elements of personhood. The process for such understanding is not highly featured in modern psychiatry; consequently, when they have presented themselves as having the capacity for understanding thoughts and feelings and their association with action, other areas of inquiry that might have led to more creative methods for determining individual subjective qualities have received little or no encouragement from psychiatry. As we will see shortly in the *Estelle* and *Barefoot* cases, the psychiatric basis for arriving at notions of remorse is a framework of understanding that deals with only one basic cultural group derived from one historical context, and from a unique micro event.

RULES, SANCTIONS, PROSCRIPTIONS, AND LAW

As far back as the 1920s, F.E. Williams, an Australian government anthropologist for Papua New Guinea, assured the world that "despite full-blooded passions, amongst these primitives we do not find license and anarchy" (Williams, 1930, p. 308); nevertheless, one has to deal not with statutes as we know them, but with "native morality and rudiments of law." The latter are distinguished from the former in that they serve as insurance for good conduct. They are one step removed from a set of social norms that define acceptable and ideal behavior.

In primitive groups such as those Williams documented, a distinction is made between those towards whom an individual has a particular and more intense set of moral obligations (such as through lineage and/or clan), and those outsiders from whose group he may take a wife or with whom he may wage war. Among cannibals, exophagy or "eating out" is the rule. With those in an ingroup, respect or avoidance (as a form of respect) is the rule. For outsiders, a member of the group has only invective; defiance and all of his hostility, both personal and collective, may be heaped on these. There is even an art to this "strong talk" and ritualized phrases for certain occasions. Such language would be abhorred for in-group behavior, but commendable when used toward the outsider groups. Pride in identity is reserved for the in-group. Later we shall examine attitudes in our own culture towards the deviant and the immigrant, who would be viewed as a deviant until a certain degree of acculturation has been achieved. Those of us who have lived for considerable periods of time in native villages have noted how peace and harmony, relatively speaking, dominate interpersonal relationships within clans or lineages, and, contrastively, how quarreling escalates as one observes relationships between individuals and groups over a wider spectrum of kinship groups.

One carefully documented case concerned two half brothers, who, representing two different lineages in a dispute over ownership of land and hunting and fishing rights, drew others into a bitter quarrel that lasted for years (Romanucci-Ross, 1966). Recognizing that the legal system of the Australians presaged future forms of litigation and resolution of conflict, these Admiralty Island natives were trying to establish past landownership and usufruct, and to have these registered in administration records. Interestingly, because a child in this bilingual village usually spoke the language of the mother first and that of the father second, these two young men—born of different mothers—spoke different first languages. Their differences were amplified by their not sharing similar traditional customs such as totemic allegiance, or religious values such as dedication to the Catholic church. Factors that influenced the decision about landownership came from many sectors of the society. First and foremost was the reckoning of rights by kinship rules. These rules went far back in time to totemic beginnings, even to the mythological creation of "the place." Both intervillage and intravillage disputes were routinely argued with quasi-historical statements. Validations of land claims relied on genealogy rooted in mythological and historical narrations, complete and exclusive knowledge of which gave title if the content was favorable to the claim. Each litigant had a story favorable to his own claim, of course, so that validation of status and status differentiation needed to be adduced as proof. For example, the history of ancestors' large ceremonial exchanges were cited as proof of the validity of land claims by the present generation; long-accepted claims were challenged by contesting a version of events of several generations ago. It is interesting that the new claimants now argued from a standard of the contact culture, claiming strict patrilany against the traditional reincorporation of the sisters' son, and *now* said that the status-validating payments in dogs' teeth and shell money of yore were worthless. Even more interesting to the anthropologist was the Australian administration trying to make the point that what was traditionally valid *then* had to be respected now.

The distinction between a civil and criminal offense in the in-group is not clear. Wife-beating, for example, involves a perpetrator and a victim, who really belong to different clans or kin groups since both have "married out." Disputes over land or sea rights, or other possessions, would rarely occur between two who are really one and the same in terms of group identity. But, to take one example of treatment of in-group immoral actions, among the Pere group of Manus (Admiralty Islands) illness is believed to be caused by a moral infraction by one member of the group to which the "patient" belongs. A child may be ill because the parents quarrel, or because a closely related person has committed adultery or left a debt unpaid within a ceremonial exchange. All can be set right by a public confession by the guilty party, payment of the debt or termination of the adulterous relationship. This may occur after a medium (a woman past her childbearing years who has borne a son now dead) has consulted with the ghost of her dead son to learn from the world of the dead the moral diagnosis of the disaster (Fortune, 1935). Reversible illness, physical or mental, has played a major role in the native system of moral sanctions: each event contained both the punishment and the illness—the judgment in the diagnosis and the reward for rectification in cure (Romanucci-Ross, 1969, p. 207).

In primitive societies there is no concept that moral codes would appeal to "rational man," for there is no disjunction between the "rational" mind and the "irrationality" of the universe. In these societies one can be a man or woman of virtue and still be struck by sorcery or break a taboo against one's totem *without knowledge or intent*. Intentionality as a concept that is basic to much of criminal law, particularly as regards specific intent to a crime, is also a modern notion. Primitive societies do not conceptualize personhood as including the qualities of mental processes such as intentionality, rationality or even free will. In the early period of Greek history, as represented in epics such as the *Iliad* and the *Odyssey*, personhood also lacked definition. To the Greeks, much individual decision making was attributed to the desire of the gods, and persons were not perceived as possessing control over their lives or having a sense of identity separate from the community as represented by the realm of the gods (Harrison, 1966).

There is a radical shift in notions of morality and law in peasant societies throughout the world. Peasant cultures are small "pocket cultures" existing within larger societies with their own historical great traditions. These isolated folk groups are not as exposed to "cultural exchanges" as are their compatriots in urban areas. However, in our time they are becoming increasingly aware, to some degree through the media, of what touches their sophisticated conationals. The urban sophisticates often dip into peasant culture to rediscover their own traditions and borrow them from time to time.

Consider the following contrast. Primitive societies are an excellent field to survey. Their acceptance of conflict, conflictual situations and stylization are instructive about proscriptions and mechanisms for conflict avoidance. Let us examine the paradigm of a peasant village in rural Mexico (Romanucci-Ross, 1986b). In this setting, involvement *meant* conflict, and in this selected village in the state of Morelos, Mexico, morality consisted mainly of avoidance, rather than action. The local moral code counseled extreme avoidance of social activity and group membership. Yet the code of manliness urged members of the community not to yield or to "give in." A village leader, who established his ability to dispense patronage by profiting from community resources personally, could legitimize his position and mitigate its aura of immorality by sharing some of the personal benefit he derived (Romanucci-Ross, 1986b, p. 94). While socioeconomic factors took precedence over all others in reckoning status, moral status had its own components and could act as modifier, although this was more true for women than men.

Sanctions, especially for transgressions that were emotional or sexual in nature, took the form of witchcraft. Violence was resorted to only by males (with one exception), and moreover only by males from the *macho* (manly) subgroup or the subgroup of alcoholics and heavy drinkers. The "manly" who would not yield were almost always alcoholics or heavy drinkers, and were considered deviant by the village. Others considered deviant were women thought to be witches. There were, of course, shades and degrees of deviance: among women, those who had had extramarital or premarital "affairs" or an abortion, two who were thought to be lesbians, the unchaste, the unreserved, the lazy, etc. were considered deviant; among men, those who did not work hard, and who did not discipline their children. The "mad" of both sexes were considered deviant. Although no one in the village had been put away in a mental institution, there were those who were considered deviant because they were "away" from the village. This group included the young teenagers who had been sent to a high school in a small urban center, for advanced studies. Many of these teenagers developed "attacks" which were diagnosed by physicians as being purely hysterical in nature; the young villagers usually returned without finishing school.

Sanctions and rules were powerful socializing agents, with gossip as a forceful handmaiden. At the same time "the law" in the village was often talked about. The law was distant—it was associated with Mexico City. It was considered negotiable and corruptible, but where landownership rights were concerned, all believed there was an ultimate solution to disputes. Such solutions were the gains of the Mexican Agrarian Revolution (1910–1917) and were considered inviolable.

Experience told them otherwise. Illustrative is a case that spanned many years and concerned the rights of an *ejido* (owner) to commercialize a sulphur spring on his property. (*Ejidos* were a part of a post-revolutionary concept of landownership which stipulated that a man could have his *ejido* or farmland as long as he worked it.) Legal issues did not center so much on whether or not the individual in question worked his *ejido* but whether the sulphur spring on his *ejido* "belonged" to him or to the village. Legal issues, although they were unclear, became irrelevant as the individual employed lawyers from Mexico City and the villagers did likewise. Visiting politicians were soon asked to take a stand on the issue and opted "for the people," using the only phrase that gave them political credibility and viability. In short, no one, neither those involved nor those passing through, was interested in a proper legal solution to the problem. Public opinion rallied against one person, which revived an ideology that seemed to revitalize the body politic of a small village. Individuals who had sustained long-standing hatreds towards each other became "as one." Even class distinctions, for a time, melted away. In the euphoria, conflictants believed that the law coming down from the nation's capital would be on their side. No one in the village noticed at the time that there was no particular interest in what the "points of law" were, not even among their attorneys. The solution was political: the individual who had wanted to do something constructive for himself—and, he claimed, for the village—was ejected from the system. An order came from somewhere in Mexico City asking him to take up *ejido* in another part of Mexico. In a more recent visit to the village the investigator found a commercialized "pool" and recreational building "developed" by certain wealthy persons in Mexico City. Reflecting on the outcome of this case, villagers assured the anthropologist that the law has nothing to do with them; it should not be resorted to again, and should be avoided when at all possible (Romanucci-Ross, 1986b).

In Western cultures, particularly the United States, we also see the negotiable features of the law and their impact on the community. The criminal process, from the discovery of a crime to the identification of a potential offender and the resolution of societal and individual interests, offers much opportunity for negotiation between individuals and the community. The most conspicuous example of this is the plea-bargaining process itself, by which the prosecution negotiates with the defendant for information regarding a crime or a series of criminal actions, and the defendant negotiates for a lesser sentence or mitigation through early parole.

The involvement of psychiatry in the criminal process is further testament to the negotiation that occurs between the offender and the state or the community. In many respects the psychiatrist is interposed between the offender and the state to mitigate and to negotiate the dominance of the community over the rights of the individual. Unfortunately the role of the psychiatrist is not clearly defined, and this ambiguity has the perverse results of allowing the psychiatrist to be sensitive and responsive to the needs of society in certain circumstances, and in other circumstances to be relatively protective of the needs of the individual being brought to trial. The use of the psychiatrist might be seen as a method of dealing with those situations where negotiation between the prosecution and the defense is hampered by the incompetence, or the reputed incompetence, of the defense. The psychiatrist is usually brought into a case when there is a question of the competence of a defendant to stand trial, for example, or when there is an allegation of insanity as the basis of the criminal act. In the question of competence to stand trial, the psychiatrist's role is to assure that the defendant or putative defender is competent to assist in his own defense, and to understand the nature of the charges against him and the principal actors involved in the court drama. But one can also look at this situation from the perspective of negotiation, and argue that the psychiatrist's role is to assure that the defendant is in the best possible position to interact with the prosecution in the courtroom and, if need be, to enter negotiations toward resolution of the case.

However, there are many difficulties in seeing the psychiatrist as purely the modus operandi for fair negotiations between the various parties in a criminal case. There is, in actual practice, much ambiguity regarding the role of the psychiatrist. He participates in the power struggles between the parties, but his bias or particular theoretical perspective may allow for distortion of his "scientific" information to the benefit of one party over the other. Rather than being a neutral force towards the actualization of negotiation or the balancing of mutual interests, the psychiatrist has the opportunity to act as a third power force to influence the outcome through his own devices, which may be a distortion of the basis of his psychiatric knowledge. The problematic aspects of having the psychiatrist serve a function between the prosecutor and the defense, or between the community and the individual, have been most evident in recent years in cases which have involved the psychiatrist in the sentencing process.

The first such case was *Estelle* v. *Smith* (1983), a Texas case which reached the United States Supreme Court. This case dealt with psychiatric testimony at the sentencing phase of the trial of an offender who had been indicted for a murder that occurred during an armed robbery when his associate fatally wounded a grocery store clerk. During the sentencing proceeding, according to Texas law, the jury is instructed to resolve three critical issues which will determine whether the death sentence is to be imposed. The issue that is of particular relevance to psychiatry deals with the potential dangerousness of the defendant. In this case, the psychiatrist had conducted a 90-minute pretrial psychiatric examination of the defendant to determine whether he was mentally competent to stand trial. During the sentencing proceeding the testimony of the psychiatrist was used for the purposes of resolving the issue as to future dangerousness. The psychiatrist, during the pretrial examination, had concluded that the defendant would continue to be a serious threat to society. In fact, he testified that he (a) "is a very serious sociopath," (b) "will continue his previous behavior," (c) suffers from a sociopathic condition which will "only get worse," and (d) has no "regard for another human being's property or for their life," and (e) that "there is no treatment, no medicine . . . that in any way at all modifies or changes this behavior," (f) the defendant "is going to go ahead and commit other similar criminal acts if given the opportunity to do so," and, finally, (g) the defendant "has no remorse or sorrow for what he has done" (1983, p. 454). This evidence allowed the jury to conclude that the defendant was in fact a serious future danger to society. Having resolved all of the three required questions in the affirmative, according to the Texas law the defendant had to receive the death penalty.

This case went to the United States Supreme Court, not on the issue of the appropriateness of psychiatric testimony at the sentencing proceeding, but on the issue of violation of the defendant's Fifth Amendment privilege through the psychiatrist using his pretrial evaluation of the offender to provide information at the sentencing proceeding without having informed the defendant that he might do so. It was determined in this case that the defendant's Fifth Amendment privilege against self-incrimination and Sixth Amendment right to the assistance of counsel were violated by the psychiatrist's testimony.

But the more significant question is why this testimony was allowed at all: may the psychiatrist use his evaluation of a patient based on what scientific information exists to substantiate his opinions or perceptions, and to provide information to a jury to determine whether the death penalty should be imposed? The psychiatrist in such a situation is faced with a serious conflict of interest, amplified by the ambiguity of his role. Although he is hired by the court to assist in decision-making around evaluation and disposition of an offender, there are still elements of a physician/patient relationship in the way he relates to the defendant. It is not unlikely that a patient talking with a psychiatrist, even if informed that the psychiatrist is an agent of another party, will lapse into moments of undefendedness and provide critical information which is interpreted by the psychiatrist and which may be used against the offender.

In having such a role, the psychiatrist becomes a final arbiter on the issue of the death sentence. To the extent that he resolves one of the most important questions for the jury—whether the patient is still dangerous— and establishes the remorselessness of the offender's reaction to his crime, the psychiatrist provides weapons, by way of "information," which help the jury and judge to arrive at a decision that they may not otherwise reach comfortably. To further complicate the situation, studies suggest that psychiatrists and other behavioral scientists are not reliable in their determinations of the potential future dangerousness of an individual (Monahan, 1981). Information that allows us to abstract social and behavioral parameters to predict future behavior simply does not exist.

The third critical issue involving the role of the psychiatrist in proceedings of this nature is that the psychiatrist serves in a way to exculpate the judge and the jury from having to address the hard questions. If the psychiatrist is able to provide some scientific basis for a decision, he has effectively absolved the jury and court of the responsibility of carefully examining the grounds on which this defendant should be executed for his acts. The psychiatrist, in many respects, can only offer the merits of pseudoscience in this decision-making because of the limited research and information that is available on the issue of potential dangerousness. Some would argue he has more to provide than the average juror or court judge in determining whether or not an individual is likely to be dangerous or whether he possesses the requisite guilty conscience to have some remorse, but this difference can be only marginal. Unfortunately, the psychiatrist's testimony can be very powerful at this stage in the trial of an offender. Its power derives from the stamp of scientific validity, albeit of questionable merit. Hence we see in the sentencing process a very clear conflict of interest: the psychiatrist in many ways is serving the purpose of the state with limited basic information available for arriving at an informed opinion, while at the same time ostensibly trying to appear neutral on the issue of the litigation between the state and the offender, but ultimately clearly favoring one party over the other.

The "hypothetical" was introduced as a way to avoid some of the conflict that the psychiatrist experiences during an examination of an offender to obtain information for either competence to stand trial or sentencing. In this method of inquiry, the lawyer for either side presents a hypothetical case to a psychiatrist at a court proceeding, and then asks him to comment on it. The hypothetical case may resemble the description of the legal case at hand, but it is felt that the hypothetical format allows the psychiatrist to remove himself to some extent from the offender, and thereby to be more "objective" in his assessment of personality characteristics, such as potential dangerousness. To a large extent this is true; it is a more objective approach to the issues of future dangerousness. But the problem is that the affect of both the defendant and the investigator are very important in the assessment of the defendant's capacity to experience remorse or guilt, and of the potential for change in his behavior. Affect is not accessible to a psychiatrist when he is only presented with a hypothetical case. Nonetheless, the Supreme Court in the case of *Barefoot* v. *Estelle* (1983) upheld the use of the hypothetical question, adding that it should be deduced from facts that are not disputed in the case. The court went on to say that the hypothetical question may be deduced from facts in the case and that it is not necessary that these facts be founded upon personal knowledge. This means, in effect, that the psychiatrist could be provided with a hypothetical case involving information that is relevant to the defendant, and on that basis be asked to comment on the likelihood of dangerousness and the remorsefulness of the "patient." In part it is felt that protection for the defendant exists to the extent that each side can bring in its own psychiatrist and ask him to respond to the hypothetical question. On the other hand, as in the case of *Estelle* v. *Smith*, only one psychiatrist's testimony may be used at the sentencing phase of the trial. Even more importantly, faced with a dispute between psychiatrists, a court and jury are likely to respond more fully to the position that closely represents their own views of the outcome of the case. The psychiatrist then has simply provided additional and perhaps critical fuel to propel the jury and the court to find an individual guilty or to impose the death penalty.

These cases and the role of the psychiatrist in competency hearings, in insanity defense arguments and even in the commitment process show the extent of the use of psychiatry as an interface between the community and the individual. The danger in this, as we have already suggested, is that conflicts of interest preclude reliance on meaningful guidelines that can be systematically applied to all cases in which certain testimony based on well-conceptualized and clinically recognized psychiatric information holds weight. The importance of these examples of the use of psychiatry is that they demonstrate that the role of the psychiatrist may be to shift the burden of decision-making, or to absorb the burden of decision-making from those who are in the best position to make the decisions—the judge and the jury, which represent community morality. They represent the legal and regulatory arms of the community or society and therefore should be critical enough to arrive at their own decisions regarding the defendant, using the psychiatrist at most as only one source of input towards that end. Oftentimes, however, the psychiatrist's input is given significant weight and relieves the decision-makers from having to struggle with the difficult question of individual responsibility.

MADNESS AND DANGER TO OTHERS

The definition of "madness" as a negotiable event has cross-cultural analogies in many societies of a similar level of complexity. We offer the example of a small Italian town in 1913, and the fate of Adalgisa Conti (Conti, 1978). At the age of 26, Conti was confined to a madhouse by her husband and his family because after several years of marriage with no children, no sexual congress with her husband, no career and no friends, she had become "melancholic," somewhat too "religious" and had lost her desire to do housework for her in-laws. The medical justification for her institutionalization was that she was "melancholic" and "suicidal." Later she became "schizophrenic," and at times, "erotic" (Conti, p. 80). By 1940 she was "disorderly, dirty, demented, hardworking" (Conti, p. 83). In 1978 a group of psychiatric social workers decided to look closely at her career in the asylum, for she had lived into her 90s. Their investigation included conversations with many from her hometown who had known her and her situation. In addition the social workers examined her autobiography written for her physician and her many letters over the years to her physician and family. What emerged was the profile of an intelligent, passionate, respected woman who happened to live in a sexually phobic society. It was also learned that her husband, having tired of her in a divorceless culture, and enjoying considerable influence as a businessman and politician, had asked for a collusion of opinion to rid him of a barren and "now melancholic" wife.

There are some interesting minor event similarities in several cases mentioned earlier. Both the Melanesian husband in the case described above and the Italian husband had another woman "waiting in the wings," with children to be legitimized in one way or another. Both women, when taunted, happened to ferociously bite a finger of one who came too close to them;

and tragically, each woman eventually accepted the fact that she "must be mad" because of the manner in which "people stare at me, and act as if I am not a person," and because each was driven to "lacerating" tendencies. Both thought they must have sinned excessively to be punished in this way.

That the two women were in a state of mental disequilibrium cannot, perhaps, be asserted without contradiction. What is being asserted here is that both were an inconvenience of some magnitude to their husbands, their husbands' families, and relatives of the "other woman" in the social spaces of daily interactions. Both deteriorated in *behavior* during the period of the *negotiation* of their madness and even more rapidly during subsequent institutionalization. Although there were many differences between a small "primitive" group in the South Pacific and a small peasant group in northern Italy, similarities in social structure and notions of deviance coalesce in both places to eject from the system a troublesome, powerless person through confinement.

One does not have to look too far into the history of institutionalization of the mentally ill in the United States to discover similar scenarios. One of the most important cases in the history of commitment of patients in the United States was the *Packard* case in the mid to late 19th century. On the petition of her husband, Mrs. Packard spent nearly three years in a state mental hospital in Illinois. She had been wrongfully involuntarily committed to serve the interests of her husband and members of the family. Once released, she became very active in a nationwide campaign to enact legislation for the protection of the civil rights of the mentally ill. Her efforts were very important in the early part of the history of commitment in this country because they brought about significant changes in many state laws. These changes included the requirement that a notice be sent to a patient regarding the possibilities of commitment, fair hearings on the issue of commitment and, in some cases, even the right to a jury trial if the patient requested it. As in Melanesia and in northern Italy, the actors in the *Packard* and many subsequent cases used the mental health system as a way to eject the unwanted individual from the social system.

CONTEXT AND NEGOTIATION OF IDENTITY: PARADIGM OF A CULTURAL PROCESS

Identity can be defined as self-conscious self-percepts which are derived from events and event constructs (De Vos & Romanucci-Ross, 1982). The self shapes identity. It does this by processing information from the behavioral environment, thereby generating a self that is from and for social contexts which may or may not signal back the acceptance of the presented self. An ethnic group looks at other groups as contrasts with itself, and then decides what not to eat, what not to wear, what not to say and what not to become. We will employ here, as a paradigm for any other definition of self as "deviant," the historical experience of an immigrant ethnic class in the United States. We refer to that period in American history, the end of the 19th and beginning of the 20th centuries, which was characterized by great waves of European migrations.

Investigators who have considered these immigrant groups and this period, have written as though there did not exist a culturally dominant group established in the United States, which defined acceptable and permissible behavior. We take as our example Italian immigrants, who in frequently cited studies (e.g., Glazer & Moyniham, 1963) are described as overwhelmed and defeated by their "need" to huddle in cities, "villagers" who were "fatalistic."

Italian immigrants came to the United States in large numbers between 1900 and 1914, at a rate of from 100,000 to 285,000 per year. From a Senate Report of 1896 we learn they were "from among the illiterate races" who "remain in the cities to lower the standards of the already crowded Atlantic Territory"(Nelli, pp. 7–11, 66). They were sufficiently culturally diverse from their immediate predecessors, the Irish and the Germans, to be isolated and burlesqued. Earlier groups of immigrants had always been fare for comedy or opprobrium, as residents attempted to remove the newcomers from the competition for opportunity space.

Italians came here in large numbers during those years in which abstinence had become public morality. Populist anti-intellectualism reigned and traditional Protestant society had taken a stand against the urban industrial lifestyle. In the South, these immigrants accepted work reserved only for blacks, and did not know that in the white American South this made them substitutable for blacks, hence lynchable.

Before 1900, Lincoln Steffens, the biographer of cities, had already described Chicago as violent and filthy. Shortly after Steffens made this observation, Italians in Chicago, though only 528 in number, were routinely described by many journalists and commentators as violent and living in filth. Nelli (1970) has shown that at the turn of the century, those 528 Italians lived rather well through honest work and business.

In a 1936 study of Italian immigrants in San Francisco it was noted that interviewer characterizations were neither logically nor operationally derived from the data collected by the interviewers, but were like the Chicago caricatures (Radin, 1936). Actually, in the American West, as Radin demonstrated, these immigrants were spectacularly successful, both economically and culturally.

Early studies of East Coast Italian immigrants featured another type of *observation*. The Glazer and Moynihan (1963) and Gans (1962) studies suffer, as did Banfield's (1958), from the cogito of the authors, who portrayed Italian immigrants as "deviants," in their hypotheses concerning cooperation and socially conscious participation in community affairs. (Banfield used an Iowa model as standard.) Gans (1962) typed Italian immigrants as to behavioral styles and found them maladapted mobile action seekers. Like Glazer and Moyniham, Gans found them to be "villager, traditional," Banfieldian amoral familists who avoid community action.

Reporters and social scientists were not aware, of course, that when Italian immigrants celebrated their own identity amongst themselves, they were much involved in church and neighborhood activities, religious and patriotic festivals, mutual aid societies, their own immigrant banks (one of which, Bank of America, is now nationally prominent), and their own literature. For the researchers and journalists however, these immigrants *manifested* an identity in any instance, no matter how rare or trivial, which met the expectations of the observer.

All of this prepared this immigrant group for the "scientism" of the 1930s that asserted that Italian immigrants had *an aptitude for crime*. Journalists reveled in "instancing" criminal behavior, real and imagined. Six Italians were lynched in Denver in 1893, three in Hahnsville, Louisiana, in 1896 and five in Tallulah, Mississippi, in 1899 (Gambino, 1974). In New Orleans in 1896, 6,000–8,000 people, led by a committee of 50 for law and order, lynched and shot nine Italians who had been *acquitted* of the death of police lieutenant Hennessey. Two hundred were driven out of Altoona, Pennsylvania, in 1884. Those who engineered this movement (like those who led the lynching in New Orleans) were respectable citizens and men in high political office extolled by prestigious newspapers for their community service in this regard (Gambino, 1974).

In denials of the criminality and the incapacity-for-collective-behavior concept, the Italo-American press published statistics continuously through the decades. But the only people who could and did read them were those who *were* the statistics, so the news of confirmation or denial went to those who needed neither.

A similar information dissemination failure occurred with the "Italian-immigrants-need-to-be-redistributed solution" to the "Italian problem."

The context into which the immigrants arrived defined the problem. In the context of American "abstinence" during that period, as imbibers of wine they were evil. In contrast to verbal and "rational" Protestantism, the ritual, liturgy, iconicity and festiveness of their Catholicism appeared mindless and idolatrous. In contrast to the American nuclear family, devotion to the extended family indicated lack of desire to be part of the larger community. Involvement in a larger community existed, but lay within scotomized "observer" fields of vision.

It has been at least 40 years since mainstream America has experienced the Italian problem. This "problem" niche is being filled, however, and not surprisingly, by other ethnic groups in various parts of the country (e.g., Mexican and Southeast Asian in southern California and other large cities elsewhere), and of course, by our new and growing group of the homeless, a significant component of which are the deinstitutionalized formerly mentally ill.

CONCLUSION

The process of labeling individuals and groups, ethnic or otherwise, as "strange," brings into play the same mechanisms that operate in the dialectic of "self and other." As we pointed out earlier, the self shapes identity by processing information inputs, and is aided by the presence or absence of restricting or amplifying mechanisms of information flow. As in the example above, competition for diminishing opportunity space would amplify the need and quicken the process of estrangement. An individual has a historically generated self, but this self might not be operational in a new environment. In the case of the immigrant ("the strange") it is the ascendant dominant culture that defines (by instancing behaviors of the newly arrived as positive or negative) the tolerable or assimilable limits of behavior. One might say this manner of indicating logical classes and relations in hierarchical form has the properties of a lattice structure. It is the ascendant culture into which the strange arrives, and which, in admitting and absorbing or refusing to absorb, defines the set. The members of such a group may decide to adopt external "ways" and retain something of their own identity, or to disappear in total assimilation—if they are able to do either. This holds true for any set defined by any dominant group through its mediators. "Strange behaviors" by which such sets are defined are reinforced through the media, the cinema and popular literature, so that the strange will know how to act when they have assumed a role. Such a process was dramatically acted out in one evening when a male group of primitives, imbibing alcoholic drinks for the first time, learned from the expectations of the audience how to behave while inebriated (Schwartz & Romanucci-Ross, 1974).

In our attempts to classify behavior, binary oppositions and the mediators of such oppositions are very important to a society. In primitive societies it is the shaman (physician-psychiatrist-priest) who mediates the dystonic episodes associated with deviance and replaces order between the categories. In complex societies it is the physicians, psychiatrists, and men of the law who usually, in some sort of not-totally-conscious collusion, define and restore this order for the sane: insane, healthy: sick and criminal: noncriminal. The difference between the two societies, primitive and modern, lies not in the presence or absence of a mediator but the qualifications that are necessary for acceptance of the mediator in each case and the extent of the mediator's involvement in a set of societal functions. As a consequence, in contemporary society, the psychiatrist by virtue of his grounding in medical science supersedes the shaman as the appropriate mediator. And, because of his expertise, his involvement in various societal decisions is far more pervasive. So, as evidenced in cases such as *Estelle* and *Barefoot*, the psychiatrist is involved not only in decisions dealing with the attribution of guilt or innocence, but also in decisions about the way society will deal with the infractor of its moral order. The mediator's role, therefore, in the interpretation of oppositions through the dialectical process, appears to be like that of a weaver attempting to reestablish social and political harmony.

Societies do not differ as we observe them in our analyses of how they order information and engage in communication. What must be examined is the manner in which consensus is achieved; for example, how, in our culture, unproven theories become decisive in life-and-death issues in a court of law. A political party in power always has a stance toward "mental illness" because it deals with control, with thoughts and feelings, with basic attitudes about "rational man" and hence with the role of the state in the private life of an individual. Grant (1983, pp. 336–343) considers the implications for governmental abuse, and notes that liberals in the United States are concerned with desegregation and civil rights while conservatives want less government, less taxation and less regulation. These views include underlying concepts of "man in society" that differ. When the liberals are in power, the overriding values of the society support the notion of the ideal man as interactive, concerned about the welfare and rights of others. In contrast, the conservatives see the ideal man as highly individualistic, thriving best when unencumbered with responsibilities for others in the social system. By virtue of their differing views and the influence that they exert within the whole social system when they are in control, they inevitably affect the objectives of psychiatric intervention. Grant emphasizes that psychiatry as a medical discipline is inextricably tied to the values of a culture and may change in its operational presuppositions when there are changes in those broader cultural values.

Italian psychiatrist Franco Basaglia was aware of this as he planned his program of deinstitutionalization (see Lovell & Scheper-Hughes, 1986). Trying to syncretize the contributions from the social psychology of George Herbert Mead and other symbolic interactionists, he put into motion what might be called a modelic psychiatric "critical theory," aimed at altering the consciousness of actors in a society so that they might all help in restructuring that society in a manner that would address their collective frustrations. Change, he averred, was hampered by the existence of "repressive institutions"; men are governed not by their environment but by their interpretations of their environment. He transformed these assertions into a sort of theatre by having inmates destroy parts of the institutions and having outsiders enter to use parts of such buildings for purposes other than the incarceration of the mentally ill. The long-term effects of his efforts have yet to be determined, but on the discourse level of deuterolearning (e.g., the task was for all actors to renegotiate a new identity), there is something to be retained from the experiment.

As the uses of fantasy are also important in the process that classifies and labels the deviant, it would be well to note that although fantasy is an intrapsychic process reflecting both the inner and outer life of the individual, it is also sociocultural in many respects. Much of the fantasy material used by an individual is furnished by "fantasy producers," and there are cultural premises inherent in the product which may not be shared by the larger society. As Gregory Bateson and Ted Schwartz (Schwartz, 1968) have noted, whole realms of fantasy have been created through literal-figurative transformations in communication both within and between cultures. What this means is that which is asserted or presented literally may be taken as figurative, and the figurative as literal. An instance of this may be seen in recent mass cult murders in the United States, in which the defense attorneys frequently point to records of songs exalting death and extinction that "possessed" the mind of the murderer for whom myth has become a reality construct. Occasionally, some will argue (in textbooks or courts of law) that bringing about violence and destruction (for grievances unaddressed) by acting out personal or cultural fantasies of power and redress is "rational." The mediator must be concerned not only with the negotiation of social status and role, but the exchange function of the mythical and the real which compete for the social definitions of "normalcy" and "deviance."

Mappings of structure of behavior in one's group put into relief the failure to map in characteristics of other groups, and these mappings tell individuals as well as groups that there are boundaries to behavior that will be acceptable. Consequently, the frequency of deviance will increase as the contact with groups dissimilar to one's own group increases. Mediators have an important role to play in this negotiation of conformity and deviance in historical periods of much culture contact and rapid culture change.

Psychiatrists as mediators, then, not only make decisions about life and death and who shall be homeless ("set free") and who shall be institutionalized or on welfare, but they actually decide whether there will be an arena at all for such decisions. Their role has become more pronounced, for "planning" itself is becoming increasingly a part of our current complex cultures, even though there is much lip service given to "free market forces."

The anthropologist too is a mediator in cross-cultural understanding and is often referred to as a cultural broker. He is a participant-observer, and (lately with many other instruments and accessories) studies another culture with a dual purpose. The first is to learn of the variety of human responses to problems faced by any human group in terms of ecological adaptation, survival in the face of disease and death, and the evaluation of social systems making it possible for individuals to live with one another. The second purpose is to better understand our own society with the insight gained from anthropological researches to see deep structural similarities in what is a great surface structure diversity as all groups attempt to solve similar problems.

Psychiatry and the fieldwork of anthropology have informed the fields of culture and personality, enriching our understanding of "normal" and "deviant." These two fields of inquiry have increasingly influenced deliberations in the courts of many countries in the Western world.

NOTES

1. Forensic psychiatry has been historically concerned with psychiatry in the criminal process. Increasingly, the work of forensic psychiatry has been expanded to include many aspects of the civil law. General psychiatry is concerned with the psychiatric needs of patients, irrespective of the criminal process.

2. There appears to be increasing evidence of a genetic basis for antisocial behavior and other complicated conditions such as alcoholism. See Bishop, J. E. (1986, February 12). Probing the cell: Researchers close in on some genetic bases of antisocial behavior. *The Wall Street Journal*, pp. 1, 19.

REFERENCES

Banfield, E. (1958). *The moral basis of a backward society*. Glencoe, IL: Free Press.
Barefoot v. *Estelle*. (1983). 103 S. Ct. 3383.
Biasin, G. P. (1975). *Literary diseases: Theme and metaphor in the Italian novel*. Austin: University of Texas Press.
Brooks, A. (1974). *Law, psychiatry and the mental health system* (pp. 165–171). Boston: Little, Brown.
Brudner-White, L. (1986). Order and its Shadow: Delinquency as reproduction and resistance. *International Journal of Law and Psychiatry*. (*Special Issue: Anthropological Reflections on Forensic Psychiatry*. L. Romanucci-Ross and L. Tancredi, eds.) 9:3:321–334. New York: Pergamon Press.
Conti, Adalgisa. (1978). *Gentilissimo Sig. Dottore: Questa e la mia vita*. Milan: Mazzotta.
Devereux, G. (1967). *From anxiety to method in the behavioral sciences*. Paris: Ecole Pratiques des Hautes Etudes; The Hague: Mouton.
De Vos, G., & Romanucci-Ross, L. (1982). *Ethnic identity in cultural continuity and change*. Chicago: University of Chicago Press.
Diagnostic Statistical Manual of Mental Disorders (DSM-III) (3rd ed.). (1980). Washington, D.C.: American Psychiatric Association.
Eaton, W. and Kessler, L. (eds.) 1985. *Epidemiologic Field Methods in Psychiatry: The NIMH Epidemiologic Catchment Area Program*. Orlando, FL: Academic Press.
Erickson, K. T. (1966). *Wayward Puritans: A study in the sociology of deviance*. New York: John Wiley & Sons.
Estelle v. *Smith* (1983). 441 U.S. 454.
Fortune, R. (1935). *Manus religion*. Philadelphia: American Philosophical Society.
Foucault, M. (1965). *Madness and civilization: A history of insanity in the Age of Reason*. Tr. Richard Howard. New York: Random House.
Gambino, R. (1974). *Blood of my blood, the dilemma of the Italian-American*. Garden City, New York: Doubleday.
Gans, H. (1962). *The Urban Villagers*. New York: Macmillan.
Glass, R. & Freedman, D. (1985, October 25). *Journal of the American Medical Association, 254*, 2280.
Glazer, N., & Moynihan, D. P. (1963). *Beyond the melting pot: The Negroes, Puerto*

Ricans, Jews, Italians, and Irish of New York City. Cambridge: Harvard University Press.

Grant, I. (1983). Psychotherapy: Brave new world or requiem for misguided idealism? In L. Romanucci-Ross, D. Moerman, & L. Tancredi (Eds.), *The anthropology of medicine: From culture to method*. South Hadley, MA: Bergin & Garvey.

Harrison, J. E. (1966). *Epilegomena to the study of Greek religion and themis: A study of the social origin of Greek religion*. New York: University Books.

Kleinman, A. (1977). Depression, somatization, and the new cross-cultural psychiatry. *Social Sciences and Medicine, 11*, 3–10.

Kleinman, A. (1980). *Patients and healers in the context of culture*. Berkeley: University of California Press.

Lévi-Strauss, C. (1966). *The savage mind*. London: Weidenfeld & Nicolson.

Lewis, O. (1957). *Five families: Mexican case studies in the culture of poverty*. New York: Random House.

Lovell, Anne M. and Nancy Scheper-Hughes. 1986. Deinstitutionalization and Psychiatric Expertise: Reflections on Dangerousness, Deviancy, and Madness (Italy and the United States). *International Journal of Law and Psychiatry* (Special Issue: Anthropological Reflections on Forensic Psychiatry. L. Romanucci-Ross and L. Tancredi, eds.) 9:3:361–382. New York: Pergamon Press.

Monahan, J. (1981). *Predicting violent behavior*. Beverly Hills, CA: Sage Publications.

Moss, L., & Cappanari, S. (1960). Folklore and medicine in an Italian village. *Journal of American Folklore, 73*, 288, 95–102.

Nelli, H. S. (1970). *The Italians in Chicago 1880–1930: A study in ethnic mobility*. New York: Oxford University Press.

Obeyesekere, G. (1976). The impact of Ayurvedic ideas on the culture and the individual in Sri Lanka. In C. Leslie (Ed.), *Asian medical systems: A comparative study* (pp. 201–226). Berkeley & Los Angeles: University of California Press.

Palgi, P. (1983). Mental health, traditional beliefs and the moral order among Yemenite Jews in Israel. In L. Romanucci-Ross, D. Moerman, & L. Tancredi (Eds.), *The anthropology of medicine: From culture to method* (pp. 319–335). South Hadley, MA: Bergin & Garvey.

Radin, P. (1936). The Italians of San Francisco: Their adjustment and acculturation. (Abstract.) *Sierra Project 2*, 2–98.

Rieff, P. (1959). *Freud: The mind of the moralist*. New York: Viking Press.

Rolle, A. (1968). *The immigrant upraised: Italian adventurers and colonists in an expanding America*. Norman, OK: University of Oklahoma Press.

Romanucci-Ross, L. (1966). Conflits fonciers à Mokerang. *L'Homme: Revue Francaise d'Anthropologie, 6*, 2, 32–53.

Romanucci-Ross, L. (1969). The hierarchy of resort in curative practices in the Admiralty Islands of Melanesia. *Journal of Health and Social Behavior, 10*, 3.

Romanucci-Ross, L. (1985). *Mead's other Manus: Phenomenology of the encounter*. South Hadley, MA: Bergin & Garvey.

Romanucci-Ross, L. (1986a). Creativity in illness: Methodological linkages to the logic and language of science in folk pursuit of health in central Italy. *Social Science and Medicine, 23* (1):1–7.

Romanucci-Ross, L. (1986b). *Morality, conflict and violence in a Mexican village*. Chicago: University of Chicago Press.

Romanucci-Ross, L., Moerman, D., & Tancredi, L. (1983). *The anthropology of medicine: From culture to method*. South Hadley, MA: Bergin & Garvey.

Romanucci-Ross, L., & Tancredi, L. R. (1987). The anthropology of healing. In R. Bulger (Ed.), *In search of the modern Hippocrates*. Iowa City: University of Iowa Press.

Schwartz, T. (1968, July 16–25). *Beyond cybernetics: Constructs, expectations and goals in human adaptation*. Paper prepared for Symposium no. 40, Wenner-Gren Foundation for Anthropological Research.Burg Wartenstein, Austria.

Schwartz, T., & Romanucci-Ross, L. (1974). Drinking and inebriate behavior in the Admiralty Islands, Melanesia. *Ethos*, *2*, 3, 213–232.

Slaby, A. E., & Tancredi, L. R. (1975). *Collusion for conformity*. New York: Jason Aronson Publishers.

Slaby, A. E., & Tancredi, L. R. (1977). The economics of moral values: Policy implications. *Journal of Health Politics, Policy and Law*, *1*, 20–31.

Slaby, A. E., Tancredi, L. R., & Lieb, J. (1981). *Clinical psychiatric medicine*. Philadelphia: Harper & Row.

Sontag, S. (1977). *Illness as metaphor*. New York: Farrar, Straus & Giroux.

Tancredi, L., & Volkow, N. (1986). AIDS: Its symbolism and ethical implications. *Medical Heritage*, *2*, 12–18.

Tseng, Wen-shing. (1972). On Chinese national character from the viewpoint of personality development. *Symposium on the Character of the Chinese*. Toipu: Institute of Technology, Academica Sinica.

Tseng, Wen-shing. (1974). Traditional and modern psychiatric care in Taiwan. In A. Kleinman, P. Kunstadter, E. R. Alexander, & J. L. Gale (Eds.), *Culture and healing in Asian societies*. Cambridge, MA: Schenkman.

Tseng, Wen-shing. (1975). The nature of somatic complaints among psychiatric patients: The Chinese case. *Comprehensive Psychiatry*, *16*, 237–245.

Wallace, A. F. C. (1970). *Culture and personality*. New York: Random House.

Wang, Jen-Yi. (1983). Psychosomatic illness in the Chinese cultural context. In L. Romanucci-Ross, D. Moerman, & L. Tancredi (Eds.), *The anthropology of medicine: From culture to method* (pp. 298–318). South Hadley, MA: Bergin & Garvey.

Williams, F. E. (1930). *Orokaiva magic*. London: Oxford University Press.

14

Ideology and Power:
Epidemiology and Interpretation
in Law and Psychiatry

Laurence R. Tancredi and
David N. Weisstub

In recent years there has been an increasing emphasis on the use of epidemiological research to obtain an information base for formulating as well as understanding problems in forensic psychiatry. Studies of the determinants of individual competence or threat to self or society have proliferated, and their results are influencing policy and legislative decisions as well as buttressing certain positions and holdings in court cases. Ennis and Litwack (1974), for example, strongly affected policy and court cases dealing with the role of psychiatrists as experts in civil commitment proceedings. Their review of empirical studies on the reliability of psychiatric judgments emphasized the conceptual difficulties in predicting dangerous behavior. This found its way into numerous court cases and influenced policy regarding the role of the psychiatrist in such proceedings.

Court cases involving forensic psychiatry have increased in number in recent years and, as noted by Appelbaum (1984), the U.S. Supreme Court has become substantially engaged with the practice of psychiatry, whereas until 1975 no Supreme Court decisions had involved "the practice of psychiatry in a civil setting." Since then there have been at least six such decisions. Although psychiatrists and behavioral scientists often testified on forensic matters with limited data to support their opinions, the court and the public now demand more than simple reliance on theoretical constructs such as psychoanalytic principles. One response has been the use of epidemiological studies that, by producing numbers easily packaged into statistical statements, give at least the appearance of relating to the real world. The intellectual position behind such a response is not incompatible with positivism, for example, which sees empirical science as a means of ordering statements that essentially satisfy such logical criteria as verifiability and meaningfulness (Popper 1980). On the other hand, one problem with relying on epidemiological research may be that data or numbers are often used to avoid the truly hard questions that address broader and perhaps more important conceptual issues. Such a criticism is consistent with the views of Karl Popper; it perceives as a distinguishing characteristic of empirical statements and theories their susceptibility to revision due to critical intellectual evaluation and likely supersession by superior statements and theories (Popper 1980).

This chapter will explore the issues of interpretation of epidemiological findings, particularly the role of ideologies in epidemiological research, and examine their ethical implications.[1] In assessing the validity of a study, two levels of analysis are possible. First, does the research meet the statistical and epidemiological requirements for a reliable study? This involves an examination of the study design and methods for gathering and interpreting data. Second, what is the underlying framework: the perspectives and values of those conducting the study, dominating ideologies (if any) both explicit and implicit, and the extent to which the research is shaped to reaffirm such ideologies? This discussion will seek to demonstrate through a critique of selected studies that the first level of analysis alone is insufficient to establish the meaningfulness of results. The second level is essential to elucidate the influences of ideologies, or preconceived values, on the results of a study and especially on the way data are interpreted.

This discussion will treat epidemiological studies in forensic psychiatry as texts with their own metaphors (Lakoff and Johnson 1980) directed at specific readers aware of basic expressed and unexpressed assumptions, discursive ideologies or concepts, ideas, beliefs, and systematically connected propositions (Romanucci-Ross and Moerman 1984; see also Chapter 18 in this volume). This type of critique is particularly relevant to ethics, since the content of information being subjected to ethical analysis is shaped by values that affect the formulating and gathering of epidemiological data and the ways in which the data are applied to the treatment of patients.

IDEOLOGIES AS SUBSCRIPT

"Ideology" is a difficult term to define mainly because it is embedded in a history starting in the eighteenth century that imbued it with pejorative connotations which remain a basic characteristic of the concept (Thompson 1984). However, it is possible to define it less substantively by focusing more on how it functions as a neutral process of intellection than on historical usage. To that end, ideology can be considered a body of notions that unites values and action. By this definition, ideology becomes an essential condition of knowledge. It is a belief system, not one fragmented into categories such as political or social but one that is basically and necessarily inconsistent or incomplete in the sense that it cannot prove or disprove anything about a social or scientific hypothesis. On the other hand, ideologies are able to live with such inconsistencies while at the same time demonstrating distinctions between theirs and other belief systems (Romanucci-Ross and Moerman chapter 18). Hence in its most ameliorative sense, the clash of conflicting ideologies (belief systems) may result in higher-order ideologies whose explanations of observed events have fewer inconsistencies (Fleck 1979).

In more recent times, ideology has retained (in our American culture) a pejorative aura with the writings of Marx, who, in works such as *The German Ideology*, introduced the idea of *"falsches Bewusstsein"* (false consciousness) to attack liberal bourgeois ideas. Those espousing Marxist doctrine continue to use "ideology" as an attribute of political and economic positions clearly different from their own and, therefore, subject to ideological corruption. Basic in the nature of this type of ideological critique is the notion of what is incorrect, *"falsches Bewusstsein."*

The Frankfurt school of philosophy elaborated considerably on the concept of "false consciousness" and constructed its own ideological critique with three primary theses. First, radical criticism of society is inseparable from criticism of its dominant ideologies. According to this basic thesis, social research should have as an ultimate goal the application of critical theory to society. Second, a critique of ideologies must be seen not just as "moralizing criticism" (Geuss 1981; Habermas 1968) but also as a method for obtaining knowledge. The critique is not, according to the Frankfurt school, designed primarily to establish morality. Third, such critiques must not follow the epidemiological method characteristic of some research aspects of the natural sciences but, instead, must focus on disclosing pseudo or illusory objectivity, make individuals more aware of the origins of their beliefs, and unearth unconscious determinants of behavior. Hence, the ideological analysis strives for self-reflectiveness as a means of going beyond the limitations of objective or empirically derived information to the elucidation of the true interest underlying values and the critical determinants of behaviors and beliefs (Geuss 1981).

Ideology can also be viewed in a more nonjudgmental sense. Some involved with the Frankfurt school (Mannheim 1955) recognized that social thought exists interdependently and coterminously with the political, economic, and anthropological constructs prevailing at a point in history. When viewed from this perspective, ideology becomes a nonvaluative term; any social thought encased in a particular time and space becomes inherently ideological. Under these terms the objective of an ideological critique becomes less concerned with evaluating the correctness of a particular position or frame of reference and more with elucidating the values, beliefs, and other underpinnings of the society of a period (Gurvitch 1971; Edlund and Tancredi 1985).

VALUE-LADEN CONCEPTS IN FORENSIC PSYCHIATRY

Basic concepts such as "competence" and "rational consent," which are found in many legal psychiatric studies, lend themselves easily to ideological characterizations. How are these to be defined and by what criteria? What constitutes autonomous decision making and what must be present for that to occur? Similarly, what is meant by notions such as self-determination and criminal responsibility? These questions address highly value-laden theoretical concepts. For example, the term "rational" alone opens up a variety of ideological perspectives. A strong scientific orientation might lead to a view of "rational" as meaning the capacity to construct a logical sequence of events leading to a particular outcome. Hence, rational consent would mean that a consenting individual is capable of arranging information in a preconceived logical sequence from which consent naturally follows. However, to others "rational" might require that decisions be approached in a manner that fits within the norm, that is, the decision maker behaves in a way consistent with expected majority behavior. The value-laden nature of these theoretical concepts creates almost insurmountable problems for those conducting studies on these questions because so much of the research must be based on meanings and interpretations of terms pertinent to various belief perspectives.

Research in other areas of medicine often depends on measurement as well as the concrete counting of events and is therefore less broad-based and theoretical than research in forensic psychiatry. For example, a study to determine the usefulness of a hospital service from the number of individuals in a community who are using the service would be a well-defined project, simple in design and relatively concrete. Such a research study would present significantly less conceptual difficulty than, for instance, a study of competence in a segment of a Medicare population. The latter is more problematic because it has to do with issues of power over and coercion of the individual. That is, the ideology of mental illness, which governs which medical concerns can justifiably override personal preferences or encroach on legal rights, results in studies that deal with broadly based and largely subjectively derived meanings because the ideological framework can be constricted or expanded to slant data toward a particular objective compatible with the ideology.

The evaluation of epidemiological studies in forensic psychiatry must consider both external and internal meanings fundamental to the research. In a critique restricted to external meanings, for example, one might wish to treat empirical studies like a text, perhaps in the sense of a closed text, as discussed by Eco (1984). In such a closed text, the intrinsic interpretation or meaning is so embedded in the ideological base and in the culture of the reader that other interpretations or meanings not only do not enhance the intrinsic meaning but also may exist separate from or concurrent with it, or even clash with it. Eco speaks of a text as needing to be understood within the context of codes that may be very different from the one assumed by the author of the work. If the author does not take into account the codes of different readers, or intends to arouse a precise response from a relatively specific group of readers, then the text is susceptible to a variety of reader interpretations. Similarly, epidemiological studies can be interpreted in various ways that may ultimately be independent of each other. In "open" texts, on the other hand, the multitude of readers' interpretations are interdependent, and one set of interpretations constructively supplements others (Eco 1984). Many of the epidemiological studies that deal with highly value-laden or ideologically ambiguous notions are similar to closed texts, and their interpretations depend strongly on the nature of the reader. Furthermore, this variation in textual interpretation with reader predilections may create major distortions in terms of the scientific validity of the results.

A critique restricted to internal meanings searches for basic expressed concepts and examines the ideological coherence of the framework of the research. Such an "internal" critique includes, at the most concrete level, an examination of the methodology of the research, such as the statistical aggregate, the arrangement or cluster of numbers, and the accuracy of mathematical manipulations and interpretations. In the broader sense, an internal critique is concerned with the coherence of the prevailing ideologies from the beginning to the end of the study. Such a critique is also concerned with the consistency of these ideologies from time to time throughout the course of the research.

Few if any epidemiological studies dealing with broad concepts, such as competence and autonomy, seem to address their ideological foundations. Rarely, if ever, is there an explicit accounting of the beliefs underlying a study, which may in fact vary as information becomes available to deconstruct the ideology responsible for the initial design. Despite this lack of explicit identification of the underlying ideology, its nature can usually be estimated by speculation, but closer examination is necessary for greater certainty. Implicit assumptions are usually not apparent. Once past the first sentence of a statement of purpose, the reader is unlikely to engage in a critical reading of underlying presuppositions.

Most studies begin with a presumption of the truth of their underlying ideology or belief system; it is their raison d'être. In addition, some research involves other theoretical beliefs that, although rarely expressed as assumptions, are presented as self-evident. Under scrutiny, however, they emerge, and in any one instance may be sufficiently ambiguous so that they fuse with other ideologies and meanings. The first of these unexpressed assumptions is "identity of the framework." This refers to the study's consonance or compatibility with some characteristic of truth and reality, especially psychiatric truth as it relates to society (Geuss 1981). From a pragmatic perspective, one could argue that the assumption of identity of framework is essential for the conduct of any empirical study. If each time research questions arise, one must reexamine the underlying framework of the information system used to structure the questions, empirical research is unlikely ever to be completed. On the other hand, once the empirical research has been done, the findings and conclusions should be examined against a backdrop of questions regarding the identity of the framework. Rarely if ever is this done in the examination and disclosure of epidemiological research data.

Another unexpressed presupposition concerns normative beliefs about the intrinsic aspects of studies. This involves at least four subcategories of issues. First, the framework is the needed means for the gathering of information. That is, the symbols of meaning in mental health—disease, competence, instability, threatening behavior, and autonomy—provide specific examples from the universe of considerations affecting the information to be obtained.

A second subcategory holds preconceived notions about what constitutes a good decision by research subjects in any particular instance. For example, research by psychiatrists on why patients refuse treatment would start with a belief by psychiatrists of what is a good decision by the patients. Where a patient deviates from that "good" decision, the researchers are likely to request the patient to justify the "deviation." Two underlying assumptions apply here. One is that psychiatrists have a clear idea of what justifications would convert the deviant choice into a "good decision"; the other is that refusing treatment requires justification. In keeping with this, acceptance of treatment would not require special justification, because acceptance is more consistent with the dominant power framework, and would appear "reasonable" and "good" to the investigators.

The third subcategory issue mandates that research statistics, evaluations, and conclusions are coherent and reasonable. This belief rests on the more primary assumption that the basis for and conduct of the research are truly valuable, and that the framework for interpretation complies with the normative beliefs behind the design of the study.

The fourth subcategory includes the assumption of "integrity," that is, the "mind" state of the researcher and the extent to which it is maintained in the text or presentation of the data, the evaluation, and the ultimate conclusions. Some points in the presentation of an empirical study parallel the conducting of it, where internal inconsistencies may reflect ideological incoherence. When this occurs, the "test of integrity" is not met.

Another important broad category of theoretical beliefs about specific research efforts is the "doctrine of error," that is, an intrinsic concept of what constitutes false ideology. To be effective, the positive or normative beliefs of an ideology require that error be clearly identifiable. A doctrine of error has its own ideological basis, which may or may not be consistent with the ideology of validity in the research. For example, one study examined denials of mental illness from the perspective of whether the denying patient is truly legally competent to refuse to consent to treatment (Roth et al. 1982). The underlying arguments concerned the precision and accuracy of mental illness diagnoses and of assessments of competence. The authors recognized that denial of illness per se does not necessarily reflect incompetence, that patients may be able to "handle" their everyday affairs adequately and to assess the risks, benefits, and alternatives of the proposed psychiatric treatment reasonably well in all respects but one: they cannot agree that treatment is relevant because they do not agree they are ill. The question raised in such a case is whether a patient who denies illness despite signs and symptoms to the contrary should be evaluated as incompetent to decide about proposed treatments.

The labeling of mental illness and the ideology of treatment create a doctrine of clearly opposing ideologies—that of the treating psychiatrist versus that of the patient who, according to the researchers, may admittedly understand substantive information but deny personal illness. When applying the ideology of psychiatric treatment, one of the two opposing ideologies (the psychiatrist's and the patient's) must be dominant. When applying an ideology of what constitutes competence, the ideology behind the refusal should be closely aligned with the issues of competence. Here it is subtended to the dominant ideology: no ideology or doctrine of error exists to assist the researcher or report reader in the power play of competing ideologies. Denial of illness, despite psychiatrically acknowledged symptoms, cannot always reasonably be judged as incompetence. In fact, a test that requires patients to "appreciate the nature of their situation," that is, to accept illness and thereby have no reasonable grounds for refusing treatment, would always assure the success of the dominant ideology. Nonacceptance of treatment would be deemed irrational.

ON STUDIES OF "COMPETENCE"

Creating a similar dilemma, Appelbaum and Roth (1981) did research on fifty newly admitted psychiatric patients to assess their competence to consent to psychiatric hospitalization. Researchers using several alternative definitions of competence tested this sample of patients shortly after admission and found that the majority appeared to have severe impairment of competence. The patients were asked fifteen questions on such subjects as their appreciation of the nature of their condition, awareness of the nature of hospitalization, comprehension of the reason admission was recommended, ability to decide to cooperate with the treatment plan, ability to protect themselves in a hospital environment, and awareness of their rights as outlined in materials given at the time of admission. Some examples of the questions demonstrate why a doctrine or ideology of error has been precluded from consideration in this study:

* Do you think that you have psychiatric problems?
* Do you think you need some kind of treatment for your problems?
* Do you think that you need to be in the hospital to get that treatment?
* Why do you think the doctor you saw recommended that you come into the hospital?
* What will the medication do for you while you are in the hospital?

The researchers, in discussing the results, pointed to the fact that half of the newly admitted patients did not think they needed to be hospitalized for treatment and that "only 46% could clearly acknowledge that they had psychiatric problems" (Appelbaum and Roth 1981:1464). This, they concluded, indicated that these patients "were not engaged in the rational manipulation of information that is a desirable element in any definition of competency" (Appelbaum and Roth 1981:1465). Again, the framework of the questions inevitably led to the conclusions expressed by the researchers. However, the questions themselves precluded an assessment of the error in the research project itself. Consistency existed once the questions were delineated, but the ideological basis for the questions remained relatively hidden though critically important in defining the questions. A negative response to the first three questions and an oppositional response to the last two (attacking the doctor's judgment and denying benefit from the medication) cannot automatically be taken as conclusive evidence that the patients could not engage in the "rational manipulation of information," unless one is so ideologically bent as to assume that only one range of responses under these circumstances evidences competence. If such an extreme position is taken, then logically patients will be given only the option of voluntarily accepting recommended treatment. If they refuse, they are judged incompetent and their rights can be overridden for psychiatric treatment.

Looking at the question of competency to give informed consent for medical procedures constituted another study; it reviewed the Roth, and Appelbaum and Roth criteria for determining competency (Weinstock, Copelan, and Bagheri 1984). The authors discovered that these criteria, first described by Roth, included the notion that a patient's decisions would be determined to be competent if they possessed the following qualities: (1) evidence of the patient's capability of editing his choice, (2) reasonableness in the outcome that results from the choice, and (3) demonstration that choice is based upon "rational" reasons; a patient demonstrates an ability to understand and in fact has actual understanding. Appelbaum and Roth subsequently expanded these criteria with the requirement that there be awareness of a patient's mental status over a period of time that would include the assessment of what may be the underlying dynamics for refusal by a patient.

This study involved thirty consultation requests that dealt with refusal of medical procedures, and psychiatrists were asked to assess the competency of the patients to give informed consent (Weinstock, Copelan and Bagheri 1984). In this study, the Roth and Appelbaum, and Roth criteria had not been placed into an operational matrix that would involve prioritizing among the various elements to establish whether a patient is competent. As a consequence the researchers developed their own method, which involved determining a threshold level of competence based on the assessment of the risks and benefits of the medical procedure. The patient was allowed to make decisions that the researchers would consider unwise unless there was a life-death situation. They were also allowed to disagree with the doctor if they were capable of weighing the risks and benefits. In the event of a life-threatening situation, there was a rebuttable presumption that a competent patient would accept the treatment. To effectively refuse treatment, a patient would have to provide some justification. Where the recommended procedure was risky and offered possibly uncertain benefits, the presumption was rebuttable that a competent patient would refuse the treatment. However, an opportunity existed for the patient who provided "good reasons" to accept even the risky and questionably beneficial procedure.

The criteria for choice presented by the authors were based essentially on Roth's earlier criteria (see Carnerie 1987). The authors added another criterion concerning the patient's ability to understand and to retain the understanding: they claimed that any patient who failed any of the four tests should be declared incompetent. In applying these criteria they discovered that only patients with organic brain syndrome were actually found to be incompetent, even though the study included patients who were depressed, exhibited schizophrenic symptoms, or suffered from personality disorder—or even had no psychiatric disorder. The researchers also found that in spite of the various criteria that were used, the patients who were ultimately judged incompetent demonstrated an inability to understand risks and benefits, or to retain that understanding. Some of those patients with these deficits were also judged incompetent because their choice did not seem to be based on "rational" reasons. However, the authors conditioned this by adding that there were no patients who based their decision on what the researchers viewed as "irrational" reasons who also did not lack the ability to understand or to retain the information. It is interesting that of the thirty patients assessed for competence to give informed consent or to refuse treatment, ten were viewed as incompetent.

One of the difficulties of this study is that the determination of competency included in its criteria highly value-laden terms such as that a choice be made on "rational" reasons, that the patient "understand" the specific procedure, and, finally, that he be able to "retain" the understanding. Again, the authors avoided addressing the "doctrine of error" relevant to these terms. It has already been discussed amply in the literature that the concept of "rational" reason is highly value-laden, if not wholly subjective (Tancredi 1984). The "rationality" of a reason to refuse treatment in any one situation is most often judged on how it comports with what the researcher or treating physician would view as "rational." There are no sharply defined criteria for assessing what is rational. A patient may have good personal reasons for refusing treatment, but from the perspective of the treating physician who has certain beliefs about medical care, these reasons might be seen as irrational. More important, whether a decision is judged rational is often based on the verbal capacities of the patient. A patient who is well educated and has a good vocabulary can justify his particular preferences in "rational" terms. A less educated patient, or perhaps one with some cognitive defects, may not be able to articulate clearly the reasons for not desiring treatment, though in fact the intensity of belief and desire may be as strong and as valid as in the former case.

The concept of a patient's ability to understand is problematic because we have no clear notion of what is to be understood. Does this mean the ability to repeat the specifics of benefits and risks? How did the authors determine that patients really understood in any "meaningful" way, which would be their ability to apply the information provided to their own situation? Similarly one gets into difficulties with the requirement that the patient demonstrate an ability "to retain understanding." This last criterion is particularly important because it addresses something philosophically troublesome about competency: the vagueness of the interests we are attempting to preserve with regard to individual rights.

Much attention since about 1975 has been devoted to autonomy and self-determination to justify redistributing the power in the physician-patient relationship. The ideas of autonomy and self-determination have something to do with "personhood," that is, the individual's integrity as a person, which may or may not have anything to do with the ability to "retain" understanding. For example, one could ask a seventy-year-old patient who displays some evidence of senility—especially an inability for recent memory—if he would accept a particular treatment. Despite his organic defects, the patient may know on some deep emotional and intellectual level that he does not want the treatment. As a result he may say "no" but ten minutes later forget the specific details of the benefits, risks, and alternatives of the treatment that was recommended to him. Can one reasonably assume that his inability to "retain" understanding empowers us to give no weight to his considered response to a question regarding what is to be done with his body? In other words, to what extent is it important that this individual be able to "retain" understanding beyond the immediacy of his decision making? One does not have to go very far into the literature of informed consent to discover that even highly intelligent, non-psychiatrically or non-neurologically disabled patients have difficulty retaining understanding about the benefits, risks, and alternatives of treatment (Tancredi 1984). Why, then, should we levy a strong test regarding this capacity on patients who diverge from expected conduct in the medical context?

REVIEW OF A SPECIFIC EPIDEMIOLOGICAL STUDY

From the various epidemiological studies on issues of competence, we have selected one to examine closely. We shall abstract certain ideological themes to demonstrate how they are fundamentally integrated, not only in defining the purpose of the research but also in its design and implementation. One of the important underlying considerations is the apparent existence of a critical point at which the internal inconsistencies of an epidemiological study (or text, by the Eco analogy) reflect ideological inflexibility.

The study, entitled "Clinical Judgments in the Decision to Commit: Psychiatric Discretion and the Law" (Schwartz et al. 1984), was conducted in response to several New York State and national court cases and legislative changes that addressed the reconceptualizing of "objective" criteria for dangerousness to self, dangerousness to others, and ability to care for self. The researchers reviewed decisions to commit or release ninety voluntarily hospitalized patients in a leading academic center in New York State and determined the extent of compliance with the state commitment laws. The study specifically examined the basis of psychiatrists' decisions to seek commitment of voluntarily hospitalized patients, decisions made when such patients filed notice of intent to leave. The study screened every formal request for discharge from July 15, 1982, through November 15, 1982. Individual episodes were considered ended when the patient eloped, was discharged, was held beyond seventy-two hours with the filing of commitment papers, or retracted the letter requesting release. Nineteen psychiatric residents were primary therapists for seventy-six of the patients, three psychology interns for five cases, and three attending psychiatrists for at least eight cases.

The first part of this study requested that each therapist fill out a questionnaire containing twenty-one items that rated patients from 1 to 7 on legal, clinical, social, and interpersonal variables. The questionnaire also allowed notation of any other factors that influenced the commitment decisions with a rating scale indicating the importance of each factor. The second part of the study consisted of an independent rating of the demographic and clinical characteristics of each patient by the principal investigator.

The results showed that the majority of the patients (sixty-six or 73 percent) retracted their sign-out letters. Twenty-one would have been held for commitment had they not retracted. Of the remainder, eighteen were discharged against medical advice, three were discharged with medical advice,

two eloped, and one was held for commitment. The researchers then compared twelve patient characteristics with decisions to commit or release patients. These included three legal variables: inability to care for self,
dangerousness to self, and dangerousness to others; six clinical characteristics: mentally ill, "in need of further treatment," "understands the need for
treatment," "psychotic-not psychotic," "acute-chronic," and "would be a
reliable outpatient"; two psychosocial factors: "a place to live" and "support
on the outside"; and a single interpersonal characteristic: argumentativeness.

The researchers claimed that the study revealed a high correlation between
the three legal variables—"dangerousness to self," "dangerousness to others," and "inability to care for self"—and decisions to seek commitment of
voluntary patients, and that the legal criteria carried more weight than clinical, psychosocial, or interpersonal factors. They also pointed out that at least
one legal factor appeared in every cluster of factors cited by clinicians as
having special influence in their decisions. The researchers saw this as convincing evidence that the legally mandated criteria governing suitability for
involuntary commitment were uniformly considered and were among the
most important determinants of the decisions. It was concluded, therefore,
that the therapists had complied with the law and relied more on legal than
on medical criteria.

The authors assessed the degree to which clinical criteria might parallel
requirements of the law. Here the reasoning became complex and arguably
ideology entered into the description and analysis to assure a particular result
and interpretation. The researchers saw the legal and clinical criteria as
parallel, whereas, if anything, they are more accurately described as conflated,
interactive, and perhaps strongly overlapping. The authors' logical error may
be that of false cause (*non causa pro causa*), that is, mistaking the wrong cause
for the real cause of a given effect. More likely, the researchers committed
a hysteron proteron, the logical fallacy of assuming as a premise something
that follows from what is to be proved. In this case, clinical criteria are the
false cause, and legal criteria are the improperly assumed premise that probably follows from what is to be proved. The imprecision and potential ex-
pansiveness of the description of legal criteria make this fallacy possible,
that is, the clinical criteria in the minds and judgments of the decision makers
actually preceded or coincided with the legal justification. The researchers
did include in the study a control mechanism, the independent clinical/
demographic rating—presence of delusions, paranoia, command hallucinations, anger, belligerence, assaultiveness—to check the validity of the clinicians' finding of dangerousness, but these are clearly medical, not legal,
criteria.

Also, while in the hospital, those patients who were committed required
neuroleptics, maximum observation, and seclusion. This would seem to
substantiate the authors' argument that legal criteria dominated the decisions
to commit. But of course the dialectic could continue endlessly as to the

ideological basis of the decisions to seclude and medicate. That is, did others not classified as dangerous to self or others receive the same treatment? Or, stated another way, the criteria used to prescribe seclusion and medication do not necessarily mean that the recipients of such treatment have met the legal criteria for commitment.

Finally, how the distinctions were made between what is legal and what is medical are unclear. The ideological base biases the distinction. The dominant ideology of the researchers (that psychiatric justifications for commitment begin with legal criteria) fixes the meaning of the results as a chemical reagent fixes a stain. It artificially creates differences where none may exist between what the clinicians conceptualize as "legal" and "clinical" criteria in order to establish a relationship between "legal" criteria and the reasons for commitment of patients. The ideology, therefore, fixes the instant diacritical view. It enters into the study with an impact on meaning, even, if necessary, to distort the results so as to support the dominating ideology. Hence, it shapes the results in a way that is compatible with affirming the basic ideology.

In this and similar studies, the objective of the research is adapted to create the illusion of absorbing the ideologies which dominate within the confines of the specific study and data so that the data in fact lead to proof of the hypothesis articulated at the initiation of the epidemiological research. This is an illusion of "difference" created by a specific focus or plane of analysis that, if looked at diachronically (over time), or perhaps from a different viewpoint, would reveal the impact of the ideology on the internal consistency, or lack thereof, of the epidemiological effort. As an illustration of the importance of perspective, a lawyer concerned with civil rights issues would be equally justified—if involved in the same research project and using similar data to perceive the clinical criteria as including the legal criteria in the minds of the clinicians—to argue that truly legal criteria are not operating as the basis for commitment.

IDEOLOGY OF ERROR

Thus far, this discussion has dealt with some general notions of ideology, especially the way in which particular beliefs function dynamically to create distortions in epidemiological studies in forensic psychiatry. We would like now to focus more closely on three broad topics that elaborate the findings from this analysis of epidemiological research: the role of the reader and the notion of the ideology of error; perceptions of the functions of social research and its implications for this analysis; and the importance of assessing interpretations derived from epidemiological research in forensic psychiatry and examining their ethical implications.

Two broad questions underlie a discussion of the relevance of an ideology of error. The first is whether it is an ideology; the second, who should make this judgment. We submit that an ideology of error exists if there is a system of belief which includes criteria for delineating error. More specifically, in assessing the accuracy of research, the perceiver (researcher or reader) will have an ideology of error to the extent that means are provided to recognize inaccuracy or inconsistency. Karl Popper, the noted historian of science, claimed that a theory is scientific if and only if a full range of observational statements, including the "negations of singular existential statements," can be appropriately and logically deduced from it (Kuhn 1977). When a theory fails in its attempted application, Popper would view this as evidence of falsification. He also stated that the logic behind the accretion of knowledge consists of the investigation of the methods used to systematically evaluate every new idea. From this investigation emerge conventions for testing new ideas. One rule, of course, would be that of evaluating the new concept from the perspective of falsification or doctrine of error.

It may be argued that the application of an ideology of error is simply a mechanical task, similar to applying a doctrine of mistake to any study requiring objectivity where statistically defined parameters exist for measurement—that is, if inappropriate statistical methods are used, errors will ensue. When the results of a study do not seem to fit into a rational pattern or logical sequence, they may simply suggest mechanical error. On the other hand, when broadly based philosophical concepts such as competence, autonomy, and criminal responsibility are involved, it is necessary to identify what would constitute an error in thinking or in the actual design or construction of the study.

The more germane question might be whether a belief system within the text of a study even includes the notion of error. It seems that one could conceptualize the doctrine of error as ideological, that is, different groups in a population interested in a specific type of data might have different notions of error, depending on their perceptions of the concepts underlying the studies. Hence, epidemiological studies by psychiatrists for psychiatrists may involve different beliefs regarding errors in research than studies by nonpsychiatrists aimed at nonpsychiatrist readers. For example, in a study dealing with denial of treatment and issues of competence, psychiatrists and lawyers will probably view error differently, for obvious reasons.

Who should assure that an ideology of error is taken into account in assessing the validity of research? The argument is compelling that this role is primarily the reader's. By the same token, a researcher, such as a psychiatrist doing a project based on a particular ideology, must have an ideology of error in order to be other than simply a polemicist presenting a seemingly rational discourse on a particular position. To offset the instinctual stacking of the deck in favor of certain conclusions, an ideology of error with regard to the specific substance of information is essential. But a too strongly defined ideology of error may constrain the researcher from engaging creatively in an epidemiological study and taking necessary conceptual risks.

From the perspective of assuring the complete understanding of empirical studies, the reader acting as critic stands to benefit most from the application of an ideology of error. The researcher, on the other hand, is forced to anticipate, in both the conduct and the final reportage of the study, who the reader will be. That is, when a study report is presented, the researcher must inevitably direct the results to a specific reader. Moreover, the reader is left with the obligation of defining the underlying meaning systems present in any piece of research, in order to be able to perform an ideologically factual analysis. Hence, the reader does more than just gather statistical data presented in a study and attempt to link the data with particular policy positions. He must also identify the underlying perspective or thrust of the study, which requires an ideological critique.

NATURE OF SOCIAL RESEARCH

Examination of the nature of social research touches on many of the issues already discussed in connection with the relevance of a doctrine of error. The revealing of "social reality" is presumed to be the end purpose of much of what is called social research. Some thinkers, such as Popper (1964), would not necessarily take the position that there is likely to be an improvement in our understanding of social reality or of human knowledge. Others, like Kuhn (1970), who posited more directedness in the development of ideas, give considerably more weight to the importance of the process of thought itself in the mechanism of knowing. Categories, relationships, and decisive examples constitute the paradigm that structures the scientist's personal view of reality, of truth (Romanucci-Ross and Moerman 1984; Elstein 1978).

Intentionality is therefore basic to a phenomenological interpretation of what occurs even in medical research; it is even more crucial in social research (Heller 1984). From this point of view, social research is concerned not merely with describing and analyzing the reality of social phenomena, but has a proactive role geared toward actually constituting that social reality. If this latter function is granted to social research, it strengthens the argument that a high degree of researcher sensitivity to error and incoherence may disserve the purposes of social research by inhibiting the constitution of social reality in a freely creative way. In a sense, ideologies are stagnant and protective, not expansive and flexible for creative reshaping of the social reality.

Ideological dissonance among different epidemiological studies, or even within studies of the same type, affects and transforms social consciousness. It changes perceptions and creates a redefinition of the objects of experience. If an accepted central function of social research is to reconstitute social reality, then the issue is not so much ideological incoherence in relation to the apparent accuracy of the research but, rather, a question of power balance, that is, whether the ideological thrust of the research, in its clash with existing ideological positions, creates such dissidence as to overthrow existing paradigms (Romanucci-Ross and Moerman 1984). Where social research creatively constitutes social reality, the argument can be made that a doctrine of error has little use except, at the most, to check social research that may reconstitute the social fabric in totally unacceptable ways.

This is not to say that a doctrine of error lacks all usefulness in a system where social research is expected to reconstitute social reality. However, if limited to the existing paradigm, the doctrine of error may prevent the adoption of any shift in perspective simply because it is a shift and not because it actually produces a more useful reconstitution of social reality. Some checking mechanism has to be provided both for the researcher in the design of experiments and for the reader in the interpretation and application of the results. Therefore, in accordance with the somewhat teleological Kuhnian model, a doctrine of error is applicable to the extent that it provides, albeit minimally, some control of the reconstituting powers of the supervening ideology. For example, if a research project finds that psychiatrists given sufficient historical information can accurately predict the potential dangerousness of patients, the project cannot totally reconstitute social reality with respect to this particular finding without being subjected to an ideological critique.

This discussion has addressed the extent to which ideologies directly influence the structuring of epidemiological research. The discussion also examined the ways in which ideologies are translated into the practical world of research design, the conduct of studies, and the interpretation of the derived information and how it is applied. In this way, the relationship between theory and practice was bridged at least to the degree that an ideological critique was demonstrated as a method for examining epidemiological research.

REFLECTION ON INTERPRETATION AND ITS ETHICAL IMPORTANCE

An examination of the nature of underlying ideologies and the extent to which they affect the context, arrangement, and interpretation of data is critical at this point in the development of forensic psychiatry because epidemiological studies are playing an increasing role in informing and shaping policies in this field. Furthermore, ideological critiques are an essential means of understanding when an ideology in this field is false or delusional because of some epistemic property of the constituted beliefs. They are also essential in examining epidemiological studies in order to reveal unconscious and otherwise hidden determinants of the explicitly described research objectives.

Along the same lines, the importance of an ideology of error should be emphasized. A study that does not include an ideology of error in its design is likely to be less an empirical, scientific effort than a polemical exercise. The ideology of error is a type of self-correcting mechanism that is an integral part of any scientific endeavor. Its presence assures some objectivity in the assessment of the validity of scientific results. Thus ideology is an essential component not only in the mind of the researcher, who must check results to detect and eliminate distortion, but also in the mind of the reader, who needs a guide to interpret the results. Anthropologist Devereux's (1967) insight that countertransference can masquerade as methodology particularly applies to epidemiological studies dealing with forensic psychiatry. Such studies inevitably involve interactions between researchers or "experts in their field" and a patient population. Hence, the potential for misperceptions and misinterpretations of data are powerful as well as serious, since the results may have major consequences in legislative policy and court decisions.

The ethical implications of the impact an ideological position can have on epidemiological studies in law and psychiatry are especially important because information from such studies frequently finds its way into courtroom and administrative deliberations on the rights of patients and criminal offenders. As stated earlier, several important Supreme Court cases involved the practice of psychiatry in both civil and criminal settings. These cases relied heavily on epidemiological information addressing questions such as the reliability of psychiatric diagnosis and the ability of psychiatrists and other behavioral scientists to predict dangerousness. *O'Connor* v. *Donaldson* (1974), the first such civil case in recent years to reach the Supreme Court, relied on information from epidemiological studies that emphasized the tentativeness of psychiatric diagnosis. *Barefoot* v. *Estelle* (1983) concerned the ability of psychiatrists to predict future dangerousness; the defendant, convicted of a capital crime, claimed that it was unconstitutional to use psychiatrists at the sentencing hearing to predict the defendant's future conduct. The court considered relevant empirical studies and cited Monahan's (1981) claims that psychiatrists accurately predict no more than one out of three cases of potential violent behavior, as well as his conclusion that there may be circumstances in which prediction is "empirically possible and ethically appropriate." Despite their relatively poor record in predicting dangerousness, the court ruled the psychiatrists' testimony admissible, arguing among other things that since similar testimony by lay persons with respect to dangerousness had been accepted, psychiatric testimony would hardly be less accurate.

In *Addington* v. *Texas* (1979), which concerned the standard of proof required at a commitment hearing to justify confining a mental patient, the Supreme Court cited the "lack of certainty and fallibility of psychiatric diagnosis and prediction of dangerousness." The court concluded that a beyond-a-reasonable-doubt standard is unrealistic for demonstrating that a person is both mentally ill and likely to be dangerous. As in *Barefoot* and

O'Connor, the Supreme Court relied on epidemiologically derived information to substantiate claims of psychiatric uncertainty and fallibility.

Studies of the uncertainty and fallibility of psychiatric diagnoses and predictions of dangerousness require the same ideological critique that was applied to the research which indicated that psychiatrists commit patients on the basis of "legally" acceptable standards. Studies of the predictability of dangerousness have not been subject to such a critique largely because they have tended to deal with incarcerated criminals rather than psychiatric patients. Also, these studies have often involved patients institutionalized for relatively long periods and thus acculturated to psychiatric expectations. These factors make it difficult to reach reliable conclusions about the actual ability of psychiatrists to predict dangerousness in psychiatric patients.

Epidemiological information enhances the power of experts in society and creates incentives for exercising paternalism; a likely consequence of this is a distortion that tips the power balance in favor of the professional over the consumer. A system of decision making based on epidemiological studies would maintain the beneficence rule articulated so effectively in the Hippocratic Oath (Veatch 1981), thereby precluding autonomy in the mental health treatment system.

From an ethical viewpoint, an ideological critique will help to achieve a balance of power between doctors and patients (or police and defendants) by ferreting out underlying, even unconscious, determinants of the overall character of a research project. Hence, the ideological critique tends to enhance patients' autonomy by revealing knowledge about relevant studies and to diminish the exercise of beneficence and paternalism in areas where law and psychiatry come together.

In the study examined in depth above, a logical conclusion of the researchers' results would be that psychiatrists generally abide by legal commitment statutes. By adhering to ostensibly "legally" defined criteria, they are meeting the overall goals of society as translated into legislative enactments. A secondary conclusion would be that mounting concerns over the rights of patients in the mental health system, particularly regarding commitment, are probably not warranted at this time. Furthermore, the study might justify a reduction in the attention paid by the legal and ethical community to psychiatric decision making in the involuntary commitment of patients. The study also implies that psychiatric discretion in areas of individual rights is probably not as unresponsive to ethical considerations as some have suspected. By extrapolation, even in other areas of patient care, such as the right to refuse psychotropic medications, the psychiatric community may well be obeying the requirements of the law.

However, a critique of this study raises doubts about all these conclusions. It suggests that results are relatively meaningless unless all the elements that go into the construction of a research study, particularly a study that touches on social problems, are carefully examined. Awareness of this is particularly important at this point in the development of psychiatry as a medical science. The period since 1975 or 1980 has seen a powerful shift from the psychoanalytical and other verbal therapies of the 1930s through the 1950s to an increasing reliance on biological and procedural technologies (e.g., surgery and drugs). Every year more new technologies are being introduced, many becoming important in the area of forensic psychiatry. For example, chemical castration, now felt to be an important treatment for sexually psychopathic individuals who engage in violent acts, has moved beyond research to recommended use for such offenders in state prison systems (Tancredi and Weisstub 1986). Similarly, the era of psychosurgery (the flourishing of lobotomies between 1945 and 1955 and experimental amygdalectomies to treat violent behavior in the early 1970s; Tancredi and Slaby 1981) may be upon us again in the near future.

Since these new or improved techniques are invasive and aimed specifically at behavior modification, they offer tremendous opportunities for abuse. Ideological positions regarding acceptable social behavior, individual responsibility, and the relative importance and benefits of psychiatric treatment may considerably influence the design, conduct, and interpretation of studies that might be cited to justify the use of the growing armamentarium of psychiatric treatments, not only to aid patients but also to control the behavior of "deviant" persons (Tancredi and Slaby 1981). The expansion of invasive procedures that modify mood and behavior makes it particularly urgent that studies in the behavioral sciences, and particularly in forensic psychiatry, be subjected to critiques that embody an understanding of ideological assumptions about end goals and processes by which we achieve them.

NOTE

1. We have explored these issues but with some diverse emphases in "The Ideology of Epidemiological Discourse in Law and Psychiatry: Ethical Implications," in L. Tancredi, ed., *The Ethics of Empirical Research* (New Brunswick, N.J.: Rutgers University Press, 1982).

REFERENCES

Appelbaum, P. 1984. "The Supreme Court looks at psychiatry." *American Journal of Psychiatry*, 141: 827–35.

Appelbaum, P. S., and Roth, L. H. 1981. "Clinical issues in the assessment of competency." *American Journal of Psychiatry*, 138:1462–67.

Addington v. *State of Texas*. 1979. 99 S.Ct. 1804 (see 1811).

Barefoot v. *Estelle*. 1983. 103 S.Ct. 3383 (see 3396–99).

Carnerie, F. 1987. "Crisis and informed consent: Analysis of a law-medicine malocclusion." *American Journal of Law and Medicine*, 12: 55–97.

Devereux, G. 1967. *From anxiety to method in the behavioral sciences*. Paris/The Hague: Ecole Pratique des Hautes Etudes/Mouton.

Eco, U. 1984. *The role of the reader*, pp. 8ff. Bloomington: Indiana University Press.

Edlund, M., and Tancredi, L. R. 1985. "Quality of life: An ideological critique." *Perspectives in Biology and Medicine*, 28:591–607.

Elstein, A. S. 1978. *Medical problem solving: An analysis of clinical reasoning*. Cambridge, Mass.: Harvard University Press.

Ennis, B. J., and Litwack, T. R. 1974. "Psychiatry and the presumption of expertise: Flipping coins in the courtroom. *California Law Review*, 62:693–752.

Fleck, L. 1979. *Genesis and development of a scientific fact*, ed. T. J. Trenn and R. K. Merton. Chicago: University of Chicago Press. (First published 1933.)

Geuss, R. 1981. *The idea of a critical theory: Habermas and the Frankfurt School*. Cambridge: Cambridge University Press.

Gurvitch, G. 1971. *The social frameworks of knowledge*. New York: Harper & Row.

Habermas, J. 1968. *Knowledge and human interest*, translated by Thomas McCarthy. pp. 113ff. Boston: Beacon Press.

Heller, T. C. 1984. Structuralism and critique. *Stanford Law Review*, 31:135–40.

Kuhn, T. 1970. *The structure of scientific revolutions*, 2nd ed. Chicago: University of Chicago Press.

———. 1977. *The essential tension: Selective studies in scientific tradition and change*. Chicago: University of Chicago Press.

Lakoff, C., and Johnson, M. 1980. *Metaphors we live by*, pp. 159–94. Chicago: University of Chicago Press.

Mannheim, K. 1955. *Ideology and utopia*. New York: Harcourt, Brace and World.

Monahan, J. 1981. *Predicting violent behavior*. Beverly Hills, Calif.: Sage Publications.

O'Connor v. *Donaldson*. 1974. 422 U.S. 585.

Popper, K. R. 1964. *The poverty of historicism*. New York: Harper & Row.

———. 1980. *The logic of scientific discovery*, pp. 49–60. London: Hutchinson.

Romanucci-Ross, L., and Moerman, D. E. 1984. "The extraneous factor: Research paradigms in Western medicine." Paper prepared for the symposium Comparing Epistemologies of Medical Systems Cross-Culturally and Through Time. American Anthropological Association, Annual Meeting, Denver.

———. 1988. "The extraneous factor in Western medicine. *Ethos: Journal of Psychological Anthropology*. 16(2): 146–66.

Roth, L. H., Appelbaum, P., Sallee, R., Reynolds, C. F., and Huber, A. 1982. "The dilemma of denial in the assessment of competency to refuse treatment." *American Journal of Psychiatry*, 139:910–13.

Schwartz, H. I., Appelbaum, P. S., and Kaplan, R. D. 1984. "Clinical judgments in the decision to commit: Psychiatric discretion and the law." *Archives of General Psychiatry*, 41:811–15.

Speigelberg, H. 1972. *Phenomenology in psychiatry and psychology: Studies in phenomenology and existential philosophy*. Evanston, Ill: Northwestern University Press.

Tancredi, L. 1984. "Competency for informed consent: Conceptual limits of empirical data." *International Journal of Law and Psychiatry*, 5:51–63.

Tancredi, L. R., and Slaby, A. E. 1981. "Ethical issues in mental health care." In *Medical ethics and the law (Implications for public policy)*, ed. M. E. Hiller. Cambridge, Mass.: Ballinger.

Tancredi, L. R., and Weisstub, D. N. 1986. "Technology assessment: Its role in forensic psychiatry and the case of chemical castration." *International Journal of Law and Psychiatry*, 8:257–61.

Thompson, J. B. 1984. *Studies in the theory of ideology.* Berkeley: University of California Press.

Veatch, R. M. 1981. *A theory of medical ethics,* pp. 296–305. New York: Basic Books.

Weinstock, R., Copelan, R., and Bagheri, A. 1984. "Competence to give informed consent for medical procedures." *Bulletin of the American Academy of Psychiatry and Law,* 12:117–25.

15

Psychosomatic Illness in the Chinese Cultural Context

JEN-YI WANG

Recent visitors to China have reported that the incidence of mental illness in the country is extremely small (Sidel and Sidel 1973). Indeed, for many years, the Western stereotype of the Chinese has been that of a calm, self-restrained, and even phlegmatic people (Veith 1955). This characterization neatly fits the so-called Apollonian type, but it is an assumption not to remain unquestioned. What makes the Chinese relatively less prone to mental illness than others? Does Chinese culture provide people with more adaptive strategies? Or have mental problems been disguised for outsiders, and expressions of mental illness been interpreted as purely physical problems?

Some of the recent studies by both Chinese and Western psychiatrists have focused on psychosomatic symptoms among the Chinese (Tseng 1975; Kleinman 1977, 1980). It was found that many Chinese are inclined to somatize their psychological problems and to express them through physiological disorders. Not purporting to exclude other possibilities, the following discussion will center around the psychosomatic phenomenon of the Chinese people and will show how the culture interacts with the social structure to influence ideas and behavior relative to mental disorders.

The Chinese have long believed in the relation between one's mood and physiological state. A study of Chinese classic novels explicitly demonstrates the belief that strong emotion always leads people to sicken or to die. The following sentences from one of the most famous classic novels, *All Men Are Brothers*, written in the sixteenth century, are typical:

He was so angry that several times he fainted from his anger. . . . His anger has risen so that he is ill of it and lies upon his bed, and his life cannot be long assured. . . . "Today I am killed by anger"—and when he had finished speaking he let his soul go free. [Klineberg 1938]

Not only anger, grief, sorrow, and regret may lead people to sicken or die. In classic love stories lovers are always sick because they miss each other; once they are heartbroken, they die very soon. These themes of sickness and death appear repeatedly. In the Ching Dynasty, the great novelist Tsao Sheh-ching (1715–1763) created a female figure who, in his work *The Dream of the Red Chamber*, has influenced generations of Chinese. The girl in the story has a very sensitive nature; she is smart, but also narrow-minded. Ever angry at others for unimportant matters, and innately weak, she is always sick. As in other love stories, as soon as she knows that her lover has to obey his parents' order to marry another girl, she dies. Many Chinese view her with great admiration; for over two centuries, the girl's name is a symbol of all smart, beautiful, and weak women. Sickness here is not a shortcoming; on the contrary, it is a virtue possessed by characters of traditional Chinese beauty. Though the Chinese, influenced by Western ideas, have started to appreciate healthy girls today, it is still common to show fainting caused by grief or even death caused by anger in contemporary television programs or movies in Taiwan.

A study of traditional Chinese medical literature reveals an early awareness of the mind-body relationship and a profound understanding of psychosomatic medicine (Veith 1955). One example can be drawn from the diagnosis made by a doctor for another woman in *The Dream of the Red Chamber*, which shows that the patient's sickness is caused by worry. Her anxiety is damaging her spleen[1] and results in the imbalance of yin and yang and five elements (gold, wood, water, fire, earth) in her body. The doctor believes that the patient can be cured by medicine. Interestingly, although Chinese traditional doctors are aware of the relationship between affective problems and illness, they treat the mental illness by the same methods used to combat physiological sickness. Therefore, in one Chinese acupuncture book the writer claims that even mental illness and neurasthenia, which are caused by affective disorders, can be treated by acupuncture (Chuang 1972). Even now, mental hospitals in China use traditional Chinese medicine and acupuncture in addition to all Western psychiatric methods.

One might argue that perhaps physiological causes are implicated in mental disorders. Freud refrained from generalizing too widely from his observations because of his uncertainty about the extent of the constitutional or somatic component in melancholia (Mendelson 1960). Cannon (1940) conjectured that underlying such conscious feelings there may be actual physiological disturbance, as exemplified in voodoo death, or that the physiological patterns of people with and without psychiatric symptoms may be different.

However, the "twin studies" that focus on heredity in affective disorders do not exclude the significance of environmental factors (Price 1968). Among these factors, cultural influence plays a significant role.

CHINESE RESPONSES TO ILLNESS

In Chinese cases, many people have a strong fantasy about their illness. Although they are totally well, they deeply believe that they are sick, and ask doctors to do all sorts of check-ups for them (see Appendix, case 7 [Tseng 1975] and case 4 [Kleinman 1980]). On the other hand, we find that the family members of patients with major mental illness have a strong tendency to deny the fact. They either keep patients at home for prolonged periods[2] or take them to visit physicians (Lin et al. 1978). Many studies suggest that the severe stigma attached to mental illness by the Chinese may be responsible for this duality (Lin et al. 1978; Kleinman 1980). This kind of denial occurs not only with major mental illness, but also with minor emotional problems. In one study 70 percent of the patients who were later documented as suffering from mental illness initially presented to the psychiatry clinic at the National Taiwan University Hospital with somatic complaints (Tseng 1975). Another study carried out in the same clinic found that among 25 patients with the depressive syndrome,[3] 88 percent initially complained only of somatic complaints. Contrasted with this, among a parallel group of 25 patients assembled at the Massachusetts General Hospital, only 4 percent of 25 depressive patients presented somatic complaints in the absence of dysphoric affect, whereas 16 percent reported somatic complaints along with dysphoric affect as their chief complaint (Kleinman 1977). Li's survey of the shrines of Taiwanese shamans also shows that, of the 126 clients who visited for physiological illness, 65 percent had psychophysical problems (Li 1972). All these studies demonstrate clearly that Chinese people are inclined to express their mental problems in a physiological way. Kleinman has noticed that it is extremely difficult to elicit personal ideas and feelings from the Chinese, because they reduce the intensity of anxiety, depression, fears, and the like, by keeping them undifferentiated in language. However, he thinks that the vagueness in expression is a socially legitimized and usually "un-self-conscious" cognitive mechanism for coping with disordered or difficult emotions, which "function[s] to reduce or entirely block introspection as well as direct expression" (Kleinman 1980). I do not agree that indirect expression arises primarily from "un-self-conscious" mechanisms, but rather from social relationships or culturally shared attitudes that "consciously" hinder people from direct expression of their affective problems.

We now focus on the various reasons for the Chinese practice of manifesting their mental problems as physical problems. First let us define our range of discussion. Since depression, neurosis, hysteria, schizophrenia, etc., are all psychopathological terms used by Western psychiatrists, and since the Chinese do not classify mental problems in such detail, I will use here the more general term "affective disorder" to include all sorts of mental problems of the Chinese people, ranging from non-psychopathological, emotional disorders to major mental illness. All of these share a common feature: they are masked by physiological complaints and are hardly accepted as purely psychological problems by the people. Although some people are conscious of the possible relations between their affective and somatic problems, most of them are not.

CHILD-REARING PRACTICES

Findings from studies of Chinese child rearing are helpful to our discussion. The Chinese pattern of socialization is characterized by oral indulgence, interdependence and lack of privacy in bowel training, emotional control, and respect for authority; the early years are also marked by indulgence as compared to the strict disciplining that begins at school age. Generally speaking, the birth of a child, especially a male, is cause for much satisfaction and celebration in a Chinese household. Parental cares and anxieties about the survival of their offspring are expressed in oral indulgence, "for liberal feeding is about the only recourse beyond prayer that exists for a people with pre-modern notions about medicine and hygiene" (Solomon 1971). As soon as the child cries, Chinese parents give him food. Solomon (1971) suggests that the considerable indulgence in infancy and early childhood, and the affection expressed through the giving of food, "seem to be the basis of an 'oral calculus' in the way that Chinese approach interpersonal relations throughout life" (p. 42). This "oral calculus" might be related to the Chinese liking for medicinal tonics and their tendency to somatize psychological problems and treat them with medicine (Tseng 1972).

Chinese culture does not emphasize traits of cleanliness, order, and punctuality, which are seen by Freudian psychologists as proceeding from strict bowel training. On the contrary, Chinese parents are rather permissive about toilet training. They take care of a child's eliminative activity for him/her before a child can walk by anticipating his/her needs and encouraging movement through whistling. Later on, little children are often seen wearing bottomless trousers. Solomon thinks that because elimination is such a "public" function (the child has a bowel movement with the help of an adult or older sibling), failure to perform properly creates anxieties about the child's relation to the adult or sibling who was helping. One develops a sense of the interdependent quality of even the most personal activities, and, with it, a basic concern for how one performs before others, a sensitivity to shame (Solomon 1971). The interdependent relationship exists not only between parents and children, but also between close friends. Moreover, sensitivity to shame partly accounts for the powerful force of conformity in Chinese culture. The studies of both Solomon and Wolf, conducted primarily in different social classes[4] among the Chinese people, suggest that there is considerable reserve in the expression of affection between parents and children (Solomon 1971; Wolf 1970). Parental models from which children learn tell them that inner feelings are not to be expressed, except in highly guarded ways, and that, in public, emotions should be masked behind the forms of propriety. Teasing and bullying also teach the child the virtue of defense through emotional impassivity. Therefore, to a Chinese, an important aspect of social identity is self-discipline. A person must exercise self-control, especially of the emotions. This restraint of feelings is even more important than improper behavior, especially where one has been taught to depend on external authority for guidance as to what is correct or incorrect behavior (Solomon 1971). Thus, direct expression of strong feelings is seen as rude and disgraceful. This explains the serene quality found in classic Chinese painting and music. Furthermore, due to the cultural stress on emotional control, Chinese children gradually learn to be sensitive to the feelings of others and to be sophisticated in expressing their own. If the child fails to learn this, troubles arise from neglecting others' "real" feelings behind their mask.

When a child, particularly a male child, reaches school age, he encounters an abrupt change in treatment. The years of indulgence are all over; now parents start to see him as reasonable, and harshly demand good school performance from him (Solomon 1971; Wolf 1970). Solomon believes that the tension between the indulgence of infancy and the subsequent harsh discipline of youth creates the contradiction between individual and group life. The attitudes of strong self-esteem and self-worth developed in early oral gratification run counter to the parental goals of developing in their children a strong commitment to the purposes of the family group.

In the foregoing paragraphs, we have briefly discussed the relation between Chinese child training and the Chinese personality. The "oral calculus" and the stress on emotional control might be associated at an unconscious level with the psychosomatic phenomena in our discussion. However, besides the more individual experiences we have also seen the emphasis on nonprivacy, interdependence, and group conformity. The following discussion of the Chinese social structure will provide us with another dimension in understanding the forces that play upon the Chinese early in their experience, and that lead most Chinese to conform, consciously or subconsciously, to their social norms.

SOCIAL STRUCTURE

The Chinese anthropologist Hsu has suggested the concepts of psychological homeostasis and the Chinese idea of *jen* as complementary tools for understanding "personality." Because the idea of personality is a Western concept rooted in individualism and stressing what goes on in the individual's psyche, the word has obscured the understanding of the human being's relationships with others. However, the word *jen*, or personage, puts emphasis on interpersonal transactions. It sees the nature of the individual's external behavior in terms of how it fits or fails to fit the interpersonal standards of the society and culture (Hsu 1971). In nonindividualistic societies, the proportion of one's characteristics that comes out of social pressure might be no smaller than that of early child experience. Therefore, individual behavior is greatly influenced by status and role.

Familism

One of the significant features of Chinese social structure is familism, i.e., the individuals' places in life are closely associated with parents, siblings, and relatives. Therefore, most of the social ethic centers around how to be a child, a sibling, or a parent. The pattern of father-son interaction is the basic model for others, and it also extends to the relationship between superiors and inferiors in the political sphere. However, outside the primary family, the boundaries of one's kin group and other social groups are vague. All behavioral norms for the interactions in this vague area are based on personal relationship, namely, what degree of closeness is established between two individuals. Therefore, interpersonal transactions are guided not by absolute rights and privileges, but by reference to the relative intimacy of the parties. It has been suggested that the social network in Chinese society is like concentric circles[5] with oneself in the center. Beyond the primary kin group, social relationships are very flexible. Thus, for the Chinese the only concrete and controllable moral entity is the self (Fei 1948). From this point of view, the significance of self-control and self-cultivation in Chinese society can be better understood. Figure 15.1 is a diagram of the basic social network of a Chinese individual as a guide for interpersonal transactions. In Figure 15.1, Circle A represents the primary family; Circle B represents the kin group; Rectangle A represents close friends (sometimes treated as fictive kin); Rectangle B represents friends. Except for Circle A, which has a firm boundary, all the boundaries of the groups are flexible.

Kleinman has noticed correctly that ideas and feelings of the Chinese are frequently divided into those held to be superficial and public and those held to be deep and private (Kleinman 1980). As to the former, society demands that individuals act properly according to their social status; as to the latter, they are carefully controlled and revealed only to the most intimate friends. Social status not only defines one's public conduct, but one's emotions as well. Hence in the classic *Book of Filial Piety*, one reads, "... when they [parents] are ill, he [the filial son] feels the greatest anxiety; in mourning for them, he exhibits every demonstration of grief; in sacrificing to them, he displays the utmost solemnity" (Veith 1955). In contemporary Taiwan,

Figure 15.1
"Heaven Is Round; Earth Is Square"

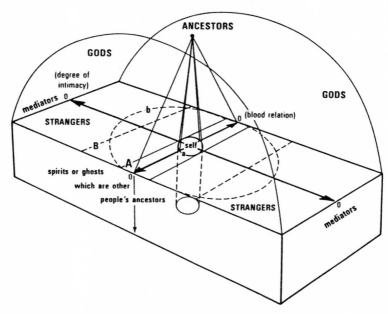

we can still find those who hire crying professionals for their parent's funeral
and amplify the cries through speakers to exhibit their deep grief.

SELF-CONTROL IN CHINESE MORALITY

The foregoing discussion on socialization practices and Chinese social
structure has led us to the focus of emotional self-control, which has been
one of the basic moral criteria for thousands of years. Although we are not
clear about the origin of the emphasis, the central ideas of the great Chinese
tradition, Confucianism, can be seen as being fostered in the same cultural
background, interacting with the folk tradition[6] and enhancing what the folk
culture stresses. Therefore, a discussion of the Confucian concept of human
nature will elucidate further the reason why self-training and emotional control are emphasized.

Confucius had an idea that men are by nature alike; but they grow wide
apart in their actions. He did not explicitly talk much about human nature,
but he admitted that both hunger and sex are inherent in human nature
(Analects). Later on, the argument about human nature was raised between
two main Confucian philosophers. Mencius asserted that human nature is
essentially good, because human beings have an innate sympathy, which

drives people to be humane. Hsun Tzu declared that all human beings are born greedy, jealous, hateful, and lustful, so that life is full of competition, cheating, distrust, and debauchery (Tseng 1975).

Starting from different premises, Mencius held that people should cultivate and develop the good aspects in their nature, whereas Hsun Tzu advocated that they should repress their inborn evil by propriety and music. Most of the later advocates of Confucius followed Mencius' thinking; therefore, for centuries the most popular book of enlightenment starts with the sentences: "In the beginning of life, all men are by nature good. It is the practice that makes people who are naturally alike apart" (*Book of Three-Words*). Probably because of this book, many scholars have claimed that the Chinese believe human nature to be good (Weber 1951; Hu 1944; F.L.K. Hsu 1971.) However, one point should be clarified. Mencius did not deny the powerful evil part, nor did Hsun Tzu deny the subtle good part, of human nature. Classic studies show that their disagreement is based more on the emphasis of each on the good and the bad, than on the quality. Both admitted the good and evil features in human nature[7] and, most importantly, both stressed the significance of emotional control and self-cultivation to remove the evil human nature and to maintain the "supreme harmony." Therefore, instead of further analyzing human nature, traditional Chinese scholars worked on how to practice the inner *kung-fu* of the mind by self-cultivation. Fulfillment of obligation to parents is still highly valued by the Chinese. Besides being morally filial to one's parents, the child should strive to achieve the parents' expectations and try one's best to honor them. De Vos's (1967) discussion on the relation between guilt and obligations toward parents among the Japanese can well be applied to the Chinese. Guilt feelings and shame feelings are more like the ends of a spectrum than a dichotomy. It is likely that the spectrum corresponds to the self-centered, concentric-circled social network. Only toward the most intimate family members can one feel guilt.[8]

Failure of Self-Control

What happens if one reveals affective problems to others? First, if the problem stems from an interpersonal relationship, it implies a moral weakness; i.e., the person has failed in self-cultivation, or, if the conflict is between family members, there is no harmony in the family. Second, if the problem arises from the relation between a man and his affairs, it implies that the person may be incapable of solving problems and that his ability to fulfill family obligations is questioned. All these implications bring shame to him or even increase his guilt toward his parents. Therefore he would rather hide his personal problems, in conformity with the Chinese saying, "Do not let out the ugly things of your family."

Many cases in Tseng's and in Kleinman's studies reveal that those with psychosomatic disturbances have talked about their problems only to their closest friends. (Tseng 1975:241, Kleinman 1980: cases 5 and 6). It is possible that the sense of shame and the behavioral rule of acting towards others according to one's intimacy to another prevents people from expressing their inner problems freely, even when they are in the presence of the Western-trained psychiatrist. This might account for the "heart-to-heart talks" reported to be the most significant method of psychiatry in China.

CAUSES OF MENTAL ILLNESS DISTINCT FROM PHYSICAL ILLNESS

With this understanding, we can turn to the Chinese concept of the individual's responsibility for getting sick. In traditional medicine, most physiological sickness is thought to be caused by a disequilibrium of yin and yang. For example, the disequilibrium of yin and yang in nature may result in wind, which causes headache, apoplexy, and dizziness; or cold, which causes cough, heartache, and stomachache; or hot, dry, wet, and so forth. Besides these causes, moral transgressions, attacks by spirits, and punishment by the gods or ancestors for wrongdoing are also cited (Morse 1934; Veith 1955; Gallin 1978). In modern times, there is a wide acceptance of Western scientific knowledge, and people easily find all sorts of reasons for their illnesses. However, relative to the broad range of explanations on physiological illness, the Chinese seem to put most of the responsibility for psychological trouble on the individual. Because the culture demands self-control, if a person fails in this, and thus develops psychological troubles, no one can really help except the person involved. That probably explains why traditional Chinese doctors do not treat the patient's psychological illness directly, but rather treat the physiological disorder which they realize might be related to the mental disorder. On the other hand, in cases of severe mental illness, blame might come to other family members. People may suspect that the illness is caused by harsh treatment by the patient's family members, or, at the folk level, by the gods or ancestors, as punishment for wrongdoing. All these ideas might contribute to the stigma attached to mental illness by the Chinese people.

Some studies have focused on traditional psychiatry in Chinese culture (Tseng 1974; J. Hsu 1974; Li 1972). Tseng listed them as shamanism, drawing *chien* (signs engraved on bamboo strips) in the temples for divination, fortune-telling, and physiognomy (Tseng 1974). One interesting finding is that the biographical sketches of a Chinese traditional doctor show that geomancy, physiognomy, palmistry, and oracular consultations with the *I-Chin* (*Book of Change*) were all included in his professional training (Chuang 1972). *Book of Change* is one of the seven classic books arranged by Confucius. In traditional times, some elites were capable of learning from the book how to do the divination for themselves through a highly complicated manipulation of linear symbols. Confucius learned it in his late life, when he was very frustrated by his political encounters. It seems that the oracular consolation found in the book is the traditional way for Chinese elites to handle their own psychological problems. The philosophical basis of *I-Chin* is Yin and Yang; therefore it matches well with the rational Chinese elites' idea of an unknowable, nonanthropomorphic cosmology.

Although fewer educated people learn *Book of Change* in contemporary society, other methods of divination have not fallen into disrepute. On the contrary, people still go to fortune-tellers for instructions, and increasingly ornate temples are being built in Taiwan.

By analyzing traditional Chinese modes of psychiatry in terms of interpersonal relationships, we may gain insight into the question under discussion. In most cases, shamans, fortune-tellers, physiognomists, and *chien* interpreters are not acquainted with their clients. Rather, the relationship is usually one of strangers. Consulting these specialists on personal questions thus avoids shame and embarrassment. Besides, all of them are mediators between humanity and supernatural beings; hence they should know and give instructions on people's problems without any intimate relationship.

Although the popular concept of mental problems implies that human beings are responsible for their sicknesses, most of the divination attributes causes to nonhuman sources, such as bad luck, attacks by spirits, ancestors' anger, etc. Nonetheless, these supernatural mediators always provide advice on how to act and how to change one's own temper. As a Chinese psychiatrist said, "It [*chien*-drawing] encourages a person to do as much as he can to improve his life; however, it puts the final responsibility on Heaven. So if the person fails and becomes depressed [the time when he would most likely go to the temple], divination puts the responsibility for failure on Heaven, and thus the person can better accept the frustration with less damage to his self-esteem" (Hsu 1974, p.137). Traditional psychiatry not only transfers the responsibility for mental problems to a more acceptable source, but actively tells people how to deal with their troubles.

To summarize, the Chinese postulate more sources for physiological illness, and the early oral indulgence might be unconsciously associated with a fondness for taking medicines. Taoism also reveals a strong tendency for people to seek immortality through magical potions. All kinds of advertisements for tonic medicines appear in the newspapers in present-day Taiwan. The traditional image of the student as the "white-faced scholar"—elegant, gentle, and nonmuscular—remains undimmed in the popular minds.

In terms of sick role, physiological sickness is the legitimate occasion for people to show affection. One of the typical ways for Taiwanese elementary students to describe how their mothers love them is to say that "When I am sick, my mother is very worried; she takes care of me day and night." It is always during one's sickness that one receives expressed concern and sympathy from others.

Therefore, when people discover that their social obligations are too hard to bear, some unconsciously escape to avoid their obligation (Tseng 1975, cases 2, 3, and 8; Kleinman 1980; case 4, are all examples; see Appendix). Physiological illness can also be a severe protest used by an indignant person, much like suicide. Since someone could be blamed for treating him badly and causing the illness, the sick man succeeds in silently making his charge by being sick (Tseng 1975, cases 4 and 7 illustrate this point very well). In addition, displacement is another function of psychosomatic symptoms. When some people are undergoing severe psychic conflicts, which are not acceptable to themselves, they displace them by somatization in order to disguise the real problems. (For example, Tseng 1975, cases 1, 5, 6; Kleinman 1980, case 6, also p. 158.)

SUMMARY

In the foregoing discussion, we have seen from three perspectives how Chinese culture gives meaning to experience and influences the handling of affective disorders. The characteristics of socialization, the Chinese social structure, and shared ideas all contribute to our understanding of the psychosomatic phenomena. Because of the impact of Western culture and the force of modernization, traditional Chinese methods of socialization and the indigenous social structure are undergoing drastic changes. However, the basic ideas about human nature have persisted, interacting with other dimensions of Chinese culture and functioning as a filter for foreign culture. Thus, the emphases on emotional control and self-cultivation, carried by all three dimensions, play significant roles in channeling the Chinese affective experience.

APPENDIX

The following cases are from Tseng (1975) and Kleinman (1980).

Psychosomatic Illness as an Excuse to Get Away from an Excess or Undesirable Obligation

Case 1. Mr. Chen, an 18-year-old high school student, visited the psychiatric clinic complaining of dizziness, poor memory, and difficulty in concentration for the previous 6 months. He requested a "brain wave examination" for his "worn-out brain."

History revealed that the patient was the eldest son of a well-to-do family, who was expected by his family to go to college after graduation from high school. The entrance examination for college in Taiwan is so difficult and competitive that he knew well that it would not be easy for him to pass the examination unless he studied extraordinarily hard. Under such pressure he studied day and night, but the more he studied the more he found it difficult to learn anything. Finally he began to experience dizziness, poor memory, and difficulty in concentration, which worried him a lot. Since, according to what he was told by a herb doctor, these symptoms are signs of a "worn-out brain," the brain is in need of a rest and "brain tonic" for recovery. His consultation at the psychiatric clinic ("brain hospital") was therefore to find out his brain problem, rather than how to deal with his pressures. With such an orientation he presented his "brain" symptoms and consequently was only anxious to have a brain-wave examination (Tseng: case 2).

Case 2. Mrs. Liu, a 28-year-old housewife and bank teller, visited the University Psychiatric Clinic presenting her problems of "pain over shoulders, easy tiredness, and insomnia" for about 2 months. In addition to medicine for her symptoms, she asked for medical certification, as she felt that she needed to take a rest at home for a short period of time. She explained that she and her husband were living together with her husband's parents' extended family. Two months ago her father-in-law had an attack of apoplexy and had been confined to bed since then. She, as the eldest daughter-in-law, had to take care of him in the evening even though she worked at the bank during the day. Being overburdened by such daily work, but with no way to avoid the present situation, she felt unhappy and became irritable. Frequently she quarreled with her husband and gave her children a difficult time.

The patient visited the psychiatric clinic to complain about her somatic discomfort, since it was a socially accepted way for her to obtain relief from her difficult situation. She explained that she dared not complain to anybody that she could not take such a great burden or cope with such responsibility. If she did she would no doubt be criticized as a vulnerable person, and not filial to her parents-in-law, etc. It would be much safer for her to complain of somatic illness, since somatic illness is considered something beyond her own control and is really in need of special consideration (Tseng: case 3).

Case 3. Mr. Sung, an 18-year-old man, was brought by his mother to the psychiatric clinic seeking a clinical evaluation and medical certificate excluding him from the draft. This thin and pale-looking young man presented multiple somatic symptoms of dizziness, lumbago, abdominal discomfort, etc., even though all his physical check-ups in the past had been negative.

The patient's mother insisted that her son was really physically weak and unable to tolerate life in the Army. According to her, her boy was born weak, and easily caught cold as an infant. In spite of her protective care he suffered frequently from illness. When he first began to go to school he asked the teacher to excuse him from classes in physical education, as she felt that he was too weak to attend such classes. The boy would use any slight discomfort as an excuse to avoid examinations and thus he was asked finally to leave the school before he finished the sixth grade.

When advised by his father to work in a factory he began to complain of many somatic symptoms such as back pain, dizziness, chest pain, etc., for which he would consult the herb doctor as well as the Western doctor for medication and treatment.

Now that he was 18 years old he was eligible for 3 years service in the Army. This worried both the patient himself and his mother very much since both of them believed that life in the Army would torture the patient. Accompanied by his mother, he visited several hospitals and clinics for physical checkups, hoping that some physical ailment would be detected that would prevent his being drafted. However, all the examinations revealed that he was physically sound. Therefore he and his mother finally followed the doctor's advice and requested a psychiatric evaluation (Tseng: case 8).

Case 4. Mr. Wang is a 26-year-old unmarried Taiwanese male, a government telegraph operator and night student in a junior college, who complains of dryness of throat of more than one year's duration. He has been to Western-style and Chinese-style doctors for his complaint without any relief. Recently he was referred by the Ear, Nose and Throat Clinic at National Taiwan University Hospital to that hospital's Psychiatry Clinic because his physical examination, X-rays, and blood tests have disclosed no abnormalities. Mr. Wang notes his chief symptom either begins or worsens when he is psychologically upset. But it is his physical symptom, not his psychological problems, that worries him. He is preoccupied by this complaint. He blames it for difficulty studying, poor school performance, lack of close friends, and family problems. It embarrasses him. He does not like to socialize with peers, date girls, or talk with others because of this problem. It makes him feel inferior to others and also leads him to fear losing face.

Besides this symptom, he reports insomnia with early morning wakening, weight loss, and periodic bouts of dizziness, rapid heart rate, sweating, and tremor of hands when he is under stress. In addition to these physical complaints, he reports some psychological complaints, which he feels are unrelated to the physical problems, including low self-esteem, feelings of shame and guilt, frustration with his job and schooling, chronic tension, and periodic feelings of sadness, hopelessness, and helplessness.

The third of six sibs, he is the only one who has not done well in school and who is neither in a profession nor studying to enter one. His academic performance has been so poor that he knows he cannot get his college degree, but he keeps attending classes because he fears his family will be ashamed of him and reject him if he cannot complete his studies successfully. He feels constantly frustrated, faced by an untenable situation that he declares "cannot change." He already believes that his parents and sibs look down on him, and he fears they don't really care about him. But he does not relate his personal and family problems to his physical complaints. Even though he recognizes that as the former worsen, the latter also become more severe, he rejects a psychophysiological explanation. When the dryness in his throat is most severe he thinks of nothing else but this "physical" problem. At such times, he worries continually about whether or not he can be cured.

On examination Mr. Wang is a thin Chinese male, appearing quite anxious. His speech reveals a partial impediment: he frequently uses the sound "ong," which he describes as a meaningless habit and which increases in frequency and loudness as he becomes anxious and feels under stress. Whenever he is asked to define or express his feelings or to talk about his school and family problems, he hesitates for long periods of time, looking off in space with tears in his eyes and repeating this same sound. The rest of his mental status exam is remarkable only for the feelings of sadness, hopelessness, and helplessness he reports. There are no delusions, hallucinations, evidence of thought disorder, phobias, or paranoid ideas. He has little insight into his problem and is able to characterize his feelings only with great difficulty and after receiving considerable help from the psychiatrist, who has to constantly prevent him from jumping directly from labeling his feelings "upset," in vague terms like *hsin-ching pu-hao*, to talking about his physical symptoms or social problems.

Psychiatric evaluation led to a diagnosis of mixed anxiety-depression syndrome with somatization and serious family and school problems. The patient rejected this diagnosis, refused to return to the Psychiatry Clinic, and discontinued his medication (a minor tranquilizer and an anti-depressant) after several days (an inadequate course of therapy) because of no symptomatic relief (Kleinman: case 4).

Psychosomatic Illness as a Way of Protest

Case 5. Mrs. Wei, a 50-year-old housewife, was brought to the psychiatric clinic by her husband. She complained of fatigue, poor appetite, emaciation, and insomnia. According to her husband she developed these symptoms several weeks previously when their son, against their advice and their attempts to interrupt it, decided to go abroad for study and left immediately. The patient was very angry and upset, as she felt that her son had deserted them. She very soon became depressed, experiencing the symptoms just described.

When asked why she did not more directly present her problems of depression and anger over her son's leaving, and instead complained about her somatic symptoms of fatigue, poor appetite, etc., she explained that she wanted to let every one know how much she was hurt by her son through such suffering from (somatic) illness. According to her it was not serious to become depressed when someone in the family has "deserted." But if she were so depressed as to suffer from a physical illness, it signified the gravity of the hurt. By way of her somatic symptoms and complaints she was actually successful in obtaining others' sympathy toward her: her husband wrote a letter to their son abroad informing him that his mother was seriously (physically) ill, and the guilty son was finally urged to give up his study and return home (Tseng: case 4).

Case 6. Mrs.Chen, a 50-year-old woman and mother of 3 children, was brought into the University Psychiatric Clinic via the Emergency Clinic, with the chief complaint of palpitation and "weak heart." Physical examination in the Emergency Room by an internist revealed no particular physical problems, but she was referred for psychiatric evaluation. When brought to the Psychiatric Outpatient Clinic she was escorted by her two daughters and one son-in-law. When the patient was interviewed it was not only she herself who complained of palpitation, but her daughters were also anxiously concerned about this. One of her daughters inquired anxiously whether there was any possibility that her mother might have "heart disease," since she looked so weak. The other daughter meanwhile asked about the danger of apoplexy. In addition the son-in-law assured the doctor that there was no need to worry about fees as he could afford to pay for whatever was necessary to provide the best medicine for his mother-in-law's heart problems.

After taking some time to calm the whole family, the psychiatrist then began to inquire how the patient first started to suffer from palpitation. She said that it first started the night before her visit to the Emergency Room, when she accidentally discovered that her husband had secretly been spending a large amount of money fooling around with a mistress. Obviously the patient was manifesting such somatic symptoms as a way of showing her anger toward her husband, and at the same time obtaining attention from her family (Tseng: case 7).

Psychosomatic Illness as a Displacement of Deep, Unacceptable Psychic Conflicts*

Case 7. Somatization may involve several family members or an entire family. For example, one lower-middle-class Taiwanese family I studied in Taipei complained of backache affecting all the family members when they visited a shaman. This was perceived by each individual as something attached to their backs and experienced by them as a heavy weight or "burden." One month before a daughter-in-law had died in a motorcycle accident which the family feared might have been a suicide. The family members held deeply ambivalent feelings about the dead woman. She had been discovered stealing money from the family business, which she sent to her father and brothers, and subsequently had quarreled repeatedly with her in-laws, demanding that her husband leave and take with him his share of the business. On several occasions she had threatened suicide, saying that if she and her husband were thwarted her ghost would haunt the family in revenge. After her death the family became terrified that her ghost would "attack" them. They also feared the retribution of the dead woman's father, who was believed to possess knowledge of sorcery. During the period of mourning, the symptom of backache was experienced by each member of the family. They did not complain of the terror they experienced, their ambivalent feelings, or their acute grief. The backache substituted for these problems. It isolated the family's distress, strengthened family bonds, and sanctioned their desire for help. The shaman treated them in part with exorcistic rituals to drive away the ghost, but also reassured them about their fears (Kleinman: p. 158).

Case 8. Mr. Yeh, a 48-year-old veteran soldier, visited the University Psychiatric Clinic with the chief complaint of a "cold sensation over the body, and frequent attacks of palpitation and anxiety" for almost 1 year. He had migrated to Taiwan from Mainland China when young. He is not married and has no close friends or relatives. As an old soldier, he depends entirely upon the army for financial as well as psychological support. He had visited an herb doctor once and was given an herb to "raise his body temperature," but in vain. Later, he consulted internists several times and was treated for "common cold" for his symptoms of chills. As there was no improvement he was referred for psychiatric evaluation.

During the first session of diagnostic interview, when asked how he developed the somatic symptoms of chills and palpitation, he brought from his pocket a piece of paper to show the doctor certain information. On the paper, entitled "Self-analysis of the cause of illness," he reported that he had been saving money for several years for his future security, particularly for life after his retirement. Every month when he got his payment and went to the bank to deposit money in savings he would become tense and anxious without knowing why. It was one year ago when he was on his way to the bank that he met one of his friends in the street. His friend teased him, saying that no matter how much money he had saved it would be no use if he

---

*Most of these cases are associated with strong guilt feelings.

became sick. As a response to such alarming comments he immediately developed the cold sensation over his whole body, with palpitation and anxiety. Since then he has suffered periodically from such symptoms. At the end of the paper he concluded by speculating that "My illness might be related to my constant worry over the possibility of losing my money."

Surprised by the patient's own insightful interpretation of his illness, the psychiatrist asked why he had not complained about the part concerning his emotional problem, i.e., worrying about losing his money as he described in his report, and why he instead complained only of somatic symptoms. He explained that according to his knowledge, every person has emotional problems; therefore, he had not thought that he should consider this as a "problem." He was concerned about his somatic symptoms of cold sensation primarily because, according to his knowledge of Chinese medicine, this is a serious sign of weakness—an indication of deficiency of Yang, the male element—and requires urgent care (Tseng: case 1).

Case 9. Miss Lo, a 26-year-old college-graduate-secretary, visited a psychiatric clinic requesting psychotherapy for her problems. She complained that she had many problems and was in need of psychiatric help. However, she had difficulty in clearly presenting the problem bothering her. She tended to focus on the somatic symptoms she had, i.e., the feeling of trembling of her hands. This attractive and intelligent patient kept being concerned with her somatic problems for several sessions, until she was able to reveal that her shakiness would occur whenever she met any man with whom she was acquainted. She described her shaking symptoms as having first begun three years before, when she met one of her previous classmates on the street who, in greeting her, inquired about her recent life and particularly about her marriage.

It took a while for the patient to stop focusing on her mysterious somatic complaints and to begin revealing her actual personal life. The patient's father, a government underground agent, had left home for some place on a special assignment when the patient was 12. He had not yet returned though he had left 14 years ago. The patient missed her father very much, as he was very fond of her. But there was nothing she could do about it, except to keep hoping that her father would reappear suddenly one day. When she was 18, she became acquainted with one of her father's previous friends, a married man her father's age, with whom she eventually became sexually involved. This involvement with a married man was considered by society as the most disgraceful event that could happen to a young girl. When it was discovered by her mother, she was scolded for her promiscuousness and forced to stop the relationship immediately.

Several years later, when she was 22, she happened to meet another friend of her father's with whom, as before, she could not resist a sexual involvement. Of course, the relationship was again interrupted when it was discovered. However, after the repeated episode, she began to wonder herself why she felt so disgraced by her promiscuous behavior, but, at the same time, still had the uncontrollable desire to do such things—acting as if she were a prostitute.

From her personal history it is easy to understand the nature of the feeling of tremulousness that occurred whenever she was close to any man with whom she got intimately acquainted, with the fear of becoming promiscuously involved again. She was constantly afraid of being discovered by others for her disgraceful personal history.

Thus, she developed shaking symptoms when she was asked about her recent personal life by her previous classmate. This also explains why she took so long in being able to work on her emotional problems after focusing on her somatic symptoms during psychiatric treatment (Tseng: case 5).

Case 10. Mr. Wang, a 34-year-old unmarried man, visited the psychiatric clinic for his obsessive fear of being scratched or bitten by cats. During the initial contact with the psychiatrist he kept worrying about the possibility of being scratched or bitten by a cat without knowing it and asked the psychiatrist to give him a physical checkup again and again. Whenever he found any unusual mark on his skin, or if he experienced any slight discomfort, he complained about it and wondered whether it was caused by the scratch of a cat or not.

After struggling for some time with such obsessive somatic fears and resistances to work on his personal life, he finally revealed the story of the development of his obsessive fears. It was several months prior to his first visit to the psychiatrist that he dropped in on one of his close friends at home. When he got to the house no one answered his knock, but since he found the door open he walked right in. As he looked about the rooms to see if anyone was home, he happened to walk into the bedroom in which his friend's wife was sleeping. He found her lying on the bed clad only in very light pajamas. Surprised and embarrassed by appearing to peep into such a seductive scene, he was about to withdraw from the room when he suddenly stepped over a cat and was bitten by it.

He had been born the only child in a well-to-do family. As a child he was very much protected by his mother and was never allowed to engage in any strenuous activity or to risk any danger. Although very intelligent, he was also very timid. He was not confident about his masculinity, and was not married yet, even though nearing middle age. After the episode of intrusion into the woman's bedroom, and of being bitten by her cat, he developed an excessive fear of being scratched or bitten by cats. For him it was easier to focus his problems in this manner rather than worry directly about the troubling event of intrusion into his friends' privacy (Tseng: case 6).

Case 11. Mr. Hung is a 60-year-old retired Navy captain from the China mainland, a widower living alone in Taipei. He has suffered from the following constellation of symptoms over the past two years: weakness in all extremities; tremor of hands; unsteadiness of gait; heart palpitations; easy fatigue; profound weight loss; and insomnia. Full medical and neurological workups revealed no organic pathology on several occasions. Medical doctors told him he had neurasthenia. Since tranquilizers did not help and since Western-style medical doctors spent very little time talking to him about his problem and led him to believe there was nothing further they could do for his condition, Mr. Hung began visiting the clinic of a noted acupuncturist, a friend who had retired from the Navy. There, over the last six months, he has begun to feel much better with return of strength and appetite, increase in weight, improvement in gait, and greatly improved sleep pattern. He spends three full mornings each week in this Chinese-style doctor's clinic. He receives a half hour of acupuncture therapy and some herb teas each visit and spends the remainder of the morning sitting in the clinic talking with his friend and the patients who come there. He feels that his friend's acupuncture has benefited him, but admits also that his friend has inspired confidence in him, helped him relax, and encouraged him to socialize—things that have been problems for him since the onset of his disorder.

Mr. Hung was in good health upon retiring from the Navy three years ago. However, over the next year, he experienced severe financial reverses in his business ventures that left him without any income other than his small government pension. These reverses destroyed both his savings and the plans for retirement he had made. He found himself deeply disturbed and ashamed. He felt that he had failed in life and had brought shame on himself and his family. He feared his friends would ridicule him if they knew his plight. He felt unable to express his sadness to anyone. And he began to avoid his friends and his grown children. He experienced his depressive affect as a "pressure" on his head and chest. Whenever he felt sad or wished to cry, he associated his despondent feelings with the somatic sensations. His depression came to mean not the psychological symptoms but the physical ones:

First the bad financial problem caused my depression on the heart and brain. [He demonstrates this with his hands as a physical pressure, a pressing on heart and brain.] Then that depression pressed further on me causing my nerves to become weak and also my heart to become weak . . . Now I take tonic and get acupuncture to make my heart and brain stronger.

Mr. Hung would tell me he was depressed, but he described that in somatic terms. If I asked him about his personal feelings, he would not tell me anything other than that he was getting better. He mentioned repeatedly that his financial problems caused his sickness (which he believed to be a physical disorder), but if I asked him how this made him feel, tears would come to his eyes, which his facial muscles would strain to hold back, and he would look away for minutes at a time. He told me that these were things that were better not talked about, that he never talked about them with anyone, *even with himself*, that after all they were getting better; then he would politely but firmly introduce another topic. Even after four months, when his depression had largely subsided, Mr. Hung refused to talk about what his feelings had been like. In fact, on one occasion he told me that he himself did not know what they were like, since when they came to mind he felt his somatic symptoms greatly worsen and became preoccupied with the latter. He also admitted that he spent most of the time watching television, reading, collecting stamps, or playing card games in order to keep his "mind blank." Keeping his mind blank seemed to him important because he felt his physical symptoms less at such times. Even at the time of my last visit, he could talk about his financial reverses in detail but could not say how they affected him beyond stating they depressed his heart and brain, thereby hurting his nerves and bringing on all of his physical complaints (Kleinman: case 6).

NOTES

1. The Chinese character for "temper" (*p'i-chi*) combines the word for "spleen" and *chi*, which means "air," "spirits", "morale," or "anger."

2. Veith has argued that filial piety imposes a dual obligation upon the family which keeps Chinese mental patients from being set apart from their accustomed surroundings, and that the architecture of Chinese traditional country houses permits easy seclusion of a disturbed family member (Veith 1955).

Although architecture has changed to Western apartment style today, there are still many Chinese mental patients hidden at home. However, filial piety is not breached by the admission of physiologically ill family members to the hospital.

3. Kleinman follows Klerman's definition to characterize depressive syndrome as depressive affect, insomnia, weight loss, dry mouth, and an apparently limited number of related psychological complaints (Kleinman 1977).

4. One criticism of Solomon's study is that most of his samples are from middle-class mainlanders' families in cities (Barnouw 1979). However, Wolf did her fieldwork in a small Taiwanese village. All the methods of child training mentioned here appeared in both studies.

5. I revise the concept of concentric circles to a more detailed diagram to explain the basic social structure of traditional Chinese society. See Fig. 15.1.

6. It is a well-known fact that there is some distance between the Chinese elites and the folk culture. But one feature of Chinese society has been social mobility through education. Thus, in the past, if a poor family managed to provide their smartest son with an education, once the man passed official examinations, he became an elite and raised the social class of his family. The line between elites and peasants in traditional Chinese society was based more on education than on economic or blood condition. Therefore, the ideas of the great tradition could find channels to interact with those of the popular tradition. This might explain the reason why Chinese families always put strong emphasis on children's education, and why school performance is seen as the most important way for children to fulfill their obligation and to honor parents. Besides, in contemporary Taiwan, because of compulsory education the distance between elites and peasants has been reduced. In the Chinese great tradition it was not forbidden to the common people to contribute ideas and thoughts.

7. As mentioned before, scholars like Solomon, Tseng, and Hsu—who study the Chinese personality and child-rearing practices from a psychological view—stress the frustration, dissatisfaction, and bitterness in the socialization process. Contrasted to this, a Chinese sociologist's humanistic approach on the Chinese personality focuses on those virtues consciously emphasized in generation after generation: for example, the morally articulated feelings *ching-tsao* (情 操), which were of such concern to Confucians as being able to reduce the anxiety, fear, and grief connected to death, and which could satisfy the desire felt by all civilized people to live a high-level social, cultural, and moral life. The sociologist thinks that the process of submitting to authority was not only painful and frustrating but also involved important feelings of gratification (Yang 1972).

Metzger thinks that the argument originates from different assumptions about behavior. In the psychological approach, the assumption is mainly about one's quest for "direct gratification," that is, survival, appetitive satisfaction, wealth, power, and prestige. In the humanistic approach, emphasis is put on an individual's "basic desires" for "Knowledge of a sense-making, cognitive and moral order, involvement in feelings and symbols intimating transcendence of death, a sense of moral worth and the associated pleasures of extending feelings of affection toward others, and feelings of solidarity, including the opportunity to devote oneself to one's group" (Metzger 1977:23).

I think that this argument might also come out of the underlying different assumptions of human nature. The ideas about "basic desires" in the psychological approach seem to be derived from Freud's concept of the id. Hence, this approach stresses that the Chinese way of socialization, frustrating as it is to children, is satisfying these innate, more biological impulses. On the other hand, the sociologist's concept of human nature seems to come out of the traditional Confucianism. Thus in his discussion, not only biological desires are contained in human nature, but also drives for sympathy, benevolence, knowledge, righteousness, and so on.

8. It is likely that, in Chinese society, the sense of *pao* (報) :retribution, repayment, reward—Yang has written an excellent article on the topic [1957]) is associated with the sense of shame or guilt. As in many primitive societies, the Chinese are very concerned about reciprocity, from which I suspect that the concept of *pao* originated. It is an important virtue that one should repay another's kindness or show gratitude. One failing to do so should feel ashamed (Hu 1944). However, according to the Chinese idea, since no one can ever repay one's parents for giving life, rearing, and training one, one should practice filial piety to show gratitude toward parents. Thus, guilt feeling arises when one feels ambivalent towards one's parents, fails to carry one's family obligations, or cannot achieve parental expectations. On the other hand, the feeling of shame is always in proportion to the degree of unfamiliarity, except that before a stranger one feels neither guilty nor ashamed. That is to say, in a group of friends, one may feel more shame toward the friend with whom one is less well acquainted.

REFERENCES

Barnouw, Victor. 1979. *Culture and Personality*. Homewood, Ill.: Dorsey Press.

Cannon, Walter B. 1940. " 'Voodoo' Death." W.A. Lessa and E.Z. Vogt, eds., *Reader in Comparative Religion*. New York: Harper & Row.

Chuang, Yu-min. 1972. *Chinese Acupuncture*, trans. D.K. Shin. Hanover, N.H.: Oriental Society.

De Vos, George. 1967. "The Relation of Guilt toward Parents to Achievement and Arranged Marriage among the Japanese." R. Hunt, ed., *Personalities and Cultures*. Austin: Univ. of Texas Press.

Fei, Hsiao-tung. 1948. *Hsiang-tu Chung-kuo* [*Rural China*]. Shanghai: Kuan-char-sheh.

Gallin, Bernard. 1978. "Comments on Contemporary Sociocultural Studies of Medicine in Chinese Societies." A. Kleinman, P. Kunstadter, E.R. Alexander, and J.L. Gale, eds., *Culture and Healing in Asian Societies*. Cambridge: Schenkman.

Hsu, Francis L.K. 1971. "Psychosocial Homeostasis and *'Jen'*: Conceptual Tools for Advancing Psychological Anthropology." *American Anthropologist*, 73:23–44.

Hsu, Jin. 1974. "Counseling in the Chinese Temple: Psychological Study of Divination by *'Chien'* Drawing." W. Lebra, ed., *Culture and Mental Health Research in Asia and the Pacific*, vol. 4. Honolulu: Univ. of Hawaii Press.

Hu, Hsien Chin. 1944. "The Chinese Concepts of 'Face.' " *American Anthropologist*, 47:45–64.

Kleinman, Arthur. 1977. "Depression, Somatization, and the New Cross-Cultural Psychiatry." *Social Science & Medicine*, 11:3–10.

————. 1980. *Patients and Healers in the Context of Culture*. Berkeley: Univ. of California Press.

Klineberg, Otto. 1938. "Emotional Expression in Chinese Literature." *Journal of Abnormal and Social Psychology*, 33:517–20.

Leites, Nathan. 1977. *Psychopolitical Analysis*, ed. E.W. Marvick. New York: Halstred Press.

Li, Yih-yuan. 1972. "Shamanism in Taiwan: An Anthropological Inquiry." W. Lebra, ed., *Culture and Mental Health Research in Asia and the Pacific*, vol. 4. Honolulu: Univ. of Hawaii.

Lin, Tsung-Yi, Kenneth Tardiff, George Donetz, and Walter Goresky. 1978. "Ethnicity and Patterns of Help-Seeking." *Culture, Medicine and Psychiatry*, 2:3.

Mendelson, Myer. 1960. *Psychoanalytic Concepts of Depression*. Springfield, Ill.: Thomas.

Metzger, Thomas A. 1977. *Escape from Predicament: Neo-Confucianism and China's Evolving Political Culture*. New York: Columbia Univ. Press.

Morse, William R. 1934. *Chinese Medicine*. New York: Paul B. Hoeber.

Price, John. 1968. "The Genetics of Depressive Behavior." A. Coppen and A. Walk, eds., *Recent Developments in Affective Disorders: A Symposium of the Royal Medico-Psychological Association*. Ashford, England: Headley Brothers.

Sidel, Victor W., and Ruth Sidel. 1973. *Serve the People: Observations on Medicine in the People's Republic of China*. New York: Josiah Macy, Jr., Foundation.

Singer, K. 1974. "Society and Rights of the Mentally Ill: A Historical Retrospective in the Chinese." *Mental Health and Society*, 1:49.

Solomon, Richard H. 1971. *Mao's Political Revolution and the Chinese Political Culture*. Berkeley: Univ. of California Press.

Tseng, Wen-shing. 1972. "On Chinese National Character from the View Point of Personality Development." Y.Y. Li and K.S. Yang, eds., *Symposium on the Character of the Chinese: An Interdisciplinary Approach*. Taipei: Institute of Ethnology, Academia Sinica.

———. 1973. "The Concept of Personality in Confucian Thought." *Psychiatry*, 36:191–202.

———. 1974. "Traditional and Modern Psychiatric Care in Taiwan." A Kleinman, P. Kunstadter, E.R. Alexander, and J.L. Gale, eds., *Culture and Healing in Asian Societies*. Cambridge, Mass.: Schenkman.

———. 1975. "The Nature of Somatic Complaints among Psychiatric Patients: The Chinese Case." *Comprehensive Psychiatry*, 16:237–45.

Veith, Ilza. 1955. "Psychiatric Thought in Chinese Medicine." *Journal of the History of Medicine and Allied Science*, 10:261–68.

Weber, Max. 1951. *The Religion of China*, trans. and ed. Hans H. Gerth. New York: Free Press.

Wolf, Margery, 1970. "Child Training and the Chinese Family." M. Freedman, ed., *Family and Kinship in Chinese Society*. Stanford: Stanford Univ. Press.

Yang, Lien-sheng. 1957. "The Concept of 'Pao' as a Basis for Social Relations in China." J.K. Fairbank, ed., *Chinese Thought and Institutions*. Chicago: Univ. of Chicago Press.

Yang, Martin M.C. 1972. "Familism and Chinese National Character." Y.Y. Li and K.S. Yang, eds., *Symposium on the Character of the Chinese: An Interdisciplinary Approach*. Taipei: Institute of Ethnology, Academia Sinica.

16

Pangolins and Advocates: Vulnerability and Self-Protection in a Mental Patients' Rights Agency

LAWRENCE B. RADINE

The last fifteen years were a period of dramatic growth in the legal system's recognition of the rights of institutionalized mental patients and retarded residents. By the mid-70s, landmark federal court decisions required state-run institutions to provide mental patients and developmentally disabled (mentally retarded) residents with humane, individualized, and professional treatment.[1] By the end of the decade most states had updated and consolidated their mental-health statutes.

In many states these comprehensive mental-health codes included some kind of monitoring, regulatory, or enforcement apparatus. These rights-protection systems varied a great deal: some were complaint-receiving; others were oriented toward litigation. But some of the rights agencies had an even larger mission: to bring about fundamental change in institutions. This chapter is an analysis of one of the more comprehensive agencies.

THE BUREAU OF RECIPIENT RIGHTS

The bureau of recipient rights, a branch of the state department of mental hygiene (DMH), was a state-level rights-monitoring agency whose primary goal was to protect the rights of mental patients and retarded residents who entered the state's two dozen public facilities.[2] The bureau consisted of a central office in the state's largest city and "rights advisers" (RAs) stationed at each of the 12 mental hospitals and 12 facilities for the developmentally disabled. At the time of my research, the bureau employed about 70 people (including clerical staff), and about 15 of these people worked in the central office.

Any observer who visited the central office would have been struck by its intensity. The office was pervaded by a sense of urgency. This atmosphere was especially apparent in staff meetings, which were brisk, well organized, and informative. The director was impressive in her ability to keep track of myriad details, taking an interest in a large number of cases, often reviewing them herself. She had a rare talent for remembering the facts and issues of each of the cases. The director often discussed impending DMH policy developments along with the bureau's plans for responses. In discussing strategies for coping with new policies, the director imbued her staff with a sense of involvement and urgency. Sometimes the meetings would close with a brief discussion of the interest the agency had attracted from the federal government or a news team. The impression was one of a busy, fast-paced office doing work of real social significance.

The office's modern, modular furniture—with movable partitions and open office geography—facilitated communication within the bureau. (The director's office was the only one with floor-to-ceiling walls and a door.) As a result, staff members, already informed through meetings of developments outside the bureau, could learn more details through easy communication with other staff members.

The meetings and informal communication produced a well-informed staff and contributed to the formation of an office culture. This culture (a central topic in this chapter) included expectations of competency, commitment, and a shared sense of urgency.

The bureau contrasts with popular preconceptions of regulatory agencies: central office officials, representing no single profession, generally identified with their agency's goals. They really cared about unresolved patient complaints.

But in talking with some of the agency's field staff (RAs who were stationed at the 12 psychiatric hospitals), I found that they shared very little of this impression of the central office. Rather, for the most part, they were quite alienated from the central office. Many felt that the central office was cold, dictatorial, and naive about hospitals.

The central office was only dimly aware of this alienation of its field staff. It had its own problems of internal strain to deal with. Its relations with the department and other outside organizations created continuous difficulty for the central office. Urgency all too often became desperation. Added to its considerable internal pressure was the suspicion frequently expressed by outsiders that the rights agency was ineffective and should be done away with.

In this chapter, I will show that these demands and pressures created in the agency a sense of vulnerability and fueled a preexisting idealism that characterized the leadership of the agency. The sense of vulnerability and the agency's idealism led the central office to insulate itself from its own field staff and from the hospitals it was monitoring. This distancing interfered with the overall operation of the rights agency, reducing its capacity to supervise its field staff supportively. My purpose here is to develop a thesis about agency vulnerability and to show how a pervasive sense of vulnerability, combined with regulatory idealism, leads to dysfunctional behavior.

POLLUTION THEORY

The central office's relationship with its field staff was seriously troubled by distrust and misunderstanding, and much of this seemed to have overtones of ideological purity or "contamination." "Contamination" may seem an odd word to use, but in fact the choice (by central office staff) of this word seems very revealing.

Contamination or pollution is a central concept in the theories of the anthropologist Mary Douglas (1966, 1975). Douglas uses the concept of pollution as a key to understanding the dynamics of strains within belief systems. She links the experience of threat or vulnerability to rituals of protection and demarcation. The usefulness of Douglas's perspective for this explanation of the problems of the bureau of recipient rights lies both in identifying pollution as a central, unifying concept and in associating pollution-protective behavior (such as shunning) with organizational and cultural strains. A brief review of this theoretical perspective follows.

Anthropologists view belief systems as systems of categories; objects or events in the world are placed in one category or another, depending on the rules of correspondence in the belief system (Needham 1979). Scientific paradigms, such as those developed in physics or physiology, rely as much on systems of classification as do the beliefs of the Lele tribe in Central Africa. Both sorts of systems contain rules of correspondence that place objects and events into the categories of the classification system.

When talking about cultural, rather than scientific, belief systems, the classification system can be linked with the form of social organization. The peculiar character of each society's classification system may depend in part on organizational features, such as the extent of consolidation of political power, division of labor between the sexes, relationships with other societies, and so forth. The classification categories and the rituals that define them perform many functions for the society and may be expressive as well as instrumental in their uses.

Dealing with the Pangolin

What makes Douglas's work so interesting—and where she goes beyond other social anthropologists—is her interest in what happens when reality does not fit the classification system. This failure of the belief system to account for events or things can occur in a number of ways. For example, if the belief system describes various categories of animals in nature, then an anomalous creature would challenge the adequacy of the system of classification. Such a creature, for the Lele tribe of Central Africa, is the pangolin. This mammal, also called a scaly anteater, defies all classification by the Lele. It is an animal, but instead of bearing litters, it bears its young only one at a time, like humans. It is a mammal, but is scaly rather than furry. Although it looks like a heavy lizard, it lives in trees like a squirrel or monkey. To add to its odd character, the pangolin does not even run away if someone goes up to it to attack it. The pangolin is an anomaly—a challenge to the Lele classification system.

Categories are delineated from one another by boundaries. An anomaly, like the pangolin, could be something that is located at the boundary between two categories or even suspended in an undefined space between two categories.

Events or situations that are anomalous pose challenges to belief systems. For example, a culture may define a successful hunt as a consequence of carrying out certain magical rituals. If one day tribesmen faithfully follow these rules of magic, but the hunt yields nothing, an anomalous situation is engendered and must be accounted for in some way.

Anomalies are fairly common occurences in society and some are not necessarily threatening. Other anomalies may pose a more disturbing threat. Because a symbol system in large measure constitutes one's view of reality, a serious ambiguity can cause one's sense of well-being to be threatened. The anomaly itself can be threatening and upsetting because it seems unpredictable, unacceptable, and perhaps incomprehensible. If the anomaly is in a key area of the culture, it suggests that the belief system is seriously amiss, and that something must be done about it.

Anomalies occasion various responses. Probably the most typical is shunning or avoidance. A second response would be physical control, including destruction. A third response would be to settle for one or another interpretation, to force the anomaly into an existing category: a "monstrous" human birth, Douglas notes, might be considered a hippo and put gently in the river to join its fellow animals. Another response would be to label the anomaly as dangerous; this is less than satisfactory because it does not resolve anxiety. The fifth response would be to make the anomaly in some sense sacred: to use it to call attention to a different level of existence. Here a specific anomaly can act as a symbolic lightning rod to draw other anomalous situations to it in a safe and controlled way. Replete with ritual, the anomalous object can be used to symbolize and explain various ambiguous situations.

The pangolin elicits several of these responses from the Lele. The predominant response is avoidance, because, as an anomaly, the pangolin is dangerous. But sometimes the creature is used in a metaphorical sense as well. A prestigious secret cult turns it into a ritual object, killing it and carrying it about in the village in an elaborate ritual. By controlling the pangolin, the Lele feel that they control the anomalies it represents. This dual role—anomaly and metaphor—allows the Lele to cope with other ambiguous or anomalous situations without upsetting their belief system. (There is no certainty that the pangolin is put to this metaphorical use by the Lele—it is simply one of several possibilities.)

The responses to anomalies in nature comprise one set of cultural mechanisms that can be referred to as pollution-protective behavior. Broadly conceived, pollution may be viewed as any experience in which matter is seen as out of place. A reaction to pollution may occur when something that belongs in one category or place comes in contact with something that should be kept separate, in its own place. When the cross-category contact occurs—either as an event, like contamination of food by dirt, or by its sheer anomalous existence, like sea creatures without fins and animals that chew their cuds but do not have unitary hooves for the ancient Israelites—the reaction is commonly disgust and avoidance.

To deal with possible pollution, cultures develop rituals of demarcation, transformation, protection, and purification. These rituals function both to identify the boundaries of the categories and to express the attachment the society has for its values. Such rituals may range from simple, private activities, such as hand washing, to elaborate patterns of social action, such as graduation ceremonies.

Whereas concerns about pollution probably can be found everywhere, one might be led to ask why some societies seem to have a great deal of anxiety over pollution and go to such great lengths to protect themselves from contamination. One might also ask why such concerns are more pronounced in some areas of a single culture than in others.

Douglas assiduously avoids propositional statements such as those that might direct one to look for an intensity of pollution concerns here or there, but she does offer hints about this issue within what one anthropologist described as a volcano of insights.[3] Pollution-protection behavior is probably related to a sense of vulnerability. The insecurity that is tied to vulnerability causes more intense fears over pollution and more protective behavior. But what is vulnerability?

TYPES OF VULNERABILITY

Vulnerability occurs at various levels. One level of vulnerability involves a whole society experiencing a sense of threat from another. Vulnerability may occur in relationships between individuals or classes and may arise from internal political instability or corruption of accepted political (or other) roles. Vulnerability may be a feature of the belief system itself. Critical, central areas within the belief system may be built on contradictions that do not map reality well, and the exposure of these flaws would be a serious threat to the system. Vulnerability may arise from other sources, including individual personalities and even the technical or environmental bases of the society.

There is no reason to assume that one should look to only one level of threat. I suggest that the area of greatest concern is where the sense of threat at various levels (ideological, organizational, and so on) happens to coincide; this is where the most pronounced pollution-protective activities occur. The impetus to protect from threats is a social force, and when the social forces all point in the same direction, the effect is cumulative. Although such an unhappy coincidence may not happen often, it did occur with particular force within the bureau of recipient rights.

The vulnerability that Douglas directs us to look for was present in the Bureau of recipient rights at three levels. One was organizational: the agency suffered from a lack of support within state government and elsewhere. The second was personal: it derived from a reasonable concern over the possibility of failure that might result from an unreasonably ambitious task structure. The third came from the idealism—or, rather, lack of realism—that typified the patients' rights ideology itself. All three levels of threat aggravated the regulatory idealism that characterized the leadership of the agency. I will consider each of the three levels in turn, and, in the course of the discussion, I will describe a pattern of regulatory idealism.

ORGANIZATIONAL VULNERABILITY

The bureau's political environment was generally either hostile or indifferent. The DMH and the state legislature were continuous sources of concern for the agency. Other organizations, such as the major urban newspapers, various advocacy groups, and advisory committees, occasionally affected the agency. The bureau had little visibility outside of mental-health or governmental circles; hence very little public support could be depended on.

The political vulnerability of the agency was a consequence of its odd organizational position. When the bureau was created by legislative enactment in 1974 as part of the state's new, comprehensive mental-health code, the legislature chose to place the agency inside the DMH. The director of the bureau reported to the director of the DMH, as did the directors of the hospitals and facilities. This "internal" structure was viewed by some critics as senseless, because the agency would then be a branch of the very department it was charged with monitoring. Predictably, the most serious and continuous difficulty in the political environment came from the DMH itself.

A latent conflict of interest existed in the reporting of complaints of rights violations. These statistics of complaints at each facility were published by the agency and were a matter of public record. The bureau had an interest in seeing these numbers high, so that it could not be accused of "covering up" or some other form of ineffectiveness. The department, in contrast, faced unending public-relations problems, and these difficulties were certainly not ameliorated by reports of thousands of complaints at its facilities. Beyond remarks about the bureau wanting to use the complaint volume for "empire building," this conflict did not often come out in the open. Rather, it seemed more subtly to separate the bureau from the rest of the department, and thus created some tension.

Of more portent, however, were conflicts that arose in the process of writing departmental policies and procedures (which the facilities had to follow), and in the stands that the department took on certain issues. The bureau was not a true regulatory agency, in that it was not empowered to write rules, policies, and procedures, and in that it lacked any direct enforcement powers. Any position statement on rights could only come from the department, or the attorney general. However, the department did not support all of the patients' rights sections of the code as strongly as the bureau, considering several sections to be something of a bother, and many other sections impossible to comply with. Furthermore, many department functionaries wanted the bureau to be a purely monitoring type of agency and to involve itself less in what they felt were administrative matters. However, the bureau understood its mandate to require it to be actively involved in the writing of departmental policies[4] and it energetically—some department functionaries would have said abrasively—attempted to do just that. Despite the agency's high visibility in the department, the process of policy writing within the department eventually came to exclude the agency from participating in the important initial stages of drafting of the rights-related policies. Once the policies were in draft form, the department could then scarcely ignore the bureau, and it would be asked to comment on the policies, just like any other branch within the department. This subtle exclusion led the bureau to feel that its input was unwelcome, despite the fact that its comments had often been incorporated in final versions.

The exclusion experienced by the bureau was interpreted both as a lack of appreciation for the patients'-rights mandate of the mental health code and as a lack of departmental support for the agency. Central office staff sensed hostility from some department functionaries as they pushed for policy changes. Of course, they expected this lack of support, and consequently regarded a supportive DMH director as a sine qua non of an effective "internal" system. This they lacked, and a deep sense of vulnerability was the result.

The major urban newspapers were a source of pressure on the department, forcing it to attend to patients' rights. One newspaper published a 15-part, front-page series about an atrocity scandal involving abuse of the retarded at one of the department's facilities. This scandal resulted in the ouster of the facility director and the director of the DMH (ironically, the only DMH director who had actively supported the bureau), and, in the aftermath of various "blue ribbon committee" investigations and hearings, in a considerable expansion of the bureau staff.

The atrocity stories did not place much blame on the bureau. The RA at the facility was presented by the newspaper as "unable to clean things up," but was not shown to be a part of the administrative laxity that had allowed the abuse to occur.[5]

The scandal intensified the legislature's concern about the department. Even before the scandal, it had kept close watch, through its committee and staff structure, on conditions in the state's hospitals and facilities. The scandal and the investigations that followed intensified the legislature's belief that the department had withheld information and balked at implementing the legislature's statutory initiatives. The growth in the bureau from 70 to more than 120 officials was the result of various political pressures on the department, which would ordinarily have opposed the expansion of its bureau. In contrast, the legislature endorsed this growth, after its committee investigations revealed rights problems.

Nevertheless, the legislature could not be depended upon by the agency for reliable, long-term support. Increased size only brought increased demands on the agency. With remarkable ambivalence, the legislature continued to view the bureau as suspect because it was part of the department. It therefore did not trust bureau data about the volume and distribution of rights violations any more than it would trust department figures on other topics that might prove politically embarrassing.

Officially, the bureau could never raise an issue with the legislature directly: it could only respond to questions. The department had official channels for initiating communications with the legislature; to circumvent these channels by attempting to communicate directly with the legislature regarding a dispute over some rights-related policy could cost one one's job.

Since the legislature's suspicion of the department spilled over onto the bureau, the legislature contributed to the bureau's sense of vulnerability. Even when expanding the agency, the legislature had serious questions about the bureau's effectiveness and independence from the department.

Taken together, the legislature and the department exerted contradictory demands on the agency and created a difficult course for its leadership to chart. If it took too aggressive a stance, the department would be antagonized. Yet no proof of effectiveness would satisfy the legislature.

TASK STRUCTURE AND
REGULATORY IDEALISM

Perhaps the reactions of suspicion, coolness, and indifference expressed toward the bureau by various organizations—such as the legislature, the newspapers, and advocacy groups—are manifestations of the disappointment politically informed Americans have experienced in the past regarding regulatory agencies. The idea that regulatory agencies are "captured" by the industries they are supposed to regulate is a popular conception in American political life. Although the capture theory may be oversimplified or even misleading, there is a widespread expectation that regulatory agencies should be viewed with a jaundiced eye. This cynicism was reinforced in the case of the bureau of recipient rights because the agency was part of the departmental bureaucracy and thus not even formally independent.

This cynicism about regulation was accompanied by expectations (in the legislature and elsewhere) that the bureau should produce some rather dramatic changes in the facilities. Given the cynicism about the agency, only a dramatic impact could convince these observers that the bureau was not ineffective. This demand for strong, clear evidence of effectiveness led to the second source of vulnerability, the bureau's unbounded task structure.

Despite the central office's focus on departmental policy-making, it defined its overall task very broadly, almost insuring that it would be mostly incapable of achieving its goals. Much of the excessively wide goal structure came from the bureau's legislative mandate. According to the mental-health code, the bureau was empowered to do anything (everything?) possible to see that patients' rights were protected.[6] This meant that the agency was to be far more than a mere complaint-handling mechanism. The bureau leadership felt that all levels of the agency had to be active in all aspects of the mandate: monitoring of complaint resolution within the facility, staff education, patient information, and administrative activities, such as review of local policies.

Added to this unbounded task structure was an unboundedness along a different dimension. The bureau was expected to see that the various patients' rights as guaranteed in chapter 7 of the code were protected in the two dozen state-run facilities; but these rights encompassed about 90 different issues, including abuse, neglect, physical restraint, telephone and mail rights, confidentiality, access to money, treatment suited to the patient's condition, and "least restrictive alternative" form of treatment. No guide for prioritizing these rights was available from the legislature or the department, and the bureau itself ordinarily made no attempt to set priorities. Why did the bureau accept such an impossibly broad responsibility?

One reason is that the central office of the agency identified with the cynics' argument about regulatory agencies. It was very concerned about independence. Whereas it could not maintain independence in fact—the director of the bureau could be fired at any time by the DMH director—it did attempt to maintain it in spirit. Another reason is that it, too, wanted to produce dramatic results. The agency tended to gauge its success in terms of policy changes rather than the facilities' day-to-day practices.

"Taking Things Seriously": Regulatory Idealism

But primarily the central office took on its vast mandate uncritically, as a consequence of its way of viewing its work. The central office people took life very seriously. They wanted to do more than "shuffle papers." The inflated mandate seemed congruent with their goals: they wanted to bring change to a system that they saw as in serious need of change, perhaps fundamentally flawed. Taking things seriously is a core characteristic of an organizational style I shall call regulatory idealism.[7]

Idealism, one dimension of taking things seriously, involves not only strong attachment to values, but also commitment per se. In other words, one should believe in believing, perhaps because it is so clear that so many other people do not. Idealism and a "belief in believing" would be predictable traits in recruits for the central office of recipient rights, just as idealism, enthusiasm, and attachment to principles are traits that are highly valued and encouraged both in academia—especially in liberal arts—and in voluntary advocacy groups, such as the American Civil Liberties Union, the Sierra Club, and the Association for Retarded Citizens. But these traits are less valued in large state bureaucracies. I sometimes encountered department bureaucrats who at one time had been idealists, but who had long since been "ground down." They found that ideals and enthusiasm did not work out in the department, due perhaps to barriers to goals and a general lack of support from other functionaries. These few individuals sensed their loss and quietly regretted it. But, given the way the department worked, this was probably the more appropriate style. Generally, the way to get along in the department, they said, was to be somewhat uninvolved with goals, never to express irritation, to be ready to compromise on anything, and to work on projects that made the department look good to the legislature or the public.

But, of course, this was not the bureau's style. It strongly advocated writing policies that would more fully implement patients' rights. It appeared determined and unwilling to compromise. Many of the rules it wanted implemented would not have helped the department look good, at least in the short run.

Taking oneself seriously is costly. It blinds one to the realities of other people's goals. Change is difficult to bring about in organizations generally because other groups have other goals. The bureau's central office accepted this fact, but also tended to dismiss it, as the other groups' goals were not seen as legitimate, but rather self-serving and lazy, or simply out of date, ignorant, and paternalistic, not to speak of being proscribed by the code. Playing down the legitimacy of others' goals produces an awareness in the others that their goals are held in contempt. This impression led many staff at various levels within the department to reject the bureau and partly explains its isolation.

Taking things seriously also has personal consequences. The stance makes it difficult to distance oneself from the job: one can come to feel singularly responsible for too much. There was a sense in the bureau's central office that without the bureau, patients would be in serious trouble. Taking things seriously can lead to a kind of narcissism, an elevation of one's own importance.

Perfectionism

Regulatory idealism involves a kind of perfectionism, which, along with some optimism, can lead idealists to believe that, given intelligent strategy, they will prevail. Bureaucratic life is like a series of games, as many observers have noted, and implicit in the notion of a game is the idea that one can win. So, from the vantage point of this notion, perfectionism brooks no failure. One should be knowledgeable in the rules of the game; one should be an effective game player (or, perhaps, a jungle-fighter). Such perfectionism demands not only skill at bureaucratic maneuvers, but clairvoyance as well. It assumes that the world is predictable and rational, even in its irrationality. One who understands the forces at play can foresee what will happen and hence can prepare for it.

There is little room in this way of thinking to allow that anyone might reasonably fail. Yet, in the matter of rights protection, the forces arrayed against the bureau were so great that it is difficult to believe that any amount of foresight and skill could have led consistently to success.

The bureau leadership was not so conscious of the possibility of globally failing as it was of being *accused* of failure in one area or another. The agency was always vulnerable to such accusations of failure, and its excessively broad mandate, coupled with very limited political power, led to a sense of near desperation. For example, the bureau felt that it could not prioritize rights unilaterally, because defining some rights as less important than others might make the agency vulnerable to criticism from some quarter. The agency could not possibly accomplish all of its tasks, yet would be readily labeled as corrupt and ineffective if it did not try. The bureau was afraid lest it miss anything. RAs' complaint handling was reviewed in part to see if additional rights issues implicit in a complaint on a subject might have been missed. There was always a concern that a patient might be seriously hurt or killed, while the bureau had previously detected nothing at the facility or on the patient's ward that would indicate anything amiss. An accusation of failure could come from neglecting to "cover all of the bases" or from appearing to be insufficiently aggressive in the pursuit of patients' rights, thereby proving the critics right—"regulatory agencies are no damned good." Given the perfectionism of regulatory idealism, there is no resolution possible for this vulnerability. The unbounded task structure was congruent with the agency leadership's desire to take on all challenges.

I have established thus far that the threat to the bureau existed on two levels: one was organizational, arising from a lack of support from the department, the legislature, and others, and the other was internal. The internal threat arose from an interaction of, on the one hand, concern about accusations of failure deriving from an unrealistic and unbounded task structure with, on the other hand, the personal traits of regulatory idealism. The threat to the bureau came from yet another direction—the agency's ideology.

IDEOLOGICAL VULNERABILITY

The rights chapter of the mental-health code was more than a mandate: it formed the basis of the agency's ideology. The patients' rights chapter of the law, a statement of principles and values, provided the agency with a belief system that placed the bureau, patients, and hospitals into categories of good and evil, virtue and corruption. Its ideology was subject to disconfirmation, however, whenever it confronted the key subjects of its categories, the patients and the staff; this created an additional source of vulnerability for the agency.

"Recipients," Not "Patients"

The code demanded a fundamental alteration of the hospitals' prevailing view of patients and of what was appropriate in terms of the care, treatment, and control of patients. Rather than use the word "patient" or "retarded resident," the writers of the code, in the rights chapter, usually used the term "recipient." The connotation is that of a contractual relationship, rather than a paternalist-dependent connection. The term implies a freedom of choice and a legal equality between the provider of service and the recipient. The recipient, it would seem, may choose not to continue as a recipient, if the services proffered are not satisfactory. The conception of two contracting parties stands in stark contrast to the conventional "benevolent conspiracy" among the doctor and the hospital ward staff, where the doctor gives orders to the patient and the entire institution takes responsibility for controlling and protecting the insane—hence irrational, irresponsible, and dependent—patient.

The code views recipients as potentially able to understand their illnesses and their course, just as one might understand the course of an infectious disease. Mental illness here is no longer a fundamental alteration of identity. The image is of a citizen who happens, right now, to have this disability, which should not be taken to encompass the whole person. By partitioning mental illness, the code can render the patient "normal" in the sense of legal rights, but still admit the reality of mental disorder.

This partitioned conceptualization of mental illness is a major point of the ideology. The rights chapter of the code begins with an assertion that the

mental illness is not legally incapacitating by separating the act of commitment from the judgment of competency. Whether involuntarily committed
or not, all adult patients and retarded residents can vote and have access to
a lawyer—and some can retain a driver's license, get divorced or married,
or form any other contract, without the hospital's or the state's interference.

Hospitals as "Evil"

If the mental patients and retarded residents are uplifted and validated
in the code, the hospitals and facilities are discredited. The code contains
numerous sections that restrain the hospital staff from brutalizing, mortifying,
or otherwise degrading its patients. These include protection from verbal,
physical, and sexual abuse, restrictions on the use of physical restraint and
seclusion, the provision of a "safe, sanitary and humane living environment,"
and the overall promotion of basic human dignity. The ideological significance of these clauses lies in the fact that they need to be stated at all. The
code, in specifying these rights, acknowledges the conditions that critics of
total institutions have ascribed to hospitals and facilities for the disabled.

In practice, this ideology as adopted by the bureau contains some difficult
contradictions. At the risk of some oversimplification, one might say that the
central office's ideology placed the hospitals in the category of evil, because
the institution was seen as the source of the problem. Yet the agency felt
that its task, at its core, was somehow to induce the facilities and hospitals
to adopt the patients' rights ideology.

Despite the self-stigmatizing implications of hospitals' attachment to the
code, some potential for this identification was possible. The hospital directors I interviewed seemed to identify to some extent with the code. One,
perhaps an extreme case, exulted spontaneously in an interview, "I think
the mental health code is a tremendous document." Some facility directors
found the code was useful from an administrator's point of view, because it
provided them with a tool to upgrade care and ward attendants' behavior.

As a result of its placement of hospitals in the evil category, the central
office of the bureau did not, in my view, differentiate the facility directors'
interests from those of other staff, such as ward attendants or psychiatrists.
The fact that the facility director was responsible for the hospital but ordinarily did not treat patients directly produced potentials for many kinds of
goal conflicts within the hospitals. Similarly, goal conflicts sometimes emerged
among various professions as a consequence of differences in their professions' ethics or views of patients, and these differences could have been
used as a vehicle to institute discussions about patients' rights reforms.

Even if the central office had fully recognized the potential for support
among facility directors and others, it might not have been able to exploit
that support effectively because of the inviolable values it was promoting.
The fact that the belief system was so embedded in fundamental American

values and in state and constitutional law meant that, as a set of values, the ideology's legitimacy was beyond dispute. In consequence, this legitimacy put the central office in an unambiguously "correct" position, at least in the abstract. Knowing that one is right prevents one from questioning oneself and is a component of regulatory idealism. Being right means that one need not persuade and negotiate quite so much, because there is so little legitimacy in other points of view.

This description of central office orientation could be described as moral absolutism, but I think that that characterization oversimplifies. The bureau did not operate the hospitals, nor was it responsible for the cure of patients. Without such leavening of disparate responsibilities, its singular ideology became paramount. What appears to be moral absolutism resulted more from the task of regulation than from personal authoritarianism.

Despite the central office's firm attachment to its values and categories, it was partially aware that staff at the hospitals did not fit the categories so simply and neatly. The central office staff knew of some differences in orientation among staff members and among the facilities and hospitals. Contact with the hospitals and facilities, to the extent that it occurred, inevitably demonstrated this diversity and thereby threatened the adequacy of the categories.

Sources of Strain in the Rights Ideology

If the practical identification of evil was ambiguous and troublesome, the characterization of virtue (the partitioned concept of the mental patient) was even worse. The code's assumptions about patients and residents did not fit facility and hospital staffs' experiences with them, and staff had an endless supply of examples of patients' and residents' mental incompetency and irrationality. One staff member told me of an incident where a retarded resident wandering about the grounds of a facility drowned in a river because she literally did not know the difference between a river and a road. Involuntarily committed mental patients sometimes just walked off hospital grounds, to be later picked up by the hospital security staff hitchhiking on the interstate route. Adolescents, staff members would say, misuse the rights complaint system to harass staff members who will not give them something they want or to "get back" at a staff member they do not like. Abuse, it was said, is far more likely to come from other patients than from staff; and given privacy partitions or private rooms, patients assault each other, unobserved by ward staff.

Of course, there are answers to all the examples hospital staff brought up. There should be better monitoring, more staff, better understanding of the rules and their exceptions, and so forth. But whatever the rationale, the point is that concrete information about patients tended to threaten the bureau's ideology.

For their part, the patients provided little help for the bureau's ideology. Most were remarkably uninterested in the patients' rights system. Few identified with the system or supported it in any way. Not only were patients uninterested in the rights system, many of the concerns they did have trivialized the rights ideology. The fact that so many rights complaints seemed petty stood in stark contrast to the ideological intensity and commitment of the central office, and demonstrated a significant gap between the rather grand, ethically grounded, and therapeutically modern rights ideology and the patients themselves.

The more contact the central office had with the hospitals and facilities, the more its ideology would have been challenged. It would have been confronted with some of the untherapeutic consequences of some of the departmental rights regulations that it had helped to formulate. It would have learned in detail that hospital activities are too differentiated to fit well into categories of good and evil, and that staff noncompliance may arise as much from inability as from unwillingness to comply. A full appreciation of these complexities would have necessitated a reorganization of the bureau's ideology. The embattled bureau was under too much stress to take that on.

I now have identified threats to the bureau of recipient rights on three levels: organizational insecurity, task unboundedness leading to the possibility of failure, and the contradictions of an idealistic ideology as it faces reality. These combined to produce a pervasive sense of vulnerability as the sources of threat tended to intersect at the nexus between the central office and the hospitals and facilities.

Vulnerability and insecurity, I have argued, can be expected to generate concerns over pollution from anomalies. If the hospitals and facilities were the prime source of iniquity—and of the bureau's problems with ideology and effectiveness—the concerns over pollution should appear there. The central office's only continuous linkage with the hospitals and facilities was through its field staff of rights advisers.

ANOMALY, PANGOLINS, AND RIGHTS ADVISERS

The rights adviser (RA) is the central office's pangolin. Situated at the boundary between the central office and the hospitals, the RA does not fit fully into either category. The RA exists in a kind of undefined space, an anomalous position. The RA, officially connected to the bureau, but physically part of the hospital, could be dangerous for the central office, according to Douglas's pollution theory.

The central office's view of the rights adviser was fraught with contradiction and concern. Even the term "adviser" symbolizes the ambiguity of the position. The bureau leadership preferred that term when the rights system was originally put in place in 1975 because it did not want to be seen as an antagonist in the department, but rather a working component within it.[8]

This cooperation should extend from the main office of the department down to its hospitals and facilities. From an administrative point of view (the central office was, after all, part of the central administration), explicitly structured antagonists within a bureaucracy do not make sense; hence the bureau consistently avoided using the term "advocate."

Yet, on the other hand, the central office knew that its job, and the job of the RAs, often meant pressuring functionaries to do things they did not want to do. Of necessity, this work involved a great deal of conflict, and to keep up this pressure the rights bureau had to maintain its sense of mission and not cave in to the department at any level. So, although it was unwilling to describe itself as an advocacy organization, it nonetheless wanted to maintain independence. This meant that the central office wanted a special kind of person for its field staff positions—people with the ability to stay independent and push single-mindedly for the bureau's goals, and yet to serve as adviser, not advocate.

Central Office's Fear of RA Co-optation

The central office's concern was not so much that its field staff would fail to recognize this rather subtle distinction, but that such staff would abandon their sense of mission entirely. The central office saw its RAs in perpetual danger of being co-opted by the hospital. Co-optation, the idea that one would sell out or allow one's principles to collapse through inclusion by the opposition, is a modern pollution belief. The central office felt that all RAs were contaminated to some extent by the sheer fact of their continuous contact with the hospitals. But some could be more contaminated than others, and the central office staff used the term "co-opted" for the more thoroughly contaminated of its RAs—the ones who saw things from the hospitals' point of view, not the bureau's.

The definition of RAs as contaminated led to behavior that is quite predictable from Douglas's theories. At the very least, RAs were shunned by the central office. I do not recall seeing an RA in the central office on an informal basis during the entire year I was connected with the bureau. Central office staff did not invite any of its field staff to its parties or other social gatherings. The only times RAs came individually to the central office were for official purposes. Of greater portent, the bureau did not promote its experienced RAs into central office operations. Clearly, promoting RAs into its own midst would have polluted the central office.

Co-optation of RAs was perceived as a serious threat for reasons beyond the concern of individual pollution of central office staff. Effectiveness was one of the central office's chief concerns, and failure to be effective was an ever-present fear and source of vulnerability. The central office's definition of effectiveness rested in part on a stance of opposition to the administration, precisely because the critics and the public would expect the agency to be captured by the organization it was trying to regulate. A co-opted RA might collude with the hospital in covering up bad conditions or in not reporting some violations. If that were exposed, it would undermine the bureau.

Co-optation also meant ineffectiveness in that the co-opted RA might shrink from forcing the hospital to comply with rights rules. The central office's goals involved much more than just complaint handling, and in order for this mission to succeed, the RAs would have to share in that vision. Co-optation, then, would detract from attempting such broad reforms.

Why were RAs seen as so susceptible to co-optation? Surely the answer must extend beyond mere proximity. Part of the answer lies in central office hiring policies for these jobs. In some sense, the central office viewed many of its RAs as second rate. The Civil Service Commission restricted the bureau's choices to people already on its localized "registers" or lists. In many facilities, this meant hiring people who were already working for the facility, but who for some reason wanted a change. And some were "inherited" from the facility directors' choices for the positions. The central office would have much preferred to hire people with less contact with the hospital.

Another part of the central office's explanation for RA co-optation lies in the nature of the RAs' work relationships. The most important relationship at any facility was with the facility director, and the responsibility for correcting rights violations was the facility director's.

RA effectiveness was nearly impossible for the central office to determine. Complaint volume, a readily available measure, was notoriously unreliable as an index of RA effectiveness. Even if the central office had had meaningful effectiveness measures, the RAs would have had considerable control over that information. The central office, therefore, had to rely all the more on its RAs' dedication or attachment to regulatory idealism.

But this dedication was already suspect, and, in itself, very difficult to assess. Even if an RA were unco-opted at one point, one could never tell when, because of close association with the iniquitous hospital, the RA might be transformed. Not able to rely on confidence alone, the central office had to resort to other methods.

SUPERVISORY METHODS

The expectation of seducibility allows the use of social controls in a manner that otherwise might be difficult to justify: pangolins must be handled with caution. In general, these controls conveyed—accurately—a sense that the central office distrusted its RAs.

Central office supervision of RAs was based on two procedures: conferences held at the central office and continuous review of RA reports on recipient rights complaints. Although these types of supervision are social controls, they can also serve as rituals of protection from pollution.

Conferences

The distance between the central office and the field staff on informal matters, already referred to, was apparent in the structure of the conferences with RAs. RAs would come to the central office or a nearby conference center to be updated on new reporting procedures, changes in regulations, or similar topics. The conferences resembled large classroom lecture situations, where various members of the central office would lecture the audience of RAs. Sometimes the program included an RA talking to the assemblage on implementation of some specific issue in the code. In some contexts this lecture format is alienating, however informative it may be. It establishes distance and separation between the central office and the field staff. The RAs sit like students in the audience. Although a student can give a presentation to a class, there is little ambiguity as to who is the professor and who is the student.

The conferences not only set the RAs apart from the central office, they also set the central office as the authority, the expert. RAs either asked questions or displayed their attributes of cleverness, energy, or independence, by talking about their efforts at the hospital. Either behavior further consolidated the relationship as one in which RAs were distinctly subordinate.

These conferences did not permit the RAs to form any kind of group solidarity or to collaborate with one another.[9] Lunch was on central office terms, with central office people at each of the tables. Some RAs commented in interviews that the only time they could talk to one another privately at the conferences (held every few months) was in the restrooms.

Bureau conferences resembled the rituals of protection and demarcation that Douglas found in Central African tribes. They separate out the polluted from the pure, acting on two levels. One level is instrumental: influencing others, reinforcing social pressures, and consolidating power through the fear of danger from pollution. The rituals are an exhortation to righteousness. The other level expresses the general view of the social order.

Reviews of Complaint Processing

The central office's reviews of RAs' complaint handling also displays these elements of ritual uncleanness combined with social control. The process, in brief, worked as follows. The RA, upon receiving a complaint, would investigate and determine whether a right had been violated. This determination might lead to a request to the facility director to remedy the situation. The investigation, determination, and recommendation for action would be presented in a written recipient right report. Ostensibly, the report was the RA's response and explanation to the complainant, typically the patient. But each report was also sent to the central office for review. The central office review assessed whether all the rights issues in the original complaint had been responded to and whether the remedial action was adequate. Often the central office staff could not understand the terminology used in the report and, in a written request, asked the RA for clarification. The RAs resented this intrusion, since they felt that everyone at the hospital understood what had been said. In other reviews that rankled RAs minor technical errors were pointed out, such as mislabeling a violation, or missing an additional rights issue in a complicated complaint.

The RAs resented these reviews (called intervention sheets) out of all proportion to the number they received: some RAs (along with their assistants) processed hundreds of recipient rights complaints each month, and the interventions numbered only a dozen or two every couple of months, and, for some RAs, only a few for the entire year. Some viewed the reviews as the central office's attempt to protect itself. Further, they resented the reviews because they felt that the interventions were useless for improving their work. If shifted their reporting style away from the local audience and added to the "bureaucratic" burden of their jobs. For a time some reviewers were student interns and this fact caused tremendous resentment among the RAs because they felt that the students were completely unqualified to render judgment on the adequacy of RAs' work.

The RA as Metaphor

It may be apparent by this point that in suspecting its field staff of co-optation, the central office was accusing the RAs of precisely the same corruption of which the "public" accused the central office. The identification of the RA as the entity to be acted upon and controlled was no mere passing the buck. The response to the RA was based on a dual reaction, just as the Lele responded to the pangolin in two different ways. The pangolin was both an anomaly per se and a metaphor for all kinds of other anomalies and problems faced by the Lele. The powerless, identifiable, and contaminated RA was a convenient metaphor for the agency's larger problems. Through its control over the RA, the agency could believe that its larger, more difficult, problems would somehow also be controlled.

For example, the rights advisers could have been a primary source of ideological disconfirmation for the central office, because they faced the hospitals every day. If they spoke of conscientious hospital staff members whom they knew, that might pose a difficulty for the central office. Similarly, if the RAs expressed complaints about difficulties in dealing with patients, they risked having the central office identify them as agents of the enemy. In this manner the central office could either prevent its field staff from presenting difficult, threatening ideas, or respond with rationales that kept the ideology intact. Some RAs knew that talking of their militance toward their facility directors would put them in good stead with the central office.

Given the central office's perfectionism, it naturally assumed it was training and reviewing its RAs in the best possible way (given its crucial lack of a middle layer of management). Viewing RAs as beleaguered, it was apparently unaware that the RAs interpreted their overwork and other pressures as a consequence of excessive demands from the central office.

Central Office Misunderstandings

RAs could never be as pure as central office ideology would demand, because their work required so much cooperation. Nor could they see themselves as the sole barrier to ruin, another dimension of regulatory idealism, because they knew too much of the variety of hospital staff and the distribution of hospital staff goodwill, and may even have agreed with some of the staff's problems with the administrative rules.

RA co-optation, despite all of the central office controls, could still, therefore, occur, and that per se would be anomalous, given the central office's expectation of its own bureaucratic expertise. An explanation would be necessary. Here it could be said that outside forces intervened, just as sorcery beliefs explain tribal failures at control. The power of the facility directors to seduce the RAs was a convenient way to deal with this difficulty.

The concept of co-optation resulted in serious misunderstanding of the RAs' work at the hospital. Their effectiveness relied heavily on a good working relationship with the facility director, because the RA had no direct power to tell the hospital staff anything. So, in order to interview an M.D. or an attendant as part of an abuse investigation, the RA had to be certain that the director would compel cooperation by his staff. The RA also relied on the facility director for corrective action in response to the recipient rights complaints. Typically, the RA would ask the facility director to discipline the staff member if improper behavior (such as patient abuse) had occurred, or would write a policy memo to the staff to change some procedures that the RA had determined violated patients' rights.

In some instances, the RAs conflicted with facility directors, but much more often the relationship was more cooperative. Some rights advisers had managed to get themselves accepted as members of the hospital administrative staff and were included in a variety of administrative meetings. I sat in on several hospital administrative staff meetings where some decision was being considered and someone, usually the facility director, would turn to the RA and ask, "Well, what does recipient rights think of this?" The RAs seemed to think their involvement in meetings was a useful way to accomplish their goals. A few fought to get included in such meetings, but others attended with little fuss.

With the rest of the hospital staff, there was even more variety: at one moment the RA might be invited to train new staff or update the nursing staff on some new regulation; at another, the RA might be confronting a staff member with a serious allegation of misconduct. The point here is that the RA was cooperative at some times with some people and confrontational at other times.

The hospital RAs I interviewed were probably nearly as isolated from the hospital as they were from the central office. As much as they were a part of the border of the bureau, they were also part of the border of the hospital itself. Although they got along with the facility directors and other hospital staff for the most part, they were not part of the hospital's informal network. To describe the complexity of the RAs' negotiations and other activities, therefore, as either globally co-opted or pure is fruitless in terms of understanding their work. RAs were fairly independent of the hospital and did what was possible.

CONCERNS ABOUT POLLUTION: CONSEQUENCES

The RAs would have welcomed supportive, educative supervision. Because of their minimal informal involvement with their facilities and their difficult jobs, they needed support from the rights system, but the absence of experienced RAs in the central office meant that it literally could not effectively supervise and train its RAs.

Despite their difficulties with the central office, a few RAs were interested in a promotion to the central office. The central office's expansion and relatively high staff turnover created several openings during the period of my interviews, but no RAs were offered any of these jobs.[10] RAs generally understood that there was no chance for mobility within the bureau, but had various explanations for it. One felt somewhat charitably that any RA's attachment to some specific rights issue might jeopardize the central office's political work at a higher level. Another RA was more bitter, saying that any disagreement would put one in disfavor with the central office.

Whereas the RAs were aware that the central office was pushing them to be more militant with facility directors, their perception of their lack of promotion opportunities seemed to be tied to their view of the central office as intolerant of disagreement. Some RAs spoke of central office pressure to "order their facility directors around," whereas, they said, the central office then complained of poor relationships between RAs and facility directors. RAs never understood that the central office viewed them as contaminated by their hospitals. And, of course, the central office never understood the nature of the RAs' work.

Rights protection is a line of work that draws people with strong values, and these people also seem to have a strong need for approval and support. Although it is understood that such support will not come from one's enemies, it should come from somewhere. As for the RAs, most felt no sense of support or approval from the central office.

Options of the Central Office

It is difficult to see how the central office could have been very different, given the external forces acting on it. It was in a lose/lose situation. Its style could have been a little less abrasive, and it could have been more skilled at gaining assent, but that would not have mattered very much. It faced a highly ideological task in a nearly impossible situation of constraints and demands. It is inevitable that it would have been concerned with its own purity and with the corruptibility of its border functionaries, and that these concerns would seriously disrupt its operations.

The state, in serious financial difficulties in 1981, cut some of its services, and many of those cuts came from the DMH budget. The department, faced with a massive budget cut, decimated the bureau, cutting its staff from 122 to 34 (the only other area of large cuts was in training and development). At this writing, there are 8 staff members in the central office (6 professionals and 2 secretaries) and about 26 in the field (7 of these are stationed by court order in the facility that was the subject of the atrocity stories). The central office's sense of vulnerability and the RAs' insecurity have both proven to be well founded.

NOTES

1. For various points of view on the consequences of these "right to treatment" decisions, see Golann and Fremouw (1976). The landmark right to treatment case is *Wyatt* v. *Stickney*, 325 F. Supp. 781 (M.D. Ala. 1971). This case appears under several different references because the Alabama Mental Health Department director, Stonewall B. Stickney, was succeeded by other officials while the case was still under review, and because two parallel class actions were pursued: one for the mentally ill and the other for the mentally retarded.

2. I had served as a consultant to this agency in 1978 as a consequence of an NIMH postdoctoral fellowship at the University of Michigan at Ann Arbor. After spending nearly a year with the agency on a part-time basis, I was asked to design and direct a study to be funded by the National Institute of Mental Health evaluating the effectiveness of the rights agency. The study was a survey of about 500 patients and 600 staff members at the 12 state-run psychiatric hospitals. As a subproject within the study, I conducted in-depth interviews with the rights advisers and facility directors at the 12 hospitals in 1979. I want to express my appreciation to NIMH for funding both the fellowship and the evaluation project. I also want to thank the staff and administrators of the 12 hospitals and the rights agency for their tremendous cooperation, interest, and candor. These people provided their support and gave of their time in ways far beyond the call of duty. The cooperation of the Department of Mental Hygiene is also to be acknowledged. The names of the state agencies have been modified to protect the confidentiality of the respondents. Daniel Moerman, J. Patrick Dobel, and Geoffrey Eley were very helpful in critiquing this essay and suggesting ideas, and I am very grateful to them.

3. Personal communication from Prof. Daniel Moerman, 17 Nov. 1979.

4. The department's administrative rules require the bureau to "draft department policies, procedures, and standards required by statute or rule relating to the rights of recipients."

5. At that time, prior to 1978, the rights advisers were hired by and reported to the facility directors. Direct supervisory authority over the rights advisers was transferred to the bureau of recipient rights in May 1978, a little more than a year before my interviews. The bureau of recipient rights had replaced about half of the rights advisers by the time I interviewed them.

6. The code reads, "[The bureau] shall receive reports of and may investigate apparent violations of the rights guaranteed by this chapter, may act to resolve disputes relating to apparent violations, may act on behalf of recipients of mental health services to obtain remedy for any apparent violations, and shall otherwise endeavor to safeguard the rights guaranteed by this chapter."

7. Idealism and idealistic commitment are in no way restricted to liberal, leftist, or emancipatory points of view. A recent study of conflicts within antitrust activities in the Federal Trade Commission shows free-market economists so strongly attached to their principles as to seriously interfere with FTC lawyers' choice of cases (Katzmann 1980).

8. The person who was the department director in 1975 created the term "adviser" in consultation with the soon-to-be director of the bureau. The bureau director originally served as a consultant to the department in the writing of the administrative rules and the planning of the rights system. Once implemented, she became director of the bureau. The department directorship thereafter changed hands several times.

9. When the bureau was approaching a size of 120 staff members, it regionalized supervision. Some of these barriers were muted as a result. RAs met less formally, in regional meetings, and the bureau even hired two former RAs in regional positions. This development occurred as my field research was drawing to its conclusion.

10. Civil Service ratings of some of the new, regional positions within the bureau added an additional barrier to promoting RAs.

REFERENCES

Douglas, Mary. 1966. *Purity and Danger: An Analysis of Concepts of Pollution and Taboo.* London: Routledge & Kegan Paul.

————. 1975. *Implicit Meanings, Essays in Anthropology,* Part I. London: Routledge & Kegan Paul.

Golann, Stuart, and William J. Fremouw, eds. 1976. *The Right to Treatment for Mental Patients.* New York: Irvington.

Katzmann, Robert A. 1980. "The Federal Trade Commission." James Q. Wilson, ed., *The Politics of Regulation.* New York: Basic Books.

Needham, Rodney. 1979. *Symbolic Classification.* Santa Monica, Cal.: Goodyear.

PART V

MODERN MEDICINE: SOCIAL STRUCTURE AND RITUAL IN BIOMEDICINE

Medicine, whether we construe it as a science, a field, a discipline, an art, or a calling, is a part of culture. Like any other part of culture—be it !Kung subsistence, Aztec sacrifice, Crow kinship terminology, or academic anthropology—medicine has an element of unrecognized internal logic, and is influenced by nonmedical cultural phenomena in a multitude of ways. Since medicine is perhaps the most deliberate of applied sciences, it becomes a particularly compelling challenge to understand both the logic and the influence.

The language of discourse in any part of culture organizes what participants think, what they "see." What we "see" is the end point of what we think we see. For example, the organization of education has as much of an effect on students as does its content. Medical students necessarily view themselves quite differently from the patients under study. They have learned to solve problems with corpses. They have learned their lessons of cause and effect on static objects, developing a cross-sectional rather than a longitudinal orientation to problem solving. The ethos and mystique of a profession grow out of the transformed shadows of its cultural survivals: Corpses are passive and are not colleagues; there is the implicit expectation that the patient will assume the same attributes. Indeed, the most obvious behavioral characteristic of the cadaver is its patience. Whatever is learned from the corpse has to be learned anew from the living body, but the affect and the context of the original lessons are never erased (Romanucci-Ross 1982).

This cross-sectionalizing of the inherently longitudinal is as apparent in larger historical contexts as it is in the biographical. Felicitously for us, Fleck's (troubling, challenging, and provocative) *Genesis and Development of a Scientific Fact* (1979) is about a problem in medicine (the "fact" that the Wasserman reaction is related to syphilis) rather than one in physics or chemistry. Whatever else we may learn from Fleck, we need to keep constantly in mind his definition of a "fact" as a "stylized signal of resistance in thinking" (1979:98), a roadblock in the flow, a cross-sectionalization of the longitudinal.

Ways of seeing, or knowing, or doing, or thinking are stylizers of cultural processes in any culture. Activities and stylizers of activities are never free of the effects predetermined by the social structure with its implicit mechanisms of self-perpetuation.

Clinical decision making should be dictated only by what the physician considers good for the patient, but actually many decisions converge at this very point. Much of the decision making can occur in a hospital where technical aspects of patient care, cost of care (from staff salaries to "empty bed expenses"), and competition with other hospitals mean that these decisions are influenced by business interests. The board of trustees are advocates and surrogates for community interests (Who is bringing money and business into the community? Do we want to go into the health sciences business? Will this attract other businesses?). This does not mean that the community does not want emergency services and an assurance of medical quality, as well as decisions consistent with present medical knowledge. It may mean, however, that cost-benefit does not have the same meaning to the patient as it does to other individuals and groups. Policy decisions, then, are products not only of the sum of all individual decisions made by good doctors but also of resources, personnel, and the science and art of the possible.

The field of the art and science of medicine, then, is a culture, an island of cognition, affect, social structure and institutions, codified language; it has boundaries that include members and exclude others. As an information system, the field of medicine is a relatively closed system of knowledge; it has many vested interests in remaining that way. Physicians who stray too far from the properly defined and encoded clinical perspective, or from what is generally deemed to constitute proper basic research, are likely to be shunned, or at least ignored, by peers and superiors. This is a most serious control system since, rhetoric to the contrary, the most lauded work is done not by individual practitioners but by teams: a recent article in the *New England Journal of Medicine* listed some ninety-six authors. The rewards in this culture are for those who go deeper and deeper into the thesaurus of the medical lexicon, into the most technical aspects of diagnosis. The accomplishments that elicit the most praise are those displaying the finest motor, auditory, and visual skills, or the most ingenious measurement and quantification. That which cannot be measured is deemed, more or less, not to exist; at best it is ignored in any notions of causality. Agonies and ecstasies of scientific meetings center on complex new technologies that require ever more years of training for organ-system specialists. A physician is much more likely to receive the plaudits of colleagues for inventing a new machine than for healing a sick patient.

This culture of medicine is organized as much by these implicit structures as it is by its overt functions of easing suffering and curing the sick. And as such, it behooves us to try to understand how these structures influence the whole healing process.

Modern medicine is also characterized by its refiguration of the body image, that is, how the body is represented to the "self" of the members of the culture. We have seen, in earlier chapters in this volume, that the Ningerum of New Guinea, for example, view the body as a container or a fortress that can be penetrated by substances, such as tiny ghost arrows or sorcery packets that will cause illness and/or death. One also may ingest evil substances that have to be sucked out of the container. The Khanty shaman viewed the body as a house ("container") that appeared to have populations of migrating souls. Soul loss and soul gain as causes of illness characterize many societies throughout the world. Patients and their doctors had "black box" theories about the invisible interior of the "container" body and acted upon these theories with ritual and herbal and other natural remedies.

But with the beginnings of modern medicine in Europe, with such simple inventions as the stethoscope, for example, the problem became to bring to the surface that which is layered in depth, to make the invisible visible and to project it on a plane. Daremberg wrote, "As soon as one used the ear or the finger to recognize on the living body what was revealed on the corpse by dissection, the description of diseases and therefore therapeutics took quite a new direction (Daremberg 1865:1066). Foucault describes this period in European medicine as the beginning of mapping the territory of disease, noting that the "sight/touch/hearing" trinity defines a perceptual configuration in which the inaccessible illness is tracked down by markers, gauged in depth, drawn to the surface, and projected virtually on the dispersed organs of the corpse (Foucault 1973:164).

We have retained this body image in our Western culture, but not without a refiguration by adding new layers to the anatomy based on the study of corpses. This added metaphorical thinking can be especially instanced in the treatment of those "dis-eases" which were formerly considered nuisances or aberrations but are now medicalized. Kugelmann provides his version of the new body image as it is related to the therapy of stress. He notes that we no longer have time for grief work, for unresolved conflicts, and therefore we have adopted an "ideology of adaptation" so that we can reduce the toxic effects of stress while keeping the tension that stress provides for excitement and motivation. Kugelmann suggests that to the anatomical base of our body image we have added new layerings, specifically the "strength of materials" notions from engineering, energy concepts from thermodynamics, and the "information body" of systems thinking. In this provocative chapter he would have us consider the vampire (in a sense our cultural ideal) as the person who thrives on needing and using a system (of people and energy).

Embedded in a larger culture, the medical culture is influenced in ways no one intended, again affecting patients in unknown and, perhaps, undesirable ways. The field of medicine is meshed within a much larger and even more complex field.

To understand medicine, we must understand the culture within which it exists. In Chapter 18, Romanucci-Ross and Moerman examine some epistemes in both clinical medicine and scientific medical research, viewed as domains of experience and structured reasoning. Both the discourse of Western medicine and its nondiscursive practices stem from values and ideologies with unrecognized and unexplained consequences. Contemporary paradigms are discussed to illustrate that perceiving always involves applying concepts about "cause" to spatial matter (the body) and the nonspatial (mind). We hold that such a concept is neither useful nor accurate in today's scientific world. (For a basic philosophical analysis of the place of Cartesian dualism today, see Churchland 1986:7–23).

Social structure and ritual in modern medicine cannot be effectively considered in our times without a discussion of ethics and the impact of technology on structure and behavior. Tancredi and Romanucci-Ross explore the cultural dimensions of bioethics as well as one aspect of the now entrenched concept of patients' rights.

In our final chapter we explore the idea of a medical anthropology, and the possibility of an even more intellectually satisfying future for this necessary discipline.

REFERENCES

Churchland, Paul M. 1986. *Matter and Consciousness: A Contemporary Introduction to the Philosophy of Mind*. Cambridge, Mass.: MIT Press.

Daremberg, Charles. 1865. *La Medicine; Histoire et Doctrines*. Paris: Didier 2nd edition.

Fleck, Ludwig. 1979. *Genesis and Development of a Scientific Fact*, ed. Thaddeus J. Trenn and Robert K. Merton. Chicago: University of Chicago Press. (First published 1935.)

Foucault, Michel. 1973. *The Birth of the Clinic: An Archaeology of Medical Perception*. New York: Pantheon Books. Tr. by A.M. Sheridan Smith.

Romanucci-Ross, Lola. 1982. "Medicalization and Metaphor: Their Meanings in Culture." In Martin W. De Vries, Robert L. Berg, and Mack Lipkin, Jr., eds., *The Use and Abuse of Medicine*. New York: Praeger.

17

STRESS AND ITS MANAGEMENT: THE CULTURAL CONSTRUCTION OF AN ILLNESS AND ITS TREATMENT

ROBERT KUGELMANN

Stress is an existential condition characteristic of our age. It happens in a world that is constantly changing, chiefly from the pressures of technological change and the social dislocations that accompany it. In that technology is as much a mode of consciousness as it is a set of material things, technological innovation at times takes place without new machines. Stress happens in a world that is without form or proportion, a time–space of white noise in which temporal and spatial boundaries collapse. They collapse because time is only quantitative, and hence scarce; the future especially floods the present. Spatial limits disappear, and under stress people find themselves on the go, never dwelling. Speed provides the means to occupy the stressful world. The occupants experience themselves less as flesh and blood than as sources of energy as they consume time, money, and energy, and swim in a flood of information. They find that they desire stress; in controlled amounts it makes them feel alive, productive, important. It promises to transform them into quasi-immortal beings who cope and prosper. They do so at a price: They consume increasing amounts of energy and information to make it through the week. Then they find, some of them, that they canot take it any more. They make lists. They develop symptoms. Stress takes its toll, since despite their best efforts, their hardiness, their buffers and supports, they have not become pure energy. They are threatened with a realization that the world to which they have adapted does not nurture or sustain their lives without extraordinary effort and resources on their part. The world is alien and hostile, bombarding them with stimuli, demands, and data as if they were astronauts flung adrift in the reaches of outer space. What can they do?

They are doing two things. First, they are getting sick and tired, sick and crazy, and are dying of stress. Stress is a modern demon taking its toll on the freeway of life. It has achieved legal status by becoming the basis for workmen's compensation claims. In this way and others it proves costly to the American economy. Hence, second, the management of stress has become a profitable enterprise, for stress reduction is good for corporate health. Happy, healthy employees produce better and more efficiently than stressed-out ones. The message has penetrated deep into consciousness as people (primarily the managerial class) take up stress management as a form of self-discipline, as the spiritual exercises of the day. Stress management is a martial art, protecting people from the ravages of being under stress.

In an article in *Insurance Review*, Terry Monroe, the president of a stress management firm, stated, "The single most important cause of stress stems from our absolute depressed feelings about our inability to change—a sense of lack of control over our lives."[1] His comment is profound, pointing to the dilemma of stress. On the surface, it appears that what he says is false: All we do is change, insofar as we adapt to the new, often eagerly. At the least, even those among us who do not idolize progress seek information to help us cope. But all this adaptation is not the kind of change that would be needed to slip the yoke of stress. At the heart of stress lies a helplessness, a kind of despair over the incessant series of losses whose rapid succession does not leave room for mourning. Despite the energizing effect of going with the changes and the comforts they offer, under stress people do feel helpless, since they need to be hooked into systems beyond their control or ken. The urge, as the quotation from Monroe suggests, is to change ourselves in order to overcome the lack of control. That is what stress management invites: Change by taking charge.

Because stress is the condition of living in constant and unsettling change, it is a form of grief. More specifically, it is a kind of unresolved grief unique to the modern age. Like all grief it has the goal of reconciling past and future by tying them together in the present. Stress, I would hold, is grief in which losses are not mourned but accommodated. Moreover, the implicit dictate to take control, to adapt to the new, and to shed the familiar short-circuits the work of grief. Grief is the "work," as Freud observed, of accepting the reality of lost love. Love dies hard, especially when there are mixed feelings toward the lost object. In the course of the grief work, the bereaved undergoes a transformation. The self that loved the lost love must itself die in order to live again. "Man is but a network of relationships," Saint-Exupéry wrote, and when one of those relationships ends, the man changes. Peter Marris sees in grief two opposing impulses that account for the necessity of a moratorium, a period of stilled time, to heal the wound of loss:

Grief, then, is the expression of a profound conflict between contradictory impulses—to consolidate all that is still valuable and important in the past, and preserve it from loss; and at the same time, to re-establish a meaningful pattern of relationships, in which the loss is accepted. Each impulse checks the other, reasserting itself by painful stabs of actuality or remorse, and recalling the bereaved to face the conflict itself. Grieving is therefore a process which must work itself out, as the sufferer swings between these claims, testing what comfort they might bring, and continually being tugged back to the task of reconciling them.[2]

The resolution, Marris continues, rests upon "A sense of continuity . . . restored by detaching the familiar meanings of life from the relationship in which they were embodied, and reestablishing them independently of it."[3] This gradual reformulation of the self and its commitments is fraught with danger. Reconciliation is not guaranteed; the grief may never end, becoming chronic.

Grief is the genus; stress, the species. Stress, like grief, entails loss: loss fundamentally of the familiar (body, self, world). Stress expresses an ambivalence, a particular case of the conflict that Marris describes for all grief. Grief is an existential condition in which one's becoming has been placed into question by loss. Death has gripped what I love, so I must let go in order to live; I am pulled away by my ongoing living, which refuses to stop entirely even for death. But I face nothing when I let go. Like Orpheus, I cannot help but look back; like him, I leave the realm of death for the sunlight. This existential momentum that sweeps me up in the passion of grieving under stress is channeled into what feels like tension, pressure, and energy by demands that leave no place or time to let go and reconcile death with a viable future. Instead, since time is scarce, I divert the passion of grief into productive work and into consumption. These activities appear to fill my neediness and satiate the desire that springs from loss. This diversion is expected and enticed in various ways, not the least among them the assumption that technologically driven change is natural and inevitable and good.

Grief, intensely personal, is also predictable in its course, and resembles a disease or a wound. Cultures ordinarily provide rituals of mourning to give a place for the conflict of grief to work itself out. In the West, mourning has been progressively lost as a public custom. We do not know how to deal with loss in the time-honored ways: moratoriums and social rituals of mourning. Stress reflects and compounds the dilemma. Grief requires time, a specific temporality. Where time is money, grief is expensive. Under stress, time as qualitative, as suitable for an activity, does not exist. One constantly adapts to loss and awaits the next blow, leaving one perpetually poised on the threshold of change, being neither here nor there. Losses accumulate; the grief work is never done. This vitality of grief has been renamed "energy," upon which we feed. Stress, then, is a kind of grief in which the wound of loss is kept bleeding in order to keep the mourner energized for the work of consumption.

THE "IDEOLOGY OF ADAPTATION"

"Stress management" as a term embraces the large majority of means to reckon with stress. Essentially, it represents an ideology of adaptation:[4] By a series of measures, one comes to have the discipline both to accommodate to the inevitability of change, especially that bred by technological progress, and to gain mastery over the process of change in a variety of ways. The approach is clearly holistic, ranging through dietary measures, exercise, mental techniques of self-development, styles of social interaction, and changes in organizational systems. They all have the common end of reducing the toxic effects of stress while maintaining enough tension in the various systems to provide motivation and excitement. In particular, stress management tends to generate special attitudes toward one's own body and one's self.

The management of stress is a metaphor derived from management, and it implies that stress is one of the things to be administered. The discipline of management dates from an 1886 address, "The Engineer and an Economist," that Henry Towne delivered to the American Society of Mechanical Engineers. Towne later wrote that management's principal task is to "welcome and encourage every influence tending to increase the efficiency of our productive processes."[5] This goal remains true; a more recent author amplifies the purpose of management thus:

As a mininal responsibility, management must balance a multitude of individual efforts and keep peace in the corridors. . . . To put it in engineering parlance, a large corporation is a system in dynamic equilibrium; its parts are moving fast, and if they run in gross imbalance, centrifugal force will tear them apart.

The supervisory role is primary, then, but taken alone it is insufficient. . . . The manager is expected to be "creative". . . . Presumably what it means . . . is that management must generate energy as well as channel it.[6]

In the present day, as the scope of management has expanded, the management of employee stress has become part of the mandate. Hence the manifesto-like wording of the following:

The rapidly changing nature of work presents an unprecedented challenge for today's managers to create conditions that will release the power of a work force. For too long this group has been constrained by stress associated with change, uncertainty and insecurity. To release this stress, managers must learn to free their employees from such inhibiting forces.[7]

The terms are clear: Change and its anxiety generate stress that binds the power of the work force. Workers of the world, relax; you have nothing to lose but your stress.

An ideology of adaptation informs stress management, as May and Kruger admit: "As technology continues to alter and depersonalize the world, people will experience a need to interact more frequently and effectively with each other, particularly in the workplace."[8] That people must adapt to such a world is beyond question. That this world is depersonalized does not matter, since "events have no meaning in and of themselves. Meaning comes from how the event is viewed."[9] These frank admissions of the hostility and senselessness of the world and the need to feel comfortable within it ensure that grief over the loss of the familiar and the meaningful will never be resolved. There is yet more change to come.

MANAGING THE BODY

Work on the body is integral to stress management. Typically, the argument for such work is that because of Cartesian dualism, we are out of touch with our bodies. We need to get in touch with them for purposes of health and happiness. Stress long endured makes us ill, but fortunately there are specific things to do to stay or get healthy. Primarily these are life-style changes. The information that moves us to do these things gets us in touch with our bodies. Knowledge about cholesterol, immune systems, coronary arteries, and so forth is common, guiding action toward our bodies.

There are more direct measures to use to get back in touch with the body. They involve relaxation and visualization, and present a body image for a stress-filled world. One such technique is "body scanning," an elaboration of progressive relaxation:

Body scanning uses your inner awareness, rather than your eyes, to examine your body. This kind of scanning involves directing your attention quickly and easily to various parts of your body.[10]

The technique works, insofar as it calms and centers, while teaching its practitioners about the location of stresses in their bodies. As an anxiety-reducing method, scanning and its numerous equivalents act as so many Trojan horses, for along with quietude they ever more securely infiltrate into one's being an alienated image of the body:

When you scan, you will imagine various parts of your body and check to see if they are tense. Some people imagine a picture of their body, others imagine their muscles as they would be drawn in an anatomy book, and still others imagine parts of a stick figure. One individual found it easier to imagine an x-ray machine scanning his muscles.[11]

This activity of dissecting the felt body into its elements of tension and relaxation exemplifies "getting in touch with your body."

If I feel better when I relax and scan, why call it a Trojan horse? But what do I get in touch with? What image or set of images does stress management inculcate? It is, I would suggest, a compound image, a four-layer inscription written into the flesh. The top layer is the "information body" of systems thinking. Hence the appropriateness of the term "scan," which has acquired the meaning of reading or analyzing patterns of lights and shadows and converting them into electrical impulses for the purpose of information processing. Information processing is inseparably linked with control or "purposive influence toward a predetermined goal."[12] Hence what one reads or processes exerts an influence on experience and action. A basic insight of the Information Age is that information, tied theoretically to decision theory and to thermodynamics, is not simply "the facts," but in its current usage carries an implicit coercive force. As Barry Glassner writes of the fitness movement, so too with body management (which subsumes fitness):

A great advantage of a fit body is that it can be entrusted to perform competently and reliably.... The fit body-cum-self is cognized as an information-processing-machine, a machine which can correct and guide itself by means of an internal expert system. When information from the medical and psychological sciences or from health crusaders is received via exercise and diet instructions or the media, the self-qua-information-processor is able to use that information to change its own behavior for the better.[13]

When we get in touch with the "information body," we have the experience of feeling as "self" what is actually fragments of conceptual schemata that are purveyed by health authorities through the media for the purposes of conforming our behavior to what these authorities have decided is our "good." We are told what we *need*.[14] The information "processed" in body management derives from three scientific pursuits (at least): the science of thermodynamics, the science of the strength of materials, and the science of anatomy (which are inscription layers 2, 3, and 4). Layer 2 exerts influence by directing consciousness to questions such as How much energy do I have? How can I get more? Since energy is the ability to do work, the questions help us shape our bodies to continue to perform with improved efficiency. Layer 3 asks How much stress can I take without breaking? How can I strengthen my material? These are engineering questions. Layer 4, the basic text upon which the others are inscribed, is the anatomized body. This layer derives originally from the study of corpses, formerly of criminals; the use of these bodies for dissection was a form of punishment.

This anatomized body is, as phenomenology has taught us, an alienated body, since it is no body—no thinking, feeling, willing body. Through emblems omnipresent today courtesy of X-ray, television, and CAT scan, we have come to accept the corpse as the real body. Stress management is a form of training that further instills in our consciousness this corpse with its layers of inscriptions in order to mold behavior and experience. To what end? To the end of managing stress, that is, living with loss of the familiar without getting sick or going crazy.

Nevertheless, the image of oneself as a living corpse, though we do not usually phrase it thus, calms, reduces anxiety. There are several reasons why the image reduces stress. First, it fosters a sense of control. Since science reveals the inner workings of the anatomical image, to the extent that I live with that image, I participate in the power that knowledge brings. I take up the role of an anatomist, of an X-ray machine, of a physician. Second, knowing my body in these terms allies me with the medical community. I become an active member of the health care team when I can describe myself in such terms. Third, the very anonymity of the image provides a measure of community. As stress isolates one in white noise, so this image of the anonymous body makes me feel that I am not alone. This body image is appropriate for a stressful world, since it is not the body as lived through and familiar; it is a body I can have, not be. Finally, the image enables me to stay under stress. In no way does it negate stress and, in fact, it facilitates being under stress. The body is but one of the systems to manage, and in this image it is quite manageable. But at a price: I image my flesh as an animated corpse.

SELF-DEVELOPMENT

The distance from which the body is touched implicates the psychological techniques of self-development. Typically they promote an internal locus of control, a sense of self-mastery, effective coping skills, and other measures to offset the sense of helplessness. By taking up crises as challenges to master and as problems to solve, one develops into a person who can thrive in an increasingly depersonalized setting. In a discussion of problem-solving therapy, we learn that an inability to solve problems causes stress. The goal of the treatment is as follows: "The client is taught how to think and behave in an autonomous, flexible, and scientific manner. Indeed, Mahoney (1974) metaphorically depicts problem-solving therapy as an educational process whereby the client learns how to function as his or her own 'personal scientist.' "[15] As is true with the body, psychological techniques develop an image of the self: here, autonomous, flexible, scientific. Specifically, this image is of a person capable of recognizing a problem, of finding alternative solutions, of evaluating means and their consequences, and finally of perceiving "cause and effect relations in interpersonal events."[16] This calculative thinking of an autonomous (independent, individualized), flexible (adaptive), scientific (detached enough to see causal networks between people) self is ideally suited to manage stress, for such a self has sufficient distance from the world not to value the familiar too highly merely because it is familiar.

Flexibility and detachment are two goals of stress management. The ability to wield power is another, equal in importance. Power proves therapeutic in two forms. An inner locus of control, that is, the perception that one's own actions make a difference, reduces stress. Since, in this ideology, events mean nothing in themselves, an inner sense that one has power—illusory or not—goes a long way to ease the sense that events are out of control. In limited interpersonal spheres, such confidence is persuasive. But the situation differs when dealing with constant change demanded by technological developments and their social organization. Then an inner locus amounts to an ability to adapt to the inevitable.

Beyond inner locus, real power reduces stress. Here the whole notion of stress as literally a load that one carries collapses. The number of demands and tensions in life does not automatically translate into a level of stress. Despite the picture of the harried executive, underlings suffer more from stress than their superiors. Not the Richard Corys, but the Willy Lomans, succumb to distress. As Kets de Vries discovered, a "power effect" helps to keep managers healthy: "Reduction of uncertainty, through control over information and people can be considered a countervailing force to feelings of helplessness."[17] Moreover, in a kind of voodoo operation, stress can be delegated: "Through the abuse of power, managers can induce stress in their subordinates, and for the person in charge, control over subordinates can have a stress-reducing effect. It is responsibility without control that gives rise to stress."[18] Power operates, however, within constraints that are not only organizational.

Without diminishing the possibility of an individual making a positive difference, the possessors of power need also to adapt to the constantly changing world. In a study of computer anxiety among managers, for instance, two researchers investigated how managers respond to increasing expectations that they operate desktop computers. Change enters an organization, they write, "through technology, structure, or people," because an organization is a system that embraces even the top dogs. They concluded that "effective adaptation to computer technology is taking place in these companies," that managers appreciated the "increased efficiency" the computer offered, but that many complained that they had "less face-to-face contact" than previously.[19] Even the powerful decision makers must go with the flow or face loss of position.

Instrumental thinking and the attainment of power are thus two important tools for managing stress. A third, which touches more intimately on the human spirit, deserves attention: the management of stress through self-monitoring and meditation. "Self-observation is the first step in personal stress management," write Quick and Quick, for it helps one to learn the causes of stress in oneself.[20] It is one aspect of the introspection endemic to the control of stress, and a form of "palliative coping," in that when the world cannot be altered, one can change one's self. Meditation, alcohol, drugs, and television are ways to alter self, meditation carrying the implicit promise of doing so without producing sickness.

Meditation in its various forms manages stress by increasing self-governance and discipline. Since change is inevitable, emotional calm makes these disruptions easier to take. While noting that meditation is a "contemplative state as against a calculating or analytic state of mind," Sethi reasons that meditation is also a tool to achieve relaxation and one's goals. Meditation frees one from stress because in realizing the illusory nature of the autonomous ego, one also realizes that "The release from stress lies through and not away from the problem—and the problem is born in, and has its sole existence, in [*sic*] the mind."[21] The wisdom of ages speaks in these words, yet one may wonder at the ease with which difficult disciplines such as yoga and meditation find acceptance.

Despite the personal well-being that comes from these techniques, they are means to accommodate people to living stressfully without great pain. Stress is accepted as natural. As Ellul asks, "What can limits mean when psychological devices make it possible to push back all limits?"[22] In sum, these practices of stress management have as their goal the infinite remolding of the human being to fit a world of endlessly engineered changes. Ellul captures the essence of such techniques in observing, "It makes men happy in a milieu which normally would have made them unhappy, if they had not been worked on, molded, and formed for just that milieu."[23] This intention of stress management rarely receives overt mention; it is characteristically disguised in an argument such as the following: "Stress is a naturally occurring experience essential to our growth, change, development and performance both at work and at home. Depending on the way in which stress is managed, it may have a detrimental effect on our well-being and health— or it may have a beneficial effect."[24] If one believes that stress is both natural and essential to growth, then of course he will cleave to it as to a lover. But the rhetoric fails when he perceives stress as a product of a blood-sucking quest for efficiency.

THE VAMPIRE IN THE SHADOW OF STRESS MANAGEMENT

Stress management intends a good end, the easing of human suffering and pain. In this effort it is not without success. Yet trailing the good intentions like a shadow is a sinister presence that undoes the good by compounding suffering through miring us deeper in stress. Stress management attempts to construct a rational, powerful, creative, calm being whose body is an animated corpse. For this being, suffering, grief, illness, and even death are not inevitable. The changes to which it adapts include medical advances that sustain its life for an increasing length of time, and creature comforts that eliminate physical work and the discomforts of nature. The price that the being has to pay for these benefits, however, is enormous. It entails a craving to become the very source of energy that keeps it in the formless, abstract, disembodied realm of stress. It entails, most fundamentally, not living through the work of grief, never resolving the conflict of grief, but accepting an endless series of hammer blows of loss as the condition for receiving the benefits of stress.

Where have we met such a being before? Only in our nightmares and in tales of gothic fantasy. Is it any wonder that this being, whose name is universally known, inspires ever new and increasingly sympathetic treatment in films and novels? This being is the vampire.

Vampires occur widely in myth and legend, but it is less to its archetypal than to its cultural manifestation that I make reference. The same famous evening of storytelling that hatched *Frankenstein* conceived John Polidori's novel *The Vampyre* (1819). While Polidori did not create the vampire, his book fascinated western Europe and inspired numerous imitations, the most famous of which is Bram Stoker's *Dracula* (1897). In our own day, countless films have dramatized Stoker's novel and played with the theme. A change in attitude toward the vampire becomes noticeable if we compare the 1979 film *Dracula* with its predecessor of 1933. In the early film, the count is clearly evil despite his cultivated manners and charm, and good triumphs in the end. In the more recent film, Dracula has become a more sympathetic figure, strikingly erotic and the melancholic representative of a vanishing race. In the film's ending, good wins out only temporarily, and we are promised, in the language of mass media, sequels. In another recent film, *The Hunger* (1983), beautiful male and female vampires lead a life of quiet charm, teach music, and stalk nightclubs. This film's brilliance is in making clear that the vampire is addicted to the blood of life, that it is hopelessly helpless without getting its needs filled by transient interpersonal relations.

The most striking reevaluation of the vampire occurs in recent novels, including Fred Saberhagen's *The Dracula Tapes* and Ann Rice's trilogy of novels, *Interview with the Vampire, The Vampire Lestat*, and *Queen of the Damned*. These novels share a common device: The narrators are vampires; we experience the world through their eyes. In Saberhagen's book, the tapes were made by the count, who retells Stoker's novel from his point of view, arguing that Jonathan Harker and the others lied about him (and were certainly mistaken about the climax of the novel). Rice's trilogy also begins with a vampire speaking into a tape recorder, in this case that of Louis, who was initiated into vampirehood by Lestat (hero of the second novel). When Rice was interviewed after the publication of the third book, a reporter asked her if she would like to be a vampire. She answered that she would, in order to go into dangerous parts of cities at night, and to fight crime. To be a vampire is to "take back the night," make it possible to live without fear in the alien world that creates stress.

Two things are essential to the nature of the vampire: It cannot die, and it feeds on blood. In both regards, stress management techniques tend to produce vampires.

Its Deathless Body

To become a vampire, a person must undergo a physical transformation. Louis, the interviewee in Rice's first novel on the topic, recalls what happened after he drank the blood that initiated the process: "All my human fluids were being forced out of me. I was dying as a human, yet completely alive as a vampire; and with my awakened senses, I had to preside over the death of my body with a certain discomfort and then, finally, fear."[25] The vampire body, devoid of human flesh, has more acute senses, greater strength and agility, and perfect health, and never ages. In these qualities it approaches the cultural ideal. What is telling in Louis's account are two aspects of the transition: first, at the moment when he should die, he does not. The death of the old self, characteristic of grief, has been bypassed in this transformation. Second, the body becomes an animated corpse; during a process of change, consciousness hovers in discomfort and fear (and then in equanimity, as feeling drains with the fluids).

Let us imagine the scene again, in the quotidian: "I" sit at home, tired and frazzled, exhausted from the pressures of the day, from fighting traffic, from stemming the flow from the checkbook, from watching television in order to unwind. Sleep eludes "me." What "I" realize, in the typical story of salvation from stress, is that "my" life-style must change. Not, mind you, that "I" will refuse to participate in the noisy world. That seems unimaginable. No, "I" take up stress-reducing measures and soon feel better, more relaxed, more in control.

Rather than dying to the stressful world—whatever that could mean at this juncture—"I" have taken it on, on its own terms, becoming disciplined. Rather than give in, at the moment of being drained "I" bite back, becoming the center of the whirlwind, not its victim. Thereby "I" become more in harmony with stress, living on its purchasable substances, energy and information. The desperation that led "me" to embrace stress management is the act that transforms "me" into a vampire. Now stress energizes rather than drains "me"; "I" do not have to die (or get sick), for "I" have transformed stress into my energy.

As Rice depicts it, the critical moment has this form, as the initiator says to Louis:

Be still. I am going to drain you now to the very threshold of death, and I want you to be quiet, so quiet that you can almost hear the flow of blood through your veins, so quiet that you can hear the flow of that same blood through mine. It is your consciousness, your will, which must keep you alive.[26]

When Louis accepts, at the moment of death, the blood from the vampire's wrist, he experiences a wholeness and oneness known only by the infant at the breast. All loss has been overcome in this moment of unity. There is no longer reason to suffer or grieve when "I" becomes that which would kill "me." The moment does not make the vampire blind to its needs; in fact, the vampire honestly accepts its need for other people, and anyone will do. He thinks in terms of systems.

Its Feeding on Blood

The vampire's grotesque parody of the Christian Eucharist needs to be viewed in the context of the present age. Blood for us has undergone a metamorphosis. Blood used to be the very stuff of our selves, defining us as noble or common. As one of the four humors, blood had powerful psychological and medical properties, such that bloodletting was a necessary practice, as was the building up of blood. Now, however, blood is a commodity to be bought and sold, a "chemical soup" capable of being shared by many physiological systems. "Give the gift of life" read the ads for blood drives, revealing the symbolic equivalents of blood. Blood is life, blood is energy, the raw material for living.

The vampire is a blood addict. Blood enables it to maintain its animated corpse in the pink of health. Stress is for people what blood is for vampires. Is it any surprise to learn that people are now becoming addicted to the stress of life? The energizing effect of undergoing stress has the potential for compulsive activity, especially when it has power as its accompaniment. "I work best under pressure," or as Waino Suojanen, an authority on human resource management, observes: "There is plenty of anecdotal evidence that some executives deliberately seek out the management life because they get a high out of controlling people."[27] And some "managers become so proud of their ability to stand up under crises that they are always creating crises to stand up under, or are always starting fires in order to put them out."[28] One gets addicted to the experience of transcending normal human life in these instances: Power, a strong medicine that (as noted above) can reduce stress, becomes poison, mastering those who too often find balm for their lives in its exercise.

In recent years the phenomenon of stress addiction has arisen, in part because addiction has become a catchall term and in part because a consumer society pushed to its limits has the addict as its ideal type. The vampire dispenses with trivial commodities, sinking its teeth into the ultimate product. The psychologist and Jungian analyst Linda Leonard concurs in part in her claim that "Dracula as Demon Lover is an archetypal symbol of addiction."[29] The figure of the addict so exercises the contemporary imagination that whereas in the past the addict was an Other, now it appears as a figure of the self. Stress addiction, or "how to turn tension into energy," like the lust of the undead, goes to the source of what addiction desires: the high, that verticality which lifts us above the merely human. We addicts thus share in the vampire's fate, becoming bestial in search of the next hit, the next sublime moment, the next crisis.

Stress management produces vampires, then, to the extent that it aids in the loss of the flesh and in adaptation to a world of relentless change. As "I" lose the flesh, through the recession of limits by human engineering, "I" feel more at home in an abstract, formless, noisy space-time. Stress thus managed promises immortality as human limits are transcended, but it is the death-lessness of the vampire. " 'I've done with grief,' she said, her eyes narrowing as she looked up at me. 'If you knew how I long to have your power; I'm ready for it, I hunger for it.' "[30] So says one vampire to another. Through managing stress we trade grief for power, loss for energy. The conflict that grief would heal becomes harnessed for work.

"The Absence of Stress Is Death"

What alternative is there? The phrase that heads this section comes from Selye, and although he did not mean it in quite the way I take it, it indicates the direction. Where death has a place, stress cannot abide. The vampire narratives provide the form: Only when mortals dig up and face in the light of day what they fear becoming, and only when they dispatch the vampire in a ritual of burial, can they lay their fears to rest. The ritual slaughter of the vampire is not simply an act of violence, since the vampire craves rest; its will cannot act on this desire.

In the stories, the primary means to vanquish a vampire is to locate its grave, unearth it, drive a stake through its heart, and bury it again. Then and only then will the undead find release from this life and its soul seek its final reward. Like insomniacs, vampires cannot find peace by themselves: They cannot succumb to passion, cannot be possessed by the elemental force of death that would lift the burden of life from their shoulders. What heals the vampire informs us as to the place and the time of the action: The place is the body, the time is the mourning that begins at the graveside.

The Stake in the Heart

> Then comes a sudden jab of red-hot memory.
> C. S. Lewis, *A Grief Observed*

A loss that occasions grief is a wound. This is no mere analogy, but the painful reality that the bereaved feel. The location of the wound varies, but typically the heart centers the pain. Since stress is unresolved grief, it is necessary to recover the felt sense of the wound of loss in order to mourn. With stress, however, the sense of being struck is usually diffuse, less fo-cused, given its disembodying nature. Stress bombards; we take flak from all sides. At other times, the experience has precision: "Employees feel like we're the anvil and everybody's beating on us with a hammer."[31] But whether the wounds come as the flak of hurriedness or the hammer of criticism, the first task is to disengage these moments from the engineering mentality that asks How much can I take? Is my material adaptable enough? Can I cope? For these moments are not attacks, they are stabs in the heart of the vampire. They contain the potential to bring back to reality an old idea and perception that things which matter have their dwelling in the flesh. The work of grief that this pain facilitates can have the salutary effect of so wounding us that we realize the flesh is no animated corpse but our very selves. Loss wounds the heart (not the pump) because love and commitment dwell in the heart. When the stake is planted in the vampire's chest, blood (energy) rushes out and the corpse decays. These are the effects one seeks in order to escape being under stress. The stab wounds of loss cannot be accounted for by the animated corpse and the knowledge (anatomy, physiology) of it. Only the story of one's particular loves can express the nature of the wounds. The decaying corpse can thus begin to become flesh again.

The flesh is the body of the familiar. This definition is true to the old echoes of "flesh" from Scripture and elsewhere, which bring together the self as somebody and all that belongs with somebody: "flesh of my flesh" (children, kin), "one flesh" (husband and wife), "the flesh is weak" (desire, passion, resistance to excesses of the spirit). Like William James's notion of the "material me," the flesh is also all that is concretely mine: clothes, dwelling, possessions, land. That under stress, dwelling in the body and in places and moments becomes problematic, means that with stress, the flesh withers, vanishes, is transcended. To bring the flesh back into perception, an anti-stress meditation may prove helpful. From the *Secretum* of Petrarch comes a meditative exercise from a late medieval tradition. It is particularly graphic, even grotesque, flying in the face of our sanitized images of the healthy, anatomized body. It evokes the flesh in all its materiality. Petrarch provides a guide to the proper meditation on death that is the polar opposite of our command: Relax!

So here is a test which will never play you false: every time you meditate on death without the least sign of motion, know that you have meditated in vain, as about any ordinary topic. But if in the act of meditation you find yourself suddenly grow stiff, if you tremble, turn pale, and feel as if already you endured its pains . . . [and after meditating on the Four Final Things] then you may be assured you have not meditated in vain.[32]

Now to the meditation:

Of all tremendous realities Death is the most tremendous. So true is this, that from ever of old its very name is terrible and dreadful to hear. Yet though so it is, it will not do that we hear that name but lightly, or allow the remembrance of it to slip quickly from our mind. No, we must take time to realize it. We must meditate with attention thereon. We must picture to ourselves the effect of death on each several part of our bodily frame, the cold extremities, the breast in the sweat of fever, the side throbbing with pain, the vital spirits running slower and slower as death draws near, the eyes sunken and weeping, every look filled with tears, the forehead pale and drawn, the cheeks hanging and hollow, the teeth staring and discoloured, the nostrils shrunk and sharpened, the lips foaming, the tongue foul and motionless, the palate parched and dry, the languid head and panting breast, the hoarse murmur and sorrowful sigh, the evil smell of the whole body, the horror of seeing the face utterly unlike itself.[33]

This practice comes from a mentality alien to the modern mind, although in one way at least the late medieval period resembles our own. This type of meditation arose in a time of war and plague, when death was ever present. In our own day, when "megadeath" has been coined in the wake of two world wars, bureaucratically organized genocide, and the specter of a nuclear winter, the practice of meditation on death may not be entirely foreign to our secular mentality. I call this practice an "anti-stress" exercise because it makes us neither more nor less resilient to stress. Its aim is to pierce the "I" that lives under stress and expose it to the losses that stress as a construct makes difficult to mourn. It holds up to the imagination an image of the body as bound to loss and to death: not the anatomized body, fixated by embalming fluids, but the flesh with its feelings and frailties. This vision of the dying flesh, less experienceable today than in Petrarch's time, may move us from stress to a passion for living. As Ariès comments:

"We must leave behind our house, our orchards, and our gardens, dishes and vessels which the artisan engraved", wrote Ronsard, reflecting upon death. Which of us faced with death would weep over a house in Florida or a farm in Virginia? In proto-capitalist eras—in other words, in periods when the capitalist and technological mentality was being developed, the process would not be completed until the eighteenth century—man had an unreasoning, visceral love for *temporalia*, which was a blanket word including things, men, and animals.[34]

When we stop for death, we can grieve, and when we grieve, we can love again. To the extent we thus stop, we step out from under stress.

BURYING THE DEAD

> *Ubi caritas gaudet, ibi est festivitas.*
> (Where charity [love] gives pleasure, there is the festivity)
> John Chrysostom

Stress occurs when losses of the familiar, which happen at an accelerating pace, become problems to solve and challenges to face, when innovation and progress in efficiency fall upon the earth like manna. This peculiarly modern form of grief allows for no resolution, for the position of loss keeps us energized, pining for we-know-not-what, feeling our inferiorities and helplessness, and hence vulnerable to the demand that we take charge and flexibly adapt. So we willingly bite back on that which feeds upon us, hungry for anything to fill the void that white noise creates.

To stop for death is a first step to enable the grief to emerge from the iron bands of stress. Then to celebrate loss through mourning. But that has been rendered difficult. Nietzsche, who saw our time of stress on the horizon, observed: "The trick is not to arrange a festival, but to find people who can *enjoy* it."[35] We are incapable of celebration to the extent that we live stress as stress. Men under stress live in no-man's-land. They cannot, we cannot, stop for death, take the time to acknowledge the completeness of things as they are, which affirmation grounds celebration, even the celebrations surrounding death.[36] Vampires, the addicted, the stressed-out, cannot acclaim the goodness of things as they are.

How to celebrate mourning? How, that is, to lay the vampire to rest, cover the grave, pray for its soul, walk back to town? Laying the vampire to rest means in part easing its neediness. The constant need for fresh blood drives the vampire, and the ambivalence of its grief keeps it so needy. To begin to celebrate mourning means to celebrate the neediness rather than satiate it with fixes of energy. Mourning begins when we are exhausted, stressed-out, frazzled.

The rush of stress covers a poverty all the more profound because it is unrecognized. The energy of stress has its generator in the betwixt-and-between nature of stress. The alien world, the ambivalence toward loss, the accommodation to change: A stockpile of emptiness builds up and, not being recognized, not lived through in bereavement, feeds the frantic pace. Then, "wiped out," the cycle begins anew. To refuse energy in the name of poverty makes celebration possible. To be thus impoverished is a condition no commodity can enrich; only the gifts that come freely in celebration can answer such poverty. In this celebration of the loss of the flesh and the familiar, we find that we are reflected, not in the chrome and glass of downtown, the coffins of vampires, but in the bums and bag ladies looking in the trash cans or, hands outstretched, asking for a gift.

They teach us how to be poor. Ask for a gift. Gifts are not scarce commodities. They are always essentially plentiful. With arms outstretched, backs turned to the temples of scarcity, we celebrate: "A festival is essentially a phenomenon of wealth; not, to be sure, the wealth of money, but of existential richness. Absence of calculation, in fact lavishness, is one of its elements."[37]

Thus enfleshed and impoverished, we celebrate our losses, not nostalgic for the past, not enthralled with the brave new world. In enacting grief for our selves and our world, we take up a place, stepping from white noise with its swirling winds and fast lanes. Our place is filled with modern junk, surrounded by noise and speed, with fleshness energized calm vampires, but a place, nonetheless, in which to bury the dead.

NOTES

1. Cited in Susan Banham, "Stress in the workplace—What can be done about it?" *Insurance Review* (May/June 1985), 12.

2. Peter Marris, *Loss and Change* (Garden City: New York: Anchor Books, 1975), pp. 31–32.

3. Ibid, p. 34.

4. Peter Marris, "The social impact of stress," in *Mental Health and the Economy*, ed. L. A. Ferman and J. P. Gordus (Kalamazoo, MI: W. E. Upjohn Institute for Employment Research, 1979), p. 311.

5. Allen C. Bluedorn, Introduction to "Special Book Review Section on the Classics of Management," *Academy of Management Review 11*, 2 (April 1986), 443.

6. Carl B. Kaufman, *Man Incorporate: The Individual and His Work in an Organizational Society* (Garden City, NY: Anchor Books, 1969), p. 140.

7. Gregory D. May and Michael J. Kruger, "The manager within," *Personnel Journal* (Feb. 1988), 57.

8. Ibid., p. 65.

9. Ibid., p. 57.

10. Edward Charlesworth and Ronald Nathan, *A Comprehensive Guide to Wellness* (New York: Atheneum, 1984), p. 60.

11. Ibid., pp. 62–63.

12. James Beniger, *The Control Revolution: Technological and Economic Origins of the Information Society* (Cambridge, MA: Harvard University Press, 1986), p. 7.

13. Barry Glassner, "Fitness and the postmodern self," *Journal of Health and Social Behavior 30*, 2 (June 1989), 184.

14. Ivan Illich, "Disabling professions," in *The Disabling Professions*, Ivan Illich, ed (Boston: Marion Boyars, 1977), pp. 11–40.

15. Donald Meichenbaum, David Henshaw, and Norman Himel, "Coping with stress as a problem-solving process," in *Achievement, Stress, and Anxiety*, ed. H. Krohne and L. Laux (Washington; DC: Hemisphere, 1982), pp. 139–40.

16. Ibid., p. 138.

17. M. F. R. Kets de Vries, "Organizational stress management audit," in *Handbook of Organizational Stress Coping Strategies*, ed. A. S. Sethi and R. S. Schuler (Cambridge, MA: Ballinger, 1984), p. 267.

18. Ibid., p. 269.

19. Virginia T. Geurin and Gary F. Kohut, "Dimensions of computer anxiety among managers: A field study," *HRMOB Proceedings*, vol. 1 (1987 HRMOB Annual National Conference), pp. 305–9. Philadelphia: Association of Human Relations Management and Organizational Behavior.

20. James C. Quick and Jonathan D. Quick, *Organizational Stress and Preventive Management* (New York: McGraw-Hill, 1984), p. 266.

21. Amarjit S. Sethi, "Contemplative strategies for technostress management,"

in *Strategic Management of Technostress in an Information Society*, ed. A. S. Sethi, D. H. J. Caro, and R. S. Schuler (Toronto: C. J. Hogrefe, 1987), p. 297.

22. Jacques Ellul, *The Technological Society*, trans. J. Wilkinson (New York: Vintage Books, 1964), p. 324.

23. Ibid., p. 348.

24. Jonathan Quick, Rebecca Horn, and James Quick, "Health consequences of stress," *Journal of Organizational Behavior Management 8*, 2 (1986), 19–20.

25. Anne Rice, *Interview with the Vampire* (New York: Ballantine, 1976), p. 21.

26. Ibid., p. 18.

27. Quoted in Richard Lyons, "Stress addiction: 'Life in the fast lane' may have its benefits," *New York Times* (July 21, 1983), p. III, 1: 1.

28. Larry Pace and Waino Suojanen, "Addictive type A behavior undermines employee involvement," *Personnel Journal 67*, 6 (June 1988), 40.

29. Linda Leonard, *On the Way to the Wedding* (Boston: Shambhala, 1986), p. 93.

30. Rice, *Interview with the Vampire*, p. 270.

31. Curtis Austin, "DART's problems shake staff," *Dallas Times-Herald*, Apr. 2, 1989, p. A–23.

32. Francesco Petrarcha, *Petrarch's Secret or The Soul's Conflict with Reason*, trans. W. H. Draper (London: Chatto & Windus, 1911), pp. 34–35.

33. Ibid., pp. 32–33.

34. Philippe Ariès, *Western Attitudes Toward Death from the Middle Ages to the Present*, trans. P. Ranum (Baltimore: Johns Hopkins University Press, 1974), p. 45.

35. Quoted in Joseph Pieper, *In Tune with the World: A Theory of Festivity*, trans. R. Winston and C. Winston (New York: Harcourt, Brace & World, 1965), p. 10.

36. Pieper, *In Tune with the World*, pp. 21–22.

37. Ibid., p. 15.

18

THE EXTRANEOUS FACTOR IN WESTERN MEDICINE

LOLA ROMANUCCI-ROSS AND DANIEL E. MOERMAN

It has been noted by philosophers of science that the successes of "method" in the physical sciences were contingent upon a division of "physical" and "mental," with the relegation of the latter "to the limbo of a sort of secondary or epiphenomenal existence" (Feigl 1953:612) and the existence of the physical accepted as a fundamental empirical fact. This mind-body problem particularly concerned Descartes, who tried to puzzle out how something nonspatial (thinking) could be causally related to spatial matter. With the enunciation of this problem in the 17th century we find the roots of modern science and medicine.

Descartes' influence is considered especially notable on the empiricist philosophers who insisted that epistemology should be the starting point of philosophy. Later, the logical positivists asserted that the meaning of scientific statements cannot be identified with their confirming evidence and that the meaning of a statement is the method of its verification (Schlick 1925). In other words, a new concept is synonymous with the set of operations that determines its applications (Bridgman 1927).

Logical empiricism developed into a phase that provided "logical" tools for reconsideration of the mind-body problem. As Feigl has pointed out, it is true that relations between indicators that can be evidenced (such as language, behavior and neurophysiological data) must be interpreted in terms of "laws," and this would then make explanation and predication possible in a mind-body identity (Feigl 1953:615). Post-empiricists such as Husserl also tried to recapture the Cartesian mode; in the words of Williams (1967:354), "the problems posed by Descartes' dualism remain at the heart of much contemporary philosophical inquiry (the work of Gilbert Ryle and Ludwig Wittgenstein, for example) being aimed directly against what are still very powerful Cartesian conceptions."

In recent times, the philosophical school popularly known as "Kuhnian" has granted a more significant role to thought itself in the process of knowing. According to Kuhn (1970), one searches for the new paradigm that will revolutionize the manner in which a problem is phrased as well as "solved." Once introduced and accepted, however, the paradigm tends to stabilize thought and reinforces the architectonic of the belief system that will remain unexamined.

The philosophical "school" that focused on the thinking process was formed by scholars in a variety of disciplines. Ludwig Fleck in his analysis of the Wasserman reaction wrote that a "fact" is a "stylized signal of resistance in thinking" (1979 [1935]:98). Just a few years earlier, Gödel proved his "inconsistency" theorem, demonstrating that in mathematics no formal system of axioms could be simultaneously consistent and complete. A consistent system includes undecidable propositions, while a complete system can prove everything, for example "p is not p." (Wilder 1952:256–261). Truth, then, is a function of knowledge that is necessarily either incomplete or illogical. Such a truth is of little value and so one is forced to turn from "truth" to "belief," grounding knowledge in experience, as did Descartes.

To contrast the two views germane to our discussion, in the 17th century Descartes could affirm the possibility of knowing the "truth" without a single doubt, based on his own *experience*. He "knew," for example, that blood was pumped through the body because the heart was hot, which caused the blood to expand and to course out through the arteries.[1] Similar properties caused similar behaviors regardless of context, an inference constituting a sort of naïve realism. For Kuhn, the paradigm or "disciplinary matrix" made up of categories, relationships, and decisive examples structures the view of truth that the scientist discovers. When the paradigm changes it is "rather as if the professional community had been suddenly transported to another planet where familiar objects are seen in a different light and are joined by unfamiliar ones as well . . . nothing changes but the view" (Kuhn 1970:111). Thus, the Kuhnian view emphasizes the changing nature of knowledge as viewed through new paradigms, whereas the Cartesian view simply builds on past perceptions.

Where is contemporary biomedicine in all this? In some cases, men and women in medicine have achieved a Kuhnian view of their profession, but most share a greater affinity with Descartes. We attempt here a Fleck/Gödelian view of the "realism" in contemporary medicine, an exercise in a psychological anthropology of medicine assessing values, ideology and paradigms. We indicate and comment on what we perceive to be major developments of present-day scientific inquiry in medicine: randomized clinical trials, animal models, the psychiatric model, the chemical intervention model and diagnosis and consider how these "styles" of investigation not only reflect values and ideologies but affect our knowledge of disease and cure.

VALUES AND IDEOLOGY

Physicians learn the wisdom of the body by dissecting cadavers; they focus their attention by "draping" body parts not under immediate scrutiny. They seek order through classification although both order *and* classifications thereof are "mentifacts" (Bidney 1953); both are constructs imposed on the "real world" even though we tend to think that the order is real and the classification describes it. The physician's order (read classification) is the basis for his general procedure: to measure; to compare; to predict.

Generally these values of mastery, order and power are axiomatic; they need not be considered or thought about. They precede thought; they provide the scaffolding for it. They are good, in and of themselves, moral virtues. When these issues *are* considered, they are transformed into virtues of the highest sort as they were for the ancient Romans who equated knowledge and virtue. Consider this text, culled from the ruminations of the surgeon Selzer in his aptly titled collection, *Mortal Lessons:*

The priestliness of my profession has ever been impressed upon me. In the beginning there are vows taken with all solemnity. Then there is the endless harsh novitiate of training, much fatigue, much sacrifice. At last one emerges as celebrant, standing close to the truth lying curtained in the Ark of the body. Not surplice and cassock but mask and gown are your regalia. You hold no chalice, but a knife. There is no wine, no wafer. There are only the facts of blood and flesh. [Selzer 1976:94]

By ideology we mean that body of notions that transforms fundamental values into social action. An ideology, or belief system, is a condition of learning and knowledge. It is not fragmented into "religious," "political," "social" or even "scientific" beliefs. A belief system encompasses attitudes in all these aspects of a personal "field" and more often than not contains inconsistencies or is incomplete; but believers live with these inconsistencies and accentuate differences with other belief systems. Contemporary ideology in biomedicine includes the following values: first, causation is temporal, reductionist and essentially metonymic, that is, the part represents the whole and/or cause is taken for effect and effect is taken for cause. In general, a part, construed as "prior" and "lower," is taken to account for the whole. Occasionally, the equation is reversed. This is related to another "value": that of measurement, comparison and prediction. It yields action in a variety of forms:

1. "Myocardial infarction is usually produced by thrombotic occlusion of one of the larger branches of the coronary arteries" (Halvey 1972:376). In this case, the part causes the whole.

2. Rheumatoid arthritis is "a chronic syndrome characterized by nonspecific inflammation of the peripheral joints. . . . The etiology is unknown" (Halvey 1972:1209). In this case, the part that causes the whole is unknown, but assumed to exist.

3. "Anorexia Nervosa . . . Food aversion, self-induced, which is a manifestation of psychiatric illness" (Halvey 1972:1423). Here, the whole causes the part.

The metonymic style looms in importance as it forms the primary structure for treatment. One "treats" the "cause" of illness, not the "symptoms" of illness. This treatment is usually conceived to be allopathic; one imagines that even pediatricians (whose daily practice includes vaccinations) would vigorously deny being homeopaths. This allopathy is generally the consequence of another major belief in biomedicine: disease is natural while, in general, healing is cultural.

A general corollary to this second belief is that disease *must* be treated, even if effective treatment is not available. Culture must at least contest with nature, even if the game is already lost. Moreover, patients who do *not* respond to standard treatments (morphine for pain) were not sick in the first place; they may be classified as "hypochondriacs." Similarly, people who *do* respond to *inert* treatments (placebos) were not really sick, either. Occasionally, these two processes can interact. A study carried out in a Texas hospital showed that house officers and nurses considered some patients to be "problem cases." These patients were those who did not respond to standard treatments, leading to the hypothesis that they were not really sick. Frequently, such patients were then treated with placebos. When they responded favorably to such treatment, this was considered verification of the hypothesis (Goodwin et al. 1979:106–110).

Similarly, there is a standard reaction to the occasional cases of "spontaneous remission," in patients who have been refractory to treatment; often enough, this is explained by saying that the condition was probably misdiagnosed in the first place. These sorts of phenomena—ineffective drugs, effective placebos, spontaneous remissions—are generally "impossible" given the ideological principles under discussion; these fall into the category of "anomalies." It is a measure of the tenacity of this ideology that a phenomenon (placebos) that can account for as much as 90 percent of ulcer healing (Moerman 1983:14–16) can be considered an "anomaly."

The placebo or biomedically inert substance that produces relief also helps eliminate bias in a research protocol. It does not fit the Western master paradigm:

Many papers have demonstrated the importance and magnitude of the placebo effect in every therapeutic area. Placebos can be more powerful than, and reverse the action of, potent active drugs. The incidence of placebo reactions approaches 100 percent in some studies. Placebos can have profound effects on organic illnesses including incurable malignancies. Placebos can often mimic the effects of active drugs. Uncontrolled studies of drug efficacy are reported effective four to five times more frequently than controlled studies. Placebo effects are so omnipresent that if they are not reported in controlled studies it is commonly accepted that the studies are unreliable. [Shapiro 1968:58]

Brody argues that the physician of our time cannot deny the placebo data, "but he can adopt an attitude towards it of exclusion, that is, labeling the placebo effect so that it can be readily recognized and thus excluded from research" (Brody 1980:27)

SOME CONTEMPORARY RESEARCH PARADIGMS

We began with mention of Descartes and it is appropriate to refer again to the man and his period, the 17th century, since in the times and in the man we recognize the foundations of modern scientific thought. Descartes respected his teachers but stated that only mathematics had ever given him "certain knowledge" (Williams 1967:344). He stressed quantitative measurement and experimentation as well as taxonomy and calculable order.

Descartes accepted the notion of circulatory movement of the blood but not the independent contraction of the heart as the driving force of the system. More inclined to mathematics and deductive thinking, he looked for another mechanical cause of blood displacement: its "heating" and subsequent expansion as it entered the heart (Snellen 1984:22).

William Harvey took up and retained the mistaken idea of "heat" but also *calculated* the total volume of blood in the circulation and estimated the output of the pumping chamber of the heart per beat and per minute. He therefore was able to conclude that the blood must recirculate, driven by the heart (Harvey 1978).

This ideology, with its commitment to observation, measurement and experiments, led not only to some false starts (through Descartes), but also to productive work (through Harvey) that led to later "knowledge explosions." However, important for our purposes, unexplained ideology still thrives in the research paradigms of our day. We have typified the much valued canons of correct "scientific" behavior and give several examples:

The *randomized clinical trial* is the study of the effects of an intervention in a sizable population expected to experience abnormal events with a given frequency. Patients are assigned to treatment, no treatment, or "ordinary care." The goal is to determine whether or not a specific intervention over a period of time will reduce the abnormal event rate in a statistically significant manner. As an example we refer to the "Coronary Artery Surgery Study" known as CASS (CASS 1983). In this large study, patients were randomly assigned to either customary medical treatment of their mild to moderate angina pectoris, or to coronary artery bypass surgery. After a (mean) six-year follow-up, the groups were compared to see if the surgical procedure extended life. No significant difference was found between medical and surgical treatment. This trial was a corrective response to the emergent "ideal" of having coronary bypass surgery performed.

But such trials can have their pitfalls as shown in another recent study, for although the randomized clinical trial is the ideal method for assessing treatment allocations, there are dangers in such trials. Even when everything from the complete, carefully collected baseline data and all statistical pitfalls is taken into account, there is still a likelihood of "chance" differences achieving statistical significance when multiple subgroups are analyzed. In a study carried out at Duke University, 1,073 coronary artery disease patients were randomly sorted into two groups; there were no differences in treatment between the two groups of patients. There was no overall difference in survival between the two groups, as one would expect. However, in a subgroup of 397 patients with three-vessel disease and abnormal left ventricular contraction, survival was significantly different in the two randomly sorted groups. Multivariable adjustment procedures attributed the difference to the combined effect of small differences in the distribution of several prognostic factors. On a univariate basis, the "treatment" (that is, randomization) might appear to be a significant factor in the survival of this subgroup ($x^2 = 5.4$; p .025). When the variables were considered jointly, the "treatment" effect became nonsignificant ($x^2 = 2.4$; $p = NS$). In addition, in another subgroup a significant survival difference was not explainable even by multivariate methods. In this case of patients with three-vessel disease, abnormal left ventricular contraction pattern, and no history of congestive heart failure, the respective three-year survival rates of the two randomly differentiated groups were 60 percent and 80 percent ($x^2 = 10.0$; $p = .01$). The authors of this study caution that clinicians must exercise careful judgment in attributing results to efficacious therapy, as they may be due to chance or to inadequate baseline comparability of groups (Lee et al. 1980:508–515).

Indeed, physicians inevitably use "judgment" when they prescribe treatments; this is to say that "science" (the clinical trial) is tempered by "knowledge grounded in experience" (what we have called "belief"); these are combined into what physicians call "clinical judgment."

Some interesting clinical judgments went into the design and analysis of another recent and widely publicized clinical trial. This study used a double-blind method to test the efficacy of lowering blood cholesterol levels in reducing the risk of heart disease in 3,806 middle-aged men. The treatment group received cholestyramine resin (a drug that inhibits absorption of lipids from the intestines) while the control group received a placebo; the subjects were followed for an average of 7.4 years. The drug group was reported to

have experienced a 19 percent reduction in risk of death due to coronary
heart disease (CHD) and/or to definite myocardial infarction, significant at
the .05 level, one-sided.

This study was interesting for the fact that in these very well matched
groups, all causes and rates of mortality were similar for the two groups, with
two exceptions. In addition to modest differences in death due to coronary
heart disease, the drug-treated group had a larger number of accidental and
violent deaths. Because of this, there was only a 7 percent reduction of all-
cause mortality in the drug group (LRCP 1984:351–364).[2] The report of the
study notes that "since no plausible connection could be established between
cholestyramine treatment and violent and accidental death, it is difficult to
conclude that this could be anything but a chance occurrence" (LRCP
1984:359).

The drug-treated group reported a substantially higher rate of gastrointestinal discomfort. While severe gastrointestinal discomforts might reduce
awareness (for accidents) or predispose one to abnormal behavior, the possibility of such effects was not considered. It is well known that "many
commonly used drugs can cause serious mental symptoms, including depression and disorders in thinking that may resemble schizophrenia" (*Medical
Letter on Drugs and Therapeutics* 1981). The drug was being tested for one
purpose (which is why the authors took the liberty of using one-tailed statistics; in two-tailed tests, the differences found in this study are not statistically significant); no need to "confound" the picture with other extraneous
possibilities.

The randomized clinical trial has had an important effect in medicine.
But the design of trials necessarily reflects the assumptions and expectations
of the investigators and may provide convincing demonstrations of "obvious"
but incorrect notions (cf. Descartes 1960[1637]: 68). Statistical significance
is no assurance against design error.

Chemical intervention models are a triumph of allopathic medicine. One finds
what there is too much or too little of, and supplies it or changes the balance.
In many instances this has caused great relief to the patient, but often at
the expense of long-term effects that are noxious or lethal. Many asthma
sufferers have ended up with hypertension (generally treatable) after eight
to ten years of treatment with steroids. Those taking the phenothiazines
(such as thorazine) have acquired irreversible tardive dyskinesias. In such
cases, the effects of drugs on biological systems through time are not taken
into account. There are other examples: use of diuretics can lead to elevated
uric acid levels and development of gout. Radioactive phosphorus used to
treat polycythemia vera can lead to leukemia. Cyclosporin used to prevent
rejection of a transplanted organ may cause cancer.

Adverse interactions of drugs given at the same time or in close sequence
(often by different physicians unaware of or unconcerned with one another's
treatments) again illustrate ignorance of the time factor, of the patient's

biography, and of the synergistic effect of drugs affecting or influencing one another. The effect can also occur by combining drugs with certain foods (*Medical Letter on Drugs and Therapeutics* 1979).

Part of the problem here results from some curious notions that physicians have regarding drugs. Particularly intriguing is the classification of drug effects into "action" and "side effect." Consider the case of the antihistamine Benadryl (diphenhydramine) which, when prescribed for allergies, is said to have the side effect of causing drowsiness. When it is used as a sedative for insomnia, its antihistaminic qualities are side effects ("dry mouth").

Although Withering described the therapeutic values of foxglove extracts 200 years ago, it is only recently that some studies have provided a demonstration of mechanisms of important extracardiac effects of digitalis glycosides, such as slowing of heart rate, rise in blood pressure, and other effects mediated by the central and peripheral nervous systems (Longhurst and Ross 1985:99A–105A). Extracardiac "side effects" had long been disturbing to patients who experienced nausea and vomiting, abdominal pain, gynecomastia in men and breast enlargement in women, vision disturbances, headaches, seizures and coma. Studies such as these, revealing the mechanisms of "drug action," should lead physicians to a revisionist view of the simplistic notion that such actions can be considered in terms of "primary" and "secondary" effects, as is currently the case.

At times, the distinction between "action" and "side effect" can have strange and untoward consequences; this confusion is a result of seeing patients only partially, seeing only the "organ system" that is sick and not the whole person—a kind of tunnel vision. Consider the case of ventricular premature ectopic beats on an electrocardiogram (ECG). The parsing of patients leads professionals in both clinical and research contexts to ignore evidence that lies outside of their expertise and their prejudgment of normalcy. Gordon Moe, a well-known physiologist, noted that if you looked closely at some ECG tracings, you would see a rhythmicity allowing you to predict the sequence of the occurrence of ectopic beats, and to predict that beats could appear, disappear or become fix-coupled (bigeminal) every other beat with either slight increases or slight decreases in the heart rate alone. He compared his observations with a recently published paper that "demonstrated" the disappearance of premature beats "due to" digitalis. But Moe had shown that what was attributed to digitalis as a direct anti-arrhythmic effect could have been the concealment of a parasystolic focus by a slight decrease in heart rate. The same effect on heart rate could have been produced by "going down an elevator." The international professional audience at this lecture (in Florence, Italy, in 1978) laughed with embarrassed amusement, not wanting to recognize Moe's conclusion that hypotheses need to be enlarged to include factors generally excluded from research paradigms. It seems unlikely that this will occur generally as it requires observing and measuring behavior. Behavior, like a "side effect," is extrinsic to the action expected from the drug.

We consider here more briefly a few other aspects of contemporary medical research and practice where extrinsic factors play an important role limiting and constricting understanding: the use of *animal models*, the *psychiatric model* and *diagnosis*.

The use of *animal models* is a particularly interesting case of the use of metaphor in medicine. Similarly, it is a case that indicates the (not surprising) difficulties that can occur when people take metaphors literally. Dogs, pigs, and baboons (among others) are widely used in cardiovascular research. The pig is at times a better representation of humans for, unlike the dog, it has a large right coronary artery, and few coronary collateral vessels located primarily on the inner heart wall. The dog, however, is sometimes a good model because it has more collaterals, most on the outer wall; and a number of people with coronary heart disease develop significant collaterals on the outer walls as well as on the inner walls. The baboon is a better hemodynamic model of humans due to its more upright posture than the other animals. One must, then, match the animal to the problem at hand; although these problems have been noted in the scientific literature (Crozatier et al. 1978:H413-H421; Sanders et al. 1977:365–370; Tomoike et al. 1981:H519-H524), they have been generally ignored as investigators go through the ritual of scientific presentation, confusing the metaphorical model for the object of their ultimate concern.

Attachment to the animal model of disease transmission has long impeded careful inquiry and more correct epidemiological explanations of the spread of certain diseases. A study of historical records with modern research techniques and current medical knowledge can yield surprising results. For example, the transmission of "the plague" was attributed to the abandonment of the infected and dying *Rattus rattus* by its resident flea, *Xenopsylla cheopis*, which regurgitated the plague bacillus, *Yersinia pestis*, into its human victim. But a consideration of such factors as seasonal occurrences of the disease, the number of cases per household, comparisons with the presence of the black house rat in other parts of the world, and the sudden disappearance of the plague in Europe has led to a broader hypothesis. (Medieval physicians knew the plague quite well and described variations in great detail.) Recent research (Ell 1980:497–510) has emphasized interhuman transmission as well as several varieties of "the plague." Those who wrote treatises and texts on the exploration of the occurrence of the plague had rested comfortably on the rat-flea-human mode of transmission, which, though correct part of the time, stifled further investigation for a long period of time.

The *psychiatric model* typifies the procedures by which states and behaviors have been medicalized, traditionally rendering patients helpless as their caretakers decide on medical and surgical interventions. The nature of communication and emotional states are crucial in the diagnosis of mental illnesses. But these were not part of the general ideology of the biomedical practitioners and were considered extraneous factors. It was only after the legal battles of the civil rights era—the 1950s to the 1970s—that such sick persons were given a "say" over their patient status (Tancredi 1983:284–297). Indeed, many health professionals now *see* these factors, but still consider them extraneous, indeed intrusive and destructive (Radine 1983:366–387).

The confluence of the psychiatric model with some features of the general diagnostic process can provide us with an interesting field for the compounding of errors. In the Soviet Union a system was developed, during the 1960s, for psychiatric diagnosis. Many of the most talented psychiatrists in that country were disciples of a central theory of schizophrenia, developing a definition so exceedingly broad as to include much of whatever else might be included in psychopathology. According to this definition, schizophrenia had three possible course forms: continuous, periodic and shift-like. Patients of the continuous type experienced early onset and did not improve; the "periodics" had periods of remission during illness; and the shift-like type patient was a combination of the continuous and periodic types. This was further complicated by the additional diagnostic criterion of "severe" or "mild" for any type.

What was (or should have been) troublesome, of course, is that many became "patients" of the "mild" type who would perhaps not be seen—in another milieu—by any psychiatrist at all. There have been studies attesting to this (Hite 1974; Rollins 1972). Interestingly, however, the International Pilot Study on Schizophrenia of the late 1960s and early 1970s, noted that two of the nine centers reviewed for diagnostic activities did poorly: Washington and Moscow (World Health Organization 1973).

The goal of the computer program was to rediagnose patients originally diagnosed as schizophrenic at various centers, using the centers' own data on the patients. Moscow's Institute of Psychiatry and Washington did poorly for very different reasons, however; a large percentage of Moscow's diagnosed schizophrenics were reassigned by the computer to neurotic and depressive categories rather than the psychoses. The Washington center had many of its patients reassigned to the psychotic categories. Obviously one center "over-diagnosed" and the other "under-diagnosed."

Some have argued that psychiatric diagnoses can be a solution to human (that is, "political" writ small—or writ large) problems (Basaglia 1980, 1981). Reich has noted that such diagnoses are also used to *reassure* all of us; he gives the example of a researcher, Dr. Summerlin, who inked the skins of his mice to make it appear that grafted skin had been "taken," when others could not repeat his experiment with his dramatic results. It was important that the public not be led to think that research in general was a fraudulent activity, for great sums are donated to the research enterprise. The investigating committee "found" that Summerlin's behavior involved self-deception and aberration. Even Dr. Lewis Thomas, president of the Sloan-Kettering Cancer Center, informed reporters that "the fraud in this work was the result of mental illness" (Reich 1981:76–77). The same explanation was put forth by those surrounding Dr. John Darsee's fraudulent research in a Harvard Medical School laboratory (Knox 1983).

Such diagnoses appear to be self-validating in the same manner that it is reasoned (with the benefit of elaborate diagnostic procedures) that a criminal "must be" insane to have committed the act for which he is undergoing psychiatric appraisal. (Romanucci-Ross and Tancredi 1986).

Diagnosis (included in the example above) similarly has a variety of extraneous factors that shape and form it, making it far less than the scientific procedure it might be. Studies have consistently shown that medical problem solving is a hypothetico-deductive activity in which early problem formulations partly guide subsequent data collection (Elstein 1978:299). In a review of 50 clinicopathologic conferences, the process of achieving a diagnosis was shown to have determinable steps. First, there is an aggregation of groups of findings into patterns followed by the selection of a "pivot" or key finding (that is, the problem is metonymized). From this is generated a "cause" list that is pruned to a set of differential diagnoses—a listing of diagnostic possibilities—from which one is selected and then validated (Eddy and Clanton 1982:1263–1268). The problem, of course, is in the amount of information to be considered; one can only interpret signs and symptoms to diagnose disease, but one's medical training was learned the other way around—by disease. This medical decision-making chain has an effect on the physician's "intuitive" uses of the principle of discriminant analysis, that is, how much weight is given to clinical versus statistical factors, or how knowledge is grounded in experience.

The diagnostic process is further constrained because the "facts" are, of necessity, selected and evaluated in a temporal ordering. Decisions have to be made within a time frame and the presenting symptom does not always indicate that the patient suffers from several afflictions. As indicated earlier in this discussion, one measures what is measurable and classifies those concepts or entities for which there are categories, while masses of information slip through the cracks of elegant analytics. The diagnostic "method" is especially vulnerable to the weaknesses in such an approach.

IDEOLOGY AND REFLEXIVITY

Seventeenth-century science valued "measurement," the relating of things not to ourselves but to each other. The end of the 18th century saw the birth of Romanticism, the "transcendental," and a serious consideration of subject-object relations. But in the 19th century, what was central to medicine was clinical investigation and experimentation, critical working hypotheses, and structure, both organic and physiological. These were epitomized in the works of Claude Bernard and Rudolph Virchow. And, as Foucault pointed out in *The Birth of the Clinic* (Foucault 1975), we had the establishment of faculties of medicine and the transmission of medical knowledge into social privilege. There was a strong beginning during this period in the exercises of looking at probabilities in diagnoses and, presumably, becoming aware of "extraneous factors." Although Morgagni still specified diseases by points of origin, he began to find cells, nervous tissues in different organs, fibrous lesions, and lesions of serous and mucous membranes (Morgagni 1761). This began the search for "principles" about tissues. It appears to have been a period of exciting theoretical modeling and synthesis in clinical experience as well as research. And yet, Italian anatomists had already made essentially the same transition, from form to function, in the 16th century (Castiglioni 1934). This historical fact demonstrates that innovation does not always overcome ideology and affect mainstream science as soon as it should and in the manner it might. Principles are rediscovered centuries later because they then fit the new paradigms. Morgagni founded pathology, and in his classic work on the causes of disease, *De Sedibus et Causis Morborum per Anatomen Indagatis* (1761), he employed the best canons of inductive research. But he was in no hurry to publish his work, fearing criticism and rejection.

Most of the values of the classical period of the 17th century have remained with medical science to the current day: to make one's contribution to the total body of knowledge without inspecting the interstices and intersects of the content of that body of knowledge, to dig deeper into "nature's secrets" with little regard for the consequences, to look for causality in relatively isolated systems. In biophysics and bioengineering we find elaborate metaphors from hydraulics or plumbing (when speaking of the circulatory system) or electrical circuitry (when discussing the nervous system). While one can speak of neural "charges" or "discharges," one cannot go so far as to imagine the system as a phone system or computer. Like all metaphors, these can provide insight, and they can facilitate communication. But metaphors provide only the form for understanding; they do not imply isomorphic correspondences, that is, identical formal structures or identical relations between points.

Medical science frequently structures its research around linked propositions in which two or more concepts are reciprocally defined. We investigate the validity of linkages and, of course, usually find them. The case mentioned earlier of an effective placebo verifying a diagnosis of malingering is a good example. Similarly, we are told that early diagnosis improves survival. Of course, if mean patient survival time after contracting an illness is ten years, and if mean time at diagnosis is five years, "five-year survival" statistics will be dismal. If mean time at diagnosis can be reduced to three years, the five-year survival statistics will be dramatically improved. This change, of course, has no relationship either to the effectiveness of treatment, or to the course of the disease for any of the patients. Aggregates of linked concepts can be made as complex as you like, but, as Bateson has indicated, "the links are provided not by the data but by you" (1979).

BEYOND KUHN?

As for the scientific method, the same processes that have led us to truth have led us to error. We have been numbed by Kuhn into believing that new paradigms will be ever self-correcting in the scientific endeavor. But it is not "yet another paradigm" that will bring us into contact with the "extraneous factors." Kant, long before Kuhn, had noted that experience itself is a species of knowledge that involves understanding (1933:22). Since medical science does and must include behavior, one must apply Devereux's dictum that "the scientific study of man is impeded by an anxiety-arousing over-lap between subject and observer" (1967:xvi); therefore, perception and interpretation of data are distorted, producing "countertransference masquerading as methodology" causing even more distortion. Devereux meant that such structural "anxiety" exacerbates individual vulnerability, revives more idiosyncratic anxieties, threatens to undermine major defenses or sublimations and exacerbates current problems (Devereux 1967:45).

An example might be provided by a patient with an illness that causes the physician to react to his patient as though he were an early significant figure in the physician's life. Even more pertinent to our present discussion, however, are recently documented professional practices of certain medical scientists who publish inaccurate statements either knowingly or unconsciously and unknowingly, who describe procedures that were not followed or followed in other experiments at other times, who "lose" primary data and/or have little direct involvement with the research leading to the articles of which they are "co-authors" (see Broad and Wade 1982; Knox 1983). "Anxiety," apparently, can be detrimental to medical as well as social scientists, nor is social science the only "science" in which one may confront the occupational risk—as noted by Weston La Barre—of "feeding multiply contaminated data into . . . truth machines" (Devereux 1967:viii).

Indeed the "progress" of science is highly dependent on peer recognition and disbursement of funds by the lay converted. It is a grievous oversimplification to contrast methodology in science with methodology in the social sciences. The development of either is highly dependent on interpersonal interactions, influence and negotiation of "truth."

Some recent studies have focused on the field of medicine as socially constructed; an interesting collection of essays focuses on certain medical events as part of the social, political, economic and cultural processes surrounding such events (Wright and Treacher 1982). Other social constructionists have researched the interactions among researchers in a laboratory

(Salk Institute in La Jolla, California) to observe and analyze daily routine work. These investigators have demonstrated that, among other things, scientists create order out of disorder, impelled greatly if not exclusively by a thirst for credit and credibility (Latour and Woolgar 1979:189–197). Personal goals notwithstanding, scientists do have an ideal about their "mission":

> The myth of science as a purely logical process, constantly reaffirmed in every textbook, article and lecture, has an overwhelming influence on scientists' perception of what they do. Even though scientists are aware of non-logical elements of their work, they tend to suppress them or at least dismiss them as being of little consequence. A major element of the scientific process is thus denied existence or significance. (Broad and Wade 1982:126)

As a result of this, scientific textbooks are nonhistorical, in fact antihistorical. Any reference to the subjective experience is strictly forbidden in scientific literature, and "considered as a literary form, a scientific paper is as stylized as a sonnet. If it fails to obey the rigid rules of composition, it will simply not be published" (Broad and Wade 1982). Physicist Paul Feyerabend, in his book *Against Method* (1975), holds that not only are there nonrational elements in the scientific process, but that such elements are dominant, and that success in science depends not only on rational argument but on subterfuge, rhetoric and propaganda. Authors Broad and Wade, who have made careers of investigating fraud in medical and scientific research, hold that fraud can flourish in such enterprises precisely because scientists are unaware of their ideologies and the wide ocean between such ideologies and praxis in their endeavors (1982:212–224).

CONCLUSION

We have examined how research paradigms in Western allopathic medicine rest on the ideology that the structure of science is unassailable as the researcher moves through better and better paradigms to "complete description" of "how things really work." We have categorized most of current medical scientific research into models (randomized clinical trials, chemical intervention, animal models, psychiatric models and diagnosis) to show how Western modes of thought expressed in philosophical systems provide the ideological linchpins for these models. We have also examined values and ideological system for its believers. For scientists, any "facts" (in the guise of extraneous factors) that do not validate the ideology are ignored or explained away as irrelevant to the "method." Epistemological flaws in the major research models to which we have alluded point to the more serious problem of how "science" really works and how we *think* it works. How we think it works is a "mentifact" distilled from centuries of philosophers and historians writing about science, with raw materials on "method" provided by the scientists themselves with themselves as appreciative critics (Goodfield 1975:218). Faking data (either consciously or unconsciously), unintentional bias, the "observer effect," and the question of whether one can make a justifiable distinction between science and other modes of thought are questions that have been addressed only recently—not only in medicine, but in anthropology as well (Broad and Wade 1982; Brush 1974; Feyerabend 1975; Goodfield 1975).

Like many other disciplines, medical science and practice have been affected by two 20th-century movements, existentialism and phenomenology. Both have had similar concerns, stressing the relationship between the individual and systems, between freedom and choice, with anxiety, and with truth and belief as aspects of experience. Resonating to such concepts, there is an emergent contemporary disillusionment with incessant pressure built into the reward system constantly to produce "astounding scientific data." There is also an emergent demand for a new kind of accountability. There is a growing awareness of the lack of those virtues that generations of scientists have declared inherent in the scientific endeavor. Few are offended by Kuhn when he sees the "transfer of attachment from one paradigm to another" as "not the sort of battle that can be resolved by proofs," but rather as a "conversion experience." Confidence has been replaced by mistrust as the new fields of medical ethics and malpractice law prosper, and as a growing literature testifies to the new criticism of scientific research and its protocols.

The real challenge here is to recognize that even though science is not all that some scientists say it is, this does *not* mean that it is *none* of the things they say it is; one does not wish to throw out the baby with the bath. But scientists must recognize the extraneous factors that will define the new medical imperatives in our future cultural transformations.

It is possible that medical scientific pursuits, given world and time enough to incorporate 18th- and 19th-century philosophical trends (Burtt 1954), as well as some recent attempts to apply the phenomenological method (Spiegelberg 1960), might be able to stand outside a paradigm of all paradigms. We mean by this that consciousness of models, of process, and of the involved self—a constant vigilance against the arrogance of naive realism—will help to keep "ideologies" and "values" as generators of social action, but deprive them of their power to maim the intellect.

ACKNOWLEDGMENTS

We express special thanks to John Ross, Jr., M.D., Professor of Medicine, School of Medicine, University of California, San Diego, who provided valuable counsel on many aspects of contemporary medicine.

NOTES

1. Descartes warns his readers against casual criticism of his work: "I would like to warn (critics) that this movement (of the blood) that I have just explained follows

as necessarily from the mere disposition of the organs which may be observed in the heart by the eye alone, and from the heat which one can feel there with one's fingers, and from the nature of the blood which can be known by experience, as does that of a clock from the power, the position and the shape of its counterweights and its wheels" (1960[1637]:68).

2. Reduction of risk, based on the published results, is only 4.5 percent; the 7 percent figure is reportedly "adjusted" by a technique not described in the study.

REFERENCES

Basaglia, Franco. 1980. Breaking the circuit of control. *Critical Psychiatry* (D. Ingleby, ed.). New York: Pantheon.

———. 1981. *Scritti I: Dalla Psichiatria Fenomenologica all'Esperienza di Gorizia*. Turin: Einaudi.

Bateson, Gregory. 1979. *Mind and Nature: A Necessary Unity*. New York: Duggon.

Bidney, David. 1953. *Theoretical Anthropology*. New York: Columbia University Press.

Bridgman, P. W. 1927. *The Logic of Modern Physics*. New York: Macmillan.

Broad, William, and Nicholas Wade. 1982. *Betrayers of the Truth: Fraud and Deceit in the Halls of Science*. New York: Simon and Schuster.

Brody, Howard. 1980. *Placebos and the Philosophy of Medicine: Clinical, Conceptual and Ethical Issues*. Chicago: University of Chicago Press.

Brush, S. G. 1974. Should the history of science be X-rated? *Science* 183:1164–1172.

Burtt, E. A. 1954. *The Metaphysical Foundations of Modern Science* (rev. ed.). Garden City, NY: Doubleday.

CASS (Coronary Artery Surgery Study) Principal Investigators and Their Associates. 1983. A randomized trial of coronary artery bypass surgery: Survival data. *Circulation* 68:939–950.

Castiglioni, Arturo. 1934. *The Renaissance of Medicine in Europe*.

Crozatier, B. J., D. Franklin Ross, C. Bloor, F. C. White, H. Tomoike, and D. P. McKown. 1978. Myocardial infarction in the baboon: Regional function and the collateral circulation. *American Journal of Physiology: Heart Circulation Physiology* 235: H413-H421.

Descartes, René. 1960. *Discourse on Method and the Meditations*. (Tr. L. J. Lafleur). Indianapolis: Bobbs-Merrill. First published 1637, Leyden.

Devereux, George. 1967. *From Anxiety to Method in the Behavioral Sciences*. Paris and the Hague: Ecole Pratique des Hautes Etudes and Mouton.

Eddy, D. M., and C. H. Clanton. 1982. The Art of diagnosis; Solving the clinico-pathological exercise. *New England Journal of Medicine* 306:1263–1268.

Ell, Stephen R. 1980. Interhuman transmission of medieval plague. *Bulletin of the History of Medicine* 54:497–510.

Elstein, A. S. 1978. *Medical Problem Solving: An Analysis of Clinical Reasoning*. Cambridge, MA: Harvard University Press.

Feigl, Herbert. 1953. The mind-body problem in the development of logical empiricism. *Readings in the Philosophy of Science* (H. Feigl and M. Brodbeck eds.), pp. 612–626. New York: Appleton-Century-Crofts.

Feyerabend, Paul, ed. 1975. *Against Method*. London: Verso.

Fleck, Ludwig. 1979[1935]. *Genesis and development of a scientific fact* (Thaddeus J. Trenn and Robert K. Merton, eds.). Chicago: University of Chicago Press.

Foucault, Michel. 1975. *The Birth of the Clinic.* Tr. A. M. Sheridan Smith. New York: Vintage.

Goodfield, June. 1975. *Cancer Under Siege.* London: Hutchinson.

Goodwin, J. S., J. M. Goodwin, and A. V. Vogel. 1979. Knowledge and use of placebos by house officers and nurses. *Annals of Internal Medicine* 91:106–110.

Halvey, David N., ed. 1972. *The Merck Manual of Diagnosis and Therapy.* Rahway, NJ: Merck Sharp and Dohme.

Harvey, William. 1978. *Exercitatio Anatomica de Motu Cordis et Sanguinis in Animalibus* (facsimile of 1628 Francofurti ed., Keynes English translation of 1928). Birmingham: Classics of Medicine Library.

Hite, C. 1974. Bridging the U.S.-Soviet psychiatric gap. *Psychiatric News* 9 (part 1):6–17; 9 (part 2):30–32, 40.

Kant, Immanuel. 1933. *The Critique of Pure Reason.* 2nd edition. (N. Kemp Smith, tr.). Chicago: University of Chicago Press. First published 1781.

Knox, Richard. 1983. The Harvard fraud case: Where does the problem lie? *Journal of the American Medical Association* 249(14):1797–1803.

Kuhn, Thomas. 1970. *The Structure of Scientific Revolutions.* 2nd edition. Chicago: University of Chicago Press.

Latour, Bruno, and Steve Woolgar. 1979. *Laboratory Life: The Social Construction of Scientific Facts.* Sage Library of Social Research, vol. 80. London: Sage Publications.

Lee, K. L., F. McNeer, C. F. Starmet, P. Harris, and R. Rosati. 1980. Clinical judgement and statistics; Lessons from a simulated randomized trial in coronary artery disease. *Circulation* 61:508–515.

Longhurst, John C., and John Ross, Jr. 1985. Extracardiac and coronary vascular effects of digitalis. Symposium on William Withering and the foxglove: The 200th anniversary of his first report. *Journal of the American College of Cardiology* 5(5):99A–105A.

LRCP (Lipid Research Clinics Program). 1984. The Lipid Research Clinics coronary primary prevention trial results; 1. Reduction of incidence of coronary heart disease. *Journal of the American Medical Association* 251:351–364.

Medical Letter on Drugs and Therapeutics. 1979. 21(2).

———.1981. 23(3):9.

Moerman, Daniel E. 1983. General medical effectiveness and human biology: Placebo effects in the treatment of ulcer disease. *Medical Anthropology Quarterly* 14(3):14–16.

Morgagni, Giovanni Battista. 1761. *De Sedibus et Causis Morborum dum per Anatomen Indagatis.* (often reprinted; first English edition, 1769).

Radine, Lawrence B. 1983. Pangolins and advocates: Vulnerability and self-protection in a mental patients' rights agency. *The Anthropology of Medicine* (L. Romanucci-Ross, D. Moerman, and L. Tancredi, eds.), pp. 366–387. New York: Praeger.

Reich, Walter, 1986. Diagnostic Ethics: The Uses and Limits of Psychiatric Explanation. *Ethical Issues in Epidemiologic Research* (L. Tancredi, ed.), pp 37–69. New Brunswick, NJ: Rutgers University Press.

Rollins, N. 1972. *Child Psychiatry in the Soviet Union.* Cambridge, MA: Harvard University Press.

Romanucci-Ross, Lola, and Laurence Tancredi. 1986. Psychiatry, the law, and cultural determinants of behavior. *International Journal of Law and Psychiatry* 9(3):265–293.

Sanders, M., F. White, and C. Bloor. 1977. Cardiovascular responses of dogs and pigs exposed to similar physiological stress. *Comparative Physiology and Biochemistry* 58(A):365–370.

Schlick, M. 1925. *Allgemeine Erkenntnislehre*. 2nd edition. Berlin: Springer.

Selzer, Richard. 1976. *Mortal Lessons; Notes on the Art of Surgery*. New York: Simon and Schuster.

Shapiro, A. K. 1968. The placebo response. *Modern Perspectives in World Psychiatry* (J. G. Howells, ed.). Edinburgh: Oliver and Boyd.

Snellen, H. A. 1984. *History of Cardiology*. Rotterdam: Donker Academic Publications.

Spiegelberg, H. 1960. *The Phenomenological Movement*. The Hague: Mouton.

Tancredi, Laurence. 1983. Psychiatry and social control. *The Anthropology of Medicine* (L. Romanucci-Ross, D. Moerman, and L. Tancredi, eds.), pp. 284–297. New York: Praeger

Tomoike, H., D. Franklin, W. Scott Kemper, S. W. McKown and John Ross, Jr. 1981. Functional evaluation of coronary collateral development in conscious dogs. *American Journal of Physiology: Heart Circulation Physiology* 241:H519-H524.

Wilder, Raymond. 1952. *Introduction to the Foundation of Mathematics*, pp. 256–261. New York: Wiley.

Williams, Bernard. 1967. René Descartes. *The Encyclopedia of Philosophy* (Paul Edwards, ed.), vol. 1, pp. 344–354. New York: Macmillan.

World Health Organization: 1973. *Report of the International Pilot Study of Schizophrenia*, vol. 1. Geneva: WHO.

Wright, P., and A. Treacher. 1982. *The Problem of Medical Knowledge: Examining the Social Construction of Medicine*. Edinburgh: Edinburgh University Press.

19

The Aging: Legal and Ethical Personhood in Culture Change

Laurence R. Tancredi and Lola Romanucci-Ross

AGING, BIOLOGICAL THEORIES, AND CULTURE

"Aging" in recent years has become a source of fascination to medical and social science researchers. Therefore, we now have some theories on the aging process. Currently, leading schools of thought focus on biological events, one of which is the "Hayflick limit" of cell division that is, that there are finite and determined programmed intracellular events under genetic control. Others are the "defective enzymes due to faulty messages" theory, the accumulation of "metabolic-waste-in cells" theory, and the theory of "free radicals"—electrically charged unbalanced forms of oxygen that can be chemically destructive. Whether old age is the cause of disease or its characteristics are caused by disease is a question whose answer still eludes us. Yet we have made some progress since the early part of this century when some distinguished physicians (such as Nobel Prize winner Elie Metchnikoff) proposed that disabilities in old age were caused by syphilis, alcoholism, or a poison produced by the bacteria of the large intestine. Biological theories, however, address neither the existential problematic role of the elderly nor bioethics and its legal implications.

In technologically simple societies the elderly were and are highly respected, and growing old, an accomplishment, is the achievement of a status. The aged are keepers of the lore, the reference libraries for celestial navigation, weather prediction, migratory patterns of birds and fish, and arbiters of disputes who know the ancient laws. They know the healing powers of plants and animals and the spirits. They are the repositories of knowledge of what sustains the culture. Their counsel is constantly sought, by tribal people as well as by anthropologists. It can be good to be old in an age-ranked society. In harsh climates, with poor resources, the infirm aged were in collusion with the others to acquiesce in death-hastening behavior (cutting food and water, encouraging suicide).

In peasant cultures, much of this obtains, but one must not outlive the social definition of one's usefulness. In recent research by one of us in Italy, a high suicide rate was found among the aged. This was puzzling until it was determined that suicide occurred only among those elderly people who were poor, owned nothing, had no resources that might allow them to remain in the exchange system (Romanucci-Ross 1982b, pp. 214–15). They were those who had no family, who could not command respect because there was nothing they could contribute in any way. In Mediterranean rural culture one usually goes into old age not only with one's networks, kin, and childhood friends but also in a cultural "emotional tone" that does not make one feel apart. Young people do not jest about the gait, infirmities, memory slips, or peculiarities of the aged. In technologically simple cultures that are very dependent on their immediate ecological resources, there is certainly a concept of optimum population but the control of numbers is at the beginning of life, some of it natural (infections, infant mortality, etc.), and some of it cultural (abortion under certain circumstances and even infanticide). Such societies do not have as heavy a cultural investment in the fetus or infant as in the aged person.

As is well recognized, in American society we accent the importance of youth. See this as a metaphor for tearing away from our maternal or paternal European cultures as a young upstart nation, or see this as the desire (again as a trope) for the need for energy and hard work to build a new nation from the wilderness, but we give all importance to young bodies and young minds. This American attitude culminated in a book by Margaret Mead entitled *Culture and Commitment* (Mead 1970), in which her main thesis is that now is the time for the old and middle-aged and mature to learn from the young.

We are, in fact, a child-centered culture, in contrast with many other cultures of the world. In many countries, the child looks to adults for cues as to how to behave. In the United States, we have adults gazing at children in wonder. Here, the adults are the audience, providers of toys, watchers of children. Becoming old, then, we emphasize in every context, is to become totally obsolete: we align culture against the aged. The culture has strategies for dealing with the aged. Advertising impresarios decide *how* the old are to be made visible. Advertising in medical journals usually features aged models posing as candidates for medication, often for psychotropic drugs or for drugs to control dysfunction, both mental and physical.

We have our warehouses for the old. Private, public, or affluent, they are all characterized by impersonality and infantilization of inmates or boarders, many of them in a confused state caused by overmedication or the synergistic results of multiple medications. Owners and managers of such institutions explain that they try to abide by rules "set by the county board." But the observer can see that the liveliness of the aged annoys and the expressions of sexuality offend. Such patients are put into "noisy" sections so that they do not subvert the "good" patients. Their reminiscences appear to bore the unwilling listeners. (In many cultures it is precisely the reminiscing that makes the elderly social or national treasures, so to speak.) But we medicate them back to rationality or we silence them.

The anthropologist and psychiatrist Jules Henry in his field study of nursing homes in the late 1950s (nor can one describe them differently now) made some interesting observations that will not be unfamiliar.

Social conscience was appeased by attending to things with high visibility, such as clean floors, freshly painted walls, the smell of disinfectants, and the like. Neglected were those items of low visibility, such as personal involvement with patients, attention, and communication. The patient who gave up hope "improved" as she/he became easier to manage. Jules Henry wrote with much feeling about the data he gathered over his years of research in old age homes for the poor, the middle class, and the rich. In colorful language he describes some old people eating in a home:

Dogs, too, eat hungrily and silently, beg for food, eat leavings, lick their bowls. Pathogenic institutions cannot handle a human being, for humanness is a threat. For a cruel institution to function within its cruelties it has to redefine its inmates . . . as retarded children, as animals, as pets (Henry 1965, pp. 416–417).

Nor is Henry without understanding for the "help" he found there: "Ignorant, poorly paid, working in a human junkyard . . . they are nevertheless sound people who withdraw from distorted people". He found instances of petty conflict and spitefulness among the patients in the ever-diminishing number of frames of reference.

We are socialized, in American culture, to feel that we must not accept being cared for unless it is absolutely necessary. Those who are confined long for communion, but nothing in the culture has taught them to achieve it, for loneliness in American culture has generally been associated with deviance. Even our architecture discourages solitude. The center of a house is ideally the family room, of public buildings it is university halls, the conference centers.

By contrast, Japanese house architecture exalts loneliness and pronounces togetherness as a necessity only to continue the practical life. The Japanese tea ceremony exalts poverty, inner wealth, and true life. The tea room is stripped and its main characteristic is emptiness. It is to be filled only with movement, harmony, and tranquillity. The meaning of this is that living is an art (Okakura 1956). Poverty means not deficiency but a state that liberates you from external concerns. During the tea ceremony the mind is cleansed. It is an emptying of oneself of social norms. The art of life includes bringing the outside *in* by way of the garden. The simple and commonplace in its most trivial aspect becomes art, an art that is understood only by cultivating one's own senses through solitude and *not* mediated by "the other." Seclusion expressed in architecture is distantiation from the environment of one's fellow creatures (Engel 1987). In such an unobstructed environment your presence develops its own meaning.

A society creates the kind of personality it needs to maintain itself and accomplish its economic goals. Our mercantilist, industrialist, exchange-oriented society (Fromm 1947, pp. 70–75) needs people who will move to new locations, who will not be bound by family ties, who can repress deep needs, knowing or believing they can be satisfied later with credit cards and money. The older America that Tocqueville described was created by men and women who had values such as thrift, hard work, living in one place, monogamy, and family orientation, including the extended family (Tocqueville 1946). But our current "marketing personality" is freer with money, friendly, unsure of himself, needs sex and adventure to "feel alive." Our contemporary American looks to his contemporaries for direction, responds to signals from wider circles outside the family. We are driven by and for technology, and all of this is rewarded. This kind of personality makes possible the suggestibility of advertising—our philosophy in a new key in which the message determines the structure of response.

Old persons not only remind us we are going to get old and noncompetitive, they also remind us of certain death. Their very presence arouses anxiety–an anxiety that permeates all the "methodology" (see Devereux 1967) we employ in studying them: us-and-them, their-problems, them-as-our problem.

MEDICINE AND THE AGING

Most of us are familiar with the demographic trends: In 1980, 11 percent of the U.S. population was over sixty-five. By 2030, 25 percent will be over sixty-five. Between 1980 and 2000, the eighty-five and older group will experience a 129.3 percent increase; the seventy-five to eighty-four, a 57.9 percent increase; the sixty-five and over, a 37.1 percent increase; and the twenty-one to sixty-four group, a 24.45 percent increase (Siegel and Taeuber 1986,102–107).

In our society, we have medicalized many a behavior and state. A host of behaviors are called depression, alcoholism is a disease, inappropriateness is a sickness, and cultural marginality may get you into therapeutic hands.

In a society such as ours, old age is treated as a disease for which one can be, and eventually is, institutionalized. Mood changes will be subject to medication, and any memory loss now makes one a likely candidate for a diagnosis of Alzheimer's disease. Acting young brings accusations of denial, trying to deny one's age. Taking your problems (medical, financial, or social, or occupational) seriously will have you labeled a depressed patient, soon treated with a course of polypharmacy bringing on disorientation and confusion.

An aspect of the physician-elderly encounter for which the physician might not be prepared is countertransference. A patient in transference endows the therapist with the persona of a significant other in his/her life. A patient may suddenly react to the doctor as a child to a parent, or vice versa, and bring that affect into the encounter. The doctor often relates to the patient as though the patient were someone else in his (the doctor's life), thus blocking his own medical effectiveness. The physician sees his own senescence, relives conflicts with parents, and also, not believing he can really be of help, denies his own failure by denying the validity of the patient's complaints.

Developing an old body takes your personality, your spirit, your "self" into a ghetto. Many behaviors formerly labeled interesting, or "madcap," or stimulating will now be labeled senile. This does not mean that there is no such thing as the real physiological changes which sometimes do accompany aging and, in some individuals, sometimes do affect behavior. But aging in itself does not *necessarily* involve a significant loss of function at defined ages.

What it does mean is that what does occur is the categorizing and labeling of all elderly people as incompetent, which generates public policy decisions (such as retirement at a certain age), which influences medical practices (such as inappropriate medication), which promotes social and cultural patterns of interaction (such as the isolation of the elderly)—all of which render them incompetent.

In Western societies, physicians have a public policy mandate. With access to the most intimate aspects of personal lives and powers of intervention, they are powerful agents for culture change. Their awareness of a few well-known concepts in the psychological and social sciences would lead far beyond good patient care, to really effective patient care, far into the future.

LAW AND THE AGING

The (almost) bloodless revolution of the 1960s made us notice the young and the black and the disenfranchised. This revolution has by now included the insane, the old, and the dying—that is, in the sense that these persons have rights.

Progressive as the revolutions of the mid-twentieth century have been with regard to the elderly, the articulation of legal rights actually lags well behind cultural perceptions and bioethical principles. The rights of the mentally ill, for example, so effectively delineated since the 1970s, are not paralleled in legal development in the treatment of the elderly. The mentally ill have gained a wide range of rights in the way they are treated both within and without the mental health system. There has been an articulation, for example, of the right to privacy for the mentally ill; a right to institutional prerogatives, such as communicating with the outside world; rights to treatment; and most recently, in a series of cases, the right to refuse treatment. The case law on the right to refuse treatment has addressed one of the most fundamental issues regarding patients' rights, and that has to do with the capacity or competency of mental patients to make decisions. The landmark case *Rogers* v. *Okin* and the many cases following that decision affirm the right of competent institutionalized mental patients to have important input into treatment decisions and to refuse treatment except in cases of emergency (*Rogers* v. *Okin* 1979).

Even for those deemed incompetent, the courts have provided protection through such devices as substitute decision making, the use of guardians *ad litem*, and, in some cases, leaving the judge to make the final decision. Perhaps the only deviation from the strong move in the direction of asserting the rights of a vulnerable group such as the mentally ill was the Supreme Court case that did not require the same level of procedural due process for the right to refuse treatment in the case of those imprisoned and mentally disturbed (*Washington et al.* v. *Harper* 1990).

But the application of these important rights to the growing and increasingly vulnerable geriatric group in our population has only begun to occur. It is generally presumed that the elderly are incompetent (along with minors), and this is used as justification for denying them choices in a variety of medical and health circumstances. It is simply assumed that this segment of society is more likely than "the average" to suffer from some forms of mental disturbance or deficiency. Even applying the criteria, predicated strongly on cognitive capacities, used for young adults in determining competency, the elderly do not uniformly meet the criteria of incompetency.

More important, bases for the test of competency (assuming that such tests are valid for ascertaining cognitive capacity) are perhaps not so relevant in the elderly population as they are in young adults more actively functioning in society. Is it, for example, so important that a senior citizen, who is perhaps retired from his job, is not able to add or subtract as quickly as a young adult, or is not as facile with verbal skills or memory? Possibly the criteria for the determination of competency in later life should place more emphasis on the history of the elderly person, the expression of preferences, the capacity to maintain himself or herself in a suitable ambiance and to sustain life with some sociability and personal satisfaction (Tancredi 1987).

Perusing the statistics on the mental condition of the elderly, we find that the picture is not at all as bleak as many would presume. A study in 1985 of nearly 3,500 adults in a community in Baltimore found that only 6.1 percent of those over sixty-five years of age actually had some form of dementia (Folstein et al. 1985). Furthermore, less than 12 percent of those over seventy-five years of age had dementia—in fact, only 2 percent of those between sixty-five and seventy-four suffered from this condition. As to prevalence of depression, anxiety, and distress, some researchers have shown that age is not a major factor in the prevalence of these conditions (Feinson 1985).

Of course not all the studies have given us reason for unbridled optimism, but even those were not pessimistic. In a study conducted by Myrna Weissman and other researchers involving over 2,500 seniors living in New Haven, Connecticut, 11 percent of those studied suffered from a DSM-III disorder or cognitive impairment at some time during the study. The picture is even less bleak when one further differentiates the age groups. For example, severe cognitive impairment was shown in nearly 17 percent of all individuals over eighty-five years of age, but in only 1.1 percent of those between sixty-five and seventy-four years of age (Weissman et al. 1985).

More significant than her conclusions on the mental disorders is the fact that Weissman found that 8 percent of those studied indicated they could benefit from some assistance with their personal care and over 30 percent said they needed help in mobility. These findings indicate that the majority of individuals labeled "elderly" in nearly every age category demonstrate a capacity to make their own decisions. These studies, of course, do not focus on the institutionalized elderly, a group that by definition is more likely to be marginal in capacity than the general population. Simply being in an institution for a long period of time creates a certain dependency and induces infantilization of the individual (Goffman 1961). It may be useful to consider that in 1985 only 5 percent of the elderly population resided in nursing homes or institutions (see U.S. Dept. of Health and Human Services 1987).

Discussion of capacity (described perhaps more accurately as "decisional capacity") is important with regard to the elderly because it is this issue that has justified what appears to be a clear disinterest in advancing the legal rights of this group. We find, for example, that in many jurisdictions the elderly can be placed in long-term care with no consideration of their legal rights (Cole 1987). In contrast, during the 1960s and 1970s we saw an upheaval because of the neglect of the rights of mental patients to due process and other constitutional powers. In fact, the laws were changed so drastically that it has become virtually impossible to commit an individual for an indeterminate period of time or to justify commitment on grounds other than the presence of a serious mental disease or defect and dangerousness to self and others.

In contrast, the elderly are routinely placed in long-term care facilities, nursing homes, and convalescent homes with no regard for their individual rights. Often informally, family members with no malevolent intention conspire, essentially, to have an elderly person placed in an institution. The elderly individual may refuse this incarceration, but such refusal frequently

lacks sanctioning power and legal assistance. Being placed in an institution
may be an irreversible condition for the elderly patient. There are no lawyers,
for example, in nursing homes or long-term care facilities as there are for
mental institutions (Cole 1987). In fact, many jurisdictions, such as New
York City, require the availability of legal assistance to patients in mental
institutions. But this is not the case with the elderly, who can be placed in
these institutions and have no true advocate's presence to assure that the
incarceration is justified to begin with and that continuing confinement is
justified.

Furthermore, on even more important issues, such as the right to refuse
treatment, the elderly are not provided with the same kinds of resources
legally and in terms of advocacy that exist for mental patients. The law, in
myriad ways, supports the cultural perceptions of the elderly as dependent,
infantile and incompetent and therefore as needing the assistance of more
competent adults to assure that the proper decisions are made in the medical
care context (Tancredi 1987). Sensitization to the particularly vulnerable
position of the elderly has occurred only in recent years, so that there are
now groups advocating greater legal response to the plight of the institutionalized elderly and affirming and maintaining the rights of those who are
not institutionalized and do not desire to be (Moody 1987).

On the other hand, one aspect of the rights of the elderly has already
become the focus of much attention from the legal community. We signal
the right of the terminally ill to elect to discontinue a life-saving treatment,
with the inevitable consequence of death. The whole issue of the right to
die has undergone considerable legal change since the mid-1970s. There
has been an essential demystification of the right to die (Weinberg 1988),
particularly through cases such as those of Karen Quinlan (*In re Quinlan* 1976)
and Saikewicz (*Superintendent of Belchertown State School* v. *Saikewicz* 1977),
and more recently in New Jersey, cases such as *In re Conroy* (1985). A series
of such cases have articulated the right to terminate nutritional supports in
those who are terminally ill or irreversibly seriously incapacitated (see *In
Matter of Jobes* 1987). Because this group for the most part involves the elderly,
the right to discontinue treatment is a cornerstone of the rights of the elderly
that is gaining acceptance in most states (see Report of President's Commission 1983).

At the same time that these cases are providing increasing self-
determination and autonomy for the elderly, they offer the opportunity to
empower community goals over those of the individual (Pollock 1989). This
is not an issue where one is dealing with a competent elderly patient who
is opting for withdrawal of life support, but it can be a problem when one
is dealing with the incompetent elderly patient and determinations are made
by family or others to withdraw life support. The laws in this regard are also
changing. In the Karen Quinlan case the patient was unconscious and unable
to voice an opinion; the court therefore allowed a putative decision maker,

the father, to attest to the preferences of his daughter were she alive to make the decision. Such intellectual game strategies offer an opportunity for family and community members to impose upon the incompetent patient values and preferences that may not, in fact, reflect their true disposition.

There is increasing interest, as we have seen in the work of ethicists such as Daniel Callahan (see Callahan 1987), in reconsidering the distribution of resources when one is dealing with the aged, and necessarily emphasizing a kind of utilitarian ethic of the greatest good for the greatest number. The conflicts imposed by the assertion of individual rights and preferences and the potential for the superimposition of a social-utility standard are just beginning to unravel individual and social values grouped around best interests, social autonomy, and community benefit (Dworkin 1977).

"BIOETHICS" CONSIDERS THE ELDERLY

Jay Katz has suggested "conversation" to overcome the pitfalls of "the Silent World of Doctor and Patient," which he maintains consists of medical arrogance and patient ignorance and submissiveness (Katz 1984). But we suggest that is not enough. Conversations with old paradigms will not necessarily provide information. Conversation sometimes permits the appearance of points of real communication, but it very frequently allows for many points of mismatch of codes and messages. The physician has a body of information constantly, if minimally, transformed while going from patient to patient, and interprets this information cross-sectionally. The patient has a longitudinal experiential history of an illness and a personal calculus of mishaps and optimization strategies for resolution of the problem. The physician/patient encounter is certainly a locus for the exercise of power, but not for a symmetrical exchange of it (Romanucci-Ross 1982a, p. 179).

We have discussed the plight of the elderly in light of social change and indicated that early Americans and modern Americans are not culturally the same. We have made some cross-cultural comparisons to illustrate different possibilities in interpersonal relations and worldview, the human condition, the individual's place in the universe and in the group. Our culture prefers, in our times, segmental and impersonal relations. Our knowledge configurations in medical science train us to think of causation as temporal and reductionistic. We are very good at working with small circuits of control in small arcs of cause and effect. Where does bioethics fit in all of this?

There is little agreement on what "ethics" is, but apparently we can agree that it is about "What should we do? What should we hope for or seek? How should we treat others?"

In philosophy, ethicists work at setting forth principles of morality (excellence in behavior) and justifying them. But most people don't want to be told what is good or bad, nor do they want to be told how to think about it. Like the herpes simplex virus, preprogrammed ethical thought has been all around us all the time, in the special institutions of our culture (homes, churches, schools, clubs, etc.), or it is acquired from the last kiss of a dying grandparent. It disappears into the nooks and crannies of a nerve sheath until a crisis calls it forth to erupt and be seen and heard and noted by all, and to be disseminated to others.

Since there is no objective way to know what the correct view of the world is, societies take no chances. We are immediately socialized to view "reality" as it benefits our culture, so that it may sustain itself. To look at all the societies and cultures of the world is to be stunned by the array of possible solutions to moral dilemmas. Yet we can all recall being told to "listen to your conscience," as though it were not ready-made for you the minute you appeared on this planet.

A prevailing cultural ideology is instilled in the child before anyone is aware of it. An ideology is the way the world is viewed, and one's place within it, the future of mankind, and one's place in the present and future grounded in the past. It is about attitudes toward authority, about interpersonal relationships, the goal of an individual or of a society. These values create a "second reality" more real than what is really "there." A society has a problem when it *recognizes* that it does. And it says a great deal about our values that we now feel that that group known as the elderly pose a "problem" for us!

If we listen to our bioethicists as regards "the problem of the elderly," we can learn some very interesting things, even if we don't learn much about solving the problem. Some, such as Albert Jonson and Daniel Callahan, appear to have evolved from posing the problem as "What is our obligation to help the elderly?" They are the coiners of the phrase "intergenerational justice." (We earlier mentioned that our culture differs from most others by placing more emphasis on "within-a-generation" relationships rather than "between-generation" relationships, so of course we have the problem of "justice" rather than altruistic motivation.) Callahan concludes that society should desist from medical goals to benefit the elderly, who should shift their interest to the young rather than themselves. They should accept death, he says, for the sake of others (see Callahan 1987).

The format for discussing the elderly and medical care in our culture is for established groups to ask our bioethicists to frame a series of questions and to answer them. The frames and the questions are highly stylized and cluster around issues such as life support, living space, cost/benefit, and "is there *room* for our elderly." Implicit in the question frame is the belief that we have to make some "terrible choices."

Ethical decisions are also about what we do to ourselves as we make such decisions. It is about whether we have the courage to look at ourselves. It is about accepting the constraints of life—lives of those other than ourselves, including wildlife, and our place in the plant and animal world. There are those who proclaim or gladly acquiesce in the infinite expansion of human activity and unchecked human proliferation at the cost of the space of other forms of life—*all* other forms of life and matter.

One does not hear the bioethicists asking these or other related questions, such as "What is the relationship of person to family, family to group, and of group to ecology? Should one make decisions about who should survive and who should come into being without being accountable for the consequences? (Native healers *are* held accountable for life and death and the consequences of their shamanic rites.)

The existential philosophers, beginning with Nietzsche, followed by Kierkegaard, Heidegger, Sartre, and others, maintained that ethics *is* about values, and that people create their own values. This means, of course, that values are not handed out on stone tablets nor diffused through gamma rays during enlightenment under a bo tree. We summarize the general stance of these thinkers, for they used very different terms in their descriptions.

The world is unintelligible, man's lot is absurd. We begin with the dark night of the soul, which leads to crisis, to our making a choice—to becoming engaged. We thus create and adhere to *values*. The existentialist wants a rich texture in moral reasoning, one that transcends cost accounting (see Nietzsche 1966; Kierkegaard 1975; Sartre 1957; Heidegger 1927).

But one does not hear the bioethicists asking "What should be our ultimate values, such as the place of art in life?" or "What of the role of solitude?" or "What will making 'terrible choices' do to us?"

The basic requirement to be able to think ethically is not so much always to "understand the viewpoint of the other," which is always emphasized, but to recognize that events are framed and placed within other event frames in changing times with changing facts. The problem of the elderly cannot be solved within our current frames.

Absolute answers are pitifully inadequate, and some questions are obsolete. John Rawls in his *Theory of Justice* (1971) suggests we approach every problem (ethically or morally) not knowing our place in society, our age, our rank, our financial or social status. Only *then* can we consider how to distribute justice or resources fairly. An interesting view, because it is very characteristic of less developed societies to approach ethical problems in exactly this fashion. One is *never* an individual but only part of a collectivity. The goal—the survival of the group values.

CONCLUSION

This chapter has attempted to examine some bioethical, legal, and cultural problems relevant to the elderly. Many of these concerns are applicable to all of us who experience the health care system. What these concerns once more emphasize is that medicine, although based in science can be, and often is, used for social objectives. Conflicting values then come into play in decisions that can be beneficial or harmful to those affected. We have the law to shore up individual rights through due process, through the asseveration of autonomy and self-determination regarding principles of privacy, and we have a body of bioethical literature that likewise addresses individual rights (Rawls 1971; Walzer 1983). On the other hand, both the law and bioethics are susceptible to interpretation; and this interpretation, based on cultural values, may easily shift at any point from emphasis on community or societal values to emphasis on individual values.

Since the mid-1970s the increasing concern about the cost of health care has indicated that economic factors are pivotal in generating social and political decisions in health care. The crisis of economics in health care is being felt on all levels—the care of children, the care of adults, the care of the mentally ill, and the care of the elderly. But it is this last group that is open to the most potential for abuse. They are a growing number in our society, and they are perceived increasingly as consumers of societal goods rather than as producers. Such factors weigh heavily in the interpretation of constitutional, legal, and bioethical principles regarding self-determination, autonomy, due process, and conflicts between the individual and society. They will continue to do so unless we ask the pertinent *ethical* questions: What kind of life do we want? What kind of world do we want? What must we do, or refrain from doing, to attain it?

REFERENCES

Callahan, Daniel. 1987. *Setting Limits: Medical Goals in an Aging Society*. New York: Simon and Schuster.

Cole, T. R. 1987. "Class, Culture and Coercion: A Historical Perspective on Long Term Care." *Generations* 11:9–15.

Devereux, George. 1967. *From Anxiety to Method in the Behavioral Sciences*. Paris and The Hague: Ecole Pratique des Hautes Etudes and Mouton.

Dworkin, R. 1977. *Taking Rights Seriously*. Cambridge, Mass.: Harvard University Press.

Engel, Heinrich. 1987. *The Japanese House: A Tradition for Contemporary Architecture*. Rutland, Vt., and Tokyo: Chas. E. Tuttle.

Feinson, M. 1985. "Aging and Mental Health: Distinguishing Myth from Reality." *Research on Aging* 7:155.

Folstein, N., J. D. Anthony, I. Parhad, B. Duffy, and E. Gruenberg. 1985. "The Meaning of Cognitive Impairment in the Elderly." *Journal of the American Geriatrics Society* 33:228.

Fromm, Erich. 1947. *Man for Himself: An Inquiry into the Psychology of Ethics*. New York: Holt, Rinehart and Winston.

Goffman, E. 1961. *Asylums: Essays on the Social Situation of Mental Patients and Other Inmates*. Garden City, N.Y.: Doubleday.

Heidegger, Martin. 1927. *Sein und Zeit*. Trans. by J. Macquarrie and E. S. Robinson as *Being and Time*. New York: 1962. Frankfurt am Main: Klosterman.

Henry, Jules. 1965. *Culture Against Man*. New York: Vintage Books-Random House.

Katz, Jay. 1984. *The Silent World of Doctor and Patient.* New York: The Free Press.

Kierkegaard, Soren. 1975. *Entwerder-Order* (Trans. by George L. Stregen as *Either/ Or.* Munich: Deutscher Taschenbuchen Verlag).

In Matter of Jobes. 1987. 108 N.J. 394, 529 A.2d 434.

Mead, Margaret. 1970. *Culture and Commitment: A Study of the Generation Gap.* Garden City, New York: Doubleday.

Moody, H. R. 1987. "Ethical Dilemmas in Nursing Home Placement." *Generations* 11:16–23.

Nietzsche, Friedrich. 1966. *Beyond Good and Evil: Prelude to a Philosophy of the Future.* Tr. Walter Kaufman. New York: Vintage Books.

Okakura, Kakuso. 1956. *The Book of Tea.* Rutland, Vt., and Tokyo: Chas. E. Tuttle.

Pollock, S. G. 1989. "Life and Death Decisions: Who Makes Them and by What Standards?" *Rutgers Law Review* 41:505–40.

Rawls, J. 1971. *A Theory of Justice.* Cambridge, Mass.: Harvard University Press.

In re Conroy. 1985. 98 N.J. 321, 486 A.2d 1209.

In re Quinlan. 1976. 70 N.J. 10, 355 A.2d 647, *Cert. Denied*, 429 U.S. 922.

Report of the President's Commission for the Study of Ethical Problems in Medicine and Biomedical and Behavioral Research. 1983. *Deciding to Forego Life-Sustaining Treatment.* Washington, D.C.: U.S. Government Printing Office.

Rogers v. *Okin.* 1979. 478 F. Supp 1342 (Ed. Mass.), 1979, *Cert. granted* and case argued sub nom *Mills* v. *Rogers*, 457 U.S. 291, 102 S.Ct. 2442 (1983). See also *Rogers* v. *Okin* 738 F.2d 1 (1984).

Rolle, Andrew F. 1968. *The Immigrant Upraised; Italian Adventurers and Colonists in an Expanding America.* Norman, Okla: University of Oklahoma Press.

Romanucci-Ross, Lola. 1982a. "Medicalization and Metaphor." In Martin W. deVries, R. L. Berg, and Mack Lipkin, Jr., eds., *The Use and Abuse of Medicine.* New York: Praeger.

———. 1982b. "The Italian Identity and Its Transformation." In George de Vos and Lola Romanucci-Ross, eds., *Ethnic Identity: Cultural Continuities and Change*, pp. 198–227. Chicago: University of Chicago Press.

Sartre, Jean-Paul. 1957. *L'Etre et le Néant: Essai d'Ontologie Phénoménologigue.* Paris: Gallimard (Trans. by Hazel Barnes as *Being and Nothingness.* New York: Philosophical Library).

Siegel, J. S. and C. M. Taeuber. 1986. Demographic Dimensions of an Aging Population. In *Our Aging Society: Paradox and Promise.* A. Pifer and L. Bronte, eds. New York: W.W. Norton.

Superintendent of Belchertown State School v. *Saikewicz.* 1977. 373 Mass. 728, 370 N.E. 2d 417.

Tancredi, L. R. 1987. "The Mental Status Examination." *Generations* 11:24–31.

Tocqueville, Alexis de. 1946. *Democracy in America.* Tr. Henry Reeve. London: Oxford University Press. (First published as *De la Democratie en Amérique*, Paris: Librairie de Charles Gosselin, 1835–1840.)

U.S. Department of Health and Human Services. 1987. *Fact Sheet on Long Term Care.* Sept. 21, pp. 66–71.

Walzer, M. 1983. *Spheres of Justice: A Defense of Pluralism and Equality.* New York: Basic Books.

Washington et. al. v. *Harper.* 1990. 110 S.Ct. 1028.

Weinberg, J. K. 1988. "Demystifying the Right to Die: The New Jersey Experience." *Medicine and Law* 7:323–45.

Weissman, M., J. K. Myers, G. L. Tischler, C. Holzer, III, P. Leaf, and J. Brody. 1985 "Psychiatric Disorders (DSM-III) and Cognitive Impairment Among the Elderly in a U.S. Urban Community." *Acta Psychiatrica Scandinavica* 71:336.

20

"Medical Anthropology": Convergence of Mind and Experience in the Anthropological Imagination

LOLA ROMANUCCI-ROSS, DANIEL E. MOERMAN, AND LAURENCE R. TANCREDI

There is an uneasy fit of the biomedical into anthropological discourse. Medical discourse also finds integrating "the cultural" problematic. It often seems very difficult to translate things from one domain to the other; the organization, style, and sense of what is important differ between the two fields.

Works that claim to be biocultural anthropology seem usually to be mainly "bio" with a few inserts of the cultural here and there. The primary reason for this, we think, is that the "bio" aspect is the more quantifiable part, and thus appears more scientific, more manageable, less subject to challenge in an argument. Such quantified material is reified as data.

In the older anthropological tradition we had, in contrast, a more apparently intuitive ethnographic method, tribal studies and peasant studies. Subsequently we became somewhat more statistical, then we became ethnoscholars, and have since become interpretative. From this tradition in anthropology, how can we carry out an anthropology of biology or medicine and in that exercise emerge with a genuine appreciation of biomedical systems and, as well, learn the possible levels of integration of biomedical phenomena with cultural phenomena? A medical event is both biological *and* cultural, and since investigators are usually aligned with one aspect or the other of such an event, the simultaneity of the two aspects needs to be acknowledged. Integrating facts from the two realms of knowing has not been, and will not be, accomplished easily while we search for cause and effect. In this chapter we will first discuss the stance of an exponent of the biocultural approach as currently conceived. This will be followed by a consideration of rhetoric and intentionality in the physical sciences; we will then focus on what can be gleaned from some current research frontiers in the medical sciences to find a resolution to the biocultural dilemma.

TANGLED HYPOTHESES

We give an example that typifies the intellectual style in biocultural studies: Melvin Konner wrote a book called *The Tangled Wing* (1982) that presumably was meant to bridge the gap between the biological and the cultural. But note the subtitle: *Biological Constraints on the Human Spirit*. While he might have chosen to focus on culture as a device by which people can be liberated from biological constraints, he chose the reverse. The critical reader should be alerted.

Consider Konner's approach to one study he analyzes to illustrate bioanthropology. In a paper published in a well-known medical journal, the investigators described three intermarrying rural villages in the Dominican Republic (Imperato-McGinley et al. 1979). Over four generations, nineteen persons appeared at birth to be female and were so raised. At puberty, they failed to develop breasts, male testes in the abdominal cavity descended, voices deepened, and the male genitalia appeared. At this point "physically and psychologically they became men." They were described by the researchers as genetically male with one X and one Y chromosome but lacking a single enzyme of the male sex hormone, 5-alpha-reductase:

The most extraordinary thing is that they became completely and securely men of their culture in every sense of the word. After twelve or more years of rearing as girls, with all the psychological influences encouraging that gender role in a rather sexist society, they are able to transform themselves into an almost typical example of the masculine gender. Of course they did not make the transformation with ease; some had years of psychological anguish. But they made it. (Konner 1982:124–25)

The researchers reasoned that the testosterone circulating during the course of growth in these *machi-hembras* (male-females) had a masculinizing effect on the brain, an effect that "appears to contribute substantially to the formation of male gender identity when combined with the transforming effect of the further testosterone surge at puberty.... The effect of testosterone predominates, overriding the effect of rearing as girls" (Imperato-McGinley et al. 1979:1236).

Konner accepts this explanation without question. In fact, he places the author of this article in the company of his collection of distinguished "tough-minded" female researchers who devoted themselves "with great courage"

(Konner 1982:106) to the question of whether sex differences in behavior have a basis that is in part biological. (We are not aware of any previous inquiry that has put such an assertion, thus stated, in doubt.) But he concludes, "After sexism is wholly stripped away . . . after differences in training have gone the way of the whalebone corset, there will still be something different, something that is grounded in biology . . . because men are more violent . . . that is merely a statement of plain observable fact" (Konner 1982:107).

Yet Konner appears to hold in highest esteem the sex-difference studies of Margaret Mead. Such studies made culture the salient (but not the exclusive) determinant of behavior (e.g., Mead 1962). He also appears to know (Konner 1982:144) that knowledge of the gender of the newborn is the first and most important question asked by its parents, so that they will "know how to act" toward the child—and, we might add, to know how to *elicit the behavior* that the family and society need and want.

A culture provides the conscious models for sex role behaviors, and one learns not only one's role but the complementary sex role as well. Both role descriptors are ascribed by society and internalized by the individual, and are responsive to external signs and signals. The culture of origin of the *machi-hembras* does indeed feature powerful disincentives to continuing female development along with the presence of male organs, a cultural rather than a biological constraint. We contend that the bioanthropologists should not rush to judgment, attributing the sudden assumption of masculinity to "a rush of testosterone."

Konner's delightful (if at times less than meticulously reasoned) book presents us with many studies that find biological bases for feelings of rage, fear, joy, lust, and love. Problematic with his approach, however, is the usual bioanthropological argument in which facts and creeds from the biological and social sciences are juxtaposed, but the mechanisms connecting them are not the demonstrable causal loops found in well-controlled prospective studies, which require controlling both cultural and biological differences simultaneously. Rather, we are confronted with myriad tropes in free association. Such casual approaches to complex problems have kept us, and will keep us, dangling from a pendulum that swings from cultural and psychosocial explanations to anatomical and physiological explanations, an exercise well exemplified by the history of psychiatry that we might try to avoid.

It takes sufficient sensitivity to the details of any culture to recognize that one learns not only one's own role but also and simultaneously the roles which contrast with it. In other words, while you are learning how to act, how to speak, how to dress, how to walk and talk, you are confronted with contrasting sets of how not to act, speak, dress, walk, and talk. The opposite role model is as important as the apposite one. Romanucci-Ross was struck with this in Italian fieldwork when she noted the relationship between the saints, who literally starved and wasted away, and the believers in these saints, who died from heart attacks, overeating for decades on long pilgrimages to shrines. Some of the saints had relinquished youthful lives of gluttony and carnality to achieve their sanctified states. No one thinks it necessary to introduce a hormone to explain the change from debauchery to abstinence, from indulgence to mutilation, from dominance to obedience.

Nowhere is this reversion to biology in the name of science more rampant then in the decades of studies on male-female differences in intelligence and other kinds of performance, although accounts of racial differences might be close in the movement toward old paradigms of causality. We do not assert that physiology has no influence on behavior or that cultural explanations are inevitably complete. Rather, we note that with reckless regularity biocultural explanations heavily emphasize the biological while tossing in a few statements to the effect that culture is also important, usually in the least relevant manner.

A BLACK HOLE HAS NO HAIR

We tend to think that the cultural part of biocultural anthropology is text and rhetorical, and that it relies heavily on the usage of tropes. This is taken by some as criticism. But we suggest that bioscience, indeed any science, has *always* used tropes and that *rhetoric* has always played a central role in science, even in the most technical treatises. We give many examples from the biological sciences. (See chapter 18 in this volume.) As is inevitably the case, however, the speakers do not recognize their own metaphors as being such; one of the most powerful aspects of culture is that it appears to its bearers as "natural."

Consider an example from the work of a renowned leader of the most physical of the physical sciences. Stephen Hawking's interesting book *A Brief History of Time* (1988) has been on the *New York Times* best-seller list for nearly two years as we write this. Whether all those who have purchased a copy have read it is not clear; but if they have, they have been exposed to a wonderfully compelling, persuasive rhetorical and metaphorical argument. Here, for example, are the kernels of a series of sentences taken from the central chapter, "Black Holes." We leave out the substance of the argument, retaining only the rhetorical devices used to create what the author puts forth as logical linkages; the italics are added.

On this assumption . . . Michell wrote. . . . Michell *suggested*. . . . [P]erhaps [Laplace] *decided* that it [black holes] was a *crazy* idea. . . . How would it [a certain kind of star] *know* that it had to lose weight? . . . Eddington was *shocked*. . . . he *refused* to believe. . . . Eddington thought it was simply not possible. . . . Einstein . . . *claimed*. . . . The hostility of other scientists . . . persuaded Chandrasekhar to abandon. . . . This scenario is not entirely realistic. . . . However, we *believe*. . . . there *must* be a singularity.

... There are some solutions of the equations ... in which it is possible for ... [e.g., solutions are chosen, not proven]. There was, however, a different interpretation of [a certain] result ... *advocated* by [other scientists]. ... They *argued*. ... [Certain] calculations *supported* this view ... [while supposedly others supported another]. It was *conjectured* that. ... a black hole must settle down. ... "A black hole has no hair." The "no hair" theorem ... greatly restricts the possible types of black holes. ... A black hole seems to be the only really *natural* explanation of the observations. (Hawking 1988: 81–94)

Much could be made of the above in analysis but we confine ourselves to two emergent points in the reasoning. One, that theorems constrain nature (with which we completely agree); and two, that these analytical constructions (black holes)—inventions (fabulations, fabrications) of Hawking and his colleagues—are aspects of "nature," with which we also agree, insofar as we are prepared to argue that nature is a cultural invention.

ON BIOMEDICINE AND CAUSALITY

Physics is not without its interpretative slants and concomitant ambiguities of natural phenomena, as we have seen with some of Hawking's perceptions, but nowhere in science is the issue of causation regarding influences on natural events more problematic than in biomedicine. This can be well illustrated in the two areas of biomedicine currently representing the cutting edge of research: genetics and the neurosciences. Many geneticists would argue that the nature-nurture issue is near resolution (Wilson 1975; Paul 1988). The discovery and elucidation at this time of over four thousand diseases of genetic origin would appear to fuel the proposition that genes and biochemistry determine our destiny, parallel to Konner's interpretation of the *machi-hembras*. However, belief that genetics is the sole determinant of individual development ignores two critical factors affecting the manifestation of a genetic trait: *gene penetrance* and *gene expressivity*.

Penetrance refers to the presence of a gene that is causally related to the development of, for example, a disease; it does not mean that every individual carrying that gene will eventually develop that disease. To use Huntington's chorea as an example, it is argued that everyone who has that particular autosomal dominant gene will develop the disease—if he or she lives long enough (Chandler et al. 1960). The vast majority will develop the disease in their forties or fifties. A small tail effect will represent those who might develop the symptoms of Huntington's chorea at ten or eleven years of age or at sixty or sixty-five years of age (Farrer et al. 1984). However, Huntington's chorea appears to be 100 percent penetrating. On the other hand, many autosomal dominant conditions are penetrating in a varying percentage of cases, occasionally skipping generation(s), and may have a wide variety of expressions (Conneally 1984). For instance, neurofibromatosis

(Von Recklinghausen's disease) may feature mild conditions identified only by the presence of café-au-lait spots; it may cause seriously deforming conditions involving the presence of fibromatous skin tumors, meningiomas, acoustic neuroma, mental retardation, scoliosis, optic neuroma, and hypoglycemia (Crowe et al. 1956; Nicolls 1969; Riccardi 1981).

Why, if genetics is determinative of the individual, don't 100 percent of those with the gene develop the condition? One explanation appears to be that cofactors are essential to bring a condition into being. Such cofactors include the presence of other genes creating biochemical substances, and cultural or environmental factors interacting with genetic or biochemical determinants that either result in the penetration of the gene or impede its development. The dynamics of penetrance seen frequently with autosomal-dominant conditions such as neurofibromatosis has by no means been thoroughly understood. Schools of thought embrace various notions of which cofactors, genetic or cultural-environmental, tip the balance. Penetrance and expressivity, discussed below, may more clearly explain the instancing of a disease such as schizophrenia, which is considered not an autosomal-dominant condition but a multigenetically caused condition in which environmental and cultural factors are strongly involved in causality. In schizophrenia we find a concordance (of approximately 60 percent) among monozygotic twins, giving support to the argument of the powerful effects of environmental and cultural factors (Connor and Ferguson-Smith 1987).

The second critical factor is expressivity. Let us consider an individual with the gene for a particular condition that has penetrated, that is, the individual develops symptoms and signs associated with the genetic disease (Holtzman 1989:233–35). We have seen here that the range of the ways in which these symptoms manifest themselves is wide. Some individuals with genetic conditions, such as Charcot-Marie-Tooth disease, may have minimal symptoms and be nearly normal despite the presence of the autosomal dominant gene (McKusick 1986:no. 11820). Others may inherit the gene and manifest severe disability consistent with the typical characterization of a particular disease.

Differences in expressivity, despite the similarity of the genetic component, may reflect the presence or absence of genetic cofactors, but in some instances have been shown to be due to cultural or environmental differences. An excellent example of this is the condition phenylketonuria (PKU), a genetically autosomal-dominant condition with varying penetrance. However, even where this condition occurs and an individual is susceptible to the symptomatology of PKU, habits of nutrition can affect its expressivity in a major way. For example, in a culture relatively devoid of phenylalanine in the diet, the expressivity of PKU would be markedly diminished in intensity. Ordinarily an individual with PKU would be severely retarded. However, when the diet is modified very early, the retardation can be significantly attenuated. Cultural factors that influence diet and nutrition will directly influence whether this disease will be manifested in its most severe form. It is conceivable that an individual born with PKU in a culture in which the diet is modified as a matter of (cultural) course would be seen as simply a minor deviation from the norm.

One might argue that this example does not directly address the thesis of those who argue that genetic or biohumoral agents determine such basic elements as personality, behavior, and personal identity. But does the inheriting of a genetic condition labeled "disease" really differ from gender identity? It is a genetically transmissible condition that affects biology and behavior, just as traits of "maleness" and "femaleness" affect biology and behavior. In part, we designate something as a disease if it has symptoms and disabilities that are incompatible with cultural values of normalcy. The designation of "disease" is very fluid, particularly with regard to behavioral and psychological conditions. Even in the case of physical conditions, what is considered a disease differs in various cultures on the basis of the percentage of individuals who possess the condition and the impact of that condition on other, potentially more serious disabilities (Nelkin and Tancredi 1989).

For example, in parts of Africa the sickle cell gene reaches substantial frequencies. The homozygous condition for this gene results in sickle cell anemia, a genetic disease that is nearly always fatal. However, it has been shown that heterozygous individuals—said to have the sickle cell trait—are less susceptible to malaria, which is endemic in the areas where the gene occurs (Livingstone 1958). The biogenetic condition leading to sickle cell trait therefore is pervasive and associated with a benefit thus rendering it unlikely to be classified as a disease; it is seen as merely a variant of the normal condition. Indeed, it is easy to show that if, in such a situation, one somehow eliminated the sickle cell gene from the population, thus eliminating mortality from sickle cell anemia, the overall mortality rate would actually increase due to malaria in unprotected individuals.

Biomedical notions of causality in the neurosciences are also problematic. In recent years research on the brain has been considered one of the major frontiers of biomedical explanation of the human condition (National Institute of Mental Health 1988). Consequently the brain is rapidly being targeted as the most exciting area of biomedical investigation. Developments such as the use of complex imaging technologies—positron emission tomography (PET), single photo emission tomography (SPECT), magnetoencephalography (SQUID), and computerized electroencephalography (CEEG and BEAM), to name a few—are major advances over earlier imaging technologies in that they provide for direct evaluation of brain function in normal living humans (Volkow and Tancredi 1991)

Such technologies have reinforced observations about brain function that had been, even in the recent past, highly inferential and based on clinical observation alone. With the use of positron emission tomography, for example, it is now possible to measure the brain's utilization of glucose, a substance necessary for cellular function, and thereby to determine which areas of the brain are activated under well-defined circumstances. Through the use of this technology, principles of brain function, such as brain organization, human variability, and openness and plasticity, can be examined directly from a biochemical and biophysiological perspective. Of these principles the most important, from the standpoint of examining the interaction of nature and nurture, is that of plasticity and openness.

"Plasticity" refers to the capacity of the brain to alter itself by virtue of external stimuli. Obviously this is most conspicuously seen through the process of learning, which essentially produces a "different" individual. External stimuli result in activation and stimulation of segments of the brain that create transformations not only of neurochemical characteristics but also of structural characteristics (Kolers 1979; Rose 1981). In addition to the activity of learning, other processes are responsible for brain remodeling. These include intervention through the use of pharmacological agents (Duncan et al. 1989), endocrinological alterations (Nottebohm 1989), a range of external insults (Cotman and Nieto-Sampedro 1985), and stress (Inoue et al. 1985). In relating external stimuli to internal response, the brain must be thought of as an open system. For although in some respects the brain is limited by its physical boundaries, in terms of its ability to transform and to be transformed, it extends into both the world within and the world without; it influences the external world but at the same time incorporates features of that world in an integrative biological fashion (Gomez-Mont and Volkow 1982).

Clinical syndromes can be identified that demonstrate defects in the ability of the individual to interact with the environment. In the Kline-Levine syndrome of hypersomnia and hyperphagia (Lichtenberg 1982:344–45), a person loses the capacity to integrate the external environment effectively (Volkow and Tancredi 1991). In some variations of the syndrome, behaviors may be triggered by the external environment and dominate internal needs and desires. Such behaviors are frequently automated routines in the brain; a person may eat whenever food is placed in front of him, for example, even though he consumed a full meal only fifteen minutes earlier; the mere presence of the food activates intention and behavior. Similarly, someone with this syndrome may, when placed in a bedroom, fall asleep immediately. Here again, the environment influences and in some respects controls behavior.

A similar syndrome (but in reverse, so to speak) indicates a severe obsessive-compulsive disorder in which the internal environment elicits behaviors frequently dissonant with the external environment. An obsession becomes so compelling that it obfuscates the integrative function which normally would balance external stimuli with internal needs to inform individual action. In both of these illustrations, that of the Klein-Levine syndrome and that of the obsessive-compulsive disorder, conscious personal needs and desires give way to external or internal environmental influences (Zohar and Insel 1987).

Positron emission tomography studies have frequently documented abnormal function of the caudate and orbital frontal cortex of these patients (Baxter et al. 1987). They are in agreement with studies involving animals that have shown repetitive compulsive behavior when the caudate nuclei or orbital frontal cortex is destroyed (Kolb 1977). It has been postulated that a circuit exists involving the orbital frontal cortex, the ventral palladium, the caudate nucleus, and the medial thalamic nucleus which serves a major role in the pathogenesis of obsessive-compulsive disease (Volkow and Tancredi 1991; Modell et al. 1989).

Both clinical studies and positron emission tomography studies indicate that brain remodeling involves a complex interplay of biological and cultural factors. Furthermore, it is important to note that there have been demonstrations, both clinical and biochemical, to suggest quite convincingly that externally or internally derived stimuli can bring about remodeling of the brain not only on a neurochemical level but also in terms of structural change (Volkow and Tancredi 1991). To this process we must add the fact of human variability indicating structural and functional differences in the brains of individuals; we are left with a complex calculus.

Because of this complex circuitry, much needs to be done to show causative linkages between specific external stimuli, be they learning or the introduction of pharmacological agents, and specific structural and neurochemical changes of the brain. Fortunately, we now have biochemical and biophysiological evidence to support inferential observations from clinical studies that the outside world *does* have an impact on shaping the brain of the individual. Social and cultural factors, coupled with the capacity of the brain to integrate information and to *intend* certain activities, create a direct interactive pattern. We have, in the studies alluded to above, a scientific basis to discredit simplistic studies which imply that sex differentiation, for example, is purely biochemical and biophysiological. The openness and plasticity of the brain do not dismiss the role of the biochemical and the biophysiological as mediating processes, but suggest instead that all the outside world, including the sociocultural, has a direct impact on biophysiological structure and function.

TOWARD A NEW LEVEL OF DISCOURSE

What should be questioned, then, is the finality and authority that many of our colleagues grant to science, to biology, to nature, as we puzzle things out. We assert that, insofar as we have any sense of them, these are things that we—anthropologists, biologists, physicians, physicists—construct in much the same manner as we construct anything else—hand axes, bridges, poems, equations, rituals—as concepts/objects that "hang together," "make sense," "seem right," and generally "fit."

Moreover, we challenge the notion endemic to much biological anthropology and biomedical research that we are observing a mechanical "other" through the two-way glass, as emic observers of the etic, whether the other be a pansy, a savage, or a thought, a disease, an illness, or a gene. "The notion that a numerical result should depend on the relation of an object to observer is in the spirit of physics in this century and is even an exemplary illustration of it" (Mandelbrot 1977:26). The observer in this view may be correct, but perhaps not completely. For we are now confronted with a tangle of wide arcs of causality in negotiating "facts" about the physical world, with more emicity in the process and with a growing recognition of both trends (see Bohr 1958; see also Feynman et al. 1966).

In the biological and medical sciences, as well as in the social sciences, we find objects of the same order studying classes of objects of which they are members, simultaneously subject to self and object to others. And, as indicated in examples above, in such sciences we test theories based on complementary and converging results that come from disparate methods of investigation. Negotiating facts and truths in such problem areas as we describe above may not be too different from negotiating "correct" ethnographic description in anthropology (for discussion of negotiating ethnography, see Geertz 1973; Habermas 1984; Romanucci-Ross 1985).

NEW DIRECTIONS

The debate as to whether culture or biology is the salient vector of behavior appears to continue unabated. We have given enough examples to indicate that it is not this illusory dichotomy which should now be problematic. In Western medical culture, however, we are historically accustomed to dualistic thought; even in our popular culture we speak of the "horns of a dilemma" (two dual symbols in this phrase, one a referent to an iconic sign, one linguistic). But it is possible to escape the paradigm entirely, and for our purposes it is necessary to learn to interpret properly the epistemological fallout of our new technologies, and the possible interpretations of our studies of culture and events.

The newer technologies will give us the information (certainly not the values) to help us confront the chaos; we have alluded to several areas that provide opportunities for thinking on the frontier. In addition, again in the illustrations in this chapter, we can begin to understand that the manner in which we think about biological and physical data is not just a cultural act; the "hard data" themselves are, if you will, contaminated with, or constructed of, cultural inputs. All of this resolves itself into a question of where we situate our subjectivity.

Bourdieu asserts that we need a unified science of practice, and that such a science must describe those laws of transformation which govern the changing of different kinds of capital into symbolic capital (Bourdieu 1977:117). He refers to economic structures, of course, but we borrow his metaphor, finding it appropriate to view information from various disciplines as capital. Different systems of information translated into "symbolic capital" can lead us to better appreciate the relationship between things or objects, and those persons (agents) shaped by their culture. We shape and define the nature of those knowledge domains which we revere as reality and therefore, with our consent, they rule the imagination. We have alluded to an example in the rhetorical devices of physicists to exemplify what is characteristic of many established scientific disciplines—an intention-based semantics. The reader is driven to ascribe meaning, but the road to meaning is carefully guided by the intent of the scientist-authors, an intent to convert the reader to a belief system. This is done through a subtle shift from words conveying thoughts to words presumably conveying things: "facts," causes, relationships (Grice 1989). Nor do we think that anthropology as a discipline is free of intentional works and pronouncements. Many anthropologists have thought of culture as the ultimate explanation, which raises the interesting question of where one could stand outside of it or find a lever long enough to arrange cultural words into meaningful constellations that are also dependable maps.

Medical anthropology has indeed enriched both anthropology and medicine, and will undoubtedly continue to do so. It is also a promising area for research in those knowledge domains composing the field; these are the domains that can be restructured into a new semantic field, a new grammar for avoiding the old paradigms of either/or. We need not look to biology or to culture for the unique, "real," and exclusive cause for any of the phenomena we study. Biological events *are* biocultural; cultural events are also biological. Biological events and cultural events are equally and simultaneously biocultural. The materials we need to reach a new level of discourse are in our grasp; we have only to abandon outmoded approaches (disciplines) to achieve an enlightening beginning for a new science.

REFERENCES

Baxter, L. R., Phelps, M. E., Mazziotta, J. B., Guze, B. H., Schwartz, J. M. and Selin, C. E. 1987. "Local Cerebral Glucose Metabolic Rates in Obsessive-Compulsive Disorder: A Comparison with Rates in Unipolar Depression and in Normal Controls." *Archives of General Psychiatry* 44:211–18.

Bohr, N. 1958. *Atomic Physics and Human Knowledge.* New York: John Wiley & Sons.

Bourdieu, Pierre. 1977. *Outline of a Theory of Practice.* Cambridge: Cambridge University Press.

Chandler, J. H., Reed, T. E., and Dejong, R. N. 1960. "Huntington's Chorea in Michigan." *Neurology* 10:148–53.

Conneally, P. M. 1984. "Huntington Disease: Genetics and Epidemiology." *American Journal of Human Genetics* 36:506–29.

Connor, J. F., and Ferguson-Smith, M. A. 1987. *Essential Medical Genetics*, 2nd edition. St. Louis: Blackball Scientific Publications.

Cotman, C. W., and Nieto-Sampedro, M. 1985. "Progress in Facilitating the Recovery of Function After Central Nervous System Trauma." In F. Nottebohm, ed., *Hope for a New Neurology*, pp. 83–204. New York: New York Academy of Sciences.

Crowe, F. W., Schull, W. J., and Neel, J. V. 1956. *A Clinical Pathological and Genetic Study of Multiple Neurofibromatosis*. Springfield, Ill.: Charles C. Thomas.

Duncan, G. E., Paul, I. A., Powell, K. R., Fassberg, J. B., Stumpf, W. E., and Breese, G. R. 1989. "Neuroanatomically Selective Down-Regulation of Beta Adrenergic Receptors by Chronic Imipramine Treatment." *Journal of Pharmacology and Experimental Therapeutics*. 248:470–77.

Farrer, L. A., Conneally, P. M., and Yu, P. 1984. "The Natural History of Huntington Disease: Possible Role of 'Aging Genes.' " *Am J Med Genet* 18:115–23.

Fausto-Sterling, Anne. 1985. *Myths of Gender*. New York: Basic Books.

Feynman, R. F., Leighton, R. B., and Sands, M. 1966. *The Feynman Lectures on Physics*. Reading, Mass.: Addison-Wesley.

Freeman, Derek. 1983. *Margaret Mead and Samoa. The Making and Unmaking of an Anthropologic Myth*. Cambridge, Mass.: Harvard University Press.

Geertz, C. 1973. *The Interpretation of Cultures*. New York: Basic Books.

Gomez-Mont, F. A., and Volkow, N. D. 1982. "The Relevance of Systems Thinking for Psychiatry." In W. Gray, J. Fidler and J. Batttista, eds., *General Systems Theory and the Psychological Sciences*, pp. 91–102. Seaside, Calif.: Intersystems Publications.

Grice, Paul. 1989. *Studies in the Way of Words*. Cambridge, Mass.: Harvard University Press.

Habermas, J. 1984. *The Theory of Communicative Action*. Tr. Thomas McCarity. London: Heinemann.

Hawking, Stephen W. 1988. *A Brief History of Time: From the Big Bang to Black Holes*. Bantam: New York.

Holtzman, N. A. 1989. *Proceed with Caution*. Baltimore: Johns Hopkins University Press.

Imperato-McGinley, J., R.E. Peterson, T. Gautier, and E. Sturlo. 1979. "Androgens and the Evolution of the Male Gender-Identity Among Male Pseudohermaphodites with 50-Reductase Deficiency." *New England Journal of Medicine* 300(22):1233–37.

Inoue, O., Akimoto, G., Hashimoto, K., and Yamasaki, T. 1985. "Alterations in Biodistribution of ^{3}H Ro 15–1788 in Mice by Acute Stress: Possible Changes in *in Vivo* Binding Availability of Brain Benzodiazepine Receptors." *International Journal of Nuclear Medicine and Biology*, 12:369–74.

Kolb, B. 1977. "Studies on the Candate-Putamen and the Dorsomedial Thalamic Nucleus of the Rat: Implications for Mammalian Frontal Lobe Functions." *Physiol Behav* 18:234–44.

Kolers, P. A. 1979. "A Pattern-Analyzing Basis of Recognition." In L. S. Cermak and F. I. M. Craik, eds., *Levels of Processing in Human Memory*. Hillsdale, N. J.: Lawrence Erlbaum.

Konner, Melvin. 1982. *The Tangled Wing: Biological Constraints on the Human Spirit*. New York: Holt, Rinehart and Winston.

Lichtenberg, R. 1982. *The Psychiatrist's Guide to Diseases of the Nervous System*. New York: John Wiley & Sons.

Livingstone, Frank B. 1958. "Anthropological Implications of Sickle Cell Distribution in West Africa." *American Anthropologist* 60:533–62.

McKusick, V. A. 1986. *Mendelian Inheritance in Man*, 7th edition. Baltimore and London: Johns Hopkins University Press.

Mandelbrot, Benoit. 1977. *The Fractal Geometry of Nature*. New York: Freeman.

Mead, Margaret. 1962. *Sex and Temperament in Three Primitive Societies*. New York: Mentor Books. (First published in 1935.)

Modell, J. G., Mountz, J. M., Curtis, G., and Gieden, J. F. 1989. "Neurophysiologic Dysfunction in Basal Ganglia/Limbic Striatal and Thalamocortical Circuits as a Pathogenetic Mechanism of Obsessive-Compulsive Disorder." *Journal of Neuropsychiatry* 1:27–36.

National Institute of Mental Health. 1988. *Approaching The Twenty-first Century: Opportunities for NIMH Neurosciences Research. Report to Congress on the Decade of the Brain*. Washington D.C.: U.S. Department of Health and Human Services.

Nelkin, D., and Tancredi, L. 1989. *Dangerous Diagnostics: The Social Power of Biological Information*. New York: Basic Books.

Nicolls, E. M. 1969. "Somatic Variation and Multiple Neurofibromatosis." *Human Heredity* 19:473–79.

Nottebohm, F. 1989. "Testosterone Triggers Growth of Brain Vocal Control Nuclei in Adult Female Canaries." *Brain Research* 189:429–36.

Paul, Diane. 1988. "Eugenic Origins of Clinical Genetics." Boston: University of Massachusetts, Boston. (Mimeodraft.)

Riccardi, V. M. 1981. "Von Recklinghausen Neurofibromatosis." *New England Journal of Medicine* 305:1617–26.

Romanucci-Ross, Lola. 1983. "Apollo Alone and Adrift in Samoa: Early Mead Reconsidered." *Reviews in Anthropology* 10(3):85–92.

———. 1985. *Mead's Other Manus: Phenomenology of the Encounter*. South Hadley, Mass: Bergin & Garvey.

Rose, S. P. 1981. "What Should a Biochemistry of Learning and Memory Be About?" *Neuroscience* 6:811–21.

Volkow, N. D., and Tancredi, L. 1991. "Biological Correlates of Mental Activity Studied with PET." *American Journal of Psychiatry* 148:439–443.

Wilson, E. O. 1975. *Sociobiology*. Cambridge, Mass.: Belknap Press.

Zohar, J., and Insel, T. R. 1987. "Obsessive-Compulsive Disorder: Psychological Approaches to Diagnosis, Treatment and Pathophysiology." *Biological Psychiatry*, 22:667–87.

About the Editors and Contributors

GEORGE J. ARMELAGOS is Professor of Anthropology at the University of Florida.

MARJORIE MANDELSTAM BALZER is Assistant Professor of Anthropology at Georgetown University.

BARRY BOGIN is Professor of Anthropology at the University of Michigan, Dearborn.

LIBBET CRANDON-MALAMUD is Assistant Professor of Anthropology at Columbia University.

NINA L. ETKIN is Professor of Anthropology at the University of Hawaii, Honolulu.

MARGARET KEITH is an anthropologist for the United States Department of Agriculture's Forest Service in Ogden, Utah.

CLARA SUE KIDWELL is Professor of Native American Studies at the University of California, Berkeley.

ROBERT KUGELMANN is Professor of Psychology at the University of Dallas, Irving, Texas.

DANIEL E. MOERMAN is Professor of Anthropology at the University of

Michigan, Dearborn. He is author of numerous articles on enthnobotany and the definitive work on the medicinal use of plants by Native Americans, *American Medical Ethnobotany* (1977).

LAWRENCE B. RADINE is Professor of Sociology at the University of Michigan, Dearborn.

ALLEN F. ROBERTS is Professor of Anthropology at the University of Iowa.

LOLA ROMANUCCI-ROSS is Professor of Community and Family Medicine and Anthropology at the University of California, San Diego. A pioneer in the field of medical anthropology, she has written widely on the subject and is author of several other books including *One Hundred Towers* (Bergin & Garvey, 1991) and *Mead's Other Manus* (Bergin & Garvey, 1985).

PAUL J. ROSS is Professor of Anthropology at the University of Hawaii, Honolulu.

LAURENCE R. TANCREDI is Professor of Law, Medicine, and Psychiatry at the University of Texas Health Service Center at Houston. He is the author of numerous articles and books on these topics as well as on ethics.

LINDA M. VAN BLERKOM is Professor of Anthropology at Drew University in Madison, New Jersey.

JEN-YI WANG is an anthropologist in Taiwan.

DAVID N. WEISSTUB is Professor of Law and Psychiatry at the University of Montreal, Quebec.

ROBERT L. WELSCH is an anthropologist at the Field Museum of Natural History, Chicago.